# A LIBRARY OF LITERARY CRITICISM

# A Library
# of Literary Criticism

**VOLUME V**

## SECOND SUPPLEMENT

**TO THE FOURTH EDITION**

# MODERN AMERICAN LITERATURE

*Compiled and edited by*

**PAUL SCHLUETER**

**JUNE SCHLUETER**

*A Frederick Ungar Book*
CONTINUUM · NEW YORK

1992

The Continuum Publishing Company
370 Lexington Avenue
New York, NY 10017

Printed in the United States of America

**Library of Congress Cataloging in Publication Data**

Schlueter, Paul, 1933–
   Modern American literature.

   (A Library of literary criticism)
   Includes index.
   1. American literature—20th century—History and
criticism.   2. Criticism—United States.   I. Schlueter,
June.   II. Curley, Dorothy Nyren. Modern American
literature.   III. Title.   IV. Series.
PS221.C8 1969 Suppl 2     810'.9'005     85-981
ISBN 0-8044-3265-1


ISBN 0-8044-3046-2 Set

# FOREWORD TO THE SECOND SUPPLEMENT

*Modern American Literature* has grown considerably since its first edition in 1960; the three-volume fourth edition (1969), for example, included critical comments on some three hundred authors, and the first supplement (1976) updated about half that number and added forty-nine new authors. The second supplement follows the same principles of selection and organization found in earlier editions and the first supplement; one hundred forty-three authors from previous volumes are updated, and thirty-one new ones are included. In some cases these new authors are established or earlier writers who for one reason or another were not included in earlier volumes (e.g., Gore Vidal, John A. Williams); in most cases, however, these new authors are younger ones generally considered important enough to warrant inclusion in a "permanent" reference book such as this. Authors added for the first time are given a representative sampling of critical comment from throughout their careers, while updated entries cover material from the date of the last volume in which they were included.

We are especially pleased to be able to include criticism on so many good, newer writers, especially women and blacks, writers speaking eloquently to our time as both members of particular groupings and as significant voices in our national literature. Among women writers included for the first time are Ann Beattie, Gail Godwin, Erica Jong, Ursula K. Le Guin, Tillie Olsen, Marge Piercy, Judith Rossner, May Swenson, and Anne Tyler. Black writers — both men and women — include Maya Angelou, Ernest J. Gaines, Robert Hayden, Zora Neale Hurston, Toni Morrison, and Alice Walker. One Native American writer has been added: N. Scott Momaday. Other new additions include Raymond Carver, Stanley Elkin, John Guare, John Hollander, David Ignatow, John Irving, Arthur Kopit, Larry McMurtry, Reynolds Price, Mark Strand, Paul Theroux, and Lanford Wilson.

Updating established authors presents problems somewhat different from merely providing a panoramic overview of a writer's entire career. For those authors about whom entire critical "industries" have sprung up, such as Eliot, Faulkner, and Hemingway, excerpts have been selected to give as broad a picture of contemporary criticism as possible. The inevitable rise and fall of reputations necessarily reflects on the quantity — and quality — of published criticism, and some authors originally thought worthy of inclusion have had to be dropped simply because of the dearth of substantial criticism. In other cases there has been such a diminution of worthwhile commentary as to make gathering and excerpting of even two or three essays a difficult task. In any event, we have at all times tried to give as balanced, astute, and useful a selection of criticism as possible so that those consulting this volume will be led to ferret out the entire original article or book in order to read more extensively on their own.

One major change from earlier volumes of this set is the elimination of various nineteenth-century writers whose careers and/or reputations extended into the twentieth century. In some cases this results from a diminution of critical stature and scholarship, but more often the reason is tied in with the need to include more recent writers whose careers have thus far not prompted the kind of critical overview given in this volume. There is no shortage of collections of critical essays and reviews on, say, Mark Twain or Henry James, whereas some of the newer writers included are given their first extended critical examination in this supplement.

We have also resisted the temptation to repeat uncritically too-familiar selections, some of which pick up bibliographic errors as one volume or another reprints them. In almost every case we have consulted the original book or periodical from which material has been taken; short of that, we have had to rely on photocopies with the result, sometimes, that providing full bibliographic documentation has been difficult if not impossible. In choosing materials, we have — like our predecessors — continued to emphasize scholarly articles and book reviews. But more than ever before, we have tried to use material from as many book-length studies as we could. We have tried to include a judicious selection of material from British periodicals and publishers as well. Finally, bibliographies for most authors in earlier volumes have been updated, but with one major change from previous practice: if an author is not included in this second supplement, no updating was done.

Such a project as this could not have been possible without the assistance and cooperation of many people. Foremost, of course, are the many publishers, editors, authors, and copyright holders who so graciously permitted use of previously published material; we are very grateful to all of these and hope that the excerpts we have cited will lead readers to consult not only the complete source from which we quoted but other material by the same critics and from the same publications. We have been fortunate in that only a few items had to be omitted because of unreasonable demands or withholding of permission. In virtually every case full permission to reprint was secured, although in a handful of cases permission of the publications in which material originally appeared was all that could be granted since authors were impossible to locate. In these few cases, we extend our apologies and wish to go on record as indicating that full credit will be given in subsequent printings if the publisher is notified.

We have profited, moreover, from being able to consult the collections at several major research libraries, including those at Columbia, Princeton, and Rutgers universities, the New York Public Library, and various libraries in or near Pennsylvania's Lehigh Valley, including Allentown, Cedar Crest, Moravian, and Muhlenburg colleges and Kutztown and Lehigh universities. Our greatest debt, though, is to the excellent reference librarians at Lafayette College, in particular Ron Robbins, Richard Everett, and Mary Ann Hershman (now at the Allentown Public Library), for their unlimited help, their continuing patience, and their imaginative efforts in locating materials for this project.

We are grateful as well to the staff at Frederick Ungar Publishing Co., Inc., for their warmth and encouragement, especially to Mr. Frederick Ungar for his unfailing faith in the project and for his lifelong dedication to publishing excellence. In Dr. Rita Stein, series editor, we have been fortunate in finding a collaborator as much as an editor; her consistently incisive editing and her many suggestions have been deeply appreciated.

Finally, we thank Lafayette College for a grant that helped with photocopying costs, and a number of Lafayette College students and others who assisted us in the mechanics of this project. We extend particular thanks to Peter Bograd '83, Geoffrey Gehman '80, Arthur Lewis '84, and Caroline Verhague '84; to Jill Riefenstahl, for typing; and to our daughter, Greta (University of Maryland '87), who added her share.

P. S.
J. S.

# AUTHORS INCLUDED

*Names of authors added in this volume are preceded by a bullet.*

Albee, Edward
Algren, Nelson
Ammons, A. R.
● Angelou, Maya
Ashbery, John
Auchincloss, Louis
Auden, W. H.

Baldwin, James
Baraka, Amiri (LeRoi Jones)
Barnes, Djuna
Barth, John
Barthelme, Donald
● Beattie, Ann
Bellow, Saul
Berger, Thomas
Berryman, John
Bishop, Elizabeth
Blackmur, R. P.
Bly, Robert
Bogan, Louise
Bowles, Jane
Bowles, Paul
Burroughs, William S.

Cain, James M.
Caldwell, Erskine
Capote, Truman
● Carver, Raymond
Cather, Willa
Chandler, Raymond
Cheever, John
Coover, Robert
Cowley, Malcolm
Cozzens, James Gould
Crane, Hart
Creeley, Robert
Cummings, E. E.

De Vries, Peter
Dickey, James
Doctorow, E. L.
Doolittle, Hilda (H. D.)
Dos Passos, John
Dreiser, Theodore
Duncan, Robert

Eberhart, Richard
Eliot, T. S.
● Elkin, Stanley
Ellison, Ralph

Farrell, James T.
Faulkner, William
Fitzgerald, F. Scott
Frost, Robert

Gaddis, William
● Gaines, Ernest J.
Gardner, John
Gass, William H.
Ginsberg, Allen
Glasgow, Ellen
● Godwin, Gail
Goyen, William
● Guare, John

Hammett, Dashiell
Hawkes, John
● Hayden, Robert
Heller, Joseph
Hellman, Lillian
Hemingway, Ernest
Himes, Chester
● Hollander, John
Howard, Richard
Hughes, Langston
● Hurston, Zora Neale

- Ignatow, David
- Irving, John

Jarrell, Randall
Jeffers, Robinson
- Jong, Erica

Kerouac, Jack
Kinnell, Galway
- Kopit, Arthur
Kosinski, Jerzy
Kunitz, Stanley

- Le Guin, Ursula K.
Levertov, Denise
Lewis, Sinclair
Lowell, Robert

MacLeish, Archibald
Mailer, Norman
Malamud, Bernard
- Mamet, David
McCarthy, Mary
McCullers, Carson
- McMurtry, Larry
Mencken, H. L.
Meredith, William
Merrill, James
Merwin, W. S.
Miller, Arthur
Miller, Henry
- Momaday, N. Scott
Moore, Marianne
Morris, Wright
- Morrison, Toni

Nabokov, Vladimir
Nemerov, Howard
Nin, Anaïs

Oates, Joyce Carol
O'Connor, Flannery
Odets, Clifford
O'Hara, Frank
O'Hara, John
- Olsen, Tillie
Olson, Charles

O'Neill, Eugene
Ozick, Cynthia

Percy, Walker
- Piercy, Marge
Plath, Sylvia
Porter, Katherine Anne
Pound, Ezra
- Price, Reynolds
Purdy, James
Pynchon, Thomas

Rabe, David
Ransom, John Crowe
Reed, Ishmael
Rexroth, Kenneth
Rich, Adrienne
Roethke, Theodore
- Rossner, Judith
Roth, Philip
Rukeyser, Muriel

Sandburg, Carl
Sarton, May
Schwartz, Delmore
Sexton, Anne
Shapiro, Karl
Shepard, Sam
Singer, Isaac Bashevis
Snodgrass, W. D.
Snyder, Gary
Sontag, Susan
Stafford, William
Stein, Gertrude
Steinbeck, John
Stevens, Wallace
- Strand, Mark
Styron, William
- Swenson, May

Tate, Allen
Taylor, Peter
- Theroux, Paul
Trilling, Lionel
- Tyler, Anne

Updike, John

- Vidal, Gore
  Vonnegut, Kurt

- Walker, Alice
  Warren, Robert Penn
  Welty, Eudora
  West, Nathanael
  Wharton, Edith
  Wilbur, Richard
  Wilder, Thornton
- Williams, John A.

Williams, Tennessee
Williams, William Carlos
Wilson, Edmund
- Wilson, Lanford
  Winters, Yvor
  Wolfe, Thomas
  Wright, James
  Wright, Richard

Zukofsky, Louis

# PERIODICALS USED

Listed below are the titles, with their abbreviations, if any, and places of publication of periodicals cited in this volume.

| | |
|---|---|
| *Am* | America (New York) |
| *ABR* | American Book Review (New York) |
| *AmEx* | The American Examiner (East Lansing, Mich.) |
| *AHumor* | American Humor (College Park, Md.) |
| *AL* | American Literature (Durham, N.C.) |
| *APR* | American Poetry Review (Philadelphia) |
| *AmerS* | American Studies (Lawrence, Kan.) |
| *AS* | The American Scholar (Washington, D.C.) |
| *AnR* | Antioch Review (Yellow Springs, Ohio) |
| *At* | The Atlantic (Boston) |
| *BALF* | Black American Literature Forum (Terre Haute, Ind.) |
| | Book World (Washington, D.C.) |
| | Callaloo (Lexington, Ky.) |
| *CentR* | Centennial Review (East Lansing, Mich.) |
| *ChiR* | Chicago Review (Chicago) |
| *CE* | College English (Urbana, Ill.) |
| *Cmty* | Commentary (New York) |
| *Com* | Commonweal (New York) |
| *CLS* | Comparative Literature Studies (Urbana, Ill.) |
| *CP* | Concerning Poetry (Bellingham, Wash.) |
| *CL* | Contemporary Literature (Madison, Wisc.) |
| *ConP* | Contemporary Poetry (Bryn Mawr, Pa.) |
| | Critique (Atlanta) |
| | Dissent (New York) |
| *ETJ* | Educational Theatre Journal, now *TJ*, q.v. (Washington, D.C.) |
| | Esquire (New York) |
| | Extrapolation (Kent, Ohio) |
| *FSt* | Feminist Studies (College Park, Md.) |
| *GaR* | Georgia Review (Athens, Ga.) |
| | Harper's Magazine (New York) |
| *HC* | The Hollins Critic (Hollins College, Va.) |
| | Horizon (Tuscaloosa, Ala.) |
| *HdR* | Hudson Review (New York) |
| *IowaR* | Iowa Review (Iowa City, Iowa) |
| *JAmS* | Journal of American Studies (Cambridge, England) |
| *JML* | Journal of Modern Literature (Philadelphia) |
| *JNT* | Journal of Narrative Technique (Ypsilanti, Mich.) |
| *KanQ* | Kansas Quarterly (Manhattan, Kan.) |
| *LitR* | Literary Review (Madison, N.J.) |

| | |
|---|---|
| *MarkhamR* | Markham Review (Staten Island, N.Y.) |
| *MR* | Massachusetts Review (Amherst, Mass.) |
| *MELUS* | Multi-Ethnic Literature of the U.S. (Cincinnati, Ohio) |
| *MQR* | Michigan Quarterly Review (Ann Arbor, Mich.) |
| *MQ* | Midwest Quarterly (Pittsburg, Kan.) |
| *MD* | Modern Drama (Toronto) |
| *MFS* | Modern Fiction Studies (West Lafayette, Ind.) |
| *MPS* | Modern Poetry Studies (Buffalo, N.Y.) |
| | Mosaic (Winnipeg, Manitoba) |
| | Mother Jones (San Francisco) |
| | Ms. (New York) |
| *NER* | New England Review (Hanover, N.H.) |
| *NL* | The New Leader (New York) |
| *NR* | The New Republic (Washington, D.C.) |
| *NYM* | New York Magazine (New York) |
| *NYT* | The New York Times Book Review |
| *NYTd* | The New York Times (daily) |
| *NYTMag* | The New York Times Magazine |
| *NY* | The New Yorker (New York) |
| | Newsweek (New York) |
| | Novel (Providence, R.I.) |
| | Obsidian (Detroit, Mich.) |
| *OhR* | Ohio Review (Athens, Ohio) |
| | Paideuma (Orono, Me.) |
| | Parnassus (New York) |
| *PR* | Partisan Review (Boston) |
| | Phylon (Atlanta) |
| | Poetry (Chicago) |
| | Prooftexts (Baltimore, Md.) |
| | Salmagundi (Saratoga Springs, N.Y.) |
| *SR* | Saturday Review (New York, subsequently Washington, D.C.) |
| *SFS* | Science Fiction Studies (Montreal) |
| *SwR* | Sewanee Review (Sewanee, Tenn.) |
| | Shenandoah (Lexington, Va.) |
| | Signs (Chicago) |
| | The Sixties (Moose Lake, Minn.) |
| *SAB* | South Atlantic Bulletin, now Review (University, Ala.) |
| *SCR* | South Carolina Review (Clemson, S.C.) |
| *SDR* | South Dakota Review (Vermillion, S.D.) |
| *SHR* | Southern Humanities Review (Auburn, Ala.) |
| *SoR* | Southern Review (Baton Rouge, La.) |
| *SWR* | Southwest Review (Dallas) |
| *SAF* | Studies in American Fiction (Boston) |
| *SBL* | Studies in Black Literature (Fredericksburg, Va.) |
| | Sub-stance (Madison, Wisc.) |
| | Theater (New Haven, Conn.) |

| | |
|---|---|
| *TJ* | Theatre Journal, formerly *ETJ*, q.v. (Washington, D.C.) |
| | Time (New York) |
| *TLS* | The Times Literary Supplement (London) |
| *VV* | The Village Voice (New York) |
| *VQR* | Virginia Quarterly Review (Charlottesville, Va.) |
| *VLS* | [The Village] Voice Literary Supplement (New York) |
| *WAL* | Western American Literature (Logan, Utah) |
| *WS* | Women's Studies (Flushing, N.Y.) |
| *WLT* | World Literature Today (Norman, Okla.) |
| *YR* | Yale Review (New Haven, Conn.) |

# ALBEE, EDWARD (1928–    )

*Who's Afraid of Virginia Woolf?*—song and play—conceals fear beneath a party surface. Far from a mere *dolce vita* of offensive couples, however, the drama of four characters terminates in an act of exorcism. Though Martha claims that George no longer knows the difference between truth and illusion, he finally kills their child of illusion in the last darkly comic scene of the play. When first heard, the Latin service for the dead sounds like camp parody, but it prepares for George's outrageous tale of the death telegram, corroborated by Honey. Unlike his namesake, Albee's George can tell a lie, but he implies that lies act in the service of truth. Possibly the dawn ending signals the birth of truth in marriage, and yet Martha's final words express fear rather than hope. Finally ambiguous, Albee's drama is comic not in its conclusion but in its verbal cruelties, lively colloquialisms, and such camp effects as Martha imitating Bette Davis, George imitating President Kennedy, a Latin burial service for an imaginary death, and a familiar tune with semi-nonsensical words— "Who's afraid of Virginia Woolf?"

   After *Virginia Woolf*, Albee's humor drains away. Like *Zoo Story*, *Tiny Alice* ends in death, but Julian, the would-be apostate, lacks the self-irony of Jerry, a prophet with a nickname. The opening scene seems to continue the three comic C's of *Virginia Woolf*—as Cardinal and Lawyer fence verbally; as they lapse into such slang as diddle, pig, loot; as they seem to play at law and church, rather than belonging to these professions. With the entrance of humorless Julian, however, comedy sputters into martyrdom (Albee apparently takes the martyrdom as seriously as does Julian, since he threatened to sue ACT for shrinking Julian's dying monologue). In *Virginia Woolf*, Martha says: "I have a fine sense of the ridiculous, but no sense of humor." Unfortunately, both senses have deserted Albee in his plays of the 1970's.

Ruby Cohn. In *Comic Relief: Humor in
Contemporary American Literature*, ed. Sarah
Blacher Cohen (Univ. of Illinois Pr., 1978), pp.
284–85

Albee is far from affirming illusion as a way of life. The fact that there is a discernible—and recoverable—real self, when the layers of game play and fantasy are stripped from George and Martha, supports Albee's commitment to man's need to confront reality on its terms. Yet Albee does not without qualification decry the evils of illusion. Although ostensibly a realistic drama, *Who's Afraid of Virginia Woolf?* is supremely aware of itself as a play and manifests this awareness throughout. Where the illusion of George and Martha is dismissed as an unsatisfactory confrontation of reality, the illusion of their creator, Albee himself—i.e., the play—is upheld as a meaningful creation, for the play, unlike the escapist illusion of its central characters, leads toward truth rather than away from it.

That Albee is concerned not only with the relationship between reality and illusion with respect to patterns of life, but with the artistic process as well, is confirmed by an examination of the relationship between George and Martha on the one hand and Nick and Honey, their youthful guests, on the other, for this relationship is a microcosm of the relationship between play and audience and a statement of the positive function of art. . . .

Albee's metafictional characters, then, simultaneously deny the validity of illusion as a way of life and affirm the validity of illusion as art. Albee asks his audience to enter a world of illusion only as a means of discovery, because for Albee, the function of fiction, whether private or public, is to illuminate, not replace, reality.

June Schlueter. *Metafictional Characters in Modern Drama* (Columbia Univ. Pr., 1979), pp. 83, 87

Despite the heaviness and seriousness of Albee's concern, it is the catholicity of his vision and technique that really distinguishes this play. Albee shows himself open and sensitive to all facets of the human condition: the serious, the funny, the physical, the metaphysical, the actual, and the illusionary. All of his devices deserve commendation: his wit; the purity of his style, so magnificent in its captivation and alteration of normal speech; and his lizard fantasy, through which he reveals the human reality. . . .

*Seascape* is not only a remarkable aesthetic achievement, but it is also a highly affirmative statement on the human condition. Albee, an American writer, seems to have employed the techniques of the European playwrights Pinter and Beckett, and transformed them so that he could make a highly personal statement, one almost antithetical to their own. He seems to be saying that human life is worth living and that it is desirable to climb the evolutionary ladder in order to experience love, art, and the complexities of human interaction. It is desirable even if that means a certain loss of freedom, natural beauty, and the security possessed by the creatures of the sea. Albee has never made so affirmative a statement in his career; it is significant that *Seascape* should follow *All Over*, which dealt so heavily with death. With *Seascape*, Albee has, as if in a Lazarus-like rebirth of mind and spirit, magnificently affirmed life.

Samuel J. Bernstein. *The Strands Entwined: A New Direction in American Drama* (Northeastern Univ. Pr., 1980), pp.130, 134

## ALGREN, NELSON (1909–1981)

*The Man with the Golden Arm* is an estimable novel which occupies an important position in Algren's development as a novelist. Though not so neatly constructed as *Never Come Morning*, it is more densely packed, more intense, and in some ways more mature. The humorous scenes lead straight to Algren's last major work, the uniquely comic *A Walk on the Wild Side*, which Algren and many of his critics consider to be his best novel. . . .

*The Man with the Golden Arm* is Algren's most comprehensive expression of his conviction that America's great middle class should be made to recognize the personal worth and dignity of the socially disinherited who do not live the spurious lives of the "business cats" and the country-club set, neither of whom has been willing to recognize "the world underneath." In writing such novels as *The Man with the Golden Arm*, Algren has blended Naturalistic Determinism "with a sympathy for his people that nevertheless cannot deter him from sending them to their miserable fates." In a style and language that are drawn directly from the world he depicts, he has "managed to impart a dignity to material which would' be merely sordid in the hands of a lesser writer." He regularly insists that the "poetry" which characterizes his Realism is a natural poetry, one taken from the people themselves: "When I heard a convict who had just finished a stretch say, 'I made my time from bell to bell, now the rest of the way is by the stars,' if somebody was fusing poetry with realism it was the con, not me. My most successful poetry, the lines people threw back at me years after they were written, were lines I never wrote. They were lines I heard, and repeated, usually by someone who never read and couldn't write."

For this reason, despite the concreteness and authoritative detail of his prose, Algren is "more a singer than an explainer," one whose prose in *The Man with the Golden Arm* can become almost a "kind of incantation, like the chanting of ritual itself." In such a form, the curb and tenement and half-shadow world of Frankie and Sophie and Molly with its unforgettable smoke-colored rain, its musk-colored murmuring, and its calamitous light have brought the world underneath a bit closer to the middle-class American consciousness and conscience.

Martha Heasley Cox and Wayne Chatterton.
*Nelson Algren* (Twayne, 1975), pp. 132–33

I have never quite met Nelson Algren—we talked on the phone once—but he has been a continuing influence in my life. He is the poet of the sad metropolis that underlies our North American cities; I was among those millions who caught an early chill there. Reading Algren didn't dispel the chill, but it did teach us to live with it and to look around us with deepened feelings and thoughts.

Algren's Chicago and the people who live in its shadows are still there. Algren is their tragic poet, enabling those who can read him to feel pain. And nearly everyone can read him. He writes with a master's clarity about the complex troubles of simple people, and not so simple people. Bruno Bicek and Frankie Machine and Steffi "with the new city light on her old world face" appear to be simple because Algren presents them with such understanding.

Algren came into the full use of his talent in the early years of the Second World War, which promised to open the way for a reassessment of our society. In full knowledge of the lower depths which had to be redeemed, Algren asserted the value of the people who lived in those depths. The intensity of his feeling, the accuracy of his thought, make me wonder if any other writer of our time has shown us more exactly the human basis of our democracy. Though Algren often defines his positive values by showing us what happens in their absence, his hell burns with passion for heaven.

Ross Macdonald. *NYT.* Dec. 4, 1977, p. 62

A Depression-era naturalist who still pops up in surrealist anthologies, [Algren] never stopped believing that the human actions and emotions which make literature are inherently unclassifiable. He blew being a convincing muckraker by noticing that "people without alternatives are forced to feel life all the way," which sounded better to him than what everybody else was doing; trading not feeling for not being forced. But then he botched being a good black humorist by missing the point that an awareness of the absurd is supposed to distance feelings and not heighten them. It's no accident that he was one of the few '30s writers to greet existentialism as reinforcement instead of deviation, and it's not surprising that he was drawn to the movement by liking the people first and their ideas later. . . . But throughout the '50s, whenever it dawned on critics that Algren didn't think of his characters as social ills to be cured, he was routinely attacked, by such people as Edmund Fuller, who also disliked

*From Here to Eternity* because the hero was a "slob."

This bias must account for the comparative lack of reputation accorded *A Walk on the Wild Side*—which *is* Algren's best novel, an astonishing suspension of tragi-comedy within endlessly meshing webs of folklore, poetry, and dread. The closest analogy would be a blend of *Huckleberry Finn* with *The Threepenny Opera*, but that's only an approximation; offhand, I can't think of any previous American book that's much like it, although dozens of writers, from Thomas Berger to Charles Bukowski, have been ransacking it for years. . . . *Wild Side* is a Depression novel in which the Depression isn't an economic situation or even a definable period, but a phantasmagoria that lifts the lid off the American character. Or, as Algren later put it, back then people couldn't *afford* inhibitions. . . .

But it's misleading to approach the book schematically. *A Walk on the Wild Side* confounds genres—its emotional effects are as various, caroming, and unmediated, as humanly scrambled, as emotion itself. And yet they're worked to such a dense, lucid level of magnification that they seem, at the same time, hallucinatory. The result is a slapstick disorientation that feels, against all reason, unquestionable. Stylistically, *Wild Side* is a kind of ultimate. Algren doesn't lend himself to being excerpted; his verbal devices, which conflate atmosphere, character, and meaning into one and the same thing, are seldom discrete. They're designed to stoke and build on themselves, and they reverberate through the whole length of the best *Neon Wilderness* stories, or, later, whole sections of *The Man with the Golden Arm*. In *Walk on the Wild Side*, Algren sustains the equivalent of a single jazz solo through an entire book. . . .

What makes Algren's work ambiguous, or disturbing, or simply puzzling to many people, I think, is that he doesn't feel any obligation to adopt a depersonalized solemnity toward his material. Yet his sardonicism, whimsicality, eccentric irony, and refractory high spirits never add up to displays of intellectual superiority. He's all there for his characters, opening himself and expressing the full range of his personality as a writer in order to be in touch with the full range of their lives as people. He asserts his own identity on their level, makes himself one of them by maintaining his individuality, which forces us to see them as individuals too, in a way that precludes simply having an intellectual attitude toward them: for Algren, do-gooding concern is as emotionally inadequate as disdain.

Tom Carson. *VLS*. Nov., 1983, pp. 16–17

## AMMONS, A. R. (1926–    )

To recognize . . . Ammons's affinities with Emerson, Dickinson, and Frost is not to reduce the pleasures of his poems but to heighten them. It is also to acknowledge that beyond these direct literary influences there are powerful currents of indirection that play perhaps a more major role still, sources of a more ancient and primal kind that inform the intellectual and emotional life of poetry at its deepest. . . .

For those who have a taste for this sort of thing—for poetry as an unravelling of meaning, a coming-apart or depletion of language—"Pray without Ceasing" may sustain interest, but more often than not the poem will have a hard time of it winning the fascination or affection of readers. At its core is a painful and bewildering renunciation of all significant sense—"it's/indifferent what I say"—the whole point being, one supposes, to reach bottom in order to know, and if possible still to praise, the ache of life in total descent. This plunge downward, into a "breakdown of pure forms," is announced in the poem's opening lines, which serve as a kind of program, or statement of intent, of what is to come:

> done is to be
> undone:
> call me down from the
> high places

Yet after pondering the poems of this book [*Diversifications*]—and a very good book it nevertheless remains—it seems clear that "the high places" constitute Ammons's most proper place, that at his best he is a poet of the solitary and singular moment, that his truest translation of himself puts him, after all, on to the heights, at the farthest remove from the lowlands of communal grief.

Alvin Rosenfeld. APR. July/Aug., 1976, pp.<br>40–41

Ammons impresses me as the best American poet now writing. He is the most versatile, his range is greatest, his excellence in the subsidiary arts included in poetry is the most distinguished, he is funny, and he has been wonderfully abundant. His published work now runs to almost a thousand pages, and he is nowhere near retirement. . . .

In his best poems, Ammons chips away at the oldest obstacle confronting American writers: the thing itself. Remotely in Eliot and Pound, indirectly in Stevens and Frost, and directly in William Carlos Williams, American-born writers have sought, sometimes with a desperation approaching hysteria, to escape the fictions of language and art so as to come as close as possible to the actual physical concrete things of the earth. . . . As purely as can be, Ammons belongs to the American tradition of using language and culture to reach ends that language and culture do not seem designed to reach. . . .

Ammons has emerged as the ideal heir to the strongest fortune of American poetry, and his work synthesizes the best experiments of all of his precursors, especially the ones who stayed at home—Whitman, Sandburg, Williams, Jeffers, Stevens, and Frost. With a southerner's innate skepticism and peculiarly efficient sense of irony, Ammons is at once the flattest of writers and the fanciest.

William Harmon. In *The American South:
Portrait of a Culture*, ed. Louis D. Rubin, Jr.
(Louisiana State Univ. Pr., 1980), pp. 342, 345

# ● ANGELOU, MAYA (1928–    )

"What are you looking at me for? I didn't come to stay. . ." With these words—from a poem that she stumbled over during a church recital—Maya Angelou opens her autobiography [*I Know Why the Caged Bird Sings*] and conveys the diminished sense of herself that pervaded much of her childhood. The words were painfully appropriate. She and her brother were shuttled back and forth between their mother in the North and grandmother in the small town of Stamps, Ark. When she was 8, she was raped. She appeared in court, failed to tell the whole truth and, after her assailant was found dead, concluded that her words could kill. She retreated to silence. "Just my breath, carrying my words out, might poison people . . . I had to stop talking."

Yet, her few years of almost complete silence—she continued to speak to her brother Bailey—actually served her well; Miss Angelou—a former dancer, director and television scriptwriter who is now at work on her second novel—clearly heard, saw, smelled, tasted and seized hold of all the sounds and sights around her. Her autobiography regularly throws out rich, dazzling images which delight and surprise with their simplicity. . . .

But Miss Angelou's book is more than a tour de force of language or the story of childhood suffering: it quietly and gracefully portrays and pays tribute to the courage, dignity and endurance of the small, rural Southern black community in which she spent most of her early years in the 1930s.

Robert A. Gross. *Newsweek*. March 2, 1970, pp.
90, 90B

In [the] primal scene of childhood which opens Maya Angelou's *I Know Why the Caged Bird Sings*, the black girl child testifies to her imprisonment in her bodily prison. She is a black ugly reality, not a whitened dream. And the attendant self-consciousness and diminished self-image throb through her bodily prison until the bladder can do nothing but explode in a parody of release (freedom).

In good autobiography the opening, whether a statement of fact such as the circumstance of birth or ancestry or the recreation of a primal incident such as Maya Angelou's, defines the strategy of the narrative. The strategy itself is a function of the autobiographer's self-image at the moment of writing, for the nature of that self-image determines the nature of the pattern of self-actualization he discovers while attempting to shape his past experiences. Such a pattern must culminate in some sense of an ending, and it is this sense of an ending that informs certain earlier moments with significance and determines the choice of what experience he recreates, what he discards. In fact the earlier moments are fully understood only after that sense of an ending has imposed itself upon the material of the autobiographer's life. Ultimately, then, the opening moment assumes the end, the end the opening moment. Its centrality derives from its distillation of the environment of the self which generated the pattern of the writer's quest after self-actualization. . . . Her genius as a writer is her ability to recapture the texture of the way of life in the texture of its idioms, its idiosyncratic vocabulary and especially in its process of image-making. The imagery holds the reality, giving it immediacy. That she chooses to recreate the past in its own sounds suggests to the reader that she accepts the past and recognizes its beauty and its ugliness, its assets and its liabilities, its strength and its weakness. Here we witness a return to and final acceptance of the past in the return to and full acceptance of its language, the language a symbolic construct of a way of life. Ultimately Maya Angelou's style testifies to her reaffirmation of self-acceptance, the self-acceptance she achieves within the pattern of the autobiography.

Sidonie A. Smith. SHR. Fall, 1973, pp.<br>366–67, 375

*I Know Why the Caged Bird Sings* creates a unique place within black autobiographical tradition, not by being "better" than the formidable autobiographical landmarks described, but by its special stance toward the self, the community, and the universe, and by a form exploiting the full measure of imagination necessary to acknowledge both beauty and absurdity.

The emerging self, equipped with imagination, resourcefulness, and a sense of the tenuousness of childhood innocence, attempts to foster itself by crediting the adult world with its own estimate of its god-like status and managing retreats into the autonomy of the childhood world when conflicts develop. Given the black adult's necessity to compromise with prevailing institutions and to develop limited codes through which nobility, strength, and beauty can be registered, the areas where a child's requirements are absolute—love, security, and consistency—quickly reveal the protean character of adult support and a barely concealed, aggressive chaos. . . .

A good deal of the book's universality derives from black life's traditions seeming to mirror, with extraordinary intensity, the root uncertainty in the universe. The conflict with whites, of course, dramatizes uncertainty and absurdity with immediate headline graphicness. What intensifies the universalism still more is the conflict between the sensitive imagination and reality, and the imagination's ability sometimes to overcome. Maya and her brother have their reservoir of absurd miming and laughter, but sometimes the imagination is caught in pathos and chaos, although its values are frequently superior. . . .

The major function of the imagination, however, is to retain a vigorous dialectic between self and society, between the intransigent world and the aspiring self. Through the dialectic, the egos maintain themselves, even where tragic incident triumphs. In a sense, the triumph of circumstance for Maya becomes a temporary halt in a process which is constantly renewed, a fact evident in the poetic language and in the mellowness of the book's confessional form. . . .

The uniqueness of *I Know Why* arises then from a full imaginative occupation of the rhythms flowing from the primal self in conflict with things as they are, but balanced by the knowledge that the self must find its own order and create its own coherence.

George E. Kent. KanQ. Summer, 1975, pp. 75, 78

When Maya Angelou speaks of "survival with style" and attributes survival to the work of artists, she is talking about a function of art similar to that described by Ralph Ellison. . . .

Such an affirmation of life, a humanizing of reality, is Maya Angelou's answer to the question of how a Black girl can grow up in a repressive system without being maimed by it. Art protects the human values of compassion, love, and innocence, and makes the freedom for the self-realization necessary for real survival. Her answer, like Ellison's, skirts the reformer's question: is "the cost of that style" too high? In this sense she and Ellison are religious writers rather than social ones, for their ultimate concern is self-transcendence. It is unlikely that either would deny the practical value of the past twenty years' progress toward attainment of Negroes' full citizenship in America. But ultimately, as artists, their concern is with the humanity which must survive, and even assimilate into its own creative potential, such restrictions as these writers have encountered. For if this humanity cannot survive restriction, then it will itself become assimilated to the roles imposed upon it.

Myra K. McMurry. SAB. 41, 2, 1976, pp. 110–11

Maya Angelou . . . has achieved a kind of literary breakthrough which few writers of any time, place, or race achieve. Moreover, since writing *The Caged Bird Sings*, she has done so with stunning regularity, in *Gather Together in My Name*, in *Singin' and Swingin' and Gettin' Merry Like Christmas*. Now comes her uproarious, passionate, and beautifully written *The Heart of a Woman*, equal in every respect to *Gather Together in My Name* and only a shade off the perfection of her luminous first volume. As with any corpus of high creativity, exactly what makes Angelou's writing unique is more readily appreciated than analyzed and stated. It is, I think, a melding of unconcerned honesty, consummate craft, and perfect descriptive pitch, yielding a rare compound of great emotional force and authenticity, undiluted by polemic. . . .

Her ability to shatter the opaque prisms of race and class between reader and subject is her special gift.

David Levering Lewis. Book World. Oct. 4,<br>1981, p. 1

## ASHBERY, JOHN (1927–    )

The first few books by John Ashbery contained a large proportion of a poetry of inconsequence. Borrowing freely from the traditions of French surrealism, and from his friends Frank O'Hara and Kenneth Koch, Ashbery tried out a fairly narrow range of voices and subjects. Subject matter, or rather the absence of it, helped form the core of his aesthetic, an aesthetic that refused to maintain a consistent attitude toward any fixed phenomena. The poems tumbled out of a whimsical, detached amusement that mixed with a quizzical melancholy. This aesthetic reached an extreme with *The Tennis Court Oath* (1962), a book in which no poem makes even the slightest attempt to marshal a rational context or an identifiable argument. Line follows line without the sheerest hint of order or apparent plan; this studied inconsequence delighted some readers at the time. But this is not a book to reread; seeing it outside the context of rebellion against the too-conscious aesthetic then fostered by academic poetry, it is difficult to understand why the book was published. . . . But reading the first four books together, one is struck by how precious are those poems that do make poetic sense, surrounded as they are by the incessant chatter of the poems of inconsequence. Slowly, however, it appears as if Ashbery was gaining confidence for his true project, and, as his work unfolds, an indulgent reader can see how it needed those aggressively banal "experiments" in nonsense to protect its frailty. Ashbery's later poetry often uses the traditions of prose discourse, but instead of a poetry of "statement" he has evolved a most tenuous, unassertive language. The first four books, one feels, would have turned out insufferably banal, or perhaps would have remained altogether unwritten, if Ashbery had faced his subject directly or made too various or rigorous demands on his limited language. . . .

What stands behind Ashbery's rather sudden succès d'estime is the triumph of a poetic mode. A mode demands less aesthetic energy than a truly individual style but usually offers more gratification than the average school or "movement." Ashbery's mode has what most modes have, a distinctive blend of sensibility, verbal texture, and thematic concerns. In each of these categories, or elements, a mode must not become too rigid; its sensibility cannot turn into a set of static attitudes, its verbal texture cannot be reducible to simple matters of vocabulary and verse forms, and its thematic concerns must allow for a range of subjects. Successful modes, then, thrive on their distinctiveness, their ability to be set off against a larger, more public set of expectations. But the moment this distinctiveness becomes too rigid, the mode slips into self-parody, consciously or unconsciously. Just when and how a mode calcifies (or what is less likely, fails to achieve a distinctive feel) is hard for literary historians to measure precisely, especially in contemporary literature.

Charles Molesworth. The Fierce Embrace: A<br>Study of Contemporary American Poetry (Univ.<br>of Missouri Pr., 1979), pp. 163, 181

Ashbery's best work, like the paintings of Jasper Johns, seems an intelligent if dark confrontation with the forces of the given. For Johns, the given may be an alphabet, target, flag, or map. For Ashbery, it is the world of degraded and charming cliché, doggerel, bad taste, Hollywood convention, newspaper prose, literary pietism, and metaphysical jargon. The central metaphysical-moral component in Ashbery's verse is its deadly withdrawal of the transcendental term and insistence on individual liberty. His image of the world does not lead to a hedonism pursued along the lines of an American pragmatic, though his ideas are as clear as a pragmatist's. . . . Ashbery's poetry, moreover, leads, as we have seen, through an excruciating evaluation of the possible consolations, cognitive and sensual, that are available. The poem is a difficulty, a resistance, and a critique. The final consolation for the poet may be, as with Stevens, the imagination. An imagination not of fragrance or of stippled sensibility nor of a late, bare, philosophical, and perhaps deluded penetration to *realia*, as in early and late Stevens. The imagination in Ashbery speaks of a constantly agitated *agon*. . . .

Man is locked in the unintelligible or barely intelligible labyrinth of language; one's art is forced to remain repetitive and solipsistic, and yet somehow adventurous. In discontinuous streams, in mistranslations, in suburban resentments and urban uncertainties, in action poetry, Ashbery leads ambiguity to the verge of nonsense and keeps it satisfactorily unredeemed.

> David Shapiro. *John Ashbery: An Introduction to the Poetry* (Columbia Univ. Pr., 1979), pp. 12–13

No volume of Ashbery's is more crucially transitional than *The Double Dream of Spring* (1970). There are some poems in *Rivers and Mountains* (1966) that could have found a place in the later book: "These Lacustrine Cities" and "A Blessing in Disguise," to name two. But *The Double Dream of Spring* as a whole inaugurates a style, a mode of discourse—meditative, less harshly elliptical—that sets it off from the earlier volumes and creates a rhetoric for the subsequent poems to continue, but also to violate. (The poems of *Houseboat Days* [1977] seem to indicate an intention on Ashbery's part to complicate the style in the direction of a return to the elliptical mode.) More important, *The Double Dream of Spring* assumes a stance that Ashbery's later books have not repudiated—that of the poet of high imagination, the visionary. The stance is crossed with obliquity, no doubt: but its presence is undeniable and still astonishing to witness. We can say that in the densely charged lyrics of *The Double Dream*, and especially in its magnificent long poem "Fragment," Ashbery comes into his own and into his inheritance. . . .

Much of the difficulty readers have with Ashbery stems from problems in gauging his tone. The difficulty intensifies when it becomes a question of determining whether or not he is parodying a traditional literary *topos*. This way of posing the reader's alternatives sets up the question in a misleading way, although I think that many readers do pose these terms in oppositional fashion. I think that seasoned readers of Ashbery learn not to demand of his poems that they move in a univocal direction: he can both parody and mean "seriously" at the same time, he both sees and revises simultaneously. At times he appears to war against the very idea of received tradition, even while acknowledging, by his refusal to give them up, that the old tropes embody a storehouse of poetic wisdom still alive for us today.

> Charles Berger. In *Beyond Amazement: New Essays on John Ashbery*, ed. David Lehman (Cornell Univ. Pr., 1980), pp. 164–65

# AUCHINCLOSS, LOUIS (1917–    )

Yet American literature—as defined by the academic elite—seldom offers sympathetic reflections of home-grown aristocracies. The books of Henry James and Edith Wharton are prominent exceptions, though these writers spent most of their lives abroad. While the public enjoys upstairs-downstairs capers, most critics view money and manners as intellectually *déclassé*. Members of the top crust do not match the nation's heroic ideal: the rebellious romantic who spurns corrupting society to hunt his singular salvation in wild nature.

There are no such heroes in the fiction of Louis Auchincloss, and his romantics almost always pay for succumbing to egoism and stepping out of line. Auchincloss's novels and story collections (nearly one a year for 20 years) deal almost exclusively with New York City's white Anglo-Saxon Protestant haven of old name and old money, whose corridor of power runs from the brownstones and duplexes of the Upper East Side to the paneled offices of Wall Street. It is an influential, publicity-shy world where the rules of the game are hardened by tradition. The costs, and sometimes the rewards, of breaking these rules are the author's principal subject. . . .

Auchincloss steers confidently through the world he knows so well. He telescopes time with delightfully gossipy character sketches and crisp vignettes. His prose is clear and judiciously cool, though his attempts to pump drama into drawing-room confrontations may lead to such awkwardness as "But Ivy's words were still written like the smoke letters of an airplane announcing a public event across the pale sky of Clara's calm. . . ."

Auchincloss's true dramatic moments are in exchanges of dialogue that he expertly stages to define his characters. It is this quality of closet theater that makes his work consistently entertaining—even when his sphere of wealth and privilege may seem hopelessly remote to most readers.            .

R. Z. Sheppard. *Time*. July 11, 1977, p. 76

Louis Auchincloss sees a lot. What he catches most suggestively, I think, are the dynamics of pride (and of vanity, arrogance, snobbishness and related failings). His work offers other pleasures, to be sure—a gallery of strikingly animated and intelligent women, a beautifully unaffected responsiveness to the claims of those who were here before us. (The portraits of the author's mother and father in *A Writer's Capital* are exceptionally loving.) And it's important not to give the impression, to readers who don't know his books, that some sort of moral hectoring or casuistry lies in wait for those who try them. In his novels Auchincloss usually offers a carefully constructed story, as well as much incidental observation, unsolemnly phrased, about social attitudes—for example, precisely how men of affairs look upon academics. This concern about entertaining is equally evident in his essays, which proceed not as sermons, but, frequently, as unpretentiously developed comparisons of one artist with another. I'm merely saying that, in my view, his writing is subtlest when it inquires into the moment-to-moment complications of self-regard—especially self-regard under pressure. . . .

Gently he leads his readers toward comprehension of the nearly universal human helplessness before the passion that preoccupies him. With that comprehension come intuitions of the fundamental innocence of pride, even in lofty quarters. And the result is the banishment, unportentously managed, of the possibility—on this front at least—of moral condemnation or satiric putdown. . . .

But literature also exists to help the powerless penetrate their own simplicity and corruption, to show forth the respects in which turbulence itself is another style of pride, and to alert people to the truth that any of us—the very rich not excluded—can be ruined by the temptation to be too hard on ourselves. Humorously, unobtrusively, the best of Louis Auchincloss's books nudge the reader toward such knowledge, which is why they will remain valuable.

Benjamin DeMott. *NYT*. Sept. 23, 1979, pp. 7, 35

*Watchfires* works out its theme of liberation with such single-minded success that it carries Auchincloss out on the other side of what seems to have been a personal and artistic obsession that has consumed him ever since he started writing as a child. . . . Auchincloss writes about the rich the way Updike writes about the middle class, though without the stylistic flourishes. His own social and professional positions have given him an insight that makes his work unique in contemporary literature. . . .

*Watchfires* . . . is so strong, and in significant ways so different from his earlier work, that it is no longer possible to misperceive his achievement. *Watchfires* is warmer, more intense, more intimate than any book he has written previously. As a writer, Auchincloss seems newly open and vulnerable. Moreover, his characters all find some sort of liberation. . . .

It is true that he is not a master stylist. He is capable of using a prefabricated phrase: describing someone who knows society "like a book." And he can produce a rat's nest of a sentence: "For if the old Puritanism of the Handys and Howlands had been diluted in her to the point of excluding the sin that existed only in the mind, or at least of ranking it as less culpable than its robuster brethren, the ancient sense of guilt had been replaced by an equally sharp horror of seeming ridiculous." But he is equally capable of a phrase that is both accurate and surprising. . . .

The world Auchincloss writes about, the world of America's ruling class, is no smaller—and is, in fact, probably larger—than Faulkner's Yoknapatawpha County or Hardy's Wessex. And its influence is vast. . . .

How good, finally, is *Watchfires*? How good is Auchincloss? Adding up his assets (complex characters; a persuasive, insider's vision of a rarefied but powerful world; an entertaining sense of narrative) and his debits (occasional stylistic infelicities) Auchincloss proves to be a sound, no-risk blue-chip, with reliable dividends.

David Black. *SR*. April, 1982, pp. 24, 28

## AUDEN, W. H. (1907–1973)

His poetry alternated between socio-political and psychological modes of analysis, and he was likely to think that psychological ills are basic, political and social wrong derived from them. The process of diagnosis and healing, with which Auden was always so much concerned, had to start not with social institutions but with the human heart. Primarily he was a moralist, and the chief importance for him of psychological and sociological modes of thought was that they provided criteria of the good. . . .

The amount of Auden's poetry in the thirties was remarkable—nine volumes in ten years. In relation to this poetry, and especially in view of the original contribution he was making, the charges that have since been so often leveled against him—carelessness, manneredness, obscurity, cliquishness, muddled thinking, frivolity, glibness, and a habit of amputating his own past, so that, the argument goes, he achieved virtuosity in different roles or styles rather than cumulative growth—seem either less warranted or less important. He created a style that was completely his own. His penchant for comic entertainment and for song, his ability to write at times with open perspicuity, his informality and imperfection widened the possibilities of poetry for other writers. He was wholly a poet of the contemporary situation, not only by topical allusion and reportage, but also because he explored and expressed the ground feelings of vague guilt, anxiety, isolation, and fear that so many shared. He was never without something to say. However pessimistic the poems might be, the general spirit of his poetry was adventurous, experimental, buoyant, full of intellectual gusto. He was the most significant new voice of the thirties, and because he was so young, he seemed boundlessly promising. But Auden's poetry changed in ways that disappointed most of his readers. . . .

I have been trying to give the impression of a retreat, for perfectly understandable reasons, into the minor and unpretentious in subject matter and style. This poetry disarms criticism or else puts it on the defensive, helpless before charm and unwilling to seem to prefer "haphazard oracular grunts." And yet, intelligent, amusing, graceful, and gracious as it is, it is not very exciting. To the extent that Auden's poetry survives, it will be mainly the poetry of the thirties.

David Perkins. *SoR.* Autumn, 1977, pp. 733–34, 737–38

Hawthorne has a story called "P.s Correspondence" (*Mosses from an Old Manse*) in which an amiable madman gives an account of his meeting with the elderly Lord Byron. The letter is headed "London, February 29, 1845," and Byron, though fat and dull—a "mortal heap," in fact—is much improved morally. . . .

Byron, it emerges, is preparing a new collected edition, which is to be corrected, expurgated, and amended "in accordance with his present creed of taste, morals, politics and religion." None of the passages commended by the visitor would find a place in this new edition. P. concludes that Byron, having lost his passions, "no longer understands his own poetry.". . .

The application is plain enough, I believe; Auden came close to a point where he no longer understood his own poetry. I do not say that he exactly follows the pattern of development detected by Mr. P. in Byron and other writers; but something happened that made him close his mind, not to the earliest poetry so much as to that of the middle 'thirties. . . .

There is a genuine and sad perversity in this failure of Auden to understand himself. It is as if he came to find himself boring, or became unable to connect with himself, as in life he grew less and less able to connect with others. All those schemes and formulas he invented to systematize his views on everything from history to ethics—it was a habit early formed, as we see from some of the prose selections in this new book—served to fence him in, to prevent any real conversation with others, or with his former self. His earlier rhetoric failed later ethical tests, and in acquiring a poetic personality that could live with these faintly schoolboyish standards of truth-telling he lost all sense of the valuable strangeness of the personality it supplanted. . . .

And we old men who still think of the poems of the 'thirties as part of an almost incomparably good time for modern poetry—when you picked up the literary journals and read a late poem of Yeats, or *East Coker*, or a new Auden—are not going to sit idly by and allow it to be said that he was really in a bad patch of pretending, but eventually got it right; and that people will come to see that he did, abandoning their allegiance to the older texts and the banned poems. At least *The English Auden* will do nothing to strengthen that kind of propaganda.

Frank Kermode. *YR*. Summer, 1978, pp. 609, 612, 614

About the Long Poems, my feelings, in the mid-forties and now, are mixed. None of them, I judge, is an unqualified success. Yet to have written them augments the stature of Auden. Not afraid to fail, he is the greater poet for having attempted them. That very courage sets him apart from minor poets who are partly so because they are perfectionists. Greatness takes risks, is willing to be imperfectly large rather than impeccably small. . . .

Auden was a phenomenon, a prodigy, poet-hero who gave his name to a group and a poetic generation in his English youth, and who, after he migrated to the United States, became a public figure, almost an anonymous famous man. To survive three or four poetic generations, generations which now move so rapidly, is to pass close scrutiny, and, as any survivor must, pass the muster of sundry, and often conflicting, points of view. . . .

Auden does not lend himself to close-reading excesses. Nor does he lend himself well to brief illustrative quotations, such as, throughout writing this essay, I have wanted to produce; partly because the sentences in his poetry are characteristically long, as though, like Milton, he was deep-lunged; partly because he is not given to phrases literally memorable either for their verbal music, their visual image, or their grammatic condensation. His syntax carries him along, and his sure sense of style, which persists even through passages which are briefly flat, diffuse, or obscure. He must be taken in quantity and at speed, this mode of reading alternating with slower speed and in selection. . . .

Auden is not, either by temperament or by Christian cosmology, a tragic poet, but he is a serious one. The Just City, "Society the Redeemed Form of Man," is not to be reached by apocalyptic reversal and can never, on earth, be perfectly realized, but it is not to be despaired of by impatient, romantic utopians and other idealists. And—very unromantic of him—Auden practiced and preached a chastened cheerfulness. It was this, as well as his art, which endeared Horace to Auden. . . . Of Auden, my considered judgment is that he was, to a high degree, both a robust, loyal, and generous man and a major poet, equaled in modern times only by Yeats, Frost, and Eliot. Not such a perfectionist as the later Yeats or as Eliot, he has written no work of length which I can rank with the *Four*

*Quartets*; but he is larger in his range and scope than either Yeats or Eliot, an ampler and richer representation of the Anglo-American genius in poetry. His civilized, and civilizing, legacy remains, to challenge and to bless.

Austin Warren. *SoR*. Summer, 1981, pp. 475–78

# BALDWIN, JAMES (1924–    )

Without Wright's rage, or Ellison's intellectual distance, Baldwin is particularly exposed to hurt. He is tormented by the way he is treated, and he faces us with a chronicle of pain that is intensely personal. But his self-absorption, his intimate insights into his own anguish seem to be the sign of a final break-away from the old prison in which just such self-absorption was prohibited. In some ways, Baldwin's very personalism, with all its idiosyncrasies and neurotic ticks, comes closest of all to embodying the force that powers the liveliest thrusts in the Movement. For Baldwin is the first black writer to give real poetic depth to the polemics of black pride.

Sadly enough, his poetic powers have seemed to decline since his first novel, *Go Tell It on the Mountain*. But he gives us in that work an imaginative expression of the black struggle for self-awareness and the ascent toward self-affirmation that is both deeper and more explicit than that in either *Native Son* or *Invisible Man. . . .*

In the novels that he writes after *Go Tell It on the Mountain*— *Giovanni's Room* (1956), *Another Country* (1962), *Tell Me How Long the Train's Been Gone* (1968), and *If Beale Street Could Talk* (1974)— Baldwin seems to become more and more a spokesman for blackness and homosexuality. He moves toward the need for solutions, for a victory of darkness or light. He struggles increasingly against his early willingness to accept the mystery of his condition, and his fiction diminishes in quality accordingly. But no one can take from him his greatest achievement, the poetic interpretation of a new black consciousness and the expression of its complexities and paradoxes. Because it formulates so expressively the forces at work in the black culture during the early 1950's, because it engages social issues at a personal and emotional depth, *Go Tell It on the Mountain* will outlive most of Baldwin's essays, which have brought him, and quite justly, so much current attention.

Jerry H. Bryant. Phylon. June, 1976, pp. 184,<br>186–87

In his dramas, James Baldwin has followed both paths of contemporary black playwrights—most consciously writing for white spectators when he seems to be denouncing them (*Blues for Mister Charlie*), most effectively creating for black audiences when he seems unaware of any audience (*The Amen Corner*). Yet the varying reactions to the two plays clearly illustrate the problem of the black playwright. Sensational, melodramatic, and written for whites, *Blues for Mister Charlie* provoked controversy that increased the attention accorded to it. The more thoughtful, more realistic, more credible *The Amen Corner* waited a decade for professional production, then appeared almost without comment. The question that arises is, Can a black be respected simultaneously as an artist and as a faithful portrayer of black life if his reputation depends upon an audience that neither knows nor cares about the world depicted by that black, but is concerned only with the effect of that world on the lives of white Americans? . . .

Baldwin's theme in *The Amen Corner* is not restricted to black people. The need for love and understanding is propounded as emphatically in *Another Country*, where Baldwin shows that white, middle-class people must learn to love each other. This theme, in fact, dominates Baldwin's work: human beings must learn to give themselves totally to other human beings if humankind is to survive. Nevertheless, he seems to develop this recurrent thesis more credibly within the traditionally religious context and church setting of *The Amen Corner* than in the topical, political situation of *Blues for Mister Charlie*.

In short, in *The Amen Corner* Baldwin achieved a success in theme and characterization surpassing his effort in *Blues for Mister Charlie*.

Darwin T. Turner. In *James Baldwin: A Critical Evaluation*, ed. Thermon B. O'Daniel (Howard Univ. Pr., 1977), pp. 190, 193–94

James Baldwin has asked the most urgent and penetrating questions any modern novelist has asked about certain key patterns of human relationships. Deeply thinking and deeply feeling, he explores the possibilities of love, the inevitabilities of hate, and the bloody angles of race relations. And these fearsome interrogations are carried out in the harsh, tangible realities of urban America. Further, Baldwin treats all these confrontations as the substance of the artist's essential task—to dig into himself and into others for truths about the human condition and to report the truths accurately and unflinchingly. He has much to tell us about the social roles and the psychological and sexual identities of men and women; he reveals the meanings of blackness and whiteness, and of their commingling, in the United States. His mastery of style renders his many sad truths not palatable but palpable; we feel them on the nerve. It also colors his few joyous truths with a luminous intensity, with a thrilling energy of awareness. . . .

Baldwin's great merit, the artist's merit, as a chronicler of race relations in America is that he makes us see and feel the subjective realities of the national torment. Behind the tracts and statistics, the histories and sociologies and psychologies, there are breathing people; Baldwin takes us into their minds and hearts and forces upon us realizations that horrify and depress—but that may ultimately heal. Particularly in his two best novels, *Go Tell It on the Mountain* and *Another Country*, he examines the interior sense of race and class, driving home the implications of these blunt facts of existence. . . .

Baldwin makes vivid the consequences of racial subordination for individual behavior and for the contours of black personality. His art might be almost a dramatization of the analysis of black psychological functioning set forth by the psychiatrists Abram Kardiner and Lionel Ovesey in their provocative study *The Mark of Oppression*. They argue that the "mark" imposed by the long history of discrimination and enforced inequality contains the central elements of low self-esteem and aggression. Attempts to deal with these elements are a series of largely futile maneuvers, self-defeating in the main, as long as the social structure of injustice remains in place. Although the years since Kardiner and Ovesey's research and since the first publication of Baldwin's novels have been distinguished by some very important charges in educational and occupational opportunity and by the abolition of legal segregation, the damage and rage are still with us in significant quantities. Baldwin captures them as no other writer, black or white, has ever done.

Robert N. Wilson. The Writer as Social Seer<br>(Univ. of North Carolina Pr., 1979), pp. 89–91

What can one say after summarizing, sampling, analyzing and interpreting the work of James Baldwin and reactions to that work, except that here is a writer of exceptional range and power. What is sometimes lacking in aesthetic control over long art forms such as the novel is more than adequately made up for by concisely constructed scenes, descriptions, sentences. Some of Baldwin's habits are bound to be irritating to some readers—his use of profanity, his explicit and sentimental sex scenes, his castigation of white America, his seeming inability to rid himself of early religious training his finds bothersome but ingrained, his repetition of some ideas, phrases, scenes. But what emerges, nevertheless, from the whole of his work, is a kind of absolute conviction and passion and honesty that is nothing less than courageous.

When his work is joined with his life, the picture of courage grows. As we see Baldwin now victorious against the odds of poverty, race, stature, looks, homosexuality, publishing realities for black authors, it is needful to remind ourselves of the struggle that victory represents. We must remind ourselves because Baldwin has shared his struggle with his readers for a purpose—to demonstrate that our suffering is our bridge to one another. For an introduction to his life and work to do less than state

that ultimate purpose behind everything Baldwin has written would be, I
think, to do him a disservice.

Carolyn Wedin Sylvander. *James Baldwin*
(Ungar, 1980), pp. 148–49

## BARAKA, AMIRI (LE ROI JONES, 1934–    )

At the core of Baraka's art is the insistence upon the formlessness of life-
giving energy and the energetic or fluid nature of all form. It is no wonder
that events in his work are violent, his images often alarmingly brutal.
The only fruition or finality honored is that of death, which produces a
sudden enlargement of vision—the realization that personality, or the
"deadweight" of any fixed idea or being, is inevitably annihilated by history's progress: "The only constant is change.". . .

Yet as the revelation and exorcism of self have given way to a communal orientation, Baraka has not abandoned his theatrical sensibility.
On the contrary, he has sought an increasingly expansive theatre—the
stage of world politics. His shifts—often perplexing and contradictory—
leading from uncompromisingly separatist black nationalism to a more
inclusive Pan-Africanism, and most recently to the embrace of international socialism, may be taken partly as an attempt to gain a broader
world forum, and partly as reflecting the need to fabricate new ideological
roles for each change wrought by contemporary history.

Baraka has shown at every instant of his public career an intense
commitment to those ideas and ideals he felt were integral to his motivating vision of life. Like James Brown, he has always been "an actor that is
now." And it is by way of this ethos, with its equation of passion and significance, that Imamu Amiri Baraka creatively identifies himself with the
evolving spirit of his people. . . .

Kimberly W. Benston. *Baraka: The Renegade and
the Mask* (Yale Univ. Pr., 1976), pp. 261, 263

Perhaps more so than any other writer, Baraka captures the idiom and
style of modern urban black life. The uniqueness and authenticity of his
work is largely attributable to his thorough knowledge of the speech and
music of urban blacks. In his best work, he exploits these two powerful
and rich possessions of an otherwise weak and impoverished people. He
shows, especially in his later works, an understanding of the full range of
black speech patterns, an element which invigorates and renders dramatic even his short stories and poems. Baraka's flawless ear retained also the

sounds of modern jazz, the most important artistic creation of black America. Along with the frequent evidence of the traditional jazz framework, we see also in the poems the following characteristics of modern jazz: spontaneity of line, moving by sheer suggestiveness of impetus; elliptical phrasing; polyrhythmic thrust. Although similar musical qualities have been attributed to the work of other modern American poets, the conscious and effective employment of these qualities cannot be questioned in Baraka's case, for his musical insights are not only integrated into the artistic methods of his plays, poems, and stories. They have been articulated in a number of perceptive essays, as well as the extremely important study *Blues People*. Throughout his literary career, Baraka has been concerned greatly with the sounds of black life. During the latter 1960's and early 1970's, this concern took on even more importance in his attempts to reach a largely non-reading audience. . . .

As we inspect the corpus of Baraka's writing, we are unavoidably aware of his faults—extreme privacy of reference, frequent experimental failure, and racist dogma, to name only a few. Nevertheless, we are also mindful of his merits—daring and frequently successful verbal approximations of jazz music, vibrant recreation of black speech, and a consummate portrayal of the black middle-class psyche. In spite of some obvious short-comings, Baraka, in the brief span of ten years, presented us with work of considerable promise. It is at least this writer's hope that the artist's increasingly myopic vision does not confirm the once-premature contention that "it is now necessary to inter him as a writer, young and kicking." However, at this point in his career, Baraka seems to be doing everything in his power to prove that grim prophecy sagacious.

Henry C. Lacey. *To Raise, Destroy, and Create: The Poetry, Drama, and Fiction of Imamu Amiri Baraka (LeRoi Jones)* (Whitston, 1981), pp. viii, 195–96

# BARNES,   DJUNA   (1892–1982)

Miss Barnes's themes have consistently taken the modern world to task, but her techniques reflect her careful study of the past. She has been influenced in diction and vocabulary by the Bible, Chaucer, Shakespeare, Donne, Milton, Fielding; by the literature of Manners, Sterne, and Joyce. With some justice, we may state that she has also admired these writers and their works for structural reasons. From the start of her longer work, she became an experimenter with fictional forms which tend to fragment, superimpose, juxtapose, or intertwine her thematic and plot lines. The episodic character of both her early and later models appears in the "spatial" quality or unorthodox arrangement of her material into forms which resist the linear-as-chronological schema typical of fictional narratives. . . .

I am not entirely persuaded as to the novelty of her structure. The picaresque novel, a very old form, is both episodic and susceptible to rearrangements of time; and certain chapters recount events occurring during the same time as other events described in previous chapters. A clearer sense of Barnes's purpose is obtained by considering time thematically rather than structurally. As interested in time rearrangements as she may be, Miss Barnes is much more interested in time as it relates to the degenerating patterns of Western society. She does not write, at the expense of theme, for the sake of creating poetic language; for both theme and style are important for her creation of her desired effect.

In turn, later writers, particularly those noted less for their popularity than for their craftsmanship, appear to have been influenced in varying degrees by Barnes's writings. For example, Faulkner showed evidence that we have indicated of having been influenced by Barnes as he sought to achieve the ideal of feminine beauty in his later novels, such as *The Hamlet*, *The Town* and *The Mansion*. Barnes is cited in the introduction to John Hawkes' novel *The Cannibal* as having influenced that writer stylistically, and Anais Nin's novels have been said to reflect such an influence.

As such conventions of the nineteenth century novel as its linear plot and its "realistic" characters are increasingly displaced by the challenges of our frighteningly changing times and people, we can anticipate that discerning readers as well as writers hopeful of improving their craftsmanship will turn in growing numbers to Miss Barnes's works for instruction.

James B. Scott. *Djuna Barnes* (Twayne, 1976), pp. 141–42

Djuna Barnes's middle vision comes to its fullest expression in *Nightwood*; that . . . immaculate novel is indeed a masterpiece. To let it stand alone as representative of a full career, however, is to deprive the novel of a good share of its merit. *Spillway* and *The Antiphon*, rather than being blind thrusts in new directions, follow from *Nightwood* in a precise and logical way. It may even be argued that *The Antiphon* is a work of comparable value insofar as it gives final shape to Miss Barnes's central themes. Certainly both companion volumes to *Nightwood* in *The Selected Works* greatly amplify the themes and stylistic attainments of their predecessor. Likewise, the uneven and sometimes flawed work before *Nightwood*, if seen with attention to the emergence of qualities that finally cohere in the novel, may reveal merits that have been overlooked. Even the early popular journalism, seeming hardly to bear upon a cryptic and subjective novel of 1936, may suggest something of what was to follow. . . .

In all, *Nightwood* is Djuna Barnes's central work, if not her only achievement of distinction. The book's trans-generic mode enables Miss Barnes to focus the themes and stylistic techniques that had been forming for years into a cohesive whole. It is completely consistent with the earlier work in form and themes, only more concentrated and intricately worked within its selective range. It brings the aims of the novel perhaps as close as possible to those of poetry, particularly with respect to the poetic image. It remains to be seen whether or not *The Antiphon*, a similar attempt in the genre of verse drama, is as successful. But *Nightwood* is a masterful work architecturally and linguistically, comparable to the works of Joyce and Eliot among the moderns, and to those earlier writers quoted or echoed in the novel itself. Like Malcolm Lowry's *Under the Volcano* and William Gaddis's *The Recognitions*, equally neglected works of similar merit, nearly every phrase in it is distinctive and functional, essential to the whole.

Louis F. Kannenstine. *The Art of Djuna Barnes: Duality and Damnation* (New York Univ. Pr., 1977), pp. xviii, 126

Barnes's reputation rests essentially on *Nightwood* (1936). A powerful novel of marriage, adultery, and betrayal, it should not be mistaken for a domestic narrative in the Updike manner, where failures can be comprehended and new beginnings achieved. Focusing on bogus aristocrats and American expatriates in Europe during the 1920's and 1930's, this is a nightmarish world, off kilter and surreal. Its inhabitants lose the object of their love, Robin Vote, and are unable to find an outlet or spillway for their anguish. Almost like puppets, they are set into frenetic motion and new behavioral patterns by forces from within their unconscious. These include sudden transvestism and bisexuality, metamorphoses of personality, and schizophrenia, all placed against juxtaposed times and swift changes in setting. Complex techniques such as these, along with eccentric characters, have led critics to associate Barnes with experimental forms and especially with anti-realism. But she is not a one-book author, and therefore she should be examined in the larger context of other important works. Though more traditional, they still reveal characters and conflicts that are the foundation of *Nightwood*, as well as her dexterity in using vastly differing styles. *A Book* (1923) and *A Night among the Horses* (1928) consist of short stories, poems, and one-act plays that, unlike *Nightwood*, are concise and even traditionally narrated. But it is here that themes such as the severed self and the atomized self are introduced. . . .

Whatever the techniques—traditional or experimental—Barnes's work is concerned with ways of being reconciled to life's random misfortunes. In the stories of *Spillway* there is often an emotional "spillway" that rechannelizes feelings of helplessness and isolation. Its specific form may not be pleasurable, yet still it exists as an alternative to the completely isolated personality. For some characters who are whirled about by stimuli they never quite understand, the spillway is passivity or acquiescence, while for others it is a private fantasy, endless travel, or psychological regression. Whatever the case, the suffering begins with detachment from origins.

Miriam Fuchs. HC. June, 1981, pp. 2–3

## BARTH, JOHN (1930–    )

The typical Barth character . . . embarks upon a voyage of thought and passion whose goal is to discover the "real" self, the "real" experience, underlying the fictions in which he is imprisoned. For Barth, the novel begins when a character becomes conscious of himself as an actor, puppet, and perhaps inventor of his own life-drama. Therefore, the plot of Barth's novels is largely the plot of discovering the underlying myths, the archfictions which will allow us to live with the smaller, less satisfying fictions of everyday life and still to believe in ourselves as conscious, creative agents. . . .

Barth's career, indeed, is a progression toward precisely such a mythic vision of the inauthentic condition of modern man: an evolution of style, theme, and subject which ends—for the present—in a severe, allegorical approach that describes the modern dilemma of writer and reader most efficiently by a retelling and inversion of the most ancient and "irrelevant" of legends. There is a surprising corollary to this evolution— as Barth's fictions become more and more obsessively "mythic," they also become lighter, more truly comic, more open to the possibilities of life and to the chances of escaping the infinite vortices of self-consciousness.

Frank D. McConnell. Four Postwar American<br>Novelists (Univ. of Chicago Pr., 1977), pp. 115–16

Make no mistake: [*Letters*] is a daunting book. Amid the fabulist fictions which have, in the past twenty years, sprouted at every hand, it rises like a monument—a monument being, of course, a construction that demands attention but is not itself alive. Patience, Shakespeare tells us, sat on a monument, and that is one of the things the reader can do with *Letters*, but whatever he does with it, he had better bring Patience along for company. Again, make no mistake: this longest and most complex of John Barth's novels is really an awesome performance. Like Nabokov's *Ada*, Pynchon's *Gravity's Rainbow* and Gaddis's *J.R.*—the only contemporary novels other than Barth's own to which it may be fairly compared—*Letters* is brilliant, witty, at times erudite, and damn near unreadable as well. The reader's jaw drops in amazement, then remains locked in the yawn position. . . .

Put briefly, Barth's intention here is to write a novel which will serve as a sequel to all five of the books he had written prior to embarking on this one, and to do so in the form of an epistolary novel, a genre he well knows was exhausted nearly two centuries ago but which he will revivify by means of all manner of alphabetical, anagrammatical and numerological games. . . .

Barth cannot write a dull page and there is much here that is delightful, but by writing a great many very similar pages, and drawing so heavily on material he has exhausted before, he becomes very quickly dull. . . .

And yet: it is impossible to dislike the book. Perhaps, given the perspective a reviewer can never immediately enjoy, I'll look upon it with more affection. Barth is as inventive and as muscular a writer as we have just now. Faint-headed readers may not finish *Letters*, but no one who cares for fiction can ignore it altogether.

Peter S. Prescott. Newsweek. Oct. 1, 1979, pp.<br>74, 76

John Barth's fictions have always used male-female relationships to explore questions of identity. Barth's characterizations have escaped criticism, however, because his fictions have gradually abandoned the pretense of realism, in favor of parodic and self-conscious techniques. The "self-reflexive" approach allows Barth to explore the deeply traditional structures—the myths—that he finds at the heart of fiction, of experience, and of perception. This pursuit of fundamental form has led him to a mythic definition of male and female identities, one that underlies all the work but becomes most explicit in *Chimera*. The notions of gender identity revealed in Barth's work are important first because they *are* traditional; they reflect the assumptions inherent in a male-centered mythology. But Barth extends the myth, employing it as metaphor for the condition of the artist/perceiver. That "new" myth contains more than the dangers of the old male-female dichotomy; it is a fascinating example of the ways that contemporary subjective relativism can support a myth even more deadening to women. Thus Barth's ideas of gender identity are

important not only in illuminating his own fictional views, but also in tracing the emergence of old sex roles in new disguises. . . .

Barth wants to show the paradoxical nature of life, but keeps coming
down on one side of the paradox, unable to resolve the polar tensions
without surrender of one pole. A perspective so heavily weighted in favor
of the "masculine," conceptual, creative pole can hardly celebrate
"feminine" principles, particularly when the narrative itself displays the
triumph of idea over fact, scheme over ambiguous life. Barth's preference
for the "male" side eliminates even the power suggested by the mythic
dichotomy, reducing the potent innerness of the Earth Mother to the
"vacuum" of the not-self, and reducing the energy of the Muse to the
mimicry of the mirror-self. The result is female characters who are always
seen from outside, who are reduced to symbols, symbols moreover of the
non-human aspects of life, and who are denied power even in that area by
narrative insistence on the creative male perceiver.

> Cynthia Davis. *CentR*. Summer, 1980, pp.
> 309, 321

There is so much that is appealing, even wise, in *Sabbatical*, that if I finally
found it irritatingly cute, I hope the shortcoming is mine, not the author's.
John Barth certainly has the right stuff. He can, as Saul Bellow once pre-
scribed, put a spin on words, but it seems to me that in *Sabbatical* he has
not so much hammered out a novel as proffered a long and convoluted
academic write. Seductive here, touching there, but ultimately confusing.
Unsatisfying. Undone, perhaps, by its own cleverness, a highly refined
propensity for literary games and riddles. . . .

For all its self-consciousness, plentiful footnotes pedantic or ponderous, and showy literary references, *Sabbatical* has been built on a frame of
very stale convention. Which is to say, at the novel's end—well, no, it
doesn't end, it stops—the author and his black-eyed Susan are (wait for it)
about to sit down and write the novel we have just read with, as the blurb
writer coyly puts it (wink, wink), a little help from the author.

> Mordecai Richler. *SR*. June, 1982, p.67

## BARTHELME, DONALD (1931–    )

To turn . . . to Donald Barthelme's *The Dead Father* may induce culture
shock. This cold short narrative is written at an extreme distance from
life, out of literary models and the author's idea of a defunct avant-garde.
*The Dead Father* is God, we are told at one point, but the tyrannic author-

ity of the past will do. It seems clear only that Barthelme finds clarity simplistic and is enchanted with the attenuated jokes of modernity. Here may be found his Lucky speech, his *Watt* palaver, his Joycean flourishes, his Kafkaesque dream, etc. It's all very cynical and chic, like Woody Allen's posture of the twirp taking on the big guys once again. Here the novel itself is a *shtick*. Barthleme is adroit and must know the dangers he runs in his use of the literary forebears he fears and admires. The awe is still in him and he cannot bring himself to real parody. The book is boring and difficult to no purpose. The little snigger we get from recognizing the Beckett line is like that Model T in *Ragtime*. Real freedom, if that is what Barthelme is seeking in laying the image of the father to rest, will come in a release of his comic talent from the merely fashionable. He is ingenious in dealing with the madness of sophisticated urban life but he is not yet angry enough to dig out from under the clods of pastiche that muffle his own voice.

Maureen Howard. YR. Spring, 1976, pp. 408–9

As though to offer an alternative to our immersion in fixed roles and clichés, and our inevitable imprisonment in the fixed structures of language, he subjects the written and spoken forms of language to endless experimentation and parody. Most typically, he literalizes metaphor, which shocks the reader into an awareness of both his own uncreative use of language and its rich possibilities. Barthelme evokes through his verbal arrangements, in fact, a universe—unborn until then, untapped in his reader's consciousness. He creates, especially up through *The Dead Father*, a unique form of comedy, with language as its subject, the emblem of man's relationship to other men and to the universe. It is a comedy, moreover, that is wildly funny, as it is liberating and educative. In some of his more recent work—with either its literalizations of metaphysical issues (which create a unique form of fable) or with its new dialogue forms—he creates an even more poetic and diffuse style. One may associate the brilliant verbal collage with the earlier and main body of his writing, and the more ineffable, infinitely suggestive and polyphonic techniques of poetry and musical composition with some of the more recent material. . . .

Barthelme is wonderfully interesting and funny: more important, he is remarkably liberating. Our pleasure comes not in figuring out how his people use words, or the sources of his parody, but rather we revel in his dazzling and endlessly provocative verbal textures. He may be aware that language constricts and that the mind tends to operate in structures, but he is unique in creating for us through his wonderful elegance the great and abundant world. He demands a sophisticated reader, for the better read and more sensitive to language and style one is, the more fun he will have, since Barthelme seems to have read everything. Unlike Eliot, however, whose literariness was didactic and in many ways, an end in itself—because it pointed back to a time of former value—Barthelme's vast information is but his means of stimulating us to a recognition of the limitations as well as the meanings of past formulations. Ultimately, Barthelme wishes us to break free and take pleasure in the world his thick textures evoke.

Lois Gordon. Donald Barthelme (Twayne, 1981),<br>pp. xi–xii, 33

Barthelme can probably write any way he wants to. He has chosen to remain a comic writer whose subject matter is disorder. (This phrase will fit Voltaire, Twain, and Beckett.) He has given no hint of a predilected order, and I can't think of one that wouldn't depress him. He accepts the absurdity of everything with the clarity of a saint or the absoluteness of a nihilist. He does not bereave us of our intelligence, our wit, our material comforts. He lets us keep every advantage we have against an absurd and futile existence, and proceeds to show us the absurdity and futility of our best and brightest, especially these.

His method is simplicity itself. There are no more contexts. Every attempt at ceremony parodies itself. Barthelme relocates our world back in Eden, apple in hand, wiseacre snake hissing psychiatry, advertising, marketing, personality tips, economics, weight watching, art appreciation, group therapy, our lovely brassy swinging culture from Philosophy 700 (Kierkegaard to Sartre) to bongo drums in the subway. But we feel suddenly naked, embarrassed, and unwelcome in the garden. Barthelme doesn't know why we feel this way either, but he can focus our feeling into a bright point that can raise a blister.

Guy Davenport. Book World. Oct. 25, 1981, p. 5

# ● BEATTIE, ANN (1947–    )

Something of Updike's attentiveness to ordinary human encounters distinguishes Ann Beattie's *Chilly Scenes of Winter*, a fine first novel which records the reluctant passage into adulthood of a twenty-seven-year-old survivor of the Woodstock generation. The novel incorporates characters and situations Beattie had treated earlier in her *New Yorker* stories, nineteen of which have been gathered under the title *Distortions* and released as a companion to the novel. But the novel is a more interesting and significant performance, richer in psychological nuance and in documentary power. Though there are many isolated passages in *Distortions* that exhibit Beattie's descriptive care and her talent for truthful dialogue, only one of the stories, "Snake's Shoes," has the sustained authority of the novel. One reason for the novel's superiority is that it is less tendentious than the stories, less confined by neo-absurdist attitudes toward contemporary experience. The novel is thus less somber than the stories and registers on every page a lively, generous alertness to the antic or comic in human relations. The characters in *Chilly Scenes* are respected more consistently than their counterparts in the stories, and although their vivid idiosyncrasies are always comically before us, what is odd or distinctive in their behavior belongs to their personalities, is rooted in Beattie's powers of observation and dramatic representation. Too often in the stories, in contrast, one feels the pressure of a surrealist program, the influence of Barthelme and Pynchon, behind the author's choice of details or in the often schematic resolution of her plots.

*Chilly Scenes* is written in the present tense and relies heavily on dialogue and on a purified declarative prose not unlike good Hemingway, but much funnier. This disciplined young novelist takes care to differentiate even her minor characters, and one of her most memorable cameo players declares herself only as a voice through the telephone—a nervous, guilty mother trying to trace her wayfaring daughter in two brief conversations that momentarily distract the protagonist during this final winter of his prolonged adolescence. The hero himself is wonderfully alive: a gentle bewildered man, extravagantly loyal to old friends and to the songs of the 'sixties, drifting through a final nostalgia for the mythologies of adversary selfhood he absorbed in college and toward an embarrassed recognition of his hunger for such ordinary adventures as marriage and fatherhood. The unillusioned tenderness that informs Beattie's portrait of her central character is a rare act of intelligence and mimetic art.

David Thorburn. YR. Summer, 1977, pp. 585–86

I can think of no other American writer save Thomas Pynchon who has found so wide and respectful an audience so early in her career. No one who has a serious interest in contemporary fiction can fail to be aware of Beattie's abrupt and alarming stories. Their publication in book form [*Distortions*] marks, I believe, a genuine event in the national life.

I suppose that one first feels struck by Beattie's consummate technical virtuosity. Her frigid prose, the shocking inexorableness of her humor and narrative designs, the macabre and spare efficiency of her thought, conspire to project her tales as actual—if rather awful—occurrences of modernist existence. I have called Beattie's prose cold: but one must read this most wicked and witty writer very closely indeed. It is true that she assembles as subjects a grotesque community of dwarfs, fats, gargoyles, and sluts, a bizarre collection of the lonely, the disoriented, and the dispossessed. Never, though, does she permit her figures to seem merely apathetic or aimlessly malcontent. Nor does she ever dismiss them as freaks. Beattie constructs her stories from within a soft and subtle sensibility of sympathy, participation, and hopefulness. She understands that, however capricious or queer, her characters' pains have their origin less in the morasses of individual neurosis than in the insipidity of the culture at large, the withering vapidity of the historical processes which envelop one and with which one must manage to coexist in some sort of emotional relation. It is the sign of her extraordinary intelligence and gentleness that Beattie considers her fictionalized people to be as human as their author; that she regards her own suffering as conterminous with that of her roughly satirized characters.

Beattie comprehends, this is to say, that we are driven into our misery and peculiarity because, appropriately, we cannot accommodate the abstraction and absurdity which surround us. Her characters fervently want to feel; especially they long to love. But the rapidity and monstrousness of contemporary history, the dearth of external supports for even the minimal impulses of human life, seem to the stories' people to invalidate the very possibility of achieving affective experience.

Peter Glassman. HdR. Autumn, 1977, p. 447

The characters who populate [*Secrets and Surprises*] came of age during the 1960's. They are, on the whole, a nice-looking bunch of people who have never suffered from any of the basic wants. Most of them, for reasons often unexplained, share a mistrust of passion and conversation. . . . They exist mainly in a stateless realm of indecision and—all too often—rather smug despair. . . .

Frequently, in these stories, things are substitutes for the chancier commitment to people; things people buy or live with or give one another are asked to bear the responsibility of objective correlatives, but too often they become a mere catalogue of trends. The reader is left holding an armful of objects and wondering what emotional responses they were meant to connect him with.

Perhaps the best level on which to enjoy these stories is as a narrative form of social history. Miss Beattie has a coolly accurate eye for the *moeurs* of her generation. . . . But a sharp eye for *moeurs* doesn't add up to a full fiction any more than the attitude of irony can be said to represent a full human response.

Gail Godwin. NYT. Jan. 14, 1979, p. 14

In the six years since her work first began to appear in *The New Yorker*,

Ann Beattie has become for many readers the representative young American novelist and short-story writer. Her two collections of stories— *Distortions* (1976) and *Secrets and Surprises* (1979)—and her novel *Chilly Scenes of Winter* (1976) won the praise of critics and reviewers and of older and established writers as diverse as John Updike and Mary Lee Settle. But her cultural significance lies as much, if not more, in the devotion and self-recognition she inspires among younger readers: people in their twenties and early thirties who graduated from college as the Sturm und Drang of the 60's faded into the anxious laid-back narcissism of the late 70's.

Her new novel at once confirms her status and marks a considerable advance on her previous work: *Falling in Place* is stronger, more accomplished, larger in every way than anything she's done, and its publication is a fitting occasion for a look at both her work and her curious celebrity.

Her fiction has none of the usual gimmicks and attractions that create a cult: it's not conspicuously witty or bizarre or sexy or politically defiant or eventful; in fact, it offers so colorless and cool a surface, so quiet a voice, that it's sometimes hard to imagine readers staying with it. Her subject matter, too, is deliberately banal: she chronicles the random comings and goings of disaffected young people who work in dull jobs or drop out, and spend a lot of time doing and feeling practically nothing except that low-grade depression Christopher Lasch has called the characteristic malaise of our time. This tepid nihilism or defeated shopping-mall consumerism is depicted in a deadpan, superrealistic style: I am not a camera but a videotape machine.

Of course, banality has many literary uses. But Ann Beattie's gray subaqueous world has none of the existential terror of Samuel Beckett's seemingly banal subject matter, or the hidden menace of Harold Pinter's social banality; there's none of the esthetic delight and wit of Donald Barthelme's intentionally banal, pop-art verbal collages, or of the apocalyptic and fully orchestrated angst, the doomed banality of Joan Didion's novels and essays. Ann Beattie's sad, bleak books are a far cry from the zany, black-humored flights of such earlier cult writers as Kurt Vonnegut or Richard Brautigan. The characters who populate the works of such recent "younger" novelists as Robert Stone, John Irving, Mary Gordon or Leslie Epstein seem in comparison as brightly colored and energetic as the characters in a Verdi opera. . . .

Inevitably these studies in domestic sorrow recall the stories of J.D. Salinger or John Cheever or John Updike: Ann Beattie's world, like theirs, is a miserable surburban purgatory inhabited by grieving wraiths. But the extraordinary literary color, shape and motion that animate the work of those older New Yorker writers are qualities Ann Beattie turns away from. Her stories are defiantly underplayed and random, trailing off into inconsequentiality, ending with a whimper or, at best, an embarrassed grin. And unlike her predecessors, she has no grand conservative vision buried deep in the background of her books. . . .

Her books exhibit a kind of Quaalude schizzy artistry; they're held together by an angry adolescent's sharp-eyed, deadpan delivery—less is more, right?—by an irony so uniformly spread around the imagined world that nearly all color and feeling are leached away, an irony that becomes a kind of self-defensive verbal tic, an irony without reference to any higher, deeper, unironically embraced standards, not even esthetic standards. . . .

Yet nothing Ann Beattie has written could quite prepare us for her new novel, *Falling in Place*. It's like going from gray television to full-color movies. Not that her themes or settings have changed that much, but there's a new urgency to the characters' feelings and a much greater range and number of characters and points of view. . . .

Richard Locke. *NYT*. May 11, 1980, pp. 1, 38

Compared to the earlier stories, these [in *The Burning House*] are less grotesque, more narrowly and intensely focused, more accomplished; they are also less outrageous and less outraged and more sympathetic to their characters. The mood is not bloody-minded; rather it is sorrowful. Most of the stories are about the process of separating, but there are no causes proposed, only affects, and thus no one is seen as responsible for the pain. The result is a certain moral attenuation. This is not hell but limbo, which some writers have located on the moon: That's where the space cadets end up.

No one is better at the plangent detail, at evoking the floating, unreal ambiance of grief. I would say Ann Beattie is at her best here, except that I think she can do even better. One admires, while becoming nonetheless slightly impatient at the sheer passivity of these remarkably sensitive instruments. When that formidable technique is used on a subject large enough for it, the results will be extraordinary indeed. Still, that's like caviling because Wayne Gretsky misses one shot. If Miss Beattie were a ballerina you could sell tickets to the warm-ups.

Margaret Atwood. *NYT*. Sept. 26, 1982, p. 34

# BELLOW, SAUL (1915–    )

Most critics, I think, would agree that Saul Bellow's greatest difficulty lies in his plots. He rewrote *Herzog* thirteen times, he tells us, turning it like "a prayer wheel"; and in *Mr. Sammler's Planet* and *Humboldt's Gift*, he seems to have thrown up his hands: contrivance and improbability in these novels will do. Why? Why does the man who so brilliantly crafted *Seize the Day* now accept something rough, unsymmetrical, and even corny?

One answer is obvious: Bellow has always flirted with the loose or episodic. *The Adventures of Augie March* was a smash hit, and *Humboldt* is in many ways a return to the earlier "fantasy holiday," as Bellow called it in the 1950s. Bellow has two modes: intense, closely textured, moral; and light, energetic, open. *The Victim, Seize the Day*, and, yes, *Herzog* represent the former while *Augie March, Sammler*, and *Humboldt* represents the latter. Bellow clearly finds great pain in his plots and is tempted for good or ill to cut loose, to stop worrying about his novel's shape. Fiction should be *interesting*, he believes, and even fun, like the old Chicago cornball humor he loved in Vaudeville and gave a try at in his play *The Last Analysis*. Simply put, Bellow fears the dangers of constriction, of polishing the life out of a work. . . .

Bellow's most obvious obstacle to plot lies in the fact that he is a realist—perhaps the reason that he wants a plot in the first place. A novel such as *Herzog* reflects Bellow's need for distance from his material, which is usually autobiographical, we're told, and embodies Bellow's struggle to control what amounts to a superabundance of material, a realistic world so weighty with detail that it's most oppressive. Plot in Bellow's work is hard won, wrested from a confusing density and multiplicity of people, ideas, events, and sensation. It's so hard won that we might well claim that the struggle *is* the plot, as all the protagonists seek to move from the overwhelming richness of experience to some kind of peace and clarity.

Here Bellow's very strength creates the obstacle, for no one catches the specifics of face and light and city as well as he. His texture is so intense, so vivid, that he must be tempted continually to write for the page. At the same time, such intensity must threaten to overthrow his plot—surely he struggles to control it. And much the same might be said of his characters. . . .

So Bellow loves energetic, driven characters who have a size and vitality that make them hard to control—so hard to control that the protagonist finds himself bullied by them, shoved about, as each tries to pull him *his* way.

And then the characters are inseparable from their ideas, which also fill Bellow's pages with a confusing abundance. Bellow often has sought a plot that would contain a number of ideologies and has imagined a quest that is mental, as he seeks to dramatize nothing less than the act of thinking. And yet there are too many thoughts finally for the plot line to be easy, since it is an *idea* after all which provides the shape of a novel. . . . In a way, Bellow is a victim not only of our present distrust of any plot, but of our incredibly high demands for the ones we do accept. The New Critics have taught us to demand that a conclusion end a novel in a memorable way, summarizing all that went before and illuminating it, crystallizing the whole book in a single glowing image or scene. Never mind that such a scene near the end of a long traditional novel might well break the tone. We're perfectionists when we talk about structure and accept only an inspired unity. It's fitting, in view of such conflicts and inconsistencies, that Bellow forge his successful plots from the very obstacles that have plagued him.

Keith Opdahl. *MFS*. Spring, 1979, pp. 15, 17, 28

In his exploration of stereotypes in *Mr. Sammler's Planet*, Bellow turned away from the Jewish milieu that dominated his earlier fiction and American Jewish writing generally—Jewish immigrant life in the ghettos of America's large cities or the second and third generation move to the suburbs and assimilation. Instead, he chose a painful "other" for the Americanized Jewish community—the life of a survivor of Nazi atrocity, a man returned from the dead and the madness of the Holocaust and deposited in the insane landscape of urban America in the '60s. If the flight to the suburbs is in part a flight away from the visibility of human failure and suffering in cities, then a novel about a survivor of genocide living on the deteriorating upper West Side of New York City is bound to be disturbing to many Jewish readers, seeking more obvious images from their own lives. But more importantly, a novel about several Jewish survivors of Nazi persecution that does not present suffering as ennobling, but rather as crippling, undercuts any sentimental myths about hard won moral lessons or the spiritual rewards of tragedy. Instead, Bellow does present a vision of human community and moral accountability, but *despite* suffering, not because of it.

*Mr. Sammler's Planet* is Bellow's most Jewish novel because it deals directly with the most important events of Jewish history in this century—the Holocaust, the state of Israel, and American Jewry's relation to both. Moreover, the major values embodied in the novel are basic tenets of Jewish life, although they are not exclusively Jewish: a reverence for life and an unwavering belief in human survival under any circumstances; an emphasis on reason and human intellect, part of a long tradition of interpretation and commentary on scripture; a preference for good deed and actions over contemplation, the concept of *mitzvoth*. These values—which constitute a rejection of despair, irrationalism, or madness as illuminating and consciousness for its own sake—are the components of Saul Bellow's humanistic vision of the world and run counter to what he has defined as literary modernism.

Hana Wirth-Nesher and Andrea Cohen Malamut.

*MFS*. Spring, 1979, p. 61

Bellow's resistance to alienation has for the most part taken the form of an individual's struggle to define those qualities which identify him as human, qualities which, for Bellow, emerge sometimes in opposition to, sometimes as a function of, the belief that goodness can be achieved only in the company of other men. In exploring these alternatives, Bellow has demonstrated an overriding concern for the ordinary circumstances of daily reality. "While our need for meanings is certainly great," he has written, "our need for concreteness, for particulars, is even greater." In approaching the reality of individuals who actually live and actually die, however, Bellow has evidenced a good deal of anxiety about a facticity that smothers the imagination. "The facts begin to crowd me," Henderson complains, "and soon I get a pressure in the chest." Bellow has responded to the same pressure. American fiction, he complained not long after the publication of *Henderson* [*the Rain King*], had become characterized by a concern for documentation animated neither by the theoretical structure that informed Zola's naturalism nor the feeling or the view of fate that described Dreiser's social novels. More recently, he has objected to the accountability to fact which the society holds the demands of the artist no less than of the scientist or the technical expert in any field. Writing of the difficulty of the artist in a modern, technological society, Bellow has remarked that "the artist has less power to resist the facts than other men. He is obliged to note the particulars. One may even say that he is condemned to see them." In this shift from the artist's need to the social demand for fact as a compelling principle of composition, Bellow anticipated a tendency which, as Pearl K. Bell has recently noted, has come to extend even to the popular novel—Bell cites as representative examples Arthur Hailey's *Wheels*, James Michener's *Centennial*, James Clavell's *Shogun*, and prominently, Herman Wouk's *War and Remembrance*—which formerly defined itself by a concern for narrative movement. Though Bellow continues to insist on the importance of giving weight to the particular, such weight, he argues, need not be in quantifiable terms any more than art should fulfill a compensatory function in restoring the alienated modern individual to psychic health. Rather, factual authority proceeds from an imaginative faculty that, with Henry

James, Bellow insists must maintain its regard for the story as story and must express man's "intuition that his own existence is peculiarly significant.". . .

Accordingly, despite his concern for social conditions, Bellow has shown little interest in specific social movements or political issues. Environment has functioned less as an influence on events and characters than as a projection of their inner conflict, a symbol as well as an agent of inhuman darkness. Bellow's protagonists are thus placed in a social environment but oppressed by personal and natural forces that obscure the resulting tensions by developing them in oblique relation to their framing situations. . . .

There is, then, in Bellow's fiction a fundamental division between a moral concern for the way things look and feel and an insistence on a more meaningful ideality, antecedent to such everyday striving and projected by characters indistinguishable from the authorial voice, whose narrow consciousness of a world displaces its portrayal through an independent perspective.

Stanley Trachtenberg. In *Critical Essays on Saul Bellow*, ed. Stanley Trachtenberg (G. K. Hall, 1979), pp. xiii–xiv

The good thing about *The Dean's December* . . . is that it is by Saul Bellow, and therefore possesses wit, vividness, tenderness, brave thought, earthy mysticism, and a most generous, searching, humorous humanity; the bad thing about it, or at least not so good, is that it also is *about* Saul Bellow, in an uncomfortable, indirect, but unignorable way. . . .

Bellow believes in the soul; this is one of his links with the ancients, with the great books. At the same time, like those great books, he feels and conveys the authentic heaviness in which our spirits are entangled; he has displayed for thirty years an unsurpassedly active and pungent awareness of the corporeal, of the mortal, of human creatureliness in all its sexual and assertive variety. He is not just a very good writer, he is one of the rare writers who when we read them feel to be taking mimesis a layer or two deeper than it has gone before. His lavish, rippling notations of persons, furniture, habiliments, and vistas awaken us to what is truly there. Such a gift for the actual is not unnaturally bound in with a yen toward the theoretical; for how do we see but by setting ourselves to see? From *Augie March* on, a sense of intellectual quest moves Bellow's heroes and is expected to move his readers. The quest in *The Dean's December* is narrow enough to meet concentrated resistance. . . .

Bellow has it in him, great poet and fearless mental venturer that he is, to write one of those unclassifiable American masterpieces like "Walden." But such a book must ramify from a firm, simple center, and this *The Dean's December* does not possess.

John Updike. NY. Feb. 22, 1982, pp. 120, 127–28

## BERGER, THOMAS (1924–    )

Thomas Berger's fifth novel [*Who Is Teddy Villanova?*] is mainly a parody of detective thrillers; his well-known *Little Big Man* was a parody of Westerns. According to the jacket copy, in *Who Is Teddy Villanova?* we will recognize the familiar "seedy office," "down-at-the-heels shamus," "procession of sinister, chicane, or merely brutal men and scheming, vicious, but lovely women" and a "sequence of savage beatings." All this is true. The novel contains much that is conventional in detective thrillers. Still, one needn't know the books of Dashiell Hammett or Raymond Chandler in order to appreciate Berger's witty burlesque of their characters and situations.

Berger's style, which is one of the great pleasures of the book, is something like S. J. Perelman's—educated, complicated, graceful, silly, destructive in spirit, and brilliant—and it is also something like Mad Comics—densely, sensuously detailed, unpredictable, packed with gags. Beyond all this, it makes an impression of scholarship—that is, Berger seems really to know what he jokes about. This includes not only Hammett and Chandler, but also Racine, Goethe, Ruskin, Elias Canetti, New York and the way its residents behave. Essentially, then, Berger's style is like itself insofar as it is like other styles. And his whole novel—in its wide ranging reference to cultural forms both high and pop—is like a huge verbal mirror. Its reflections are similar to what we see in much contemporary literature—hilarious and serious at once.

Leonard Michaels. NYT. March 20, 1977, p. 1

Thomas Berger belongs, with Mark Twain and Mencken and Philip Roth, among our first-rate literary wiseguys. Savvy and skeptical, equipped with a natural eloquence and a knack for parody, he has been expertly flinging mud at the more solemn and self-important national myths for 20 years. In *Little Big Man*, the best-known of his books—for, alas, the usual reason—he brilliantly savaged the legendary American West. *Who Is Teddy Villanova?*, perhaps the funniest 300 pages of 1977, took on the world of the tough-guy detective novel. For all its clowning, it performed a serious service in deflating the bloody and rather vainglorious cult of

Bogart-out-of-Philip Marlowe. Mr. Berger's method, with these and the other mythical landscapes he has explored in his nine novels, is to set them down in his droll, relentlessly straight-faced prose, so as to empty them of romance, and let the brutal/crummy facts stare out. His pages swarm with bawdy puns and slapstick and bookish in-jokes; but even at his most absurd, his intrinsic tone is that of a hard-nosed realist who won't let the myths distort his essentially grouchy idea of the way things really are.

Grouchy, emphatically, is the word. In a review of Mr. Berger's Reinhart books—*Crazy in Berlin, Reinhart in Love*, and *Vital Parts*—Richard Schickel pointed out what is distinctive about Mr. Berger as a satirist. It is that he is more piqued by Good than by Bad. Doing good in a world that is mostly bad can have bizarre or disastrous consequences. This wry paradox is at the heart of Mr. Berger's interest in Good King Arthur and his Knights of the Round Table, and in their incorrigibly noble chivalric code. *Arthur Rex*, Mr. Berger's newest novel, is his splendid, satiric retelling of the legend of Camelot. . . .

Mr. Berger's revisions are most authentic, most profound, when the admixture of parody is strongest. At those times—a good three-fourths of the book—he is never merely a parodist after all, but also a compelling yarnspinner in his own right; a Tolkien for the worldly indeed, stripped of their 19th-century sentiment by the author's deeply anti-Romantic ways, the stories have a leaner, more strident look than they have had in a long time. Not T. H. White's *The Once and Future King*, nor John Steinbeck's mostly antiquarian version, but Thomas Berger's *Arthur Rex* is the Arthur book for our time.

John Romano. *NYT*. Nov. 12, 1978, pp. 3, 62

It is a mystery of literary criticism that Thomas Berger, one of the most ambitious, versatile, and entertaining of contemporary novelists, is hardly ever mentioned in the company of America's major writers. He is a wit, a fine caricaturist, and his prose crackles with Rabelaisian vitality. His phenomenal ear for oddnesses of speech appropriates as readily the grey malapropisms of the silent majority in *Reinhart in Love* . . . as the winning tall-tale garrulousness of *Little Big Man*, a savory reminiscence of the Cheyenne Indians in frontier days. . . .

Moreover, it cannot be said that he ever writes from a universal, or even an ordinary eye-level perspective. He is a magic realist; . . . Berger's focus, his grasp of detail, is sharper and smaller than life. He will allow something infinitesimal to catch his eye and brood upon it, even as he overlooks a larger emotion or design. In the past the disturbing effect of this was somewhat offset by the sheer cascade into his bulky novels of tangy physical images, raunchy episodes, and eccentric wayside characters with an extravagant gift of gab. In his new book, *Neighbors*, there are no such fringe benefits. This strange exasperating little story has been pared down to the taunting colloquy among four characters on a dead-end street in an unnamed suburb. We see them through a pane that is blindingly clear and yet so distorting as to make them seem demented. . . .

He is in fact terrifyingly methodical and consciously satanic in this psychological chiller whose hero is victimized mainly by his own weakness and ambivalence. The plot dramatizes a conviction Berger has held for a long time. In the fictional foreword to *Little Big Man*, the narrator observes: "Each of us, no matter how humble, from day to day finds himself in situations in which he has the choice of acting either heroically or craven." Is Berger telling us in *Neighbors* that cravenness, uncertainty about our own feelings, breeds aggression in others? That obsequiousness is really distrust, and once suspected will be returned in kind? *Neighbors* is a cool study in taking advantage, a chess game in which each move is followed inexorably by the countermove the player leaves himself open for. The victim is at the mercy of some force not larger than himself as happens in Kafka's *The Trial* but, far more grueling, exactly equal to himself. That is to say, everyone gets his just psychological deserts.

Isa Kapp. *NR*. April 26, 1980, pp. 34–35

# BERRYMAN, JOHN (1914–1972)

It is somehow fitting that his final book should find its noblest moments in a tribute to Beethoven since Berryman took seriously the idea of "the mysterious late excellence which is the crown/of our trials & our last bride" (*Dream Song*), an excellence that he admired in Yeats, Williams, and Goya, as well as in Beethoven. That his own last books are not among his most impressive is, of course, distressing, and we are left with the inevitable speculations about where his art would have taken him had he chosen to live—he was, after all, only fifty-seven when he died. Whether he would have gained "the crown of our trials" is impossible to say, though *Delusions, Etc.*, which seems to be the product of a mind at the end of its tether, suggests that this is unlikely. The only thing we can be certain of, however, is that he would have surprised us with an altogether unexpected mode—he never repeated himself, each of his books being as different from the one that precedes it as that book, in turn, is from its immediate predecessor. Who would have predicted that *Delusions, Etc.*, would follow *Love & Fame*, that *Love & Fame* would emerge from the *Songs*, that the songs themselves would be the next step after *Mistress*

*Bradstreet*? Anyone willing to speculate on the sort of work Berryman might have written in his sixties (or seventies!) is either clairvoyant or reckless.

What we do know, of course, is that his final books, whatever their virtues (and these, particularly in the case of *Love & Fame*, are considerable), represent a falling off from his strongest work. We should not regret their existence, however, disappointed as we may be that they are not more consistently fine. Nor should we, in our haste to evaluate Berryman's overall achievement, attach undue importance to these rather desperate works. To do so would be to lose sight of the fact that this man, whatever his personal and aesthetic crises, gave us the *Sonnets* and *Homage to Mistress Bradstreet*.

Joel Connaroe. HC. Oct., 1976, pp. 11–12

The "typical" Berryman poem presents a character radically at odds with his environment who, through a process of suffering and self-examination, comes to a realization of the importance of either love or work or both. In both cases it is the character's responsibility to the culture which is rescued from the threats of irresponsibility (on the personal level, usually sex, drink, aggression or the desire for death; on the cultural level, aggression in any number of forms). Stated in other terms, Berryman's characters go through a process of rebellion and submission, finding, however, in that submission a means of triumph. The world doesn't change (or changes in only relatively minor ways), but the character finds a satisfactory means of adapting to it. Mistress Bradstreet, Henry, and the Berryman of the late poems submit to the needs (and joys) of the family and the will of God.

This is grossly oversimplified, of course, and stated so simply leaves out much of what makes Berryman's poetry valuable. For such simple solutions are not and cannot be arrived at simply, and it is the presentation of the enormous and complex difficulties, caused by both internal and external factors, that distinguishes Berryman's work. . . .

Gary Q. Arpin. The Poetry of John Berryman<br>(Kennikat, 1978), pp. 10–11

Almost from the beginning of his work on *The Dream Songs*, Berryman felt urged to confer a structure upon the poem. He succeeded best in commending certain models to the interest of its unfolding. Provoked by what he took to be the conventional exigencies of the long poem, he tried to inject a plot into material which had little intrinsic narrative direction apart from that of the natural order of events. . . . He wanted to submit the Songs (the sections of the poem) to the discipline of sequence and succession. He felt it important for them to imply a story. Continuity alone, whether of form and style, or of the creative life which the Songs composed, was just not enough. His aim was to impose an absolute form on a poem constituted by multiple occasions. . . .

He could not help looking ahead, however, trying to anticipate the nature of the work. He needed to control the direction of its progress (which was a type of wanting to control his own life), not to surrender it; to project its plot (and then to enforce it), rather than to allow it self-definition. The effort to chart the poem to a determinative point was in most respects a losing one, for its true character was that of chance, of segmented insights, and of occasional lucubrations. While working on his second volume of Dream Songs in 1966, Berryman told Jonathan Sisson that *His Toy, His Dream, His Rest* "has to be composed out of whatever I save." The statement may be seen as tantamount to an admission that his structural principle was one of elimination, of chance and discovery. During the following year he gave all his time to writing more and more Songs, with the result that Book VII came to be seriously (and perhaps pointlessly) distended with sections ordered and written more on the principle of a diary. Because of that difference of approach, the work as a whole is unbalanced and desultory in structure.

John Haffenden. *John Berryman: A Critical Commentary* (New York Univ. Pr., 1980), pp. 6–7

# BISHOP, ELIZABETH (1911–1979)

Elizabeth Bishop is constantly brought back to the particularities of earth: thus she is "contemplative." Yet her poems also demonstrate a search for understanding, for transcendence, for epiphany. She is a meditative poet. "Sandpiper," then, is strangely different from Blake's poem to which it alludes. For Bishop is more likely to find in grains of sand simply the marvel of various color (as the sandpiper does at the end of her poem) than she is "the world" as does Blake. Such "worlds" as those of color and infinite variety which the sandpiper sees in the sand do become for him transcendent "minute and vast and clear." Even with her apparent search for "vision," however, Bishop is much more likely to see the properties in a wild flower in some new way which provides self-understanding than she is to see them as "heaven," as does Blake—who is certainly the more visionary of the two poets. . . .

What characterizes Elizabeth Bishop's sensibility is a coalescence of realistic description and personal imagination. Her poetry results from a careful process of "looking." Such seeing is reflected in her accurate images. Experienced as maps to her own experiences, however, Bishop's poems emerge as a record of her own manner of seeing things as they are and more often than not of the carefully evolved epiphanic insights into their particular meaning for her.

Sybil P. Estess. *SoR*. Autumn, 1977, pp. 721, 726

Admiring action, there may be behind Bishop's poems a fear of passivity in itself: the reduction of the status of the observer to that of the excluded. If one were to try to station the writer behind a movie camera in these poems, it would be hard to say from just what angle the movie was being shot. The object is everything, the viewer and the viewer's position—except by inference—the merest assumption. Yet how remarkably consistent that lens is, how particularly keen the eye behind it! There is a great deal to be said for scope, but more to be said, I think, for the absolutely achieved. These poems strike me as ageless; there are no false starts, no fake endings. None of the provincial statements of youth, none of the enticements of facility are allowed to enter. Starting with "The Map," we are in the hands of an artist so secure in the knowledge of what makes and doesn't make a poem that a whole generation of poets—and remarkably different ones—has learned to know what a poem is through her practice. She has taught us without a shred of pedagogy to be wary of the hustling of the emotions, of the false allurements of the grand. Rereading these poems, how utterly absent the specious is! There is no need to revise them for future editions, the way Auden revised and Marianne Moore revised and Robert Lowell revised. Nothing need be added, nothing taken away. They constitute a body of work in which the innovative and the traditional are bound into a single way of looking. From a poet's point of view, these poems are the ones of all her contemporaries that seem to me most to reward rereading.

Howard Moss. *WLT*. Winter, 1977, p. 33

The dignity and precision of Elizabeth Bishop's poetic delivery rely largely upon her imagery of detachment, an imagery that takes interior dilemmas and expresses them in terms of the exterior world of nature. In *Questions of Travel* such imagery draws the individual poems into a recognizable unity not only by physical recurrence, but also, more importantly, by complementing and interweaving the major themes. These themes (or, alternately, the dilemmas or questions of the title) include the permanent realm of the potential in human life, the puzzles of epistemology, and the temporary resolutions of the imagination. Corresponding to these themes, the categories of imagery are, respectively, images of transformation, of frames, and of suspension. Despite my abstract nomenclature, the imagery, by which I mean the entire physical world presented in the poem and not just its figurative language, consists of quite concrete, often ordinary objects. For instance, the imagery of transformation revolves mainly around water; of frames, around colors; and of suspension, around birds. Very rarely do the birds, colors, or water grow into deliberate symbols; instead, they serve more humbly as indicators of the interdependence of theme and imagery.

Ruth Quebe. *MPS*. 10, 1, 1980, p. 68

## BLACKMUR,   R.   P.   (1904–1965)

Blackmur was a poet. He published in his lifetime three volumes of verse and hoped that some of his work at least would stand. At present he has almost no readers. At a time when so little poetry is read, it is not surprising that a small voice like Blackmur's should not be heard. Some critics, like Denis Donoghue, in an introduction to a recent collected edition of the poems, regret that we have forgotten Blackmur and urge us to discover the poetry for ourselves. But Donoghue is a fine critic, and even he cannot persuade us that there is much in Blackmur to compel sustained attention. "Sometimes the knowledge in Blackmur's poems is not his own but what he recalls of Hopkins' knowledge," he concedes. Or one hears the music of Eliot, or Pound, or Yeats: "But mostly the knowledge is his own." Perhaps. But then, the issue is not whether Blackmur occasionally broke free of his models and wrote in a voice that sounded more like his own than theirs. The fact is that, even in his best poems, Blackmur sounds more like a man who wants to write poetry than like a true poet. . . .

For Blackmur, ideas could be as interesting as they were for another sort of critic entirely. And he showed, in his later work especially, that politics and cultural institutions could be quite as absorbing to the literary mind as poems or stories. We go on with the question of content here because it is so central to our concern with poetical thinking. The content Blackmur could not honor was a content that was nothing but a sentiment, an attitude or an idea. He was ready to accept that certain ideas were more attractive than others, or that a particular attitude would readily serve the gifts of a particular poet. But in themselves these ideas or attitudes were not the facts that could inspire a final sympathy or allegiance. Eliot's mind was a fact in the more final sense, his better poems an enactment of his sensibility that would stand, permanently, as an emblem of a certain kind of possibility realized. Call it the possibility of a mind divided against itself but working strenuously all the same at a wholeness it associated with utter singleness of purpose.

Robert Boyers. *R. P. Blackmur: Poet-Critic*
(Univ. of Missouri Pr., 1980), pp. 8–9, 64–65

Blackmur's contribution to literature may be found in the form of the critical essays he wrote during the later phases of his career. The Library of Congress essays, in particular, represent the form of the critical essay that marks his unique contribution. These essays were his attempt to raise criticism to a new plane of discourse.

Briefly put, Blackmur attempted to incorporate into these essays an expression of his aesthetic experience of literature and of culture. Thus, in effect, he tried to "open" the form of the critical essay by giving equal emphasis to the nonrational expression of his own experience. Prior to Blackmur's practice, critical essayists had always tried to be, with more or less success, proponents of rational thinking. Blackmur, however, made the irrational, the emotional, part of the critical essay. . . .

Blackmur did not mean to discount the rational understanding of his essays. Rather, he sought what he thought should be a *total* experience that included the irrational with the rational. In this desire he was seeking for the art of criticism what modern artists had sought for painting, poetry, the novel, and music. Blackmur did not want his criticism to point to an experience but to *be* an experience. In this way he extended the scope and the form of literary criticism.

In addition to raising criticism to the level of a legitimate art form, Blackmur also contributed a whole body of work that will have permanent value as long as there is a Western culture. Throughout his work Blackmur questioned the lack of standards to judge not only art but life, liberty, and the pursuit of happiness. He was against the democratic inclusiveness of the spirit that meant whatever is done must perforce be "creative." At the same time he agonized over the question of creativity and its manifestations in a democratic, romantic age. In his own work he applied the scrupulosity he admired so much in Henry Adams; that is, he took pains to give his essays a "form" as well as a content. Put another way, Blackmur thought he could control unbridled romantic effusions of spirit by insisting upon a rigorous attention to form.

All of his work has a certain tension that derives from this conflict between form and content, reason and imagination. Blackmur fought the same battle that every twentieth-century artist has fought and must fight. His particular art form was criticism, but it could have been poetry or the novel. In the last analysis, his work must be seen as his unique attempt to create order and meaning out of the undifferentiated chaos of the spirit. So Blackmur becomes one with the many who have built their own edifices of meaning through art.

Gerald J. Pannick. *Richard Palmer Blackmur*
(Twayne, 1981), pp. 155–57

# BLY, ROBERT (1926– )

The stimulus injected by Robert Bly into the poets of the Emotive Imagination has not been solely as translator, editor, and theoretician. *Silence in the Snowy Fields*, a 1962 collection of poems which had appeared earlier over a period of almost ten years in the magazines, was the first volume demonstrating extensively the realized potentialities of the Emotive Imagination. Bly's second volume, *The Light around the Body*, demonstrated his expanding interest in political poetry. The 1973 volumes *Jumping Out of Bed* and *Sleepers Joining Hands* disclose his enduring predilection for the Emotive Imagination, even as the political poems have diminished as a result of America's disengagement in Vietnam.

Bly's success as a poet depends of course on the quality of the individual poems, but . . . his own work has been indisputably shaped by his long interest in and translation of poets like [Pablo] Neruda and [Georg] Trakl. Moreover, his poetry also inevitably becomes a kind of illustration of his own poetics, outlined, as we have also seen, in scores of essays and reviews. When Bly says, for example, that a poem is "something that penetrates for an instant into the unconscious," one expects his own verse to show how that is so. . . .

In the past quarter-century of Bly's publication of poetry, he appears to have found reinforcements of and elaborations upon a fundamental method which sprang up almost at once in his work and which was clearly worked out by the time of his first volume in 1962, *Silence in the Snowy Fields*. He has not departed radically from the use of the Emotive Imagination as we have defined it, and his work, perhaps more than the other poets treated here, represents a continuing and long-range experimentation with its resources. Most of Bly's poems are whimsical and minor; they have no pretensions of being anything else. Frequently his political verse manages to go little beyond bald propaganda. His poetry finally belongs in the same context as his translations, as well as his criticism and editing. As an indefatigable man-of-letters, in the best sense of the term, Robert Bly has been a vital phenomenon in American poetry since mid-century.

> George S. Lensing and Ronald Moran. *Four Poets and the Emotive Imagination* (Louisiana State Univ. Pr., 1976), pp. 71, 85

My sense of Bly's poetry is that it exhibits the skill it does because of its author's high seriousness, but such a sense can only be averred, not demonstrated. However, we can register the characteristic energy of Bly's lyrics by exploring them as resolutions (not solutions, in the sense of problems disposed of, but resolutions, in the sense of a consciousness articulated) through which two apparently opposing compulsions redefine one another. One of these compulsions is most visible as theme, the other as style. Thematically, the concerns of meditative poetry, namely the structures of consciousness and the relation of fact and value, outline the range and subject of these poems. Poetry for Bly offers a criticism of life, but a criticism available only through discipline, by a rectification of thought and feeling. Bly's antiwar poetry doesn't settle for expressing humanistic values; rather, he alleges that the grossest forms of false consciousness are necessary for such inhumanity as a war to occur and that only through a fundamental relearning of the world can it be prevented. This accounts for Bly's aggressive, sometimes intemperate modernism: he sees the poet simultaneously as a solitary craftsman and as a moral scourge. . . .

What I think Bly's poetry enacts, especially in the strengths and weaknesses of *Camphor*, is the persistent desire of American poets simultaneously to celebrate the body and to incorporate the universal energies, thus making them available to all. How to domesticate the sublime? Bly's answer seems to be to deify the *truly* immediate, that is, the data of consciousness understood not as thought, but as bodily sensation. Bodily presence and process—the purview of natural history, with its emphasis on seeing, on turning the given into a specimen by an act of loving attentiveness to detail and change—thus become equated with bodily ecstasy—the evidence of religion, with its proffered hope that the bodies of men and women can become one body, which will manifest, in a Blakean way, the transforming and divine energies of the universe.

Charles Molesworth. *The Fierce Embrace: A Study of Contemporary American Poetry* (Univ. of Missouri Pr., 1979), pp. 116, 138

## BOGAN, LOUISE   (1897–1970)

It is [a] constant conflict between will and authority that shapes Bogan's poems. Because she herself unconsciously represented some of the strictures her spirit rebelled against, only form and symbol can express the tight, concentrated emotion of the unconscious struggling with the conscious. Although she strove always to make her poetry something beyond the narrowly personal and to cast out "small emotions with which poetry should not, and cannot deal," to be objective (a note on the worksheet indicating the poems to be published in the volume *The Sleeping Fury* says

". . . they must be as objective as possible"), it is often the personal emotion of the poet that informs the poem and gives authenticity to it. The emotion which is distanced by formal structures, sometimes distanced to the point of a "mask," a male persona, operates to illustrate the inherent conflict that the poem is really about. . . .

Her use of lyrical stanzas with second and fourth lines of rhyme or slant rhyme link the intellectual content of the poem with the subjective response to rhythm and sound. The appeal is to both the conscious and unconscious, and the imagery is of both: the images of the conscious of the first two stanzas and the images of the unconscious in the last two ("whispers in the glassy corridor" is especially wonderful in combining sound, imagery, and meaning). The tone is one of unhappy questioning rather than of being "contented with a thought/Through an idle fancy wrought." Her poem wonders about the human state that, by implication, is ruled by the same "forms and appetites" as the rest of nature, but aspires to more and therefore suffers. . . .

Louise Bogan once made the comment that highly formal poetry has always been obscure because the universe is difficult. Her own formal poetry is an acknowledgement of that difficulty, that obscurity, and of the complexity of modern truth.

Jacqueline Ridgeway. WS. 5, 2, 1977, pp. 141,<br>147–48

Louise Bogan was a poet who matured during the first half of this century and who embraced traditional forms, masks, and mythologies. Compared to contemporary women poets, she is neither direct, personal, or particular. Yet buried under the metrical decorum, the masks, the symbols, and the reticence of her poetry is a person who is painfully aware of her situation as a woman, and who tries to escape it. . . .

The strongest desire in Bogan's poetry has Emersonian overtones: she wants to recover a sense of wholeness in the face of the human passion for destructive analysis. Bogan dislikes anything that the human mind superimposes on the world because human interpretations or analyses are distortions of the unity of nature and experience. Her clearest expression of this dislike is in "Baroque Comment.". . .

"Masked Woman's Song" is extremely oblique and can only be understood by sifting it through the motifs in her other poems. . . . In Bogan's poetry men are always threatening or betraying. They try to pin women to words in "The Romantic," try to trap women in those forms "Coincident with the lie, anger, lust, oppression and death in many forms" in "Baroque Comment," and try to reduce women to heartless, emotionless servants who "return, return,/To meet forever Jim home on the 5:35," in "Evening in the Sanitarium.". . .

In ["Masked Woman's Song"] . . . Bogan writes that men have over-thrown the constructive values of life, like freedom and love, and have forced women to live, out of fear, at a distance, masked from the varieties of experience and the wellsprings of life. But such an interpretation must be made between the lines: Bogan's attitude toward men, as ever, is obscured by her restrained and elliptical style. Her true feelings are blurred by symbol, distanced by masks, muted by form.

Today, needless to say, such a style is rare, if not impossible, in a feminist poet. Where free verse is the exception in Bogan's poetry, some-thing like a sigh of relief in a wasteland of anxiety and repression, most contemporary women poets use free forms as a matter of course, for their spontaneity, directness, and freedom from objectification and unwanted literary associations. But contemporary women poets have much less to fear than Bogan did; feminism is more secure now and support groups abound. Yet Louise Bogan was one of the earlier women poets who pointed to a way out of the strangling forms and mentalities of traditional verse. If for no other reason than that, her life and her poetry deserve our interest and attention.

Patrick Moore. In *Gender and Literary Voice*, ed.
Janet Todd (Holmes and Meier, 1980), pp. 67–69,
78–79

## BOWLES,   JANE   (1917–1973)

It is difficult to imagine—especially in these days of celebrity-authors—a writer who would actually *prefer* a limited readership, but then Jane Bowles is not like other writers. She is original to the point of being unnerving, and it seems entirely possible that she wrote as much with the intention to exclude as to include. She is fated to remain a specialized taste because hers goes beyond a mere idiosyncrasy of style, an identifi-able semantic tic like Donald Barthelme's or William Gass's. One is tempted to make comparisons—to Ivy Compton-Burnett for the entrenched habit of irony, to Carson McCullers for the use of the grotesque —but they don't really hold up: she is both more human than the former and less sentimental than the latter. Bowles's voice is an uncompromis-ingly independent one and it bespeaks a vision of life so unflinching as to challenge most of our assumptions.

To read *My Sister's Hand in Mine* is to submit to a demanding pres-ence. Jane Bowles is one of those writers who can truly be said to inhabit a country of her own making. Although the specific geographical location might change, the emotional terrain is characteristically depleted, and one comes away with an unsettling image of projected solitude. . . .

Jane Bowles is a capricious weaver of spells; her stories often end as though they were about to begin again somewhere else—now you see the magic, now you don't. Perhaps that is because her fiction is conceived at such a rarified altitude; her characters are living in domesticated penal colonies. . . .

There is a persistent mystery at the heart of Jane Bowles's fiction. What is amazing, finally, is that fiction so intentionally whimsical, even perverse, should reverberate the way Bowles's does, igniting sparks of recognition on every page.

Daphne Merkin. *NR*. Feb. 11, 1978, pp. 30–31

If there is one common denominator in Mrs. Bowles's work, it is women's relentless search for autonomy and self-knowledge, for release from all conventional structures. And a demonic, frenzied search it becomes in Mrs. Bowles's hands. . . .

Of the 20th-century novelists who have written most poignantly about modern women's independence from men—Colette, Lessing, Kate Chopin, Jean Rhys, Jane Bowles come immediately to mind—the last three are consummate artists who have each spent several decades buried in oblivion. . . . As for Jane Bowles, whose oeuvre also concerns a redefinition of female freedom, a considerable silence has attended her work since the production of her play *In the Summer House* 25 years ago, notwithstanding the critical acclaim she has received. . . .

The theme of women's independence, and its frequent coefficients of solitude and potential destruction, have more often than not been limned with Lessingesque earnestness in a socio-realistic setting. So Mrs. Bowles's oeuvre is all the more unique because of its Grand Guignol hilarity, its constant surprises, and a blend of realism and grotesqueness that occasionally recalls Ronald Firbank. There is extraordinary tension between the sturdy, supernormal physical world she describes and the gloriously unpredictable, fantastic movements of the eccentric personages who inhabit it. . . .

Mrs. Bowles's acerbic genius for the *outré* does not leave it any grounds for comparison with Radclyffe Hall's sentimental tale [*The Well of Loneliness*]. Neither are her heroines' precipitous declines caused by any preference for lesbianism, for they seem as asexual as they are independent and nomadic, turning to the flesh as a symbol of independence without appearing to enjoy one moment of it. Their gloriously uninhibited carousing, their voluptuous liberation from all male discipline . . . has much more to do with a return to the permissive sexual androgyny of juvenile bonding than with any sexual preference. It is this very childlike playfulness that gives Mrs. Bowles's work its fey power and its luminous originality, and that may disconcert readers fond of predictably "female," "mature" heroines. . . .

In Mrs. Bowles's work, the traditional novelistic struggle between weak and strong characters ends inevitably in a draw. The rigorous pursuit of autonomy, and a rueful acceptance of its often tragic consequences, is the only heroic goal. For even the strongest are unmade by their failure to take into account "the terrible strength of the weak," and follow an equally drunken downward path to wisdom. There is a severe avoidance of all moralizing. It is left to the individual reader to determine whether Mrs. Bowles's heroines were better off in the shelter of their repressive marriages and inhibited spinsterhoods than in the anarchy of their libertinage.

Francine du Plessix Gray. NYT. Feb. 19, 1978,<br>pp. 3, 28

From the time she was a child Jane had had the sense of sin—a sin that she could never define except to say that it was hers and original, that which separated her from others. Her life had been spent in the doubleness of the knowledge of that sin and the evasion of the knowledge. She had been obsessed by Elsie Dinsmore and yet had mocked Elsie's obedience to her father and her even greater obedience to Jesus. She had read Simone Weil's work over and over, feeling an identity with her, but then she had laughed and said, "But I have a sensual side too." For years she had spoken about sin and salvation—no one understood it. Most people thought it was Jane being funny, as when she'd said, "Most of all I want to be a religious leader," and then laughed and said, "But of course I'm not."

That sin which she took to be her destiny was inseparable from her imagination. Her writing became both the evidence of the sin and also— by some turn within her—the religious sacrifice that was its expiation. In her work, from the beginning, the themes of sin and salvation were unrelenting: in the words of Miss Goering as a child, baptizing Mary, "Dear God . . . make this girl Mary pure as Jesus Your Son"; in the words of Miss Goering at the end of her journey, ". . . is it possible that a part of me hidden from my sight is piling sin upon sin as fast as Mrs. Copperfield?"; in the words that tell of Sadie's life, "She conceived of her life as separate from herself; the road was laid out always a little ahead of her by sacred hands. . . ."

If in the earliest works there was a double edge—the sense of belief and the other side of belief, both present and united by her wiles—as the years went on, as her work became only unfinished work, the voices of sin and salvation became more urgent. "My life is *not* my own," Bozoe Flanner screams at Janet Murphy. "Have you missed the whole point of my life?" And of a woman in an unfinished play, Jane wrote: "She believes that she has a second heart and because she believes this she can accept a lie and protect it—Her wild clinging to this false trust is a result of her not wishing to discover that she has only one heart after all. . . . She guards her false trust in order not to fall into her single heart—The single heart is herself—it is suffering—it is God—it is nothing. . . ."

Millicent Dillon. *A Little Original Sin: The Life and Works of Jane Bowles* (Holt, Rinehart and Winston, 1981), pp. 414–15

## BOWLES, PAUL (1910–    )

Paul Bowles has produced a large body of work, only a fraction of which is represented in the *Collected Stories*. He has published poetry, four novels, an autobiography and two travel essays. He has taped and translated an impressive number of oral stories in Moghrebi, a North African dialect. These translations are an achievement in themselves and also play a central part in the development of his short fiction. Bowles is moreover a composer of some standing, and has recorded a large collection of North African music. Nevertheless, fiction is the central pillar of his work, and his autobiography, poetry and journalism are only interesting galleries attached to the central structure, ornamental perhaps, but hardly essential. His novels have excellent qualities but only his first, *The Sheltering Sky*, deserves to be classed with the short fiction. . . .

The majority of the stories published in Bowles's first collection, *The Delicate Prey*, already exhibit a mature sense of subject and of technique. "A Distant Episode" is one of the best of these stories. The title reminds the reader that the events described are far removed from the west. It is an initiation story (Bowles has written a number of these), a meeting between the rule-bound west, represented by "the Professor," and the violence of North Africa. The Professor is a professor of linguistics; preoccupied by the structure of Language, he is incapable of communication. . . .

Like the Professor in "A Distant Episode," Bowles may seem to have returned to his starting point, surrealistic description having been replaced by kif dreams and automatic writing by oral texts. But to see his career as static or circular is a mistake. The early surrealism was an act of violence towards language, a literal dismembering. The stories collected here redirect this violence, allowing dismemberment an uneasy coherence. The seventeen-year-old could only appropriate a style; the intervening years have created a master capable of appropriating a culture.

H. C. Ricks. *ChiR*. Spring, 1980, pp. 83, 85, 88

[William Carlos] Williams' characteristically trenchant observation of one of Bowles' techniques is one that holds true for all the novels and short stories that Bowles has published since *The Sheltering Sky*: he is an author who works to avoid cliché by confronting his materials, not by sidling past them with the help of the codified tics and patterns of "fine writing." His work is unsettling, but rarely because of the raw materials, the content, of his stories. Rather, it is the acutely conscious attempt to deal with these materials honestly that enables him to transcend the content that, in other hands, might be the stuff of sensation or didacticism.

The language of Bowles' fiction is reticent and formal, but often brutal in its flat candor. No wonder Williams admired him. Over his work there lies a barely visible "haze" of anxiety or terror. His characters, once embarked upon the adventures that he invents for them, carry them through to the end; there is no point in a Bowles story at which one can say, with any certainty, *there* is where the story takes its turn. His stories do not take "turns," but follow strait and undeviating paths, the beginnings of which are anterior to their first words. We "come in" on them, as it were.

It is as if Bowles has made a compact with his readers, one that assumes that he and they know that people are weak, vacillating, self-serving, envious, and often base, as well as being, more often than not, irrational because of fixed and unexamined beliefs in country, class, religion, culture, and so on. Granting the existence of this compact, the stories may be seen as inevitable, their characters not so much caught in a web of problems as playing out, so to speak, their hands. In a curious way, the stories may be seen as modern variations on the Jonsonian use of medieval "humours.". . .

[He] is most at home in his work in a North African setting, usually Moroccan, and . . . most of his stories have to do with Arabs or with Arabs and their dealings with Americans or Europeans. I would say that much of Bowles' power and clarity, his freshness and eschewal of the banal has come about because he uses this material without resorting to condescension, awed delight, or sociological analysis: the specific world of Morocco is *there*.

Nowhere in Bowles do we find any hint of the exotic. His Arabs don't think of themselves as such, but as people who live the lives that have been given them. The brilliance of Bowles' work is rooted in the fact that his prose takes his non-western world for granted, and this matter-of-fact attitude is tacitly held in subtle opposition to what might be called the reader's expectations. We bring our great bag of *idées fixes* to Bowles' Morocco, and he calmly proceeds to empty it in front of us. Furthermore, Bowles' western characters are often seen to be carrying that same bag in the stories in which they appear: their reward for this cultural error is usually disaster. . . . He does what the good artist everywhere does: solves the problems he has created for himself with the same tools used to create the problems. He is responsible to his work and not to the dim flickerings of "taste." These are distinguished stories indeed.

Gilbert Sorrentino. *Book World*. Aug. 2, 1981,
pp. 3, 6

## BURROUGHS, WILLIAM S. (1914–    )

In *Naked Lunch* and its three less well-known sequels, *The Soft Machine*, *Nova Express*, and *The Ticket That Exploded*, William Burroughs weaves an intricate and horrible allegory of human greed, corruption, and debasement. Like Orwell's *1984* and Huxley's *Brave New World*, Burroughs' four works, taken collectively, seize on the evils or tendencies toward a certain type of evil that the author sees as being particularly malignant in his contemporary world and project them into a dystopian future, where, magnified, they have grown monstrous and taken on an exaggerated and fantastic shape. And like these classics of dystopian fiction, Burroughs' works are more novels of ideas that cleverly utilize the trappings of science fiction than they are what most people would consider "pure and simple" science fiction.

Even to the sophisticated reader they are troublesome puzzles; they are clearly more impenetrable than most popular literature. . . .

Significantly, this is not to say that they are without meaning or story, or that they are not imitations of life. But these elements are both realized differently here than they are in more conventional fiction. Although they share the same themes, metaphorical images, characters, and stylistic approach, this quartet—Burroughs' most serious novels—becomes more bizarre and takes on more of the appearance of science fiction as the novels progressively clarify and develop the author's thought. Each volume contributes to a single plot—or rather combines with the others to suggest the elements of what little plot there is. Thus, they may each be considered sections of one large work that encompasses them all.

Burroughs experiments with a style that has its closest analog in the cinematic technique of montage, although that technique is here most radically employed. He juxtaposes one scene with another without regard to plot, character, or, in the short view, theme to promote an association of the reader's negative emotional reaction to the superficial content (sexual perversion, drug abuse, senseless violence) of certain scenes with the implied narrative content (examples of "addictions": to drugs, money, sex, power, i.e., the allegory) of others. One clear instance of this technique is Burroughs' treatment of homosexuality, a practice that, while it is repeatedly equated with excrement and death (and is likely to have a negative connotation in the minds of most readers), is also endlessly juxtaposed to various addictions, particularly heroin addiction. The theory is that if such juxtapositions recur often enough, the feeling of revulsion strategically created by the first set of images will form the reader's attitude toward the second set of examples.

Donald Palumbo. *Extrapolation*. Winter, 1979,
pp. 321–22

William Burroughs' novels provide the most graphic and extreme expression of anarchic idealism and rage in contemporary literature. His characters are incessantly beset by forces of exploitation which push them into lives of addiction, self-destruction and progressive dehumanization. Rarely do they perceive either what is happening to them or their own participation in their degradation. Most accept uncritically the propaganda broadcast by the media, the institutions of social control, the "Time, Life, Fortune Monopoly," the "reality studios," or the political groups of *Naked Lunch*—the Liquifactionists, Divisionists and Senders, all of whom are intent on replicating themselves through their victims or dominating people's thoughts by instilling a single pattern of cognition and expression in society.

But Burroughs also suggests that to struggle against social control means to battle against one's prior identification with it—and, even more distressing, that to actively oppose the enemy insures that one remains defined by them: for as long as one is obsessed with fighting the opposition, one is not free of it. In Burroughs' novels, the greatest danger is thus to allow oneself to become rigidly defined by something external to oneself, for then one's identity is restricted and vulnerable. Consequently, the individual must not only disrupt the reality studios, but continuously disorient himself and his language to prevent his life from being controlled by anything except immediate, personal will. Against the institutions of control, Burroughs sends his anarchists, terrorists and the "Nova Police" who expose what is taken for reality for the grotesque horror it is. Against the three political parties of *Naked Lunch*, he pits a fourth, the Factualists, whose job it is to reveal in the most brutal—and often pornographic—terms the truth of our normal lives. The Factualists, however, cannot substitute an alternative vision, for Burroughs trusts no codified message or program, which might then be co-opted or become an authoritarian voice in others' lives. All the Factualists can do is disrupt and expose reality to force people to recognize themselves for what they are both before and after they accept a version of the "reality film"—

"dying animals on a doomed planet." Paradoxically then, precisely what sends people into addiction—their fear of chaos and pain, their sense of personal fragmentation and insignificance—becomes the means and the basis of their cure. Disruption, chaos, violence and exposure are what one must learn to live in. Only those strong enough to exist without external support, without a rigid identity, will survive.

Charles Russell. Sub-stance. No. 27, 1980, p. 321

The truth is that the attempt to rescue Burroughs for literary respectability by representing him as a satirist is hard to carry through convincingly.

It entails an insistence that the erotic and violent materials in the novels, and perhaps also the drugs, are generally there to instil disgust (a word Burroughs uses and invites the use of) and fear. But when these motifs are so widely distributed in the book, with such invariant wording, it is hard to feel that a strong local meaning attaches to them. . . .

As Burroughs implies, disgust is irrelevant to the sexual effect of a motif. An erotic context will subdue a disgust that might otherwise have arisen. Erotic imagery is a poor weapon for the satirist, for its tendency is not to sharpen our aversion to, but to reconcile us with, what is morally or physically repugnant. In fact all three of the kinds of material in Burroughs which excite desire and subdue disgust—sex, physical violence, and drugs—are at various points in the novels used affirmatively.

*Cities of the Red Night* perhaps carries Burroughs's utopianism further than do any of its predecessors. A change in history is fantasized whereby "pirate communes" (of a kind pioneered in reality by Captain Mission in the early eighteenth century) successfully establish themselves in Central America, and with their fraternal, egalitarian doctrines dislodge the Spanish, and are posed for a global expansion. The commune leaders are vigorously active homosexuals; their military successes are due to an early invention of the cartridge and the explosive shell (suddenly envisaged by one of the characters at the climax of an act of buggery), and citizens are kept loyal and resilient through an efficient distribution of opium (so much for the execrated "junk pyramid" of *Naked Lunch*).

The utopian narrative cannot sustain itself, and is shown to collapse back into something more macabre, disorderly, and recognizably Burroughs. What follows is perhaps more "satirical," but the juxtaposition with the earlier chapters, and the characteristic libration between horror and relish, produce the true Burroughs manifold of feeling: that ambivalence of the libertarian versus the eccentric and misanthropic. . . .

It is part of the abrupt and disconcerting sense of design which can crop up in a Burroughs novel that the final journey through the cities follows a progression which is announced many pages, and many hallucinatory episodes, earlier. Similarly, the quite orthodox first chapter of the book, which seems to have been lost sight of, is all at once referred to ten pages from the end. In *Naked Lunch* Burroughs undoubtedly developed a remarkable technique (whether by recording his dreams, using cut-up methods, or however) for getting on paper a very special kind of connected but free fantasy. It is essentially the repetition of that technique which *Cities of the Red Night* and the other novels have to offer. Burroughs's books, for all their afflatus, have a way of making the reader sit back and ponder, quite coldly: "How was that done?" The technique is not that new, either. It has very little to do with Jonathan Swift, but much to do with another Irishman. The present-tense, pantomimic rendering of the gruesome fantasy exemplified in the hanging sequences—and indeed their content—was first explored (and in this instance set in a thoroughly designed context) by Joyce in the "Circe" episode of *Ulysses*.

Michael Mason. *TLS*. March 27, 1981, p. 333

## CAIN, JAMES M. (1892–1977)

Though Cain writes out of the social and literary milieu that produced the deliberate attacks of the proletarian novelists, Cain never deals directly, as we have noted, with society's ills. While in several novels the relevance of Cain's characters to a larger social context is fairly intimate, his most effective social criticism emerges from his treatment of another interest—character portrayal, handled statically in the essays; dramatically, in the dialogues; narratively, in the novels. But, in all three genres, it is the dramatic thrust of characters in action that intrigues him; and they add up to an impressive gallery of American public types. . . .

While there seems to be no serious intention nor artistic conception at the heart of any of his sixteen novels, [Cain] does exhibit in his work a strange mingling of serious and of popular elements which he has made his own; and he has always, in his own way, been serious about craft. A writer of unfortunate faults, he is an interesting example of the author who often lets his journalistic temperament blur his creative field of vision. But, if his vision of life never becomes sharply focused, controlled, or conceptualized, it is obviously heightened and exaggerated to create effects that are often poetically compressed. While Cain seldom rises above certain commercial elements and never seems quite to step over the threshold into novelistic art, as it is normally conceived, his novels are valuable illustrations of the concept of the "pure" novel.

Certainly Cain's art, more than anything else, moves even the serious reader to almost complete emotional commitment to the traumatic experiences Cain renders; and this artistic control convinces me that without his finest novels—*The Postman* [*Always Rings Twice*], *Serenade*, *Mildred Pierce*, and *The Butterfly*— the cream of our twentieth-century fiction would be thinner. Straddling realism and expressionism, he often gives us a vivid account of life on the American scene as he has observed and experienced it; and, in his best moments, he provides the finer vibrations afforded by the esthetic experience. Cain the entertainer may fail to say anything truly important about life, but he takes us through experiences whose special quality is found in no other writer's work.

David Madden. *James M. Cain* (Twayne, 1970),
pp. 164, 175–76

In the Twain-Crane-Dreiser-Hemingway tradition, Cain successfully made the leap from journalism to fiction although he never abandoned magazine writing. Journalism not only provided him with some knowledge of a number of career fields but, more significantly for his craft, helped him achieve the compression, tautness and detached objectivity which, coupled with his sensational and brutal subject matter, characterize his writing and link him with other "tough guy" writers of the period. . . .

Cain's L.A. novels, drawing on this tradition, express the collective and destructive fantasies of the depression decade and turn these fantasies into nightmares. All of his heroes and heroines are self-destructively driven by sexual passion, a too-consuming love or an overpowering desire for material possessions. Such hunger is always the force driving them to desperate acts. Cain's pattern is to give his protagonists the temporary illusion of victory and then to take everything away from them. . . .

What defeats Cain's heroes . . . is not what defeats Fitzgerald's: the truth that the dream, once realized, can neither be preserved nor recaptured. For Cain the characters are defeated because their dreams are in direct conflict with those of others. Each character is yoked to, and set against, another—Frank and Cora, Mildred and Veda, Walter and Phyllis—and destroyed because the other is more ruthless, more clever or simply more determined. The pairs are suicidally tied to each other by passion, greed and jealousy. . . . There is never a chance they will get away with anything. . . .

For Cain, who arrived in Los Angeles soon after the Crash and remained through the Depression, the city came to represent the betrayed dreams of the whole nation. In the boom years hundreds of thousands had come seeking their fresh starts and new beginnings—a detached house, open space, mobility, good climate, renewed health and a piece of the wealth. The dream seemed within grasp. Fortunes, real and rumored, were being made in real estate, restaurants, oil and movies. Where the dream was most fervently believed and seemed closest to fulfillment, the collapse was more painful. Cain gave us a sense of what it was like to live, work and dream in Los Angeles in the thirties. His restless, driven and self-destructive heroes and heroines remind us of the hunger and the desperation that were a part of that not-so-distant past.

David M. Fine. *AmerS*. Spring, 1979, pp. 27–29, 33–34

# CALDWELL, ERSKINE (1903–     )

When all is said and done, how significant a writer is Caldwell? The critical consensus, as of 1979, was that he is an interesting, but unquestionably minor figure, whose work never fulfilled his early promise. And yet, as we have seen, this consensus is largely a result of a consistent failure on the part of Caldwell commentators to deal with Caldwell on his own terms. Of course, even the most careful attention to the ways in which Caldwell's aesthetic functions in his work does not negate the fact that this work has limitations, some of which are a direct result of the aesthetic itself. For one thing, there are certain kinds of reading pleasure Caldwell does not provide, even at his best. The enjoyment of re-reading a story or novel, carefully exploring its subtleties until its full implications are apparent—an enjoyment Faulkner, Hemingway, Bellow, and so many of the most respected contemporary writers give us again and again—is almost entirely absent from the experience of reading Caldwell. By and large, re-reading a Caldwell story or novel not only fails to uncover subtleties missed the first time through, it eliminates the suspense originally generated by our curiosity about what the characters might do next. To put it another way, once we've finished a Caldwell story, it ceases to be "fiction"—at least according to Caldwell's definition—and becomes memory. Secondly, since Caldwell's fiction is centered entirely on his characters' statements and actions, we do not experience the exploration of fictional forms which makes Stein or Faulkner enjoyable volume after volume. Third, no matter how many of Caldwell's books we read, we do not grow aware—as we do, say, in Eliot or Hardy or Steinbeck—of a World View, a model against which we can measure our interpretations of our own experience. . . .

In the final analysis, Caldwell has as much to offer us—despite his perfectly obvious "limitations"—as any other first-rate modern writer. Working within an unusual but cogent definition of fiction, he has created dozens of interesting stories characterized by a courageous willingness to be honest about the mysterious complexities of human lives and by a determination to communicate the fruits of his intensive observation in a form which is clear enough, direct enough, and powerful enough to be read, understood and vividly remembered for years by both trained literary critics and lay readers . . . I believe [Caldwell] . . . is a great writer, and he may be the most refreshingly unpretentious great writer we've ever had.

Scott MacDonald. In *Critical Essays on Erskine Caldwell*, ed. Scott MacDonald (G. K. Hall, 1981), pp. xxix, xxxi–xxxii

Any final assessment of Caldwell's contribution to the documentary genre in America must rest on the work he did in the 1930s, when he developed the techniques that have served him throughout his literary career. He recognized from the outset that documentary truth has more kinship with the authenticity of fiction than with scientific poll-taking and therefore never assumed a factitious air of disinterestedness about the material he recorded. Documentary and nonfiction writing has always been for Caldwell partisan, personal and highly selective; his imagination has played as vital a part in it as his conscience and observation. Yet there are clear stylistic and ideological distinctions between Caldwell's fiction and nonfiction. Despite the obvious inventive quality of much of his reporting which has led several of his critics to label it fiction, Caldwell maintains a separate persona, vocabulary, technique and even point of view in his nonfiction. While the fiction is almost consistently notable for the author's disengaged stance from the "antics and motivations" of the characters, the nonfiction permits an intrusive author, calling attention to his presence, his awkwardness, his anger and his sympathy. The more sophisticated vocabulary of the nonfiction reveals to what extent the ingenuous style of the fiction is a consciously contrived technique, while the tendency to separate comedy from degradation in the nonfiction suggests a different ideological purpose—reform rather than despair for the victims of economic and racial exploitation. While the underlying vision of human nature and society, especially as symbolically manifested in the South, is consistent in all his work, it is in the nonfiction that the intensity of Caldwell's moral purpose is most evident; by developing a carefully wrought, inventive literary method for his documentary reporting, he has succeeded in his best works, in negating the conventional distinction between effective propaganda and genuine aesthetic merit.

Sylvia Jenkins Cook. In *Critical Essays on Erskine Caldwell*, ed. Scott MacDonald (G. K. Hall, 1981), pp. 390–91

## CAPOTE, TRUMAN (1924–1984)

Readers who accept the idea that Capote's early writing should be categorized as romance can then dismiss irrelevant issues. They are the people who find Capote's second book remarkable in its voyage into the human psyche via the route of the romance. *A Tree of Night and Other Stories* is like a heavily woven tapestry of different depths that draws one from layer to layer. The collection contains stories in both a light and dark mode. Although Capote was never again to publish stories of the latter kind, some of the characteristics appear in other works, and some of the characters surface under other names in the fiction of the past decade.

Capote has spoken of his work as belonging to cycles in his development as a writer. He labels *Other Voices, Other Rooms* at the end of the first cycle, and he places *A Tree of Night and Other Stories* in the second. During the ten-year period of his second cycle, his most varied and prolific, he wrote the autobiographical story, "A Christmas Memory"; *The Grass Harp*, a novel which he also turned into a play; "House of Flowers," a short story which later became a musical comedy; essays and portraits, *Local Color* and *Observations*; film scripts for *Beat the Devil* and *The Innocents*; a nonfiction, comic, book-length travel report, *The Muses Are Heard*; and finally, the very popular novel, *Breakfast at Tiffany's*.

Capote's third cycle, corresponding to the decade of the sixties, was devoted primarily to the preparation and writing of *In Cold Blood*, although during that time he also published two of his well-known pieces, "A Thanksgiving Visitor," which is a spin-off from "A Christmas Memory," and "Among the Paths to Eden," one of his best short stories, and one which led some critics to predict, incorrectly, that this was the direction his future fiction was to follow.

Much has been written about *In Cold Blood*, its genre, its style, its narrator. Every conceivable type of study of the book has been undertaken. In interviews Capote continues to explain the genesis of the book and his interest in developing a new art form. During the time that he was writing articles on a regular basis for *The New Yorker*, particularly those that became *The Muses Are Heard*, he developed a strong interest in narrative journalism. He decided he wanted to expand reporting into something more meaningful, to create a work which combined journalism and fiction. When his attention was piqued by a news story of the murder of a Kansas family, he felt that he had found the subject matter to experiment with a different type of novel. The result was Capote's most noted book and greatest literary achievement, to which he gave the designation, the "nonfiction novel." Other writers, American and European, have been using similar techniques since Capote introduced them; yet, he is bitter about the failure of some critics to acknowledge his contribution in devising a new theory of writing. One of those he singles out is Norman Mailer, who, Capote says, was disparaging of the form, yet quickly saw the value of it for his own work and wrote a number of nonfiction novels. Whether or not sufficient credit is given to Capote for his innovativeness, nobody can question the impact the book has had.

Helen S. Garson. *Truman Capote* (Ungar, 1980),<br>pp. 7–9

*Music for Chameleons* consists of a brief autobiographical introduction, then six short stories followed by a novella; and it ends with seven "Conversational Portraits.". . . Despite [Capote's] claims, the technique is (mercifully) innovatory only in one or two superficial and formal ways; in many more important ones it is a brave step back to older literary virtues. He now writes fiction increasingly near fact, and *vice versa*. In practice this means that he is very skillfully blending the received techniques of several kinds of writing. . . .

If all one required of a writer was high stylishness, a marvelous eye and ear, a far from contemptible degree of self-honesty, and a piquant readability in all he attempts, then one cannot fault Mr. Capote. He is as good as sheer literary intelligence can make a writer. What he seems to me to lack (and what raised his French models above being *only* great stylists) is a literary heart, which requires not only magnanimity but a patience with ordinariness, the gray muddle of average existence.

He speaks in his foreword of wanting to assimilate into his new style of writing all he has learned from "film scripts, plays, reportage, poetry, the short story, novellas, the novel." The odd man out here, the awkward fit, is surely that last thing. It is the very length and diffuseness of the novel that allows the growth of deeper feelings in both writer and reader; and creating such feelings in the short story is the most difficult Indian ropetrick in fiction. Yet all the truly great masters (most famously James Joyce in *The Dead*) have accomplished it, and as I read these glittering and always entertaining stories I found myself wondering why Mr. Capote came close at times, but never quite made it. . . . Of one thing I am certain: Contemporary literature would be much, much duller and poorer without him.

John Fowles. SR. July, 1980, pp. 52–53

Much of Capote's work is marked by a kind of concealed documentation. F. W. Dupee's comment about *In Cold Blood* is to the point: "the documentation is, for the most part, suppressed in the text—presumably in order to supply the narrative with a surface of persuasive immediacy and impenetrable omniscience." All three of Capote's longer fictional works, *Other Voices, Other Rooms*, *The Grass Harp*, and *Breakfast at Tiffany's*, are veiled, loosely autobiographic tales that reflect to some limited extent the author's personal history. The sketches in *Local Color* also contain this veiled documentation of the author's having lived in the places about which he writes: New Orleans, New York, Brooklyn, and other similarly colorful locations. *The Muses Are Heard*, "The Duke in His Domain," and *In Cold Blood*—all three of which were written for *The New Yorker*—are pieces in which "facts" are handled at the same time both literally and impressionistically. . . .

Whereas it is sometimes possible to view the writing of other authors as a unified whole, the numerous and varied products of Capote's literary career tend to resist categorization and thematic generalization. However, certain thematic patterns can be identified, if not universally applied to everything he has written in the past thirty years. . . .

Capote writes most often retrospectively, with attention to childhood and adolescent adventures that relate to problems of initiation, of coming of age, of growing up in a world beset with danger and insecurity. Certainly, these generalizations apply to his longer and more acclaimed pieces such as *Other Voices, Other Rooms*, *The Grass Harp*, *Breakfast at Tiffany's*, *A Christmas Memory*, *The Thanksgiving Visitor*, and even *In Cold Blood*; for in each of these is the problem of childhood or adolescent mentality in its uncertain struggle to somehow "adjust" to the demands of approaching adult "responsibility." To fail in this crucial adjustment is to be victimized or to victimize others. To succeed in the adjustment process is to live a life that is relatively satisfying because it is free, unrestricted, and directed from within.

Kenneth T. Reed. *Truman Capote* (Twayne, 1981), pp. 123, 129–30

● **CARVER,  RAYMOND  (1938–    )**

In most of these 22 short fictions [*Will You Please Be Quiet, Please?*] the objects of Raymond Carver's close attention are men and women out of work or between jobs, at loose ends, confused and often terrified. If they are kids, they play hooky. Husbands and wives lie beside each other in bed, touch cautiously, retreat, feign sleep, lie, each bewildered by what has just happened and by what might happen next. The stories themselves are not at all confused; they have been carefully shaped, shorn of ornamentation and directed away from anything that might mislead. They are brief stories but by no means stark: they imply complexities of action and motive and they are especially artful in their suggestion of repressed violence.

No human blood is shed in any of these stories, yet almost all of them hold a promise of mayhem, of some final, awful breaking out from confines, and breaking through to liberty. . . .

In his choice of plots and materials Mr. Carver is in the modernist train of Kafka. Odd and threatening messages come as though by magic through the mails or by telephone. Strangers invade one another's lives and offer preposterous challenges to one another. In the customary literary execution of such procedures, identities shift, characters are misled into taking enemies as friends, conspiracies develop or are, at the least, apprehended. Mr. Carver, by contrast, anchors his men and women, his children, even his dogs and cats, in stable identities. With a speed common to all his stories he fixes the special tic or manner he wishes to develop: "I was out of work," says the narrator of "Collectors" in the story's first sentence. "But any day I expected to hear from up north. I lay on the sofa and listened to the rain. Now and then I'd lift up and look through the curtain for the mailman."

Geoffrey Wolff. NYT. March 7, 1976, pp. 4–5

Compared to the more "mannered" writers of the sixties and seventies—Barth, Pynchon, Barthelme, for example—Carver's style seems ingenuously simple, almost photo-realistic. Even the prose of Grace Paley and Leonard Michaels, both considered exemplars of lean, taut language, seems positively lush, almost Baroque in resonances and allusiveness, when held up to that of Carver. The temptation is to classify Carver as a throwback to an earlier era, say, of Anderson, Lardner and Hemingway. Although he derives from and to some extent reminds us of these earlier writers, there's a crucial difference. The sensibility here is clearly post-modern: beyond the flat quality of the Hemingway hero struggling to preserve an identity in the drear vastness of the wasteland, beyond the psychological frameworks of Anderson's stories, beyond the comic satire of Lardner. Carver's simple language is a disguise, as is Harold Pinter's, for the emotional violence lurking beneath neutral surfaces. . . .

Like most of us, his characters aren't heroes. They don't teach us how to behave nobly or honorably or even intelligently in moments of crisis. Like the voyeurs they are or resemble, Carver's characters shy away from dramatic confrontation, they avoid existential tests of character. These people are completely removed from Mailer's or Hemingway's preoccupation with masculine assertion. Although there are showdowns in these stories, no one really wants them to occur. Betraying wives are threatened with bodily harm, but rarely do their husbands actually make good on their threats. . . .

Nothing happens because in the main Carver's dissociated characters prefer it that way. Living in a world of unarticulated longing, a world verging on silence, they may even, like the couples in "Neighbors" and "Will You Please Be Quiet, Please?," consider themselves "happy." But such happiness is fragile, Carver tells us. Something or someone always happens along to disturb the uneasy equilibrium, forcing a sudden confrontation with a hidden or suppressed part of the self. The disturbance itself acts as a trigger to larger revelations of self-alienation.

David Boxer and Cassandra Phillips. IowaR.<br/>Summer, 1979, pp. 81, 83–84

Raymond Carver's America is helpless, clouded by pain and the loss of dreams, but it is not as fragile as it looks. It is a place of survivors and a place of stories. People live to tell their tales and the tales of others.

"Things are better now," they say. "I am sitting over coffee and cigarettes at my friend Rita's and I am telling her about it." "That was in Crescent City, up near the Oregon border. I left soon after."

Mr. Carver is the author of two volumes of short fiction and two books of poetry, as well as other works in limited editions. His writing is full of edges and silences, haunted by things not said, not even to be guessed at. He has done what many of the most gifted writers fail to do: He has invented a country of his own, like no other except the very world, as Wordsworth said, which is the world of all of us. It is an American world, of course, littered with place names, credit, convertibles, Stanley Products, sunburst clocks, shopping centers, Jell-O, motels, Almond Roca, baseball caps, trips to Reno, Elks, Indian reservations, beckoning spaces of Western country and children with names like Rae and Melody. But there are simple, central solitudes and bewilderments here too: local enough, but not the property of any one nation. "I could hear my heart beating. I could hear everyone's heart. I could hear the human noise we sat there making. . ." . . .

Mr. Carver's first book of stories [*Will You Please Be Quiet, Please?*] explored a common plight rather than a common subject. His characters were lost or diminished in their own different ways. The 17 stories in *What We Talk About When We Talk About Love* make up a more concentrated volume, less a collection than a set of variations on the themes of marriage, infidelity and the disquieting tricks of human affection. . . .

"Things change," a character says in [one] story, and this is the dominant note in the book. People lose track of who they were and what they wanted, mislay their lives and are startled by their memories. . . .

In other stories it is the failure of speech, rather than its absence, that does the talking: "He wanted to say something else. But there was no saying what it should be." "There were things he wanted to say, grieving things, consoling things, things like that." In the last story in the book a husband leaving home insists that he wants to "say one more thing. . . But then he could not think what it could possibly be."

The point is not that words are inadequate, or that actions speak louder. It is that the desire to talk can be perceived as a need, and that need has its fluency, makes use of any language that comes to hand. This is a troublesome fact for a writer, but Mr. Carver does not dodge it. "She seemed anxious, or maybe that's too strong a word." Only a very delicate stylist would worry about the strength of "anxious" and the milder, perhaps unnamable quality of feeling that hides behind this attempt at description. In Mr. Carver's silences, a good deal of the unsayable gets said.

Michael Wood. NYT. April 26, 1981, pp. 1, 34

Mr. Carver has been mostly a writer of strong but limited effects—the sort of writer who shapes and twists his material to a high point of stylization. In his newest collection of stories, *Cathedral*, there are a few that suggest he is moving toward a greater ease of manner and generosity of feeling; but in most of his work it's his own presence, the hard grip of his will, that is the strongest force. It's not that he imposes moral or political judgments; in that respect, he's quite self-effacing. It's that his abrupt rhythms and compressions come to be utterly decisive. . . .

*Cathedral* contains a number of similar stories, very skillful within their narrow limits, written with a dry intensity, and moving, at their climaxes, from the commonplace to the unnerving. . . .

These stories yield neither the familiar recognitions of realistic narrative nor the ambiguous motifs of symbolic fiction. They cast us adrift, into a void on the far side of the ordinary. Ordinary life is threatening; ordinary life is the enemy of ordinary people.

Behind Mr. Carver's stories there are strong American literary traditions. Formally, they summon remembrances of Hemingway and perhaps Stephen Crane, masters of tightly packed fiction. In subject matter they draw upon the American voice of loneliness and stoicism, the native soul locked in this continent's space. Mr. Carver's characters, like those of many earlier American writers, lack a vocabulary that can release their feelings, so they must express themselves mainly through obscure gesture and berserk display.

It's a meager life that Mr. Carver portrays, without religion or politics or culture, without the shelter of class or ethnicity, without the support of strong folkways or conscious rebellion. It's the life of people who cluster in the folds of our society. They are not bad or stupid; they merely lack the capacity to understand the nature of their deprivation—the one thing, as it happens, that might ease or redeem it. When they get the breaks, they can manage; but once there's a sign of trouble, they turn out to be terribly brittle. Lacking an imagination for strangeness, they succumb to the strangeness of their trouble.

A few of Mr. Carver's stories—"They're Not Your Husband," "Where I'm Calling From" and "A Serious Talk"—can already be counted among the masterpieces of American fiction; a number of others are very strong. But something of the emotional meagerness that he portrays seeps into the narrative. His art is an art of exclusion—many of life's shadings and surprises, pleasures and possibilities, are cut away by the stringency of his form. . . .

I think Mr. Carver is showing us at least part of the truth about a segment of American experience few of our writers trouble to notice. Neoconservative critics, intent upon pasting a smile onto the country's face, may charge him with programmatic gloom and other heresies, but at his best he is probing, as many American writers have done before, the waste and destructiveness that prevail beneath the affluence of American life. . . .

*Cathedral* shows a gifted writer struggling for a larger scope of reference, a finer touch of nuance. What he has already done makes one eager to read his future work.

Irving Howe. *NYT*. Sept. 11, 1983, pp. 1, 42–43

## CATHER, WILLA (1876–1947)

We have seen that in her earlier novels Willa Cather explored the archetypal modes of the imagination—epic, pastoral, satire—and that the three novels written at the height of her career form something like a "mortal comedy." But what of the last four volumes, *Obscure Destinies, Lucy Gayheart, Sapphira and the Slave Girl, The Old Beauty and Others*, which most critics agree mark the decline of Willa Cather's art? Are these books, from a writer of such depths, as undistinguished and insignificant as has been suggested? The answer, I believe, is at once affirmative and negative. With the exception of the long story "Old Mrs. Harris," the later writing lacks the same kind of imaginative energy which found expression in the earlier novels. The last fictions are subtle, intelligent, and artfully contrived, but the vision which underlies them is one which questions the old urge to expression through art. I believe the author came to feel in her later years that not art but life mattered most now; consequently, her last books occupy the paradoxical position of works of art suggesting their own devaluation.

As a romantic Willa Cather had believed strongly in the absoluteness of the artist's vocation, an attitude most directly expressed in *The Song of the Lark* and in "Coming, Aphrodite!" In this light her major novels might be described as the egotistic expressions of an individual consciousness seeking both self-knowledge and recognition from others. But the last novels and stories posit quite a different relationship between art and its creator. No longer driven by the same urge to create, Willa Cather, I feel, came to view her lifetime dedication to art as placing selfish limitations on life, particularly on human relationships. Again the author was following a path well worn by (to use one of her favorite metaphors) the "pilgrims" of the imagination. Many writers before Willa Cather reached a point in their lives when they no longer felt art to be so very important. Some dramatized that feeling emphatically by arresting their work early or in mid-career: Rimbaud, for example, went to Abyssinia to make his fortune in the slave trade; Tolstoi turned his back on the world and the novel to become a recluse and social pamphleteer; and Hart Crane, in his quest for a transcendental ideal, despaired of the limitations of poetry and committed suicide. For Willa Cather the implications of her vision were never so definitive or tragic, yet instinctively she moved toward that same juncture where art terminates in the mute acceptance (or, in Crane's case, hopeful transcendence) of life.

David Stouck. *Willa Cather's Imagination*
(Univ. of Nebraska Pr., 1975), pp. 206–7

In . . . much of her fiction, Cather connects sexual passion with self-destruction; this remark suggests that the creator's passion, by contrast, thwarts death. The artist may "die of love" in the process of creation, but he is "born again." Cather's romantic apostrophe to the Nebraska soil in the concluding paragraph of *O Pioneers!* also promises rebirth for Alexandra, the novel's artist, after she has "faded away" into the land: "Fortunate country, that is one day to receive hearts like Alexandra's into its bosom, to give them out again in the yellow wheat, in the rustling corn, in the shining eyes of youth!". . .

In speaking of *O Pioneers!* Willa Cather provided support for those critics who have found the novel's structure loose, insisting that she made no effort to impose form on her material: the book formed itself without her conscious intervention. The "cold Swedish story" had simply "entwined itself" with the Bohemian story, she told Elizabeth Sergeant, and "somehow she had on her hands a two-part pastoral." She struck a similar note in her preface to the second edition of *Alexander's Bridge* (1922), explaining that when the artist found "his own material" (as she had in *O Pioneers!*) he would have "less and less power of choice about the molding of it. It seems to be there of itself, already molded." But to trust the tale rather than the teller is to find that the two parts of Willa Cather's pastoral are carefully intertwined; these contrasting and counterpointed explorations of creative and sexual passion with their opposed heroines give the novel both thematic and structural unity. Willa Cather quite likely believed her statement that she did not consciously shape *O Pioneers!*, but in drawing on creative and psychological energies beneath consciousness she produced a novel whose structure may even seem overly controlled and balanced.

Sharon O'Brien. *SAF.* Autumn, 1978, pp. 168–69

*My Ántonia* (1918), Willa Cather's celebration of the American frontier experience, is marred by many strange flaws and omissions. It is, for instance, difficult to determine who is the novel's central character. If it is Ántonia, as we might reasonably assume, why does she entirely disappear for two of the novel's five books? If, on the other hand, we decide that Jim Burden, the narrator, is the central figure, we find that the novel explores neither his consciousness nor his development. Similarly, although the narrator overtly claims that the relationship between Ántonia and Jim is the heart of the matter, their friendship actually fades soon after childhood: between these two characters there is only, as E. K. Brown said, "an emptiness where the strongest emotion might have been expected to gather." Other inconsistencies and contradictions pervade the text—Cather's ambivalent treatment of Lena Lingard and Tiny Soderball, for example—and all are in some way related to sex roles and to sexuality.

This emphasis is not surprising: as a writer who was also a woman, Willa Cather faced the difficulties that confronted, and still do confront, accomplished and ambitious women. As a professional writer, Cather began, after a certain point in her career, to see the world and other women, including her own female characters, from a male point of view. Further, Cather was a lesbian who could not, or did not, acknowledge her homosexuality and who, in her fiction, transformed her emotional life and experiences into acceptable, heterosexual forms and guises. In her society it was difficult to be a woman and achieve professionally, and she could certainly not be a woman who loved women; she responded by denying, on the one hand, her womanhood and, on the other, her lesbianism. These painful denials are manifest in her fiction. After certain early work, in which she created strong and achieving women, like herself, she abandoned her female characters to the most conventional and traditional roles; analogously, she began to deny or distort the sexuality of her principal characters. *My Ántonia*, written at a time of great stress in her life, is a crucial and revealing work, for in it we can discern the consequences of Cather's dilemma as a lesbian writer in a patriarchal society. . . .

In order to create independent and heroic women, women who are like herself, the woman writer must avoid male identification, the likelihood of which is enhanced by being a writer who is unmarried, childless, and a lesbian. In the case of *My Ántonia*, Cather had to contend not only with the anxiety of creating a strong woman character, but also with the fear of a homosexual attraction to Annie/Ántonia. The novel's defensive narrative structure, the absence of thematic and structural unity that readers have noted, these are the results of such anxieties. Yet, because it has been difficult for readers to recognize the betrayal of female independence and female sexuality in fiction—their absence is customary—it has also been difficult to penetrate the ambiguities of *My Ántonia*, a crucial novel in Cather's long writing career.

Deborah G. Lambert. AL. Jan., 1982, pp. 676–77,<br>690

## CHANDLER, RAYMOND (1888–1959)

Chandler was a naturally gifted and fluent writer, but for nearly fifty years he was unable to find a medium that suited him. He endured continuing disappointments and frustrations and, already sensitive, he became withdrawn and introverted. When at last he began to write stories for the pulps and published his own novels, he pulled together the opposed aspects of his nature and created something extraordinarily vital and original. Chandler tended to deprecate his own importance as a writer, but he had a clear idea of what he had achieved, and he knew that his writing held him together. . . .

His double vision—half-English, half-American—enabled him to see the world he lived in with exceptional insight. His vision of America has become increasingly fulfilled, although twenty-five years ago few people could have imagined the relevance of his work today. He was a prophet of modern America; out of the European literary tradition he wrote about a world that both repelled and delighted him. He did not generalize or theorize. Rather, he trusted his impulses, and like Chaucer or Dickens he wrote about the people, places, and things he saw with scorn and also with love. This has made him one of the most important writers of his time, as well as one of the most delightful.

Frank MacShane. The Life of Raymond Chandler<br>(Dutton, 1976), pp. 268–69

Now if in comparing the tender and the tough conventions one is looking for "real life" in the verifiable sense, one must conclude that although the first kind of story will not bear sceptical examination, the second is—as Shakespeare says apropos of two liars—"an even more wonderful song than the other." Nor is this all that Raymond Chandler's essay ["The Simple Art of Murder"] brings to mind. The tender school aims at producing a denouement having the force of necessity, as in Greek tragedy. All the facts (clues, words, motives) must converge to give the mystery one solution and one only. That by itself is a good reason for making the crime occur in a law-abiding circle, where the habits of the *dramatis personae* are by hypothesis regular and reasonable. In such a setting the violence of murder is the more striking, and stronger also the desire to manacle the offender. Murder among thugs and drug addicts is hardly unexpected, and the feeling that in this milieu anything can happen does not increase but rather lessens the interest. Hence the artistic need for the tough writer to involve some innocent, whose ways *are* peaceable, and to put steadily in peril the detective-defender of that lump of virtue. In short, in murder à la Chandler, murder is not enough to keep us going—and neither is detection, since it is never a feature of the foreground.

Chandler as artist is so aware of these lacks that he reinforces the dam-sel-in-distress motive with what is nothing less than a political motive. He makes it clear in his essay that the hero of the new and improved genre is fighting society. Except for the favoured victim, he alone is pure in heart, a C-green incorruptible. The rich are all crooked or "phonies," and cowards in the end. Since the police, the mayor, the whole Establishment are soon shown as a conspiracy to pervert justice and kill off troublemakers, we naturally share the detective's smothered indignation and are powerfully driven, like him, to see the right vindicated.

Jacques Barzun. In *The World of Raymond Chandler*, ed. Miriam Gross (A & W, 1977), pp. 161–62

Chandler's uniqueness—and the source of his popularity—is the product of a wide variety of personal traits and talents, circumstances and coincidences. He brought to his work a European sensibility and education supported by a bedrock of childhood experiences in the American Great Plains of the late nineteenth century. He arrived in California while the pioneering spirit still thrived and witnessed the rise of the movie studios and the attendant exploi-tation of glamour and illusion. He barely survived the First World War and was just achieving the peak of his writing career as Western civilization threatened to fall apart in the Second.

Given his far-ranging experience, it is perhaps remarkable that he maintained the conviction throughout it all that "the best way to comment on large things is to comment on small things." The "small things" that preoccupied him were character and language. By concentrating on the motives of individual characters, he approaches such larger themes as the unpredictability of human emotion under pressure and the manner in which changing times appear to alter one's ethical possibilities. He illuminates the way in which characters are alternately responsible for the world in which they live and trapped by that world. As Dostoevsky reminded us in *Crime and Punishment*, "this damnable psychology cuts both ways." The reactions of Chandler's characters to their psychic binds imply the pervasive instability at the core of modern society. And the language by which these characters reveal themselves allows the author to convey a sense of the delicate web by which we are all bound together.

The most significant "small things" that occupy Chandler are the mind and actions of his detective, Philip Marlowe. Marlowe is a microcosm of both Chandler's concern for character and his concern for the language by which that character is expressed. It is Marlowe's voice, of course, that is the constant ground of Chandler's stories. It is the detached, ironic, frequently alienated tone of that voice that holds our attention and provides an interpretive framework for the tales.

But while we may feel we know Marlowe's voice almost instinctively, a close examination of the novels reveals very little of a "factual" nature about the detective. We know a few details about his surroundings, almost nothing about his past, and very little about his personal motives. We almost never see his mind working, except as that mental activity is translated into dramatic action. And yet, we identify with him.

Understanding that identification may be as close as we can come to appreciating Chandler's power and uniqueness as a writer. And comprehending what Chandler called his "objective method" is essential to that appreciation.

Jerry Speir. *Raymond Chandler* (Ungar, 1981),
pp. vii–viii

# CHEEVER, JOHN (1912–1982)

The fictional landscape of Cheever's art includes the social pretensions and moral implications of modern suburbia, the larger patterns of human experience, such as the loss of innocence and the deep spiritual hunger for a golden simpler past, and the discovery of beautiful moments to celebrate within the contemporary wasteland. These themes and ideas occur again and again in the short stories and novels. The way they are organized and detailed reveals the form in which Cheever's fictional landscape is created. . . .

The emotional center or vision of Cheever's fiction remains somewhat elusive. His light, ironic style can cut both ways. On the one hand, he seems to be a romantic, yearning for the good old days of yesteryear, far from the madding crowds of the aimless, tasteless contemporary world. On the other hand, he seems to realize the essential futility and unreality of such romantic notions and seems determined to find moments of beauty within the chaotic and graceless contemporary world. . . . In either case Cheever's style can both illuminate and avoid the implications of the situations he writes about. He seems to want his style to be both disarming and protective at once. He seems, finally, to be celebrating his own ability to find delight in both the romantic past, however false, and the contemporary present, however chaotic. . . .

Cheever is neither concerned with uncovering the complexities within a particular moment of experience nor interested in sounding the depths of an episode. His is more an attempt to translate that immediate experience into the artistic opportunity to display the lyric gracefulness of his style, to focus the reader's attention primarily upon the encounter between the artist and his material.

Samuel Coale. *John Cheever* (Ungar, 1977), pp. 115–17

John Cheever is one of the few living American novelists who might qualify as true artists. His work ranges from competent to awesome on all the grounds I would count: formal and technical mastery; educated intelligence; what I call "artistic sincerity," which implies, among other things, an indifference to aesthetic fashion. . . .

Cheever's *Falconer*, though not long or "difficult," not profound or massive, devoid of verisimilitude's endless explanations on the one hand, and of overwrought allegorical extension on the other—though in fact merely a dramatic story of character and action accessible to the most ordinary sensitive reader—is an extraordinary work of art. . . .

No one is simply good in *Falconer*; the novel convinced us that in point of fact no one in the world is really good. Yet *Falconer* has nothing in common with the typical contemporary novel about how life is garbage. Life, for Cheever, is simply beautiful and tragic, or that's how he presents it, and both the beauty and the tragedy in *Falconer* are earned. Cheever finds no easy enemies, as William Gaddis would, no easy salvation for the liberated penis and spirit, as Updike would. He finds only what is there: pathos and beauty, "the inestimable richness of human nature." . . .

Cheever proves what we are always forgetting: that great art is not technical trickery, novelty of effect, or philosophical complexity beyond our depth, but absolute clarity: reality with the obfuscating wrappings peeled away. The reason Cheever is a great writer—besides his command of literary form, impeccable style, and unsentimental compassion—is that what he says seems true.

John Gardner. *SR*. April 2, 1977, pp. 20–21, 23

Cheever is not a sociologist; he is an artist. A social scientist's concern is to so concentrate on particular instances that, accumulatively, a general pattern for understanding the behavior of some segment of society might emerge. The artist, too, begins with the concrete particular, but he *enters* it; a particular experience is thus transformed by his imaginative and compassionate feeling in order that the humanly universal, not the statistically general, might emerge and engage our feeling and imaginative response. The findings of the social sciences are, almost by definition, statable. The results of art elude such definition since the art of fiction, at its best, engages mystery, the mystery of the human and its corollary, the mystery of language.

These twin mysteries are the key to the magic of John Cheever. . . . His narratives move swiftly and almost in linear fashion from one glimpse, one incident, one snippet of conversation to another. What is sacrificed here in terms of organic fictional unity—always the stuffy critic's touchstone when he has little else to say—is redeemed by exceptional inventiveness, flexibility and versatility. This apparently loose structure gives his stories the qualities of a yarn and, *sans* dialect and sentimentality, places him firmly in the American tradition of Mark Twain, Ring Lardner and Damon Runyon. Furthermore, a Cheever dialogue is unique in that, while it remains true to our realistic ear, it is always heightened beyond realism to a peculiar brand of poetic speech—and it is this that sets him apart from the genial accuracy of a John O'Hara or Philip Roth. . . .

Just as Cheever is not a strict satirist, he is not a moralist either. And yet, his work, as his last novel *Falconer* made evident, is deeply Christian in sensibility. Few of his stories, apart from cleverly inserted Biblical allusions, are obviously religious in design. But Cheever's sympathy with his characters' fallen state together with their vague yearnings for personal rebirth, for a virtuous life possibly untrammeled by life's more sordid confusions, betray his sincere Episcopal beliefs.

George Hunt. *Com.* Jan. 19, 1979, pp. 20–22

# COOVER, ROBERT (1932–    )

Robert Coover's fictions demonstrate how diverse perceptions combine and recombine to create meaning. His work, from the early *Origin of the Brunists* (1966) to the recent *The Public Burning* (1977), does not employ language to refer to a fixed set of meaning behind which lies a central, unifying order. Rather, his fictions suggest that meaning resides everywhere and nowhere. It can be located only by a fiction—perhaps the reader's, perhaps the narrator's—constructed in language. Of course, even there, new meanings accrue as we sally into the world of the imagination, a world where interpretation mounts on interpretation and perceptions can constantly shift.

Coover plays with the many possibilities and alternatives contained within language and narrative structures. At the same time, fictions which open a labyrinth of meanings do not therefore imply an absence of ethical strategy or even moral vision. The world of experience exists despite our fictions, and it is a world to which we must always return, even if it is fundamentally incomprehensible. Yet, the imagination gives us our sense of the world, and Coover enjoins us to become aware of the various relationships and perspectives in constant need of reformulation. To live, we choose whatever fictions best sort out our perceptions and sensations. Yet, we often and conveniently forget that our point of view, itself fictional, implies an element of choice. In our forgetfulness, we allow our fictions to overtake our lives. . . .

Coover does not, therefore, dispense with the notion of consciousness or imagination but rather underscores need for balance. Neither narrator nor character, writer nor reader, self nor environment create independently. On the other hand, he does not go as far as the French objectivist novel, for example, or Donald Barthelme, for another example, in the reduction of the self to the level of all other surfaces. Coover's stories present the mind at work, discovering the contiguous relations amidst a network of alternatives. . . .

[A] metaphor for the place of imagination—neither here nor there—appears in *The Universal Baseball Association*. Creative renewal ocurs on the playing field. In this novel, Coover suggests that realms of the actual and of the imagination interpenetrate but must remain autonomous as well. For Coover, life bears on our fictions and fictions bear on our lives. The interdependence of imagination and actuality, however, assumes their separation. One realm must not be totally submerged by the other. Henry Waugh submerges himself so completely in his fiction that he not only becomes lost to life, but his invention fails him as well. We need our fictions to cope with life, and we need experience to keep our fictions vital.

Brenda Wineapple. *IowaR*. Summer, 1979, pp.<br>66, 68–69, 71

Coover's fictions clearly emphasize their author's interest in providing his readers with the kinds of metaphors that are necessary for a healthy imagination. Unfortunately, Coover says between the lines in every story he writes, people today have lost their desire for the thrill of discovery. They have become comfortable with having their conventional viewpoints confirmed through a limited range of artistic forms that have outlived their usefulness. Each of Coover's stories, then, invites its reader to relinquish one or more of his traditional approaches to art and participate with its author in an exercise of wit that frequently juxtaposes what is fantastic in life with the everyday.

The principal method through which Coover liberates readers from sensibilities that have been deadened by the familiar is irony. Irony enables Coover and his readers to distance themselves from traditional forms without isolating themselves from the human content of those forms. As a result, Coover's readers have the opportunity and pleasure of tearing down many of society's inherited approaches to art and life without losing their concern for humanity's condition. The result is a healthy sense of humor and the awareness of a developing consciousness. . . .

Reworking history, as he has done with myths, legends, and fairy tales, may represent a new arena in which Coover can explore further the interests that have been of primary concern to him since *The Origin of the Brunists*: "Like in the creation of myths, I sometimes transpose events for the sake of a kind of inner coherence, but there's a certain amount of condensation and so on, but mainly I accept that what I'm dealing with here is a society that is fascinated with real data, facts and figures, dates, newspaper stuff. I can't mess around too much with the data here lest I lose contact with that fascination.". . .

However Coover chooses to reinterpret history, his readers can be assured of accomplished and inventive stories that deal absurdly and metaphysically with the human condition without losing their sense of humor.

Richard Andersen. *Robert Coover* (Twayne, 1981), pp. 141–43

## COWLEY, MALCOLM (1898–    )

In a sense *A Second Flowering* represents a part of a long struggle on Cowley's part to redeem the American writer from his condition of alienation. It would be misleading to say that this struggle has dominated Cowley's wide-ranging work as a literary critic. It is hardly too much to say that it provides a strong unifying theme in his complex and varied achievement. But in the same breath we must observe that it is a struggle Cowley has never intended to win. When we add to his criticism Cowley's small but important body of poetry, we see running through the whole range of his work as a twentieth-century poet, critic, and literary and cultural historian a basic motive of alienation. As both a creator and an interpreter of the literature of the lost generation, Cowley is a contributor to one of its leading aspects: a myth or a legend of creativity which is definable as a poetics of exile.

Lewis P. Simpson. *SwR*. Spring, 1976, p. 225

What is perhaps most impressive about Cowley as a literary and cultural commentator is his ability—most clearly demonstrated in his earlier writings—to sense and report the psychic weather, the dominant moods and styles, the subtle forces that shape the collective state of mind of the historical moment very often while the moment is still in the process of being formed and he himself is being formed by it. This is what gave *Exile's Return* its special quality of seeming to be almost magically evocative of his generation's experience at the same time that it arranged that experience into a pattern of tonal and thematic development which was more fictive than historical. . . .

But although Cowley had something of Dos Passos' historical perspective and wrote a prose that at times uncannily resembled Hemingway's, he was most like Fitzgerald in seeing his personal experience as a sort of microcosmic version of what had happened to them all, as emblematic of their common fate and fortune. . . .

Cowley's literary contemporaries did indeed have a remarkable awareness of shared experience, and his own career is not only . . . representative but almost seismographically reflective of the changes that have occurred in the literary life of this country over the past sixty years. During that time he has lived through nearly all the evolutionary phases of the modernist movement in literature, and he has made his own significant contribution to each. More than any other historical critic except possibly Edmund Wilson, he has been persistently alert to the complex interplay of cultural and intellectual forces which have helped shape the character of modern literature even as they provided the collective history from which his generation of writers derived their strong sense of united creative purpose. . . .

If now in his old age Cowley cannot enjoy the satisfaction of spectacular triumph, great reputation, or large public accolade, he does have behind him more than half a century of working honorably and successfully at the writer's trade, retaining a devotion to the high calling of literature that is now very nearly extinct in the world, and keeping alive the works and days of his generation whom he now lives on to commemorate and represent.

John W. Aldridge. MQR. Summer, 1979, pp.<br>482–83, 489–90

## COZZENS, JAMES GOULD (1903–1978)

It is . . . harder to write about Cozzens than it is to write about the romancers who form the majority of our authors, whether Poe and Hawthorne back then, or Pynchon and Ellison and Updike now. . . .

Almost all of Cozzens's best work is laid in small towns or communities with urban values. . . . In each case you have a center which is yet a provincial center, which has firm traditions of its own, and which has little or not desire to drop its own values for those of the big city. On the contrary, representatives of big-city culture . . . tend to be seen as threats and even as corrupters. In our prevailing literary view, they ought, of course, to be seen as bringers of enlightenment. . . .

But in his fiction what produces that sense is the difference in values between the provincial center and the metropolitan center. The metropolitan center is, of course, pluralistic. It is the place where roots matter least, and oneself now matters most. . . .

By contrast, both the pastoral milieu and the town milieu tend to carry a single set of standards, which express and contain the whole history of the place, which all accept. There is one network—and maybe one hierarchy— of which everybody is a part. . . .

To my taste, he is one of the supreme stylists in American literature. I mean, he writes well. But what he writes is the periodic sentence, the highly wrought paragraph, the book which is clearly the product of the whole history of English and American literature. Such a style is exclusionary. It's not difficult to read, in the way that almost any important work in social science is difficult, or in the way *The Sound and the Fury* is difficult. But it does withhold itself, at least in part, from the reader whose ear is not attuned to the cadences of language, and perhaps from the reader whose past has not included considerable reading of classical English literature—books in the high style. Perhaps a better way to put it would be that Cozzens seems to assume consistently that there still *is* a high style, and not merely a lot of different ways of writing, which there is no way to grade or rank or sort. As opposed to the ingratiating openness, the friendly looseness of the American casual style, which invites the reader in ("come as you are"), a chapter of Cozzens makes demands, puts the reader on his mettle, may even shut doors in his face. You can do that in the pastoral milieu, as Frost did, but not so readily in the town milieu.

Noel Perrin. *NR*. Sept. 17, 1977, pp. 44–45

James Gould Cozzens is the least-read and least-taught of the major American novelists. It cannot be said that his work has suffered from inadequate exposure; but not even six Book-of-the-Month Club selections have attracted a broad readership. Except for *By Love Possessed*, no Cozzens novel has had a substantial mass-market paperback sale; and none has become a college classroom standard text. Although he has staunch admirers, one of the master American novelists is in some ways a cult-author. The resistance to Cozzens's work has been blamed on his refusal to make concessions to inattentive or unintelligent readers. Yet he is not difficult to read. His prose is precise; his meanings are clear; and, before *By Love Possessed*, his style is unembellished. The increasing dignity of style enforces Cozzens's objectivity. The "coldness" that critics have cited in Cozzens's observation of his characters is the stoical detachment of a writer trying to achieve "the stability of truth" in dealing with profound matters of human conduct. The periodic sentences and heavy subordination of *By Love Possessed* and *Morning Noon and Night* can intimidate only those who have not mastered the structure of the English sentence. The by-no-means overwhelming use of uncommon words achieves exactness of statement. Such words are intended to fix the reader's attention and, if necessary, send him to a dictionary. Cozzens's developed style is the natural expression for a highly literate writer with a traditionalist's respect for language. The complexity of sentence structure is appropriate to the complexity of his thinking. His use of open or concealed literary allusion in *Guard of Honor, By Love Possessed,* and *Morning Noon and Night* does not exclude the much-cherished general reader. The allusions are there for readers who recognize them; but the meanings of the books do not depend on that recognition. Cozzens is not a mandarin author; his work is far more accessible than that of many novelists currently in critical favor. He does not, in fact, make extraordinary demands on readers—beyond requiring them to pay attention.

The concept of vocation is central to Cozzens's representations of general nature, but he fully credits the determining factors in human conduct—education, social position, intelligence, training, luck, and what used to be called "character." The mark of Cozzens's people is that their values and behavior are developed in terms of their professions. You are what you do and how well you do it. This recognition may partly account for the denigration of his work among humanists who hold the job of teaching literature. Believing that success is a sign of corruption, they endeavor to persuade students that the real business of life is to live in accordance with one's feelings. Cozzens alarms proponents of the higher failure.

Cozzens has been called a conservative, an aristocrat, and a classicist. He rejects all of these identifications, insisting that he tries only to render life and people accurately as he sees them. He respects intelligence, moral firmness, and self-discipline. He rejects emotions as guides for conduct while recognizing the force of "Man's incurable wish to believe what he preferred to believe."

Matthew J. Bruccoli. Introduction to *Just Representations: A James Gould Cozzens Reader* (Southern Illinois Univ. Pr. and Harcourt Brace Jovanovich, 1978), pp. xviii–xix

The burden of Cozzens's fiction is that man must recognize and accept his condition and still bear the responsibility of action. . . . To act in the full awareness of the irony of the conditions within which he must act is, for Cozzens, the dignity of man.

If this is Cozzens's theme—and it is, I think, present in all the major novels—then he may now have found his own moment in time; until now Cozzens has been neglected, but there are signs that this neglect is about to end. History has finally prepared for him an audience that can share his angle of vision. Until it did, Cozzens went his solitary way, writing fine novels, pursuing his own sense of what life is about, undeterred by the almost total absence of recognition.

John William Ward. In *James Gould Cozzens: New Acquist of True Experience*, ed. Matthew J. Bruccoli (Southern Illinois Univ. Pr., 1979), pp. 15–16

## CRANE,  HART  (1899–1932)

Not only is *The Bridge* constructed according to Crane's theory of organic poetry, and hence to some extent explicable in terms of his poetics; but also, *The Bridge* is a poem about the creation of a poem, one that can embody the truth of the fictional poet's imagination in "one arc synoptic" ("Atlantis"). The poem, then, not only results from a process of organic creation, it also continually celebrates and re-enacts that process as its proper subject. Thus to propose a goal for, or a critical appreciation of, *The Bridge* which is based on categories or intentions not inherent in Crane's poetic purposes is to run that risk of a confusion of categories. In the American tradition of Emerson and Whitman, Crane was not concerned with society except insofar as it proceeded from the life of the individual, which for the poet means the life of the individual's imagination. Such poetry "teaches" society by evincing that life. . . .

There are three major aspects of Crane's poetic theory which bear on the nature and direction of *The Bridge*: the process by which a poem is created, the kind of poem resulting from this process, and the function of the poem in relation to the reader. The creative process is an organic one in which the poet submits to experience, assimilates and unifies it, then represents to the world the evidence of this unifying of experience within a poem. . . . Thus . . . the poem is . . . a celebration of the power of the imagination, the harp that engenders the chord, and hence a celebration of the life and act of the imagination. The dream of act is the dream that the poet-persona will, in the life of his particular imagination, be able to unite diverse materials, reach a state of unity and absolute innocence, symbolized by Atlantis, and then cast a "mythic spear," meaning write the poem, *The Bridge*, that will urge others (the audience) to the same kind of activity, the same kind of life, that engendered the poem. It is within this context that *The Bridge*, Crane's epic of the modern consciousness, must be described.

Richard P. Sugg. *Hart Crane's "The Bridge"*
(Univ. of Alabama Pr., 1976), pp. 4, 7

The Romantic tradition in which Crane is writing has been profoundly antidogmatic from the beginning. In Crane's poetry the balance between circumstantial or contingent truth and its dissolution in random occurrence is never given over in favor of some answer from Beyond. Crane celebrates the possibility of meaning, faith, and work in individual circumstances, while he demonstrates through the dramatic contexts of the poems that "meaning" is a temporary product of an always creative-destructive mind. This is why seeing Crane as a "redeemer" must be seriously qualified. I do not believe that Crane's poems represent an attempt to reassert the religious consciousness in an unreligious age. Their honesty and skepticism continually see through the efforts of the mind to redeem the world. What Crane has discovered is that the power of the mind never has depended on the absolute truth of its beliefs. Instead, the flexibility of the mind, its genius for disagreeing with itself, is its greatest strength. . . .

Crane's poems work toward a revelation which could be characterized as seeing through an experience without surrendering or demeaning a naive sense of its reality. Absolute knowledge for him is a momentary recognition of what is naive about the experience *and* what is wonderful about it. Such a recognition is absolute in the sense that it is both undeniably real and free of the biases of the poet and of the reader. Crane accepts the problematical nature of its interpretation and the precarious state of its existence as challenges to expression. . . .

The special character of Crane's lyrics was produced from a sensibility passionate and simple, by a mind as brilliant as Eliot's. Crane could glean from a magazine article or an offhand conversation the essence of a current of thought too advanced for most to grasp with the best education. His poetry begins with the complete and honest indulgence of personal feelings; then a most penetrating introspection pushes these toward what I have called absolute knowledge. The result is an intensely personal lyricism cast in the light of an awareness of the deceiving nature of thought and feeling themselves. But neither the feeling nor the awareness is surrendered. Crane's difficult style is his solution to the problem of sustaining tension between the two. It involves exploiting the ambiguity of sense experience under the direction of the sense of value. His willingness to destroy the comfortable individuation and public aspect of experience results in a Dionysian art which rejects optimism but transcends pessimism. And it results in a uniquely Romantic lyric which celebrates life without pretending to correct existence. His poetry is thus unabashedly personal, confessional, proud, and relentlessly self-conscious.

Robert Combs. *Vision of the Voyage: Hart Crane
and the Psychology of Romanticism* (Memphis
State Univ. Pr., 1978), pp. x–xi, 39, 106–7

## CREELEY, ROBERT (1926–    )

Both Creeley's poetic "posture" and his pacing of the line are more complex aspects of his work than critics have so far indicated in their brief studies. Indeed, it is difficult to make general statements about Creeley's poetry that are both useful and valid. A close examination of any one of his volumes reveals a wide range of personal attitudes and methods of expression. In *For Love*, for instance, Creeley uses an impressive variety of poetic voices, only one of which strikes the note of colloquial ease. In other poems he sounds nervous or hesitant—conspicuously antiidiomatic—and in still other poems he uses "Elizabethanisms," and in still others, childish pratter. Similarly, Creeley's poetic stance changes often even in the course of a single volume. Now he is shy, now arrogant, now poignant, now contemptuous. Thus it is of limited value of speak of a typical Creeley poem. His leap from genre to genre in his other literary work may dramatize the fact that Creeley does not stay with one technique, voice, or viewpoint in his poetry in any systematic sense.

> Cynthia D. Edelberg. *Robert Creeley's Poetry: A Critical Introduction* (Univ. of New Mexico Pr., 1978), p. 15

I believe that Creeley's major accomplishment will be technical and that he will be remembered primarily as a craftsman. Time and again I have been impressed with the total control he exerts over the rhythms, especially, of his prose and poetry. The line, the pauses, the hesitancies, the syntax and ellipses usually mirror precisely the statement of the poem; in fact, in his best poems and in his best short stories, these elements become the statement itself. What he says is relatively less important than how he says it, or at least I believe that that is what future generations will say. . . .

Creeley has chosen, or as he might say, it has been chosen for him, to write poetry that constricts itself to a small point of intensity, with the emphasis on small as well as intensity. His poetry and fiction avoid the grand statement and the grand method; in fact, they accept technical limitations in the same way that they accept thematic limitations. His work is minimal in that it functions more by what is excluded than by what is included. The question then is not so much whether Creeley is or will be known as a major writer, but rather whether minimal art itself can ever be major. In other words, has Creeley, by the course he runs, removed himself from consideration as a major writer? Although any answer to this question can be argued endlessly, I suspect that the answer is yes. So far in his career at least, Creeley's work lacks both the thematic and technical scope to qualify as major. Within the self-imposed limitations of his poetry and fiction, the achievement is impressive; however, those self-imposed limitations are still limitations. To the literary historian, that evaluation is both justifiable and understandable; however, to the poet such a statement remains fortunately irrelevant.

Arthur Ford. *Robert Creeley* (Twayne, 1978), pp. 137–38

## CUMMINGS, E. E. (1894–1962)

Whose poems are E. E. Cummings'? Antitheses beckon in reply. Are they the poems of an arch classicist, radically concerned with formal balance and traditional decorums, or those of a radical modern, archly delighted with scattered typography, omitted punctuation, and bawdy puns? Are they songs of the lyrical sonneteer, chivalrously singing his love and his lady, or blasts of the indignant satirist, savagely caricaturing the fools he saw everywhere? Are they poems of an eternal romantic, lover of nature, selfhood, and organic wholeness, or those of a contemporary realist, knower of fear and fragmentation? Replying to another dichotomous question, Cummings answered as he would have for the alternatives just offered: "And why not both?" The poet—certainly this poet—is many selves. . . .

Modification is what Cummings sought. He is among the company of poets who tell us always, either explicitly or by implication, how to live; though of course for these as for any poets, the way of saying is an essential part of the thing said. Further, Cummings sought modification through intensity—he tried to board his readers at a station deeper than intellect—and thus, whether we deal with the tricky but overt instructions of the "sonnet entitled how to run the world" . . . or the unspecified commitments that underlie "All in green went my love riding" . . . we must pay particular attention in his poetry to the unity of idea and expression. Though it will sometimes be expedient to talk of these as if each had independent existence, this *caveat* must right that notion. Cummings' intensity lives almost entirely in the marriage of spirited conception and linguistic flesh; divorce these or make one subservient, and what vanishes is poetry.

Gary Lane. *I Am: A Study of E. E. Cummings'*
*Poems* (Regents Pr. of Kansas, 1976), pp. 4–5

Many of the writers and painters we study . . . composed their works in an unwalled landscape, in a crosscurrent of impulses coming from the traditions and artifacts of many *métiers* besides their own.

Cummings was just such an eclectic. From the outset, reviewers and critics were quick to point out that he was a "visual" poet. . . .

Where Apollinaire and the Dada poets strove to make visual art out of words in much the same way a draftsman makes a picture out of lines, Cummings always made *poetry* out of words—although he borrowed as much as he could from the visual arts without abandoning his responsibility to language. And where his contemporaries in poetry rarely thought to violate the sanctity of lines and words and the conventions of the printers, Cummings broke open words, scattered letters across the page, intruded punctuation where it had never been before, and generally (as one of his later reviewers was to say of his paintings) "flabbergasted the Rotarians" by his insistence that poetry is not only words and punctuation but also— and most emphatically—the matrix of empty space in which they hang. One is hard pressed to think of another major poet who looked as deeply into the interrelations between these arts and who incorporated into poetry his findings.

At his best . . . Cummings was able to bring into poetry, in a way which Stevens never attempted, the aesthetic discoveries of the Cubists and their contemporaries. A brief glance through the poetry periodicals of the past twenty-five years indicates that it is not the theoretical endeavors of Stevens but the applied experimentation of Cummings which has had the greatest impact. The effect has not always been salubrious, for few poets have had Cummings' understanding of the principles of painting. But it is safe to say that no poet can avoid the implications of Cummings' discoveries: even the poets who choose not to follow his lead must constantly defend their allegiance to traditional forms. Stevens, and a host of thinkers before and after his time, showed that there ought to be an aesthetic common to poetry and painting. Cummings, almost alone, labored to prove in his practice as a painter and poet that there was one.

Rushworth M. Kidder. JML. April, 1979, pp.<br>255, 257, 291

# DE  VRIES,  PETER  (1910–    )

The opening chapter of *Madder Music . . .* is as sustained a piece of comedy as anything De Vries has ever achieved. His effects cannot properly be conveyed by quotation since the dazzling edifice he builds depends upon his unique capacity to pile one witticism precariously on top of another. Like Oscar Wilde he believes a good remark is worth repeating, but there is enough fresh material for the reader to overlook such lapses as "she was one of those women you don't give a book because they've already got one." Just occasionally he reveals too much of the stage machinery; a character called Betty Tingle remarks to the hero as he fondles her breasts "You're making Betty Tingle"—worth it for the triple entendre?

*Madder Music* is the story of the events that forced the hero to escape into the character of Groucho Marx. De Vries makes play with those reversals of the natural order of things that occur so often in everyday life. In his own house, the hero chances upon his wife making love to someone else. He desperately tries to hide and to his everlasting shame is discovered by the lovers crouching in a cupboard: "He had been caught in the act of catching in the act lovers who were rendered thereby vastly less guilty than himself, since his offense was the pettier though theirs the graver." As in his previous novels, De Vries delivers numerous homespun insights of this sort into the curious workings of the human mind: they are always expressed with deft economy—"Nothing will make a man a model husband faster than infidelity."

De Vries's satire is as accurate as ever: he successfully derides many contemporary American institutions, including modern art, psychiatry, and real estate business and of course current sexual mores. But his satire lacks passion—and one suspects he would not really wish the world very different from the way it is for then there would be less to laugh at.

In some of the novels of his middle period, such as *Reuben, Reuben*, Peter De Vries combined a feeling for the comedy of the human situation with genuine feeling for its victims. *Madder Music* and its immediate predecessor, *I Hear America Swinging*, revert to the style of earlier novels such as *Mackerel Plaza*. The characters are mouthpieces for De Vries's own witticisms—a nice device for disclaiming a bad joke. He has moments of sympathizing with them, but even then he holds them at a considerable distance: his hero is "unfit for either marriage or adultery, being restless in the one and remorseful in the other." When De Vries's verbal inventiveness flags, his lack of serious interest in his characters makes for the occasional dull page, but he remains one of the most stylish of living novelists and much, much the funniest.

Stuart Sutherland. TLS. March 24, 1978, p. 337

Nineteen eighty marks the publication of Peter De Vries' twenty-fifth book, *Consenting Adults*, and his seventieth birthday. A retrospective is in order for one of our most gifted but neglected comic writers. . . .

A little religion, a good deal of sexual warfare and then victory-making, a cast of unbelievable but effective satiric characters all go toward fleshing out *Consenting Adults*. De Vries' major theme remains constant too. One of the characters says "We must sooner or later be trundled into surgery for . . . an illusionectomy," and in investigating human relations and the relations the individual must have with those institutions around him, De Vries has composed his latest novelistic lesson on the text of growing up in modern America, on the necessity of separating workable illusions from those that defeat the individual. . . .

The book ends touchingly, perhaps forewarningly, as Peachum envisions his deathbed scene. The elegiac note here might remind us that De Vries is himself seventy years old, that perhaps here in Peachum's comic acceptance of the cosmos with all of its flux and paradox is also De Vries' own, that De Vries, like Prospero, may soon be ready to give up his particular brand of magic. Like the world of De Vries' early and masterful fictions, the world of Peachum is comic and positive rather than darkly absurd as in De Vries' later novels, a world that, with all its confusion and chaos, as Peachum learns, beckons commitment, not avoidance.

Taken together, the novels of Peter De Vries form a fascinating investigation into the mores of America over the last thirty years. We tend to neglect De Vries' artistry and insight because of the sheer wealth of his comic virtuosity—a typical De Vries novel contains enough wit for other authors to salt judiciously throughout their canons. But the exuberant comic display masks the unity of comic vision and technique. De Vries' most serious comic devices—fallible narrators, character role-playing, stylistic parody and burlesque, and word play—typically serve dual purposes. They entertain—at times almost overwhelmingly so—but they also reinforce and support his major theme of the illusion-making propensities of the individual, especially when rebelling against tradition or institution. There is a purposeful confluence, then, between idea and form in De Vries' work, a deft union of language, style, wit, and theme that creates an enduring comic vision of the way we live.

T. Jeff Evans. AHumor. Fall, 1980, pp. 13, 15–16

Peter De Vries . . . is a dedicated Puntheist, which is why he is rightly shameless. There is a character in this latest novel [*Slouching towards Kalamazoo*] who nudges his listener so violently every time the point of a joke comes looming up ("She was disappointed in love. She got married.") that the hero is jested black and blue: I'm sure we are meant to notice that the author does the same. It will come as no surprise to De Vries's admirers to be told that in this novel someone does slouch to Kalamazoo, Michigan, and there is a birth there; the baby is named Ahab, after one of the rougher beasts in American Literature, which this novel continuously and joyously celebrates.

It isn't just a baby that gets born either. The baby is the product of a brief liaison between Maggie Doubloon, a spirited English teacher, and the eighth-grade, thirteen-year-old, hero, the "star underachiever" of the town they agree to call Ulalume, North Dakota. The lad, Tony Thrasher by name, has a rash which reveals not only that he is itching to get out of town but also that his mother is taking a prurient interest in a dermatologist.

Class has been studying Hawthorne's *Scarlet Letter*, and when Maggie discovers that she is pregnant with meaning (and Tony is unhelpful: sent off to the chemist to get hold of some pills to get a girl out of trouble, he comes back with the Pill, woefully confusing cause and effect) she defies the overly virtuous townsfolk by appearing on a public balcony wearing not a scarlet A, but a scarlet A+, the sexual grade her pupil has accorded her. She thereby gives birth, De Vries suggests, to additional offspring: the sexual revolution and the modern tee-shirt. . . .

There is a subplot, of course. Tony's father, a silver-tongued preacher, given to reading the great monuments of American literature at length to his cowering wife and son ("'If you just wouldn't read with expression,' she blurted out") takes on in public debate the dermatologist, his rival and the town unbeliever, the subject the existence of God or sense in the universe. The debate is a draw, each convinces the other, and they exchange extremisms. The Preacher leaves his church and takes up television commercials; the infidel becomes a born-again knocker-on-doors and utterer of texts. Concerned relatives manage to stage a rematch, after which both speakers are converted to Christian Atheism, which I take to be De Vries's own theological stand. If there is a meaning in the scheme of things it is a double meaning.

There is a certain quality of homogeneity in Peter De Vries which his fans welcome, though non-fans, and I can imagine with an effort that such people might exist, would regard it as a certain sameness. This is the reliable product once again, the real McCoy; and if it must be said—and it must—that the whisky is a little watered to make a longer drink (some of his neater books would have had a dozen subplots) there is still enough to quench one's thirst. And there's still an artesian outpouring of parodistic and mimetic felicities, of literary nudges and verbal and nominal wheezes.

Eric Korn. TLS. Aug. 26, 1983, p. 898

## DICKEY, JAMES (1923–    )

For all his collections of poetry, James Dickey came closest to capturing his personal mythopoeic vision in the controversial novel *Deliverance*. That his vision was admittedly masculine seems unnecessary to justify, and that the novel was filled with violence, gore, and sport imagery is also defensible. For what Dickey was creating in his novel was a *Pilgrim's Progress* of male egoism, complete with all varieties of masculine fantasy—physical power and prowess, sexual expectation and satisfaction, and above all, contest, competition. What he achieved in the execution of the novel was a resolution far different from his characters' expectations—whether those of Lewis Medlock, the greatest achiever, or those of Ed Gentry, the follower. Dickey's resolution was an understanding beyond fantasy, an understanding of the reality of life, and an acceptance. . . .

Perhaps the chief weakness in *Deliverance* is the fact that all its parts do mesh so well. The explicit leads of the opening—with the charged dialogue between Ed and Lewis, even though it may be ironic dialogue, speech that we as readers understand as naive and indulgent—leave very little for the reader to come to alone. Once into the story, however, the demands of the plot keep Dickey from repeating his theme excessively; the movement of the book is apt for this twentieth-century river story. Dickey's is an incremental yet never leisurely rhythm, based on moderately long sentences which often branch with unexpected modifiers, and come up short in a simpler structure. . . .

Viewed as a masculine initiation story, set on a river, *Deliverance* can be considered a kind of gothic, even bitter, *Adventures of Huckleberry Finn*. That the story is no idyll is part of Dickey's theme: the simple tests, the primitive encounters, may be almost beyond civilized people—not out of their own deficiency, either physical or moral—but from the exigencies of common sense. Just as Dickey's comments on the seemingly pastoral life are scathing in their satire, and the doctor echoes them, so his notion that civilization *has* brought humanity pervades the "After" section. . . .

The three days of Dickey's *Deliverance* have seemed like an eternity, and in some ways they are. But they give Ed, and Lewis, and perhaps Dickey himself, the kind of freedom from the stereotyped male image, and from the pride, that blinds so many would-be powerful men. It is no simple journey; rather it is a contemporary descent into hell, modeled on the exploration-of-self through exploration-of-river that images a peculiarly American, masculine quest for identity. . . .

Linda Wagner. SCR. April, 1978, pp. 49, 52–55

Dickey does not always allow the idea of poetry to control the poem. . . . His self-consciousness, his desire to appear poetic in spite of himself is abandoned in the fine poem that gives <i>Falling</i> its name. Dickey gives himself up to the cadence of his own voice entirely, with brilliant results. The elision of images, muffed in the branches of "To the Last Wolverine," is convincing in "Falling" because it is pure and unconfused. Unembarrassed about form, he breaks his speech into natural units. Unconcerned about dividing his statement into traditional metrical or rhythmic units, he leaves syntax alone and lets it speak. We hear image occur and recur as the mind of the falling woman mixes with the mind of the poet. The awful, inexorable fall is matched by an almost inevitable use of language. In the end both the poem and the tragedy of sudden death are transformed into a beauty that is both uncommon and unmistakable. . . .

That Dickey himself understood the strength of his poetic gift is clear in the way he has approached pretty since <i>Falling. The Eyebeaters, Blood, Victory, Madness, Buckhead and Mercy</i> is a collection of unusual poems that not only are considerably longer than the early lyrics, but also are conversational in syntax. The most powerful among them, poems like "Living There" and "Looking for the Buckhead Boys," avoid the structure of poetic convention that Dickey finds intimidating. The "memorable language" that Dickey admires in poetry, the search for the "unusual word in a sentence," is left to the speech of the provincial South. He does not attempt to create images that are wild in the hope that they might be expressive, but expresses hope in the speech of the men he has known. As he himself admits, it is not a compressed image but the expansiveness of language that is needed. His process of writing is to "cut down from six, seven, eight times longer . . . I like to write long."

It is in this realization and in the freedom of the later poems that Dickey unites his voice with a poetic form that is its complement. His struggle is not to find an end, therefore, but to remain uncomplicated by the pretensions of his craft, a temptation not always resistible. He wishes closure on his own terms. The final verdict, as he writes in "The Firebombing," is not yet clear. . . .

James M. Haule. In James Dickey: Splintered<br>Sunlight, ed. Patricia De La Fuente (Pan<br>American Univ., 1979), pp. 42–44

## DIDION, JOAN (1934–    )

All of Didion's heroines have trouble with history, personal and otherwise, and each of her novels is an attempt at travelling backwards in search of various historical explanations. It is a tentative operation—she only grudgingly appreciates "all the opiates of the people, whether they are as accessible as alcohol and heroin and promiscuity or as hard to come by as faith in God or History." A willingness to seek explanation in the past, and to invite disappointment, is the impetus of each of her novels, as well as the basis for their narrative structures. All three books open immediately after a disaster— Everett's murder of Ryder Channing and his subsequent suicide in *Run River* (1963); Maria's breakdown and hospitalization in *Play It as It Lays*; Charlotte Douglas' death in a Central American revolution in *A Book of Common Prayer*—and then take the reader backwards in time to show him what triggered the catastrophe. The effect of the technique is not only to erase immediately any grounds for optimism in the reader—he knows that the book can only take him back to the bad end he has already glimpsed— but to prepare him for an historical test: is the view of the past he is about to get sufficient explanation of the disaster he has already witnessed? This question is one that Didion repeatedly asks of history in these books. Her faith in her own exploration and method is much tried and ultimately very limited, but her looking backwards remains compulsive.

The heroines of all three novels share an unusual number of similarities. Physically, each has what is called for Lily Knight McClellan in *Run River* a "compelling fragility" or for Charlotte an "extreme and volatile thinness." An inability to cope with the day-to-day, a dreaminess, forms a large part of their sexual attraction.

Thomas Mallon. Critique. 21, 3, 1980, pp. 43–44

In both her essays and her fiction Didion seeks to render the moral complexity of contemporary American experience, especially the dilemmas and ambiguities resulting from the erosion of traditional values by a new social and political reality. To this end, she violates the conventions of traditional journalism whenever it suits her purpose, fusing the public and the personal, frequently placing herself in an otherwise objective essay, giving us her private and often anguished experience as a metaphor for the writer, for her generation, and sometimes for her entire society.

In her fiction, on the other hand, Didion has found that a traditional form and structure better suit her purpose. Unlike many other contemporary novelists, she creates real settings, characters that behave with some consistency, plots that have a beginning, middle, and end. In her few pieces of literary criticism Didion defends these traditions against the "new fiction" of

Kurt Vonnegut, Joseph Heller, and Bruce Jay Friedman. Lacking plot, structure, or consistent point of view, the new fiction, Didion feels, allows the author to abnegate his responsibility to make a moral statement. . . .

Implicit in Didion's view of the writer's responsibility is her conviction that, however multiple and ambiguous it may be, truth exists and can be approached by the writer with the courage and skill to project a coherent, realistic vision. Her own vision reveals to us the moral condition of contemporary Americans, living by illusions as fragile as fine china, clinging to shards of broken dreams, yet often redeemed by an immense potential for love and commitment.

Katherine Usher Henderson. *Joan Didion*
(Ungar, 1981), pp. vii–viii, 143, 146–47

No contemporary writer has more successfully carved the symbolic properties of emotional inertness into a territory of her own than has Joan Didion, and nowhere more so than in the style she has pursued with a discipline wholly to be admired. Of her work it can truly be said its substance is the sound of the author's voice. . . .

In Didion the insistence of atmosphere over character in transparent. People are given liquid injections of attitude and placed firmly on a monochromatic landscape the prose insists is the color of interior light. No Didion character will ever surprise either the author or the reader. . . .

In Didion, the antisocial and the spiritually malevolent have been given metaphoric meaning. Her people are not dangerously lost and damaged; rather they are the holy scraps of existential survival. Her men are nihilists whose sexual brutality is an inverse mark of Cain: sensitive souls mangled by murderous life. Her women are thin, crushed-mouthed, silent: Magdalene-madonnas pushed willingly around by the nihilists for whom they suffer gladly because they, too, know living is an alien business. These nerveless, hollowed-out, childlike women stare wide-eyed into the joyless Don Juanism of their men, and they do not turn away. Floating in unanchored space, arrested in emotional time, they are in thrall to spiritual loss.

For Didion, modern life is a wound from which there is no recovery. In her novels, abortion, infant mortality, and cancer are symbolic inflictions. Because there is no escaping fatal loss, nothing matters. Nothing mattering is a recurrent assault on a woundedness as undefended as a child's. We who, accidentally and only apparently, survive the siege of life understand this. Deeply. We walk through our meaningless days and nights, mad and battered, our cruel, corrupt behavior the stigmata of the permanent hellishness that is the only condition we will ever know.

Didion's contribution to the literature of the walking wounded is a rhythmic use of ellipsis devoted to capturing the taste and feel of this ultimate piece of understanding. Volumes of unspoken message are trapped inside her sentence repetitions, her broken-up paragraphs, her tight-lipped juxtapositions. She inserts repeatedly, endlessly, throughout her novels, in puzzling, inappropriate silly places, certain sentences that carry the burden of her insistence. . . .

She gives texture to the prose of nothingness, enriches the distance, lends dimension to the etherizing numbness, and insists on the legitimacy of the Corrupt Innocents in the Alien Promised Land with a relentlessness no other American writer can equal. . . .

Yet skilled as this writing is, it does not feel genuine. There is a space between the pain it alludes to and the expression of that pain. That space seems occupied by a stylish kind of American hip, derived from Hemingway and adopted by an adolescent camp culture, an existential macho swagger whose characteristic economy of expression is duplicitous. . . .

Vivian Gornick. *VV*. Feb. 18–24, 1981, pp. 36–38

## DOCTOROW, E. L. (1931–   )

When a novel like *Ragtime* comes along, bucks the trend and breaks the mold, we are confronted with a cultural case which encourages us to consider several interesting questions about art and its audience. What is there about *Ragtime* that has allowed it to cross the border and close the usually unbridgeable gap between "high" and "popular" culture when the same author's previous novels—like those of most novelists—could not? . . .

The answers are to be found in both the form and content of *Ragtime*: a form that is experimental and accomplished enough to appeal to critics who demand innovation and yet familiar enough to attract the common reader, and a content that grapples with the fundamental issues confronting the contemporary fictionist yet never ceases to entertain and engage. This is the combination which Doctorow's previous novels—like most of the seven thousand or so published each year—lacked. . . .

Doctorow's third novel, *The Book of Daniel* (1971) . . . most certainly is an exceptional book worthy of the National Book Award nomination it received. It is a critic's delight because of its structural complications, its use of multiple points of view, the complexity of its character development, its imaginative juxtaposition of reality and fantasy, and its political stance. But it is also exasperating to the common reader—and for exactly the same reasons. . . .

In *Ragtime* Doctorow found both the story and the techniques which would allow him to capitalize on these strengths and reach a broader audience as well. *Ragtime*'s point of view is stabilized, and that eliminates much of the confusion; there is, to make the point simply, something for everyone in the *story* of three families caught up in the events of the first decade-and-a-half of this century—the era when America lost her innocence and suddenly found herself naked in the modern world. . . .

To the reader weary of self-conscious explorations of the individual psyche, then, *Ragtime* offers an exuberant journey through the storehouse of our common memories. In addition, it offers much more to a popular audience. To the reader intimidated by the increasingly common use of unfamiliar mythological references in contemporary fiction, it offers the creation of a new mythology out of the familiar images of our shared past. To the reader inundated with novels of complicated character, it offers a return to narrative and story; to the reader confused by contemporary experimentation, accessible innovation; to an age in the grip of nostalgia, another time; to an audience captivated by the rhythms of Scott Joplin's "The Entertainer," a verbal equivalent of ragtime.

Bernard F. Rodgers, Jr. ChiR. Winter, 1975–76,<br>pp. 138–41

Doctorow reminds us that writing history is a very creative activity, and that the professional historian would not claim that it is possible to write history *objectively*. . . . Doctorow's own brilliant imagination has given us not only some rather compelling—and disturbing—versions of America's past, but in addition his skillfully crafted narratives confront us with the terrible wisdom of great art, altering us in a manner that perhaps even the best historical discourse cannot do.

Doctorow points out that history exists for most of us as sets of images—the more remote in time, the fewer the images. The images in Doctorow's novels often clash violently with those that have seized the popular mind. *Welcome to Hard Times* demolishes the romantic view of the Wild West and its adulation of the "social bandit," reminding us that we have lionized individuals whose only mark of distinction was plunder and murder. In the nineteenth century the American West functioned as the nation's "safety valve," promising a new start for those fleeing from failure or personal tragedy in the East. Aggressively promoted as Arcadia, the frontier enticed many with its lure of "free land"; "the myth of the garden" even suggested that rainfall would follow the plow. Unfortunately the harsh and unrelenting climate of the arid Great Plains refused to yield to the myth, and many who journeyed West, faced with the lack of timber and water so bountiful in the East, found the American Dream a mere mirage, their hopes evaporating into disappointment, failure, or disaster.

No one who reads *The Book of Daniel* will succumb to the recent nostalgia for the "Fabulous Fifties.". . . . Like Doctorow's earlier novels, *Ragtime* indicts our complacency and admonishes us that we continue to indulge in an uncritical nostalgia at our peril. Doctorow's novels suggest that by refusing to analyze our own responsibility for our past failures—not infrequently projecting evil outward onto other nations—we ensure that periods of mass hysteria like the McCarthy era or the burning of the nation's cities in the sixties will haunt us again.

Daniel L. Zins. *HC.* Dec., 1979, pp. 2–3

The excitement caused by *Ragtime* five years ago was so great that, long before its European publication, we who live on the Mediterranean were itching to get hold of a copy. Summoned to Hollywood for a script conference, I made straight for a Los Angeles bookstore and bought one. Jet lag abetted my decision to read the book before even making amicable contact with my temporary masters at Universal. I was, of course, disappointed. Literary reality has never yet lived up to literary expectation. But that E.L. Doctorow was a genuine experimentalist I did not doubt. The aim of *Ragtime* was as purely aesthetic as that of *Ulysses*: The joy lay in the manipulation of the crass elements of history. Houdini and Scott Joplin and Freud and Jung and certain of their less reputable contemporaries were drawn into a kind of ballet. Bernard Shaw had done something similar in his *In Good King Charles's Golden Days*, but Doctorow's achievement didn't seem derivative.

Rereading *Ragtime*, I find that most of the initial impact has been blunted: Literary shocks are subject to the law of diminishing returns. I find, too, a certain vacuity of literary display. What once seemed verbally startling is now revealed as mostly tinsel. But that Doctorow was superior to most of his American fellow-novelists in his concentration on fiction as form, not as a vehicle for special or ethnic preaching, is made very clear. A rereading of *Welcome to Hard Times* and *The Book of Daniel* has confirmed Doctorow's special status. *Loon Lake* exhibits a new formal direction. It is a difficult book and I don't think it is a successful one. But it is a very honorable attempt at expanding the resources of the genre. . . .

I am happy to learn that *Loon Lake* is already a popular book, in that it is a Book of the Month Club choice and eighty-odd thousand copies have already been printed. Happy because, whatever the faults of the work (nearly always the admirable faults of the overreacher), serious students of the novel must recognize here a bracing technical liberation, and such a recognition is being forced upon a readership probably happier with *Princess Daisy*. The bulk of our popular fiction is the work of either cynics or simpletons. The serious novelist's problem is to be uncompromising and yet to find an audience. Doctorow has found an audience and nothing could be less of a fictional compromise than *Loon Lake*. Like most writers who consider the craft to be primarily an exploration of the nature of human consciousness, he is brought up against such damnable problems as the validity of memory, the truthfulness of the senses, and, more than anything, the ghastly dilemmas of style. And, behind the epistemological agonies, there rests that basic obligation of all but the French antinovelists—to invent living personages and a convincing spacetime continuum to hold them. Doctorow's characters—Joe, Penfield, Clara, even the grotesque Fat Lady of the carney—are alive, unrefracted by the often wayward medium. That *Loon Lake* breaks new technical ground and yet possesses so many of the traditional virtues of fiction must be accounted its peculiar distinction.

Anthony Burgess. *SR*. Sept., 1980, pp. 66–67

# DOOLITTLE, HILDA (H. D., 1886–1961)

Why is her poetry not read? H.D. is part of the same literary tradition that produced the mature work of the "established" artists—T. S. Eliot, Ezra Pound, William Carlos Williams, D. H. Lawrence. She in fact knew these artists well; she had known and almost married Pound while the two were students in Philadelphia (H.D.'s intensely absorbing recreation of their lifetime friendship, *End to Torment*, is being prepared for publication); her friendship with Williams goes back to those student days; but most important, she was an active member of the London literary circle that spun out the dazzling succession of artistic "isms"—imagism, dadaism, vorticism, futurism—before the catastrophe of the First World War smashed this coterie into the confusion of a spiritual wasteland. Like these artists, H.D. began writing in the aestheticism and fascination for pure form characteristic of the imagists; and like them, she turned to epic form and to myth, religious tradition, and the dream as a way of giving meaning to the cataclysms and fragmentation of the twentieth century. Her epic poetry should be compared to the *Cantos*, *Paterson*, the *Four Quartets*, and *The Bridge*, for like these poems, her work is the kind of "cosmic poetry" the imagists swore they would never write.

The pattern of her poetic development not only paralleled that of more famous artists, but it was also permeated by major intellectual currents of the century. In 1933 and 1934 she was psychoanalyzed by Freud, an exploration deep within her own unconscious that ultimately linked for her the personal with the universal, the private myth with the "tribal" myths. At the same time that she studied with Freud, the convinced materialist, she was a student of comparative religion, of esoteric tradition, and, like Yeats, of the occult. The forces perpetually at work to bring a directionless century to war were a constant preoccupation in her work. Consciously rejecting the mechanistic, materialist conceptions of reality that formed the faith of the empirical modern age, H.D. affirmed a "spiritual realism" and the relevance of a quest for intangible meanings. Her growth into a poet exploring the psyche or soul of humanity and reaching out to confront the questions of history, tradition, and myth places her squarely in the mainstream of "established" modern literature. But still, outside of a few poets like Denise Levertov, who wrote "An Appreciation" of H.D., Robert Duncan, and the aficionados who circulate a pirated edition of *Hermetic Definition*, few people read her poetry. . . . H.D. was a serious prolific poet exploring the same questions as her famous counterparts and thus inviting comparison with them. It is something of an understatement, I think, to say that in our profession artists do not have to wear the badge of greatness in order to have articles and books written about them. The simple relevance of her work to the issues and experiments of modern poetry demands that it be studied. . . .

The answer is simple enough, I think. It lies biographically and factually right in front of our critical noses—too close perhaps to be seen easily. It lies in what makes H.D. and her work different from a long string of more studied poets like Eliot, Pound, Crane, Williams, and Yeats. And it lies in the response of her critics. She was a woman, she wrote about women, and all the ever-questioning, artistic, intellectual heroes of her epic poetry and novels were women. In the quest poetry and fiction of the established literary tradition (particularly the poetic tradition), women as active, thinking, individual human beings rarely exist. They are instead the apocalyptic Pocahontas and the demonic prostitute of *The Bridge*, the goddess in the park sought by the poet Paterson, the superficial women walking to and fro talking of Michelangelo. They are the static, symbolic objects of quest, not the questors; they are "feminine principles," both threatening and life-giving, and not particularized human beings. Women are dehumanized, while the quest of the male poet is presented and understood as the anguished journey of the prophet-seer for the absolute on behalf of all humankind. For "mankind" they may be the spokesmen, but for "womenkind" they are not. As a woman writing about women, H.D. explored the untold half of the human story, and by that act she set herself outside of the established tradition.

Susan Friedman. *CE*. March, 1975, pp. 802–3

*Helen in Egypt* is an epic poem of great depth and beauty; it is H.D.'s finest achievement. . . . As an impersonal poem *Helen in Egypt* is a meditation upon the cause of war. War takes place, says H.D., because someone (or some group or culture) will not bend to the will of someone else (or some other group or culture).

H.D. sees the war between the sexes as primal and believes all wars follow the same logic. A person or culture attempts to enforce his will on another person or another culture. Who, then, is to be blamed? The one who attempts to force his will on another or the one who refuses to submit? In H.D.'s experience men had attempted to force their will upon her; resistance leads to strife. Do we then blame the woman for resisting? Or do we blame her for provoking the attack? Or, suggests H.D., is it not the case that men ought to take responsibility for war? They are, after all, the aggressors. Why should women be blamed for simply existing? These are some of the larger questions that prompt the strophes of *Helen in Egypt*. . . .

While it is true that H.D.'s vision was informed by far more than Aldington, Pound, and Lawrence, she was always deeply aware that the particular traumatic events involving them had precipitated her coming to consciousness. Her work with Freud enabled H.D. to bring these events into consciousness on an epic scale and to understand the transpersonal nature of her experience. The Helen-Iphigeneia realization is not a mere metaphor for a personal event; rather, the event was the efficient cause, the precipitating occurrence from which the conception was realized. But the efficient cause is not the sufficient cause. The conception was informed by the entire body of circumstances of the poet's life and mind.

Janice S. Robinson. *H. D.: The Life and Work of an American Poet* (Houghton Mifflin, 1982), pp. 362, 369, 378–79

# DOS PASSOS, JOHN (1896–1970)

What is crucial to the judgment of political novels is not only the extent to which a novelist's politics are intrinsic to his work, but the extent to which in his work he is incapable of transcending them—for to that extent, if one does not share these politics, one is scarcely likely to bear to read the work.

A case very much to the point is that of John Dos Passos, America's most unrelievedly political novelist through his long career till his death in 1970. No other literary career in America has been so subjected to extra-literary, to essentially political, judgment than Dos Passos's. Perhaps no other novelist suffered in his lifetime so precipitous a drop in literary esteem. Dos Passos was one of the four major novelists of the 1920's—the other three being Sinclair Lewis, Ernest Hemingway, and F. Scott Fitzgerald—and of them all, time has dealt most harshly with Dos Passos. Hemingway and Fitzgerald are still large items on the cultural agenda of the young as well as of those who read them when young. If this is less true of Lewis, he yet remains an established author in university curricula, and *Main Street* and *Babbitt* continue to be taught for their documentary interest.

Dos Passos, though, is largely ignored. Although his productivity did not fall off appreciably, he was in fact neglected over the last three decades of his life. No Nobels, no Pulitzers, no academic revivals came his way. Neglect so complete must have been especially embittering to a novelist who in his younger days was considered central, and not by Americans alone. D. H. Lawrence wrote of Dos Passos's novel, *Manhattan Transfer*, that it is "the best modern book about New York that I have read." Jean-Paul Sartre came forth with heavier praise. "I regard Dos Passos," he wrote in 1938, "as the greatest writer of our time." After 1940 no names of equal weight offered similar endorsements. Even in death, Dos Passos was partially ignored: having the bad luck to die on the same day as Colonel Gamal Abdel Nasser, he was deprived of the Great American Writer obituaries that might otherwise have been his. As a character in one of his novels says: "Funny t'ing a man's life."

It would be an exaggeration to say that Dos Passos was a modernist master, but no one was more adept than he at applying modernist techniques to politically radical purposes, and nowhere did he succeed more securely at doing this than in *U.S.A.* Whitmanesque in approach, Gibbonian in scope, it is a book that sets out to tell everything about America (its protagonist, as Alfred Kazin once pointed out, is American society itself) and it is the most ambitious single literary work ever undertaken in this country. Its influence, though obviously momentous, is perhaps impossible to gauge precisely. The novelists of the 1920's, whether they wished the role or not, were important teachers, each with a specific lesson. Sinclair Lewis taught loathing of the small town, business, and the middle class. Hemingway taught a narrow yet enticing code of manliness. Fitzgerald taught style in social and personal life, even if his teaching was often riddled with the snobbishness of a Middlewestern Irish Catholic. Dos Passos taught how to think about politics, and his instruction featured hatred of large organization, sympathy for the underdog, and the belief that society is a machine that twists and crushes, forcing some men to sell out, others to knuckle under, while grinding most face first into the slime. Such at any rate was the catechism *U.S.A.* provided.

*U.S.A.* is a young man's novel—written by a then-young Dos Passos and best read when young. A distinct recollection of when they first read it, and under what conditions and with what effect, is very common among people who read it between the ages of sixteen and, say, twenty-four. So furious is its energy, so passionate its sympathies and hatreds, that it is all but impossible not to be swept up by it, captivated, hypnotized, enthralled. In later years one may forget the characters and the working out of its five separate plots, but one never forgets its impact. It is the kind of book that changes people's lives.

Joseph Epstein. *Cmty*. Jan., 1976, pp. 63–65

He did not have time before he died to polish *Century's Ebb*. But neither the incompleteness nor the bias in what he told Harold Weston was his "last forlorn Chronicle of Despair" is what matters about the book. What matters is that it is the final work of a major American writer of the twentieth century who had struggled throughout his literary career to convey a panorama of twentieth-century society. Although his work, especially books like *Adventures of a Young Man*, *The Grand Design*, *The Prospect Before Us*, and *The Great Days*, may strike readers as too polemical, anyone wanting to dismiss Dos Passos should remember that he was not a crank, but an intelligent, thoughtful man who agonized about politics. He was not alone when he shifted from Left to Right, and his sorrow about his chosen country was akin to that of literally millions of his countrymen who despaired—as he never did—about their nation. *Century's Ebb* is not so much a diatribe from the Right as a final statement in which Dos Passos, who had devoted his career to observing America, hoped to awaken other Americans with his words. If, like his earlier chronicles, it often paints a dark, even a savage picture, it also reflects his pleasure and amusement in his fellow men, who might scurry about foolishly and self-importantly, but who have as well their moments of tragedy, of compassion, and of greatness. The book rounded out his vision of American life and marked the end of his lover's quarrel with the world.

Like Whitman, Bartolomeo Vanzetti was one of Dos Passos's heroes. What Dos Passos had said about the Italian anarchist in 1926— what John Chamberlain in his 1939 review of *Adventures of a Young Man* reminded his readers was the author's own stance—was still true of Dos Passos when he died. Vanzetti's politics, Dos Passos had written, were "less a matter of labels than of feeling, of gentle philosophic brooding." Vanzetti hoped, Dos Passos believed, that "somehow men's predatory instincts, incarnate in the capitalist system, can be canalized into other channels, leaving free communities of artisans and farmers and fishermen and cattle breeders who would work for their livelihood with pleasure, because the work was itself enjoyable in the serene white light of a reasonable world." All that need be added to this to be an intellectual portrait of Dos Passos at the conclusion of his life was that he had come to believe that the capitalist system might function for the good of everyone; yet we should remember that even in later works like *Midcentury* he portrayed corruption and greed under capitalism. He thought it the best possible system, but it was constantly being abused because, as he had told Lucy, "there is a great deal more evil than good in the human character." In fact, it may be that the substantial difference in Dos Passos early and late was his final conviction that evil was not a part of some of us, but of us all. He had become, as he himself claimed, a disillusioned moralist and as a result a more complete—and ever harsher—satirist of the American scene.

Townsend Ludington. John Dos Passos:<br>A Twentieth Century Odyssey (Dutton, 1980),<br>pp. 506–7

Aesthetic purists notwithstanding, politics is not inimical to art, and for Dos Passos it is in fact its very essence, what makes his art possible. A criticism that fails or refuses seriously to engage itself with the political content of Dos Passos's work—and the point, of course, is not to pitch more baseballs at it—will miss what makes his fiction so often exciting and valuable.

Central to Dos Passos's achievement as a political novelist is the ambitiousness of his quest—to chronicle and analyze twentieth-century American society. Though broad in scope, his fiction is never abstract or mystifying. He persisted in trying to explain human conditions; he did not simply bemoan and reify their seeming irrationality. And he succeeded in dramatizing, often with extraordinary clarity and power, how great historical forces shape the lives of individuals. Further, the technical experimenting through which he sought to expand the scope of his fiction is not only exciting in itself, but also sheds much light on the complex relationship between political ideology and literary form.

A careful examination of Dos Passos's political thinking—expressed most unambiguously in his letters, diaries, journalism, historical writings, and the many causes he gave his name and time to—is obviously essential to a full understanding of his art. Moreover, his views, though not necessarily original, are themselves worth studying, for through them Dos Passos—as he becomes successively a youthful pacifist rebel, a libertarian socialist, a Jeffersonian democrat, and finally a conservative Republican—emerges as a sort of emblematic figure. The evolution (or, perhaps, devolution) of his ideas epitomizes, in many ways, the difficulties, the contradictions, and ultimately the fate of radical idealism in America; once he turns away from the left, he becomes one particularly articulate representative of a whole generation of ex-radicals. In addition, since he is an artist, a careful look at the entire range of Dos Passos's activities raises a whole series of still very important questions about the relationship between political passions and literary efforts.

Robert C. Rosen. John Dos Passos: Politics and<br>the Writer (Univ. of Nebraska Pr., 1981), p. x

# DREISER, THEODORE (1871–1945)

Dreiser's basic tendency as a novelist was to establish a clear central structure (Hurstwood's fall and Carrie's rise; Cowperwood's alternating business and love affairs; Clyde's parallel life in Kansas City and Lycurgus; Solon's double life as businessman and Quaker), to pursue this structure to its seeming conclusion (death or an emotional stasis), yet to suggest both by authorial commentary and by a powerful symbol within the narrative (a rocking chair, deep-sea fish, a street scene, a brook) that life is essentially circular, that it moves in endless repetitive patterns. Frequently this circular pattern involves a seeker or quester—sometimes driven by desire, sometimes by other motives—who finds at the end of the novel that he has returned to where he started: Carrie still seeking beauty and happiness; Jennie once again alone despite her immense capacity to love; Cowperwood's millions gone; Clyde still walled in; Solon returning to the simplicity of absolute faith. It is possible to visualize Dreiser's novels as a graphic irony—the characters believe they are pushing forward but they are really moving in a circle. . . .

Another pervasive structure in Dreiser's novels is best illustrated by "Butcher Rogaum's Door." The three principal figures in the story—Rogaum, Theresa, and Almerting—can be characterized as a well-meaning but ignorant and authoritarian parent, a youth seeking the wonder and excitement of life, and a seducer who takes advantage of the conflict between parent and child. Rogaum, blind to the needs of youth, drives Theresa to rebellion, and she is almost seduced by Almerting. This triangle and the narrative which derives from it constitute an archetypal structure within the world of Dreiser's novels, though it is a structure which appears in increasingly complex and displaced forms. . . .

A third significant characteristic of the form of Dreiser's early stories is their tendency toward the parody of sentimental or hackneyed narrative patterns. . . . Throughout his career as a novelist Dreiser was to rely on similar formulas, particularly those of the seduced country girl in *Sister Carrie* and *Jennie Gerhardt* and the Horatio Alger myth of success in the Cowperwood trilogy, *The "Genius,"* and *An American Tragedy.* In most instances, he both used the myth and reversed some of its traditional assumptions. Carrie "rises" not only despite her seduction but also because of it, and Clyde finds neither luck nor pluck in his attempt to succeed. Like many major American novelists, Dreiser used the mythic center of American life as a base from which to remold myth into patterns more closely resembling experience as he knew it.

The various overlapping structures which I have been discussing constitute in their totality the formalistic expression of Dreiser's basic cast of mind, a cast which can best be called ironic. For though Dreiser seldom engages in verbal irony, he habitually relies in his fiction on an intricately interwoven series of narrative or structural ironies. That is, he constantly juxtaposes the true nature of a situation and a character's estimation of it in order to reveal the weaknesses either in the character's values or in ours, a revelation which is at once theme and form in his work. . . .

On the one hand, these are the conventional ironies of all fiction. Fiction—because it is a temporal rather than a spatial art, and because it dramatizes the difference between what characters believe and what the author knows—is inherently ironic. On the other hand, Dreiser's ironic formulas in his short stories look forward to a bolder and more intense reliance on this particular characteristic of fiction than is usual in most novels. Like Stephen Crane, Dreiser translated an uneasy mixture of iconoclasm and unconventional belief into a structural principle. But whereas for Crane this principle was a subtle and complex modulation in authorial tone, imagery, and diction, for Dreiser it was an equally sophisticated ordering of events within an extended narrative. Dreiser labored to perfect this technique throughout his career as a writer of fiction, and after some twenty-five years he achieved in *An American Tragedy* a novel whose structural approximation of his deeply ironic view of life results in a work of complex beauty.

Donald Pizer. *The Novels of Theodore Dreiser*
(Univ. of Minnesota Pr., 1976), pp. 25–27

It is by his style that Dreiser must stand or fall. We may speak of a novelist's ideas, but ideas in novels are real only in so far as we can feel them, and feelings are evoked by style. When Dreiser wrote about gasoliers or a cold winter's day, he was able to re-create the states of feeling that went with them, and such moments, repeated again and again, created the illusion of character, a Carrie or a Hurstwood. He could make you share Clyde Griffith's sudden awareness of the lake, the still water, the trees on either side. He could make you see how much depended on a new jacket, the heat emanating from a radiator, the cold on the open platform of a trolley. Dreiser had discovered Flaubert's secret: immersion. The way to get a style is to immerse yourself so thoroughly in the physical life of your character that everything you write has an air of experience. Once you have been immersed in Charles Bovary, have travelled with him drowsily on the road to the Bertaux, at one and the same time looking at the horizon and hearing the curtain rings jingling around the marital bed, you understand pretty well what Charles will be thinking for the rest of the novel. . . .

Dreiser does not so much create character as states of feeling. His characters, viewed only from outside, are always less than we—we can see all around them. Their states of feeling, however, enclose us—sometimes so painfully that we hurry to the end of the chapter. We are relieved when Hurstwood turns on the gas and when Clyde's long agony in the death-house is concluded. One does not merely finish a book by Dreiser—one escapes from it.

Louis Simpson. TLS. Dec. 3, 1976, p. 1502

## DUNCAN, ROBERT (1889–1979)

Where most postmodern poets are content to render dramatic instances of the mind satisfied in process, Duncan has grander ambitions. His aim to reinterpret the aesthetics of presence in terms that can recover the contemporary significance of the Romance and hermetic imaginative traditions. . . .

When critics notice [Duncan] at all, they comment on his weaknesses as a lyric poet, for his verse is often diffuse, boring, and without vitality in language or imagery. Moreover, like Olson, his work is often difficult and apparently remote from contemporary concerns because his mythic enterprise requires that he incorporate a good deal of abstruse learning into his work. Yet once one accepts him as a poet whose primary task is to reflect on what others express directly, one can, I think forgive some of the lyric weaknesses and learn to read him for his intellectual interest and for those moments when he develops those interests into intense lyrical passages. Duncan is at the least a very important influence on other poets like Creeley and Levertov and at best he rivals his stylistic master, Pound, in integrating historical and mythic meditations with lyrical exaltation. . . .

Sympathetically read, Duncan's work then has greater imaginative scope than that of his peers. By reflecting on what other poets are reflections of, he achieves a generality and abstractness that articulates the value schemes shared by most postmodern visions of Romanticism. He makes self-reflexive and systematic the analogical nature of [much of his poetry]. . . , and he defines the analogical process in a rich restatement of the Romantic dialectic between creative mind and creative nature. But his ambitiousness creates serious aesthetic problems, exacerbated by the fact that he is more deductive and allegorical in his use of myth than the great moderns and consequently exhibits little doubt or struggle. One cannot simply read Duncan dramatically: one must understand and work to share the beliefs before one can really participate in the poetry. In this skeptical age . . . readers find it difficult to pursue abstractions they see as hard to understand and impossible to trust—especially when Duncan's immediate surfaces are so thoroughly conceptual and remote from ordinary existential problems and needs.

Charles Altieri. *Enlarging the Temple: New Directions in American Poetry during the 1960s* (Bucknell Univ. Pr., 1979), pp. 150–51, 163

In his poetry and prose, Duncan grapples (much as Whitman did) with the meaning of America, not as political entity alone, but as the generative source for poetic and personal endeavor. It is undoubtedly the native American literary line to seek the basis of poetry in antipoetic or unpoetic material and to redeem the creative potentiality of mundane subjects. Emerson had invited poetic expression equal to the qualities and characteristics of the evolving nation. Whitman answered the invitation repeatedly. In his essay "Slang in America" he found an inherent piquancy in socially nontraditional language which captured his imagination and provided intimations of a mythic past. . . .

Duncan holds a far less sanguine view of America than Whitman, but his desire to call up its presence, despite inherent contradictions, is equally imperative. At the political level Duncan can work less on faith than Whitman, and he is too honest to fool himself that Whitman's egalitarian optimism remains viable for *all* men in the twentieth-century. . . .

Whitman is as much a formative influence on Duncan's work as Dante or Blake, providing him with a special legacy that answers Duncan's imaginative needs. . . . Duncan has called the Romantic movement in poetry "the intellectual adventure of not knowing" . . . and he is firmly grounded in that tradition. Striving to extend the thematic and formal boundaries of the poem, Duncan goes beyond a concern for the poem itself into a total and often mystical participation in the rites of the "evolving and continuing work of poetry [he] could never complete—a poetry that had begun long before [he] was born and that extended beyond [his] own work in it." His most characteristic poem in this vein, "Passages," can end only with his life—the process of the entire venture more important than the product. Again we hear Whitman, this time from the 1872 preface to *Leaves of Grass*: "But what is life but an experiment? and mortality but an exercise? with reference to results beyond. And so shall my poems be. If incomplete here, and superfluous there, *n'importe*—the earnest trial and persistent exploration shall at least be mine, and other success failing, shall be success enough.". . . The premise of incompleteness, the weight of the "never achiev'd poem" . . . is a heavy burden indeed, but one which Robert Duncan, of all our contemporary poets, is best able to carry to fruition.

Mark Johnson and Robert DeMott. In *Robert Duncan: Scales of the Marvelous*, ed. Robert J. Bertholf and Ian W. Reid (New Directions, 1979), pp. 228–29, 231, 239–40

## EBERHART, RICHARD (1904–    )

Richard Eberhart . . . is perhaps the most distinguished survivor of a tradition that remained potent well into this century but that has been partially eclipsed by the nihilist tendencies of the day, the tradition of religious romanticism whose greatest modern exemplars are Yeats, D. H. Lawrence, Dylan Thomas, and Roethke. If Eberhart sometimes strikes readers as an anomalous figure, it may be because his closest affinities have been not with his contemporaries, whatever their stripe, but with earlier Romantics—Wordsworth, Blake, and Hopkins in particular. I shall seek . . . to indicate the direction of the poet's spiritual development and to probe critical stages of it as they become manifest in representative poems.

[Eberhart's] most impressive early meditation on mortality is "The Groundhog.". . . Indeed most of the verse initially collected in *Reading the Spirit* (1936) seems important now mainly as evidence of his struggle to find the voice and point of view perfected in that poem. The question he poses is whether the animal's demise represents, not just physically but also spiritually, a "senseless change." Eberhart treats death most effectively when he is able to gain a certain, though not too great, distance on it.

One finds a characteristic instance of Eberhart's recoil from transcendence in "I walked out to the graveyard to see the dead.". . . With a wryness not much evident in the earlier poems but fairly common in the later work, he rejects the golden pheasant's invitation to contemplate the mysteries.

Richard K. Cross. *CP*. Spring, 1979, pp. 13–15

At seventy-six Richard Eberhart stands apart, as ever, belonging to no school of poetry, going his own way without apology. An irrepressible voice in American poetry for more than five decades, in *Ways of Light* he remains ebullient, quirky, brilliant and uneven. Not counting his large *Collected Poems* of 1975, this is his first book of poems since *Fields of Grace* (1972); readers familiar with his work will find Eberhart reworking his usual themes: the fragility of existence, the finality of death, mutability in its various aspects and guises. These are subjects which found their classic expression in his early work: "The Groundhog," "The Fury of Aerial Bombardment," "For a Lamb," and "Cancer Cells" come to mind, all widely anthologized. What is new in this book, or freshly seen, is the central but intractable nature of love; Eberhart rejoices in his love, not only of humankind, but of the earth as well, "The wildness of the thicket, the order of the garden,/And the apples, O the red apples of the orchard." He writes with poignancy, and with the peculiar angle of vision characteristic of his work.

Eberhart is perhaps the last genuinely Romantic poet not to suffer unduly from what Harold Bloom calls "belatedness." He is unabashedly vatic, believing in "inspiration" as innocently as any poet ever has. His work contains little of the ironic distance so common in American poetry in the past decades. This allows him to confront his subjects with an oddly affecting naiveté. . . .

Eberhart sounds [an] astringent, elegiac note throughout the volume. The mood of a New England autumn, with its traditional associations of brilliance in decline, predominates, this "Season of bliss and yellow wistfulness,/The corn going down with the sun late afternoon.". . .

It would be wrong to suggest that *Ways of Life* is a gloomy book because of Eberhart's fascination with mutability and decline. The second elegy for Lowell, "Stone Words for Robert Lowell," ends with defiance in the face of Death, personified as Goliath. And in a central poem, "Survivors," the poet celebrates the ancient ladies of the Maine coast who, in their nineties, can still "Drive from Boston to Maine," and who are "clear/In mind and body," sharp-tongued, sporting, very much alive. . . .

To praise what remains mysterious, to fight back at death, and to acknowledge decay with a certain sorrow but no final bitterness, requires both an autumnal serenity and in indomitable spirit. Eberhart has come upon both honestly, and their mixture informs this late product of a life dedicated to the art of poetry.

Jay Parini TLS. Sept. 26, 1980, p. 1060

# ELIOT, T. S. (1888–1965)

Yeats and Eliot made opposite public uses of romanticism to define their own poetic stances. While Yeats projected himself as the last romantic, Eliot posed as an anti-romantic modern; and whereas Yeats strove to rescue romanticism from its own defects, Eliot worked to purge literature as a whole of the contamination of romanticism. Both these postures exaggerate, for Yeats' rescue meant transformation and Eliot's overt wreckage masked covert salvage. Like the speaker of Stevens' "Man and

Bottle," Eliot destroyed romantic tenements only to clear the ground for new pleasure domes. To have been told this in his youth would have horrified him; by old age it might not even have surprised him.

In one important respect the patterns of Elliot's and Yeats' long careers share the same relation to the romantics: a tripartite division of strong initial attraction and identification (a theme little heard of among Eliot's more devout admirers), violent rejection in order to form an independent identity as poet, and final if incomplete reconciliation. But here the parallel ends, for three main reasons. First, Eliot's romantic phase stops with his teens rather than with the onset of middle age. . . . Second, Eliot's grasp of romanticism was superficial compared to Yeats'. He never studied Shelley or Blake as intensely as Yeats and never understood them as well. . . . Finally, Eliot did not reconcile himself to the romantics while still primarily a practicing poet. His rapprochement coincided with his emergence as dramatist, Christian sociologist, and institution; in none of these identities did the romantics threaten him, and in some of them Coleridge was a positive help. . . .

Eliot unmistakably adopted a world view not just dependent on unhuman powers but requiring repudiation of both nature and imagination, as *The Cocktail Party* elsewhere makes clear. Blake repudiated all hypostatizations, Shelley adhered to a visionary skepticism, Keats was certain of nothing but the holiness of the heart's affections and the truths of imagination, and even the more orthodoxly religious Wordsworth and Coleridge saw both nature and imagination as positive. Eliot did not, and his refusal generated the conflict between the overt and covert mental action of his poems. Unlike Shelley, who equally recognized the dangers of imagination, Eliot could never see "all that faith creates, or love desires" as ultimately human, although he, too, perceived "Terrible, strange, sublime and beauteous shapes." He was romantic against the grain, illustrating in his own career the contention of his essay on Baudelaire that in a romantic age a poet could not be anti-romantic except in tendency. The saint repudiated the swordsman, although not without subterranean vacillation.

George Bornstein. *Transformations of Romanticism in Yeats, Eliot, and Stevens* (Univ. of Chicago Pr., 1976), pp. 94–95, 161–62

There should be no question that Eliot seeks a middle ground, that he is concerned with poetry both as a lonely, uncompromised act of definition and as an act of speech that is eloquent to other men. The dialect of the tribe is purified by insight; but those insights in turn are given substance by their entry into the dialect. Among the many progressions which can be charted in *Four Quartets* is the movement from the personal to the public, from the enclosed garden to the historic community. Parallel to this movement is the reconciliation of the poetic with the commonplace, of the lyric with the meditative and discursive, of the moments of insight with the institutions of understanding, of doctrine with the experience that seeks it and finally forms a creative relationship with it. Not all these consorts can be made to dance perfectly together, but Eliot strives for the right interplay between them with craftsmanship, commitment, and intelligence. . . .

For Eliot, the peril has always been that we condemn ourselves to the worst by not seeking the best. It is a choice of either the vision or the desolation. Commitment to the vision may result in a scorn of the desolation that can be anti-poetic. Acceptance of the desolation can mean a refusal of the search for meaning which is the basis of the poetic effort. In this most fundamental of dilemmas, *Four Quartets* represents the finding of a middle ground. It is the fulfillment of a long endeavour that keeps the shape of that endeavour in balance, so that the weight of futility does not overwhelm our final understanding of what can be heard in the "moderate usual noises." We begin with discontinuity, a deep sense of the cleavage between vision and desolation. We end with a tentative continuity, the impossible union of spheres of existence, made real in the poetic enterprise. The poem which Eliot writes between these points is a poem which tells us that self-renewal is endless and that in this rented house we do not reach conclusion once we discover the nature of our tenancy. Through the persistence of its hunger for meaning it attains eligibility for its own forward movement. Achieving the longed-for turn from chaos to design, it nevertheless continues to fare forward, recapitulating and reopening its history in a further circle of recurrence and reversal. It is both a meditative poem of the mind and a heroic poem of the human journey, brought into being with a depth of craftsmanship that can originate only in a resolute openness to experience. For that craftsmanship Pound sets down the exacting standard: "The poet's job is to *define* and yet again define till the detail of surface is in accord with the root of justice." Eliot has defined and redefined, making the detail not only consistent with the root but the main means of discovering what the root is.

Balachandra Rajan. *The Overwhelming
Question: A Study of the Poetry of T. S. Eliot*
(Univ. of Toronto Pr., 1976), pp. 133–36

*The Waste Land* has seemed to be from the beginning a kind of incredibly complicated ink blot designed for a Rorschach test, confirming whatever is already present in the eye of the beholder. Whether Marxist, Christian, or merely aesthete, readers could hail the poem as summing up the attitude of a generation. And the poem's "meaning" became embodied not only in criticism, sociology, and history, but also in other works of art. Take, for example, three American novels: F. Scott Fitzgerald's *The Great Gatsby* (1925) presents a waste land in miniature in the valley of ashes that lies between West Egg and New York; Ernest Hemingway's *The Sun Also Rises* (1926) presents an impotent hero as spokesman for a lost generation living meaningless lives; William Faulkner's *Sanctuary* (1931) presents still other impotent (both psychically and physically) characters living and dying in a world of purposeless, pointless violence. These are but three instances that could be multiplied endlessly of works directly or indirectly influenced by *The Waste Land*—and the very influence suggesting an interpretation of the poem.

Thus making *The Waste Land* mean has been a task pursued with determination over a half-century by critics, poets, and novelists, with a conspicuous lack of unanimity as to what that meaning is—and with the bemused dismay of the poem's author. It would be difficult to find in all literary history a poet whose poem appeared abandoned so completely to others for revision and interpretation. It is almost as though it were snatched from the author's hands and cut, shaped, and read to fit the needs of an ailing modern age. And before his very eyes, his poem was metamorphosed into another identity, another existence, with which he himself would eventually need to come to terms.

James E. Miller, Jr. *T. S. Eliot's Personal Waste Land: Exorcism of the Demons* (Pennsylvania State Univ. Pr., 1977), p. 159

The poetry concerns us all, not because it is true or false, but because Eliot's mastery of our language makes his life-work a potent fact in the culture of the English-speaking world. His poetry has a power in our minds, through the authority of its diction and rhythms and images, to enforce certain meanings and feelings, and to suppress others. It has this power, of course, only because it is drawing upon meanings, and habits of feeling and perception already established in the language, and so in our mentality. Its potency is for animating a deep-rooted tradition of the common mind. We may like to think that Eliot's Mind of Europe is not ours; but very few of us can call our minds altogether our own. When Eliot writes of "heaven and damnation/Which flesh cannot endure," we know immediately and inwardly what he is saying whether we share his beliefs or not. It is the same with his "spirit" which he would have enter "that refining fire/Where you must move in measure, like a dancer": we may prefer Yeats' (and Valéry's) vision of the unified being of the dancer; but I suspect that Eliot's lines impose themselves upon us with weightier authority. We can become free of him—free to accept his vision, or to seek another—only by seeing his poetry as in itself it really is. . . .

Because he was a master of the actual experience of the ideal, Eliot's poetry can speak for and to this civilisation. His poetry articulates the woe that is in the marriage of alienated neurotic egos; the atrophy and perversions of spirit in the crowd that flows over London Bridge; the pitifulness of its recreations, and the depressed resignation of humble people who expect nothing; the waste of living and partly living, of loving and partly loving; the sense of life turning to dust and ashes in the mouth; the anxiety, and fear, and sick loathing; the conscious impotence of rage at human folly, and the consequent self-contempt; and the death-wish. He had a certain real knowledge of the world. . . .

The essential experience of Eliot's poetry is the essential experience of an actual state of civilisation, but in an extraordinarily refined and intelligent form. The interpretation he put upon it, and the cure he recommended, may seem out of touch with the common way of thinking. Yet by thus connecting the current form of the drive for the absolute and ideal with its relatively recent origins, and with a traditional form, he has rendered it the more intelligible. He is a true voice of our Western world.

A. D. Moody. *Thomas Stearns Eliot, Poet*
(Cambridge Univ. Pr., 1979), pp. xv, 298


# ● ELKIN, STANLEY (1930–    )

Gustiness, let me say, is just about all [*Boswell*] has in common with *Catch-22*. That, and a sense of satirical fantasy. In point of style and of intellectual grace, the author of *Boswell* is to the author of *Catch-22* as a jeweler to a primitive potter. Nor have I any basis other than happenstance on which to justify this ramble from the old master to the late arrival as if they did in fact belong in the same box. The thing about happenstance, however, is that it does happen. I did find myself thinking of the two together. And what I found myself thinking was that I remain at least as grateful to *Boswell* for its wacky satire as I am to the [John] O'Hara shelf for its memory banks. . . .

*Boswell*, as it turns out, is nothing less than a satirist's diary of the ego. Have we not all sat with kings and captains inside our own reveries?—sat with them and found them wanting? This world is the ego's oyster and Jim Boswell is time's shucker.

From Stanley Elkin, moreover, Jim Boswell has an intellect both learned and honed, a perception forever ready to burst into its own sort of wild and wacky poetry and a well-mastered pen with which to keep his diary. It is a mad fantasy that rises from the pages of that diary. But in

Boswell's world only fantasy can begin to describe reality.

As for the poetry, let me recommend to any reader that he turn first to pages 137–52, to the account of Boswell's wooing of William Lome, "a rrrrrich man." And especially to the final encounter with Lome, in which he turns pitchman and sells bits of colored clay on the sidewalk. Elkin, to be sure, does not maintain an equal altitude throughout. I suspect the reader would die of anoxia on such a sustained flight. But glory to the heights in such moments as we can reach them.

Or it may be that *Boswell* is the hoax of the year, though it if is, it would be so only as one more semblance of the world as Elkin sees it. For the essence of this world, as seen, is exactly in the fact that it is a contrivance. But it is still that sort of contrivance we all more than half suspect our own world may turn out to be. A city of paper dragons. But add, too, that at its best it crackles around those weaving and bobbing grotesques like a Chinese New Year.

John Ciardi. SR. Aug. 15, 1964, p. 6

After finishing this zany, experimental short-story collection [*Criers and Kibitzers, Kibitzers and Criers*], one will probably be able later to recall a few ticklishly funny lines. . . .

If Elkin has the good grace to avoid ritual dramas stressing the "need for love" and the "essential brotherhood of all mankind," he compensates for it by playing back to the reader another unconscionably overworked literary theme and such institutionalized ideas as the downtrodden shopkeeper in his waning little store (the title story), tragedy at a New York mountain resort ("Among the Witnesses"), a teenage gang of mediocre misfits in the Bronx ("Cousin Poor Lesley and the Lousy People"), a petit bourgeois trying to cope with a terminal illness ("In the Alley"). Elkin, the dust jacket avers, is "a deadly serious satirist." Often, indeed, he actually seems ready to belittle the cant phrases and stances of our climby, commerce-ridden society, as only a Bruce Jay Friedman at his best is capable of doing. Then, like a driver's license candidate using someone else's car in heavy traffic, he loses control, and there's rather a nasty mess.

The Elkin protagonist is lonely and isolated because he is bereaved or abandoned and has nowhere to turn. Greenspahn, the desolate merchant in the title story, mourns his recently-dead son Harold, who had not yet even married or settled down; after a period of unappeasable grief for his beloved son, he discovers that Harold had stolen from the store's cash register. Ed Wolfe, a cruel, self-centered orphan ("I Look Out for Ed Wolfe"), withdraws entirely from society, hoarding all his money; one night he meets a Negro at a bar, forces him to be sociable, and winds up with him at a Negro key club, where he insults a girl and offends everyone else, finally throwing his remaining money away at the audience. The dying Mr. Feldman ("In the Alley"), who didn't know how to spend his last days, ends up annoying two women at a bar. In the weirdest, least successful story, "On a Field, Rampant," a fairy-tale prince of obscure origin tries vainly to establish his identity in the great world outside; finally even his talismanic medallion can't help him and the mob closes in for the kill.

Perhaps the most disappointing features of Elkin's tales are the monotony of his "inability to communicate" theme and his straining for effect by means of unreal, unsuitable settings and plots. Often the perverse protagonist winds up addressing an assembly so alien to him that his message is ludicrous and pointless. . . .

So pitifully ill is the ego of the Elkin protagonist that he must do or say some hideous thing just to compel the proper kind of attention from his ignorers. . . . To Elkin himself, one wants to shout: "Be more natural and stop speaking your own private language. What's the matter with you? The writer must serve!"

Samuel I. Bellman. SR. Jan. 15, 1966, p. 41

"Though hypocrisy can take you far, it can only take you *so* far," says Dick Gibson, the protean-enriched radio personality of Stanley Elkin's third novel [*The Dick Gibson Show*]. It is one of those ebullient statements that instantly sprouts provocative questions: How far do you want to go? Who will you be when you get there?

The Dick Gibson of the title, a seriocomic straight man in a burlesque mythology of mass culture, wants to go all the way. But not vertically (to a network presidency), or even horizontally to become one of those tympanic coast-to-coast voices that always "seem to speak from the frontiers of commitment." Instead, like the wrestler in Elkin's first novel (*Boswell*) and the department store owner in his second (*A Bad Man*), Gibson craves the all-points dimension of human need.

An itinerant early media man, he has worked for dozens of small-town radio stations. As the perpetual apprentice, whetting his skills and adopting names and accents to suit geography, he evolves into part of American folklore. As Dick Gibson, the paradox of his truest identity is that he is from Nowhere, U.S.A. . . .

Gibson hits his peak as the star of *Night Letters*, a telephone participation show. Audience feedback creates a web of involvement and expands radio to almost mythic proportions. Spinning his dials and monitoring the tape delay device that censors callers' obscenities, Gibson is a McLuhan obfuscation made flesh—a benevolent witch doctor in an electronic village of the lonely, the sick and screwed up.

*The Dick Gibson Show*, like *Portnoy's Complaint*, contains enough comic material for a dozen nightclub acts. Yet it is considerably more than an entertainment. The banal and the profound, the vulgar and the touching, are humanely juggled into a vital blur—a brilliant approximation of what it is like to live with one's eyes and ears constantly open.

R. Z. Sheppard. *Time*. March 1, 1971, p. 82

I enjoyed "The Bailbondsman," the first and longest of Stanley Elkin's three novellas in *Searches and Seizures*. It's a mordant, deeply bitter and intermittently funny story about Alex Main, a middle-aged Cincinnati bailbondsman who plays God to a stream of petty criminals and their families. He is "one dreadful sonofabitch" and prides himself on shafting his clients openly.

A cross between Nathanael West's Miss Lonelyhearts and W. C. Fields in *Never Give a Sucker an Even Break*, widower Alex is a scholar-humanitarian gone slightly mad. He gets his kicks from self-hate and manic stoicism in the face of universal agony. . . .

The second novella, "The Making of Ashenden," is a fantasy satirizing Brewster Ashenden, an idle wastrel in love with Jane Loes Lipton, a kind of Baby Jane Holzer with a Schweitzerian yen to do good. The "shocking" climax, within the dream landscape of a rich Englishman's private zoo, has Brewster interminably screwing a bear which I *think* he does to prove to Baby Jane his manly virtue.

I'm almost certain I missed the point of this story and also of the slightly better "The Condominium" ("about the relationship of the houses people live in and their bodies," says the author). Elkin talks his way out of these stories with patly unconvincing endings.

I say "talk" advisedly. Whether or not you like Elkin's stories depends on how generous you feel toward his ferocious, sometimes pointed but often mindlessly gruesome stream of masochistic repartee which I suppose is "Jewish.". . . Elkin's monologues, at which he excels, are the alienated patter of a brilliant, but turned off, stand-up literary comic. I'm very suspicious of it in large doses. . . .

How very tired I'm becoming of "absurd" humor, except in a master's hands. If technical virtuosity implied mastery Stanley Elkin would be home and dry. What spoils the stories for me is an absence of *relation*, of genuine emotion. Even while laughing at Elkin's many funny one-liners, I yearned for causality, for the author to relax a moment and play straight man to his effervescent wit.

This is not to deny the force of Elkin's talent for baroque. But placed alongside, for example, the genuine morbidities of Algren or Yurick or Lenny Bruce himself, his stories seem limp, exploitative and curiously commercial.

Clancy Sigal. *NR*. Nov. 24, 1973, p. 31

Elkin's protagonists are ordinary men with extraordinary purposes and

singular dreams, men who become obsessed with the improbable possibilities of the self's expansion. Isolated by their obsessions, these manic
heroes mount single-minded assaults upon the world and force themselves toward ultimate fulfillments. Although development is their end,
plot becomes the compulsive repetition of action and complex situation is
reduced to simplicity by their obsessions. Even setting is defined by the
radical subjectivity of the obsessive inhabiting it. Sellers of singleness,
pitchmen of transcendence, Elkin's narrators and heroes have a high-
energy, repetitive rhetoric, an exclamatory prose that intensifies the ordinary, presses the impossible, and registers the urgency of their fixations.
The result is a unity of effect, a Siamese connection of substance and
style.

It is probably a truism that characters in contemporary American fiction are obsessional, but Elkin's heroes, unlike those, say, of Mailer,
Hawkes, or O'Connor, develop their obsessions from natural authorities,
common needs, or the promises of a popular culture rather than from
some social, psychological, or religious ideology. Elkin's are not the exotic products of a subculture nor the constructs of an experimental theory
but the distortions of the American almost-ordinary. Because their obsessions arise from areas of mass fascination and because they expend their
energies within recognizable—if sometimes dislocated—systems of
value, their private thoughts and public careers reveal truths particularly
relevant and available to the American present. Theirs is the singleness
that illuminates multiplicity, the focus that creates perspective, and Elkin
uses them to examine both the normalities and aberrancies of our
time. . . .

Elkin's favorite performances are oral—tales, reminiscences,
speeches, harangues, directives, lectures, routines, jokes, patter—and
singular, repartee and dialogue somewhat detracting from the rhetorical
effect of monologue. Elkin loves to let his obsessed characters, major and
minor, talk, and since the qualities of their voices carry over into the style
he uses to describe, analyze, and narrate, this style may also be called
obsessive. Although Elkin's narrational style has the individuality,
exuberance, and extremity of his obsessives, it is not experimental (or
obsessive) the way Beckett's or Burroughs' is. Because Elkin's purposes
are the pressurized expansion of sense and the executed appeal to a felt
audience—not the music of randomness or song of solipsism—he mixes
high and low elements, vernacular and literary, to achieve a charged communication.

Thomas LeClair. CL. Spring, 1975,<br>
pp. 146–47, 156

All of Elkin's novels have dealt with the by-now familiar modern issues of isolation, alienation, and the existential construction of value systems to help fill the void, pass the time in the face of mortality and an absurd but potentially destructive exterior environment. Like many modern characters, Elkin's heroes all have the same primitive need to say, like Bellow's Henderson, *I want, I want*, but unlike Henderson or Huck or Hemingway's characters, and unlike Nabokov's Kinbote and Humbert, Coover's J. Henry Waugh, or Kesey's McMurtry, Elkin's characters find their transcendence and freedom not in lighting out for some literal or imagined territory, but in seeking out the familiar, in filling themselves with the drek and ticky-tack of modern America. . . . Elkin's heroes are moved by these kinds of excesses because they are obsessively aware of death and because they are isolated in the midst of a world of plenty. . . .

Elkin's heroes are also outcasts and outsiders, men who typically operate on the fringes of society even as they control it, and who even prefer it that way for fear that they will have to share their bounty with others. Such basic selfishness may help explain why no truly significant women or satisfying love affairs occur in Elkin's fiction. . . .

Elkin's claims that his novels have a "well-defined structure" are rather misleading and were probably induced by his simply getting tired of critics blaming him for something that does not have anything to do with the success of what he is aiming for in his novels. When we examine the way his books work, they really *do not* have a tightly woven structure, at least not in any usual notion of plot. Oh, they have a development of a sort, although Elkin's books develop more by a principle of repetition than by subtle shifts in personal motivation or by the gradual introduction of narrative complexities; and they usually have a sense of progression . . . although even it is created more by accretion than anything else. If we really take Elkin's books apart paragraph by paragraph, we hardly find the carefully balanced blend of elements and subtle interrelationships among significant details that we would find, say, in Nabokov's novels. Quite the contrary, we find constant digression, tall tales, jokes, and descriptions, none of which seems to lead anywhere. Above all, we discover that Elkin loves to stop the action of his novels to present what is his most singular and successful stylistic feature: his catalogues and lists. These catalogues do not contribute to the action nor even directly assist in illuminating anything related to the plot except insofar as they demonstrate the incredible vitality of the characters' rhetoric and imaginations. If we complain that Elkin has stopped the action "merely" to create a catalogue, tell a joke, or make a sales pitch, we are missing the point.

Larry McCaffery. *Critique*. 21, 2, 1979, pp.<br>40–42, 47

*The Living End* is Stanley Elkin's comic fable of Heaven, Hell and the Last Days, a small book big in every way but length. And I should say at once that this "triptych," as Elkin calls it, composed of three sections entitled "The Conventional Wisdom," "The Bottom Line," and "The State of the Art," is the work of a master, a story eloquent in its gestures and amazing for the ease with which it moves from a liquor store hold-up in Minneapolis to the "wall-to-wall Wall" of damnation, from Heaven as a "theme park" to Hell as "the ultimate inner city." Half farce, half morality play, *The Living End* puts God himself on trial, the Lord faced off against the damned who in their countless number equal Everyman. Quite possibly only Stanley Elkin possesses the exact blend of irreverence and care, of hardcore realism and fabulous invention, to have pulled this off.

Elkin knows that clichés are the substance of our lives, the coinage of human intercourse, the ways and means that hold our messy selves and sprawling nation intact. To exploit their vigor and set them forth with unexpected force has been the basis of his success as a novelist; no writer has maneuvered life's shoddy stock-in-trade into more brilliantly funny forms. Long before he wrote *The Franchiser*, Elkin appropriated the notion of the franchise—the idea that we Americans borrow our being from the staples of quotidian culture, the banal, the vulgar, the cartoonlike and mean, all our packaged dreams and gaudy perks, accumulating thereby some concoction of clichés which, for each of us, constitutes our "story."

But if our stories are private they are in no way new. Our predicament, as a nation dedicated to exploring frontiers and starting fresh, is not only our rising sense of limits, but our fear of predictability, of stuckness, of *old* wine in old bottles, as if sameness were inherently ridiculous. And maybe it is. Originality is at best displacement of the ordinary. Our most outlandish moments are the stuff of public domain. In *The Bailbondsman*, Elkin's protagonist judges the jailed, sizes up the risk of posting their bail, merely by listening to their stories. At the end of *The Dick Gibson Show* the MC of a late-night talk program cannot bear to listen to yet *another* "story of my life": he knows by heart their silly pathos, their ludicrous outcomes, the garbled grief of options foreclosed.

Something of this desperation, relieved by raucous humor, slips into *The Living End*, where Elkin takes on the ultimate cliché, death and the preposterous protocol of Hereafter. To see how the mighty are fallen, to bring high things low, is a comic ploy as old as Aristophanes, accomplished in Elkin's case by setting standard myths of immortality within the low-rent clutter of ordinary life. So the angel of death talks "like a cabbie with an out-of-town fare." The crowd around the Lord's throne looks like the snapshot of a summit conference. Christ and his Dad don't get along, and the Virgin Mother never liked sex in the first place. As for sudden death, "all that wrath, those terrible swift sword arrangements, that's the M.O. of God Himself!". . .

There is a kind of vulgate glory to Stanley Elkin's prose, and much of the power of *The Living End* depends on how things are worded. Elkin is the *magister ludi* of American vernacular, and for sheer stylistic brilliance no other writer can top him. The American novelist he most resembles is Nathanael West, but whereas West allowed us to feel superior to life's lunacy through savage irony, Elkin refuses us this distance, this illusion. And unlike others of his generation, Thomas Pynchon and William Gaddis for example, Elkin does not identify with the laughter of the gods, he does not dissociate himself from the human spectacle by taking out a franchise on the cosmic joke. Hard and unyielding as his comic vision becomes, Elkin's laughter is remission and reprieve, a gesture of willingness to join the human mess, to side with the damned, to laugh in momentary grace at whatever makes life Hell.

Terrence des Pres. Book World. July 1, 1979, pp.<br>1, 4

In seven volumes of fiction published since the mid-Sixties, Stanley Elkin has made clear claim, by reason of the quality inherent in his work, to consideration as a major contemporary American writer. Yet though his books have inspired a following of devoted readers—both in and outside of the academic community—Elkin can be said to have largely missed out on the recognition due him. I should like to make a gesture towards righting that wrong by attempting a necessarily brief survey of Elkin's fictional works, and by making some general observations about his style and themes. For if Elkin seems to be some sort of spiritual descendant of Nathanael West in the ways in which he attaches out-loud, falling-on-the-floor humor to reflections on the human state as a steady downward plunge to death, he is nevertheless very much his own man in the manner in which he explores and develops that tradition. . . .

Stanley Elkin's characters' contemplations of their situations have always been informed by the inevitable facts of their own deaths and those of others, giving his fiction an eschatological emphasis uncommon in contemporary letters. In *The Living End* (1979), Elkin moves beyond the point of death in an assault on received notions of theological order. That a lonely author of the universe should find confirmed by the behavior of his creatures the notion that his ways are not our ways, nor ours his, seems the suggestion of this short volume described on its cover as a "triptych." The allusion to paintings in panels of three, particularly altar panels, is fitting. The book is as crowded with scenes from the far side of the grave as something by Bosch or Grünewald. . . .

What next for Elkin? He is nearly through with a novel to be called *George Mills*—from excerpts I have heard, another *Bildungsroman*—which is to be published in 1982. It promises to be long, perhaps the most ambitious product of Elkin's career. One wishes him well with it, expecting full well that like its predecessors, it will be wrought with extraordinary care and love for the unleashed English tongue, and that like them it will also confront the human species trying to fasttalk itself into an understanding in the face of pain and of mortality. Most certain of all is that it will be, like them, full of the sound of a savage and infectious laughter. "So grotesque," concludes a woman newly risen from the dead in *The Living End*; "death grotesque as life. All, all grotesque."

John Ditsky. *HC*. June, 1982, pp. 1–2, 10–11

Elkin's taste . . . is not as lowbrow as he claims. His greatest strength is the ability to combine high art and pop culture without shortchanging either one. His frequent subject is the regular guy with an all-American dream of making it big, but his sentences are often convoluted enough to give a Jamesian pause. This density of language may have kept Elkin off the best-seller list, but his natural audience is the one that appreciates John Irving and Kurt Vonnegut.

*George Mills* is not his most affecting book, and certainly not his funniest, but it is quintessential Elkin in style and substance. His five previous novels and two story collections not only capture Middle America; they embrace it. . . . Elkin deflates intellectual pretensions by recognizing that most people are perfectly comfortable in a fast-food world.

*The Living End*, Elkin's last novel, sets us up for *George Mills*. God puts in an appearance, and even he turns out to be a regular guy—part storyteller, part standup comic, part practical joker. *George Mills* takes this idea even further: it is about 1000 years of guys who are so ordinary they hand it down from father to son as a family tradition. From the first George Mills, servant to a nobleman during the Crusades, to the last, a working stiff in contemporary St. Louis, these are men who live under the curse of their "blue collar blood," pass on to their sons the story of this heritage, and always seem to be the butts of God's practical jokes. . . .

George's rejection of history is not necessarily a triumph. Faulkner's stylistic influence on Elkin suggests their common concern with the power of history and myth. (Elkin's Faulknerian voice runs through the novel, at times overwhelming his characterization of George. Learning that a brother and sister live in a car parked outside the Glazers' house, George thinks of "the poor's special charters and manumissions, their little license and acquittals, all law's exonerate laxity and stretched-point privilege.") Elkin substitutes Middle America for the South and one-liners for Gothic darkness; the Millses are ironic equivalents of the Comp-sons. George is like Quentin, reconciling himself to his family history by sifting through its legends. *George Mills* suggests that however inflated and distorted its history, the past cannot be dismissed. . . . For Stanley Elkin, the greatest curse is not having a sense of humor.

Caryn James. *VV*. Oct. 26, 1982, p. 52


## ELLISON, RALPH (1914–    )


A kind of critical commonplace has grown up around *Invisible Man* to the effect that it is a novel centering on "the problem of identity." Certainly this seems a valid observation, but too often it serves to terminate rather than to begin a discussion of the book's basic concerns. The result is a bat-tery of statements that would lead one to believe that by the novel's end the narrator knows who he *is*, when in fact it is more accurate to say that at that point he only knows who he *isn't*. His "state of hibernation," we should recall, is simply "a covert preparation for a more overt action." It is by that action that he must finally achieve identity.

The book, then, may be said to deal most essentially with considera-tions which precede identification; that is, with ontology itself. In making this point Ellison has said that "*Invisible Man* is an attempt to describe reality as it really exists rather than in terms of what [the narrator] has assumed it to be. Because it was the clash between his assumptions, his illusions about reality, and its actual shape which made for his agony." What Ellison's protagonist finally comes to see is that the "actual shape" of reality is wholly protean, ambiguous, and chaotic. He realizes—even as his tormentors do not—that any attempt to deal with such essential dynamism in terms of fixed and static phenomena is not only to delude oneself but ultimately to deny the possibility of any genuinely meaningful existence. *Invisible Man* carries its hero to the point of such realization, but not beyond. He comes to grips with the nature of reality; identity will be achieved only when that understanding is put to active use. . . .

The [bulk] of the novel, I believe, is structured around a series of encounters in which that sense of certainty is repeatedly challenged, proven inadequate, and supplanted by yet another. In each case the terms of the encounter are basically the same; someone embodying a particular institution of tradition imposes his fixed and rigid vision of reality upon the usually acquiescent narrator, thereby rendering him at once "invisi-ble" and ignorant of his invisibility. Chronically failing to apprehend the basic flux of reality which disqualifies all such prescriptive visions, he is tossed from one set of certainties to another, until his mounting disillusionment finally exposes him to a perception of fundamental chaos and to a recognition of the primary sources of his invisibility. He is helped toward this perception, moreover, by other encounters with individuals who provide—deliberately or otherwise—certain strategic "clues" regarding the true nature of reality. The novel can be seen, then, as a succession of episodes which finally strip the hero of his illusions, either through a painful process of trial and error or by providing strategic glimpses of that essential fluidity which erodes and distorts all static formalizations of experience.

Jeffrey Steinbrink. SBL. Autumn, 1976, pp. 1–2

Ellison is by no means the first writer to inlay his work with the silver and gold of Afro-American folklore. Mark Twain, Charles Chesnutt, James Weldon Johnson, William Faulkner, Zora Neale Hurston, Sterling A. Brown, and Langston Hughes used it before Ellison, often with supreme skill. But Ellison's case is special, because of the sheer virtuousity of *Invisible Man*, which, replete with its "inside" use of black folklore, is also very modern in its technique. In this contemporary novel, the vital transformation from folk item to written literature seems wonderfully complete. The language is consistently astir with actual Afro-American speech, as well as with the tales, songs, and games of folklore. What Ellington and Wagner achieved in music is here achieved in fiction: the transmutation of folk materials into a fully orchestrated masterpiece. . . .

Ellison's artistic vision is always ironical, complex, ambiguous. And easy answers prove troubling. He points out, for instance, that paradoxical as it may seem, blacks are in certain ways the freest of Americans. Living at the bottom of the American social hierarchy, blacks have been left alone to experiment with new styles of expression. Echoing James Weldon Johnson, Ellison has observed that much that the world knows as uniquely American (particularly with regard to language, music, and dance) was created by black slaves and their offspring. . . .

It is ironic that James Weldon Johnson's fictional character, the Ex-Colored Man, retreats from the black world into the white one, but nonetheless narrates one of the most affirmative novels about black life. It is odd that the Invisible Man, who ends by escaping into a dark hole, tells a tale full of hope. In Ellison's fiction, especially from the forties on, the portraits of such strong black characters as Jefferson, Mary Rambo, Trueblood, and Hickman have been diverse and affirming. Characters are cheated, tricked, left for dead, beaten, and even lynched. But certain powerful figures, aware of roots in a sustaining tradition, manage to persevere with heroism and high style. The insistence on the heroic impulse in black life has contributed to Ellison's influence.

He has had a lasting impact on many younger writers, notably Al Young, Ishmael Reed, Leon Forrest, Toni Morrison, Alice Walker, and James Alan McPherson. His special contribution to the new wave of black writing is his unceasing insistence upon connections between the contemporary writer, and not only the American realistic tradition, but the symbolist tradition that nourished Melville and Faulkner, and the vernacular tradition, rooted in American language and lore.

Robert G. O'Meally. *The Craft of Ralph Ellison*
(Harvard Univ. Pr., 1980), pp. 3–5

Although he does not write a historical novel in [any traditional] vein, he uses the career of his protagonist to suggest the history of the southern black who has moved from slavery to Booker T. Washingtonism, to the migrations north, to Marxism, to (it is hoped) a viable position as a free human individual. . . . *Invisible Man* suggests that these experiences offer understandable meanings if we will but see them. Like [Ellen] Glasgow or [Henry] James, Ellison creates a social history that, while not always narrowly realistic, certainly captures satirically—and frequently humorously—the social manners he wishes to attack; and like Faulkner, Warren, Styron, and other southern authors, Ellison uses contemporary novelistic techniques masterfully to body forth the symbolic meanings he sees in his protagonist's experiences. Moreover, he creates a cyclical structure for his novel that in itself is a comment on the nature of man's experience in time. Ellison's evidence of the past's continued presence is embodied in the shadow it casts through folk elements—the songs, the extravagant language, the tall-tale, the evangelical Protestantism—that make up the shared experience of the southerner, both black and white. In [Hugh] Holman's terms, his message is Hegelian. There is meaning in history: the past is revealed through process, not replication. His voice is southern. His *Invisible Man* is worthy indeed to claim a place among the great southern novels of this or any other century.

Ladell Payne. *Black Novelists and the Southern
Literary Tradition* (Univ. of Georgia Pr., 1981),
p. 98

## FARRELL,   JAMES   T.   (1904–1979)

Farrell's work, like that of other writers, is uneven from book to book and exhibits both weaknesses and strengths, the weaknesses sometimes being the defects of the strengths. For example, it may be said that at times Farrell depends too exclusively on dialogue for characterization, yet that technique dramatically reveals the mentality behind the words and thus carries and verifies the thematic indictment of what city life does to people. His writing can be doggedly repetitive and wordy, but again it is often so for thematic purposes—just as Walt Whitman, Henry James, and William Faulkner can be repetitive and wordy in their ways to achieve their effects. Such flaws of his style, if that is what they are, are in any case minor compared to its virtues in his best work: its over-all thematic suitability, its expressive adaptability to the speech patterns of many characters, its frequent attainment of a natural eloquence. . . .

Farrell has not realized the full potential in his vision. But his vision is large and single, and step by step he has created a single world of ample proportions. His cycles of novels with his other fiction approximate a sequence, a rarity in American literature. At its best, the American past he creates is deeply authentic as art and as social history, like Faulkner's South. Farrell's re-created and recorded past is especially meaningful to us because, through its rich details of urban manners, it shows the heavy cost exacted of people and institutions by the modern city. His characters' lives expose social process; time slowly brings change, and the making of personality and the formation of society merge. His Lonigans, O'Flahertys, and O'Neills are deeply immersed in their time and place—interesting contrasts to Hemingway's disengaged Americans—and his work is exceptional in our fiction for the number of its living characters. The contrast between their often blind groping for a better future and the grimness of their present, flowing inevitably out of their past, is a subject with tragic power.

Edgar M. Branch. James T. Farrell (Twayne,<br>1971), pp. 169, 171

If Farrell had not possessed a major talent and a major subject, his feat of endurance would be less interesting if still significant. The inheritor of a largely unscrutinized American literary tradition represented by Dreiser, Anderson, and Lewis, Farrell had both the talent and the subject. He was a master in the creation of mass scenes: raging, hilarious, bitter family quarrels with a cast of dozens, piously organized civic and religious festivities, violent, protracted New Year's Eve parties. Few have been better chroniclers than Farrell of that particularly American experience and subject, the mood: the endless series of frightened adjustments called living, the lunging and inching toward attention by each individual psyche within a hopelessly blurred crowd, the troubled intimacy with which one tentatively fixes and appropriates one's alien *persona*, the confusion in which one haphazardly sorts the fragmented hurtful thoughts one wakes up to and goes to sleep with. No one has equalled Farrell's sustained delineation of second- and third-generation Americans: women who must live too often as stereotypes within the minds of would-be stereotypes, men who are fans and outsiders in their adopted land, incarnations of social anxiety.

With Farrell's death, we have lost our finest literary perspective on the meaning of assimilation and ambition in American life, and a writer uniquely and admirably free from that most malignant form of cultural life: audience dependency. Farrell was always ready to fulminate about the critics' neglect and misunderstanding of him, but in the last analysis, he wrote for himself. Writing for Farrell was the only postponement of the inevitable, a definition that covers most of life as Farrell portrays it that admits what it postpones, and thus genuinely *happens*. For Farrell, writing was still a synonym for self-sufficiency; and this was the most radical self-definition possible to one who believed that America was becoming a nation of consumers and spectators. We possess, as he meant us to, his example and his books. Farrell's work constitutes the last important experiment to date in American literature with what can be viewed as deliberately unedited material. The malice he drew from censors and critics was out of proportion to the boldness, or the awkwardness, of his enterprise. The censorship battle is over; the critical one has barely begun. Others will honor James Farrell; they will read and sort and care for his works if we do not.

Ann Douglas. *Dissent.* Spring, 1980, p. 216

# FAULKNER, WILLIAM (1897–1962)

I interpret Faulkner to be saying that time does not exist apart from the consciousness of some human being. Apart from that stream of living consciousness, time is merely an abstraction. Thus, *as actually experienced*, time has little to do with the time that is measured off by the ticking of a chronometer. Such a conception of time, however, did not impel Faulkner to destroy his own watch as Quentin Compson did (in *The Sound and the Fury*). Though clock time, as an abstraction, might be deemed to be in some sense unreal, Faulkner, like Henri Bergson himself, conceded that clock-and-calendar time had its uses and that no human life of the slightest complexity could get along without constant reference to it. . . .

To come at the problem from another direction: in spite of Faulkner's acceptance of Bergson's conception of time as fluid and continuous (time as "duration"), it is hard to think of a novelist who exceeds Faulkner in his careful attention to the details of clock time and calendar time. I am thinking here particularly of the chronology of his novels. Each conforms not only to a generally consistent time scheme; the details of the time scheme are often very precise. Indeed, it is a revelation to go through a Faulkner novel, giving special attention to its chronology, and so discover how many unobtrusive but specific time-clues Faulkner has planted. Though such clues often do not call attention to themselves, yet when noted and put together, the chronology that they plot is much too consistent to be unpurposed. Even if Faulkner did not mean for every reader to be aware of these buried chronologies, we may be sure that he was himself in command of the sequence of events. . . .

To sum up, though Bergson may have confirmed some of Faulkner's notions about time and about the ways in which human beings can know reality, and though Bergson may have stimulated Faulkner to experiment with the verbal presentation of motion and action, I find little in Faulkner's narrative treatment that can be certainly attributed to Bergson's influence. Many of Faulkner's techniques turn out to be simply skillful and imaginative adaptations of traditional narrative methods, but if one were to specify particular influences it would not be Bergson's so much as Conrad's, the early Eliot's, and Joyce's. Whatever Faulkner's indebtedness, his handling of time reached perhaps its most brilliant achievement in *Absalom, Absalom!*

Cleanth Brooks. *William Faulkner: Toward Yoknapatawpha and Beyond* (Yale Univ. Pr., 1978), pp. 254, 258, 264–65

Like Thomas Hardy's Wessex, William Faulkner's Yoknapatawpha County originated in the imagination of a young writer reared in a provincial community. In both instances a youthful mind, endowed with literary genius, discovered that the small, remote world of his nativity embodied the major experience of modern Western civilization: the world historical differentiation of a novel society of history and science from a sacramental order of myth and tradition. In either case a youthful writer entered into the knowledge of this phenomenon through an unacademic but intense and sustained process of reading in varied literary and philosophical works; and in either case, during the struggles of his self-education, a youthful writer began to conceive of himself as a member of the cosmopolitan realm of poets and literary prophets that for five hundred years or more has sought to give moral and spiritual guidance to the long process of societal differentiation in Western civilization. . . .

Implied in Faulkner's serene, retrospective vision of Yoknapatawpha as a transcendent autonomy of the artist is all the pathos of the literary myth of modern history—of the drama of the artist and the historical differentiation of the self. The vision reveals what it denies: the unremitting tension between self and history. Yoknapatawpha is in truth no sublimation of the actual but the embodiment of the profoundest reality: the terrifying modern internalization of history—which in its ineffable and pervasive dominion comprises man and nature, God, world, and universe—in the self. Faulkner hid the truth of Yoknapatawpha from himself at times, particularly in his later career. But he acknowledged it all the same—in the term that he used to describe Yoknapatawpha: "my apocryphal county." Sometimes he called the Yoknapatawpha stories "my apocrypha." He meant more than "my fictions." He meant my stories in which there are "hidden things," and notable among the things he hid in the tales is the story of the artist and his struggle against modern history. In this struggle Faulkner followed the defiant Joycean dream of sacramentalizing the role of the artist by means of grace self-bestowed. But Faulkner knew, perhaps more surely than Joyce knew, that dreaming his biography was only a part of his being as a creature of history. He understood this irony as an American, and especially as a southerner. He grasped it so well that in his final novel, *The Reivers*, subtitled *A Reminiscence*, though trying not to do so, he virtually surrenders to the pathos of history: creating a Yoknapatawpha existing neither in the *was* of Quentin Compson nor in the *is* of Gavin Stevens but in a mingled *is-was* that, transcending all tense, is yet the truest tense for Americans, the tense of nostalgia—the tense Americans use when they speak of America as "home sweet home," the place beyond all grief and sorrow.

> Lewis P. Simpson. In *The American South:*
> *Portrait of a Culture*, ed. Louis B. Rubin, Jr.
> (Louisiana State Univ. Pr., 1980), pp. 227, 244

Faulkner's fondness for the tall tale or anecdote, humorous or otherwise, has a bearing upon the form of his fiction. Throughout his fiction, the basis of his art is the single episode. As a result, his books seem to divide into brilliant but very loosely unified stories at times ingeniously yoked together. For example, after reading *The Sound and the Fury*, the reader is likely to remember the work not as a single story but as at least four separate stories relating to the Compson family. Such works as *Sartoris*, *Sanctuary*, *Light in August*, and *Absalom, Absalom!* similarly contain multiple plots, while there is serious question if *The Unvanquished*, *The Hamlet*, and *Go Down, Moses* may not be more properly called volumes of short stories than novels. In Faulkner's great outpouring of superb fiction during the 1930s, perhaps only *As I Lay Dying* was conceived and written as a single story. . . .

The perspective of literary history today helps Faulkner's reader to grasp the implications of his work far more clearly than they could have been understood in the author's lifetime. Presently, Faulkner's fiction seems more a continuation or logical development from the American nineteenth century than the outpouring of a radical innovator or experimenter. Currently, as in the future his contribution to American literature rests not so much upon his ideas about artistic form, his narrative skills, the devices of his fiction, or even his stylistic accomplishments— important though these matters are—as it does upon the intensity and sincerity with which he has depicted the complexities of human experience measured by the progression of history. No other writer since Henry James has identified so directly and expressed so forcefully as Faulkner the truths that govern man's success or failure in right living.

Like many other Southerners of the 1930s, Faulkner held the Southern economic system based upon tenant farming and sharecropping, legacies of the Civil War and its aftermath, responsible for much of the unhappiness and poverty of the South. When administered by dishonest and unscrupulous landowners, the "economic edifice" locked both races into bondage to the land, depressed their living standards, and stifled ambition. Although nominally free, the Negroes (and poor whites) were still bound in a vicious round of debt from which they might never be free. Although Faulkner had great admiration for the endurance and strength of the Negro race, in the 1930s, the decade of the Great Depression, he saw little evidence of immediate change in their prospects for the better.

Harsh and oppressive as the economic system of the South seemed to him and regardless of his awareness of the depths of man's folly and his propensity for evil, Faulkner yet asserted that man could "prevail." Like millions of his countrymen, past and present, Faulkner believed in the possibility of reform and progress. One has only to consider the lives of Jason Compson, Temple Drake, Gail Hightower, Thomas Sutpen, Flem Snopes, and others to understand that Faulkner believed that man's greatest enemy lay within himself and that man must reform himself from within before he can defeat those forces that undermine the quality of his life. Man's pride, hate, self-interest, greed, and willingness to purchase material possessions at the cost of private integrity inhibit his enjoyment of the good life. Insofar as he can, man must replace these traits with the virtues Faulkner names in his Nobel Prize Speech of Acceptance, "the courage and honor and hope and pride and compassion and pity and sacrifice which have been the glory of his past." To Faulkner, these are the verities of human experience. More and more, as time passes, Faulkner emerges as an advocate of traditional humanistic values. At the heart of Yoknapatawpha lies Faulkner's vision of man in a moral universe.

John Pilkington. *The Heart of Yoknapatawpha*
(Univ. Pr. of Mississippi, 1981), pp. 293, 295–97

# FITZGERALD, F. SCOTT (1896–1940)

In all Fitzgerald's thinking there is a consistent pattern, a habit of mind which asserts itself in every situation. His ideas on any subject tend to arrange themselves into a system of opposed contraries. We have just seen how strongly this is reflected in his conception of the artist, but it is equally apparent in all the other matters discussed in this chapter: he regarded wealth and social status from both a middle-class and an aristocratic standpoint; he acted as spokesman for a new freedom in morals and manners and yet possessed a puritan conscience; and the Jazz Age fascinated him because he saw in it a capacity for delirious excitement balanced by equally strong potentialities for disaster. He was fully conscious of this tendency in his thought and assigned a very high value to it: as he remarks in "The Crack-up," "the test of a first-rate intelligence is the ability to hold two opposed ideas in the mind at the same time, and still retain the ability to function." It is no exaggeration to say that this is the essential element in his gift as a social novelist, but it implies a creative tension which can only be maintained at the cost of an enormous and unremitting effort. It provides the ground for the most fruitful kind of complexity in art, but must often lead to uncertainty and disorder in actual living. . . .

His intense self-awareness and the complexity of his reactions made it almost impossible for him to be spontaneous and natural, and his social life had the character of a series of complicated manoeuvres or theatrical tableaux. Sometimes these were hasty improvisations like the bus incident: often they were contrived in advance with the forethought of an impresario or a film producer. . . . Fitzgerald's feeling for the right thing was matched by an uncannily precise instinct for the worst possible behaviour: the quality of insight which enabled him to charm and captivate, could also be used to devise peculiarly subtle punishments for people who bored or irritated him. . . .

What appears as confusion and error in his life is transformed into an ideal clarity of vision in his art. While this is the case with many great artists, it is true of Fitzgerald to an unusually marked degree. It is the main reason why the critics and biographers who see his life and his work as alternative, almost interchangeable, versions of the same story are so completely misled.

Brian Way. *F. Scott Fitzgerald and the Art of Social Fiction* (St. Martin's, 1980), pp. 19–21

All of Fitzgerald's characters start off with romantic expectations, with a heightened sense of self that eventually comes into conflict with the outside world. Amory Blaine gives way to postwar cynicism; Anthony Patch to a sense of drift in a work-a-day world; Jay Gatsby to a world of established money that he never understands; Dick Diver to an emotionally sick and sterile society; and Monroe Stahr to a materialistic world that cannot accommodate the fated idealist and quickly exhausts him. Like Monroe Stahr, Fitzgerald's characters create a sense of the lavish and heighten it further through the vitality of imagination. But it is imagination that is severed from everything but its own vision. Alone, detached, aloof, their dreams are exhaustible because they feed on themselves and are cut off from the resources of a vital culture. In Fitzgerald's fiction, a sense of romantic possibility plays itself out in a cultural wasteland. Fitzgerald's sense of opportunity warred with a Spenglerian sense of destiny; and if Fitzgerald found in Spengler a historian whose idea of the modern augmented his own, as I believe he did, he also brought to Spengler a sense of romantic possibility that challenged these historical assumptions at the outset.

Richard Lehan. *TCL*. Summer, 1980, pp. 154–55

*The Great Gatsby*'s image patterns and even the workings of its plot show more than a general family resemblance to classical tales of flying men. The legend of Phaeton is the one which echoes in this novel most persistently and strongly—so strongly that there is cause for wondering whether Phaeton isn't as deliberately called up here as Odysseus is in Leopold Bloom's wanderings around Dublin. . . .

There is no proving that Fitzgerald consciously turned to Ovid in designing *The Great Gatsby*. He apparently never said a word about doing so; and we can be sure that if Phaeton was on Fitzgerald's mind, other tales were haunting him too. One of his working titles for the novel, *Trimalchio in West Egg*, certainly makes the case for *The Satyricon*, but there are also shadows of *The Waste Land*, and recently some interesting parallels have been turned up between passages in *Gatsby* and lines in *The Golden Bough*. The point, then, of looking at the Phaeton tale in *The Great Gatsby* is not to make an argument for one literary debt and one alone, or to arrive at one pat explanation of how the novel works and what Fitzgerald meant by it. If *Gatsby* borrows something from Phaeton, it might very well be an unconscious borrowing. But one way or the other we are left with the fact that parallels between the stories turn up in uncanny profusion, that the implications of those parallels need to be followed out, and that the closeness of the new myth to the old one helps us understand better how Gatsby's story *is* a myth, how the rise and fall of a deluded and childlike gangster turns into a vital classic of *our* time. . . .

At the end of the novel the "American Dream" is alive because Nick's imagination is still under its spell. If Gatsby has lived that dream to an inevitable, disastrous conclusion, he has done so in a fashion as much classic as American, and Nick has been classic in telling of it, not simply in allusion and metaphor but in condition of mind. Phaeton may be here in Gatsby by contrivance, or he may not; but *Gatsby* is certainly more akin to Ovid than it is to the Fuller-Magee case or Ben Franklin's *Autobiography* or *Hopalong Cassidy* or the Alger stories or any other rise or rise-and-fall tales that Fitzgerald ever knew of. The story is ancient in more than one way, and that is precisely why it stays with us, not only powerful, but invincibly new.

Bruce Michelson. MFS. Winter, 1980–81, pp. 566–67, 577

## FROST, ROBERT    (1875–1963)

Let there be no confusion about the particular relationship that I claim for Frost and the modern tradition. Though Frost read William James, and through James came into contact with a number of the salient themes of modernist philosophy and aesthetics, I doubt that Frost was "influenced" in the sense that historicists used to say that imaginative writers were influenced or "shaped" by the "intellectual backgrounds of the times." My understanding is that writers are rarely influenced in that way; they learn almost nothing from philosophers, aestheticians, and literary critics. What happens is that they sometimes read a philosopher (or even a literary critic) and find their own intuitions about things reflected discursively, and hence in that sense confirmed. Modernism becomes the historical ambience of Frost's work in the sense that it is what one comes to conceptually if one moves outward from his poems in an attempt to define the intellectual milieu of the kinds of experience found there.

Frost is not modernist because he holds self-consciously to certain ideas which we identify with this or that modern philosopher because there are few ideas as such in his poetry (modernist or otherwise). Properly speaking his poems do not "belong" to the intellectual environment we call "the modern mind" because "the modern mind" does not have independent, Platonic existence. It is a thing that the poems themselves have helped to create. The perspectives of modern philosophy and aesthetics are conceptual abstractions from that dense, pre-ideational, primary data of human experience which Frost renders from the inside, as lived.

More than most modern poets Frost needs to have some sort of historical context deliberately constructed for him. Unlike Wallace Stevens, Frost rarely deals directly with the issues of post-Kantian epistemology; unlike Hart Crane, William Carlos Williams, and W. H. Auden, he rarely situates us in the modern urban environment; unlike Ezra Pound and T. S. Eliot he does not measure in any richly allusive way the modern moment against tradition and the past. And, from the point of view of language and metrical experiment, Frost looks very traditional. In two of the best books about him, he is presented as inhabiting a sort of timeless world. John Lynen sees Frost in the venerable tradition of pastoralism. Reuben Brower, drawing his comparisons from the range of world literature, relates him to the tradition of tough-minded, unflinching writers who see things as they are and do not hesitate to tell the score. Lynen and Brower are both persuasive. Frost inhabits a timeless world as do all poets of high quality. Yet Frost did not exist in a vacuum, and his poems do not present an ahistorical consciousness. What I would call his "implicit poetics" is a regulative principle which does not help much in explicating the poems, but which does help us to "generalize" the experiential patterns of those poems, and hence to extend their significance for our times.

Frank Lentricchia. *Robert Frost: Modern Poetics and the Landscapes of Self* (Duke Univ. Pr., 1975), pp. 18–19

Frost is a poet of genius because he could so often make his subtleties inextricable from an apparent availability. The assumption that he is more easily read than are his contemporaries, like Yeats and Eliot, persists only in ignorance of the unique but equally strenuous kinds of difficulty which inform his best work. He is likely to be most evasive when his idioms are so ordinary as to relax rather than stimulate attention; he is an allusive poet, but in a hedging and off-hand way, the allusions being often perceptible only to the ear, and then just barely—in echoings of earlier poets like Herbert or Rossetti, or in metrical patternings traceable to Milton; he will wrap central implications, especially of a sexual kind, within phraseologies that seem innocent of what they carry. . . .

Frost seems to me of vital interest and consequence because his ultimate subject is the interpretive process itself. He "plays" with possibilities for interpretation in a poetry that seems "obvious" only because it is all the while also concerned with the interpretations of what, in the most ordinary sense, are the "signs" of life itself, particular and mundane signs which nonetheless hint at possibilities that continually elude us. . . .

His poetry is especially exciting when it makes of the "obvious" something problematic, or when it lets us discover, by casual inflections or hesitations of movement, that the "obvious" by nature *is* problematic.

Richard Poirier. Robert Frost: The Work of<br>Knowing (Oxford Univ. Pr., 1977), pp. x–xi

Frost's most powerful inspiration seemed to take shape in visions of struggle. The speakers in his three score greatest poems, regional and nonregional alike, are explorers, seekers, questioners. What they long for is understanding, confidence, and a sense of form or order: what he called a "momentary stay against confusion." All his great works draw on this vision. As a young man (in fact, until he was approaching forty), his personal lack of confidence was so great and his sense of uncertainty and aberrancy so strong that he could hardly find effective ways to express his imaginative impulses. His quest for an attractive and imposing vantage point led him to adopt a variety of essentially Romantic poses; yet they elicited no sincere commitment and provided no satisfactory stance from which he could objectify his visions and give voice to his inspiration. . . .

To read or hear or recite Frost's great poetry is to share in the pursuit of a profound vision of human life. As we observe his speakers undertake physical, intellectual, and imaginative exploration, the power of their words and the beauty of their song persuades us that they deserve not only our attention, but also our commitment and fullest appreciation. Few modern American authors have more to offer us. Whether in America, or around the world in Europe, Africa, or Asia, we may find rewarding fields for our own exploration as we turn and turn again with increased understanding and enjoyment to those poems in which Frost made best use of his literary gifts and his extraordinary imagination, his special sensitivity to life in New England and his insight into human nature.

John C. Kemp. Robert Frost and New England:<br>The Poet as Regionalist (Princeton Univ. Pr.,<br>1979), pp. 230, 235

A number of Frost's best-known early lyrics are made of a language from which distinctively formal words are largely excluded. But it is equally true and important—although for this, etymological breakdowns cannot provide objective corroboration—that the language of these poems is lacking in words and expressions of distinctively colloquial quality. . . .

The regionalisms so paradoxically lacking in poems so thoroughly regional are but one subclass of the distinctively literary elements, are by
and large excluded. Frost's elected norm of discourse here, and the key to
his verbal artistry, is the common level of style, which represents a selection from the spoken language rather than a reproduction of it. . . .

In setting himself up as the exclusive "guide" ("And put a sign up
CLOSED to all but me") to a truth he has hedged about with verbal and symbolic obscurities, and in proceeding to imply that only those who can
interpret this poetically mediated truth are worthy to be saved, Frost, one
may well think, has his nerve. The teasing and testing, the archness and
complacent whimsy, will always alienate a certain number of readers, and
long familiarity will not render them any less irritating. But though "Directive" is flawed in part by the arch-avuncular pose of the elderly Frost,
it is not seriously damaged. The ideal it upholds—the encompassing of
Puritanical grimness and strength by a saving joy and imagination—is
powerful and viable in this as in the other poems which make up Frost's
New Testament. And, in "Directive" particularly, we must admire the
brilliance with which so great a range of resources—rural Americana,
American-style humorous understatement, legend, history and fairy tale,
the literary past, the chivalric and Christian traditions—has been drawn
upon and forged into a stylistic whole. Here, as in all Frost's best poems,
what is literary and elevated seems not to impose itself upon, but to rise
naturally from, basic simplicity—the everyday things of country life,
lucidly and concretely rendered in common language—which is Frost's
primary and most memorable poetic world.

Marie Borroff. *Language and the Poet: Verbal
Artistry in Frost, Stevens, and Moore* (Univ. of
Chicago Pr., 1979), pp. 29, 40–41

Although Frost is reported to have joked once that "Directive" is his
"Eliot poem" because it mentions the Holy Grail, the religious trappings
are not throw-aways. Allusions to the Crucifixion ("tatters hung on barb
and thorn") and to God as the final source ("Too lofty and original to
rage") are offered seriously to those readers who would experience the
poem as a religious statement. Frost himself pointed to the word "source"
as the center of "Directive": "the key lines, if you want to know, are 'Cold
as a spring as yet so near its source,/Too lofty and original to rage.' . . .
But the key word in the whole poem is source—whatever source it is."

Despite the importance of the religious tone, the poem is indispensable because it nudges the reader to consider sources beyond religion.
Frost hints as much when he comments on "whatever source it is," thus
suggesting an extra-religious dimension. . . .

"Directive" ends with the word "confusion": "Here are your waters and your watering place./Drink and be whole again beyond confusion." A significant word in the Frost canon, "confusion" is probably best known as part of the memorable phrase in his essay "The Figure a Poem Makes" when he talks about "a momentary stay against confusion." Although the literal meaning of the phrase is that the completed poem stays the confusion which the poet experiences when he first begins to write, the context of the entire essay suggests that any consciously created form, but especially poetry, is a momentary stay against the permanence of confusion. Form stay chaos, but only for a while. Poems must be written again and again.

If this suggestion has merit, then the last great poem of Frost's career is as much about poetry as it is about religion. The source that helps mankind to be "whole again beyond confusion" will be different things to different people, but for Frost himself the source is poetry—it always was. The technique of "Directive" testifies to his artistic prowess in old age; he was seventy-three when *Steeple Bush* was published. One can only marvel at the stately blank verse, the sudden opening line of monosyllables, the metaphors of quest and home and child. But "Directive" is a major poem by any standard because it insists on the close relationship between artistic creation and religious faith. Those familiar with the Frost biography know how his commitment to poetry clashed with his commitment to family. Frost was a survivor. He would not be beaten down by anyone's death but his own. When pressure threatened and chaos called, he always had poetry to go on with. Art was his source. To create it was to affirm wholeness.

Affirmation of creativity is the heart of Frost's canon. Even in his darkest verse, those lyrics and dialogue poems that unsettle the reader with glimpses of universal terror and portrayals of domestic fear, the affirmation of technique balances the pessimistic theme. He lodged so many poems in American literature that his best work will be forever necessary to the cultural health of the nation. The phrase "the indispensable Robert Frost" thus cuts two ways: it describes the stature of a major author, and it invites a discussion of those parts of his canon that the reader who would understand his work should know. Frost himself might not have agreed with the choices examined here, but eager to hold the spotlight he would have been pleased that the examination was taking place.

Donald J. Greiner. In Critical Essays on Robert<br>Frost, ed. Philip L. Gerber (G. K. Hall, 1982), pp.<br>237–38

# GADDIS, WILLIAM (1922–    )

Much of what strikes the casual reader as "excessive" in [*The Recognitions*]—its length, the virulence of its satire, the wide and esoteric range of its allusiveness, the improbability of certain incidents—suggests the extreme lengths to which William Gaddis was prepared to go to create an art commensurate with all reality rather than some limited aspect of it. . . . *The Recognitions* is an obsessive book, in that both author and characters seem driven to extremities of experience, perception, and thought. . . .

It is through the focal character of Wyatt that *The Recognitions* carries on a continual and insistent debate. That debate, which might be termed the obsession of the novel as a whole, revolves around the following double question: *What is the nature of, and what are the conditions for, genuine art?*

That in *The Recognitions* "reality" and "art" are interchangeable metaphors for each other is, I think, clear to every thoughtful reader. The cheap tourist art of Montmartre, the upside-down painting of Max, the distorted portrait of Recktall Brown—each symbolizes and epitomizes the context of life that surrounds it. For Gaddis, art is the touchstone by which the genuineness of life is judged, and the purity of human motives measured. Wyatt is not only an individual artist, but an Everyman whose concerns are universal; his art—and art in general—is no mere adornment or addition to life, but life itself in the deepest and truest sense. This is part of the achievement of the novel: it succeeds in turning the simple analogy of art and life into a baffling and frightening identity. In *The Recognitions* questions that ostensibly deal with aesthetics actually are questions that probe to the very core of the human condition. . . .

Here indeed is the aesthetic which lies at the core of *The Recognitions*, both as a work of art and as a statement *about* art. The words of Stanley that "the Devil is the father of false art" take on an ethical, even metaphysical meaning in this light. The creation of art is an act of atonement, in that it constellates true significance in the midst of falsity, redeeming that falsity just as the cross redeems sin. In point of fact, Gaddis's position seems to be that genuine art atones not only for false art, but for false life as well. Stanley's work expiates the falsity of Wyatt's and that same work is the instrument of his martyrdom. This martyrdom . . . is actually that of Stephen-Wyatt, for Gaddis has deliberately created a "mystical participation" between these two characters, corresponding to the relationship of Redeemer and Redeemed. Art is the ultimate expiation, for through it not only suffering, but the falsehood which lies at the core of existence is transfigured beyond the pettiness and sordidness of its context and origins. Thus, as Stanley's music "soared in atonement," the shaky edifice of falsehood trembles and falls, and this final counterpoint of upward release and triumph and downward collapse and fatality is art's perfect image of both man's implication in falsehood, and his capacity for redemption.

Joseph S. Salemi. Novel. Winter, 1977, pp. 127–<br>28, 136

Like other novels of excess, *JR* is aggressively rhetorical, risking the reader's refusal while offering pointers to its own intentions. In *The Public Burning*, [Robert] Coover uses chapters on *Time* and *The New York Times* to comment on his own novel. The narrator of [Thomas Pynchon's] *Gravity's Rainbow* bobs and weaves among his characters, mixing charitable omniscience with insults to the reader. There are several episodes in *JR* that reveal the desperation of the communication breakdown that is a central subject of the novel and the methods—what I call recording and redundancy—Gaddis uses to prevent breakdown between his novel and its reader. These methods are risky: although realism and repetition are at first aids to clear communication, in excess they become an assault as Gaddis insistently and thoroughly manifests what a runaway is. Messages among the characters in *JR* fail for many reasons: the sender's intellectual shortcomings or lack of interest, duplicity in language itself, the receiver's distraction or ignorance of the code, interference in or overload of the channels of communication. Throughout the novel sirens, loudspeakers, radios, televisions, and other agents create noise against which communication has to struggle. These problems inspire several experiments by a minor character named Vogel. One of these, teleportation, reflects Gaddis' method in the book, for teleportation attempts to send the messenger rather than just the message. Adopting the roles of recorder, collector, and transmitter rather than narrator, Gaddis "sends the messenger," allows his characters to present themselves as voices. This I call recording because Gaddis does not use certain conventions that would suggest authorial mediation or the transformation of speech into writing. Contexts and speakers are not identified in *JR*. There are no quotation marks in the text; the punctuation within sentences is irregular, usually suggesting the arbitrary pause of a voice rather than the formality of written discourse. The filler, solecisms, false starts, fragments, and repetitions of speech are left in. To further this sense of raw recording, Gaddis includes reproductions of newspaper advertisements, a handwritten school essay, a series of logotypes, and a writer's note cards. Playing back the stupid, pathetic, and ugly noise we hear in our work, media, families, and in our own throats, Gaddis assults us with an excess of verisimilitude, what is called over and over again in the book "the real." The single most dominant quality of this reality is its instantaneousness. As the clocks splinter into seconds, money-making minutes, the characters are always behind, late, making an abrupt change, rushing, trying to keep up with life that has been pervaded by the quantitative values of the runaway economic system. Fragmentation and trivialization of speech are the minute-to-minute effects of this speeded-up system.

Thomas LeClair. *MFS*. Winter, 1981–82, pp. 598–99

● **GAINES, ERNEST J. (1933–   )**

I can think of no other contemporary American novelist whose work has produced in me anything like the sense of depth, the sense of humanity and compassion, and the sense of honesty that I find in Gaines's fiction. It contains the austere dignity and simplicity of ancient epic, a concern with man's most powerful emotions and the actions that arise from those emotions, and an artistic intuition that carefully keeps such passions and behavior under fictive control. Gaines may be one of our most naturally gifted story-tellers. . . .

From the beginning, Gaines has worked to put into an appropriate form his own sense of history, a sense which has both dictated and arisen from his central subject, the blacks and the whites who live in and around his imaginary town of Bayonne, near Baton Rouge, and who work the land of the plantations that still survive. Gaines has the special feeling for these people and this land that comes from having grown up among them, and having absorbed the quality of their lives without exercising any analytical selectivity as to what he absorbed. Thus, his feelings are strongly attached to the sheer physical texture of this country, and it pervades his fiction: the hot summer sky filled with a hazy sun; the freezing, sleet-ridden days of winter; the monochromatic hues of a brilliantly white sky meeting a brilliantly white earth; the winter darkness in whose heavy overcast the distinction between the earth and the sky are obliterated. Gaines has the intuition of D. H. Lawrence and Thomas Hardy. Like them, he feels a permanent spirit residing in the land, which transcends time and space. His characters are born with the past in their bones, and their lives, whether they stay or leave this place, are dominated by it—this "place" in which the past is embedded. . . .

Whether it is intuitive or learned, Gaines's perception of the world resembles that of a biologist, who sees each living organism passing through time, occupying stages, crossing boundary lines into new and unfamiliar territory. Organic life is postulated on the oscillation between life and death, and these are the realities which Gaines fastens on to.

Jerry H. Bryant. *IowaR*. Winter, 1972, pp. 106,
110, 119

While his lands and subjects are consistent, there is an evolution of Ernest Gaines's vision through his four works, as he becomes increasingly concerned with black history and black community. The movement from *Catherine Carmier* to *Miss Jane Pittman* is from personal and racial history rendered as a kind of bondage, a solitary existential nightmare of dead ends and blasted families, toward history sensed as a natural cycle, wheeling slowly through the rebirth of a *people*, toward their inevitable collective liberation. As his vision matures, there is an accompanying shift in Gaines's use of materials and fictional techniques. He moves away from a personal version of the white "existential" novel, later assimilating and adapting folk forms—popular sermons, slave narratives, folk tales, oral histories—re-making the long fictional forms to his own unique ends. . . .

With *Bloodline*, Ernest Gaines sounds a very different emphasis on black history and community. The vision of history as fate, as a cycle from which one cannot escape, is expanded. As the title *Bloodline* suggests, the book is concerned with the living, the organic, and Gaines is writing with a vision of the natural history of a people. The dominant concern through these five stories is with natural patterns of growth and decay, the evolution from childhood to maturity to old age as seen in the lives of people, races, generations, eras. In the shapes of these stories, and in the recurrent images and metaphors, the past, present and future are all of a piece; history is part of a natural process, and humans who live within it find their lives infused with significance.

Jack Hicks. *BALF*. Spring, 1977, pp. 9, 13

When Ernest Gaines published *The Autobiography of Miss Jane Pittman* in 1971, he secured his footing within the American literary world as an important artist. The critical acclaim was nearly unanimous, and the transformation of the work into a popular television drama embellished that success. But Gaines' quiet vision of endurance was no sudden occurrence. With the patience of a journeyman becoming master of his vision, his view of life had been worked out in three previous books; of these earlier works, *Bloodline*, a cycle of short stories published in 1968, is a minor-keyed masterpiece. This is so, despite an age in which easy praise inflates achievement.

To discuss *Bloodline* properly, one must grant that a writer need not strain with an overreaching ambition to create significance in his fiction; he may instead make his mark by accurately recreating the texture of ordinary life, and leave it to us to discover the subtleties of the specific milieu he knows thoroughly. In this sense, *Bloodline* is a worthy descendant of Turgenev's *Sportsman's Sketches* and Joyce's *Dubliners*. It is equally evocative of ordinary life. Within the specific tradition of Afro-American literature, however, *Bloodline* is of even more pressing importance.

*Bloodline* has significance because it is in line with, though still different from, past landmarks of Afro-American short fiction. Charles Chesnutt's *Conjure Woman and Other Stories*, Jean Toomer's *Cane*, and Richard Wright's *Uncle Tom's Children*—all, like Gaines' *Bloodline*, concern themselves chiefly with the South, that "old country" of racial memory. In these works, successive generations of particular writers, each with some tie to the South, wrestled to divine the significance of that "old country." The works are important for that reason. Further, with regard to their importance and place in an ethnic short-prose tradition, these works are outstanding precisely because they are very much more than collections of separate pieces. Each writer in his own way—Chesnutt by undermining the Plantation Tradition, Toomer by evoking the mysteries of racial memory, Wright by the programmatic ordering of horror—constructs a whole with far greater significance than that of its separate pieces. In the regard, *Bloodline*, too, urges us beyond the bare sum of its parts, while, even more than its predecessors, accepting the ordinariness of the lives it sketches.

Todd Duncan. *Callaloo*. May, 1978, pp. 85–86

Ernest Gaines's fiction has been characterized from the first by its quiet force. The characters in his several fine books often raise their voices, but the author declines to raise his. These characters are mainly poor, and mostly black; their lives are seldom far removed from the threat of violence, physical or emotional or both. Sooner or later the violence arrives, and the characters cry out at one another, or to the heavens. Their pain, struggle, bewilderment, joys and agonies are registered with precision and sympathy, but the strong prose that carries their stories is not affected by the fevers or the biases of those it describes.

A swimmer cannot influence the flow of a river, and the characters of Ernest Gaines's fiction—from Catherine Carmier to Miss Jane Pittman, and from Miss Jane to the Rev. Phillip Martin of *In My Father's House*—

are propelled by a prose that is serene, considered and unexcited. It is the force of Mr. Gaines's character and intelligence, operating through this deceptively quiet style, that makes his fiction compelling. He is, pre-eminently, a writer who takes his own good time, and in this case [*In My Father's House*] the result of his taking it is a mature and muscular novel. . . .

Not the least of the book's virtues is the variety and richness of its minor characters. Phillip Martin's guilty search into his past takes him, internally, down a long road of memory. Externally it brings him into contact with a number of people—his godmother, an old girlfriend, a former gambling buddy and an embittered young black guerrilla—whose portraits are done with Flaubertian economy but equally Flaubertian vividness. The dialogue is spare, but unerring, and humor will keep slipping in subtly, despite the tragedies behind these lives. The tone of the book is determined by Mr. Gaines's decision—a brilliant one—to set the novel not in the expected context of a sweaty, dripping Louisiana summer, but in the miserable, frigid, sunless Louisiana winter. The sun never shines on this story, and the metaphors that describe the doom of Robert X are, appropriately, metaphors of chill.

There are few blemishes on the book. Now and then a character strays into polemic; once or twice the tone breaks. Perhaps Robert X should not have been allowed to speak at all, for his condemnatory silence is far more eloquent than the little that he eventually says. But these are small blemishes indeed on a book that attempts a large theme, and is fully adequate to it.

Larry McMurtry. NYT. June 11, 1978, p. 13

*In My Father's House* is an important work, showing significant development in Gaines's art and thought, especially in light of his depiction of and reaction to the 1970s. . . .

Gaines's distancing of his readers—and himself—from this novel may not indicate a change in his philosophy, but it does, I think, reflect a change in his attitude toward his characters' potential development. Considered in sequence, Gaines's first three novels show a gradual development in his characters' ability to grow, change, and prevail. All the characters in *Catherine Carmier*, his first novel, are victims of social or environmental forces, while in *Of Love and Dust* Jim Kelly and Marcus Payne achieve growth through fighting the inertia of southern black life and, within limits at least, gain the capacity to shape their lives. Gaines's sense of this power on the part of his characters culminates in the depiction of Jane Pittman, who prevails over seriously adverse circumstances. The *Autobiography* reconciles the dichotomies of the earlier novels: past and present, young and old, man and woman. In *In My Father's House* the reconciliation falls apart. . . .

Gaines's first three novels culminated in Jane Pittman, a character who embodies the positive values in his world. Perhaps he was then faced with the problem of how to create a story which would represent a significant development from such a powerful, heroic figure. In *In My Father's House* Gaines implies that Miss Jane's triumph, both personal and social, may be atypical, that Martin's fall is the more usual human fate. Burdened by a past he cannot escape, by overweening pride and self-esteem, Martin is defeated. Whether he can rise again, as is characteristic of traditional tragic heroes, is problematical. The ending of this novel suggests the ending of his first novel, *Catherine Carmier*, in that the characters are in stasis, immobile, unable to move and break out of the pattern in which they are trapped. The novel ends *we just go'n have to start again*.

Frank W. Shelton. *SoR*. Spring, 1981, pp.
340–41, 345

# GARDNER, JOHN (1933–1982)

A puzzling absence of criticism attends the works of John Gardner. He has published five novels since 1966: *The Resurrection* (1966), *The Wreckage of Agathon* (1970), *Grendel* (1971), *The Sunlight Dialogues* (1972), and *Nickel Mountain* (1973); he has also published a long poem, *Jason and Medeia* (1973), and a collection of stories, *The King's Indian* (1974). His works have been praised in an impressive number of brief reviews; his experiments with novelistic form have won him recognition as an innovator. But as prolific, well-received, and innovative as he may be, Gardner has not yet received the serious critical attention which his works merit. . . . One can consider the five novels as a group of works written at the beginning of his career and suppose that they were written in the following phases: the "very early" phase—*The Resurrection* and *Nickel Mountain;* the "early" phase—*The Sunlight Dialogues* and *The Wreckage of Agathon;* and the "late" phase—*Grendel*.

*The Resurrection* and *Nickel Mountain* share a concern with the affirmation of life in the face of death. . . . These two novels from the "very early" phase of Gardner's career resemble each other in several ways. They share an upstate New York setting, which Gardner will replace with more fabulous realms in the later novels. They share an omniscient narrator, presenting plausible characters who speak convincing dialogue; Gardner will use self-conscious and unreliable first-person narrators in the later novels. They share a conventional chronological structure, which will be modified to more experimental forms in the last three novels. *The Resurrection* and *Nickel Mountain* share a large, philosophical focus on the question, posed bluntly and emphatically to James Chandler, *"What is the meaning of life?"* . . . Just as the first two novels share similar themes and techniques, they also share a similar flaw. At their worst, they are sentimental; the affirmations made by the protagonists are not earned nor are they fully credible. . . .

Gardner's last three novels are his best and are distinguished from the first two by their inclusion of the figure of the alien, developed to its fullest in *Grendel*. Gardner's three most compelling characters are aliens: the Sunlight Man, Agathon, and Grendel. Each is an eccentric, estranged from a society he improves through the biting wit of his alienation; each is pitted against righteousness and complacency; each is an artist of sorts: the Sunlight Man with magic, Agathon with fictionalized narrative, and Grendel with poetic myth. Finally, each is a joker, a sad clown, whose jokes emerge like black humor from a mood of despair.

*The Sunlight Dialogues* and *The Wreckage of Agathon* share a similar theme, in which the metaphysical focus of the earlier novels is replaced by a social focus. Both novels are about the inadequacy of law and the need for justice, the narrowness of codified rules and the need for a broader human understanding.

Susan Strehle. Critique. 18, 2, 1976, pp. 86–88

John Gardner is one of the few American novelists who has remained fascinated by the man who acts, who wills one thing intensely enough to get it. A medievalist, Gardner seems to have kept his faith that "except in the life of a hero, the whole world's meaningless." *October Light* is a stunningly written tragicomic novel that searches through the operative myths of national greatness for a surviving American heroism. Sally, an 83-year-old feminist, and James, her 70-year-old farmer brother, mirror two heroic strains in the American consciousness, the one intoxicated by progress; the other devoted to the land and deriving its values from the endless repetitions of nature. Belief in progress and change and willingness to work the land opened up the American wilderness. . . .

Missing in his novels is a sense of masculine purpose, of the hero as the man who can put his power in the service of a worthwhile cause. Gardner's heroes are willful, self-absorbed narcissists who see determination and merit as the same, and whose heroism involves only the willingness to follow their obsessions wherever they might lead . . . In not making distinctions between the value of one obsession and another, Gardner stalemates his novels.

Gardner's irresolution takes the form of an irony so pervasive it seems to stem from that well of American bitterness that made Herman Melville and Mark Twain, creators of distinctive American heroes, finally black about America's possibilities. Gardner presses his ambivalences into *October Light*, forcing his chauvinism and his nihilism against each other like monuments to two American civilizations. He achieves a disturbing, utterly original novel that gets as close as any book can to that acid cartoon, Grant Wood's "American Gothic."

Josephine Hendin. *NR*. Feb. 5, 1977, pp. 31–32

*On Moral Fiction* . . . will probably be quoted as widely as [William] Gass's *Fiction and the Figures of Life* was a few years ago, not because Gardner's formulations of the new fictional conservatism are particularly brilliant but because he articulates feelings and tastes many disgruntled readers share. Gass's essays had an elegant uselessness; Gardner's appeal is plain talk and righteousness. I have heard "Kill the Aestheticians" murmured in my university library. Gardner responds to this kind of frustration with academic jargon by using words, such as Beauty, Truth, and Goodness, that most critics walked away from years ago. These abstractions come to have a sludge-like quality, Gardner's distinctions often lack precision (a favorite pejorative is "creepy"), and his readings of recent fiction are sometimes militantly unimaginative. But *On Moral Fiction* is still a necessary book because its earnest force requires even the reader who resists it page by page to examine his assumptions about fiction and because no other writer—Tom Wolfe in *The Painted Word* excepted— has reminded us recently that art is by and for human beings.

Gardner finds most contemporary American fiction and its criticism mediocre or worse. Authors lack belief, so they follow the cult of style, fancy surface. If they have values worth communicating, their fiction is too often programmatic and didactic. Criticism accepts this diminished state of fiction while trifling with finer and finer-gauged descriptive categories. What we need, argues Gardner, is a moral fiction, one that improves life through its sane and healthy vision and through its creation of character models for our imitation. The moral artist is the poet-priest who creates by a process of careful imitation, testing his fiction against the larger reality of human experience. A true criticism would judge fiction, at least partially, on moral grounds. This summary does little violence to Gardner's positions. While they are filled out with some explanation of central terms, with references to classic authorities, and with discussions of contemporary writers (John Fowles as hero, William Gass and mostly unnamed nihilists as villains), Gardner's arguments are meant to be fundamental. He insists on a common sense view, an enforced simplicity, and he has the Platonic assurance that we—always it is "we"—know the good but just can't find it.

I think Gardner's assessment of the current literary scene is substantially accurate if our contemporaries are measured against classic or even classic modern writers. His judgments would also be true of the fiction written in the 1870s. Still, we do need to recognize that very few of our writers have the heart or ambition to be a Melville or a Pynchon. Even Gardner's prescriptions could be persuasive had he not vitiated the basic force of his argument with an inconsistent definition of moral fiction, with narrow assumptions, inflated claims, and limited sympathies. Gardner defines moral fiction both by the exploratory, mimetic process of its composition and by the healthy effects it has without fully considering that a "moral" process can and sometimes does produce a negative, even a nihilistic work. His assumptions—that ordinary language is adequate for interesting fiction, that art communicates very much like other discourses, that the reader should fall into fiction as into a dream—are insistently naive, but even more difficult to accept is Gardner's pride. He proclaims that art and criticism are the only ordering agencies left in our culture, that "true" art—and not just the best art—is necessarily moral, and that the artist is the only true critic. As a reader of his fellow novelists, Gardner is sometimes pettish (his comments on Bellow and Updike), occasionally sloppy, and at least once flatly wrong—when he mistakes what happened in Heller's *Something Happened*. There is little sympathy for satirists, creators of indirect affirmations, and makers of imaginative ornaments. In a world where everything and everyone is used, ordered for a purpose, Gardner would make fiction one more operation, the most efficient persuasion. He forgets fun.

*On Moral Fiction* does not collapse through its many weaknesses because, ultimately, Gardner sides with great art, an ambitious humane art that displays the writer's love for his craft, his world, and his readers.

Thomas LeClair. *CL*. Autumn, 1979, pp. 509–11

The garden and the machine confront each other anew in Gardner's fiction. The voice of the garden, linked to the pastoral impulse with its love of nature and poetic longings, confronts the voice of the machine, linked to the darker Manichaean belief that the world is mere accident, brute force controls all history, and only outright manipulation will keep things running. The basic pattern of dialogue between the classical/medieval hope for regeneration and redemption, linked to light and often magic, and the modern nihilistic certainty of gloom and despair, linked to darkness and often black magic, informs the basic narrative structure of Gardner's fiction. These voices set off against one another—the human heart in conflict with itself—set up a counterpoint in his fiction, which slowly works itself out in the process of the confrontation itself. Fiction becomes a "dream unfolding in the mind," a spell cast by both opposing camps, defining each other by the pattern of dialogue and conflict between them. . . .

In *The Sunlight Dialogues* Gardner achieves that equilibrium between "radical disunities," that fully wrought balance between the pastoral idyll and Calvinist/Manichaean melodrama, which lies at the heart of the greatest of American literature. Here Clumly, the benevolent watchdog, and Taggert Hodge, the Babylonian anarchist, confront one another in a series of dialogues representing the contradictory impulses of western and, in particular, American culture. The dialogue, in fact, becomes Gardner's basic narrative structure, his basic aesthetic form, in the book. The Babylonian holiness of matter confronts the Judeo-Christian holiness of spirit. The Babylonian love of substance opposes the Judeo-Christian "idle speculation" about abstract relationships between soul and flesh (p. 413). An impersonal universe confronts that "grand American responsibility" for right and wrong (p. 323). Clumly finally realizes that "'we must all be vigilant against growing indifferent to people less fortunate. . . . We have to stay awake, as best we can, and be ready to obey the laws as best as we're able to see them. That's it. That's the whole thing'" (pp. 670, 672). No winners or losers but a constant juggling of contraries, a balance of irreconcilable positions, a continued vigilance in the unrelenting encounter between the "radical disunities" of American culture. The Manichaean interpenetration of each becomes the only certainty, although the pastoral vantage point points the way toward armed reconciliation. . . .

What Henry James referred to as American literature's "rich passion for extremes" can be found in Gardner's fiction. Gardner's hope for human communion and love, however fragmentary and diminished, remains undaunted. He is clearly reworking the American fable for our own troubled contemporary times and not merely delighting in structuralist and "post-modernist" techniques for their own artificer's delight. Like Hawthorne, Melville, and Faulkner before him, he seems intent on dispelling anew the notion of a special American innocence, yet at the same time recognizing the pull and enchantment of the pastoral impulses implicit in that American myth. He's aware of the precariousness in that farther darkness and uses his pastoralism as a vantage point from which to observe and re-create the American heart's unrelenting conflict with itself.

Samuel Coale. In *John Gardner: Critical Perspectives*, ed. Robert A. Morace and Kathryn Van Spanckeren (Southern Illinois Univ. Pr., 1982), pp. 20, 23, 26–27

In recent years, Gardner has been dogged by charges of plagiarism—he was accused of twigging his popularized biographical book *The Life and Times of Chaucer* (1977) with unattributed borrowings from more-serious

Chaucerian scholars—and in a foreword to this new book, he conscientiously reels off his sources and influences, perhaps hoping to fend off further charges. He needn't have fussed. The novel *is* patchy and derivative, but that's the least of its worries. . . .

His new novel, I'm afraid, is a whopping piece of academic bull slinging. With *Mickelsson's Ghosts*, John Gardner hasn't so much composed a novel as he has used his mind as a vacuum cleaner to suck up a lot of serious reading and then dump the scruffy contents on the reader's carpet. Gleanings from Nietzsche and Luther and Wittgenstein, ruminations on the significance of Dadaism, trendy little velleities about nuclear strife. . . , deep-think musings on the sovereignty of music, morbid broodings on the lingering shadows of Nazism—time and time again Gardner empties his mind, burying the reader in foothills of lint. . . . What is *Mickelsson's Ghosts* about? Name it: love, guilt, history, family ties, entropy and doom, God's enigmatic silence—the whole shebang. But magisterial themes call for a magisterial style, and the writing in *Mickelsson's Ghosts* is all slap and dribble, a trickling spill of irrelevancies. . . .

*Mickelsson's Ghosts* . . . is . . . one of those big, noisy books that tries to be about everything and, because of its incoherence, ends up being about nothing. Nabokov describing Pnin's tongue at play among his craggy teeth gives one more to live for than does John Gardner prowling through the mists of history, trying to slip the handcuffs on Heidegger. . . .

Literary critics aren't the only ones thrown from the sled by highbrow slumming; trying to play philosopher in this new novel sends John Gardner for an inglorious spill. As *Grendel* proved, Gardner is at home with myth and legend—he can make you feel the heat of a beastie's breath, the crack of wood on stone. But as a thinker he's hopeless. *Mickelsson's Ghosts* simply won't do.

James Wolcott. *Esquire*. June, 1982, p. 134

# GASS, WILLIAM H. (1924–    )

Like all metafictions, *Willie Masters' Lonesome Wife* deals with writing and its own construction in a self-conscious manner. The work proves to be especially complex and ambitious, however, because Gass brings to it not only a literary viewpoint, but a background in the philosophy of language (a subject in which Gass received his Ph.D. from Cornell). *Willie Masters'* deals with the building-blocks of fiction—words and concepts—

in a more direct and sophisticated fashion than most other metafictions; it is more explicitly experimental than just about any other work of fiction which comes to mind and can serve as a virtual casebook of literary experimentalism, since it appropriates almost every experimental device used by writers in the past and suggests a good many possibilities for future development as well. . . .

As the best metafiction does, *Willie Masters' Lonesome Wife* forces us to examine the nature of fiction-making from new perspectives. If . . . Gass [has] succeeded, our attention has been focused on the act of reading words in a way we probably have not experienced before. The steady concern with the *stuff* of fiction, words, makes Gass's work unique among metafictions which have appeared thus far. At the end of the book, we encounter a reminder from Gass stamped onto the page: "YOU HAVE FALLEN INTO ART—RETURN TO LIFE." When we do return to life, we have, hopefully, a new appreciation—perhaps even love—of that lonesome lady in Gass's title.

Larry McCaffery. *Critique*. 18, 1, 1976, pp. 23–24, 34

In *The Pleasure of the Text*, Roland Barthes sexualizes the pleasure of reading contemporary fiction and calls for "writing aloud". . . . William Gass' *On Being Blue* is the writer's companion to Barthes' reader's guide, an erotics of writing that defines the productive relation of lay and lie for the novelist. Gass both argues and displays "the use of language like a lover . . . not the language of love, but the love of language, not matter, but meaning, not what the tongue touches, but what it forms, not lips and nipples, but nouns and verbs." Throughout *On Being Blue* is the kind of "writing aloud" we get from no other American novelist or critic. . . .

At once metaphor and metaphoric, *On Being Blue* is an elegant extension of Gass' plea for the medium of fiction articulated in the essays of *Fiction and the Figures of Life* and in the fictional essay *Willie Masters' Lonesome Wife*. He asks the writer to "give up the blue things of this world in favor of the words which say them" because sex—and most other charged subjects—lacks a sufficient vocabulary, disrupts esthetic form, and turns language into a transparency on a world we only think we know. Blue books come to signify every kind of fiction that makes its reader a voyeur peering through the lens of language, never noting it no matter what its color, to see the supposed subject—politics, city life, the perils of being female, whatever. . . . *On Being Blue* [is] a book no person who loves writing and the sound writing makes should be without.

Thomas LeClair. *NR*. Oct. 9, 1976, p. 38

Mr. Gass is hardly a structuralist philosopher, but he has written works of fiction—*Omensetter's Luck* and *In the Heart of the Heart of the Country* are his best-known works—that give heart to the structuralist enterprise, and his essays may be said to promote the attack on realist aesthetics. . . . [The essays in] *Fiction and the Figures of Life* (1972) . . . constitute the most vigorous anti-realist literary "programme" we have had in our time. His new collection of essays, *The World within the Word*, not as dedicated to system-building as the first, but no less teasing and brilliant, sustains but does not substantially develop his theory. When the earlier book first appeared, a reviewer for the *New York Times* called it "a defense of 'poesy' in a time of need." The time is always needy, of course, and it is more than "poesy" that Gass defends, but the reviewer was not mistaken to state that Gass "calls our attention to art." To do so, need we say, is to remind us as well of all the things that art is not, and ought never to be asked to be. Gass calls our attention to art not by instructing us in the decipherment of signs or in the chastening of sentiment but by underlining all of the things art will not do, and celebrating the very special things it has to do.

Gass's books are wonderful books because they raise all of the important aesthetic issues in the starkest and most inventive way. The writing is informed by a moral passion and a love of beautiful things that are never compromised by the author's compulsive addiction to aestheticizing formulations. We all know what Gass is writing against, including the tiresome use of novels for purposes of unitary moral uplift and penetrating "word-view." What he detests is the goody sweepstakes, in which works of art are judged not by their formal complexity or nuances of verbal texture but by their ability to satisfy easy moral imperatives. Gass has had some hand in discrediting the kind of righteous moralism that so corrupts ordinary apprehension of the literary arts. That is good. But the essays in his two collections have also served to confuse some readers about the art of reading. In so far as the essays suggest that realism is necessarily a debased aesthetic, they encourage a view of reading as a specialized activity to which we bring special passions—like the passion for form—and from which we rigorously exclude others. That is not, it seems to me, an entirely useful way to record what really goes on when we read a book. Strange to say, I think William Gass knows better than the rest of us what goes on; and one day he may even decide to tell us.

Robert Boyers. *TLS*. Nov. 3, 1978, pp. 1274–75

## GINSBERG, ALLEN (1926–   )

Ginsberg insists that the study of consciousness is the primary legitimate tradition in poetry. . . . Ginsberg vowed to dedicate his life and poetics to the realization of Blake's demand that the poet must cleanse the doors of perception. . . .

Ginsberg's poetics, then, must be approached from the angle of his Blake visions, since these visions dominated his theory and practice of poetry from 1948–63. The visions, in turn, should be understood as the point of departure for his studies of consciousness. Out of his visionary experiments, Ginsberg emerged with many of the primary theories and practices of his poetics. From his discipleship with Blake . . . he has developed a complicated and often misunderstood theory of composition, which he has labelled "First Thought, Best Thought"; a notion of his role as a poet; several ideas on the concept of prosody as a record of the movement of the meditative mind; a messianic identity, and a commitment to writing poetry as a record of the minute particulars of quotidian reality—as well as the minute particulars of the mind itself. . . .

Ginsberg's prophetic quest had a significant influence on his poetics, as demonstrated in his use of physical surroundings, the breath notation of his line, and the use of the catalogue. Each of these innovations was a part of his artful devotion to the study of consciousness. His decision to follow Blake's statement that every man was a prophet led him to a practice of writing that involved deep absorption in meditation. The meditation, in turn, focused on many of the elements discussed in this section. His ultimate prophetic ambition was not only to retrieve the heightened awareness he had experienced in his Blake visions, but to learn how to induce higher states of consciousness in his readers. . . . Ginsberg's quest for extraordinary or mystical states of being were to prove self-defeating. In fact, after re-examining his fifteen years of devotion to his guru, Blake, he came to the point of having to renounce his visionary master. He felt himself too much under Blake's domination. The obligation he had labored under to follow what he conceived as Blake's "instructions" had led to his denying the here and now. He felt he had denied himself the freedom to be just himself.

Paul Portugués. *The Visionary Poetics of Allen
Ginsberg* (Ross-Erikson, 1978), pp. 4–5, 89

Robert Lowell and Allen Ginsberg, arguably the best poets of their generation, have perhaps succeeded most notably in surviving their own publicity. They have been able to write good poetry for thirty years in part because the publicity that surrounded them was generated by others who were quick to attend not so much to talent as to popularity. Lowell and Ginsberg became well known in different ways, of course, but both ways grew out of their talents for an endless, often *driven* form of speaking that at one and the same time clarified itself and grew more inclusive of the historical complexity it recorded. This speaking—one often thinks of both poets as "commentators"—has a confessional cast to it, and both men have made the private order into public occasion more than once. But their fullest voices were achieved through their ability to make the public events they often deplored into something like private musings. The languages they discovered to enable this transformation are sometimes similar; for all the apparent differences in their sensibilities, it might be interesting to see just what lies behind, and inside, their distinctive modes of speech. . . .

The source of Ginsberg's sensibility . . . is the affinity group rather than the nuclear family. In contrast to Lowell's historical burdens, Ginsberg's social and political consciousness, and even his conscience, seems looser and yet more extensive. Lowell's political awareness takes shapes in key epochs, or even key moments, that serve as measures of values, tests of true progress, while at the same time hinting that all is devolutionary. Ginsberg's polis is always a future, utopian one; though he shares Lowell's sense of America's massive failure as a political "experiment," that failure has a different texture, a different moral weight in his poetry than it does in Lowell's.

Charles Molesworth. *The Fierce Embrace: A Study of Contemporary American Poetry* (Univ. of Missouri Pr., 1979), pp. 37, 39

Allen Ginsberg, in "Wichita Vortex Sutra," seems to have managed both the articulation of particulars and their imaginative transcendence. It appears that Ginsberg's powerful emotional response to the inhumanity that war represents, as it is reflected early in the poem, allows him finally to negate that war, to eliminate it entirely from his system of recognitions. No poem that I have seen dealing with the Vietnam period in American life is so packed with angry details at the beginning—the minutiae of newspapers, radio reports, advertising slogans, all of which tend to falsify reality—and so blithe and ethereal at the end. The personal and poetic transformation Ginsberg works in "Wichita," from almost total submersion in and obsession with political and military detail and dishonesty to final disbelief and liberation from such detail, is most unusual.

Perhaps even more unusual is the fact that this poem was written with the greatest "projective" rapidity—actually composed on tape-recorder as the poet traveled southwest through Kansas by car. The transformation occurring at the end—the transcendence of the personal— . . . is effected not through the adoption of *persona*, dramatic projection, or the subordination of present ills by a philosophic consideration of the past, but rather through the ritual act of *mantra*, in which Ginsberg, having described as many civil and military evils as possible, calls upon a rich pantheon of Indian, Christian, and Jewish gods to exorcize those evils and flatly declares the end of war. Surprisingly, the mantra seems to work, not just for Ginsberg, but for the reader as well. . . .

In this work of Ginsberg we have, to my mind, that rare integration of visual and aural, phenomenal and personal attentions which somehow eluded both Denise Levertov and Robert Duncan in their various strivings to personalize and politicize their poetry. We also have a remarkable instance of the success of modern organic/projective poetry from a writer who, for all his uplifted spontaneity, refuses to shut himself off from the validity of the outside world—particularly the natural and human world—and its insistent claim to reality.

William Aiken. *MPS*. 10, 2–3, 1981, pp. 232, 240

## GLASGOW, ELLEN (1874–1945)

In the history of Southern literature Ellen Glasgow's place is assured. She was, simply, the first really modern Southern novelist, the pioneer who opened up for fictional imagination a whole spectrum of her region's experience that hitherto had been considered inappropriate for depiction in polite letters. From the very beginning she meant business, and she had no patience with those who would have literature be anything less or other than an honest portrait of human experience and human meaning. Decades before Faulkner, Wolfe, Warren, Caldwell, Welty, and the others, she did her best to write about Southern experience as she actually viewed it, not as her neighbors thought she ought to be seeing it. In the words of the historian C. Vann Woodward, "When eventually the bold moderns of the South arrested the reading and theatrical world with the tragic intensity of the inner life and social drama of the South, they could find scarcely a theme that Ellen Glasgow had wholly neglected. She had bridged the gap between the old and the new literary revival, between romanticism and realism."

Louis D. Rubin, Jr. In *Ellen Glasgow: Centennial
Essays*, ed. M. Thomas Inge (Univ. Pr. of
Virginia, 1976), p. 4

Ellen Glasgow, . . . who died in 1945, is not at all highly regarded at present; yet she was a distinguished American novelist and the first of the Southern women writers . . . to repudiate the "willed heroic vision." Her primary theme, indeed, is the way in which grand ideas and facile goodwill interfere with the capacity to perceive ordinary miserable truths. . . .

What fascinates Ellen Glasgow is the paradox involved in the correlation between integrity and dissembling; in her novels it is always those of the highest moral character who are most reluctant to take account of domestic or social ills. They become adept at pretending. She makes the point over and over: "Her higher nature lent itself to deceit"; ". . . both clung . . . to the belief that a pretty sham has a more intimate relation to morality than has an ugly truth." The characters—most of them at any rate—are not at all critical of society's arrangements, but the author is: she is openly a crusader for social reforms, but she avoids a haranguing note by keeping her tone sardonic rather than impassioned. Benign obtuseness, willed or otherwise, is her target; but she understands how this quality can make life more agreeable for those who possess it. . . .

Ellen Glasgow's objective . . . is to underline the harm occasioned by self-deceits and wilful delusions, and to suggest, as far as possible, a wider social parallel for the personal failures and tragedies her novels depict. At best, her work is authoritative and graceful; and her social observation is always acute.

Patricia Craig. *TLS*. Nov. 13, 1981, p. 1319

## ● GODWIN, GAIL (1937–    )

Back in the days before the Women's Liberation Front changed everything it used to be possible to think of women who wrote novels as a different order of beings from male novelists. Now, we are supposed to think of all women as essentially identical with men, except for some slight variations in plumbing, etc.

Yet the desire to think of women who write as dissimilar in some real and important sense to men who write persists, and Gail Godwin's first novel, it seems to me, has to be thought of in relation to this difference. Her book is very much a woman's novel, and I want to discuss it in those terms. But let me say first that it is an excellent piece of work, shrewdly observed and carefully crafted, deserving of the praise that such established writers as Kurt Vonnegut, John Fowles, and George P. Elliot have already bestowed on it. *The Perfectionists* is, in fact, too good, too clever, and too finished a product to be patronized as a "first novel." It deserves better; it deserves criticism. And that is what I will try to give it.

*The Perfectionists* is a novel of domestic life or, more accurately, of sexual partnership. The "perfectionists" of the title are an English psychotherapist, Dr. Empson, and his American wife, Dane, who come to Majorca for something like a belated honeymoon, along with the doctor's three-year-old illegitimate son and one of his female patients. The relationship between husband and wife, as complicated by the strange little boy, is the central concern of the novel, and it is developed with a satiric and symbolic vigor that suggests a combination of Jane Austen and D. H. Lawrence. The eerie tension that marks this complex relationship is the great achievement of the novel. It is an extraordinary accomplishment, which is bound to attract and hold many readers. . . .

My principal criticism of these proceedings has to do with the resolute femininity with which they are presented. By this I mean not that metaphysical womanhood which Dickens perceived behind the pseudonym of "George Eliot" when he reviewed her amazing first novel, *Adam Bede*, but a narrower and pettier kind of thing. The women in this novel are, all of them, more or less interesting, more or less sympathetic. The men, starting with the doctor . . . are all fatuous and self-centered creatures.

This is, then, a woman's novel in a narrow and constricting way. I suspect that Miss Godwin can extend the range of both her sympathy and her satire. I hope that she will want to. From Jane Austen to Iris Murdoch, the great women of our fiction have been metaphysically female and not merely feminine.

Robert Scholes. SR. Aug. 8, 1970, pp. 37–38

Gail Godwin's *The Odd Woman* (1974) does not at first glance seem to be in the currently popular mode of self-conscious fiction—and perhaps for this reason has not attracted the critical attention it deserves. Neither a work as involuted as one by Borges nor a *Kuenstlerroman*, *The Odd Woman* centers on the relation between literature and life, especially on the effect that literature—and the lies it often tells—has on those who believe it. Of special interest is the novel's focus on fiction's traditional portrayal of women and its effect on women's relations with and reactions to men. . . .

To Jane, a professor of English, literature serves as far more than simply vocation or avocation. It is not just an object of perception but conditions her very mode of seeing. She views her own life through the refracting filter of literature. . . .

The full insight that the literary world has no necessary correlation with the actual world bursts on Jane. Villains in art need not be villains in life. Moreover, her insight confirms the truth of Jane's early wondering whether or not the concept of the self is itself a myth—"Characters were not so wholly good or bad, heroes or villains, anymore," whether or not the very notion of personality—the staple of fiction—is itself false. As the concepts of personality and of heroes and villains die, so does "all the stuff of novels" on which Jane depends to give meaning to her life.

Unfortunately, *The Odd Woman* does not end on an optimistic note of lessons learned. . . . The novel closes with the snow falling, reminding us of Jane's retreat when writing her dissertation, and pointing to another such frozen retreat from the actual world.

Godwin seems to offer a forceful indictment of literature and the harmful effects it can have on its readers. Jane can never be happy except, perhaps, in the safe world of the imagination, the only world which can begin to fulfill the expectations literature has fostered in her. We must go on to ask how Godwin can escape her own indictment of literature, whether her message does not undermine the very novel in which it is embodied. . . .

As Jane notes, Gissing's novel [with the same title] displays his "unrelenting pessimism. It was one of the few nineteenth-century novels she could think of in which every main female character who was allowed to live through the last page had to do so alone. The book's ending depressed her utterly." Godwin might find her defense against the charge she, too, levels against literature in pointing to the pessimistic ending of Jane's story as an example of the truth-telling that we must require from contemporary fiction. Godwin, however, has some of the Jane Clifford in her, and her novel still embodies some of the old attractive lies.

Susan E. Lorsch. *Critique.* 20, 2, 1978, pp. 21, 31

Gail Godwin's newest novel, *Violet Clay*, [is] a terrifying example of sentimentality in the disguise of contemporary sensibility. . . .

None of the novel's characters has been translated by Godwin's imagination into credibility. They speak to each other in prolix and tendentious conversations, so unedited by personality that they are droll. . . .

Well, to be fair, a lot of this is the fault of bad writing, an inability to describe exactly or to transcribe the sound of different voices into anything resembling living language. . . .

But there is worse than this, the basis from which the flabby language, the insubstantial characters, the odd lapses of taste seem to spring; the novel is simply half-baked, half-created, and so far from inevitable that one reads it constantly reminding oneself that it could easily have been avoided. . . .

If the book carries any conviction with it, it is that Violet's esthetic is pretty much molded by her author's, a schoolgirl sensibility in search of vocation. Gail Godwin has been regarded highly as a novelist for some time, certainly since *The Odd Woman* was published in 1974, and I wonder unhappily how much of that regard is due to the fashionable nature of her themes, which can create, without feeling for character, language, ambience, or moral significance, a job lot of current concerns that passes as "Women's Fiction."

Edith Milton. *NR*. July 8–15, 1978, pp. 40–41

Gail Godwin, on first reading, seems to stand apart from contemporary women writers. She appears immune to experiments with style and the contemporary raw language of sexuality. Her works are plotted symmetrically in the manner of George Eliot, whom she admires, and at a time when many women writers are primarily concerned with woman's emerging sexuality as well as with her active participation in the outside world, Godwin maintains that the demands of the inner woman are much more complex than this. Inner life, says her heroine, Jane Clifford (*The Odd Woman*, 1974), is as important as outer life. But it is obvious that the author considers the inner life even more important. Her first two novels, *The Perfectionists* (1970) and *Glass People* (1972), are clever, well-executed works about women who attempt to grapple with the domestic life and with sexual partnership. More specifically, the heroine of *Glass People* is confronted with what she comes to regard as the awful responsibility of freedom.

How to achieve freedom while in union with another person, and impose one's own order on life so as to find self-fulfillment, is the theme which runs through Godwin's works and becomes the major theme of exploration in her third novel, *The Odd Woman*. . . . Where some other women writers maintain a pessimism about the man/woman relationship, Godwin has her heroine doggedly affirm that man and woman can be a unit; man and woman need each other. Yet it is worth noting that the heroine is alone in the end. The open ending, however, indicates that the author is still the writer of freedom, marriage, love, children, and the relationship between generations. Her subsequent work, *Dream Children* (1976), continues these themes with variations.

Anne Z. Mickelson. *Reaching Out: Sensitivity and*
*Order in Recent American Fiction by Women*
(Scarecrow, 1979), p. 68

Gail Godwin's heroines have abandoned their soapboxes, and thank goodness for that. Godwin is by now an "established" writer; she has four novels and a collection of short stories to her credit, not to mention a National Book Award nomination. Her complex and fascinating characters, like Jane Clifford in *The Odd Woman* and Violet in *Violet Clay*, have until now suffered from two crippling flaws: they have repeatedly indulged in long, often boring, interior monologues—"meandering and distinctly tedious," huffed novelist Larry McMurtry of an earlier novel— and they have had no sense of humor whatsoever.

However, the news of Godwin's latest novel, *A Mother and Two Daughters*, is good, in fact, very good indeed. Nell, Cate, and Lydia Strickland, the three women who dominate the stage, are—like Violet Clay and Jane Clifford—thoughtful, well-educated, self-analytic people, but Godwin hustles them along at a brisk pace through this long, but definitely never tedious tale. They don't opine about the meaning of love or the perils of George Eliot, but do share with us their attempts to make a good job of an ordinary daily life familiar to us all. . . .

Only a few times in this long novel does Godwin falter. A digression on contemporary fiction seems jarringly self-conscious. The requisite eccentrics are skillfully drawn, but show up right on cue: the overbearing, curious spinster aunt Theodora and the disfigured Uncle Osgood with his heart of gold and his redemptive role for latter-day sinners. The middle-class black couple seem plopped down in order to stir up a few thoughts on prejudice and change. All the characters take themselves very seriously, but it is part of their astonishing strength that they persuade us to do likewise.

Anyone from an average family will find themselves drawing a breath and muttering: "Yes, that's how *I* felt, that's how it always is." Godwin wrote of Jane Clifford in *The Odd Woman*: "Her profession was words and she believed in them deeply. The articulation, interpretation, and preservation of good words." She could have been describing herself. She pilots her cast of characters with infinite care, through turbulence, clouds, and sparkling skies. The smooth landing at the novel's end is deeply satisfying: not a neat tying up of loose ends, but a making sense of the past and a hint of the possibilities of the future. Gail Godwin is not just an established writer, she is a growing writer.

Brigitte Weeks. Ms. Jan., 1982, pp. 40–41

In general, Miss Godwin's gifts (like Margaret Drabble's) have been best served by the spacious dimensions of the conventional novel. Her talent lies in creating intelligent woman protagonists—usually middle-class and imaginative, often with artistic aspirations—who struggle to lead examined lives in the face of self-imposed as well as cultural constraints. Blessed with humor as well as perceptiveness, they are nearly always sympathetic, even when they behave badly. (Their amiability can be irritating. I sometimes wish Miss Godwin's characters would behave worse more often; her women often suffer from the excess of politesse common to children of the 1950's.)

In any case, her reflective characters come to life slowly, emerging as much from thought as from action, and Miss Godwin's novels have generally accommodated them. I especially liked the edgy perversity of *The Perfectionists* (1970) and the irony and insight of *The Odd Woman* (1974), as well as the gentler but widening vision of *A Mother and Two Daughters*.

I wish I could be as enthusiastic about *Mr. Bedford and the Muses*, a short novel and five stories. The stories have the more obvious problems, which are at least partly due to brevity and partly to their tucked-in edges. Shapeliness is deadly in short fiction. At best, it creates an excess of charm; at worst, it kills the story on the page. . . .

On its own terms, which are not those of Miss Godwin's larger novels, *Mr. Bedford* is a memorable portrait of the kind of people who might have known Scott Fitzgerald during their "better days." It is wry, haunting and sharp.

Judith Gies. *NYT*. Sept. 18, 1983, pp. 14, 37

## GOYEN, WILLIAM (1915–1983)

It is hard to believe that these two books were written by the same man. One, the *Selected Writings*, shows William Goyen to be an extraordinarily rewarding and exciting writer. The other, *Come, the Restorer*, is an embarrassingly bad echo. Of course, Goyen's fiction technique is by its nature a fail-safe gamble. He approaches the problem of fiction in such a way that he can only win or lose—he cannot produce a middling good book.

William Goyen is one of those writers whose reputation has always outrun his sales. When I first read him some 10 years ago, I was told that he was like Malcolm Lowry. Well, I don't see the resemblance—except perhaps in the fervor of his devoted readers. The *Selected Writings* collection brings together some of his out-of-print works, from the years 1950–1963; its intent clearly is to present Goyen as a kind of classic. The book actually includes a short bibliography, articles in three languages to show what a fine and valued writer he is. Now that is a pretentious bit of scholarly trivia—but don't be put off by it. The *Selected Writings* is a book well worth reading. It is not, as the English would say, a "good read." It is dark, mystical, hypnotic, grotesquely powerful. It will probably haunt your dreams. . . .

Goyen is usually classified as a Southern writer, but his regionalism sits lightly on him. He superficially resembles Flannery O'Connor and the early Truman Capote ("Other Voices, Other Rooms"). But the similarities are misleading. Capote and O'Connor were truly regionalists, drawing their support from their background. Goyen is very nearly a completely placeless writer, his landscape the mind's interior.

The *Selected Writings* shows Goyen to be an eccentric, difficult writer. Because of his great concern with his own inner perspective, he is often jumbled in his words and tangled in his wildly grotesque visions. He is primarily a writer of despair, of hopelessness, of pain. There is no relief, no shadow of comfort in his vision, only a kind of frenzied dance of death performed with a curious desperate elegance. A stylish apocalypse, as it were.

Goyen always seems far more interested in expression—the recording of his own visions and thoughts—than in communicating with the reader. And this is basically the reason for the failure of his new novel.

*Come, the Restorer* is a long private dream of good and evil, of the life and death, of man the angel and man the beast, of creation and destruction. It is like a canvas of Hieronymus Bosch but without Bosch's unifying esthetic tensions. *Come, the Restorer* is a novel without pattern, without plot (except in the crudest sense), without forward motion. Everything is symbolic, and every symbol alters its meaning many times. It is a book in which conventional logic is of no use, no value. This fragmentation is of course quite deliberate. In his freewheeling fashion Goyen pyramids his shifting symbols (a white rattlesnake, a grave in the Garden of Eden, an exploding chemical factory, etc.), relying on their cumulative effect, their overall impression on the reader's emotions rather than his intelligence. Randomness produces unity—at least in theory.

*Come, the Restorer* is a foolish novel. There is, for example, a long passage in a tropical Garden of Eden (where elemental male and female forces engage in a battle of sexuality) that is embarrassingly silly. It is as if *Green Mansions* were being replayed with Xaviera Hollander in the part of Rima the bird girl.

The novel suffers, moreover, from being too clever. It dies of its own intricacy. Its grotesques are just impossibly exaggerated. . . .

Still, in this day of written-to-order novels, of fiction tailored to meet the expected demands of the market—like a new breakfast cereal or an after-shave lotion—it is encouraging to find a novelist who has enough faith in himself as a writer to be difficult and obscure and inevitably limited in his sales. The serious American novel is still alive!

Shirley Ann Grau. *NYT.* Nov. 3, 1974, pp. 73–74

As befits an age of universal solitude, in which art often is *about* art, William Goyen's stories are a testament to the essentiality of telling. He regards such communication as a form of love, a process including seeing and saying: to tell one must know; once one knows he *must* tell. . . .

Goyen's sense of his own work is just as serious: "story telling is a rhythm, a charged movement, a chain of pulses or beats. To write out of life is to catch, in pace, this pulse that beats in the material of life." His affirmations that he wishes "to write out of life" and "record as closely as possible the speech as *heard*" show that he sees himself as a medium of a heritage. Like many of his characters, he passes on an assimilation of actual and imagined material. Though the proportions of the mixture would be impossible to measure, Goyen's concentration on rendering the "true music" in the "marvelous instrument of language . . . *given* to me" is the most distinctive feature of his work.

The willingness to discipline himself in the use of language underlies his entire achievement as a writer. His stories ring with precision because they are language told to someone, not simply private, inchoate voices. . . . *The Collected Stories of William Goyen* (1975) . . . presents his ideas with remarkable continuity and seems to have been his means of experimenting in form and of finding "a language I thought I could use." Whether he writes of homelessness, fragmentation of individuals, elusiveness of the past, or the miracle of human love, Goyen is playing his main themes—the essentiality of telling—and orchestrating speech to render the "marvelous reciprocity" of a genuine relationship. . . .

Goyen has always written of human relationships—solitary people who fail to connect, solitary people who succeed in loving. The latter have been Goyen's hope: they are alert to surroundings; they have patience and imagination to comprehend others.

Jay S. Paul. *Critique*. 19, 2, 1977, pp. 77–78

*The House of Breath* is unique in our literature, owing no debts to any literary antecedents. One reason for such uniqueness is that Goyen almost always writes in the first-person singular, and the voice is unquestionably his own—Southwestern, sensitive, searching, deeply rooted in Old Testament locutions. Goyen, exiled in body from the Southwest, can never absent himself from that locale. He has the almost morbid sensibility that comes from the feelings of exile and suppression. . . .

A second reason his work is unique is that his books seem composed through a sort of double process—that of the photograph and that of the poem of the fact and the vision. . . .

Thirdly, Goyen's imagery is often dreamlike, unreal to the point of surrealism, and always intensely personal. He draws upon a personal mythology of rattlesnakes and oil wells, tightrope walkers and flagpole sitters, which is distinctly his own. Goyen is in point a fabulist, making his own myths and creating characters much larger than life. His dreamlike imagery and mythic characters are but two facets of his distinctive style. His stories and novels are all written in prose, but in prose which has many of the characteristics of poetry. It is a style which yokes the exaltations of poetry with the ordinariness of spoken prose. His books are dramatic, but they are not plays. . . .

Like poetry, they give the outlines of life rather than the whole of it (as in many novels). In this respect, Goyen's fiction bears little relationship to the sociological novel, or the novel of environment. . . . Goyen's novels break with the things which *are* in order to merge with those things which *may be*, including even spirits, which figure prominently in his second book, *Ghost and Flesh*. . . .

From the first—that is, roughly from 1949 onward—his fiction has been of the most intimate kind, surpassing the physical realities in favor of the subjective ones. Events, when they occur in his fiction at all, are related not to character so much as to sensibility. His concern is not for concrete truths, but poetic truths—for the dream, the fantasy, the outrageous. It is this engagement with *all* things, not merely the physical things of this world, which is a part of Goyen's real achievement. . . .

Overall, his work is consistent and at a very high level. And *The House of Breath* is perhaps a masterpiece—still in print twenty-five years after publication.

Nevertheless, it is doubtful that Goyen's fiction has been a creditable influence upon any other writer of note today. His concerns and his style are too highly individual to be of use by others. (Anyone who has attempted to copy his style will find that task near impossible.) Rather than being famous as the founder of a school or a following, Goyen should be noted as a highly individualized voice. He is a fabulous original, like Carson McCullers and Flannery O'Connor and not many others. In an age of mechanization, he devotes himself to poetry. In an age of plastic, he celebrates the ghost and the flesh.

Robert Phillips. *William Goyen* (Twayne, 1979),
pp. 33–35, 112, 114

William Goyen, who died in August, will be remembered as one of the great American writers of short fiction. Tapestries of storylike scenes form his famous first novel, *The House of Breath* (1950), and the later ones. His special success with the short form grows essentially from his language, which grips the reader with an Ancient Mariner's powerful hand while speaking of both the everyday and the uncanny. Though Goyen was often labeled a Texas writer, his language was a stylistic accomplishment rather than a regional or period manner, utterly individual, neither typically Southern nor, as some would have had it more recently, magic-realist. What may appear at first to be a colloquial narrative often becomes an intense, songlike prose utterance with verses and refrains. Goyen himself once remarked that some of his stories were really anthems.

*Arcadio*, his only major published work since *Collected Stories* (1975), is the most intense of these visionary songs of life. Set in his native Texas, like many of his previous works, it opens with a typically Goyenesque narrative of a "visitation"—Goyenesque in that the author characteristically filtered a story through one of its characters, a witness slightly apart who hears someone else speak of what happened, and Goyenesque also in that what interested him most of all was passion and intensity of experience. . . .

The apparition has been evoked by the narrator's memory of his taciturn uncle, who on another hot night had told him of seeing a person bathing in secret in the nearby river, someone who seemed both man and woman. That was Arcadio, a living war and a reconciliation of opposites, half man and half woman, half "Mescan" and half Texan, half saintly and half wanton, half truth teller and half blatant exaggerator.

Framed by the narrator's reminiscence, the novel becomes Arcadio's account of himself (he seems slightly more male than female), delivered on a long day to a silent listener—our narrator—in the shade of an abandoned, vine-tangled railroad trestle over a dry riverbed. Jesus consorted with publicans and sinners, and Arcadio recounts a life of spiritual quest in a world of brothels and jailhouses.

This is a work of profound sympathy for the lost, the displaced, the crazy, the imprisoned, the homeless, the deformed, the loveless—all the turned-away, whose light we tend to put out by our fear of them. Amazingly, Arcadio also touches on the reigning social problems of our day: the environment destroyed, the family broken and dispersed, loveless sex. He does this in passing, offering the viewpoint of the outcast, the sinner, whose sense of the world around him is both true and naïve. Neither Arcadio's ultimate confrontation with his long-lost family nor the apocalyptic destruction of cities and people he has witnessed can redeem his travails or solve the problems around him. Instead, he tells his story to a silent listener, and his extended aria transforms pitiable sadness and crazy misdeeds into a reconciliation of violent opposites. His remembering and singing of others who are gone makes peace with them and, through his being heard by his listener, makes peace for them. An early story, "Ghost and Flesh," is perhaps the most important statement of Goyen's belief that the situation of the storyteller and the listener is a spiritual one in which guilt, suffering and sorrow are finally redeemed.

Arcadio's parables and paradoxes restore meaning to the lives he recounts. His song may be Goyen's finest achievement. The work of a master fabulist, it was one more courageous foray into fiction unlike anyone else's, haunting the reader with its tenderness and ferocity.

Reginald Gibbons. NYT. Nov. 6, 1983, pp. 14,<br>36-37

# ● GUARE, JOHN (1938–    )

Although steeped in Ibsen (frequent references to *A Doll's House*) and Chekhov (one notably funny diatribe against *The Three Sisters*), [*Marco Polo Sings a Solo*] recalls nothing so much as the play Kurt Vonnegut would have written if he could write plays; the same affectionate loathing for humanity, the same manipulation of preposterousness in event and language, the same comic ability to grab a cliché and twist it into life by taking it literally. Above all, the same despair, splashed across an otherwise good-humored farcical entertainment, too thinly to rank as a deep artistic vision but strong enough to put a chill on the jollity, to scatter it across the stage in tiny beads of freeze-dried horror. You feel that, packed into a test tube, Guare's view of life would indeed be powerful enough to freeze the whole world, like Vonnegut's ice-nine. We probably ought to be grateful that he has the kindness to dilute it with sheer playfulness, that his mind cannot resist a purely comic or nonsensical diversion, that he follows so many tracks off in so many directions that returning to the main point becomes a tour de force.

The forces that keep *Marco Polo* from falling apart are the characters' obsessions, carried almost to the degree of Jonsonian humors: one with heroism and planthood, one with the glow of someone else's family life, one with his stature in the pop-political world of diplomacy. And the glamorous female around whom these three creatures revolve, drained of any feeling at all, sublimates her disgust by going to endless productions of *A Doll's House*. The end is stasis, an emotional icing over that reflects the ice-palace setting. The characters wait, frozen, for the new century, wondering if they have actually lived through any of this one.

Michael Feingold. *VV*. Feb. 14, 1977, p. 43

*The Landscape of the Body* is quite simply the best work Guare has ever done. It is the play Guare's supporters have always wanted to see and the one which skeptics, pointing to the brilliant flashes contained within plays that never seemed to find a final structure, doubted Guare could write. With *Landscape* "the world's oldest living promising playwright" (the quote is from Guare's *Rich and Famous*) hands in a masterpiece. . . .

Guare has always defined his plays as being about the conflict between dreams and the world. But it strikes me that Guare at his best is about much more than that. He is a man at once furious at the imperfections of the world—he actually does find it disgusting, as Holahan says in the play, that Joseph Welch made a movie for Otto Preminger—and thoroughly compassionate about what people must do when in battle with this world.

This compassion is not always present in Guare's work, but when it is there, it makes Guare unique among current satirists. Guare is not a social critic standing on the outside and laughing with slight disdain. He is *inside*, and it is from this particularly painful vantage point that the laughter comes. It brings not only criticism but complicity, not righteous anger but a desperate struggle against despair. Guare is an idealist and realist both.

Terry Curtis Fox. VV. Aug. 15, 1977, pp. 34–35

*Muzeeka* shows Guare's inventiveness and facility. Unrealistic monologues alternate with direct address to the audience as violence erupts out of domesticity. The titular Muzeeka is the canned music of conformism, which overtakes Jack Argue (whose name is an anagram of Guare). Although inspired by the Dionysian dances of the Etruscans, Argue becomes a junior executive for Muzeeka, marries a nice girl, has a suburban house and a baby. On the night his baby is born, he goes to a whore in Greenwich Village for a "Chinese basket job." Glad to be drafted, Argue is soon in Vietnam, where the soldiers fight for television coverage of their skirmishes. When his soldier buddy offers Argue a share in his father's business and marriage to his sister, Argue stabs himself. At home his wife intones patriotic platitudes, the Greenwich Village whore intones hip platitudes, his Vietnam army buddy intones military platitudes, and a stagehand pours the ketchup of Argue's blood. . . .

*The House of Blue Leaves* . . . [is] a marriage of Feydeau and Strindberg, or a painful domestic situation played as farce. The House of Blue Leaves is an insane asylum, and the inhabitants of a Queens, New York apartment convert it to an insane asylum when they step in and out of three doors and a window. . . .

In marrying Feydeau of the precipitous doors to Strindberg of the restraining straitjacket, Guare complained: "Who says I have to be confined and show a guy slipping on a banana peel? Why can't I take him to the next level and show him howling with pain because he's broken his ass?" Guare hasn't learned the simple answer: because a broken ass on stage is funny, and the audience will not believe the pain.

By 1972 Guare did not have to think of pain. Not only did *Blue Leaves* win an Obie and the New York Drama Critics Circle award, but also his adaptation of *Two Gentlemen of Verona* (with music by Galt MacDermott) was voted the best musical. Rich and rather famous, Guare wrote *Rich and Famous* about a Broadway playwright with the farcical name of Bing Ringling. One actor plays Bing, and another plays all other male parts, while an actress plays all female parts. . . .

*Landscape of the Body* (1977) parodies another aspect of New York City, but Guare sees the play as "people fighting against the death in all our lives." Death is grisly soon after the opening scene in which a disguised passenger on the Hyannisport–Nantucket ferry apprehends a woman for beheading her adolescent son. . . .

After these sallies Off-Broadway, Guare returned to Broadway with the small cast, reined fantasy, but unsubdued wit of *Bosoms and Neglect* (1980). His most skilfully constructed plot—a prologue and two acts on three realistic sets—and clearly delineated characters were soon swept off the Great White Way, but they have graced several other theatres in the very year of opening. . . .

Like Neil Simon, John Guare endows his characters with wit at the expense of credibility. Tending to self-indulgence at the expense of drama, Guare seems most recently to be in control of wit and farce. In *The House of Blue Leaves* we were barely introduced to Guare's Strindbergian characters before they were slammed by Feydeauian doors. A decade later farce simmers down to neurosis in *Bosoms and Neglect*, and the Strindbergian note sounds only in a loveless mother-son family, a loveless daughter-father (offstage) family. True to Broadway desire, a new couple finally forms, and yet the coupling bristles with psychological peril. The contemporary avatar of happy endings is person-to-person warmth, however fragile, however improbable. Sentimentality has a new hard edge.

Ruby Cohn. New American Dramatists: 1960–<br>1980 (Grove, 1982), pp. 36–41

John Guare has just run his second horse in the Lydie Breeze Sweepstakes, while a third is being saddled up for the next race. At this rate, he will soon have the largest stable in the American theater. Let's wish him luck with his final entry. The first two nags haven't shown the stamina to finish the course, and they are being led to the starting post in confusing chronological order.

*Gardenia* . . . takes place in 1875 and 1884; *Lydie Breeze* . . . is set in 1895. A few of the events remembered in the latter work are dramatized in the former, while some characters only mentioned in *Lydie Breeze* now constitute the central figures of *Gardenia*. That history is happening in *Gardenia*, rather than being recalled, should result in a more active play. It doesn't. Guare is more controlled here, because less distracted by the progress of spirochete bacilli through his characters' veins, but *Gardenia* remains basically undramatized, a disunified sketch in search of another draft. . . .

It is maddening to find this gifted playwright continually betraying his own talents through a failure of craft. Guare usually provides enough material for a dozen plays. I think his dramaturgy would benefit by his settling on one (how much more powerful *Bosoms and Neglect* would have been had he not diluted a black comedy about death with an irrelevant second act about a cute meet in a psychiatrist's office). We should be grateful that at least one American playwright is willing to create an historical context for his work, but perhaps he should think more about supplementing his readings in revisionist history with some study of Aristotle's *Poetics*. . . .

I await the third play in the trilogy, less out of expectation that it will produce something significant than out of hope that John Guare will finally have gotten this damned Lydie Breeze business out of his system. Perhaps then he can settle down to write a coherent and consistent play—preferably one that observes the unities.

Robert Brustein. NR. May 19, 1982, pp. 24–25

## HAMMETT,  DASHIELL  (1894–1961)

The works Hammett didn't write must give way to the ones he did. To move from surmising about what never happened in favor of discussing the real and the achieved is to clear a path to the art of fast-paced adventure and intrigue. Hammett has the craft of good narration well in hand. He writes fresh, muscular prose; he controls his materials; he knows how to seize and then hold the reader. . . . Much of Hammett's best work sustains this vibrancy by means of color, concreteness, and a sharp eye for both social detail and historical change. Sometimes, he wins the day by avoiding vibrancy. The precision of flat, bald factual statements recounted in toneless sequence conveys menace. . . .

Most often, Hammett stirs our imaginations by using forms and norms traditionally associated with crime fiction. He knew the aesthetic limits of his medium and kept within them. . . .

What other writers grope for, Hammett knows instinctively. He doesn't narrate. Instead, he makes things happen to people. Then he makes us wonder where the excitement came from and what it meant. There is little in his plots to stretch on the rack of literary theory. Hammett puts forth a personal vision that expresses itself in movement and conflict. There is little moral struggle, the characters having already lost their battles with conscience. Before they come to us, they have decided to rob, deceive a husband, wife, or business associate, steal—even kill for—the falcon. Hammett heightens but won't brood or analyze, showing the effects rather than the development of psychological drama. Vivid in both conception and execution, these effects translate well to radio and screen. . . .

Hammett avoids giving insights into his characters' thoughts and feelings in order to compel greater reader participation. The Op reacts neither morally nor emotionally to the twin discovery of a corpse alongside him and the apparent murder weapon, an ice pick, in his hand when he wakes from a drugged sleep in *Red Harvest*. His composure creates a high degree of intensity, yoking form to content while forcing the reader to question motives. But it also blocks expansiveness. If Hammett's people change or grow, they keep it to themselves. Rarely do we see a character converted or reborn. Experience teaches little in Hammett, even the experience of terror. . . .

Hammett's first-hand knowledge of crime-stopping gave American detective fiction both a freshness and a command it never enjoyed before. The narrative drive resulting in part from his brisk, colorful documentation has also earned him acceptance as the founder of modern American detective fiction—the tough, realistic mystery centering on a lonely, cynical private eye.

Peter Wolfe. *Beams Falling: The Art of Dashiell Hammett* (Bowling Green State Univ. Popular Pr., 1980), pp. 9, 18–20

[There are] a number of features or incidents in Dashiell Hammett's novels which seem to break sharply with previous conventions of the detective story. I do not refer to the important changes of direction brought about by the "hard-boiled" school and instanced by such matters as the professional detective, organized crime, dark urban streets and a spare, colloquial, "tough" style. Rather, I wish to concentrate on features which are unexpected even *in* the context of "tough-guy" writing and which occur unexpectedly in order deliberately and provocatively to remind the reader, in the midst of an easily-identifiable style, of other styles and methods of enquiry into human behaviour and, ultimately, of another and very different world-view which must be placed against the world-view of the rest of the novel. By adopting this technique, Hammett succeeds in drawing attention not only to the limitations of his particular kind of popular fiction but also to ways in which these very limitations can be used. The aspects of Hammett's novels to which I began by referring are not separated stylistically from the rest of the novel. But they nonetheless suggest to the reader that the first-person narrator might have to be viewed in a context other than that in which he normally presents himself for the reader's judgement (and, frequently, approval). . . .

Hammett's detectives do indeed rely on their own strength and invention to maintain their security, yet their strength resides not in a stable personality but in the ability to change like a chameleon to meet the needs of a fluctuating world, to hold to the security of the present moment, and their invention is always powerfully destructive in human terms. They operate not from the base of a recognizable interior self but from a deliberately created void. They cannot be seriously damaged because there is nothing there to damage. Hammett has often been likened to Hemingway, but Hemingway's heroes, in a non-teleological universe, adopt a concrete style as a mimetic representation of physical action allied to narrow but recognizable rules (bull fighting, big-game hunting) or physical action whose consecutive, non-idealized function is a healing coalescence with natural rhythms ("Big Two-Hearted River"). The Continental Op and Sam Spade adopt self-generative language allied to the creation of their own rules and the rhythms of their work are anything but natural. Even when Hemingway's heroes retreat from the illusions of the past and the impotence of the present to the narrowest possible area of light ("A Clean, Well-Lighted Place") they harm no-one. Hammett's heroes persistently do harm without ever leaving themselves the chance to feel guilty.

John S. Whitley. *JAmS*. Dec., 1980, pp. 443, 454

## HAWKES, JOHN (1925–    )

*Travesty* is a difficult work. Not that it is difficult to read, for it is on the surface the clearest of Hawkes's novels, easily gone through in one sitting. The plot is a relatively simple one, lacking in those abrupt shifts of time and place that often blur the action of Hawkes's other fictions. It is, in effect, a one-character novel. While Papa presumably talks to his passengers, we hear them only as they are filtered through his consciousness. He extends words of comfort to Chantal and Henri as they suffer respectively from spasms of hysterical retching and asthmatic wheezing, but we cannot be certain the two are even present.

Which begins to suggest the real difficulties of *Travesty*. It is not surprising that one reviewer found the novel "disturbing" because, as he put it, "we cannot know how to 'read' it in any one stable, reassuring way . . . we cannot 'frame' it." Though *Travesty* is surely a disturbing novel, deeply disturbing, we can "frame" it. Indeed, we must. The last novel of a triad—preceded by *The Blood Oranges* (1971) and *Death, Sleep & The Traveler* (1974)—*Travesty* in great measure depends on the design which embraces the three parts into a coherent whole. That design is the pulse of comedy.

Travesty is a form of low burlesque; that is, it treats elevated themes in a trivial manner. The themes of Hawkes's travesty are the great subjects of comedy—death, sex, and the imagination. In high comedy, in the exquisite vision of *The Blood Oranges* for example, these are woven into a triumphant celebration, but *Travesty* turns the comic festival into a farce. Ultimately, the meaning of the triad is expressed neither in the sweet rhapsody of *The Blood Oranges* nor in the raucous counterpoint of *Travesty*, but in the strange melody achieved by their harmony.

Enid Veron. In *A John Hawkes Symposium:
Design and Debris*, ed. Anthony C. Santore and
Michael Pocalyko (New Directions, 1977), pp.
64–65

*The Owl* is one of the very best of Hawkes' fictions, and probably the best introduction to his work. His method has always been to work with strong images that can be developed into scenes of nightmarish power and vividness, and then to seek some means by connecting these scenes in a coherent and developmental way. Because he starts with images rather than with a story, his work *is* different from conventionally plotted fiction, though this is not the same thing as being without plot altogether. Over the years, as his work has developed, he has turned more and more to the unifying voice of a single narrator as a way of giving coherence to the events of his narrative. At the same time, his fiction, which began with an emphasis on terror, violence, and death, has moved from those horrors toward a lush eroticism, initiated in the closing section of *Second Skin* and continued in *The Blood Oranges* and *Death, Sleep & the Traveler*. Even *Travesty*, which moves toward death, draws most of its strength from its slightly over-ripe eroticism—what the French, in speaking of the decadence that brings the grapes of Sauternes to their highest pitch of sweetness, call *la pourriture noble*. . . .

The point of this immersion in the abhorrent is to force readers to acknowledge a kind of complicity, to admit that something in us resonates to all sorts of monstrous measures, even as we recognize and condemn the evil consciousness for what it is. As a literary strategy this requires great delicacy and control. Both the horrible complicity and the shudder of condemnation must be actively aroused by the text and maintained in a precarious balance. In *The Owl* Hawkes manages this feat as well as anywhere in his work. . . .

This portrayal of repressive fascism is . . . at once terrible and comic, bizarre in its extremity but profoundly accurate in probing the philosophical and emotional roots of this mentality as embodied in the Hangman. It is of course an imaginative construct rather than a case study, an emblem rather than a portrait. In saying that plot, character, setting, and theme were the enemies of the novel, Hawkes was hyperbolically and provocatively protesting against certain traditional ways of approaching the construction of fiction. But the only true justification for surrealism in art is that it destroys certain surface plausibilities in order to liberate realities that are habitually concealed by habits of vision attuned only to the surface itself. And this is precisely what Hawkes accomplishes in *The Owl*. It is time to recognize that achievement.

Robert Scholes. HC. June, 1977, pp. 2–3, 10

Setting in Hawkes' fiction has always been both specific and approximate: the Germany of *The Cannibal* (1949), the American West of *The Beetle Leg* (1951), the Italy of *Lunar Landscapes: Stories and Short Novels*

(1949–1963), and the England of *The Lime Twig* were drawn with apparently authentic detail but were unmistakably no reader's "real" Germany, America, Italy or England. Specifically named and, thus, given a connotative "history," these settings were inserts, props, backdrops as real as a Magritte sky in chunks and cubes or, perhaps more appropriately, as real as a Tanguy "lunar landscape," glossy and always reproduced. But with the trilogy, countries have lost both their names and their historical associations. Cyril in *The Blood Oranges* is a cerebral Hemingway-expatriate, having more to do with Roman orgies of centuries ago than with the southern France he inhabits. Allert in *Death, Sleep & The Traveler* is more the Flying Dutchman of legend than a former denizen of Holland, and his cruise takes place somewhere in pagan mythology and *The Tempest* of Shakespeare. And the southern France of *Travesty* is as much a pretext as the plot: the narrator remains at the wheel of a speeding car from start to finish, and the exterior landscape does not influence the core situation of the fiction at all. . . .

Hawkes' fictional characters have moved from named countries and popular culture to myth and dreams, from unexplained horror to ominous and unfathomable sexuality, but the ultimate failure of eroticism in the trilogy points to the same existential condition in all of Hawkes' fiction. His characters are "damned souls," doomed to playing out preordained tapestries that can only end badly, because there is no avenue of escape, no idea of salvation, no way of attaining "grace."

William F. Van Wert. *LitR*. Fall, 1980, pp. 37–39

# ● HAYDEN, ROBERT (1913–1980)

The two finest poems by Negroes (not the two finest Negro poets) both draw their subjects from the epic history of Negro suffering: Richard Wright's "Between the World and Me," which celebrates an imagined lynching; and Robert Hayden's "Middle Passage," which tells the story of the slave ships and their black cargoes. They have, in the literature of the race war, positions analogous to *Invisible Man* among the novels and *The Dutchman* among the plays. The effect they produce is irresistible and entire, the hurt they give is lasting. It inheres in part, this pain, in the very hell of their subjects, in each case so completely evoked. The effect is certified, though, by the satisfying, spherical fullness of the design, the exactness of the craft.

Both are long poems, in which one could scarcely change a word with any hope of increasing the rightness or the power. Both are bloody, graphic, even documentary in their detailing of the horror; but so certain and controlled one can *use* the torment. The urge to quote in both cases is irresistible, and appropriate; nothing less than extensive quotation, in the case of Hayden's piece, could acknowledge the brim-full rightness, the necessary alternation of mode and effect. . . .

Hayden, a "major" Negro poet, has written many other poems, professional and stylish: Communist and African-memory poems, war poems, Negro hero poems, poems overfilled with a sort of decadent delirious excess of hallucinatory imagery. But it all now seems, in unfair retrospect, apprentice work for "Middle Passage."

David Littlejohn. *Black on White: A Critical Survey of Writing by American Negroes* (Viking, 1966), pp. 83-84, 86

The recent publication of Robert Hayden's *Angle of Ascent* is something of a troubling and problematic event for the student of the Afro-American tradition in poetry, for while it gives us occasion to review and pay homage to the best work of one of our finest poets, it insistently calls to mind the appalling tardiness of our recognition of his achievement. A meticulous craftsman whose exacting standards severely limit the amount of his published verse, Robert Hayden has steadily accumulated over the course of three decades a body of poetry so distinctive in character and harmonious in development that its very existence seems more fated than willed, the organic issue of a natural principle rather than the deliberate artifice of a human imagination. . . .

Robert Hayden is a poet whose symbolistic imagination is intent on divining the shape of a transcendent order of spirit and grace that might redeem a world tragically bent on its own destruction. And his memory, assailed by the discontinuities created by its own fallibility, is equally determined to catch and preserve every shadow and echo of the actual human experience in which our terribleness stands revealed. In poem after poem Hayden deftly balances the conflicting claims of the ideal and the actual. Spiritual enlightenment in his poetry is never the reward of evasion of material fact. The realities of imagination and the actualities of history are bound together in an intimate symbiotic alliance that makes neither thinkable without the other. Robert Hayden's poetry proposes that if it is in the higher order of spirit that the gross actualities of life find their true meaning, it is also true that that transcendent realm is meaningful to man only if it is visibly incarnate on the plane of human experience.

Wilburn Williams, Jr. *MR*. Winter, 1977, pp. 731–32

"Middle Passage" is a deceptive piece, a perfectly modulated pastiche of voices contained in diary, deposition, and reminiscence, that has for its subject the slave trade between Africa and America. The poem exhibits a toughness of language and a variety of method, including prose, parody, and prayer, that create effects of horror and anger in service of a passage through history, the "voyage through death/to life upon these shores.". . . "Middle Passage" is the best contemporary poem I have read on slavery. It is a singular performance, one which Hayden's later poems have not matched, in part because it is a poem whose special construction does not invite imitation.

Hayden has not discovered other methods rich enough to encompass public or private history so well. The defects which mar his poetry include compositional tics (repetition, for example: "the name he never can he never can repeat") and, especially in the newer poems, occasional opaqueness. Some recent poems are contrived from feelings so momentary that only a fleeting satisfaction is achieved. At worst, in the new work the phrases break up, the words fly apart, and the associative structure holds no meaning. The poems may shatter into component images, individually attractive but fragmentary. There are a few first-rate metaphors; the poems that remain in the mind persuade by narrative, not image. As one moves through the book, it is disconcerting to find the older poems last. Such an ordering places the newer poems, whose methods are smaller, and which should be seen as the product of development, at a disadvantage; as the older poems drape themselves in description and narration, the newer work seems insubstantial.

William Logan. *Poetry*. July, 1977, p. 228

Hayden is a poet of many voices, using varieties of ironic black folk speech, and a spare, ebullient poetic diction, to grip and chill his readers. He draws characters of stark vividness as he transmutes cardinal points and commonplaces of history into dramatic action and symbol.

The slender, potent *American Journal* is well named. For here we peruse, at close range, portions of America's visible (public, documented) and—to use Octavio Paz's term—"invisible history." We ascend "The Point" at Stonington, Connecticut, and in the brilliant air, alive with wild swans and terns, we salute the revolutionaries who repelled the British there: "we are for an instant held in shining/like memories in the mind of God."

The Afro-American past is of special concern here. In "A Letter from Phillis Wheatley," Hayden uses understatement to reveal what historians have recently discovered: that Phillis, the 18th-century slave poet, viewed slavery and prejudice with horror, wonder, and well-guarded humor. . . .

The title poem is a tour de force framed as the jottings of an other-worldly visitor reporting on the American people during the bicentennial. The visitor, in earthling disguise, finds Americans noisy, vain, wasteful, and cruel worshippers of machines; yet the "charming savages enlightened primitives brash/new comers lately sprung up in our galaxy" are attractively vigorous and ingenious. Doubtful he could survive for long in this violent nation, the visitor is nonetheless lured by Americans' "variousness . . . their vital elan and that something essence/quiddity I cannot penetrate or name."

The most compelling section of this book is the sequence of poems ironically called "Elegies for Paradise Valley," named for a tough Detroit neighborhood of yesteryear, a place vividly recalled from the poet's boyhood, and captured in terse, sometimes gritty language. . . .

*American Journal*, by Hayden the "poet of perfect pitch," is a book of unforgettable images of America and her people, a prayerful report from one of our most hauntingly accurate, and yet hopeful, recorders.

Robert G. O'Meally. *Book World*. June 25, 1978,
p. G6

[Hayden] has attempted to portray all human activity as essentially a spiritual journey, often grotesquely distorted, towards sanctity. The evils in his poems are scientific rationalism, materialism, and the failure of universal love. That mankind will ultimately triumph, Hayden seems certain, and equally certain is his belief that the preparatory trials will be harsh and prolonged. The optimistic note is sounded in the title itself: *Angle of Ascent*. In many poems, spiritual revelation is the obvious intention; but many other poems would seem to express unqualified cynicism, much like Christ's despairing cry just before his death, if taken out of context. . . .

*Angle of Ascent* is Hayden's *Leaves of Grass*. Like Whitman's work, it contains the possibly final version of poems regularly revised. More importantly, *Angle of Ascent* possesses something like epic form, largely by means of unifying subjects and themes. Whether writing about religion, poetry, history, or other subjects, Hayden attempts to portray the essential oneness of the universe. In Hayden's view, all religions acknowledge powers beyond natural ones; that is to say, all religions confirm a belief in the spiritual nature of reality. Even the grossest superstition contains the germs of spiritual enlightenment. Similarly, Hayden believes that true art, whether or not the artist consciously intended it, helps men to glimpse the underlying reality of existence. The apparent diversity of physical reality, the seeming contradictions in the visible universe are shown to be apparent and not real. Finally, the history poems also survey human experience, especially the Afro-American experience, not as meaningless and chaotic but as a necessary evolution, a progressive development towards freedom. But this is not to say that the evolution is uniform in all times and places. Much struggling and suffering will be necessary before spiritual enlightenment is universally achieved.

William H. Hansell. *BALF*. Spring, 1979, pp. 24, 31

The gift of Robert Hayden's poetry is his coherent vision of the black experience in this country as a continuing journey both communal and private. This journey begins in the involuntary suffering of the middle passage and continues across land and into consciousness. His poems are full of travelers whose imagination transforms the journey. In the striking sonnet, "Frederick Douglass," Hayden names the journey "this freedom, this liberty, this beautiful/and terrible thing, needful to man as air." He celebrates Douglass's dream that makes "lives grown out of his life." These lives become the various dreamers of Hayden's canon. From his earliest published volume, *A Ballad of Remembrance*, to the last, *American Journal*, a traveler's perspective of our American experience is his most striking theme.

The black epic journey, a "voyage through death," is the subject of his complex, brilliant early poem, "Middle Passage." An anonymous narrator controls the tone of the poem from horror to celebration. The narrator is concealed as a witness, yet his is the ironic intelligence that judges, condemns, celebrates. He hears and reports the testimonies of those oceanic voyagers who are the poem's European voices. The epic black journey is recounted in a collage of white voices: hypocrites hymning in New England of Jesus walking upon the waters, scoundrel shipowners, deck officers, maritime lawyers, sick seamen. Into this sequence is threaded Shakespeare's song of Ariel in a fine double irony. It parodies the European civilization's great poet while it extends Shakespeare's text to emphasize the profound rage of the enslaved.

Vilma Raskin Potter. *MELUS*. Spring, 1981, p. 51

# HELLER, JOSEPH (1923–    )

It is one of Joseph Heller's several virtues as a black humorist that he has been able to avoid this problem [i.e., that while the responses may be powerfully rendered, the concrete events and specific social circumstances that induced them are seldom identified or objectified] and dramatize his steadily darkening vision of contemporary life through an evocation of the experiences responsible for it. In the fiction of Pynchon and Donald Barthelme, for example, virtually everything and everyone exists in such a radical state of distortion and aberration that there is no way of determining from which conditions in the real world they have been derived or from what standard of sanity they may be said to depart. The conventions of verisimilitude and sanity have been nullified, and the fiction itself stands as a metaphor of a derangement that is seemingly without provocation and beyond measurement.

Heller, by contrast, derives his materials from the actualities of the observable world, portrays them with much greater fidelity to realism, and achieves his effects through comic exaggeration and burlesque rather than hallucination—which is perhaps to say that he descends from Dickens rather than Beckett. His characters are almost always grotesques, but they are presented as grotesques, and with no suggestion that grotesqueness is the natural and universal state of being. One is always certain, furthermore, precisely to what degree they and their situations are absurd or insane, because his narrative point of view is located in an observer with whom we can identify and who is rational enough to be able to measure the departures from rationality in the people and situations he encounters. . . .

But the deeply lodged suspicion in both *Catch-22* and *Something Happened* is that there is no one at all in charge, that Kafka's castle is in fact empty, that there is no crime for which one eternally stands condemned, no order behind organization, no system behind bureaucratic structure, no governing principle behind government, that what is happening is happening for no reason, and that there is absolutely nothing to be done about it because the causes responsible cannot be located and the very idea of responsibility may have lost all meaning.

This is the radically nihilistic perception behind Heller's new novel, *Good as Gold*. Yet in spite of it he has been able to generate what is at times an almost joyous comedy out of the depths of apocalypse and to identify and engage some of the specific social conditions that have caused the vision of apocalypse to become a defining feature of the present. Heller has accomplished this through his particularly effective use of two seemingly different kinds of narrative materials—the Jewish family experience (his first attempt in fiction to draw on this experience) and a wildly phantasmagoric rendition of the Washington political scene. His protagonist, Bruce Gold, is a minor Jewish intellectual, academic, and essayist who plans to write an "abstract autobiography" based on the history of Jewish life in America, a book that is never written, but which the novel, in effect, becomes. . . .

As he did in *Catch-22*, Heller tends here to ring too many changes on what is essentially one good joke. And the satire much of the time is so lightheartedly outlandish that it very nearly neutralizes one's awareness that the kind of insanity Heller makes laughable has also in the real world had the most destructive consequences. Yet there is more than an edge of anger in Heller's portrait of the Washington political scene, just as there are extremely ominous implications in his vision of American culture. His novel is indeed comic, often hilariously so, but it is also comedy of the bleakest and blackest kind. It is all about a society that is fast going insane, that is learning to accept chaos as order, and unreality as normal. The horror is that the time may soon come when the conditions Heller depicts will no longer seem to us either funny or the least bit odd.

John W. Aldridge. Harper's. March, 1979, pp. 115–18

It's obvious that Heller wrote *Good as Gold* more quickly than either *Catch-22* (1961) or *Something Happened* (1974). If he used up his military experience in the first book and his corporate experience in the second, why not his Jewish experience this time, meager as it may have been? After all, a writer has only so much capital.

In any case the wisecracking voice we hear in *Good as Gold* is familiar from the two earlier novels, and uniquely Heller's own, however threadbare the material. Though the people in those books were deliberately *not* Jewish, their cast of mind bore unmistakable traces of the post-Kafka Jewish literary sensibility: nervous, agile, hilarious, paranoid, fatalistic. . . .

In his first two novels Heller seemed radically gripped by his material, exorcising his obsessions by working them into the form and language. This scarcely happens in *Good as Gold*. Heller's literary genius showed itself especially in a certain rhythm, a subtle but needling texture of repetition which is simply absent from the new novel. *Catch-22* took shape not in chronological sequence but around the unfolding mystery of the death of Snowden, the catch of Catch-22 itself, the raising of the bombing missions, and a hundred other intricately developed leitmotivs. . . .

Like Beckett and Pinter, Heller at his best knows how to make the trivial feel ominous through reiteration. This web of repetition makes the first 100 pages of *Something Happened* particularly brilliant; it locks us like helpless prisoners into Slocum's petty mind, and stirs up a terrific swirl of verbal energy that is not zany and explosive as in *Catch-22*, but burrowing, sinuous, and relentless. Slocum is all of us at our most grasping, selfish, and devious; but by confining us to his mean viewpoint for 592 pages, the book finally becomes as hollow and unbearable as its protagonist. The point about *Something Happened* is that hardly anything does. No one could accuse Heller of trying to be ingratiating.

*Good as Gold* picks up neither the bleakness of *Something Happened* nor the burning intensity of its writing; but it does borrow some of the negative qualities of its hero, its theme of middle-aged compromise and disappointment. . . .

*Good as Gold* offers as many belly-laughs as *Catch-22*; there are pages we can barely resist reading aloud, gags we'll want to retell. But it's all too uneven, and when the satire ebbs, in the last 100 pages especially, the book turns slack and plotty, with little of real human interest to hold our attention. . . .

Heller's runaway riffs of surreal satire and winged fantasy are as brilliant as ever. But much of *Good as Gold* is too earthbound, too leaden, to really take off.

Morris Dickstein. SR. March 31, 1979, pp. 49–52

Heller's novels identify, as in Faulkner, the creative and ordering potency of consciousness, but Heller begins to modify naive, objectivist emphases. In the phenomenon of *déjà vu* in either novel, Heller accounts for both a content—the ontological status of *Catch-22* and *Something Happened* must be regarded as the human consciousness—and an epistemological technique. But—especially in *Catch-22*—he leaves open the answers to questions concerning where the phenomenon is to be assigned most prominently. It seems sometimes to operate traditionally, within the mind of an invisible narrator, but at other times it seems inside created characters, and, eventually, perforce, in the mind of a reader, in much the same well-known way that Joycean techniques of epiphany and narrative disjunction work. . . .

Heller, in contrast to Faulkner, has now identified a stable base in the archetypes of consciousness. Both manifest in and identified by literary constructs, these archetypes permit Heller [and others] now to project a more determinate fictional form than a naive existentialism would permit. The archetypal pattern of romance, which becomes the projected frame for Heller, offers his novel a construct within which he—projecting through the consciousnesses of his characters—can determine form and meanings. Discrete, disjunctive details of imagery and events begin to draw together around the archetypes at the core of consciousness—author's, character's, and reader's. So that despite the large gaps locally in Heller's novel, the overall form has revealed itself as rather more insistently determined than one might otherwise expect.

James M. Mellard. The Exploded Form: The<br>Modernist Novel in America (Univ. of Illinois Pr.,<br>1980), pp. 104, 106

## HELLMAN, LILLIAN (1905–1984)

*Scoundrel Time* bring[s] back, with extraordinary pain, the sorrow and disorder of those years when, under similar circumstances, thousands of Americans suddenly found themselves on planes, buses, and trains, wandering the streets of strange cities, with a voice inside screaming "What am I doing here? How did I get here? What is *happening*?"

What is, of course, distinctive about *Scoundrel Time* is the voice behind the words—that voice we first heard with such startled pleasure in *An Unfinished Woman*, then with deepening gratification in *Pentimento*, and now with moving intensity in this third volume of Hellman memoirs. It is the voice of a writer who seeks to describe in measured sentences as precisely as possible the imprecise flow of life as it has moved through her and all around her. It is the voice of a writer who reveals great courage of spirit because that voice, quite plainly, says: Make no mistake, there is much about myself I do not know, much that remains a dark and painful mystery I cannot face unflinchingly because if I do I will lose control and fall apart all over these pages, and that I'm damned if I'll do. But much that seems painful is often merely difficult. I know the difference between pressure and pain, and pressure I can take. I will force my pen, my actions, my life down on those pressure points to the utmost of my ability—even unto the point of pain.

It is this quality that makes Lillian Hellman the remarkable writer she is. The measured gravity of her sentences coupled always with the sudden, earthy directness reveals a steadiness and independence of mind, heart, and spirit that induce nothing but uncritical admiration: a welling-up of warmth and gratitude in the face of such a civilized intelligence. . . .

*Scoundrel Time* is a valuable piece of work. The kind of work that stands alone, untouched, in the midst of foolish criticism and foolish praise alike.

Vivian Gornick. Ms. Aug., 1976, pp. 46–47

Such a value system as Hellman's, whether in the plays or the memoirs, with its clearcut criteria of good and evil, has a reassuring emotional appeal; it makes us nostalgic for a child's world (where the worst crime is to tattle on your friends) and for the make-believe world of fiction and drama, of despoilers and bystanders, where such a system flourishes. But the adult realm of politics and history demands complexities of knowledge and fact, in which value judgments are painfully arrived at. We must do more than ask Sophronia.

Lillian Hellman's insight is sharpest when it is most personal and specific. If some of her plays seem dated now it is probably because of their "well-made," realistic mode and their two-dimensional, good-or-evil characterizations. But three plays (and perhaps others) have had current repertory revivals—*The Autumn Garden*, *Toys in the Attic*, and *The Children's Hour*. These are the less structured ones, more concerned with psychology than plot, and with moral ambiguity rather than moral definition.

As a memoirist, Hellman was able to present her materials dramatically, without the limitations imposed by the stage. The memoir form allowed, too, for subtlety in the exploration of character; for unanswered questions, and for a certain mysterious quality that evoked a response from readers who knew that mystery for their own.

The personal, the ambiguous, were not appropriate, however, to the politics of *Scoundrel Time*, and Hellman has taken some punishment for that mistake. But she formulated her philosophy of survival when she was fourteen: "If you are willing to take the punishment, you are halfway through the battle."

Lillian Hellman is still producing, still battling, still surviving, still performing. Whatever we may think of her politics or temperament, we must rejoice in the energy, ingenuity, and skill of the performance.

Doris V. Falk. Lillian Hellman (Ungar, 1978), pp. 156–57

The central figure of this strange short memoir [*Maybe: A Memoir*] (if it can be called such) is not its ostensible subject, Sarah Cameron, nor the memoirist, Lillian Hellman, but the elusive, mutilated, often reeling character of memory itself. Again and again Miss Hellman tries to corner memory, forcing it to reveal the truth about the people and events she is trying to make sense of. Important epistemological questions are suggested: How valid is what we know—or think we know—about the people who dropped in and out of our lives in the past? How can we tell where memory blends into fantasy, producing a composite that takes on different shapes at different times, according to our needs? At the end of Miss Hellman's struggle with these questions, we have to settle for some very dusty answers; meanwhile we have been entertained, dismayed and, above all, tantalized.

Though few dates are given, one can, with the help of two of the earlier memoirs (*An Unfinished Woman* and *Pentimento*) and with close attention to some extremely vague sequences and contexts, assemble a rough chronology for the fragmented story that is being told. Some time around 1929 or 1930 Lillian Hellman met—at a *New Yorker* magazine party or at a Paris restaurant—a beautiful, uninhibited, alcoholic, dope-taking, chronically untruthful woman named Sarah who went to Foxcroft and married a rich lawyer named Carter Cameron; the Camerons had a son, Isaac, whom Sarah insisted on calling "Som." Sarah may or may not have taken Lillian Hellman's first lover away from her; this malicious young man, Alex (also mentioned in *An Unfinished Woman*), had devastated Miss Hellman on their fourth and final session in bed by recommending that she take a bath because of her strong female odor. . . .

I shall myself withhold the bizarre revelations or possibilities concerning Sarah and Som that bring *Maybe* into the 1970's and instead comment upon the very interesting persona Lillian Hellman has created for herself in these pages. She portrays herself as truculent, sardonic and (better than most around her) able to hold her liquor. Sexually independent herself, she is nonetheless caustic with her long-time lover Dashiell Hammett for letting strange ladies drift casually in and out of his whiskey-soaked Hollywood existence. The conversations of this sharp-tongued, easily angered woman tend to be sparring matches that modulate into gentle banter when she is with someone like "Dash," for whom she feels strong affection. The recorded or reconstructed talk is permeated with a fine period flavor, full of goddamns and wisecracks, with situations referred to as "nutty" and people as "nuts.". . .

But absorbing as this autobiographical material is, it does not compensate, in my opinion, for the emptiness at the heart of the book. Miss Hellman fails to bring Sarah Cameron into existence as even a remotely comprehensible woman. The evidence is so scattered, so inconsistent, so blurred by time and alcohol, that we are left with a wraith too insubstantial to evoke even a sense of mystery, much less to support a valid point about the ultimate unknowability of figures in our past. Miss Hellman is aware of her problem. "One of the strangest things about heavy drinkers, me among them in those days," she writes, "is that much that seems clear to you as you drink, in sober periods will never seem clear again, because of course it never was." Halfway through *Maybe* she admits that she doesn't know much of what really happened and "never tried to find out.". . .

I prefer to accept Miss Hellman's word that she is trying to get at the truth—and assume that the truth she has in mind is not of some novelistic or symbolic·variety. Even if it were intended as fiction or as fictionalized memoir, the Sarah-story still would not add up to anything significant. Facts and dates do not constitute the "truth," but they are useful in anchoring an otherwise free-floating subjectivity. By surrendering prematurely to the impossibility of getting things straight—or at least straighter—Lillian Hellman has, I think, lost a chance to make *Maybe* the fascinating encounter with memory and time that it might have been. Despite the subtleties of its voice, its strong period quality and its brave forays into the self, the book remains, disappointingly, less a memoir than a shaggy-dog story.

Robert Towers. NYT. June 1, 1980, pp. 3, 36

# HEMINGWAY, ERNEST (1899–1961)

Characteristically, Hemingway's fictional protagonists finish alone, a pattern which becomes increasingly dominant in his later writing. The fear of loneliness implicit in these final fictions reflects what Erich Fromm calls the "deepest need of man . . . the need to overcome his separateness, to leave the prison of his aloneness." Hemingway as an individualist refused to subdue that separateness by blending into the herd or by following a numbing, nine-to-five work routine. He also found bumpy and dangerous the alternative route to integration, that "fusion with another person, in *love*," which Fromm calls the "full answer" to the terror of aloneness.

In defining his terms, Fromm distinguishes between *symbiotic* love and *mature* love. In symbiotic love, one partner normally assumes a passive, masochistic, inferior role to the other's active, sadistic superiority. Most of Hemingway's love stories, which usually assume a dominant-submissive relationship, focus on this kind of love. Mature lovers, on the other hand, share equally: they give and gain by giving. In a process which Fromm defines as "union under the condition of preserving one's integrity," the paradox occurs "that two beings become one and yet remain two." In this paradox resided Hemingway's dilemma. Like all men he dreaded aloneness; he dreaded it more than most. But he also feared that love would deprive him of his own individuality, of his own inmost self.

Among his fictional counterparts, Robert Jordan in *For Whom the Bell Tolls* comes closest to achieving the Frommian state of mature love. Like Frederic Henry with Catherine, he resists Maria's desire to become exactly like him, to passively submerge herself in him. "I would be thee because I love thee so," she says, but he counters, "It is better to be one and each one to be the one he is." Unlike Frederic, though, during his three days among the Spanish guerrillas, Jordan comes to understand the beauty of giving and the importance of selflessness to those in love. "He knew he himself was nothing, and he knew death was nothing. . . . In the last few days he had learned that he himself, with another person, could be everything."

At least once in his fiction, then, Ernest Hemingway created a hero who loved maturely and selflessly without giving up his own integrity. The evidence of his life and of the bulk of his writing, however, suggests that he himself kept barriers standing against such total commitment.

> Scott Donaldson. *By Force of Will: The Life and Art of Ernest Hemingway* (Viking, 1977), pp. 173–74

Hemingway's first and last truths are remarkably akin to the dominant themes in Albert Camus and, from a quite different angle, to those in

Boris Pasternak. These three so various novelists come together in celebration of a purified sensibility, an innocent love of being in the world. Cutting through grand phrases and empty syllables, they exalt in the plain confrontation of man with nature and with other men. Serge Doubrovsky, writing about Camus's reception in the United States, argues that American readers applaud the element of existential struggle and unremitting effort in his novels but often overlook the "solar joy." So with Hemingway, we perhaps pay too much heed to the hero's battle, which is of unquestioned salience, and attend too little to his poetic joy, his sheer aliveness and sensual alertness. Hemingway sends us precise messages to, about, and through the senses; much in the manner of T. S. Eliot's "objective correlative," his writing makes us experience as his hero experiences and recreate for ourselves his being and "isness." We are told how things look, feel, taste, smell, sound. And never for a moment can we forget that the individual is a physical being in a physical universe. Existence for its own sweet sake, in a world of colors and textures, shadows and curves, is what we are enjoined to relish. The necessary but artificial fabric of values and concepts, vocations and ideals, is underlain always by the naked pleasure of sensory transactions. In the dense symbolic and institutional environment of modern society, we need to be reminded that we sweat and sleep, get rained and sunned on, feel shapes and see movements—and that our enjoyment of all these requires no justification, but does require recognition and praise. . . .

If Hemingway is firmly bonded to the first half of this century and if many of his assumptions are now unfashionable, we must still recognize that the universal qualities of his themes and perceptions outweigh the time bound. Regardless of changes in a society's values or in its conceptions of social roles, the key issues of being human and living a life persist. Whatever the specific lineaments of the social universe, one can scarcely envision a model of the good life that is not instinct with Hemingway's virtues. The individual cannot move through this world, cannot count himself fully alive, without the sense of solar joy, without the exercise of competence, without some deep apprehension of fidelity to himself and others. William James said that the true gentleman was the person who, in sure knowledge of life's brevity, yet conducted himself as if he were going to live forever. This the writer must do, especially in the conduct of his writing. So the best part of Hemingway lives on in the clear language, if not forever, at least for a very long time.

Robert N. Wilson. The Writer as Social Seer<br>(Univ. of North Carolina Pr., 1979), pp. 43–44,<br>55

One of the most powerful sources of Hemingway's enduring appeal is the irresistible combination of lucidity and elusiveness in his writing. The surface is as clear as a trout stream, perfectly simple, indubitably there, the thing itself—caught and held and defined. Yet underneath, as every reader senses, strange unnamable monsters lurk: the swamp into which Nick dares not venture at the end of "Big Two-Hearted River."

The lucid-elusive phenomenon is most present and most immediately obvious in the short stories, although the technique is used in the novels also. The shorter the work, the more disturbing to the reader is the tension. We have fewer clues, less evidence. Every word counts. We sense, in fact, that some words are missing. Evidence has been withheld. Something is desperately wrong. . . .

As various critics have pointed out, the missing center is often connected with both physical and psychological wounding—Hemingway's dominant theme—and, as a consequence, much has been written from a biographical viewpoint about the wounding at Fossalta (and all the subsequent woundings in his life, culminating in the climactic suicide). Meanwhile, Freudian critics have leapt with cries of joy over all of the evidence that suggests castration fears—and the evidence is abundant.

More than any other work, the Nick Adams stories hold the clue. And especially the Nick Adams stories that present the relationship between father and son. . . .

Ann Edwards Boutelle. JML. 9, 1, 1981–82, pp.<br>133–34

## HIMES, CHESTER (1909–1984)

Himes, with his taut, upbeat prose, is more than a master stylist. Through a career that spans four decades, Himes moved toward the mastery of four distinct types of novel in a way that distinguishes him as one of the most versatile as well as one of the most enigmatic of modern writers. Himes's novels are not for the timid; they are bitter, structured around scenes of pervasive unpleasantness, rely heavily upon the symbolic implications of nightmares, and are filled with violence: fists crunch into jawbones, ballpeen hammers drop like weighted darkness, switchblade knives click open, pistols blast flame into the Harlem night, and murdered men lie sprawled among the cigarette wrappers and broken glass on the ghetto sidewalks. But this is not violence for the sake of morbid thrills only; it is based on Himes's conviction—arrived at in prison, expressed in all of his books, and reinforced by a hundred turns of plot—that people will do anything. The result is a singular kind of tension: reading a Himes novel is like standing on an electric grid, blindfolded, waiting for the current to be turned on, and knowing that it will be. Reading Himes is also an education in social history by a master of mayhem who specializes in powerfully individualized portraits of black men literally being driven crazy by white society and themselves. Himes gives us a vision of a racially obsessed and decadent America. But more important than that picture—as terrifying as it is—is his ability to coolly achieve, in his best work, an effective union of social protest and art. . . .

Whatever vision Himes chooses to express, his writing is icily incisive in its penetration of the American racial scene, so incisive that he is often frightening in his ability to evoke the terror of situations from which there is no exit other than desperation. But then he is also able to evoke the strange beauty inherent in desperate acts. What T. M. Curran wrote of *Black on Black* certainly holds for all of Himes's major work: "[These] writings are powerful and, indeed, bear the authentic impress of a master. Himes is in absolute control of all moods and all forms. He can be tragic or hilariously funny, poignantly ironic or savagely vicious, absurd or coldly logical." But it is more than his range that makes Himes unique; there is no other writer like him because he is hard-edged and uptempo, a rule unto himself—articulate, durable to the point where even his failures are impressive, and always making the disturbing demands upon his readers that only mastery of form permits.

James Lundquist. Chester Himes (Ungar, 1976),<br>pp. 2–3, 146–47

Himes, it seems clear, did not consciously choose to be controversial—he wanted to be popular, even extremely popular—but, he was in fact controversial. His books spurred readers to think about and react to subjects that invariably inspire anger. Something deep within himself—Baldwin's use of the word *integrity* seems an apt choice—had chosen for him the roughest road available, and he could hardly blame the critics for that. But, as a novelist, a man in the business of making verbal scale models of the world as he has known it, felt it, and lived it, as a constructor of elaborate extended metaphors designed to guide readers into his own unique and private realm of experience, Chester Himes did, fairly often, have legitimate grounds for complaint against critics who refused to accord him his full share of artistic license, refused to respect fully his need to write subjectively in one of the most highly subjective of literary genres. . . .

Racism, the hurts it inflicts, and all the tangled hates, is the dominant subject of the literary works that Chester Himes actually did produce. He did not choose the subject. It was thrust upon him. He did not at first even choose the literary forms that he used. But he drove deeper into the subject than anyone ever had before. He recorded what happens to a man when his humanity is questioned, the rage that explodes within him, the doubts that follow, and the fears, and the awful temptation to yield, to embrace degradation. If you lock up a first-rate literary talent for a lifetime in a small box, it will give you a complete statement of how it feels to be locked up in that particular box. It is a simple situation, but a complex experience. And being caught in a trap, boxed-in, in one way or another, is perhaps the essence of the modern experience. Himes has had the advantage—dubious but real—of a highly visible trap. Racism was Chester Himes's box, and he has produced, in the form of a long series of novels, both heavy and light, what was, arguably, the most complete and perfect statement of the nature of native American racism to be found in American literature, and one of the most profound statements about the nature of social oppression, and the rage and fear it generates in individuals, in all of modern literature.

Stephen F. Milliken. Chester Himes: A Critical<br>Appraisal (Univ. of Missouri Pr., 1976), pp. 305–7

Far more, however, than the informing vision and design of *If He Hollers Let Him Go* has been contrary about Himes. Nearly every novel and short story he has written since "His Last Day" explores one or another aspect of a world made violent by racial oppositions and inversions. Yet though his writing has been chided as often diagrammatic or obsessive, it has actually been pretty various—lyric, or acerbic, or of late, boldly satiric and surreal. Despite differences of texture, his "serious" fiction, the five novels he wrote between 1945 and 1954, has especially been thought to need leavening, even though hints of *Pinktoes* (1961), an eloquent piece of bawdy, and of the later thrillers, lay there all along. By a nice point of contrast Himes's detective stories, which began in 1957 with *For Love of Imabelle*, and in which Himes brought into play quite astonishing feats of plot-making and wit, were thought by some reviewers altogether too playful, the invention verging on showmanship, the wit giving in to mere display. Just as the earlier fiction was neither as solemn nor monotone as had casually been supposed so Himes's use of the thriller genre, ostensibly all pantomime and knock-about, could be seen to mask serious and long-held preoccupations. In changing from high to popular form Himes hadn't altered his basic sense of direction.

But if his themes have arguably been of a piece, Himes's overall achievement presents more difficult problems. His very best writing can give way to weaknesses of a quite blatant kind. He can sound clumsy, flat-footed, too strident. His style has often been uneven and the pressure of his own feelings has shown through. Yet within writing which exhibits all of these deficiencies, as well as others, he has scored clear and attractive triumphs. If Himes isn't major in the sense that we speak of Ellison or Wright, to cite two contemporaries, he assuredly amounts to far more than a passing minor talent. And if his achievement has seemed contrary,

even contradictory, so too has the reputation of his work. Shifts of attention, of praise and disapproval, have dogged his career. . . .

As to his reputation: despite occasional good notices like Wright's,
Himes's work has either been ignored altogether, or lambasted from the
Right for doing racial dirt on America (*If He Hollers Let Him Go* was
thought particularly to offend), or, as in a novel so resolutely individual in
its political line on race as *Lonely Crusade* (1947), indicted by the Left for
selling short the cause. Over time other evaluations have made their way
to the surface. When not under scrutiny for his politics, Himes's racial
concerns drew attention. If he persisted in writing on black life and
themes, he was narrow, insufficiently universal; if he wrote "raceless"
(meaning white) fiction, as in *Cast the First Stone* (1952), he had turned
his face from his own heritage and condition.

A. Robert Lee. JAmS. April, 1978, pp. 99–100

## ● HOLLANDER, JOHN (1929–    )

John Hollander's poems [in *Moviegoing, and Other Poems*], even at their
most frivolous and perverse, explore the shifting barriers between
semblance and reality with a sort of chuckling irony, but never with a very
high inner seriousness. His irony has no satirical thrust behind it, little
melancholy, no compelling joy. These are poems whose major emotion
lies in their own cleverness. It is worth taking poetry more seriously—as
in their ways Creeley and Levertov do—and perhaps in his third book
Hollander will find his way.

Peter Davison. At. Nov., 1962, p. 87

John Hollander's *Visions from the Ramble* . . . uses the New York locale.
From that area of Central Park known as the Ramble, the poet sees visions, past and present, inner and outer, real and fanciful, "remembering
treacheries of remembrance." Unfortunately, too often the images won't
stand up under examination. I am not thinking of the occasional faltering
to be expected in a book of poems. It is rather that with Hollander the
images are an exercise of the will, not a hatch of the imagination and the
unconscious. Adjectives and adverbs clog his verses. He mistakes bad
prose for poetry:

> The slowly-dropping summer sun
> Lowers a reddening yolk into
>    its cup in New Jersey.

He mistakes bad puns for wit: "ballads made to their mistresses' highbrows" and "on the foggy road Harvey rode westward." Nevertheless, poems like "Sunday Evenings" and "From the Ramble" show what Hollander is capable of. And one must respect the ambitious concept underlying his book, whose Poem and fourteen poems inviting comparisons with Hart Crane's *The Bridge* have the unity of a musical suite. Few poets today are ready to risk failure and disappointment by undertaking so long and sustained an effort.

Samuel Yellen. NYT. Nov. 21, 1965, pp. 26–27

With the exception of James Merrill (in a poem like "The Summer People") I don't know an American poet better at turning out sophisticated, hard-nosed (but good-hearted too) social verse than John Hollander, and it ends up not feeling "light," like light whiskey, at all. This volume [*Town and Country Matters*], published in 1972 in a handsome edition by David R. Godine, is made up of Erotica and Satirica, "translations and fresh creation" of "a world of classical urbanity" says the blurb. John Hollander's dirty mind is excellently displayed throughout, and Anne Hollander has provided appropriately feelthy and not so feelthy pictures as illustrations. The idea of setting out to be dirty and daring is a depressing one, but in fact these poems don't let themselves get locked into lubricious points. For me the best things in a never less than interesting collection are eighteen "Sonnets for Roseblush". . . . But the gem of the volume, and I would claim the best poem Hollander has ever written, is a long one called "New York," spun off from Juvenal, the friend "Rus" leaving town for good because living in the city has grown impossible, the poet staying behind to reflect on the meaning of living there. Written in strong couplets the verse twists and moves rapidly through the junk and glories of urban life. . . . "New York" is neither a speciality nor a sport, just an admirable piece of work.

William H. Pritchard. HdR. Autumn, 1973, pp.<br>590–92

Hollander has written his *Reflections on Espionage* in the form of a single long poem composed in strict eleven-syllable lines, except for twenty-one lines at the very end which contain a clever cipher carefully explicated in the author's notes. . . .

The basic power of Hollander's conception . . . lies in the way in which he has maintained the literal details of his fable: the "Terminations" of failed agents, the tortures, the deceptions, the sordid traps, the fears, the suspicions, the frustrations of a world in which "Scattered outbreaks of terror do not abate," while he transmutes the details into a parable of the efforts of a creative seeker, a tragicomic saga of the human effort to explore the workings of ultimate truth, to probe the depths of one's own consciousness, and to discover the springs of human motive in others. The effort, we learn, can only hope to succeed through stout mental discipline (symbolized by the eleven-syllable grid). . . . And with discipline comes the hoped-for liberation: one must admire the flexibility and ease with which Hollander moves within his chosen grid; there is no sense of straining; the language, though frequently colloquial, moves with dignity and grace toward a measured eloquence. . . . With such a book, if we had not known his stature before, John Hollander surely stands forth as one of the two or three best in his generation of American poets now in their forties or early fifties. Indeed, I would say one of two.

Louis L. Martz. YR. Autumn, 1976, pp. 118,<br>121–22

In the group of essays which composes Vision and Resonance, Hollander explores questions of poetic form as it were after the fall. "Music" can no longer be trusted to explain anything, but must itself be explained. The critic must try to clarify a hazy relationship between the sister arts, as well as both the aural and spatial dimensions of poetic form.

Hollander's tastes are eclectic, which enables him to write cogently on poets as disparate as Donne, Jonson and Campion, Marvell, Milton and Pope, Wordsworth and Blake, Whitman, Pound, and William Carlos Williams. Since his cultural range includes European music and graphic art, classical literature and literary theory, and contemporary linguistics, the rifts of this volume are quite filled with ore. And his ear and eye are fine, so that his readings are usually reliable, which is more than one can say for many critics who attempt to write on prosody. He has excellent chapters dealing with contrastive stress, with enjambment, with rhyme. Each, if applied historically, would yield discoveries about ideas of order in English poetry over the last four centuries. The question of line-break has particular significance for modern poetry, where it serves as the single most important formal signal for a great number of poets (go back to Pound and Cummings, move up to Creeley), opening doors in hitherto plain blank walls. Here Hollander makes some brilliant observations about how the relations between line-break and syntactic juncture in the twentieth century consistently direct attention, create drama, produce meaning. There are also good chapters on the role of meter as frame, and on formal experimentation, both theory and practice, in Romantic and modern American poetry. . . .

A . . . serious flaw concerns the ghost of sphery music haunting Hollander. He seems to occupy himself excessively with efforts to lay this ghost—belaboring poets and prosodists who have made misleading poetry-music analogies, extensively demonstrating, as if it needed demonstration, the inadequacy of musical settings to Donne's un-songlike "songs," recounting at length the differences between Greek meters, which were music-based, and English, which are not. We may all suffer from a nostalgia for primal harmony which we recognize as a fiction, but Hollander's repeated digressions from poetic to musical matters practically entitle this book to be called *The Elephant and the Music Problem*.

Finally, and unfortunately, both Hollander's organization and his prose leave much to be desired. This is a meandering, repetitive book, in which most of the essays read like occasional pieces or even worked-up footnotes, and the writing style is as stuffy as an overheated, overfurnished, close-windowed lamplit room. The possession of vast learning should not exempt an author from the lucidity and grace required of other mortals. In this case, non-specialists should brace themselves. Nevertheless, the ideas in *Vision and Resonance* deserve a wide audience for their solid discoveries and for their provocative suggestions, and for reminding us again, as at the outset of his first volume, that "particularly in the case of poetry, the functional relationship of form to content continues to pose the most demanding critical questions."

Alicia Ostriker. *PR.* 44, 4, 1977, pp. 634, 636

It is exactly 20 years since the appearance of John Hollander's first book of poems. I read the book then, soon after I first met the poet, and was rather more impressed by the man than by the book. It has taken 20 years for the emotional complexity, spiritual anguish, and intellectual and moral power of the man to become the book. The enormous mastery of verse was there from the start, and is there still, so augmented that only James Merrill in his own generation seems to me Hollander's peer as an *artist*, as a stylist equal to Auden and to Wilbur. But there seemed almost always to be more knowledge and insight within Hollander than the verse could accommodate. . . .

As a poet, Hollander was not truly Hollander until the volume, *The Night Mirror*, published in 1971, when he was past meridian. His book of selected poems [*Spectral Emanations*], now published is strongest in his work of the 1970s, in the sequence or long poem "The Head of the Bed," in the title sequence of "Tales Told of the Fathers," and in "Spectral Emanations," the superb and difficult long poem that should make a new beginning for him.

Hollander began as an Audenesque poet of the 1950s, merging the American Auden back into the Jonsonian line of measured wisdom. But from *The Night Mirror* on, Hollander surprisingly blends Jonson and Shelley in a single body, with Stevens inevitably displacing Auden as central precursor. Quite explicitly, Hollander has developed into an American-Jewish High Romantic, esoteric and elegiac, and daring to write long poems in the Sublime mode.

Harold Bloom. NR. Sept. 9, 1978, p. 42

John Hollander does not become easier as he goes, nor does the somewhat frustrated pleasure of reading him grow less. He is always on the point of being fully comprehensible and never quite arrives at that point. The poems [in *Blue Wine*] are poems with beginnings middles and ends; not parts of a continuum you could hack into pieces, without its mattering where you hacked, here would do as well as there, and call the pieces poems. Hollander's poems have not only structure but subject and substance, but even if I know what he is talking about, please do not ask me to tell you exactly what he is saying about it. Then what makes them admirable? It is easy to take examples of his artful combinations: from "Anonymous Master, 'Standing Figure'": "Of course, the painting, full of the rich/Light of contrivance, could hardly have/That for a name"; "The literalness of shaping a/Mass is like a kind of/Groping around in a/Midnight of thick fact"; "That would mean/Marble clanging out in sweet pain." But this is to break up the sequences, and there are sequences, if not exactly of thought, of a dreamlike train of ideas which in an assured order keep turning into something else. . . . Put it briefly, Hollander is a master poet with an eye for image, a sense of line (and a sense of humor), and a rightness of composition; all of which qualities makes him a delight to read, whether or not we come out more fully informed than when we went in.

Richmond Lattimore. HdR. Autumn, 1979, pp.<br>443–44

## HOWARD, RICHARD (1929–    )

There is a scheme behind the publication of Howard's books. After the appearance of *Untitled Subjects*—a cycle of long poems—came *Findings*—a gathering of shorter unrelated ones. *Fellow Feelings*, the present volume, is for the most part work brief and varied. It follows *Two-Part Inventions*, six long dramatic poems obviously conceived as a book and not a gathering. With Howard shorter is not slighter! *Fellow Feelings* contains some of his most impressive work. These include "Venetian Interior, 1889," a remarkably full rendering of the sad world of Pen Browning; "Decades"; and "The Giant on Giant-Killing." The latter two utilize Hart Crane's history and Donatello's bronze of David, respectively, to illumine Howard's own life. Both poems openly explore homosexuality: indeed, the book is the most out-of-the-closet collection since Howard's own *Two-Part Inventions*. Rather than being sensational, Howard's poems convey tenderness, and seek understanding. He movingly pictures both himself and Crane as on "permanent short-leave from the opposite sex." In "The Giant on Giant-Killing" we are given a defense of homosexuality, yet are reminded that the name Goliath, while meaning *destroyer* in Assyrian, means *exile* in Hebrew. Throughout the volume there is a feeling of singularity and alienation.

Howard's most felicitous gift is for the well-turned epigram. Some are worthy of Wilde: "Ripeness is hell"; "The tiny is the last resort of the tremendous"; "Kissing is not cosmetic, merely cosmic"; "We are what we see"; "The sacred and the suburban often coincide"; etc. The danger Howard risks is that he displays too much wit. Verbal pyrotechnics call attention to themselves, rather than to the meaning they are employed to convey. . . .

Yet all wit and wordplay are employed to extremely serious ends. If the book has two misfires ("Compulsive Qualifications" and "Howard's Way"—poems in which questionable subjects seem paraded rather than contemplated), it also has many direct hits on fascinating and difficult targets. Howard is one of our most original poets.

Robert Phillips. *Com*. Sept. 10, 1976, p. 597

Like Good and Bad Angels, two spirits of very different kinds are at work in Richard Howard's six books of poetry to date. One is genial and generous, and shows itself in the two best known of the volumes, *Untitled Subjects* (1969) and *Two-Part Inventions* (1974). To the prominence of these, the third and the fifth of the books, the former's having been awarded the Pulitzer Prize in 1970 and the latter's having been nominated for the National Book Award in 1975 attest, but the measure of the heights to which the books rise can best be taken in terms of *pleasure*. There is an ampleness about the books that is perhaps the sine qua non of pleasure itself. For the reader of the poetry entire, however, the surest guide to their genius (or angel) is the relief felt in coming to them, particularly since we cannot help but sense that this feeling was the poet's before it was ours—his Good Angel was at work. . . .

But the two books are haunted by their successors, *Findings* (1971) and *Fellow Feelings* (1976), the fourth and the sixth of the volumes, in which the Bad Angel shows itself. These two are demanding where the other two are open-handed, compelling where the others are attractive; if we sense the poet's ease in *Untitled Subjects* and *Two-Part Inventions*, we will feel the constraints under which he works in *Findings* and *Fellow Feelings*. The measure of the depths to which the latter two sink, as it is perhaps the Bad Angel's name, is *will*. Since the books are not given to the poet or the reader, they have to be taken by each.

If *Untitled Subjects* and *Two-Part Inventions* were better books than *Findings* and *Fellow Feelings*, if the difference between them were that the former achieve what the latter fail to achieve, Richard Howard's poetry would be easier to understand. But *Findings* and *Fellow Feelings* are no less accomplished than their predecessors in the oeuvre; their success is different in kind. (A Good Angel differs from a Bad Angel in terms other than that of accomplishment). It may be possible to think of the poet's first two books, *Quantities* (1962) and *The Damages* (1967), as the bases for, without in any way being anticipatory of, the high ground of *Untitled Subjects* (the book comes as a surprise), but what I am contending here is that the first two books must be seen as preparation for the depths of *Findings* as well. And, for the reader, the delight in pleasure should be no less enjoyable than the admiration of will.

Henry Sloss. Shenandoah. Fall, 1977, pp. 85–86

An important force in contemporary American poetry, Richard Howard has grappled again and again with issues which haunt the twentieth-century American psyche. Confronting the passage of time in poems of notable elegance and finish as well as vigor and vitality, he has grown from an urbane young sophisticate obsessed with age into a poet of vision. Central to his development has been his emergence as a poet of "otherness," one whose understanding of the lives of others has enabled him to transcend the limitations of a time-bound self. In response to a question about autobiographical passages in his historical poems Howard told Sanford Friedman, "I am not sure whether you could call it a way of attaching other lives by injecting my own memories into them, or of achieving my own memories by articulating them in other lives." Howard's movement from a narrow self-absorption toward an apprehension of the continuity of human experience may be a result of his mature understanding of the limits of our individual lives. "I am aware of alternatives the lived life does not suggest," he remarked to Friedman; and he added, "I am somewhat intimidated by the notion that the life lived has to be that life and no other. . . . I should like the life to be thought of as, well, that life but other possible ones as well." His identification of himself with fellow feelers, his effort to rejoin the fathers after all, is not only a statement of human continuity, but also a recognition of shared values bridging the narrow spaces of individual lifespans. When an interviewer suggested that he was perhaps too "generous" in his evaluations of his contemporaries in *Alone with America: Essays on the Art of Poetry in the United States since 1950*, Howard protested, "No, it's not that I'm generous—I think that's a mistake, unless we trace the word back to what it originally

meant, which is that I recognize my kind." It is precisely this ability to recognize his kind which Howard posits as a solution to the existential loneliness of an individual life limited by the exigencies of time. To transcend
these limits by rejoining the fathers, by identifying with fellow feelers, by
recognizing one's kind, is simultaneously to affirm and to escape the self.

Claude J. Summers and Ted-Larry Pebworth.<br>
ConP. Winter, 1978, pp. 32–33

## HUGHES, LANGSTON (1902–1967)

Hughes was primarily a social poet, and recognized himself as such; but
he was also a lyricist of the first order. His lyric, apolitical poems, for the
most part built on the techniques of Imagism and the poetic conceit, are
rich and original. His love poems, for instance, compare with the best in
the language for their freshness, tenderness, musicality, and evocative
power.

Hughes's poetry is both surface-simple and deep, both lucid and profound. It glitters with laughter—the understated, ironic humor of the
blues. In his blues and jazz poems, and in the black sensibility which,
against the opposition of his "respectable" readers, he succeeded in infusing into contemporary free verse in general, Hughes is a technician and
innovator of the first rank and a seminal figure in American literature. . . .

Langston Hughes is quite possibly the most grossly misjudged poet
of major importance in America. The American literary establishment,
their lenses ground to formal complexity and trained on "mainstream"
culture, when they acknowledge Hughes's existence at all, typically view
him as a poor misguided soul laboring in an unrewarding "ethnic province," searching for an illusory "racial art." Hughes is dismissed as too
simple, too quaintly humorous, unserious, unreflective, parochial,
limited in scope, without a metaphysic and without profundity. . . .

Hughes's poetry exhibits many of the characteristics of oral poetry
the world over. It is marked by an economy of means, by an almost ruthless exclusion of extraneous embellishments, resulting in a lean, spare,
uncluttered style, and in efficient structure and logistics that permit no
tedious or unnecessary diversions. Its commitment to the auditory, which
in oral poetry is primary and definitive, and to a popular mass audience,
makes indispensable a lucidity of surface, normal syntax, a contemporary
and colloquial rather than archaic or learned idiom, and vivid, concrete,
and evocative imagery—in short, felicitous speech and mellifluous

motion. Hughes's poetry is to be commended both for its fidelity to traditional forms and themes and for its transposition, manipulation, and adaptation of them. . . .

In Hughes, black folk culture is the weapon, black social and economic sufficiency the prize fought for. By utilizing the black heritage so fully in his work, Hughes preserves and transmits that heritage and thereby aids the survival of Afro-Americans as a distinct people. One of the far-reaching effects of his esthetic, and of its elaborations and extensions by others, is to compel us, in evaluating a black writer, to take into account his attitude to himself and his people and heritage, and what use he makes or fails to make of that heritage. In other words, we must consider the presence, balance, and power of the positive compulsions in his work. Perhaps more than any other writer of his generation, Hughes permits these positive energies the most uninhibited, prolonged and unified play.

Onwuchekwa Jemie. *Langston Hughes: An Introduction to the Poetry* (Columbia Univ. Pr., 1975), pp. xvi, 187, 196–97, 199

[There is] a basic ambiguity in some of Hughes' "dream" poems: on the one hand his satiric expose of the deferred dream in Black America is invariably couched in terms which taunt White America about the essentially non-revolutionist nature of its Revolution; but, on the other hand, his identification with the Black American's rebellion does not go beyond protest to any revolutionary ideology of his own. Indeed, one may speculate that it is easier for Hughes to demand that White America make good on the promises of its Revolution precisely because a satisfactory fulfillment of these promises, from Hughes' point of view, would not necessitate that fundamental restructuring of the social order, which even an historian like Bernard Bailyn associates with revolution. The point is not that Hughes is being hypocritical, or even muddle-headed, rather that his interest in socio-political reform is sharply defined by his basic loyalty to the unfulfilled promises of the American Revolution. So that in the final analysis his overall protest is not that the deferred dream is non-revolutionist but, quite simply, that it has been deferred. . . .

The poetic insights of Hughes' "Freedom's Plow" insist on a frank, if unflattering, admission of the gulf between the artist/intellectual and the masses, a gulf which Hughes as poet deliberately crosses in order to share a popular faith in the American Dream. On the other hand, the current trend in Black revolutionary literature assumes a rather easy identification of the artist with some mass revolutionary taste, a taste, one should add, that is often postulated but never really demonstrated as fact. Hughes' admission may very well irk the revolutionary enthusiasts among us, but in the absence of any obvious enthusiasm for radical revolution (as distinct from rebellious impatience) among those masses, one is left with the suspicion that Hughes is perhaps more realistic about the actual relationships between the Black American masses and the American Dream, and that, conversely, [LeRoi] Jones' prophetic vision of Black people as Black poets, Black poem as Black world is another dream legacy—that is, another revolution as dream.

Lloyd W. Brown. *SBL*. Spring, 1976, p. 18

Langston Hughes's final book of poetry, *The Panther and the Lash*, was assembled prior to his unexpected death on May 22, 1967, and published in July of that year. In many respects it is a somber book, devoid of racial comedy or humor. Within its pages there are no black folk characters luxuriating in the warm richness of the black experience; there are no happy blues singers, no Simples and no Madame Alberta K. Johnsons— no poems that celebrate the vibrancy and color of the black life-style. Instead, the emotional tone of the poems reflects the temper of the times. Between the publication of *Ask Your Mama* and *Panther*, America and the world had teetered on the brink of revolutionary racial change. Not only had the Montgomery miracle occurred in the late 1950s to give black America its first organized victory against racial segregation, but sit-in demonstrations had flared throughout the South and extensive riots seared the congested urban black ghettoes of the North. As a consequence, America and the rest of the world became aware both of the plight of black people and the ever increasing menace of widespread racial violence and revolution. The Reverend Martin Luther King, Jr., astride his unicorn, had spread his doctrine of nonviolent social change for all to hear. His message appealed to people everywhere, but the roots of racial hatred ran so deep in America and elsewhere that many racists were never touched by the sunlight of Christian charity. . . .

His title, *The Panther and the Lash*—such a far cry from the black life-style titles given his other poetical volumes—suggests the bitter racial strife which was then shaking America from stem to stern. The "lash" symbolizes overt and covert white hostility to the black man's thrust for civil rights and first-class citizenship; and the "panther," political symbol of America's most militant racial group, symbolizes black anger and black separatism. Significantly enough, the volume is also subtitled "Poems of Our Times," and of the eighty-six, twenty-six had been written and published at an earlier time. "Christ in Alabama" and "Justice," for instance, were first published in *Scottsboro Limited* in 1932. Intended at that time to give an accurate appraisal of the brutal inequities of southern justice, the poems were still, in the 1960s, "poems of the times," suggesting that despite the passing decades, nothing much had changed. Similarly, several poems of racial protest, previously published in *One-Way Ticket*, *Fields of Wonder*, and *Montage*, acquired a new meaning and significance during the turbulent years of challenge and change in the 1960s. Thus, in his last volume of poetry Hughes earned an accolade bestowable on few of his fellow poets: he emerges as an artist who not only had the gift for trenchant analysis of the present but who, at the same time, could contemplate future vistas and read the wave of the future. In other words, even though he was the poet of rapid insight and fleet impressions, he rarely became so immersed in the particularities of a given moment that he forgot the future's debt to the present and the present's debt to the past. . . .

> Richard K. Barksdale. *Langston Hughes: The Poet and His Critics* (American Library Association, 1977), pp. 119, 121–22

# ● HURSTON, ZORA NEALE (1901–1960)

Only to reach a wider audience, need [Zora Neale Hurston] ever write books—because she is a perfect book of entertainment in herself. In her youth she was always getting scholarships and things from wealthy white people, some of whom simply paid her just to sit around and represent the Negro race for them, she did it in such a racy fashion. She was full of side-splitting anecdotes, humorous tales, and tragicomic stories, remembered out of her life in the South as a daughter of a travelling minister of God. She could make you laugh one minute and cry the next. To many of her white friends, no doubt, she was a perfect "darkie," in the nice meaning they give the term—that is a naïve, childlike, sweet, humorous, and highly colored Negro.

But Miss Hurston was clever, too—a student who didn't let college give her a broad *a* and who had great scorn for all pretensions, academic or otherwise. That is why she was such a fine folk-lore collector, able to go among the people and never act as if she had been to school at all. Almost nobody else could stop the average Harlemite on Lenox Avenue and measure his head with a strange-looking, anthropological device and not get bawled out for the attempt, except Zora, who used to stop anyone whose head looked interesting, and measure it.

> Langston Hughes. *The Big Sea* (Knopf, 1940), pp. 238–39

Out of her abundant stores of vitality Zora Hurston fashions an autobiography [*Dust Tracks on a Road*] which shoots off bright sparks of personality. . . . A woman of courage and action, she would scorn any academic retreat from the touch and feel of ordinary life. Not only is there nothing of the recluse in her nature, but there is, to state it positively, a preference for the jostling of the crowd. She feels a challenge to elbow her way along her traffic-jammed road with a roving eye for adventure. Tracks she leaves behind her in the dust, witnesses of her presence which only she among all those people can make. Mixing with others only enhances her individuality. . . .

Free of many routine moral obligations, Zora Hurston busies herself with unwrapping the happiness contained in each moment. She engenders an atmosphere of surprises both for herself and others who know her. Shrinking from the dullness of dogmatism, she blossoms out with an originality of thought and conduct. Although the author can hardly inform us that this originality is the secret of her charm, we can quickly detect it on each page of her autobiography. Even her literary style shows an out-of-the-ordinary quality, a concrete and earthy imagery, an uneven rhythm which reflect imagination, warmth, and impulsiveness. It is a safe guess that few people were bored in her presence. Angered sometimes, amused often, at least they must have responded positively to the unexpected course of her behavior. Sustained by her unflagging spirit, Zora Hurston is enabled to present a strong case for the doctrine of individuality in her own person.

Rebecca Chalmers Barton. Witnesses for Freedom<br>(Harper, 1948), pp. 101, 114

*Jonah's Gourd Vine* has style without structure, a rich verbal texture without dramatic form, "atmosphere" without real characterization. . . . The style of the novel is impressive enough. Zora Neale Hurston, whom Langston Hughes has described as a rare *raconteuse*, draws freely on the verbal ingenuity of the folk. Her vivid, metaphorical style is based primarily on the Negro preacher's graphic ability to present abstractions to his flock. . . . The danger is that . . . folk sayings may become the main point of the novel. Overdone, they destroy rather than support authentic characterization. In *Jonah's Gourd Vine* they are too nonfunctional, too anthropological, and in the end merely exotic. Miss Hurston has not yet mastered the form of the novel, but her style holds promise of more substantial accomplishment to come.

The genesis of a work of art may be of no moment to literary criticism but it is sometimes crucial in literary history. It may, for example, account for the rare occasion when an author outclasses himself. *Their Eyes Were Watching God* (1937) is a case in point. The novel was written in Haiti in just seven weeks, under the emotional pressure of a recent love affair. . . . Ordinarily the prognosis for such a novel would be dismal enough. One might expect immediacy and intensity, but not distance, or control, or universality. Yet oddly, or perhaps not so oddly, it is Miss Hurston's best novel, and possibly the best novel of the period, excepting *Native Son.*

> Robert A. Bone. *The Negro Novel in America,*
> rev. ed. (Yale Univ. Pr., 1965), pp. 127–28

Despite the psychological limitations which color her works, her novels deserve more recognition than they have received. While publishing more books than any Afro-American woman before her—four novels, two collections of folklore, and an autobiography—she was one of the few Southern-born Afro-American writers who have consistently mined literary materials from Southern soil. Gifted with an ear for dialect, an appreciation of the folktale, a lively imagination, and an understanding of feminine psychology, she interwove these materials in deceptively simple stories which exhibit increasing artistic consciousness and her awareness of the shifting tastes in the American literary market. . . .

Her relative anonymity may be blamed on two causes. First, during her most productive period—the 1930s—widespread poverty limited the sale of books. Second, her tales of common people form a seemingly quiet meadow overshadowed by commanding, storm-swept hills on either side. To the rear, in the twenties, stands the exoticism of the Harlem Renaissance—Claude McKay's lurid depictions of Harlem, Wallace Thurman's satirical invective, Langston Hughes's jazz rhythms, and Countee Cullen's melodious chauvinism. On the other side, in the forties, stands the lusty violence of Richard Wright, Frank Yerby, Ann Petry, and Willard Motley. Most of Zora Neale Hurston's stories, in contrast, seem to be quiet quests for self-realization. . . .

Because of her simple style, humor, and folklore, Zora Neale Hurston deserves more recognition than she ever earned. But, superficial and shallow in her artistic and social judgments, she became neither an impeccable raconteur nor a scholar. Always, she remained a wandering minstrel. It was eccentric but perhaps appropriate for her to return to Florida to take a job as a cook and maid for a white family and to die in poverty. She had not ended her days as she once had hoped—a farmer among the growing things she loved. Instead she had returned to the level of life which she proposed for her people.

> Darwin T. Turner. *Zora Neale Hurston: The*
> *Wandering Minstrel* (Southern Illinois Univ. Pr.,
> 1971), pp. 98–99, 120

Miss Hurston's awareness of the uniqueness of her experience, the ways in which it sets her apart from the rest of the rural Deep South as well as from the growing experience of blacks in the Northern cities—Chicago or New York City's Harlem—. . . is apparent everywhere in her work. It is clear that she sees herself, in her fiction and in the occasional articles she wrote specifically on racial matters and the experience of the American black, as someone particularly qualified to see the truth. Further, in the self-conscious use of a "down-home" idiom—"hitting a straight lick with a crooked stick"—which she quickly explains in her next two sentences, we can recognize whom she conceives her audience to be. It is an audience not familiar with the circumstances of the South, nor with the idiom she draws from it. Her audience is white. And she is attempting to charm that audience, both with her authenticity and with her good cheer. It should not surprise us that *Dust Tracks on a Road* "won the Anisfield Wolf Award for its contribution to improving race relations.". . .

*Jonah's Gourd Vine* is in large part the story of Miss Hurston's parents, as we learn when we read her autobiography. Her father's history closely parallels that of the protagonist of *Jonah's Gourd Vine*, John Buddy Pearson; the account of her mother's death in the autobiography could have been taken from the novel. The plot of the novel is that of a man's full growth and failure, but it is probably fair to say that our interest is not focused on the plot, anyway. It is focused on the breathtaking recreation of a particular and specified dialect, and, through that, the particular and intensely realized life of a Southern black man, removed from the world of overt racism halfway through the novel, struggling against the weaknesses of his nature—and losing. . . .

The vitality of the book comes entirely from its folkloristic reporting of a language, a dialect, of the black rural South. The plot construction, the sense of time in the novel, the acting out of imagined scenes—all these qualities are deficient, which is not surprising in a first novel. . . .

It is finally the immediacy of these details of the novel which makes *Jonah's Gourd Vine* worth reading; it is hard to find sources which convey more directly the particular quality of black life in the rural South in the first half of the Twentieth Century.

James Rambeau. MarkhamR. Summer, 1976, pp.<br>61–63

To herself, she was a failure. Fortunately, no critic wholly supports this view. While a few lampoon her for what they consider her lack of social consciousness, her tendency to transcend racism and prejudices by disallowing them a major role in her works, and for technical and narrative deficiences in her fiction, most praise her for her ability to tell a good story well, for her vivid and unforgettable figurative language, for her staunch individualism, and for the sense of "racial health" that permeates her fiction. . . .

What really made her premature, however, was all the beauty and struggle of *Their Eyes Were Watching God* where marriage is largely defined in sexual terms; where one mate must remain petal open and honest for the other; where mere sex may take place without consummation of the marriage since consummation only takes place when the right dust-bearing bee comes along; where the quality of one's life counts more than the quantity of it; where poetry is more essential than prose, love more essential than money, sharing paramount to dominating; where one's dream is the horizon and one must "go there to know there." All that and more made Hurston extraordinary; all that makes the beauty of *Their Eyes Were Watching God* almost unbearable today, makes one wonder if even today the world is ready for Zora Neale Hurston.

Her works are important because they affirm blackness (while not denying whiteness) in a black-denying society. They present characters who are not all lovable but who are undeniably and realistically human. They record the history, the life, of a place and time which are remarkably like other places and times, though perhaps a bit more honest in the rendering. They offer some light for those who "ain't ne'er seen de light at all."

Lillie P. Howard. Zora Neale Hurston (Twayne, 1980), pp. 170, 174–75

# ● IGNATOW, DAVID (1914–    )

David Ignatow takes few pleasures with himself. His poems describe a world of unresponsive faces and emotions. In place of people, guilt; in place of light, brick tenements, and a wall. Ignatow hammers against the wall flatly, undramatically. Yet he carries odd shaped stones out of his inner life, and piles them in place. The wall has no style, and the poet hates it. But he takes an odd comfort in knowing it is there. . . .

As a poet of the city, Ignatow has little in common with other New York poets like Frank O'Hara, Kenneth Koch or Paul Blackburn. For O'Hara and his followers, the city has become a web of short-circuited images: places, people, objects thrown together, as in a surrealist poem, by the violent energy of the street. The city takes on a shape of unreason; it is not a place to live, but a kind of rundown fairyland in which the poet is always a tourist, never a resident. The natural rhythms which the city lacks are replaced by a chaotic frenzy, a portrait of the *id* made of jagged lines and interesting associations, the whole extremely refined, and almost dandyistic.

Ignatow, however, is a New Yorker in another sense. He is not playful enough to be a tourist. He is condemned to be a resident: to be wholly consumed by the crowds and the money-making; to face a raw, unpoetic world with all the spiritual need of man who has never learned to respond to anything else, and yet who is too flatly lucid to find in the city a satisfaction which it can never give him. . . .

David Ignatow speaks to us from a comfortless underground. His isolation is not simple, nor is it the gilded, half-public isolation of the Beats. His poems are like letters from a prison, where he has always lived, and which he himself has partly built. They are profoundly simple, expressing, at their best, the authority and the spiritual grace of a man who has had much time to think, in his prison, and more to feel. Whenever the smells and shapes of the world flood, momentarily, through the angular window of his cell, they reverberate in the emptiness, taking on a terrifying presence.

Crunk [pseud. for Robert Bly]. The Sixties.<br>Summer, 1968, pp. 10, 16, 23

A poet as adept as Ignatow at managing shifts in perception and the levels of perception, as well as committed to levelling collective experience, can expect, in turn, to have the open structures of his short poems eventually compared to that most levelling of popular media in his day—the motion picture—especially in the manner in which the personalism of his poetry enlists a comparable participation and personalism on the parts of his readers. This personalism which has been the active goal of the generation of poets after Jarrell and which Ignatow's work allows to an unusual degree may provide the most intelligent explanation why these younger writers, as Bly has asserted, have insisted so strongly that Ignatow's "poetry be reviewed and published.". . .

Ignatow's near-mirroring by its very stylization and compression is different from both life and the self-congratulatory tone of the criticism it has received. Silence is often more than its verbalization, and Ignatow is one of the last poets about whom it may be said that he is not simply a poet of sensibility. Ignatow derives from a culture which has traditionally regarded silence with special awe, particularly as it approaches and reveals Deity, but equally, as his review of [James Dickey's] *Buckdancer's Choice* makes clear, Ignatow has himself thought long on the problems of silence and its impact: "I have read and reread ["The Firebombing"], fascinated by what it omits to say. I have been seeking to make out the meaning of this gap and have come to believe it is the poem itself, as the holes in [Henry] Moore's sculpture determine its form." An audience that would recognize what Ignatow has to offer will have to seek meaning, too, in silence, gaps, and their manipulations.

Jerome Mazzaro. Salmagundi. Spring/Summer,<br>1973, pp. 184–86

Ignatow has a storyteller's gift which is rare among American poets. Instead of psychology and introspection, he gives us mad tales, hallucinations which tip us off to their sly, self-dramatic quality with a wink of exaggeration. . . . The poems become homemade myths which the mind invents to console itself for the savagery of its days. They reflect the agitated experiments we try out on ourselves day after day, with only rare times out for repose: the lunges of fantasy, the inner conversations, the voices and faces performing the busy play in our heads which we call "thinking.". . .

The best of these poems—and there are many "best"—are characterized by a sort of uncluttered authority which one hasn't experienced in American poetry since William Carlos Williams. The language is undecorated. There are no side effects, no tapestry of consoling images. This is not a cultural matter, Ignatow's tone of voice tells us. These poems have got to keep talking: it's a question of sanity, of life. But the urgency is not frantic either. It is like breathing and eating. The result is what we have come to call "unliterary." The poems refuse to redeem the painfulness of experience from a distance, they refuse to create an ennobling framework into which the reader agrees, for the duration of the poem, to be transposed. Instead, they use an opposite guile. They pretend to be talkative, half-educated. Few novelists have grasped the voice of the neighborhoods as Ignatow has: the complaints, the garrulous philosophizing, the straight-out talk of ordinary, unlovely existences. If you can't make sense right here in the stink of the world, Ignatow says, then you're not making sense at all. . . .

Ignatow's poems are as sparse and rhetorically exact as any being written today. They are closely argued, subtle; they think with luminous precision. Only in the narrowest sense can they be called "unliterary." They are exactly what we mean by literature: formed utterances which help us to make sense of ourselves, and of each other.

*Facing the Tree* displays all of the qualities one has come to expect of Ignatow's work: the "unliterary" simplicity, the obsession of fathers and sons, the bad dreams of a man talking to himself in our presence. But there is another element which has become increasingly present in Ignatow's recent work: a note of amazed reconciliation, as of a survivor who has begun to look around him, and notices that he is walking, seeing; that a lifetime of wrestling with his inner ghosts, has spewed him miraculously forth, older now, closer to the last act of his life, but full of wonder, and a stranger clear-sighted peacefulness. The doors and windows of his room have been thrown open, and he is flooded with the permanent, silent presence of outside. . . .

There is a moral resilience in Ignatow's poetry which makes it unique among contemporary American poets. It's about time more of us listened, and understood that a "master" is indeed among us, as James Wright accurately puts it in his comment on *Facing the Tree*.

Paul Zweig. APR. Jan./Feb., 1976, pp. 29–30

Ignatow was not really recognized as a major writer until the 1960's with [the] publication during that decade of three collections, *Say Pardon*, *Figures of the Human*, and *Rescue the Dead*. Today Ignatow continues to be both one of the most curiously rewarding and perhaps most unrewarded poets of his period. . . . Ignatow has been a kind of watchdog of the American conscience and consciousness (not to mention his own conscience and consciousness) for some 40 years now. It seems increasingly a kind of modest tragedy in the history of American poetry that critically the poet received little attention until the 1960's. . . .

Ignatow [in *Tread the Dark*] in the midst of a certain sadness, is not above making a recognizable and sensible joy, even to the point of making fun of himself. Such a poem is surely the one in which the poet equates the act of continuing to go on living, with the watering of his plants, "knowing that the world would end with the demise of all plants" (#77). Perhaps the ultimate gesture in this direction, for the reader of Ignatow's poetry generally, occurs in "I'm a Depressed Poem" (#86), in which the poet says with finality: "You probably understand [this], from experience; gone through something like it yourself which may be why you hold me this long. I've made you thoughtful and sad and now there are two of us. I think it's fun. . . ."

Michael Benedikt. *ABR*. Dec./Jan., 1978–79, pp. 4–5

● **IRVING, JOHN   (1942–    )**

John Irving is twenty-seven years old. A native of New Hampshire, he attended Phillips Exeter Academy and the University of Pittsburgh, then went to Vienna, where he stayed long enough to become thoroughly hung up on Europe before returning home. At some point during these adventures Irving conceived a novel that would combine the horrors of World War II with the far gentler troubles of a youth stumbling into self-awareness and manhood. *Setting Free the Bears* is the result, and it represents a puzzling, often astonishing literary debut.

The puzzling—and completely unresolved—aspect of the book is its lack of identity with either the Jamesian tradition or the American mainstream of the 1960s. *Setting Free the Bears* simply isn't a contemporary American novel; the language could almost be a European translation from an original by a European writer.

There are no Americans in the book at all, and the few references to racial troubles in the United States, obviously drawn in as parallels to the inhumanity of the war, seem curiously out of place. The tone of the novel, in short, is determinedly consistent with its setting—Vienna and the Austrian countryside.

This would be no problem were it not for nagging reminders throughout the book that something important—apparently the author's American identity and sensibility—is missing. . . .

After an unfortunate beginning, Irving proves in *Setting Free the Bears* that he is a writer of uncommon imaginative power. Moved by what must have been the awful reality of Vienna's memories, he has transcended, though not without serious difficulties, the limbo of his European years. He is back in America now, teaching at a small college in New Hampshire; perhaps he will decide on an identity and produce an American novel. Whatever he writes, it will be worth reading.

Henry S. Resnik. *SR*. Feb. 8, 1969, p. 26

John Irving is a young, eccentrically talented novelist with a singular rage to instruct. His books—funny, cleverly written, sometimes oddly endearing—provide a wealth of information about subjects one hardly expects to encounter in works of fiction. . . . [In *The 158-Pound Marriage*] the title and many of the episodes derive from wrestling, a sport that, as far as I know, has been unnoticed by contemporary authors. From Irving's previous book, *The Water-Method Man*, one learned a great deal about a rare ailment of the male urinary tract, and that particular pain in the human condition has also been neglected by novelists in droves. In each case, of course, Irving's pedantic exposition is eventually linked to a subject that does indeed interest novelists—marriage, with all its devious sexual and emotional permutations—but one must wade through a lot of words about wrestling and urology before coming in sight of the human heart behind these awkward symbols. . . .

But although he can graphically convey the special ambiance of a college gymnasium, his characters elude him; for all their sexual energy, they remain bloodless, ghostly lovers without bone and muscle. If, in the end, Irving seems to spell out his lesson. . . , along the way he has lost control of the affirmations his story is presumably meant to offer. Swathed in a tangle of irresolute hints and guesses, neither the wrestling nor the sex bestows sufficient substance or meaning to *The 158-Pound Marriage*, and one is left with a mood of shambling inconsequence.

Pearl K. Bell. NL. Nov. 25, 1974, pp. 13–14

*The World According to Garp* is a book of dimensions. It is entertainment on a grand, anyway stylish, scale. It is bravado transfigured into bravery—or maybe the other way around. In fact, I think quite often the other way around—which is not to damn, but to wonder. . . .

Murder is a frequent occurrence in *Garp* (both Garp and his mother die in this fashion), but it isn't about murder really, it's about how to breathe life into life. Mayhem and mutilation are on every other page, but the theme of the book is addressed to making things whole. The Ellen Jamesians can't speak (and Garp himself smashes his jaw and must communicate by notes), yet the novel is concerned with articulation as perhaps the only saving grace. One of the most unforgettable characters is a football tight end turned transsexual (there is homoerotic awareness everywhere), yet *Garp* is profoundly centered on heterosexual urges and itches and relationships and fulfillments, and, out of these *and* beyond them, on families and children. Garp is a true romantic hero: he wants the world safe, not for himself, but for them. . . .

Garp's world is so bizarrely and completely dangerous that while one nods how true, how true, one never quite suspends disbelief. Like the accident, everything awful *could* happen, but that it does is somehow too neat. Part of the manipulation is disarmament by irony—for an awareness of ironic possibility accompanies every disaster, every shock. . . . Garp's second son was conceived as, in a sense, a reserve—in case the first son became a victim of the unsafe world. It is the second who is killed.

So, the world (Garp's) is horrendous; yet his struggle to make it sensible—accountable, as it were, to a human sense of order—is strangely unnecessary. For the world (Irving's) works just fine: It is a marvelous invented contraption. . . .

With *Garp*, however, it's the reader who pulls aside the curtain, and it is not Garp who is revealed at the controls, but John Irving. He is a master magician, and the show is great. But we see too much, and both Garp's dread and Irving's optimism fade away into what one too sharply realizes is an illusion. A grand illusion, very powerful; the book can freak you out. But, in the end, the interest of *The World According to Garp* lies not in that world, but in the wondrous mechanics of its invention and the deft manipulation—while the show goes on—of our awe and tears and laughter.

Eliot Fremont-Smith. VV. May 22, 1978, pp.<br>77–78

*The World According to Garp* was, of course, 1978's *Ragtime*, which is to say that it is the most recent manifestation of the greatest-novel-of-the-decade. . . . *The World According to Garp* does indeed have "extraordinary" qualities. Its plot, for one thing. Like so many extraordinary things, the story lacks, shall we say, credibility. That is not necessarily a criticism: John Irving has never been able to construct a believable plot, but he has always tried to make a virtue of this chronic deficiency. Which is to say that, like other formless novelists—Pynchon, Barth, Doctorow—he abandons any pretense at narrative (and therefore psychological) realism, and seeks instead to attract and maintain the reader's attention with random monstrosities and grotesque occurrences, chiefly sexual or violent in nature, frequently both. The idea, in other words, is to horrify or titillate the reader to such an extent that he or she will be compelled to continue reading, even without the promise of any realistic development of story or explication of character. . . .

Irving's talent is primarily comedic, and his purposes are best served by his dialogue, which is well done and often amusing. It is important to note at the outset that his style as a whole is *not* exhibitionistic, not even mildly tortured: it does not seek to function as a smokescreen for the author's views and perceptions. More than anything else, however, Irving's prose is the prose of a poorly educated man—his vocabulary is uninspiring, his knowledge of the grammatical proprieties is severely limited. He is a child of his time in his lack of respect for lucidity ("Garp was an excessive man," and "Garp felt a peculiar feeling of unfairness overwhelm him"). In Irving's case, however, the sporadic incoherence and the syntactical sloppiness seem to be simply the consequence of the author's unwillingness—or, perhaps, his inability—to polish his output, rather than a deliberate smog-policy. The carelessness, in other words, is in the expression, not in the sentiments which seek that expression. Like all other Major American Novelists, Irving says his ambition is to write "accessible" fiction, and he has done so. His style is simplistic, almost childlike—it is, in other words, what has come to be referred to as "readable." What *Garp* is, is a funny book. Or rather, it tries to be. But it is a low humor, based chiefly on the prepubescent assumption that conscientious vulgarity is by definition amusing.

The immature quality of John Irving's comedic sense is worth mentioning primarily because of its subsidiary effect, which is to conceal, or at least to disguise, the novel's more fundamental flaw. What we are talking about, of course, is Irving's obsession with kinky violence (or violent kinkiness, it is hard to say which), and what concerns us here is the perverse enthusiasm with which many American critics have embraced that eccentric quality.

Bryan Griffin. At. June, 1979, pp. 50–51, 55

John Irving's first four novels suggest that to him structure is *nearly* everything. All his novels are structurally complex, and they all incorporate remarkably similar settings and experiences, somewhat like those in Irving's own life. Writers, former wrestlers, New England colleges, Vienna, Iowa—we find them in all the books. Similar characters appear in all four works, and the same characters also appear. The same aging but elegant Viennese prostitute, for instance, with a fur muff to hide her sparkling ringed fingers, appears in *The Water-Method Man* and *The World According to Garp*—only her name has been changed. Yet these novels are worlds apart, as different from each other as their main characters are from the author. Irving uses his own experiences ruthlessly to create self-contained worlds within each novel—worlds of exaggeration populated with bizarre, sometimes absurd characters—in order to compel us to recognize the truths that underlie human existence. Regardless of the world in which we find them, the truths Irving magnifies are unchanging. . . .

Like Garp, Irving has been trying to find a personal vision, a way to tell his stories with his imagination and not his memory. In a large sense, the narrative techniques and perspectives that Irving employs in his first three books are all included in *The World According to Garp*, but the narrator in that novel is omniscient, unlike the others who are involved in the stories they narrate. . . .

*The World According to Garp* is the closest that Irving has come to writing a selective autobiography—which is important in one very strong sense. By exaggerating events and characters from his life, Irving has made them more interesting and better adapted to his own needs. He has found both his personal vision and celebrated its arrival in *The World According to Garp*. Through an omniscient narrator, Irving has imposed order and structure upon the "lunacy and sorrow" of the world within the novel. . . .

Despite his remonstrations and attempts to espouse traditional literary values, Irving has up to now written a combination of modern and traditional fiction. In *The World According to Garp* he combines traditional story-telling and literary modes (chronological sequence, omniscient narration, and the epilogue) with modern techniques (writing-within-writing and self-reflexive narration). All four of his works contain writing which Irving uses to explain his own intentions and explicate his own text.

Michael Priestley. *Critique*. 23, 1, 1981, pp. 94–96

It's extraordinary what a little feeling can do for a novel. To prepare for *The Hotel New Hampshire*, I read *The World According to Garp*, and disliked it intensely, not for its slapstick sex or for its "comic and ugly and bizarre" preoccupation with mutilation and death, but for its shallowness, its quality of energy without feeling. The novel conveyed only one emotion—self-love. Garp, Irving's writer-hero, was so taken with himself that the title of the last chapter jarred: how could there possibly be "Life After Garp"? Who would want to go on living without that paragon? I frankly hated *Garp*, and picked up the new novel expecting to hate it too. Instead I liked it. Feeling made the difference. In *Garp*, it all flows back on Irving's alter ego; in *The Hotel New Hampshire*, it flows out, bringing a whole family to life on a wide current of care.

John Irving is a talented but facile writer. His prose never encounters those resistances—emotional, moral, epistemological—that energize memorable statement. It never strains at meaning; it just sweeps you along, its easy momentum lulling your critical faculty and rocking you back to a childlike state of wonder. In this 400-page book, for example, I can find only one moment of verbal felicity: "Harold Swallow, darting through the trees, guiding us like a hush up the path. . . ." One pauses over that "like a hush up a path," to admire it. But that is just what Irving doesn't want, for if we stop we might start asking questions that would undermine our pleasure in a novel so willfully unrealistic. So Irving keeps us moving, sacrificing rhetoric to pace, as in the most primitive narrative forms, the fable and the fairy tale. In fiction like this, meaning lies near the surface of the story and in the voice of the storyteller.

*The Hotel New Hampshire* is a family saga; the storyteller is John Berry, the middle child, a brother and sister fore and aft. Not a novelist like Garp, he is the family annalist, the compiler of its collective story. . . .

The novel has the manic rhythm of a cartoon; crisis follows crisis in a spiral of woe; and, at each crisis, the Berry family comes together in a moving tableau of solidarity. Family is one of the novel's values; imagination is the other. That faculty is seen in a double light. On the one hand, it is a defense, a way of coping with troubles. The lack of it can be disabling, and one character commits suicide when her imagination fails. On the other hand, the attempt to realize everything you imagine can be dangerous. . . .

Someone calls John "a weight lifting maiden aunt"; in another vocabulary, he would be a *mensch*. His moments of caring, together with the larger set pieces of family solidarity, make the human element in a novel otherwise unbearably farcical. John Berry and John Irving remind us that the imagination is not simply a Rube Golberg faculty of invention; it is also a moral force, a way of sharing others' lives, others' burdens. We all want to check in to the Hotel New Hampshire. It is "the sympathy space" where we can be fully known and yet fully loved, and where a powerful imagination holds us fast and won't let us die.

Jack Beatty. *NR*. Sept. 23, 1981, pp. 37–38

## JARRELL, RANDALL (1914–1965)

While no Miniver Cheevy (his reputation as a nondrinker would preclude that), Randall Jarrell seems in some respects more suited to the heroic days of "iron clothing" than to the computerized society he reacted against in *A Sad Heart at the Supermarket*. His sensibility leads him to prefer a Renaissance mask just as surely as Pound in "Histrion." Like his nineteenth-century idol, Goethe, he looked backward in time, at least in these analogies with art, for his inspiration. He is no more just a voice of his own age than Goethe's *Faust* is an exponent of the *Sturm und Drang* period wherein it was written. Jarrell's fondness for the Renaissance as incarnated into art caused him to cherish its works, such as Uccello's *The Battle of San Romano*, . . . brought back to him in a good reproduction by his friend Robert Lowell after a trip to Italy. As for Brueghel, he kept a copy of *Hunters in the Snow* in his office, in addition to the one in "the little house in the woods."

Like Goethe, Randall Jarrell had almost superhuman versatility, a mark of that intelligence which was the wonder of all his associates, and a Renaissance curiosity as well as desire for excellence, ranging from athletics, fashions, and sports cars to classical ballet, music, and painting. He fits the passage wherein Ophelia recalls the Hamlet she knew before his mission of revenge disordered his princely qualities. Harold Jantz in *Goethe's Faust as a Renaissance Man: Parallels and Prototypes* quotes the German writer as saying in 1826: "As long as the poet merely expresses his own few objective perceptions, he cannot be called a poet but as soon as he knows how to make the world his own and to express it, he is a poet." Jarrell knew how to, and was. . . .

No reason for Jarrell's devotion to *Faust* strikes one as more relevant than this further comment by Harold Jantz: "We should turn to it [*Faust*] not to learn precepts for life but to learn life." Goethe had an uncanny ability to enter into the Renaissance. The heart of the Renaissance is Man; and into the heart of Man, in poem after poem, Randall Jarrell also enters.

Bernetta Quinn. *Randall Jarrell* (Twayne, 1981),
pp. 90–91

As critics have variously noticed, much of Jarrell's poetry springs from the conflict between intellect and imagination. His remarkable genius for articulate form is felt to be struggling with the desire to yield to an upsurge of unconscious images and dreams. This tension between consciousness and the perilous realm of the unconscious—central to Jarrell's oeuvre—is not unrelated to the poet's lifelong concern with psychology and strongly colors his use of images and symbols. In fact, many poems directly enact this tension through the device of contrasting pairs like darkness/light, sea/island, forest/clearings, sleep/waking. The beginning of "The Märchen" is a case in point. . . . The reader quickly notices the structural opposition between forest, sea, and night on the one hand, and clearing, island, and sunlight on the other. The two groups of images (interchangeable in each set) clearly represent the underlying antithesis of the conscious and the unconscious. While the reference to the history of tools used by primitive man alludes to the phylogenetic evolution of the human mind, the ontogenetic development is implied as well: each individual clears his own space in the forest ("We felled our islands there") encouraged by the illusory belief in the permanence of his achievement. However, at the end of day (both in terms of individual life and of human history) original darkness will once more prevail. In Jarrell's work, correlative pairs of this type always betray a latent instability; light, island, clearing, and their variants precariously maintain their existence against overwhelming odds. To Randall Jarrell the conflict between consciousness (form) and the unconscious (energy) is the very essence of the poetic process. In the act of writing the poet bravely attempts to win archetypal images from the dark source of the unconscious: ". . . well water/ Pumped from an old well at the bottom of the world./The pump you pump the water from is rusty/And hard to move. . . ." The poet appears as a mythmaker, and his creative act as a ceaseless struggle between unconscious drives and the conscious control of form. . . .

It has often been observed that Jarrell's poetry abounds with motifs from myths and fairy tales, as well as with psychoanalytic casebook studies and dreams. Like C. G. Jung, Jarrell regards myths, fairy-tales, and individual dreams as revelatory of the nature of the human psyche in general and of the creative act in particular. . . .

In his poetic world no child can rely on maternal help in a moment of distress or danger, for the mother is invariably depicted as either absent, dead, fainting, crazy, or thoroughly hostile. Throughout his life Jarrell was painfully aware that his character had largely been determined by his childhood experiences, in particular by the unbringing he received from his mother. Since his father left the family when Randall was still a little boy, his mother became his chief influence. And yet, the biographical evidence is not sufficient to explain the predominance of the mother figure in

Jarrell's work. Although he repeatedly asserts that man cannot escape his own mother, whose image he carries forever with him, it is clear that the poetic significance of the mother figure far transcends that of any individual woman: "Back far enough, down deep enough, one comes to the Mothers."

Helen Hagenbüchle. In *Critical Essays on Randall Jarrell*, ed. Suzanne Ferguson (G. K. Hall, 1983), pp. 101–3

## JEFFERS, ROBINSON   (1887–1962)

The value of Jeffers's poetry to the Sierra Club, both for the illustration of its books and for the confirmation of its philosophy, has contributed to the increase of his reputation. In celebrating his own "Inhumanism" he had proclaimed a "transhuman magnificence"; the negative of his philosophy found its positive in modern conservationism. In a sense he prophesied the modern movement. But in a deeper sense his poetry had also been prophesied by the naturalism of George Santayana more than two generations earlier. The strangely eloquent address delivered by the Spanish philosopher to a University of California audience in 1911 has often been quoted at length, but one sentence is crucial. Invoking "your forests and your Sierras," Santayana proclaimed that "In their non-human beauty and peace they stir the sub-human depths and the superhuman magnificence" of Jeffers. But the phrase "sub-human depths" has often been forgotten. In his most characteristic narrative poetry Jeffers explored the sub-human depths below as well as the trans-human beauty above. And modern criticism has focused increasingly on these sub-human depths. . . .

In all his mature poetry Jeffers sought to explore the realm beyond good and evil. In *The Women at Point Sur* his Barclay specifically announced this purpose. But in this realm there are no roads or reasons, and half-way through this poem Jeffers proclaimed that "these here have gone mad." In their belief that they could live beyond evil, these characters became alienated from the world of reason and law. And this is the fate of all who believe that to go beyond evil means to deny the reality of evil. . . .

The world which Jeffers's poetry explores is not beyond evil, but beneath (or before) evil. In *Tamar* her heroine proclaimed: "Time stands still, old man, you'll learn when you have lived at the muddy root/Under the rock of things." All his poems, in Santayana's phrase, "stir the sub-human depths of the spirit." They recall those impulses which primitive myth once celebrated, and which early civilization sometimes practiced (the early Pharaohs practiced royal incest), but which modern civilization has put down. Buried beneath the level of modern consciousness, these impulses still exist beneath evil, "at the muddy root of things." Only if the author fails to distinguish between the two realms do problems develop. Jeffers's early poetry had distinguished clearly: "for goodness and evil are two things and still variant, but the quality of life as of death and of light/ As of darkness is one, one beauty. . . ." ("Point Pinos and Point Lobos"). But his later poetry concerned itself more with the "one."

Modern criticism has done much to discover the distinctions of "voice," style, and structure which these later poems include. Depth psychology and myth criticism have offered clues for exploring the depths. But whatever the "voice," Jeffers continues to speak to us today.

Frederic I. Carpenter. *AL.* March, 1977, pp. 89, 95–96

In his best poetry Jeffers provides us with a world that is beautifully and sometimes terrifyingly real—or real in the sense that any artistic creation is real; the world of every artist is, of course, visionary; the degree of his success is in proportion to the reader's or viewer's or listener's being convinced that the "world" is real and, in addition, has meaning for the auditor. . . . Certainly no other American poet has approached him in the ability to endow character with life; his people, tormented and tormenting creatures, haunt the memory like grisly phantoms or spectral shapes rising from some atavistic depth of which we were unaware. Passing before the mind's eye, they reveal those gulfs over which we daily pass. In their strengths and weaknesses we see ourselves; they reveal to us, above all else, how slippery is our hold on reason and how tempting are the lures of irrationality in all its forms. Which is to say, Jeffers did what all great writers have done: he provided insight into the human condition.

Insight, above all else. And that insight does not stop with the human condition, but extends outward into the larger and, for Jeffers, more important natural world. No other poet of this century strove more successfully to "catch the inhuman God" in his lens. In this area, indeed, Jeffers had few peers in all of literature. The violence and extreme passion of the natural world color his lines in an unforgettable fashion. . . .

The human drama, whether comic or tragic, is little more than a relief against what he called in an early poem the "divinely superfluous beauty" of the natural world. And "if the great manners of death dreamed up/In the laboratories work well" and humans do succeed in killing themselves off, that beauty will certainly remain. The poetry of Jeffers enables us better to see and understand both ourselves and the shining glory of the world.

William H. Nolte. *Rock and Hawk: Robinson Jeffers and the Romantic Agony* (Univ. of Georgia Pr., 1978), pp. 199–201

# ● JONG, ERICA (1942–    )

Erica Jong's first novel, *Fear of Flying*, feels like a winner. It has class and sass, brightness and bite. Containing all the cracked eggs of the feminist litany, her soufflé rises with a poet's afflatus. She sprinkles on the four-letter words as if women had invented them; her cheerful sexual frank-ness brings a new flavor to female prose. Mrs. Jong's heroine, Isadora Wing, surveying the "shy, shrinking, schizoid" array of women writers in English, asks, "Where was the female Chaucer?," and the Wife of Bath, were she young and gorgeous, neurotic and Jewish, urban and contem-porary, might have written like this. *Fear of Flying* not only stands as a notably luxuriant and glowing bloom in the sometimes thistly garden of "raised" feminine consciousness but belongs to, and hilariously extends, the tradition of *Catcher in the Rye* and *Portnoy's Complaint*—that of the New York voice on the couch, the smart kid's lament. Though Isadora Wing, as shamelessly and obsessively as Alexander Portnoy, rubs the reader's nose in the fantasies and phobias and family slapstick of growing up, she avoids the solipsism that turns Roth's hero unwittingly cruel; nor does she, like Holden Caulfield, though no less sensitive to phoniness, make of innocence an ideal. She remains alert to this world. . . .

Isadora Wing should be recognized as a privileged case, with no sub-stantial economic barriers between her and liberation, and—by her own choice—no children, either. Edna Pontellier, the heroine of Kate Cho-pin's elegiac novel of female revolt, *The Awakening*, was a mother as well as a wife, and drowned herself to escape the impasse between her per-sonal, artistic identity and her maternal obligations. Childless, with an American Express card as escort on her pilgrimage and with a profes-sional forgiver as a husband, Isadora Wing, for all her terrors, is the heroine of a comedy. . . .

The novel is so full, indeed, that one wonders whether the author has enough leftover life for another novel. Fearless and fresh, tender and exact, Mrs. Jong has arrived non-stop at the point of being a literary per-sonality; may she now travel on toward Canterbury.

John Updike. *NY*. Dec. 17, 1973, pp. 149–50, 153

Erica Jong's first book of poems, *Fruits & Vegetables*, was one of those things rare in poetry: a new experience. I read these poems the way you watch a trapeze act, with held breath, marvelling at the agility, the lightness of touch, the brilliant demonstration of the difficult made to look easy. The poems were brief, swift, sure of themselves; they combined a cool eighteenth-century detached wit and a talent for epigram with a virtuoso handling of that favourite seventeenth-century figure of speech, the conceit, with body as fruit as body, poem as food as poem, man as Muse, Muse as man. They did not pose as straight-from-the-soul confessions; rather they posed as artifacts, beautifully *made*: china figurines which were really Iron Maidens, the spikes hidden beneath the painted foliage. They were literate without being literary. They toyed with the reader, refusing to reveal the extent of their seriousness—whether they *meant* it. . . .

In *Half-Lives* the tongue is out of the cheek, at least part of the time. This book's cover is not lush pink but stark black. The wit is still there, but it's less like a flirtation than a duel. There's less fun, more pain. . . .

Jong's poetry is sometimes tricky, like a well-performed conjuring trick; the props show only occasionally. But a good magician's best trick is to leave some doubt in the minds of the audience: perhaps the magic is real, perhaps the magic *power* is real. And in Jong's best poems, it *is* real. We may find the fool more entertaining, but the magician is, finally, more impressive.

Margaret Atwood. Parnassus. Spring/Summer,<br>1974, pp. 98, 104

In striking contrast to the fears of the body expressed in the fiction of Joyce Carol Oates, both novels by Erica Jong—*Fear of Flying* and *How to Save Your Own Life*—end with a kind of symbolic ritual baptism in celebration of the female body. . . .

As with all patterns of language, the writer after a while is imprisoned within a rigid enclosure of words in which, as in *How to. . .*, love is reduced to cunt and cock. We don't have a man and woman experiencing a warmly human relationship in which ultimately there is a sense of rebirth and a feeling of unity with the living universe (as that post-sexual love dialogue between Isadora and Josh would have us believe). There is only an impression of disembodied genitalia in which dripping cunt meets hard cock. . . .

In using this kind of sexual vocabulary, there is a sense of the writer beggared for expression and falling back on a vocabulary of male street usage. Woman needs a sexual vocabulary of her own—not one borrowed from men's street language. Such language is always self-limiting, because it is more geared to voicing frustrations than fulfillment. . . .

The world of *Fear of Flying* and its sequel *How to. . .* offers us a heroine who appears to be far more intrepid and confident than any of Oates's women. Yet, ultimately, we see that Jong's Isadora Wing is as helpless as the most timid of Oates's women characters—in the common avowal that man has the power. True, Isadora's discovery comes out of sexual need and not fear, but her conclusion is basically the same as the one affirmed in book after book by Oates. Woman is helpless. Man is powerful.

Ann Z. Mickelson. *Reaching Out: Sensitivity and*
*Order in Recent American Fiction by Women*
(Scarecrow, 1979), pp. 35, 46–48

Erica Jong is too fine a writer to care much about the accidental categories of the activists, categories that are a product of crippled imaginations. If Ms. Jong wrote a novel with a male protagonist-narrator, I would pick it up with respect and in the expectation of entertainment and even of enlightenment. If she said, in effect, "Men are like this," I would know her to be right. I trust her insight and her imagination. So far, in *Fear of Flying* and *How to Save Your Own Life*, to say nothing of her poems, she has presented the pains and occasional elations of the Modern American Female. With the confidence in the exterior validity of introspection that marks the true poet (Keats for instance), she has extrapolated from her own life and her own fear an archetype that has had immense appeal, not only with the MAF, but also with the Modern European Woman.

In her new novel, Erica Jong has refused to capitalize on an outlook and an ambience that a less scrupulous writer could have exploited forever. She has gone to the British 18th century and contrived an authentic picaresque novel with a female protagonist. Her title *Fanny*, as well as the afterword, acknowledges a measure of indebtedness to John Cleland's erotic masterpiece, *Fanny Hill*, but the book is neither a pastiche nor a parody. It is, despite its allegiance to an antique genre, a genuinely original creation.

This brings me to an aspect of Ms. Jong's work rarely considered by her admirers or her detracters—its stylistic distinction. Style, indeed, must be regarded not as an aspect of a book but its totality: The intention, or pretension, to produce literature—as opposed to the book of a possible film—depends on verbal competence more than knowledge of "life," whatever that is. Ms. Jong's first two books are highly literate. They show mastery, or mistressy, of language; they depend for their effects on verbal exactitude and the disposition of rhythm. Subject matter apart, they are models of what orthodox, as opposed to experimental, fiction ought to be in this final phase of the century.

Ms. Jong's concern with language has led her to a genuine experiment—the composition of a full-length novel in a mode of English no longer in use, though still capable of expressing a modern sensibility. She has gone further than Joyce, who merely, in the "Oxen of the Sun" chapter of *Ulysses*, played brief passages in ancient style. Her 18th-century English is not a matter of restoring the second person singular, using tags like *prithee*, or slavishly following old orthography (*musick, logick*, capital initials for nouns). It is a matter of vocabulary, and also of rhythm. . . .

The female liberationists are going to be angry with Ms. Jong because she has not repeated what she has already done so well. Instead, Ms. Jong, who is a literary scholar and a specialist in the 18th century, has transmuted her learning into literature, a very laudable thing to do.

A few critics will condemn what she has done because the writing of 18th-century literature is the task of 18th-century men and possibly women, and there is nothing to add to what, by its nature, has already been completed. There are answers to that. The romantic movement began with a pastiche of the past—the Rowley and Macpherson fabrications—but also with *The Ancient Mariner*, which used the vocabulary and metric of the old ballads. Most of our best-selling novelists write, because they know no better, in a calcified Victorian style. But Bernard Malamud, with *The Fixer*, wrote a 19th-century Russian novel that literature needed, and Ms. Jong may be said to have filled a gap in the great tradition of the picaresque novel. *Fanny: Being the True History of the Adventures of Fanny Hackabout-Jones* had to be written, and Erica Jong was the right hermaphrodite to write or endite it. I am delighted to belong to her sex.

Anthony Burgess. SR. Aug., 1980, pp. 54–55

## KEROUAC, JACK (1922–1969)

Kerouac's characters are separated from the community and have no interest in social reorganization, much to the disgust of many of the author's critics. But to the Kerouac hero the world and its institutions are too absurd for personal involvement. Nature offers no lasting relief either. Essentially, it is blind and uncaring. The only answer seems to be to get beyond time and desire, either through annihilating the senses with sensation or by freezing them in mystic contemplation. Neither method is satisfactory, and Kerouac's focal characters oscillate endlessly between the two states until, with the publication of the last novel, *Vanity of Duluoz*, it is evident that the quest for ecstasy and oneness with God has perpetuated an incorrigible loneliness, the final position of the quintessential Beat.

What relief there is in mystical belief is due to Kerouac's study of Buddhism superimposed upon his early Catholic training. He longs to accept the dance of life, the play of the illusion that most consider their waking reality, while at the same time seeking contact with the spiritual center of existence. . . .

Fascinated by the play of his own mind, Kerouac tried to get down all of his experience into words, first in the manner of Thomas Wolfe and then more in the manner of Henry Miller and William Burroughs. . . .

He has left us a body of work including the novels of the Duluoz Legend, his poetry, and his long unpublished treatise on Buddhism, but it is probable that little of it will survive. Because of continuing interest in the Beat generation, *On the Road* will no doubt remain the novel to be read to get at the quintessence of Beatness. Complementary works on the Beats will also retain a certain appeal. *Dharma Bums* contains some of the memorable minor characters, such as Japhy Ryder and Sean Monahan, and some of the best description of nature. It also treats the hero's mystic quest with the greatest degree of detachment. *Big Sur* is the novel that sums up the futility of Beat existence.

Whatever the merits of Spontaneous Prose, and we might wish for prose better honed or more thoroughly revised in a number of his books, Kerouac's prose method did produce at least one remarkable book, *The Subterraneans*, in which the spontaneity of style is largely responsible for the strength of its effect. It is a novel that is unique in its intensity, not only in all of Kerouac's work but in the work of the New Romantics generally.

Robert A. Hipkiss. *Jack Kerouac: Prophet of the New Romanticism* (Regents Pr. of Kansas, 1976), pp. 133–35

Striding above the constraints of society, beyond sin, doubt, and complexity, Kerouac's heroes, who are in a state of grace that precludes any experience from soiling their souls, exhibit an antinomianism that in American literature is usually simply labeled innocence. But Kerouac's men are profoundly subversive of the tradition of Western innocence in one crucial respect—they are opposed to and commit no violence. Kerouac ignored the blood-soaked world of American literature and the notion of the saintly killer who is "regenerated through violence." Guns hardly exist in Kerouac's novels. His characters do not even get into friendly barroom brawls.

Kerouac's males would prefer to live outside society, but they are inexorably entangled within it. Marriage, divorce, speeding tickets, even jails encroach upon their lives, but they continue to search for a permissive, individualistic society, such as they believe existed in the nineteenth-century West. In *Visions of Cody*, that search appears fruitless. . . .

Above all, Kerouac should be remembered as a seminal and major contributor to a contemporary myth of the West. Conjuring up a free territory in which gentle, spiritual people live in harmony, this latest version of the Isle of Fair Women had an incalculable influence on Americans in the 1950's and 1960's. For dreamers of a Western paradise, Jack Kerouac's books proved as indispensable (and often as inaccurate) as the guidebooks of the 1830's and 1840's had been for the original settlers. Finally, after a veritable epidemic of "Donner parties," the myth was discredited, although some survivors continue to intone its dogmas.

Harry Russell Huebel. *Jack Kerouac* (Boise State Univ. Pr., 1979), pp. 30, 43

# KINNELL, GALWAY (1927-    )

Kinnell was . . . faced with the problem of how to bring his poetry out of the modernist cul-de-sac of irony into a postmodernist aesthetic. He did this in large measure by two actions, which may appear contradictory but are in fact complementary: self-discovery and self-destruction, the heuristic and the incendiary actions of poetry. Kinnell became a shamanist, rather than a historicist, of the imagination. . . .

Destructive though the element of fire may be, Kinnell's forms are always instructive. There is an almost didactic tone in some parts of this book [*The Book of Nightmares*], a didacticism close to the evangelical. (That alone should make the book distinct from the dominant modern mode of irony.) But the poet draws back from priesthood because he continually rediscovers himself, and discovers in himself "the hunger to be new." Proposing new visions, like Adam he awakes to find them true: "The witness trees heal/their scars at the flesh fire." Nightmares are incendiary, but the book is heuristic. Or, to put it another way, what we see in our nightmares will surely char us unless we can transcribe it. The shaman-speaker of the last poem in *Body Rags* ends his days wondering; but in this later book, the shaman-speaker is closer to the answer to that question, "what . . . was the rank flavor of blood . . . by which I lived?" Again, it is through dream that the answer is formulated. . . . Once more the human face and the poetic text coincide to register the vision. Learn, he tells his child, "to reach deeper/into the sorrows/to come," anticipate the "still undanced cadence of vanishing." Then, with the child soothed and put back to sleep, he adds a promise. The promise is to learn, even if the lesson is preceded by destruction, and the promise constitutes Kinnell's testament.

Charles Molesworth. *The Fierce Embrace: A Study of Contemporary American Poetry* (Univ. of Missouri Pr., 1979), pp. 99, 110

Galway Kinnell's career gives the impression of continuity despite his transformations of style and tone, perhaps because he has held fast to a certain idea of the possibilities of poetry. Throughout his career he has minded his matter first, in the faith that feeling sincerely will produce words adequate to experience, and has seemed pretty much content to cast his material in the received style of the day. Kinnell addresses the great and eternal themes in a contemporary idiom, convinced, it seems, that familiar emotions need only be rephrased with passion to be made new.

The poems in *Moral Acts, Mortal Words* partake of the autumnal mellowness that now threatens to become the standard for the poets of Kinnell's generation as they enter the "late period." These new poems are as muted and personal as much of his previous work was hyperbolic and overscaled. That their burden is lighter does not mean, sadly, that Kinnell has succeeded any better at carrying it. He seems, as always, to arrive at resolutions he ultimately falls short of earning. Kinnell continually announces the familiar in the rhetoric of discovery; there is much of the inexplicable oddity of birth and death, and other such topics, in these poems. . . .

Kinnell hopes, by taking on the great, intractable facts of love and loss, to achieve the kind of embattled radiance associated with the line of grim realists exemplified by Robert Frost. Yet the ruthless skepticism that such a stance demands is not among the weapons that Kinnell brings to the struggle; too often he resorts to rhetoric as a substitute for imaginative energy. The result might be likened to a fixed fight; no matter how good the show, and much of Kinnell is not without a certain power, the outcome rings hollow in the end.

Vernon Shetley. Poetry. Feb., 1981, pp. 298–99

# ● KOPIT, ARTHUR (1937–    )

With Arthur Kopit's *Oh Dad, Poor Dad*, the avant-garde fashion turns chi-chi. Jerome Robbins has obviously poured a fortune into his production, possibly to hide the thinness and immaturity of the play. But though the cash tinkles too loudly sometimes, let us be grateful for the things that money can buy. . . . As for the play—which Robbins has correctly directed like a cartoon—the final scene has a grisly humor, revolving as it does around a corpse which keeps falling on a girl while she is trying to make love; but the rest of the work is inadequate and derivative. Mr. Kopit shares with Broadway psychological playwrights an abiding distaste for mothers and potential mothers, expressed by displaying females in possessive, smothering, and emasculating attitudes. With Tennessee Williams, he evokes a predatory world populated by man-eating fish, man-eating plants, and man-eating women. And with a growing number of aspiring young dramatists, he has a tendency to ape the techniques of the avant-garde without adding anything original of his own. It is this desire to join a parade rather than to communicate a unique vision that tends to reduce the Absurd to the ridiculous. And though it offers excellent copy for journalists, it threatens to make the American Absurdist movement as arid a cultural phenomenon as the late, unlamented Generation of the Beats.

Robert Brustein. NR. March 19, 1962, p. 31

*The Day the Whores Came Out to Play Tennis*, the second of Arthur Kopit's pair of one-acters . . . , is a farce about the invasion of a Jewish country club by eighteen of the tennis players. The action takes place in the nursery of the clubhouse, and, with the exception of a snide English waiter who looks like a wax dummy, all the characters are members of the club's executive committee, which has been summoned at dawn to deal with the emergency. The ladies, according to a stumbling and over-wrought report by the son of the president of the club, arrived in a couple of Rolls-Royces with one-way mirrors for windows, and immediately made for the courts. They never put in an appearance on-stage, but they make themselves felt in a number of ways.

The play is Mr. Kopit's first major entry since *Oh Dad, Poor Dad*. There is no plot. Again he makes use of all kinds of old movie and burlesque stunts for his effects. The club president's son spends much of his time rocking on a hobbyhorse. A couple of exploding cigars explode, and the wrapper on a chocolate bar conceals a pop-up butterfly. A panel in a door opens and a bottle of tequila flies in. Tennis balls bounce through the win-dows, and later bang rhythmically against the closed shutters. The tone of the comedy is more mocking than satirical (at least, I could see no indica-tion that Mr. Kopit wants to change or do away with Jewish country clubs), and the targets of his mockery are varied. A lot of what is said is coarse and indecent, but it didn't strike me as vulgar or out of keeping, and some of it is funny. *Oh Dad* dealt in part with a namby-pamby young man and his rapacious mother. This time, we have a namby-pamby young man and his contemptuous father. The son is much more overtly sissy, as the part is written—and, God knows, as it is played by Anthony Holland, who is nothing if not overt in everything he does. *Oh Dad* was farce, too, but as performed by an expert and subtly directed company it was farce with an undertone of horror. In *The Day the Whores*, there is no under-tone of anything. The play is better written than it sounded . . . —some of it is as harsh and unsparing as a tape recording—and perhaps Mr. Kopit's intentions (assuming he had any) would have become clearer if the acting had been better, which is to say less muffled, more on target, and not so distractingly and disagreeably broad.

Edith Oliver. *NY*. March 27, 1965, pp. 146–47

*Indians*, in its approach to history, is wildly unprofessional. But in its boldness and its surrealism, it may get us closer to historical and psychological realities than "factual" histories about Indians. *Indians* is perhaps our domestic *Slaughterhouse Five* in its focus upon racism and genocide in the American character and experience, now and in centuries past. And like Vonnegut's novel, or Heller's *Catch-22*, *Indians* uses sur-realistic technique to deal with certain American realities because no other technique—certainly not realism—will do. And that is because cer-tain American realities are surreal. . . .

To object that *Indians* distorts history is to miss the point. Kopit has said, in his use of dramatic technique, in his stage directions, in interviews, that *Indians* is not at all about historical Indians. *Indians* is about whites. About what they have made of Indians. About white myths. Perhaps the central message of the play is that bad as American actions have been in dealing with technologically weak minority and alien cultures—Indians or Vietnamese—worse yet is that white Americans have lied, not so much to others, but to themselves in insisting that their ends, their motives, were pure, pure enough to redeem their tainted means. . . .

Kopit's point is that Americans insist that what they do—whatever they do—is for the good of those to whom they do it. And this is because the superior mental and technological qualifications of white Americans enable them to see farther and deeper than "primitive" or "underdeveloped" peoples. If Kopit can somehow penetrate our psychological defensiveness and our historical defenses to that fundamental truth, then the validity of his unhistorical surrealistic method, and his deliberate and public distortion of historical facts in a morality play, will have been established.

Bruce Curtis. *AmEx*. Winter, 1973, p. 5

The language of the mind losing hold of words as it drifts off to sleep was first explored by Joyce in *Ulysses* at the end of the Ithaca episode. But it was Beckett who, in his plays and novels, evoked states bordering on, or representing, aphasia, albeit not literally reproducing clinical cases. [In *Wings*] Kopit pushes farther in that direction, but for all his research into and re-creation of actual defective speech by patients, he too keeps the verbiage within literary boundaries. Thus the work's master metaphor is wings, flying—symbolizing both speech winging its way from person to person and the psyche setting forth on perilous voyages into life and eventually, out of it.

The play has many virtues. The opening scene, which evokes a stroke by the simple flickering of lights and fading of sounds (the ticking of a clock) until there is both terrible silence and frightening clatter, is magisterial. So too is the use of several revolving black panels—now transparent, now opaque—combined with mirrors that distort and mislead to suggest the labyrinthine world of hospitals, sickness, inability to understand be understood. By various verbal and visual means, Kopit achingly conveys the humiliations of a disability that isolates a mind from its peers and makes of cross-purposes a spirit-breaking cross to bear. He gives us both charmingly wistful moments where patient and therapist become fellow ignoramuses before the mystery of words and moments of nervous humor when a speech-therapy group session yields funny contretemps amid tentative successes.

But, finally, the language of the play, especially in its supposedly most rapturously aerobatic moments, does not quite sustain the poetic flights and dramatic impact demanded from it. Moreover, the tragic conclusion, after strong promises of recovery, seems, though clinically possible, dramatically forced. Most serious of all, the several implications of the "wings" image never interlock completely with the blessed click of everything falling into place.

John Simon. *NYM*. July 10, 1978, pp. 66–67

On 13 October 1969, two days before the first national moratorium to end the war in Vietnam, Arthur L. Kopit's play, *Indians*, opened in New York. Walter Kerr, in his review of *Indians*, wrote, "We do not deserve a play in which the argument is unorganized, in which the conflict is undramatized." Indeed, to a nation plagued by upheavals at home and a surreal war abroad, *Indians* may have seemed as confusing as the milieu which helped to shape its theme and form. Between the London premiere of the play and its American debut in Washington, D.C., however, *Indians* had undergone numerous changes until Kopit had perfected a form which Lewis Funke described shortly after the Broadway opening as "a sort of collage." Largely because of this non-traditional, collage-like form, *Indians* has emerged as one of the most accomplished plays of the Vietnam era. . . .

Dialectics, both on stage and off, were characteristic of the decade. It is a measure of the achievement of *Indians* that in seeking to develop a new dramatic form Kopit managed to avoid the excesses of the avant-garde of the period, shaping a play which is neither historical drama nor representational in a traditional way. Whereas once-heralded works such as Megan Terry's *Viet Rock* (1966) or the musical *Hair* (1967) now seem firmly anchored to that time in terms of both theme and structure, *Indians* remains vital. Kopit offers in the play a portrait of Vietnam-era America which interprets history theatrically to describe the cumulative effect of that history—contemporary life—in a new, dramatically viable way. Through Kopit's imaginative response to drama and to history, he discovered in *Indians* what Robert Brustein has called the truest poetic function of the theatre—"to invent metaphors which poignantly suggest a nation's nightmares and afflictions."

To do so, Kopit created a play which he intended to be perceived as a mosaic. *Indians* transcends the artistic embroilment of its time to address the timeless issues of myth and power in the American character. The initial concept of the play conveniently accommodated itself to the synthesis of various dramatic styles and theatrical modes into a loose, but cohesive, whole. Kopit claims the idea for *Indians* came to him while simultaneously reading a statement on American policy in Vietnam issued by General William Westmoreland and listening to Charles Ives' Fourth Symphony: "In it two orchestras play against each other. One plays chamber music, the other distorted marching band music. The idea and form for the play seemed to come to me in a flash." Organic from its inception, then, *Indians*, despite both its title and critical explanation of the play as a sharp attack on white America's treatment of the red man, is exclusively about Indians as much as Ibsen's *Ghosts* is about venereal disease. The play explores Buffalo Bill Cody's contrary impulses to help the red man and to destroy him—a situation analogous to the effect of an American presence in Southeast Asia on the people of Vietnam. The plight of the red man in *Indians* indicates, as does Oswald's disease in *Ghosts*, a larger, more destructive force embedded in the entire social structure. "I wanted to expose the madness of our involvement in Vietnam," Kopit said of his intentions in *Indians*. "I had believed for some time that what was happening was the symptom of a national disease.". . .

By using poetic license with history, Kopit makes an equation between the American past and the American present, while simultaneously placing *Indians* in a realm beyond the confines of a documentary drama, or the so-called "theatre of fact.". . . "I wanted to capture the nightmarish confusion of being bombarded by statements, by justifications, by historical references," Kopit has stated. "The only way to present this in a play was to create a sense of disorientation in the audience." The earlier *Chamber Music* anticipates this approach. Like *Indians*, it blurs the distinction between the "now" of the play and the "then" of history. By reincarnating different epochs and different movements in art and politics through each inmate's mad delusion in *Chamber Music*, Kopit blends all of history into the single world of the play, a world which becomes theatrically viable because each member of the audience is forced to make referential connections, to step into history and back out as part of one continuous response, and thus complete the artifice of the play.

Michael C. O'Neill. *TJ*. Dec., 1982, pp. 493–94,<br>498

# KOSINSKI, JERZY (1933–   )

[A] quality found in all of Kosinski's novels [is] a dispassionate rendering of the human condition, sometimes for the sake of possible correction, sometimes for the sake of simple understanding. One of the most fascinating outcomes of reading the modern parables that make up *Cockpit* is our insight into the ambiguities of the self. The very title, *Cockpit*, serves to point up man's ambiguous state. An actual airplane cockpit, the heart of a controlling mechanism designed to destroy people, appears only once in the entire novel, but one finds it a number of times in disguise. From that high perch, Tarden [the protagonist] can look down upon the rest of mankind: he considers himself to be free because everyone is his potential victim. He can act rather than he acted upon. On the other hand, the word "cockpit" is a sexual pun which ultimately suggests Tarden's entrapment in the human condition, part of which is death. . . .

According to Kosinski, the act of remembering operates in uncontrollable spurts with little linkage. He once suggested that one can create a montage of memories in much the same way that one can create a montage of celluloid shots. He noted that "the cinematic image has become the key to modern perception." In *Cockpit*, the Eisensteinian theory of montage, shot A plus shot B creates a shot C of the imagination, is what the author counts on to structure both the novel and our recognition of its truths.

Gerald Barrett. MQR. Summer, 1976, pp.<br>357, 359

Jerry Kosinski is not *moraliste*. He is one of the post-modern novelists passed on by Dostoevsky as Evil, and turned Indifferent by Camus and Robbe-Grillet. Well aware of rejecting the Christian moral universe, Kosinski is not signing up with the affirmative traditions in literature, in which a man and his transcendence count, as they did even in the works of such nonbelievers as Jean-Paul Sartre, and as they still do in Saul Bellow's "holy" fiction. . . .

Jerzy Kosinski's novels lie in the area between the post-war European emotional lucidity and the hip coolness of American mid-generation. His is a non-judgmental, morally permissive fiction, in which action is meant not as salvation, but as making the most of life. In Kosinski's novels, man does not have a character by which he is doomed; he adjusts himself to reality by denying his civilized self and his moral judgment. He forms a personality-free character in a personality-free world.

Kosinski's novels are agitated, ghoulish yarns, told in dispassionate, icy language. They are void of realistic linearity and of emotional temperature. The untitled "chapters" form the unconnected units of narration, space and time are fragmented, little actions follow like digressions, the plotless plot converges rather than continues; words do not burn, as in passionate texts, but are lucid and conniving.

Kosinski's characterless characters have no fixed personalities, yet they do have consistent ego. Like a Pirandellian hero (it was Pirandello who finally got rid of characters, as Joyce did away with recognizably continuous storytelling), the Kosinski protagonist exists from moment to moment. Continually creating himself anew, he never achieves a solidified, hard-core reality of a continuous hero. The story line is the unfinished and unfinishable business of life; thus, it is not accidental that every novel ends inconclusively, with the hero looking out of the window into future spaces. . . .

As a "vile" Romantic, already acknowledged as a legitimate character of many authors who have declared war on the bourgeoisie, Kosinski is entitled to a denial of tragedy and suffering as useless; the best writers did that. Even Brecht in his Marxist period did not postulate that the conflict of the diseased business ethics of our times and decayed Christian morality was reconcilable through sacrifice. But he convinced us of the existence of a connection between people that goes beyond guilt, by the creation of vivid realities and vivid characters. The writers of the massive masterpieces, such as Balzac, Tolstoy or Melville, as well as authors of existential works such as Camus or Mailer, fleshed out the dangerous realities of consciousness and conscience. They created live people out of the dead matrix of words, endowed them with affective life, supplied them with gestures of desire. Without desire, without ecstasy, without failure purified in death (the death of the rebel, as well as his victim), the literature of cruelty does not restore the reader or renew society's vision. The most nihilistic texts, brimming over with lacerating despair and rage, were informed by emotional fullness. Even when nothing could satisfy the desire, the repetitious pattern of desire sustained the life of the characters, the life of the novels.

Krystyna Prendowska. JNT. Winter, 1978, pp. 11,<br>13, 23–24

The five-book cycle from *The Painted Bird* to *Cockpit* has explored the relative values of personal security and power, from the orphan Boy cast loose upon the battlefield of World War II to the supremely confident agent controlling life from his self-contained cockpit. Kosinski's subsequent novel, *Blind Date*, is closest in spirit to *Cockpit*, for it details the similar adventures of another mature protagonist—this time named George Levanter. However, Kosinski has made this newer novel the closest record to his own experiences since *The Painted Bird*. . . .

The themes of Kosinski's novels, then, have shifted since *The Painted Bird*. In the social context of that novel, personal self-sufficiency was the goal. *Steps* tested this goal against the social union of two persons, who could best meet as equals within their own selves. But with *Being There* the problematics of life—especially life in America—began to assert themselves, and Kosinski's next three novels present a series of protagonists each more calculating and austere than the last, from Jonathan Whalen through Tarden to George Levanter. Yet the development was not entirely negative, for in *Blind Date* a new philosophy was offered.

Jerome Klinkowitz. *Literary Disruptions*, 2nd ed.
(Univ. of Illinois Pr., 1980), pp. 214, 216

The issue of violence in Kosinski's work . . . is a complex one, and one which he knows touches the center of his achievement as a writer. Whatever that achievement is, his books are not so much a preoccupation with violence as they are complex studies in the shifting identity of victim and oppressor. Power, not violence, is what fascinates Kosinski. All of his main characters—the boy in *The Painted Bird*, Tarden in *Cockpit*, Levanter in *Blind Date*, Fabian in *Passion Play*, indeed Kosinski himself—have known powerlessness and victimization. Their natural impulse (and here is where Kosinski is most compelling as a writer) is to transform themselves from victim to oppressor. . . .

In the world of Kosinski, there are no other options open to the victim: he must seize power through deception or remain powerless. Divesting one's self of the identity of victim means assuming the identity of the oppressor. Or, as Mitka the Cuckoo explains to the boy in *The Painted Bird*, "Man carries in himself his own justice, which is his alone to administer." Since each person is intensely alone, everything that is outside the individual self—political structures, nation states, business institutions, friends, lovers—represents a potential enemy, and must be constantly deceived or destroyed before it transforms that person into victim. . . .

Kosinski's personal vision, his insistence that we should develop "an awareness of life as it happens in each of its moments, and that man must treat each of those moments as unique," is consistently and convincingly portrayed in his novels. But if the vision is new, it is not a moral one. A code of behavior that treats each moment as unique but excludes an evaluation of the meaning of that moment, especially the moment's possible ramifications of pain and suffering for others, can not also be a moral code. Granted, the moment is unique, unrepeatable; the question, and one which Kosinski begs continually in his fiction, is what to *do* with the moment. Rape Nameless? Help a refugee from a police state? Photograph Valerie being raped? Arrange to have an imprisoned writer released? The problem with the vision, and with the code of behavior derived from the vision, is that it is too simple: life is reduced to a series of unique moments that elude evaluation. Human relationships are reduced to power plays between victim and oppressor. But a moral vision implies awareness of complexity, the presence of doubt, ambiguity, involvement, despair, joy. Kosinski offers sequences of moments, each unique and powerfully narrated, but with all the complexity of life simply abstracted (Tarden's words came back: "I could abstract myself from its power") until the moment is nearly a hollow shell.

Paul R. Lilly, Jr. *LitR*. Spring, 1982, pp. 390–91, 400

## KUNITZ, STANLEY (1905–    )

Through all the particulars of this volume [*A Kind of Order, a Kind of Folly*], a uniform quality of mind pervades—a quality marked by reasonableness, sensitivity, lucidity, and balance. One thinks inevitably of Aristotle's Magnanimous Man, of Camus' *homme du midi*. His materials he has arranged into associative groups which, like the stanzas of a poem, proceed processionally from one to the next. Just as in a poem we almost invariably have favorite passages, favorite isolatable lines, individual readers will no doubt find their sympathies unequally distributed among the components of this book. . . . Yet the volume, for all its diversity, is one. It is made so by Mr. Kunitz's persistent conceptualization of the nature of art, and by the tough and unfailing elegance of his style. . . .

It is no doubt a judgment of our age that we find good sense astounding. Mr. Kunitz has it, and to an astonishing degree. He says a great many things which, in this late frantic hour of our art, need desperately once again to be said—which is to say of course that they need desperately once again to be heard. . . . The spirit by which Kunitz's book is informed— the spirit of simple truthfulness, lucidity, and compassion—will survive to perpetually generate new works and new voices out of its ache.

Richard Vine. *Salmagundi*. Winter, 1977, pp. 120–21, 123

All of Kunitz's poems . . . , early and late, are lyrical, personal, emotional, and intense. None of his poems is public or occasional like Robert Lowell's "Quaker Graveyard at Nantucket" or "For the Union Dead." Reading Kunitz, rather, one comes to know the persona of the poet and his feelings about the "fable" of his life, though still not in the personally identifiable, anguished way one does in the poetry of such "confessional" poets as Lowell himself (in his nonpublic aspect) or Anne Sexton or Sylvia Plath.

For Kunitz is not at all a confessional poet, and most likely he would himself, too, as he said about Roethke, "vomit . . . at the thought" of being called one. As he said, "Secrets are part of the legend," the "fable" of his life. And his own "emphasis isn't on spilling everything." Hence, although he writes about himself in the main, he by no means tells "all." Neither, on the other hand, are the figures that march through his poems masks or objective creations, the Tiresiases, Odysseuses, Prufrocks, Mauberleys, Crazy Janes, Catherines, or Kavanaughs or Eliot, Pound, Yeats, and Lowell.

Like theirs, of course, some of his poetry is allusive, but not greatly so. Allusions, particularly those to the classical tradition, are rather much a well-read poet's stock in trade—especially in his youth. And so some of Kunitz's poems make references to various mythic persons, places, objects, and events: Oedipus, Odysseus, Agamemnon, Clytemnestra, Apollo, Zeus; Thebes, Point Lotus, Lethe; golden bough, laurel, and shower of gold—among others. Most of these do not seem to be obscure, are not central, and would appear to be used principally to recall eternally true stories and motifs.

In Kunitz's poetry such allusions become rarer as he turned his own life into fable and found therein such mythic parallels as the "Lilith" woman in "The Dark and the Fair" and the lost father in "Father and Son." Both of these take on archetypal lineaments, though they are grounded firmly, it seems, in experience and in the poet's examination of his own life. . . .

Kunitz's work consists already of a few nearly perfect poems of great intensity, passion, and universality and a further body of good poems that ensure his reputation. Besides all these, his book of essays and conversations, rather neglected so far, and his translations from Russian round out a long, busy life that was remarkable in its single-minded dedication to poetry. Underlying everything he has done is his conviction as to the seriousness of poetry: "Like Hopkins' bird of peace, a poem does not come to coo; it comes with work to do." Kunitz's own life has been, in his phrase about Keats's, not a career but "a life of poetry."

Marie Hénault. *Stanley Kunitz* (Twayne, 1980),
pp. 29–30, 142

# ● LE GUIN, URSULA K. (1929–   )

*The Lathe of Heaven* . . . is really a very neat performance, accomplishing what science fiction is supposed to do. The time is 2002, the hero a passive man who discovers that his dreams are out of control. George's dreams change reality. Whatever George dreams comes true as he dreams it; moreover, his dreams cover their tracks, changing the past and what people remember as well. Naturally people are reluctant to believe George's story—but George is terrified. His "effective" dreams, as he calls them, began in a small way—a relative killed, a picture changed— but in time he dreams of the alteration of the world and history. The earth's population is decimated; its wars intensified and then halted; an alien planet attacks . . . and all because George dreamed it. An ambitious psychiatrist discovers that under hypnosis George will dream what he is told and so the psychiatrist can play God, advancing both his own career and history as he wishes—except that, as we know from Freud, dreams like to play tricks.

Ursula Le Guin is extremely inventive. She shifts her continuum of the world and its past every few pages, playing expertly on alternative suggestions as to what we may expect from violence, war and overpopulation. She has a nice sense of irony, too: for all his tremendous power, George remains virtually a prisoner; for all the horror of his dreams, the world actually seems to improve. Science fiction is rarely able to offer a sustained view of an interesting alternative to the world we know, and Mrs. Le Guin does not attempt to do so; instead, she provides the brief glimpses, the partial speculations that I have suggested are essential to a story of this kind. Even her moral—that we cannot stand outside the world and direct it but must be content to be part of the whole—is gracefully developed. It is, after all, what the ecologists are still trying to tell us.

Peter S. Prescott. Newsweek. Nov. 29, 1971,<br>p. 106

Her fiction is closer to fantasy than naturalism, but it is just as grounded in ethical concerns as [John] Brunner's work, despite its apparent distance from present actualities. Though some would argue that her political novel, *The Dispossessed* (1974), is her best work, and others might favor her ecological romance, *The Word for World Is Forest* (1972, 1976), or her young people's fantasy, *A Wizard of Earthsea* (1968), today's critical consensus is still that her best single work is *The Left Hand of Darkness* (1969).

In *The Left Hand of Darkness* Le Guin moves far from our world in time and space, to give us a planet where life has evolved on different lines from our own. This world, which happens to be in a period of high glaciation, has evolved political institutions in two adjoining countries that resemble feudalism on the one hand, and bureaucracy on the other. But the most important difference between this world and our own is that its human inhabitants are different from us in their physical sexuality. All beings on the planet Gethen have both male and female sexual organs. In a periodic cycle like estrus in animals, Gethenians become sexually aroused—but only one set of sexual organs is activated at this time. These people are potentially hermaphroditic. Most of the time they are neuter, but then they may briefly become a man or a woman, and in that time beget a child or conceive one. Thus the same person may experience both fatherhood and motherhood at different times. . . . The major effect of Le Guin's imagining such a fictional world is to force us to examine how sexual stereotyping dominates actual human concepts of personality and influences all human relationships. . . .

Ursula Le Guin has been attacked by radical feminists for not going far enough, for using male protagonists, as she does even in *The Left Hand of Darkness*, and for putting other issues, both political and environmental, ahead of feminism. In fact, it is probably wrong to think of her as a feminist. But I know of no single book likely to raise consciences about sexism more thoroughly and convincingly than this one. And that this is done gently, in a book which manages also to be a fine tale of adventure and a tender story of love and friendship, makes the achievement all the more remarkable. There are few writers in the United States who offer fiction as pleasurable and thoughtful as Ursula Le Guin's. It is time for her to be recognized beyond the special province of fantasy and science fiction or feminism as simply one of our best writers.

Robert Scholes. *NR*. Oct. 30, 1976, pp. 39–40

"*An die Musik*" and *Orsinian Tales* are acts of imagination that transform the calamity of history that is Central Europe into a celebration of the individual's ability to survive bad times. . . . Le Guin has consistently occupied herself with her own inner life. She has always written fantasy, searching not in the outside world, but in her own creative unconscious, for the subjects of her fiction. The course of her development from the early sixties into the middle seventies has been a series of attempts to develop for herself the means of expressing her own suffering (which, of course, can be ethical and political as well as psychological) and its conquest more precisely and clearly. She would probably agree with Rilke's repeated assertion that we are "only just where we persist in praising."

But she also feels the need to blame. The strength of her convictions and her ethical principles demands that. When her fiction blames, however, as *The Word for World is Forest* does, it is less just.

Ultimately, the real subject of "*An die Musik*" and the rest of Le Guin's fiction that explores ethical problems is not a group of ethical questions. These are means, not ends. Her purpose is to ask them, not to answer them. The real subject of "*An die Musik*" is celebration; the tale is a celebration of Gaye's devotion to his art, and beyond that, a celebration of art itself. That is the meaning of its title. Like . . . many other Le Guin characters, Gaye is an "enemy of the feasible." Le Guin places so many obstacles between him and his music not merely to wrestle with questions about the duty of the artist and the function of art, but to dramatize more vividly Gaye's capacity to endure and survive, and to pursue an ideal without compromising either himself or his goal.

James W. Bittner. SFS. Nov., 1978, p. 235

*The Dispossessed* . . . has both implicit and explicit connections with anarchism and utopian tradition. Its very title recalls the English title of Dostoevsky's controversial satire (*The Possessed*) on Nechayev and his nihilist gangsterism, a movement related to anarchism through its influence on Bakunin. In its more obvious sense, though, "dispossessed" refers to the freedom from property that is central to anarchism and which is actualized in Odonian society. Indeed, elsewhere Le Guin has indicated her partiality for anarchism as a political ideal, stating that the thematic motivation of *The Dispossessed* was to accomplish for the first time the embodiment of that ideal in a novel. Similarly, the novel's subtitle ("An Ambiguous Utopia") indicates that it is to be read as a contribution to the utopian tradition, while its structure, which alternates chapters narrating Shevek's experiences on Urras with episodes from his life on Anarres, conveys the dialectic of old world and new world that is central to utopian satire and vision.

John P. Brennan and Michael C. Downs. In<br>Ursula K. Le Guin, ed. Joseph D. Olander and<br>Martin Harry Greenberg (Taplinger, 1979),<br>p. 117

It is not uncommon, as a literary technique, to employ a critical individual who narrates as the action unfolds. Ursula Le Guin takes this device one step further, making of her protagonists participant-observers; in short, she transforms them into anthropologists. Her heroes all seem to have characteristics that separate them from the worlds in which they find themselves: they are either off-worlders whose job may be explicitly that of an ethnographer, such as Rocannon (*Rocannon's World*) or Genly Ai (*The Left Hand of Darkness*), or they are the skeptics and freethinkers in their native society, as in the cases of Selver and Lyubov (*The Word for World Is Forest*) and Shevek (*The Dispossessed*). Because they are outsiders with the outsider's critical viewpoint, they are cast in the mold of anthropologists, with the perspective and unique dilemmas of the discipline. Repeatedly in her fiction we confront individuals who are of society and yet not quite a part of it. The outsider, the alien, the marginal man, adopts a vantage point with rather serious existential and philosophical implications. For Le Guin this marginality becomes a metaphor whose potency is fulfilled in a critical assessment of society. . . .

Le Guin squarely confronts the isolation and loneliness of her protagonists. Themes such as xenophobia, a suspicion and mistrust of all that is different, are developed in all her work, but reach a clear culmination in 1972 in *WWF*. Here there is an explicit presentation of the heroes (Lyubov and Selver) as anthropologists in their roles as outsiders and translators. Consistently her portrayal is pessimistic. Such individuals suffer heartily. Abandoned, misread, and psychologically disoriented, they often sacrifice themselves or are sacrificed for their understanding. Yet often they represent the only hope.

Le Guin has, essentially, two modes for presenting her protagonists as outsiders: either they are true aliens (for example, Rocannon, Lyubov, Genly Ai, and Falk-Ramarren [*City of Illusions*]) or they are natives of a society, yet their perception of social life nevertheless sets them apart (for example, Shevek, Selver, Estraven [*LHD*], Jakob Agat [*Planet of Exile*], and George Orr [*The Lathe of Heaven*]). In either case, their problems, and more importantly their solutions, are of a similar nature. Their apartness precludes their complete membership in, or commitment to, any particular society. Yet their critical viewpoint gives them an insight into the nature of social relations that eludes their fellows. . . .

In the final analysis, however, Le Guin's anthropologist-outsiders have the edge over their fellows. For all their solitariness, their convictions are strengthened by their ordeals. They are no longer mystified by differences. They can grant humanity to others because they cease to glorify or stigmatize that which is not immediately comprehensible. The irony is that in their realization that opposition does not necessarily imply impenetrable boundaries, they erect barriers between themselves and their society. Because they recognize that the task of understanding is not impossible, they contribute to their own isolation. Their perception of balance is an appreciation of differences. And it is here that the paradox ultimately resides; for if there is an aloneness in the chaos of social life, there is even greater solitariness once order is achieved.

Karen Sinclair. In *Ursula K. Le Guin: Voyager to Inner Lands and to Outer Space*, ed. Joe De Bolt (Kennikat, 1979), pp. 50–52, 64–65

In the nine novels and numerous short works which she has written between 1962 and 1976, the exploration of imaginary worlds has provided a
framework for an exploration of the varieties of physical life, social
organizations, and personal development open to human beings. At the
same time, this richness and variety suggest the ethical concept underlying her work: a celebration of life itself, through a joyful acceptance of its
patterns. This concept is expressed not only in the works themselves, but
in her vision of the artistic process which brought them forth. . . . In general, her characters are engaged in a quest, both a physical journey to an
unknown goal which proves to be their home, and an inward search for
knowledge of the one true act they must perform. The development of the
plot, then, takes on a deeper significance than is usual in science fiction,
with its emphasis on action for the sake of entertainment. The Le Guin
character often initiates actions which have personal and social consequences. . . . More important than the pattern of plot, however, is each
character's movement to an understanding of this pattern: to an acceptance both of the integrity of each individual life, and of the place of each
individual within the overall pattern of life. . . .

Le Guin's weakness is a paradoxical tendency to impose moral and
ethical patterns on her work, so that form and content work against her
philosophy. This didacticism is most evident in "The Word for World Is
Forest" (1972), "The Ones Who Walk Away from Omelas" (1972), and
passages of *The Dispossessed*. The author's statement of values precludes
their discovery, in contrast to the process, most notable in the Earthsea
books, whereby the reader shares naturally in the characters' growing
awareness of the right direction of their lives. Such a tendency is inevitable, however, given Le Guin's serious concern with human experience
and conduct. It is this concern, usually embodied convincingly in individuals' actions and perceptions, which has made her one of the most notable writers to choose science fiction as a framework for discovery.

Ursula Le Guin's work, then, is mature art: rich and varied in content, skillful in presentation, joyous in its celebration of life, and, above
all, thoughtful in approach, rooted in and developing a significant personal philosophy. The maturity is literal as well as literary.

Susan Wood. In Voices for the Future: Essays on<br>
Major Science Fiction Writers, Vol. 2, ed. Thomas<br>
D. Clareson (Bowling Green State Univ.<br>
Popular Pr., 1979), pp. 154–56

Surely one sign of the serious artist is the willingness to subordinate the
part to the whole. Somehow, through her faithfulness to the controlling
conception of the work, the artist hopes to create a whole that transcends
the sum of its parts. I think Le Guin has done this in *The Left Hand of*

*Darkness*, but that is not all of her accomplishment. The artist's desire for coherence can lead to dogmatism; in this case, unity can easily become sterility. Freud observed that life resists order, that perfect order is synonymous with death. This observation is germane to *Left Hand*, not only because the dualism it implies is thematically relevant to Le Guin's holistic vision but because the book offers us both the satisfaction of artistic unity and the richness of a complex diversity. For almost every statement she gives us, Le Guin supplies a counterstatement. No truth is allowed to stand as the entire truth; every insight is presented as partial, subject to revision and another perspective. . . .

Such subtle but pervasive insistence that every truth is a partial truth is, of course, wholly consistent with Le Guin's controlling vision for this book, since if she allowed any truth to stand as *the* truth, the sense that wholeness emerges from a tension between dualities would be lost. The delicate balance of conflicting possibilities that Le Guin posits means, for one thing, that the book is rarely in danger of becoming dogma. It also means that, for a complete expression of Le Guin's holistic vision, nothing less than the entire structure of the book will suffice. The final whole that emerges is the book itself. And this kind of unity, which encompasses within itself all manner of diversity, makes *The Left Hand of Darkness* itself an example of the creative fecundity that is possible when differences are not suppressed but used to create a new whole. For all these reasons, *The Left Hand of Darkness* is one of Le Guin's finest books, and an enduring literary achievement.

N. B. Hayles. In *Ursula K. Le Guin*, ed. Joseph
D. Olander and Martin Harry Greenberg
(Taplinger, 1979), pp. 113–15

The importance of Ursula Le Guin's contribution to science fiction lies in her ability to use a distinctly Western art form to communicate the essence that is Tao. In many of her novels, Tao is the universal base upon which societies and individual characters act. The fact that Tao exists not in rational systems but in life and the imaginative construct of life that we call art makes the critic's task of revealing the methods and materials of Le Guin's imaginative integration a very difficult one. . . . The Taoist mythos . . . permeates the three novels—*City of Illusions*, *The Left Hand of Darkness*, and *The Dispossessed*—which I think best communicate it. . . .

Le Guin is a deliberate, conscientious writer who not only creates fully developed cultures in each of her novels, but who has woven them together into an entire cosmogony, giving, in the course of all her novels and stories, a history of the spread of civilization from Hain-Davenant to the Ekumen of eighty worlds, of which Terra is a part. She weaves social and political commentary into her cultural presentation, as in the conflicts between Karhide and Orgoreyn in *The Left Hand of Darkness*, or Anarres and Urras in *The Dispossessed*, always set within the larger scale of humanity as an integral part of the balance of the cosmos. Finally, her style mirrors the balance of her themes. Her writing moves gently but inexorably. To use another analogy from Lao Tzu, it is like a deep pool of water, seemingly inactive, but actually teeming with life. She, too, like the Sage, influences by actionless activity. The value of her work lies in the combination of all these elements, and others, into a complete overview of what it means to be human, no matter on what world, in what cultural subdivision, humans find themselves.

Dena C. Bain. *Extrapolation*. Fall, 1980, pp. 209, 221

Le Guin is a seeker who uses her imagination. If she returns again and again to fantasy and science fiction, it is not only because these genres are traditionally ones that make use of journeys and marvels. It is also because they offer great scope to the creative mind. Le Guin is convinced, as she explains in her essay, "Why Are Americans Afraid of Dragons?", that we must use imagination, as long as it is disciplined by art, for our minds to be fully alive and well.

She says this in defense of fantasy. But what is true of fantasy is, for her, also true of science fiction. She recognizes that they are different forms and, after her early novels, she has tried not to mix them. But, all the same, she feels that there is a similarity between them. . . .

Le Guin is a romantic, and as a romantic she values love, nature, adventure, marvels, dreams, the imagination, and the unconscious. Like the romantics, she is aware of the dark side of things and is attracted by it, even when she prefers the light. She values the individual and his or her struggle for personal liberation. And she expresses that struggle in a language that, while straightforward, makes use of poetic metaphor. But like the Brontës, she manages to be romantic and realistic at the same time. Her early apprenticeship to the description of people's daily lives, even if those lives were led in a country that cannot be found on any map, taught her skill in handling specific detail. She uses that skill to good effect in her fantasy and science fiction.

However, it is hardly surprising that she did not find a publisher for her first novels. Romantics are not welcome nowadays in mainstream literature. It is in fantasy and science fiction that such an unfashionable attitude can find a home, since these genres offer a great deal of liberty to the writer. Certain conventions have to be observed, but within these conventions there is scope for the widest variety of outlook, approach, and style. Because of her love of personal freedom, Ursula K. Le Guin has chosen the genre that affords the greatest freedom to her mind, for which we can well be grateful.

Barbara J. Bucknall. Ursula K. Le Guin (Ungar, 1981), pp. 153–54

## LEVERTOV, DENISE (1923–    )

Levertov's poetry derives most directly from the masculine tradition that dominates modern poetry, although both its recurrent ambivalence and frequent flashes of vibrant strength seem to me to arise out of an engagement with her feminine experience. . . .

Levertov . . . occupies a significant and transitional position in the history of poetry by women because her work contains elements of both the dominant masculine and the emerging feminine traditions. She seems to see herself as poet, not as woman poet. Over the twenty-five years of her poetic career, her work has grown in skill and refinement, but there has been little change in either her aesthetic theories or the forms in which they are rendered. Writing closely within a mainstream of modern poetry—"imagistic," "organic"—she also brings to her work a spiritual, religious element and particular kind of personalism (that of her feminine experience). Sometimes these elements work together in harmony; at other times they struggle with one another, affecting the unity of a given poem. A need to abstract and to generalize upon the greater significance of an experience (a distancing movement found in both the poetic and the spiritual traditions in which she works) is sometimes at odds with an involvement and an immediacy that arise most strongly in poems that deal with intense personal experience (in particular, the feminine and the political). . . .

Levertov's poetry constantly explores the relation between the inner world of dream and the outer world of action precisely because this dynamic is the very source of poetry itself. . . .

Because she is a woman, the experience that her poems require for their existence is feminine experience. The dominant qualities of those experiences of nature, art, people, and politics that make up her poems are their personal and private nature and their circumscribed boundaries. Such qualities have come to be associated with women's experience, so on that level Levertov's poetry seems very feminine. Even when her poetry becomes more public in its involvement with political issues, such as the

Vietnam war, it continues to explore these problems in relation to every-day and private life.

Suzanne Juhasz. *Naked and Fiery Forms: Modern*
*American Poetry by Women—A New Tradition*
(Octagon Books, 1976), pp. 58–61

[Levertov's] poems have been an important part of the contemporary literary scene for twenty years. When the formalist 1950s relaxed to accept Allen Ginsberg's "Howl" and Robert Creeley's short-lined love poems, Levertov's work offered a kind of middle ground: poems in which rich sound patterns balanced "natural speech"; poems in which a humanistic credo—and the need to express it—overshadowed the mere presentation of an image. From the first, Levertov had insisted that a poet had to use all language resources available. She had also declared that every poet had firm social responsibilities. . . .

The tone of many of the poems in *The Freeing of the Dust* is quieter, more satisfied—not with the physical or social circumstances of life, but with a human being's ability to cope with those circumstances. There is much emphasis here on exploring the fullest ranges of consciousness and psyche, and I was reminded of her 1972 essay on Ezra Pound in which she praised his writing because "He stirs me into a sharper realization of my own sensibility. I learn to desire not to know what he knows but to know what I know: to emulate, not to imitate." Poems here echo with this com-pletion of earlier promise, with the sense of Levertov as person knowing herself, being, and becoming, through both life and poetry. *The Freeing of the Dust* is an amazingly rich book, giving us the image of Levertov as fully realized poet, humanist, seer and—not the least—as woman. In the process of complete engagement, a poet who is also a woman must, finally, speak with a woman's voice: any denial of that primary identity would play havoc with the self-determination of the poem. There are perhaps too many women who use the crutch of sexual identity to make bad poems effective, but when Levertov creates the feminine identity, as in the evocative "Cancion," its use is powerful. . . .

In countless other ways, this 1975 collection re-states Levertov's strengths as poet. It impresses with its versatility: there are seven groups of poems, ranging from the political commentaries to poems about love and divorce; from masterful sequences to the single-image poems that reach further than any image poems have any right to. Not a collected or selected work, *The Freeing of the Dust* gives a reader the sense that the searching vicissitudes of American poetry during the past half century have brought us to an art capable of expressing (and first recognizing) both "despair" and "wildest joy."

Linda Wagner. *SCR*. Spring, 1979, pp. 18–21

When Levertov makes myth serve humanity—that idol of prophets and politicians—it is sluggish in its duties. She is a dreamer at heart, and her best moments are stolen, solitary ones, glimpses of a landscape at one A.M. when "humanity" has long since gone to bed. Recently Levertov has used dream to diagram experience (the anguish of her mother's death, the uncertainty of a love affair); but if these are to be read as dreams at all we can be sure the superego has done a lot of work to get them into their present, analyzable shape, for again the language is more illuminating when it is aimed at the border between the human and the non-human, or into the caverns of the unconscious. In *The Double Image*, in fact, she is a little wary of dream, which does not so much clarify her relations with others as disrupt them, and draws her away from the security of familiar rooms. As the "walls of dream" close behind her, they open onto a stunning landscape of solitude. The native inhabitants of that landscape are the blind, who have been her visionary guides since *The Double Image*. Her initial ambivalence toward these "seers" is apparent in "Fear of the Blind." But in "Life in the Forest" they have become her compatriots, and she is dedicating poems to them, for wiping clean a world smudged with pain. . . .

Levertov is really a romantic poet, giving what she gazes at "the recognition no look ever before granted it." This is much the same compliment Coleridge paid to Wordsworth, and it is how Levertov identifies her archetypal poet in the lyrical "Growth of a Poet." That the poem is paired with another more discursive and anecdotal "Conversation in Moscow," which deals with the poet as social critic, suggests a continued division between her private and public selves. The two come together rhetorically in the "mineshaft of passion," but between the deep canyon of "duende" and the Black Sea of "human reality" lies a continent she is only beginning to cross.

Bonnie Costello. *Parnassus*. Fall/Winter, 1979,
pp. 201, 211

## LEWIS,   SINCLAIR   (1885–1951)

[Lewis], unlike any other major writer of his time, presents initial obstacles for the reader which are so spiky that one wonders how one is to surmount them to approach an evaluation of the enduring qualities of his work. There are, first, the books established on the mushy ground of such trivial notions as "play." There are the badly conceived books even after his apprentice days had ended—books like *Mantrap*, *Work of Art*, *Bethel Merriday*, *The God-Seeker*, *World So Wide*. In his best books there are many pages of poor prose and absurd notions. But I have tried to suggest that Lewis, born in a transitional age in American literary history and being a brash youth with few of the "standards" which in the Nobel speech he lamented were needed in American literature, had to fight his way through the appeal and the repulsion of cults and fads before he could establish a position from which, first, to direct his satire, and, second, to sustain his documentation of reality. If, now, . . . we have gained some understanding of the evolution of Lewis's imagination 'and have examined his skill in reporting some of the argument of American society and some of the concerns of American individuals, then we can ask, hasn't Lewis left us one additional gift? For it his idol, Dickens, served him well. The search for the value of American life continues—in society and within ourselves. In fact, it has intensified. His representation of it can move us by its terrible sense of pain and urgency. Furthermore, though the atmosphere of language in which his seekers wandered was noxious, by pushing his fantastic power of mimicry to the limit, he prophesied the crazier oratory of our day. The editorialist; the racist preacher; the retired militarist; the professional hireling; the rationalist for defoliation; the ad-writer for half-empty boxes; the "poemulator" who sells millions of books and phonograph records; the leering sexologist; the inciter of violence; the astrology cultist; the talkers, talkers, talkers—they all pollute the air. But whether they know it or not, they squawk through loudspeakers and gesticulate before distortion mirrors that Sinclair Lewis set up a generation ago.

Martin Light. *The Quixotic Vision of Sinclair Lewis* (Purdue Univ. Pr., 1975), pp. 143–44

If it is true, as E. M. Forster noted, that Sinclair Lewis managed to "lodge a piece of a continent in our imagination," it would be no less true to observe that in a sense this achievement required constant appeals to his image of another continent. That continent, of course, was "Yurrup," or, more conventionally, Europe. Though ranged against the entire *oeuvre* few of the novels address the European question directly, all reflect the influence of what Lewis believed Europe to be and to mean. Certainly it is not without significance that the bulk of events in both his very first book, *Our Mr. Wrenn* (1914), and his very last book, *World So Wide* (1951), should occur in a European setting, a setting not sketched in as accidental background but treated in such a way as to constitute an important strain in the novels' thematic structure. Moreover, that he should have turned at the end of his glorious decade, presumably secure in the feeling that he was at the height of his powers—having with *Main Street* (1920), *Babbitt* (1922), *Arrowsmith* (1925), and *Elmer Gantry* (1927) persuaded his critics that his apprenticeship had made way for a certain mastery and not yet suspecting that this mastery would soon disintegrate—to a direct confrontation with Europe in *Dodsworth* (1929) testifies to a compelling interest in the subject. . . .

His Europe, never to enter his thinking totally divested of a romantic halo, was from the beginning rarely a reality objectively considered but an object of vague desires and dreams which neither the observed actuality could completely contradict nor his own maturity entirely dismiss. It is why he so often appeals to the European past, a medieval and chivalric Europe, or a Europe as incarnated in a woman, the Dodsworthian "Not Impossible She." But with the Europe, say, which, by the time he was writing *Our Mr. Wrenn*, was soon to be the muddy and bloody terrain of the First World War, or with the Europe which, by the time he was writing *World So Wide*, had recently suffered the ravages of the Second World War, he preferred not to deal. And since the needs of his inner life were answered only by an imaginary Europe, contrasting the actual Europe with his native land (a task attempted with *Dodsworth*) could scarcely result in a rationally reached conclusion in favor of one or the other. Neither as proud patriot nor as determined expatriate was Lewis to resolve that history of discontent which was his life. If a choice was made, and in a real sense it was, we must look for the grounds of that decision (and the possibilities for justifying it) in the recesses of his inner life, the psychic depths where his dreams took shape. . . .

Finally, then, Lewis's romantic dreams, indisputably adolescent, inevitably frustrated, did issue in—and are somehow validated by—a vision of America which, however dimly glimpsed and weakly articulated, was at bottom maturely conceived, a vision no longer the result of fanciful dreams but the result of a struggle to define an ideal, a vision which, proceeding from our actual past could point to an actual future, a vision of a potential America whose realization might be unlikely but whose inspiration would immeasurably improve the quality of American life. If in his imagination, if not in his person, Lewis *did* ultimately affirm America, he did so on the basis of that ideal vision of its possibilities. Though no "promised land," America remained for Lewis the land of promise.

Meanwhile, Europe, no longer significant for him as a place either where one's dreams of a romantic life might be enacted or where a genuine alternative culture had its life, became for him a sort of asylum, a retreat where weary Americans like Sam Dodsworth (and himself) could drift toward death with a minimal amount of external disturbance.

Dick Wagenaar. *AL*. May, 1978, pp. 230, 235, 249

# LOWELL,  ROBERT  (1917–1977)

Robert Lowell is a poet of politics in this largest sense; as such, he is now commonly and, I think, justly acclaimed as the best, the most inclusive, the most deeply intelligent American public poet of his time. He is *the* poet of our advanced—or late—industrial civilization: of the iron bestiary of Victorian Boston fading into the pure geometries of New York; of the manic energy of presidents, and the obscure sadness of the citizen coddled and threatened as never before; of the intelligent mind enmeshed in institutional commitments that no longer automatically justify themselves as right and human, or even as harmless. In Richard Poirier's words, Lowell is "our truest historian."

Lowell's preeminence can only partly be explained by those external enabling factors he shares with many narrower writers: his close personal involvement in politics, both Establishment and non-Establishment, at several crucial moments in recent history; his gifts as a poetic realist, his eye for detail, his historian's grasp of the past. What gives life to these events, these faculties, is the complexity of mind and personality that "sees" the world by means of them; a complexity which—even if we ignore its personal side for the moment and speak only of ideology—is rather unusual. Lowell harbors within himself an Eliot-like conservative's insistence on forms of integrity lost in historical "progress"; a revolutionary's vision of apocalyptic community and hunger for poetic justice; and a liberal's sharp, impersonal scruples (blunted to an essentially conservative *laisser aller* in so many lives, but not in this one). By his faithful recording of himself (or his selves) responding to history, Lowell records a history that is never easy, one-sided, or blinded by the temper of his times. But neither does it conduce to quietistic withdrawal; Lowell continues, almost desperately, to seek images of ethical action, even when the world he perceives gives a compelled, impersonal, and guilty shape to almost every emphatic action it contains.

Lowell's vision of civilization—being a product both of the man he is and of the time he lives in—is particular, painful, and dark. It is redeemed neither by an Eliot's faith that an adequate, if authoritarian, utopia may have existed in the past, nor by a revolutionary's faith that one can be abstractly yet accurately designed for the future. Consequently, Lowell must necessarily leave more questions of value, of cause and responsibility, of fundamental "human nature," open to poetic inquiry than did his nearest predecessors. But it is this very appalling fundamentalness of Lowell's questions, combined with his honesty about historical terror, that make him a modern epic poet, and (to my mind) a more satisfying poet of history than Eliot or Pound, Auden or Berryman or Olson.

Alan Williamson. *Pity the Monsters: The Political Vision of Robert Lowell* (Yale Univ. Pr., 1974), pp. 1–2

To no little extent . . . Lowell seems already to have achieved what he once admired in the work of Eliot. Not only have all his poems become one poem—both in the broad sense that they make up a context that serves a maieutic purpose for any one of them and in the narrower sense that they have all in effect contributed to *History*—but his one poem has increasingly become his life. The latest books point the difficulty: the achievement groans under its own weight. Precisely because his career has developed in a manner comparable to that of one of his poems or one of his volumes, each new work labors directly under the burden of the past. How almost inconceivably difficult it must have been to reshape this burden as it appeared in *Notebook* into *History*. Nor does it seem—not that there is any indication that he would prefer to be able to do so—that there is any easy way for Lowell to retrench at this point. Given the vast echo chamber that he has constructed, every word that he utters must reverberate on and on for him, and consequently it is no wonder that he sometimes sounds as though he were sealed off from common experience by his ordinary personal experience. He has used virtually all the available material in weaving the net in which he is enmeshed; and yet he is convinced, this unlikely Penelope of the littoral, that it is his obligation to go on knotting and undoing the tarred rope.

Stephen Yenser. *Circle to Circle: The Poetry of Robert Lowell* (Univ. of California Pr., 1975), pp. 322–23

Writers have used lyric verse to write oratory, diaries, prophecies, natural history, philosophy and theology. Since Lowell is using it to write autobiography, we expect from him what we ask of all literary autobiographies—subjectivity, vivid self-presentation, subtlety of analysis and some detachment (whether scientific or ironic). On these counts alone Lowell ranks very high. He has largely given up one of the most solacing aspects of conventional lyric—that transcending of past and future in favor of an intense present moment of love, or grief, or happiness. Lowell forces us to read the emotions of the moment in the knowledge of emotions past and anticipated. Nothing is unshadowed; nothing is forgotten; no moment but reaches out to another on the farther shore. The burden of reading *Day by Day* comes from this weight of autobiography everywhere pervading a verse which is itself, paradoxically enough, almost transparent. . . .

Even in Lowell's most obscure moments, the presumption of story and sentence held fast, no matter how murky the story nor how rapid the utterance. He did not adopt those discontinuities of the modern poem and the modern line—collages, fragments, typographical dislocations and unpunctuated reveries—which were the external signs of an attempted mimesis of inner, rather than outer, reality. Lowell was wedded, like Milton, to syntax, and was unwilling to forgo that powerful resource for the weaker glue of Poundian associativeness. *Day by Day* seems to me to have broken the hold of tidy narration and chronological sentences without abandoning conventional English writing—an altogether remarkable sleight of hand.

Helen Vendler. *NYT*. Aug. 14, 1977, p. 1

To borrow one of his own metaphors, Lowell's poetry "clutches only life," for it is based on his belief that "art and the life blood of experience can't live without each other.". . . [His] major poetic changes . . . grew out of his deepening sense of the relationship between art and experience. In his youthful period, under the direct tutelage of Allen Tate and the pervasive influence of T. S. Eliot, Lowell fit his personal experience into impersonal mythic patterns. He conceived of his life as being in service to the poetic idea, as needing to be depersonalized and transformed into art. He constructed verbal icons out of his experience, the most ambitious and powerful of these being "The Quaker Graveyard in Nantucket." In his second, "revolutionary" phase, he learned, under the approving eye of William Carlos Williams, to bring his undisguised personal experience to the forefront of his poetry. Exercising a brilliantly original art, he produced an album of "photographs" of experience, his Confessional masterpiece *Life Studies*. In the third, long period of his maturity, Lowell continued to explore the domain along the boundary where life meets art. He now conceived of experience as being more inward than in his *Life Studies* stage: not isolable events from the past but a fusion of immediate impressions with consciousness itself. Experience in this sense, as T. S. Eliot wrote long ago, is indefinable except that it is "more real than anything else." In the great poems of this period—"For the Union Dead," the "Near the Ocean" sequence, and *The Dolphin*—Lowell revealed the truth of a human heart and mind, his own.

Lowell's poetry of experience presents both danger and opportunity. The very word "experience"—signifying a trial, a putting to the test, an experiment, in Lowell's phrase a "working through"—implies risk. There is point in the fact that "peril" lies half-hidden within it. Yet the peril is redeemed by the reward: a poetry that unites the values of artistic creation with more universal human values. Lowell's poems plunge into, and thereby affirm for himself and for us all, the infinite possibilities for human life in the actual world. They embody a complex process of clarifying and thus culminating his experience; and then, since poems are themselves real, they take their rightful place within experience, leaving author and reader alike altered. Lowell once said of Thoreau that the most wonderful and necessary thing about his life was the courageous hand that wrote it down. The words apply equally to himself.

Steven Gould Axelrod. Robert Lowell: Life and<br>Art (Princeton Univ. Pr., 1978), pp. 11–12

Though Lowell is without question a poet of large talents, and also of large achievement, though he was much honored and reasonably widely read during his lifetime, and will never be forgotten now that he is dead, though some called him a great poet and almost no one was ever able to ignore him, or ever will be able to ignore him, he was from the start impossible to classify in any simple way. And as he moved through the stages of a forty-year career, he changed more than most men, or most poets, are likely to change. Lowell's life, like his career, swung between poles separated by immense distance, and that too is typical of the man and of the poet. He can be viewed—as I myself view him—as a great poet who for the most part refused to write great poetry. He can be viewed—as others have seen him—as unquestionably the leading poet of his generation, the moulder and maker of forms and approaches followed and depended upon by a host of lesser writers. Or he may be viewed as a poet thrust into prominence, unjustifiably on the whole, by critics and publicists in search of "greatness" to write about. . . .

Lowell's life, intensely dramatic in an inner sense, was plainly undramatic in the usual meaning of the term. Fiercely honest, deeply intellectual, he lived in the world without being entirely of the world. His talents, in any objective overview, were as ample and compelling as those of any poet of our time, but his achievement did not measure up to his capabilities. But that is to denigrate his achievement only in some ultimate, absolute sense, for Robert Lowell—flawed, incomplete, tormented and sometimes tormenting—has left us a body of work that we who are his contemporaries have not been able to ignore, nor will it be ignorable by those who come after. There is, to use a frequently abused word, a special magic in Lowell's poetry, and in his plays, and in his translations and imitations, that forces us into attention, if not always into admiration or agreement.

Burton Raffel. Robert Lowell (Ungar, 1981), pp.<br>1–2, 12

## MACLEISH,   ARCHIBALD   (1892–1982)

It is to the art of poetry that Mr. MacLeish has given the best part of his mind and heart, and it is to the poetry that we must turn—and return—for a sense of his true accomplishment.

Yet even in this sacred precinct, in other writers so distant from the hurly-burly of public affairs, it is sometimes difficult to know exactly what kind of poet is addressing us. For in his poetry, too, Mr. MacLeish is often a public figure, easily lured into debate on the issues of the day and frequently tempted to construct those elephantine historical scenarios that have so often proved to be the graveyard of noble literary intentions. The writer who gave us the lengthy *Conquistador* and *Frescoes for Mr. Rockefeller's City* and *America Was Promises* will always, perhaps, have a place in the cultural history of the 1930's, but it is not primarily as poetry that such works survive today. . . .

One has no doubt that it was in the lyric mode, with its inward examination of private experience, that Mr. MacLeish found his true vocation. The poems addressed to public issues are simply not in the same class, and not only those of the 1930's but the recent ones, too. The voice of civic rectitude in his verse is pious, stentorian, false—less so in the later poems, perhaps, but it is still a voice that is a poor surrogate for action or impotent rage. And the odd thing about Mr. MacLeish's career is that two of his most famous poems—"Ars poetica," written in the 20's, and "Invocation to the Social Muse," written in the 30's—are eloquent warnings against precisely this sort of tendentious sermonizing. As he wrote in the latter poem: "The things of the poet are done to a man alone/As the things of love are done—or of death when he hears the/Step withdraw on the stair and the clock tick only." The wisdom of these lines was, for some years, little heeded by the poet himself.

Archibald MacLeish is, then, a contradictory and paradoxical poet, and his *New and Collected Poems, 1917–1976* is a book, a big book, very much divided against itself. One would like to see some day a slenderer volume of short lyrics culled from this large book—a book made up of the poems of the "man alone"—for it looks very much as if it will be by those poems that this writer will live.

Hilton Kramer. NYT. Oct. 3, 1976, pp. 27–28

Ten years ago Archibald MacLeish published a prose collection called *A Continuing Journey*; it was a public book, addresses and essays on topics ranging from literary theory to the fate of the nation. Now he has published a new prose collection, *Riders on the Earth*; this one is a private book, filled with MacLeish's reminiscences, meditations, and convictions. They reveal behind the fine mind a generous spirit.

There are two kinds of essays here. In the more formal ones MacLeish examines the course of humanism in the last decade and makes a case for its future. In the others he discusses, fondly but with unsoftened clarity, his own past and the lives and careers of some of his friends and colleagues. He is the last of the race of literary giants that created modernism, and he has had to write these eulogies for some time now. . . .

MacLeish has, and has long had, a bad name in literary circles that call themselves sophisticated because he is an optimist. Indeed, examining the events of the late sixties, MacLeish finds grounds for hope where many have seen despair. The resentment of the young was valuable, he says, because it was "not a resentment of our human life but a resentment *on behalf* of human life." He makes an essential distinction between this spirit and any of the particular forms rebellion may happen to take, some of which threaten the order necessary for a human life. . . .

MacLeish's optimism is not born of naiveté; we should be naive to presume it of a man whose close friends have included not only Ezra Pound and Ernest Hemingway but also Niels Bohr and Franklin Roosevelt. The very range of his experience is astonishing. Perhaps the best reason we might have to take heart about our own futures is the optimism of a man such as this.

Tom Johnson. *SwR*. Fall, 1978, pp. cxxvi–cxxx

## MAILER, NORMAN (1923–    )

In essence, Mailer sees the machine technology and those who contribute to the furtherance of its power as the villains and the whole man as the victim. Leo Marx has shown us that the theme of the machine in the garden has been present in American literature since its inception, but in Mailer's version the machine has a human face, for finally the machine is man himself, product of a lengthy technological process, whose mind is divided into a complex of isolated compartments, whose senses have all but atrophied, and whose instincts are all but extinct, whose body functions at a remove from its mind, and whose spirit can scarcely be believed to exist. Through a revolution of his own making, in the manner of the God of Genesis, Mailer wishes to breathe life into this robot, to change it back into a man with all of his faculties reintegrated who is once more capable himself of producing life. While analogues to this "new man" may be found in the Renaissance, in frontier America, and in Romantic literature when human possibility seemed limitless, the Mailer hero will emerge from the crosscurrents of his times. The recreation of the human consciousness which Mailer envisions is to be accomplished through a series of small but meaningful victories over the death impulse. The basis for this view is Mailer's self-developed existentialism, considered by him and well documented to be American rather than European in nature and origin, which can be summarized as follows: since death is the end of our lives both biologically and as the product of the process which moves our culture, the only way to live is to face the fact of that death and fight it off with all of one's resources. . . .

Mailer, . . . like many a hero in modern literature who must create the value of his own life, conceives of life as constructed on an existential plane from a series of moments, with growth taking the form of a line of movement which he has described as drawn by "going forward until you have to make a delicate decision either to continue in a different situation or to retreat and look for another way to go forward." The line has breadth as well as length, for growth is expansive: it pushes back the boundaries of consciousness and enlarges meaning and possibility. And "in widening the arena of the possible [for oneself], one widens it reciprocally for others as well". . . . In this sense the Mailer hero has more in common with the traditional hero than the contemporary antihero or nonheroic protagonist: he embodies what he believes the normative behavior of his society ought to be.

Laura Adams. Existential Battles: The Growth of Norman Mailer (Ohio Univ. Pr., 1976), pp. 5–7

Whatever his talents as a journalist, he needs the novel. Even if he wishes to continue exploring the interstice where fiction and history, or reportage, or biography, meet, he must plunge into fiction, with all the risks that implies for him, or lose the excitement that is a hallmark of his style. One wonders—and here the judgment is perhaps unfair and certain to strike to the heart of Mailer's vanity—if he has become afraid of the risks of fiction. Since his first two novels, every one of Mailer's works, fiction or nonfiction, has been written at top speed (so that he could avoid confronting himself in the activity he was engaged in?) or under the influence of stimulants or drugs of some sort, or, what has become his normal pattern, under the external pressure of a deadline. Sitting down to write a novel, to write it as well as he can, seems at present beyond Mailer's psychological capabilities. Yet if he is to be the extraordinary figure in American letters which he wishes to be, he has to turn once again to that frightening blank page that must be filled with the verbal outlines of his imaginative world. . . .

There is hope that Mailer will write another fine novel, perhaps even one that surpasses previous efforts. *Marilyn* reveals an understanding of the growth of the human psyche and a sensitivity to the complexities of womanhood, which Mailer had never demonstrated before. This, conjoined with his insights into the nature of society and the struggle of individuals who must cope with their personal and social existences, and with his splendid prose and sense of verbal mood and balance, may yet enable Norman Mailer to become the outstanding novelist of our age.

Stanley T. Gutman. *Mankind in Barbary: The Individual and Society in the Novels of Norman Mailer* (Univ. Pr. of New England, 1975), pp. 195–96, 198, 200–201, 203

The fiction of Norman Mailer up to and including *The Deer Park* concerns man trying to achieve a self-fulfilling autonomy that takes into realistic account the social and biological forces of life and guards against the delusive security of conventional moralities. The early fiction asks: what is the world that man may understand it? But when the mixed reception of *The Deer Park* turned Mailer into an impassioned outlaw, his fiction underwent a radical change. The emphasis shifted. A new question was asked: what is man that the world may understand him? In the early fiction, reality acted upon consciousness. In the later fiction, consciousness acts upon reality, or rather transforms it through the egocentric imagination. The direction of Mailer's fiction, then, has been from the mimetic to the expressive, from a world described to a world envisioned. . . .

Whatever formal or artistic differences we find among Mailer's works, we should not imagine a thematic difference when, in fact, none exists. An essential conflict undergirds all Mailer's books and makes them indivisible: the conflict between will and external power.

The real moral power of Mailer's writing derives from his depiction of human will and human imagination battling against the forces of constraint. The only thing that operates for good in Mailer's world is the individual fighting alone against the institutional powers that be. . . .

A spiritual fervor kindles the heart of Mailer's rebellion; for ultimately it is not what men make or do that evokes his opposition, but the very terms of human mortality itself. He insists on believing that man is supernatural, not natural. His struggle, then, has been mythic, epical. On the basis of *Advertisements for Myself, An American Dream, Why Are We in Vietnam?, The Armies of the Night,* and *Miami and the Siege of Chicago,* a fair claim can be made: the magnitude of Mailer's imagination and his extraordinary powers of expressiveness have restored to English literature the fertile, energetic grandeur it has seldom known since the seventeenth century.

Philip H. Bufithis. *Norman Mailer* (Ungar, 1978), pp. 131–33

When we consider that Mailer's themes focus on the battle between Life and Death, when we see that the dream is the foundation of his concept of robust art, when we understand that Mailer's concern over the survival of the human race urges him to write books that are intended to generate action, it should not be improbable that Mailer writes allegorically. . . .

It is in his recourse to the dream, to perceptions generally termed *visionary*, and to the allegorical mode that Mailer's work is to be distinguished from realism as well as from the fabulism (the conscious or mechanical appropriation of specific parables, epics, or myths) associated with many of his American contemporaries. . . .

Like Jung, Mailer is interested in the unconscious as a primitive source of psychic truth and a potential source of psychic integration or wholeness. Both Mailer and Jung believe that the self (the total personality) has both somatic and mental bases, and that psychic phenomena are rooted not only in body and mind and not only in conscious and unconscious mind, but in the personal and transpersonal psyche. . . .

After *The Naked and the Dead*, Mailer began to emphasize the unconscious elements of his work, just as he continually disparaged the reductive, mechanical appropriation of psychological theory in some of his contemporaries. Mailer admits that in writing *The Naked and the Dead* he thought in terms of symbols, forms, allegorical (or rational) structures, and classical myths and that he could barely write a sentence without convincing himself it was on five levels. But as soon as he jettisons such "lower academic literary apparatus" in favor of simple writing without "a formal thought" in his conscious mind, he starts writing what I believe to be true (or archetypal) allegory, though he gives every reason to believe he is unaware of it. . . .

Mailer's opposition to the dominant values of our culture during his lifetime is precisely what places him in a major American literary tradition. He has joined the long lineage of writers who have sought to awaken the moral consciousness of their people, who have sought to attach words, through image and symbol, as Emerson said, to visible things, who have allegorically depicted the journey of the individual soul as somehow connected to the journey of America—as both an existence and an ideal—itself.

Robert J. Begiebing. *Acts of Regeneration:*
*Allegory and Archetype in the Works of Norman*
*Mailer* (Univ. of Missouri Pr., 1980), pp. 5, 7–8,
200–201

At least since the appearance of *Advertisements for Myself* more than twenty years ago, we have come to expect an aggressively personal and flamboyant voice in Norman Mailer's writing. In *The Armies of the Night*,

*Of a Fire on the Moon*, *Marilyn*, and other works he has gone for a self-consciously ambitious style which pits the resources of his formidable imagination against the great figures, myths, and issues of our time. Mailer has tried to make his words into the matrix of modern life, so that his work does not simply comment on the contemporary; it shapes our sense of what is contemporary and significant. Furthermore, in writing about himself, and about the process of his interaction with his subjects, he has produced keen theoretical insights about the nature of writing and interpretation. For example, in *The Armies of the Night* he ingeniously writes history, historiography, and fiction while shrewdly reflecting on the nature of all three. In *Marilyn* he writes a biography about biography, and the character of the biographer, as viewed by the novelist. Nearly every subject he manages suggests new facets of meaning and surprising ambiguities. Whether or not we are always convinced by Mailer's imaginative probing seems less important than his compelling demonstration that his subjects and his style are inseparable and indispensable.

Set against this background of self-reflexive writing, *The Executioner's Song* seems to be a startling book. Its sentences are simple and clear, with an occasionally striking but not elaborate metaphor. Absent from the narrative is Mailer's characteristic sentence or paragraph, which is long and comprehensive—an encyclopedic attempt to gather all of reality in one magnificent statement. . . .

*The Executioner's Song* is for Mailer biography in a new key, since we hear as never before the author attending to the integrity of individual lives without quickly elevating those lives into symbolic significance. At the same time, the continuity of Mailer's concerns over the last twenty years is apparent in his ambitious desire to show that true life must be mediated through the imaginative power of a singular intelligence. He understood that *The Executioner's Song* required a voice, flexible and comprehensive, in order to embody the myriad voices that make up reality. The book hinges on that old philosophical problem: how to understand the many and the one, how to interpret the parts by a sense of the whole, how to interpret the whole by a sense of the parts. There is no resolution to this problem, and no resolution to the dialectical tension of the book. We must read the work in the spirit of its contrarieties, and absorb both its sounds and silences.

Carl E. Rollyson, Jr. *ChiR.* Spring, 1980, pp. 31, 39

Swiftly *Ancient Evenings* pulls its reader inside a consciousness different from any hitherto met in fiction. A soul or body entombed is struggling to burst free, desperate not alone for light and air but for prayer and story—promised comforters that have been treacherously withheld or stolen.

Dwelling within this consciousness we relive the "experience" of an Egyptian body undergoing burial preparations, sense the soul's overwhelming yearnings, within an unquiet grave, for healing that no physical treatment can provide. All is strange, dark, intense, mysteriously coherent.

A second voice speaks. Offering a kind of taunting succor, it commences a story of the gods—the myth of Isis and Osiris which in this telling is made utterly new, indeed seems to have been given utterance by the strewn bones and limbs themselves. I looked up at the end of this section of the book, simultaneously moved and (I am speaking seriously) ashamed—troubled by my own habitual skepticism, my trained resistance to whatever is heavily promoted. Would it not prove impossible for a work so well begun to be anything but magnificent over all? Was not the book in my hand certain to prove the truth of its author's contention that he was capable of producing a masterpiece totally unique and incomparably splendid?

The answer to both questions is no. *Ancient Evenings* turns out to be neither magnificent nor a masterpiece. What is more, describing the book simply as a failure—a near-miss earning respect for noble ambitions and partial triumphs—will not do. The case is that, despite the brilliance of those first 90 pages, this 700-page work is something considerably less than a heroic venture botched in the execution. It is, speaking bluntly, a disaster. . . .

The farther one proceeds in *Ancient Evenings* the longer one lingers over any page or passage bare of embarrassments. Here is a carefully researched chapter on the tactical maneuvers preceding the Battle of Kadesh: Pause, speculate about its sources. Here is a chariot charge, vigorously evoked: Pause, savor. Here the Nile rises and the river-bank folk sense the change: Stiff old school historians, such as J. H. Breasted, had their own eloquence on the subject, but Mailer's eloquence is at least not negligible. Here is the Charioteer catching his first glimpse of the Pharaoh: Concentrate on the fine phrases.

But in truth release and escape are elusive. Arguably the obsessions that control this work, considered abstractly, possess dignity. The writer who gives himself up to them is, at the minimum, a challenger—someone admirably scornful of the diminution of his humanity that arid decorum, politic timidity and the like seek to enforce. . . .

The ambition to teach has often been visible in Mailer's books, and it has seldom stifled either wit or self-awareness. The writer's ruling assumption has been that, regardless of subject or form, all his feeling and remembering, inventing and reporting, must be accompanied by critical activity. In *The Armies of the Night* the hero's contempt for others is set under examination—shown to be a feeling traceable not just to their fatuity and self-delusion but to the hero's own vanity, arrogance and snobbism. In *The Executioner's Song* the heroine, risking her life in her murderous male's apartment to recover an Electrolux and attachments, is seen by herself as courageous, and seen by the reader, owing to the critical activity in progress, as someone perilously naïve, tranced, victimized by commodity fetishization, and so on. The surprising perspective—the leap offering instant release from bondage to cliché—is what we have come to expect in even the shortest piece from this pen. But that expectation is nowhere satisfied in *Ancient Evenings*.

Benjamin DeMott. *NYT.* April 10, 1983, pp. 1, 34–36

## MALAMUD, BERNARD (1914–   )

Because he is so vitally concerned with matters of conscience, the allegorical use of character is especially important in Malamud's fiction. The use of a character near the protagonist to represent conscience, a device commonly used by Malamud, is nearly as old as literature itself, and there is ample precedent in the American tradition. . . .

In Malamud's fiction objectification by character operates on two levels—for the central character by other characters, and for the reader by the central character. In most of his fictions, there is at least one character who provides "the test," who brings the lingering internal question to the surface, who forces the central character to the question of conscience: bumbling innocence is caught up by the collar and vague, good intentions are not enough—"Who are you?" and "What do you stand for?"

Malamud uses several different patterns in dramatizing this confrontation, each presenting to the reader a slightly different moral. One sort of test is that presented by the "loathly lady," as Edwin M. Eigner and others have labeled this figure. Many, if not nearly all, the women that Malamud central-character males have romantic encounters with show themselves to have some severe defect. The test, which is among other things a criticism of the "girl-of-my-dreams" syndrome, consists of a challenge to the depth of the protagonist's love—will he reject the woman because she does not match his superficial criteria? . . .

Our culture holds that happiness and security come from wealth and the acquisition of goods. Malamud's fiction suggests that the struggle to acquire wealth or to keep it makes us insensitive, selfish, and unloving, and that there is no joy except in loving. There are not very many wealthy people in Malamud's fiction. . . .

Malamud's best work shows us the human soul in conflict with itself on a stage stripped bare of cosmetics, media myths, and the junk of affluence. He cuts away, cuts away, down to the bone, through flesh and bone to essence of human need, agony, and joy. Everything is so minimal—so little is needed, and yet so little is given. Just a "little living," just a little mercy, for Christ's sake. He can tear the reader's heart out for the pity of it.

Jackson J. Benson. In *The Fiction of Bernard Malamud*, ed. Richard Astro and Jackson J. Benson (Oregon State Univ. Pr., 1977), pp. 21–22, 38–39

At the heart of Malamud's fiction is a reverence for the family, a fragile unit forged from affection, loyalty, and above all duty. Malamud's perspective reveals the importance of his own immigrant Jewish background. In a personal letter, he pays tribute to his parents as "compassionate" people who influenced him. Although he emphasizes that his "father always supported" them, he describes both his parents as "hardworking." Reminiscent of the Bobers in *The Assistant*, the Malamuds worked together in the store and developed something of a partnership in their marriage as well as in their business. His father fulfilled the role of a gentle patriarch. He guided and supported the family with the assistance of his well-meaning but somewhat protective wife (whom the author remembers as fearful of "gypsies"). In their compassion, in their dedication to the family, and in their perseverance, the senior Malamuds resemble some of the author's couples who, despite difficulties, are bound to each other in relationships evocative of European Yiddish life. . . .

In America the Jewish father's power is eroded. No longer the distant scholar, the fountain of wisdom, he does not inspire awe as he used to. Toiling alongside him, his wife is emboldened to assert herself more openly. Instead of quietly advising him, she may loudly nag him. Nevertheless, at least in Malamud's fiction, the man still makes the important family decisions. In *The Assistant* Morris Bober quietly determines the family's fate. He hides unpleasant news from his wife, continues to operate the store the way he wants to, and ignores her complaints and demands. Ida realizes that the grocer is "a hard man to move. In the past she could sometimes resist him, but the weight of his endurance is too much for her now." When he decides to shovel snow, she cannot stop him, nor can she persuade him to take advantage of an unsuspecting refugee. Despite her fears, Morris retains his Italian assistant, Frank Alpine. But the grocer rules with a gentle hand. He accepts the changes initiated by his ambitious assistant, who remodels the store to improve profits. But even in this enterprise, Morris has the ultimate veto and refuses to sanction deceptive business practices. He is clearly the family head, mourning for his dead son, worrying about his daughter's future, guiding his young helper, and operating the store. Though an American citizen for many years, Bober resembles many Eastern European Jewish men in his idealism and in his relationship to the family. A poor provider, he nevertheless retains their compassion and loyalty. As the practical wife, Ida complains, but she also loves Morris and blames herself for his failure to become a druggist. Helen's daughterly devotion makes her sacrifice her education to help support the family. It also makes her initially avoid Alpine, a non-Jew, so as not to hurt her parents. Despite poverty and suffering, the Bobers remain a family. Not surprisingly, then, Bober's death creates a vacuum, which will need to be filled by Frank Alpine, who becomes a surrogate father. . . .

In Malamud's fiction it is rare, though not impossible, for men to desert or abuse their families. In "The Mourners" Kessler is an aging recluse who had abandoned his family years before. Oskar Gassner, "the German refugee," had fled Hitler and left his wife behind to die. In *The Assistant* the tough, brutal Detective Minogue, who nearly kills his warped son, is probably Malamud's worst father figure, but he is also an exception. Most of Malamud's male characters learn to be responsible family heads. Those who do not, suffer severely. Kessler makes a pathetic figure as he confronts his past sins and hopeless future. Oskar Gassner, unable to forget his gentile wife, gasses himself to death. And Detective Minogue is tormented by his son Ward, a hard-core criminal resembling Bigger Thomas.

Evelyn Gross Avery. *Rebels and Victims: The Fiction of Richard Wright and Bernard Malamud* (Kennikat, 1979), pp. 58–61

Bernard Malamud sometimes gets obscured by flashier American writers. He isn't a formal innovator, he doesn't construct what one might call fictional "fortresses," those huge novels bristling with erudition which have intimidated critics and readers alike. He isn't "zany" or exquisitely sensitive or grandly perverse. But he writes superbly most of the time, at least as well as any living American writer of fiction, and time will pardon him for violating the categories.

For he does do that, and reviewers, whose categories they largely are, are often uncomfortable with him because of it. His narratives, which we are told ought to be shapely and lucid, are often lopsided and indistinct. He can be abrupt, impatient with the demands of plot without being willing to scuttle plot altogether; so he'll take shortcuts. His situations sometimes fail wholly to convince on sociological grounds—*The Tenant* is an example—and his tense, loving, troubled appreciation of life, with its concomitant of occasional desperation, can lead him to sentimentality, an excess of willing; *The Fixer* suffers from that. In short, he isn't a tidy novelist, but loose and erratic, someone struggling.

But how well he writes! His great gift is that of using language so as to bring about the narrowest possible spaces among experience, thought and utterance, to come as close as one can to eliminating the discrepancy between experience and its recovery as literature. This near unity of instrument and object results in a quiet eloquence, a nearly inaudible one at times, since to be determinedly eloquent is to weight language toward a celebration of itself, with a consequent diminution of actuality. And Malamud's fiction, even the seemingly fantastic short stories, is one of actuality, which is to say that it esteems and mourns what exists, without wishing to add to it. He is a realist in the sense of Dostoevsky was, a writer true to the structures of experience.

I find all this necessary to say because there are things wrong with Malamud's new novel, *Dubin's Lives*, but I don't think they matter. They are malfeasances only from the perspective of an educated, reasonable notion of fiction, a notion of elements in their proper relation: plot, structure, style, everything in balance, everything "convincing," no room for dubiety, incompleteness, disjunction. But it isn't through satisfying a preexisting set of standards that fiction triumphs. The "felt life" of Henry James's dictum is what counts: life sensed deeply, made conscious, within such structures as are necessary for its more or less rough shape. The best fiction spills over, protrudes; heretical as it may sound, the best fiction has nothing much to do with the critic's categories. . . . One of [Malamud's] great strengths . . . is his ability to move the reader by an alternation of tones, a subtle passage from statement to evocation. The world of his fiction emits a glow of consciousness; things making themselves known, gamely, lovingly. No other writer we have celebrates so well the hard-earned nobility of the literary imagination as it makes its conquests.

Richard Gilman. NR. March 24, 1979, pp. 28–30

Bernard Malamud is a writer who early on established an emphatic paradigm for his fictional world and who ever since has been struggling in a variety of ways to escape its confines. His latest novel [*God's Grace*] is his most strenuous strategem of escape, moving beyond the urban horizon of his formative work into an entirely new mode of postapocalyptic fantasy—with intriguing though somewhat problematic results.

When I say "paradigm," I am not referring to the explicit Jewish themes or to the morally floundering Jewish protagonists that have been trademarks of Malamud's fiction, with the exception of his first novel, *The Natural*. In fact, *God's Grace* is the most self-consciously Jewish of all his books. . . .

Gore Vidal's *Kalki* (1978) provides an instructive contrast to *God's Grace*. It is also a post-apocalyptic fantasy, though the bulk of the novel is devoted to a brilliantly suspenseful account of the plot to bring about the apocalypse. Here, too, the relentless egoism of some of the survivors ends by subverting the possibility of survival. There is, however, a kind of purity of witty misanthropy in Vidal's treatment of this whole subject. No "prophetic" or moralistic claims are made for the story; it is an end-of-the-world thriller that reveals the essential nastiness of the ingenious human animal, something about which the author has never been seriously in doubt. This is probably too glib and too limited a view of mankind to generate anything like major fiction, but it does give the work in question a certain consistency, even a kind of circumscribed integrity. *God's Grace*, by contrast, invites us to take it as an impassioned plea for kindness and pity for all living creatures in the face of man's enormous capacity for murderous destruction. The moral message is unexceptionable, but the vehemence with which the brutish counterforce to kindness and pity is imagined at the end is disquieting. Instead of holding a prophetic mirror to the contorted face of mankind, the novelist—at least so it seems to this reader—has once again taken his lovingly fashioned creatures, bound them hand and foot, and begun to play with axes, knives, tearing incisors, and other instruments of dismemberment.

Robert Alter. *NR*. Sept. 20 and 27, 1982, pp. 38, 40

In his fiction Malamud considers the moral evolution of his characters. They grow in ethical depth through various kinds of suffering, intellectual as well as physical. Using such techniques as mirror images, symbiotic pairs of characters, and the double vision of Jewish humor, Malamud often succeeds in showing us the human soul, stripped bare of romantic dreams, pretense, and materialistic aspirations, in conflict with its own divided nature. It is no exaggeration to say that spiritual conflict dwells at the center of Malamud's moral universe. Freedom can be achieved, but only through moral awareness, which, paradoxically, binds a person to others in a web of commitments.

Each of the protagonists of Malamud's novels faces a trial of conscience or a spiritual test and triumphs only by accepting fatherly spiritual guidance or by listening to his own troubled conscience, an acceptance that must be accompanied by an expression of mercy, love, charity, or forgiveness. . . .

The implied lesson is, quite simply, that people can change. Their circumstances may remain the same but spiritually they transcend their surroundings. This recurring theme in Malamud's writing is simple but efficacious. For example, as a corollary Malamud implies that life is relative. A store can become a prison for one man and a means of deliverance for another. Things, in and of themselves, are neither good nor bad; they are what we make of them. In the world of Malamud's fiction compassion, love, and understanding—the humane values—rather than physical circumstances give meaning to one's life. It is a world that blends hope with despair, pain with possibility, and suffering with moral growth. Out of the everyday defeats and indignities of ordinary people, Malamud creates beautiful parables that capture the joy as well as the pain of life; he expresses the dignity of the human spirit searching for freedom and moral growth in the face of hardship, injustice, and the existential anguish of life in our time.

Sheldon J. Hershinow. Bernard Malamud<br>(Ungar, 1980), pp. 145–46

● **MAMET, DAVID (1947–    )**

*Sexual Perversity in Chicago*, the first of two one-acters by a remarkable writer named David Mamet which are now playing Off Off Broadway, is one of the saddest comedies I can remember, but it is a comedy, all right. It seems at first to be just a series of absurd, sexy blackouts, but one gradually becomes aware that a quite substantial theme is in progress— the growth and subsequent disintegration of a fragile love affair between two young people who were formerly anchored (whether aware of it or not) in homosexual partnerships; after a period of intense happiness they break up, as much because of inexperience and bewilderment at the small abrasions of daily living as because of the unceasing disparagement of their new lovers by their former ones. In the last scenes we see the downcast young woman back home with her bitchy roommate, who gives her a short, brutal lecture on her young man, and the young man with *his* roommate, girl-watching at a beach, to the accompaniment of the roommate's equally brutal, dirty, monosyllabic observations on the girls being watched. Boy and girl have taken a chance and muffed it; they may or may not get a second chance, but their confidence has been impaired.

Looking back I can see I've made everything sound too glacial and too solemn; actually, the subtly pointed incidents are so unobtrusively put together that for quite a while the audience is unaware that any story is being told at all—or even, perhaps, that these couples are homosexual. Also, one spends so much time laughing at the funny lines that the underlying sadness of the play comes as an aftertaste. The piece is written with grace. . . .

The second piece, *Duck Variations*, is, strictly speaking, a poem in the guise of the desultory conversation of two old Jewish men . . . pottering around a bench in a park presumably facing Lake Michigan. There is a marvellous ring of truth in the meandering, speculative talk of these old men—the comic, obsessive talk of men who spend most of their time alone, nurturing and indulging their preposterous notions. There is more here than just geriatric humor; there is also imagination and understanding, as these old parties grow impatient with each other, quarrel, make up, reveal their need for each other, and talk glorious nonsense with impassioned solemnity. They never become ridiculous or pathetic; their dignity remains intact from beginning to end. Mr. Mamet is a true and original writer, who cherishes words and, on the evidence at hand, cherishes character even more.

Edith Oliver. NY. Nov. 10, 1975, pp. 135–36

There's a new generation of unheralded playwrights about to burst forth with major works . . . but most of us felt that only Mamet had done work worthy of major critical recognition at this point, and recognition not so much for his plays as for the potential they represent, especially in his careful, gorgeous, loving sense of language. In fact, I'd go so far as to say that at the age of 28 Mamet is the most promising American playwright to have emerged in the '70s and that he has the most acute ear for dialogue of any American writer since J. D. Salinger. . . . Mamet's extraordinary promise resides not so much in his insights into male-female relationships, or in the comic manipulations of his understanding, as in the exhilarating perfection of the language with which he expresses it. It's a rarity in theatre to find the insights, the action, so deeply embedded in the dialogue itself.

It's a terrible burden to place upon a writer, but if Mamet can continue the astonishing advance in achievement from *Duck Variations* (1971) to *Sexual Perversity in Chicago* (1974) to *American Buffalo* (1975), I feel confident his next leap forward will give us nothing less than an American masterpiece. . . .

It's a rare writer indeed who by the age of 28 has *both* such a distinctive voice and such a wide range of subject matter (from metaphysical reflections on death to sexual farce to an exploration of the relationship between money and violence in American culture).

Ross Wetzsteon. VV. July 5, 1976, pp. 101, 103

From the beginning, Mr. Mamet's most notable and noticeable quality was his extraordinary use of speech. He concentrated not upon cultivated expression but upon that apparent wasteland of middle American speech.

It was the language of the secretary, the salesman, the file clerk, the telephone linesman, the small-time crook, the semiliterate college kid.

It was grotesquely realistic. . . . Spoken, it sounded both more natural and funnier. But there is something beyond realism there. There is a desperate energy behind these apparent incoherences, a passion for speaking that is so intense as to become authentically lyrical. (In Mamet's later plays . . . the lyricism is even more apparent without ever being anything but completely authentic. Among other odd thoughts that come up in wondering where Mr. Mamet may be heading is the notion that—if this process of intensification and refining continues—he might just possibly become our first true verse dramatist). . . .

His characters are not hopeful, though they are trustful. Their world is full of distorted wisdom, of lessons learned but learned wrong because of the unreasonable ferocity, the lack of shape or instruction of middle American life.

They have the kind of skewed philosophy that ants might evolve in the generations after the destruction of the anthill. God exists, He is dangerous and capricious, and He is a giant Foot. And just as ants keep surviving their precarious worlds, Mamet's characters barely preserve their damaged humanity. They yearn and hatch schemes; their feelers wave delicately in the wreckage. . . .

Mamet's language is pared down. There is humor and awkwardness in the speeches but it is stripped of virtuosity or self-consciousness. It grows naturally and expressively. He has never written better.

It is more than an ear for speech. It is an ear for heartbeats, evidence of his character's state of life and its constant transformations. The evidence is often indirect and evasive. In its awkwardnesses and silences, speech can testify to the opposite of what it seems to say. The gun flash is precisely not where the bullet lodges. Mr. Mamet reports the flash and shows us where the wound really is.

*The Water Engine* is less intense, more complex and more spacious. It is Mr. Mamet's most beautiful play though not necessarily his best, nor his most powerful. It has a story, many characters, a melodramatic plot. . . .

Even his best work has defects. *The Woods*, strong as it is, has problems of structure and clarity. The changes are perhaps too exclusively internal; apart from a rainstorm, nothing outside happens to test or stretch the couple. There is some airlessness there.

Mamet seems to reach out farther with each new play, but he has only begun, in *Water Engine*, to test his extraordinary command of mood, character and language—poetic and specific—with the real changes and stresses of a plot and external reality. But for what he has done already, and what he shows every sign of going on to do, his return to Broadway is another candle in what could turn out to be a long celebration for the American theater.

Richard Eder. *NYTMag.* March 12, 1978, pp. 40, 42, 45, 47

Structurally, *The Woods* is hack formula: a build to crisis for the act curtain, then escalation to a climax and final resolution. (Five minutes into Act II, I called the rest of the action: "They're gonna goad each other for a while, then he'll hit her, and then we'll get the tearful reconciliation.") Mamet creates the illusion of form and direction in the play mainly by bringing back snatches of early speeches later on, culminating in a monologue of facile, "meaningful" nonsense about a bear that can't open its jaws to speak.

But *The Woods* is not just a benignly lousy play by an overrated playwright. It is deeply infested with misogyny disguised as an enlightened, even feminist, examination of couple interactions. Nick is a self-centered taker with concerns like "I can not sleep," "I want to fuck you." Ruth is a giver, who tries to love Nick and place their relationship in a great cosmic scheme of human interaction. ("This is the best thing two people can do—to share things that they have gone through before.") The only sex scene consists of Nick grabbing Ruth to the ground, ripping open her pants, covering her face with her poncho, and forcing his way in (ignoring her pleas to go indoors and "get some stuff"), then grumping away when it doesn't work well—while she protests that the fact that she "wasn't wet" doesn't mean she doesn't want him. So we have woman as sensitive and abused, man as cad. Feminist, right?

Wrong. The play presents Ruth as an imbecilic, needy giver, and then vindicates that role by making it facilitate Everycouple's first real communication. It affirms female as victim. But, more disturbing, Mamet ultimately *dismisses* the woman. *The Woods* is not really about a couple: It is about a man. It's he who has the grand emotional breakthrough, he who has the center-stage finale speech. Ruth's function in the play's structure parallels her role in the relationship: She's the wifelet, the steady, self-effacing, supporting figure that nourishes the primary one. On every level, *The Woods* suggests that a couple consists of a man *with* a woman rather than a man *and* a woman.

Eileen Blumenthal. *VV*. May 7, 1979, p. 103

"Woman lives but in her lord/" wrote Dorothy Parker, "Count to ten, and Man is bored/" and she concluded, sourly, "With this the gist and sum of it/What earthly good can come of it?" This question is the central focus of David Mamet's painful, sardonic, and engrossing new play, *The Woods*, and his outlook is, if anything, bleaker than Parker's for being less glibly cynical.

The play's elements are few. Nick and Ruth, about whom we know virtually nothing except that they have been seeing each other "in the city," spend half a weekend—long enough for young love to turn rancid and finally explode—at a summer house owned by Nick's family. The woodsy area they go to is brilliantly designed by John Lee Beatty: Trees (made from bundles of ropes) dominate the stage, while Nick's cabin is nothing but a few slats nailed between two posts and a porch, surrounded by more trees. In metaphoric terms, there is no inside to escape to. . . .

It is the man who gets the worst of Mamet's critique. The woman's sentimentality about nature and about relationships is comic, but there is also a sense in which it is deep and sincere, while the man's pretense of being a skilled backwoodsman and experienced lover is a flat-out fraud. At the end, when her threat to leave has reduced him to a whimper and a fetal position, she stays to mother him, and the play ends with an unfinished sentence, continuing a fairy tale she has previously started about two little children lost in a wood, which brings out what their relationship has been all along but hardly bodes well for its continuing.

For a play which is half personal and specific, and half abstract parable, Mamet has made a dangerous choice in his language. His words are naturalistic—there is no single line in the play which you could not hear someone say on the street—but they are all selected from those horrible moments when, reaching for a simple phrase, we seize pomposity. Human beings often ring false, and this is part of the failure *The Woods* details. I suppose it is possible to believe, alternatively, that the junior master of Chicago bad-mouth who could compose a symphony of slang and swearwords like *American Buffalo* has aspirations to the Maxwell Anderson-Archibald MacLeish loftiness league, but I personally doubt it.

Michael Feingold. *VV*. May 7, 1979, p. 103

In any assessment of *American Buffalo* Mamet's use of language must be regarded as an achievement. If the vocabulary of men such as Bobby, Teach and Donny is impoverished, Mamet's rendering of it reminds us that vocabulary is only one of the resources of language. Teach does have an eloquence when expressing his sense that he has been abused. . . .

The urban nature of the language in *American Buffalo* is a matter not just of its street vulgarity, or expressions such as "skin-pop" and "He takes me off my coin. . ." but also of an abbreviation characteristic of urban pace. . . .

Besides the play's language, a second critical issue which has resulted in opposing assessments of *American Buffalo* is that of its content, or lack of it. . . .

To buffalo is as American as to bake an apple pie. Notions of the American way—democracy and free enterprise—become corrupted when they enter the look-out-for-number-one rationalizations of crooks and unethical businessmen. Down-and-outs in a democracy may feel they have been cheated because "all men should be equal." Knowledge creates divisions among people, divisions of power and wealth, but such divisions can seem undemocratic, un-American. So robbing and cheating are attempts to restore justice. Or, "In America one is free to make a fortune for himself" turns into Teach's definition of free enterprise. My modest conclusion is that in satirizing such corrupt notions Mamet *has* written a play of intellectual content.

Jack V. Barbera. MD. Sept., 1981, pp.<br>271–72, 275

David Mamet is a playwright of the 1970s, and ever since his brilliant debut with *American Buffalo* and *Sexual Perversity in Chicago* he has been having a little difficulty getting a purchase on the problems of this decade. With his new play, *Edmond* . . . he has accomplished something of a breakthrough. As directed by Gregory Mosher, *Edmond* is a remarkably cruel play—ruthless, remorseless, unremittingly ugly. Written in that terse banal naturalism that has become Mamet's staccato trademark, it follows the spiritual journey of a stocky middle-class young man who wakes up one morning to tell his wife that he is deserting her. Leaving the safety of his home, he embarks on a terrifying odyssey through the urban landscape, looking for sexual and other satisfactions but instead finding violence and fraud. . . .

What Mamet has written is a version of *Woyzeck* in the modern city, displaying not only Buechner's hallucinatory power but also the same capacity to show compassion for lowly, inarticulate wretches without mitigating their awful fates. He has pushed our faces into a world which most of us spend our waking hours trying to avoid, finding a kind of redemption in the bleakest, most severe alternatives. I don't think he will be thanked much for this, but I for one want to express gratitude—for the play. . . .

Robert Brustein. NR. July 12, 1982, p. 24

# MCCARTHY, MARY (1912–    )

McCarthy's voice has always been perfectly reliable; the stirring and disturbing tone of the born truth teller is hers, whether she is writing essays or fiction. Her perspective is always feminine: Antigone grown up, her absoluteness not diminished as she takes on sex. She has never been easy on herself or her characters, or tried to make anyone look better. This is true whether she is describing her failure to best an anti-Semite ("Artists in Uniform"), her fears about traveling as a reporter in Vietnam ("How It Went"), or her heroine's response to divorce in "Cruel and Barbarous Treatment.". . .

Where are we, then, to place *Cannibals and Missionaries*, which its publishers present as "a thriller," in the context of Mary McCarthy's work? She is not the sort of writer who would toss off a book as a lark or a diverting experiment, so why has she done it?

It is clear to me that this, the most political, the least autobiographical of her novels, would have been impossible without her experience of traveling to Vietnam as a reporter. Many of the details of that experience, particularly those about physical fear and communal bonding, find their way into this novel in the accounts of the passengers' ordeal. *Cannibals and Missionaries* is the story, among other things, of a committee of liberals who are hijacked while traveling to Iran to examine the atrocities of the Shah's regime. It speaks, with McCarthy's habitually unsentimental voice, to the problem of witness and political responsibility among nonprofessional men of good will. For McCarthy, terrorism is disturbing in the same way that sexual promiscuity would have been for Emily Brontë: it is political activity without manners, without form; therefore it is incapable of yielding much meaning and is inevitably without hope. In some crucial way, it is not serious; it has no stake in the future. . . .

The most important achievement of *Cannibals and Missionaries* is McCarthy's understanding of the psychology of terrorism, the perception, expressed by Henk, that terrorism is the product of despair, "the ultimate sin against the Holy Ghost." Once again, McCarthy is asking the difficult question, confronting the difficult problem. For surely, terrorism threatens us all, not only physically and politically, but morally and intellectually as well. It postulates a system of oblique correspondences, a violent disproportion between ends and means, against which we have no recourse. She comes to terms as well with our peculiar but irrefutable tendency to see human beings as replaceable, works of art unique. For the lover of formal beauty who is also a moralist, it is the most vexed of questions. I'm not sure McCarthy has anything new to say on the subject, but she does not imply that she does.

Often, artists have responded to the prospect of atrocity by creating a well-crafted work of art. One thinks of Milton's "On the Late Massacre of the Piedmontese," a perfect Italian sonnet whose hundredth word is "hundredfold." In response to the truly frightful prospect of anarchic terrorism, Mary McCarthy has written one of the most shapely novels to have come out in recent years: a well-made book. It is delightful to observe her balancing, winnowing, fitting in the pieces of her plot.

The tone of *Cannibals and Missionaries* is a lively pessimism. Its difficult conclusion is that to be a human being at this time is a sad fate: even the revolutionaries have no hope for the future, and virtue is in the hands of the unremarkable, who alone remain unscathed.

Mary Gordon. NYT. Sept. 30, 1979, pp. 1, 33–35

*Cannibals and Missionaries* is susceptible to the recurring criticism that McCarthy is more essayist than novelist. One reader wonders why she wrote this book as a novel; another finds the long periods of inaction tedious. We may again pass over the question of genre. As the term is commonly used, *Cannibals and Missionaries* is a novel. But to say so does not clear it of the charge that it contains so many monologues, both internal and external, that the subjects of conversations and reflections, rather than action and character, sometimes dominate our attention.

There is, to be sure, a lot of talk in *Ulysses*, *The Sound and the Fury*, and *Portnoy's Complaint*. But McCarthy's fiction hardly resembles Joyce's, or Faulkner's, or Roth's. Although she exposes the minds and actions of her characters, she does not often explore their souls and invite us to *feel* with them. Indeed, we hardly even mourn their deaths—fortunately, since their mortality rate is appalling. We like many of them, but amusement and embarrassment are the emotions we are most likely to feel on their behalf; and we do not willingly identify with most of them. We do, however, judge them. We think about them in terms of what they do and ought to do, not of how they feel or why they feel that way. Our attention is directed to how their minds work, what they know, and how they explain themselves. McCarthy believes (as she says in the interview with Niebuhr) that truth is knowable; her characters are prone to err, but not with impunity and not without presenting their case. They argue and rationalize. They think in essays; sometimes they write letters and journals. And finally, we cannot believe that Sophie's journal entries and Pete Levi's letter are written to portray Sophie and Peter; rather, these characters seem at times to have been created to ponder ideas.

If a weakness of McCarthy's fiction is its essayistic tendencies, its great strength is the accuracy with which she portrays characters, particularly comic characters, giving new life and individuality to universal types. Aileen Simmons belongs to the tradition of the Wife of Bath, going on a pilgrimage and looking for a mate, gregarious, a little overdressed, out-spoken, ever-mindful of precedence. Her eye is on the clerkly Senator, an unlikely prospect if ever there was one, but she also contemplates a rich old man, Charles Tenant; like Allison of Bath, she is alert to any oppor-tunity. Frank Barber has literary kinsmen in Parson Adams and Pangloss and, doubtless, some Ur-Parson among the cavemen. Of more recent vin-tage is the wicked Charles, genuinely liberal, dauntless, and dreadful in his confessions of the human frailties that plague us all. He is a comic character and a homosexual, and the two facts have nothing to do with each other; the gay Charles is offered as character without any statement about his sexual identity, which is a problem only to Aileen. At eighty, he is in any case past his prime, but he is physically fearless and a good foil to the other men with their macho instincts.

Willene Hardy. Mary McCarthy (Ungar, 1981),<br>pp. 194–95


## MCCULLERS, CARSON    (1917–1967)


If the muse of isolation was for Carson McCullers inward-turning and at home only in the South of her childhood memories, it inspired her best writing with a rare sympathy for and insight into hidden suffering which, I think, represent the highest accomplishments of her fiction. For McCul-lers wrote of man's isolation with an understanding that was as compas-sionate as it was despairing. She spoke for people, who, in their trapped inwardness, could not speak for themselves, who loved without hope of being loved. Running throughout her works is the unstated conviction that no human being can in his inmost, truest self ever be really known, that he is doomed either to eternal loneliness or to compromise with the crass world outside. . . .

McCullers believed that only through the compassion and empathy of art could such vulnerable inwardness be freed and appreciated for the valuable and rare quality that it was. Her vision of human loneliness is a vision born of love. . . . McCullers possessed what most of her characters tragically lack, a double vision that enabled her to see the inside and the outside of people: a hopeless love for a departed friend beneath John Singer's deferential politeness, a sincere moral outrage beneath Jake Blount's loud talk and belligerent manner, an uncertainty of identity and terror of the future beneath Frankie's foolishness and irritability, and a desperate, lonely passion beneath Miss Amelia's masculine dress and crafty business practices. In her most successful works McCullers could, as she once claimed, "become" her characters, enter their lonely lives, the places where they lived. And without letting us lose sight of their awkward, sometimes frightening and often amusing outwardness, she let us see into their secret inwardness.

Richard M. Cook. Carson McCullers (Ungar,<br>1975), pp. 126–28

McCullers's is . . . the definitive use of a specific emotional effect—a pathos that at once lends a strange atmosphere to landscape and character, and helps establish an intimate, unusually searching relationship between tale and reader. This is an impressive achievement—showing the kind of subtlety and even deviousness of intent we are perhaps more inclined to associate with more "difficult" fiction—and its very impressiveness has, I believe, led one or two of McCullers's critics into overestimating her. . . .

The very perfection of McCullers's work depends, after all, upon her own level-headed acceptance of her limitations. She knows that she can describe, quite subtly, one particular dilemma or area of life and she concentrates almost her entire resources on that. There is no place in her fiction . . . for the rich "over-plus" of experience—by which I mean any aspects of behavior that cannot be included under the heading of theme, or any dimensions of feeling that cannot be reconciled with the major effect of pathos. And recognizing this she demonstrates little interest in such matters as the historical and social context, and no commitment either to the idea of a developing consciousness. Her people walk around and around within the circle of their own personalities, their inner world of thought and desire hardly engaging with the outer world at all. They seldom change, except physically, they never reflect more than one aspect of our experience (admittedly, it is a significant one); and to inflate them, their world, or indeed their creator to a major status—to suppose, in fact, that McCullers's novels and short stories are any more important to the tradition than they genuinely are—is, I believe, to be guilty of what used to be called "overkill." It is, in other words, to smother a quiet but effective talent by heaping upon it unearned and patently unacceptable praise.

As for McCullers's actual achievement, though, setting aside all such exaggeration, that surely is certain and secure. She is not a major writer. . . . But she is a very good minor one—so good, indeed, that she seems to reap a definite advantage from her minor status and turn her limitations into virtues.

Richard Gray. The Literature of Memory (Johns<br>Hopkins Univ. Pr., 1977), pp. 272–73

Mrs. McCullers's fiction, in particular *The Member of the Wedding*, can speak to the adolescent reader in very intense fashion, for what it conveys is the frustration and pain of being more than a child and yet not an adult, with the agony of self-awareness and sense of isolation thereby involved. There is the shock of recognition—something of the same kind of reassurance through identification that books such as *Look Homeward, Angel* or *The Catcher in the Rye* have been known to provide. . . .

The McCullers fiction, I believe, has at its center a fundamental premise: which is, that solitude—loneliness—is a human constant, and cannot possibly be alleviated for very long at a time. But there is no philosophical acceptance of that condition, and none of the joy in it that one finds in, say, Thomas Wolfe or even Hemingway. The solitude is inevitable, and it is always painful. Thus life is a matter of living in pain, and art is the portraying of anguish. Occasionally, a character of hers knows happiness, but never for very long. . . .

Like certain other of her contemporaries, Carson McCullers, it seems to me, constructed her art out of the South, but not out of its history, its common myths, its public values and the failure to cherish them. What is Southern in her books are the rhythms, the sense of brooding loneliness in a place saturated with time. Compare *The Heart Is a Lonely Hunter* or *The Member of the Wedding* with, say, *Winesburg, Ohio*, and the relationship with the region is obvious. Sherwood Anderson's grotesques are more simple; a few clear, masterful sentences and we get their essential quality. Carson McCullers must show her misfits, whether spiritual or physical, in an extended context; there is plenty of time for everything. The Southern quality is unmistakable, in the unhurried fascination with surfaces, the preoccupation with the setting in which the characterization reveals itself. Character is not for McCullers, any more than for Eudora Welty or William Faulkner or Thomas Wolfe, an idea, but a state of awareness. To repeat, there is plenty of time . . . and when the violence comes, as it so often does, it erupts in a place and a context, and it jars, queerly or terribly or both, the established and accustomed patterns. Before and after, there is lots of waiting, lots of time to think about everything.

Louis D. Rubin, Jr. *VQR*. Spring, 1977,
pp. 269–70, 281–82

## ● MCMURTRY, LARRY (1936–    )

Texas teen-agers complain that a small town is so dead there is nothing to do on a Saturday night except sit on the curb and watch the sewer back up. Seemingly, Thalia, as ugly and lonely as the land around it, qualifies. Its optimistic founders, though, first named it Paradise—but Texas already had a Paradise. Undaunted, they chose Thalia ("blooming and luxuriant"). Perhaps it was to their eyes, but not to Larry McMurtry's. Thalia was the general background for his *Horseman Pass By* (filmed as *Hud*) and *Leaving Cheyenne*. Now, in *The Last Picture Show* Thalia takes center stage and so does McMurtry.

The book is about the initiation of a boy, Sonny Crawford, into the mystique of manhood. Other major characters are Sonny's buddy, Duane, and Duane's girl, Jacey, who is rich, pretty and Queen Bee of Thalia High.

During the course of a year, Sonny learns a great deal from the neglected wife of an overly virile coach who reveres his mother and has a passion for guns. Another mentor is the pool-hall owner, who is the guardian of youth, particularly simple-minded Billy. Sonny also learns from Jacey's mother never to say thank you to a lady. By the end of the novel, Sonny and Duane have fought over Jacey, reconciled, and attended the last movie to be shown in Thalia. Sonny becomes painfully aware that his youth, like the picture show, is gone, and that manhood is something more than sexual pleasure.

The high school scenes are achingly familiar and include one of the wildest, funniest basketball games ever recorded. But it is the boys' preoccupation with sex that dominates the book. McMurtry takes his characters on a trip from onanism to prostitution, with a stop at every station in between. One seduction scene (surely a literary first) has Jacey being aroused by a one-man demonstration of shooting pool. Her further adventures with the rich kids in Wichita Falls are eyebrow-raisers. Another notable episode involves a gang of slightly drunken boys in a comic orgy in a cow lot. Afterward, they take Billy the idiot, shove him into the back seat of a car with a grotesque whore, and watch the results.

Offensive? Miraculously, no. McMurtry is an alchemist who converts the basest materials to gold. The sexual encounters are sad, funny, touching, sometimes horrifying, but always honest, always human.

The whole, however, is not as satisfying as the parts. The characters lack depth. The boys have no ambitions above their plated belt buckles. Duane remains shadowy, and Sonny finally becomes almost mute, victimized by a too-contrived story line. The novel loses focus when Jacey takes over. Ultimately, even pictorial accuracy and authentic language cannot sustain a plot that slicks up.

There are also some unnecessary literary clichés. The coach's persecution of the English teacher who takes boys swimming wasn't new in *Tea and Sympathy*. And the death of Billy detracts from, rather than strengthens, the fresh symbol of the last picture show. The pages of literature are strewn with the bones of slaughtered innocents. Billy and his death will cause few readers to shed a tear.

One point, however, is well-established. Though McMurtry blandly dedicates this book to Thalia, he would never recommend it as a place to live. But it's a fascinating place to visit—in a book.

W. T. Jack. *NYT*. Nov. 12, 1966, pp. 68–69

McMurtry is typical of a new breed of Southwest writers who are reacting against the tendency of an earlier generation to idealize and simplify the past in order to establish the purity of its heroism and nobility for a presumably inferior present. . . .

Because his works are more lifelike than the typical Western adventure and because he has sometimes viewed the foibles of his native state with a cold eye, McMurtry has often been regarded as having completely turned his back on the virtues of the past in order to adopt the role of iconoclast. Such is not the case. Indeed, McMurtry is one of the few Southwest novelists to understand the full potential of the Western myth as a framework for serious fiction. Certainly this myth has tremendous possibilities in an age when most urban writers are content to picture their characters as isolated figures floating weightless in a cultural and moral vacuum, and McMurtry explores those possibilities in his most significant works. . . .

McMurtry is worthy of serious study for two important reasons. First, as a craftsman he has demonstrated a remarkable ability to solve the technical problems posed by the existence of a Western mythology already known to a readership raised on *Gunsmoke*. It is the question of credibility which is, after all, most troublesome to the exploiters of myths. . . . Second, McMurtry is a social critic whose views of his region mirror the larger concerns of contemporary intellectuals. Whether one agrees with him or not, McMurtry must be acknowledged as one of the spokesmen for a climate of opinion which may soon be prevalent throughout the Southwest and which, however dissident, must be reckoned with as a cultural force. . . .

Whatever his shortcomings may be, he has demonstrated a remarkable technical skill, and his profound insights into the nature of the cowboy, both mythic and real, will provide him with all the subject matter he will need for a lifetime of productivity, should he see fit to return to his earlier preoccupation with the type. If he should choose to explore other thematic material, he will not enter a strange country without valuable resources at his disposal. For his is a considerable talent, and his contribution to the literature of the Southwest has already justified the attention he has received in the region. And if a significant Southwestern literature is to be the wave of the future, then McMurtry is one who will surely ride the crest of that wave to national preeminence.

Thomas Landess. Larry McMurtry (Steck-<br>Vaughn, 1969), pp. 1–2, 5, 42–43

Larry McMurtry's sixth novel, *Terms of Endearment*, rounds out the trilogy-adventures of a smart set of Houstonian characters begun in *Moving On* (1970) and continued through *All My Friends Are Going to Be Strangers* (1972). Though time sequences often fall out of order in the three novels, key events and characters are repeated often enough to maintain a continuous theme which, not surprisingly, has three parts: sex and its frustrations, academics and its frustrations, and something like culture and its frustrations which McMurtry has branded *Ecch-Texas* in a book of essays, *In a Narrow Grave*.

The author of three novels-made-movies, *Horseman, Pass By* (filmed as *Hud*), *Leaving Cheyenne* (filmed as *Lovin' Molly*), and *The Last Picture Show*, McMurtry has moved the setting from the wide-open ranges of the Texas cattle country to the wide-open residential sections of Houston for the second set of three novels. But what is unfortunately revealed by this newest effort is the wide-open spaces of McMurtry's imagination and stockpile of Texas stereotypes. This last book is hopelessly like the previous two, and whatever was fresh and innovative about the others is conspicuously absent from this third novel. . . .

In spite of some loose ends . . . , McMurtry seems finally to have capped off the story as a trilogy. The time of the second part of *Terms of Endearment* is 1971–1976, which suggests either that it is the last chapter to this somewhat uninteresting story, or that McMurtry desires a few more years of breathing room before attacking the next installment. In many ways the novel is lacking. In spite of its four-hundred-page length, the development of the characters is not always satisfying; the situations are often wanting for credulity or for significance, and the dialogue is sometimes "bitchy" and pointless. Occasionally the conflict is mundane and predictable, therefore dull; and time-movement is a problem throughout the book. One of the biggest problems is one which plagues all three of the novels: McMurtry knows too much about literature to allow his characters to be completely unread. The "name-dropping" of famous titles and authors is only a part of the problem; the rest centers in

McMurtry's allowing characters to speak about deep philosophical or literary problems which one might expect a Guggenheim Fellow to know about, but with an authority one would find incredible in a Houstonian socialite, even a rich and well-educated one. Also one cannot help but feel that McMurtry wrote all three novels with an eye toward Hollywood's acceptance of them for film, but in spite of his inclusion of Peter Bogdanovich in the book (at a party), one must doubt the possibility of film adaptation for any of the three.

On the plus side, the book reads well. There is humor for those who have not become inundated with McMurtry's lampooning of Texas and Texans; and the story has enough twists and turns to keep the reader's attention in spite of the somewhat trite nature of the conflict. In short, McMurtry has worn out the stereotypes. Aurora, Vernon, Rosie, and Royce are all out of a well-used stockpile, and their shopworn appearance is damaging to the book. Lack of development is not a charge to be laid lightly at McMurtry's door, and one does not wish for another eight-hundred-page monolith such as *Moving On*. In spite of these lesser efforts, however, McMurtry has demonstrated in his first three novels that he is a talented and forceful writer. One can hope that number seven will be a luckier number than was *Terms of Endearment*.

R. C. Reynolds. SWR. Winter, 1976, pp. 102,<br>104–5

McMurtry is unique among Southwestern regionalists in his use of satire and black humor in a context in which these elements have been traditionally absent—the Western novel. The mordant wit that characterizes many of his essays is intensified in his fiction, which often becomes Hogarthian in the savagery of its satire. His cynical view of marriage reaches its height in *All My Friends Are Going to Be Strangers*; the caustic portraits of Uncle Laredo and his wife, Martha, who are so antagonistic toward each other that they live on separate ranches is a monstrously magnified depiction of marital incompatibility. He caricatures sex-crazed Mexicans in the same novel, Petey Ximenes and Antonio (though perhaps these characterizations illustrate a regional ethnic bias against the non-Anglo). His personal antipathy toward the hypocrisy and tawdry icons of the small town is personified in *The Last Picture Show*, particularly in the figures of Herman Popper and Jacy Farrow. McMurtry has said that the small town derives its concept of masculinity and femininity from the examples of the football coach and the high school beauty queen, but the characterizations of Coach Popper and Jacy Farrow undermine these accepted norms for sexual identification. . . .

McMurtry's use of black humor in *The Last Picture Show* should not be overemphasized, for the novel is a highly symbolic and complex work, as well as a scathing denunciation of the spiritual stagnation of a small town. But it should be noted that the frank treatment of sex in this novel sets it apart from the stereotypes established in such typically Western books as Owen Wister's *The Virginian*, while the humorous treatment of the same subject exhibits the approach utilized by other young Texas writers, such as Donald Barthelme and Terry Southern, or by James Leo Herlihy in *Midnight Cowboy*. . . .

In Faulkner's epic saga of the South, a new breed of man, the Snopeses, arises after the Civil War to challenge not only the power but the life-styles and values of the old aristocracy. The emergence of this class signals the birth of the new South and the end of the old mythic South. Faulkner was able to chronicle the demise of the old traditions and to reconstruct the antebellum South in his art while avoiding the pitfalls of historical romance. He succeeds, ultimately, in utilizing the materials of mythology to restore the old South in a kind of living presence, one in which he was totally at home. For more than a decade, McMurtry's task has been not so much to restore the myth of the West as to lay it to rest, to escape from its hold. Indeed, McMurtry has never been fully convinced of the accuracy of the myth, but whether he conceives of it as something that was, or that might have or should have been, his conception of the old West as myth gave form to his earliest fiction and ennobles some of his most memorable characters: Homer Bannon, Sam the Lion, and Roger Waggoner. . . .

McMurtry laments that although Texas has "a few decent writers," it has had no Homer and no Faulkner. "Thus," he says, "it has no single, greatly told tragic story, no central myth." McMurtry remains preeminently a regional novelist, the finest Texas has yet produced. Should he overcome the unresolved tension he feels about his native soil, he might succeed in writing the saga the region lacks.

Charles D. Peavy. *Larry McMurtry* (Twayne, 1977), pp. 102, 105, 116–18

Larry McMurtry's fiction is noteworthy for its sympathetic and sensitive examination of present and future citybillies. *Hud*, for example, records the passing of a frontier cattleman and the attempts of his stepson and grandson at coping with modern society. The title character, in fact, is a cowboy seduced by urban ways, a ranch hand no longer satisfied with the slow periods of ranch life. But *The Last Picture Show* provides the most complete portrait of the disintegration of small-town Texas life as the larger-than-life older generation dies out and is replaced by younger people spoiled by the modern world, and thus incapable of facing the rigors of a "land so powerful that it is all but impossible to live on it pleasantly" (*In a Narrow Grave*), people for whom citybilly life is the only alternative to the emptiness of dying high plains towns.

*The Last Picture Show* operates on a series of contrasts between characters, places, and the sources of values which determine the psychological realities of each generation. The characters are differentiated not so much by age as by their sense of belonging and self-knowledge. Sam the Lion, Lois, and eventually Mrs. Popper have come to terms with themselves and with the land, whereas Sonny, Duane, and Jacy are groping for identities the country can no longer supply. The roles they attempt to play are empty both to themselves and to their companions, since roles must have some relationship to the places in which they are lived. The social gathering places of the older generation are either disappearing or no longer serving the needs of the young. With the loss of place comes a loss of identity, a loss which cannot be compensated for by the stereotypes of movies or television.

Andrew Macdonald and Gina Macdonald. In
*Larry McMurtry: Unredeemed Dreams*, ed.
Dorey Schmidt (Pan American Univ., 1978), p. 22

By his own account, Cadillac Jack McGriff, 6 feet 5 inches of Texas manhood without his boots or Stetson, 35 years old and twice divorced, is a natural scout and a natural womanizer. Having done a stint as a bulldogger on the rodeo circuit, he retired to roam the country in his big pearl-colored Caddy with peach velour interior. He now spends his days scouting—exploring back roads for antiques and collectibles, buying and selling what strikes his fancy, "too curious, too restless, too much in love with the treasure hunt" to specialize.

The double conceit of scouting and that fancy vehicle allows Larry McMurtry, the author of seven other novels, the peculiar luxury of a rambling, often incoherent, frequently entertaining tale [*Cadillac Jack*]. . . .

But every time Mr. McMurtry threatens to get into something like substantive plot or character development, Jack jumps into that dad-blamed car and drives off somewhere. The cruising is endless and serves only to connect the short, affectionate, sometimes hilarious vignettes of Americans trading and swapping that give the book its genuine eccentricity. . . .

Larry McMurtry is a problematic figure. His second and finest novel, *Leaving Cheyenne*, threatens to become an acknowledged classic. That tender love story of a strong-minded trio spans half a century but is set in only a few square miles of rural Texas. Indeed, it is crucial that Molly, the independent heroine, will not leave her land. With his third novel Mr.

McMurtry found cars and the possibility of escape; then came Houston and after that the open road. Lately, as the author has drawn on his experiences in Hollywood and in Washington, where he is a rare-book dealer and critic, his fiction has been increasingly satirical and cartoonish. It's the folks in the background of *Cadillac Jack*, the ones who live out there in the middle of America, who seem real. They are worth meeting.

Eden Ross Lipson. *NYT*. Nov. 21, 1982, pp. 13, 20

## MENCKEN, H. L. (1880–1956)

In one sense . . . Mencken was not a thinker. He was certainly not a philosopher, especially if the role of philosopher is identified with sustained linear argument or with a complicated architectonic of thought. Mencken, of course, never applied the word philosopher to himself, and preferred to think of himself as a critic of ideas. It might be still better to think of him as a dramatist of ideas, since it is not the systematic quality of his ideas that is important but their ingenious and highly stylized development. Nevertheless, his huge gifts of historical imagination could not have been possible without a strong intellectual framework to contain this imagination, to give it shape. While Mencken never used ideas in the manner of the philosopher, never wanted to be tied down to the hardness of intellectual formality and exactitude, his ideas are of no small importance as artistic vision. . . .

Obviously the enduring power of Mencken's vision is due to his wizardry with words and his large gift for simplifying and vivifying ideas, for chopping off little blocks from the vast and inert morass of human knowledge and holding these blocks up to the glare of light, featuring them in their full dramatic intensity. Mencken's greatest genius was not only that he could do this, and do it better than any of his contemporaries, but that he happened to hit upon, with fine and exact precision, most of the great verities of life in America, upon our most persistent and troublesome social conditions and disorders. The continuing interest of Americans in Mencken is due not merely to the fact that he was a vivid though now somewhat remote and alien figure of the twenties, that he captivated a generation of intellectuals who were struggling against small-town smugness and complacency, or against an impoverished cultural and social life, but that he continues to address himself to our problems today.

George H. Douglas. *H. L. Mencken: Critic of American Life* (Archon, 1978), pp. 14–16

American criticism was a dry, juiceless pursuit which threw a very dim light on the literature (principally the English literature) of the past: it considered that it was making a significant contribution to human knowledge if it counted the number of irregular verbs in *Beowulf* or located some Latin source for an obscure passage in *The Faerie Queene*. It could not be bothered, it felt that it would be beneath its dignity to bother, with the literature that was taking shape around it.

Mencken's criticism differed from this not just in degree but in kind. There had simply never been anything like it before. Though he was extraordinarily well read, he gave little time to mining the classics of earlier generations; his work is notably free of both quotation and learned allusion. He preferred to deal with the contemporary—and in his role as a book reviewer this meant dealing as much or more with the bad, the third- and fourth-rate, as with the good. Indeed, it was the attention that he gave to the bad, and the ridicule he poured upon it month after month after month in *The Smart Set*, that exposed it for what it was and so cleared the path for better and more honest work.

When he wrote about the good—Conrad's novels, for example, or Dreiser's—he illumined it superbly for the benefit of those who had read or would read it, but at the same time he was at an infinite remove from that tribe that Hemingway would later call "explainers." That is to say, however much insight he might bring to bear upon an author's craftsmanship and thought, he never looked for symbolism or two or three layers of hidden meaning. His analyses, in fact, could be read with pleasure and profit by people who had no particular interest in Conrad or Dreiser. Often—there are those who complain that it was too often—his consideration of the work of other men was only a point of departure for setting forth his own ideas; such great essays as "The National Letters," "Puritanism as a Literary Force," and "The Sahara of the Bozart" not only trace the history of American literature but are a part of it. . . .

His thought, it should be unnecessary to say, was seldom original and never profound. There is no point in making him out to have been a great thinker, and any suggestion that he was one would have evoked a violent reaction from him—either he would have burst into guffaws or disappeared quietly into a nearby ocean. "Great Thinkers" were precisely the kind of people whom he distrusted most. His ideas are chiefly notable for their solid common sense—but common sense was a rather rare commodity in the America of his time, and perhaps that is the reason why he seemed so unusual and irritatingly different. If there is a larger supply of it today, if life is saner and more intelligent and a bit pleasanter to live, he deserves much of the credit for that fact. We also have to be grateful to him for giving us a body of literature that, a generation after his passing, is still capable of reminding us that laughter is the best antidote for our troubles, and that it remains the only really effective way for disposing of the "charlatans," "mountebanks," and "frauds" which, despite his best efforts, continue in our midst.

Charles A. Fecher. Mencken: A Study of His Thought (Knopf, 1978), pp. 17, 352

Mencken was only a second-rate philosopher when he came to do a set piece, but that he was a wiser and a better writer as a journalist, and as such an original. Like all originals, he was a bad master. By which I mean that he is a dangerous model for authors of lesser talent. During the 1920s, American newspapers and magazines, even the *Smart Set* and the *American Mercury* themselves, were full of Mencken imitators, who imitated only the windy rhetoric, the facetious polysyllables, the verbosity. There must have been some awful undergraduate essays spawned by Mencken's fame. This, however, is the price the public has to pay for the appearance of any genuine original. It was the same, in his day, with Dickens. And with Mark Twain. And any year after *The Rite of Spring* the concert halls were glutted with fourth-rate Stravinskys. . . .

Intellectual clowns are wits, and Mencken could certainly by witty. But he was also, and I maintain more remarkably, a humorist, and all humorists are professional mountebanks. They instinctively (when they are good) and deliberately (when they are bad) adopt an attitude toward the facts of life that is more naive than that of their audience. This puts the audience in a superior frame of mind, which is the proper frame for the agreeable form of compassion known as laughter. However, the laughter would remain in its pure state of pity if the humorist were really naive. He is, in fact, sharper than his audience. But the successful technique of humor demands that he should throw furtive hints of intelligence to his readers, as if they were his only allies in a world of oafs. The circuit of flattery is now complete. The audience begins by chuckling at the simpleness of the writer and goes on to laugh in triumph at the sudden discovery that they and he alone form a secret society of mockers at the great mass of men.

Alistair Cooke. In On Mencken, ed. John Dorsey (Knopf, 1980), pp. 99–100, 107–8

## MEREDITH, WILLIAM (1929–    )

Since "Resemblances between the life and character of Hazard are not disclaimed but are much fewer than the author would like," we can take Hazard [of *Hazard, the Painter*] as Meredith's model of an admirable man as well as his opportunity to speak of himself in the third person—perhaps not such a surprising tactic in a poet so decorous and diffident, but a very surprising one in a poet who has spoken so beautifully for himself in his own person so often in the past.

In devising a persona through whom he will talk, Meredith places his voice at too far a remove from his experience (Hazard's experience is of course Meredith's, whether historically true or not); the voice becomes so elusive that Meredith is often in danger of vanishing from his own poetry. . . . [We] realize with acute discomfort that we're hearing Meredith talking about how Meredith talks about Hazard. Such convolution shows the seams of the art; the fiction evaporates and we're left with psychological history instead of poetry. What we finally hear is neither a whole characterization nor a whole poet, but a dispossessed consciousness shunting back and forth between the two.

Except for Hazard's equanimity in accepting age, it's hard to know why Meredith finds him admirable. . . .

The best expression of the book's prevailing mood, and one of its best poems, is "Rhode Island". . . . Quite a good poem, and reminiscent of Meredith at his quiet, cultivated best: the gentle wit; the graceful handling of a line which wonderfully replicates Hazard's lazy, random thought; that dextrously placed concluding joke whereby the enervated Hazard continues occupying a necessary space while the small frets of his life chatter on about him. But the charm of the poem derives from its inconsequentiality as much as from anything else.

That's a part of the hazard Meredith takes with his new book—the risk of making poetry out of slim occasions. But perhaps his largest risk lies in continuing to make poetry out of a sensibility which in its easy optimism, its insulating comforts, and its abiding concerns for custom and ceremony must seem to many quite at odds with the prevailing spirit of our times, not least to Meredith himself.

Alan Helms. *Parnassus*. Spring/Summer, 1976,
pp. 220–21, 224

*The Wreck of the Thresher*, published in 1964, was the book which most firmly established the nature and strength of William Meredith's poetry. It seems now, two books later, to have been the culmination of a development in certain directions from which the poet has since swerved, though not unrewardingly. *The Wreck of the Thresher* reveals unobtrusive mastery of craft traditionally conceived; it is not full of sonnets, villanelles, sestinas, or other insistent evidences that the poet is comfortable in formal cages; but beneath the steady, honest lines with their sometimes unpredictable rhyme schemes, there is a sense of assurance that for Meredith, form is a method, not a barrier. In its range of subject, tone and mode, the book consistently offers the voice of a civilized man, a man with good but not flashy manners, engaged in encounters with matters of inexhaustible interest. . . .

Meredith's most recent book, *Hazard, the Painter* (1975) [, a] collection of sixteen poems[,] seems to have been designed to provoke a number of reactions, not all of them charitable, and not all of them familiar to readers of Meredith's previous books. . . .

The style of *Hazard* appears to be more casual, less concentrated, than anything Meredith has written before. One notices, for instance, that there is not a semicolon anywhere in these poems; instead, the independent clauses tumble along over their commas, contributing to the feeling of interior life, as in the second half of this stanza from "Politics," a poem about old liberals gathering to hear jazz for McGovern. . . .

Gradually, as one rereads these poems, the accumulation of anecdote and detail provides the density that is missing from the style, and there arises the illusion of a life, a way of life, made difficult by a difficult time, but still enjoyable and cherished. "The culture is in late imperial decline," Hazard thinks in the line taken from Berryman; and in "Hazard's Optimism," considering his vision of the parachutist as he himself tries a parachute jump, Hazard concludes thus. . . .

The mask of Hazard gives Meredith, at least for the duration of this deceptively brief book, the freedom to work out of ways in which he might think he was becoming set. In the chattiness that contains more than it at first seems to, beneath the detailed surfaces, there is room here for satire as well as for a serious, loving exploration of a peculiar world.

But Hazard is not destined to take over Meredith's voice and life. He is an interesting character met along the way, and, having met him, Meredith is usefully diverted from his way. There are too few uncollected poems on which to base conclusions about apparent directions to come, except to note that in some recent "dialogue poems" responding to wittily chosen epigraphs, Meredith continues to find fresh ways of reminding us that there is joy in plucking at the hems of even the darkest mysteries.

Henry Taylor. *HC*. Feb., 1979, pp. 1–2, 14–15

The distinctive quality of William Meredith's *The Cheer* is its precision of statement, achieved for the most part without falling into aridity and abstraction. Mr. Meredith is refreshingly unafraid to *think* in poetry or to use the wide vocabulary and pliant syntax that many poets now deliberately avoid in favor of vatic pronouncement or egalitarian plainness. . . . I am struck by the narrowness of the gap between the versified quotation from Freud and the continuation in Mr. Meredith's own voice. True, it is the poet who moves from the abstractness of "attitude" and "admiration" to the more particular hospitals, tombstones and trees; but surely the most arresting word in this passage is the abstract (and Freudian) "incestuous," which is endlessly suggestive in this context.

While few of these poems are remarkable for their depth of feeling, some have memorable imagery and music. . . . If, as Mr. Meredith says in his title poem, "The cheer is hidden in the right words," this is one of the more cheerful books I've read lately.

Paul Breslin. *NYT*. March 22, 1981, p. 14

## MERRILL, JAMES (1926–    )

Merrill has absorbed into verse many of the resources of daily conversation and prose. Still, there is a special strangeness and sometimes strain to Merrill's colloquial style, a taut alertness to the meanings which lurk in apparently casual words and phrases. We may find this in all good poets, but Merrill raises it to a habit of vigilance, a quickened control and poise, sometimes bravado, which he clearly trusts as a source of power. When Merrill uses an idiom, he turns it over curiously, as if prospecting for ore. . . .

The figures who appear and re-appear in Merrill's poems have more substance than the legendary heroines who were muses to the sonneteers, but they also have the same mesmerizing force, as he considers and reconsiders their shaping impact on his life. To reread Merrill's books since *Water Street* is to discover him preparing a stage whose objects and cast of characters become increasingly luminous. They become charged with symbolic meaning and release symbolic reverberations from otherwise ordinary narrative event. . . .

Much of Merrill's interest in narrative and everyday experience has been aimed at discovering the charges with which certain objects have become invested for him. He seems in his developed poetry to be asking the Freudian or the Proustian question: what animates certain scenes— and not others—for us? Over the years Merrill's poems have used the objects and stages of daily life, the arrangements of civilized behavior, almost as if he expected to waken sleeping presences and take by surprise the myths he lives by.

David Kalstone. *Five Temperaments: Elizabeth
Bishop, Robert Lowell, James Merrill, Adrienne
Rich, John Ashbery* (Oxford Univ. Pr., 1977), pp.
79–80, 82–83

Merrill's "Mirror" is by no means his best poem. He went on in subsequent books to move in a Proustian direction which was quite original, and in *Water Street* and afterwards he assimilated the impulses of narrative autobiography to a commanding and continuing mythopoeia. His way has been that of the mirror, not the window. His mature poetry inhabits part of that region of emblematic tale-telling which Elizabeth Bishop for some decades before her death, and Robert Penn Warren more recently, have inhabited for their major poetry. I do not refer, of course, to what has been called "confessional," that shrill and pitiful mode of contemporary verse which, neither window nor mirror, most resembles the sound of breaking glass. We can hear it, but learn nothing from it except that some disaster has occurred and that our lives are full of woe, which it seems shocking to need poetry for to inform us. The first part of Merrill's most recent trilogy mythologizes what is in fact the Spirit of Involuntary Memory as a psychic "control" of a ouija board. This is partially to say that the long, astonishing poem called "The Book of Ephraim" is, in almost every way, in lieu of a novel. But the mirror poem revealed a door, a hallway, down which American poetry of the next two decades would walk, not with the purpose of leaving the house and doing something outside of it, nor indeed on a nervous stroll marked by glances out of the windows in distaste. It was a walk taken indoors in an endless house, continually being added to and restored in some of its older parts, neglected to the point of near-ruin in others. But to explore it, and to map it, was to map heaven and hell, now and then, all the overlays which enable us to read the raw sense of the physical map of life itself.

John Hollander. *YR.* Winter, 1981, p. 170

# MERWIN, W. S. (1927–    )

W. S. Merwin has become a stunning modernist. Yet his first four books have come back to remind us how "Horatian" his beginnings were and how dull. These mostly precious, waxen poems are the "classical" work of a young man for whom the classical tradition is in fact dead. They exist after the fact. The poet but embroiders on a funeral cloth while, rocking in the cradle of his talent, an unknown quality waits to be born.

Merwin commenced in the fifties not merely as a poetic academic but as a sort of ghost. This world, dragging its physical, hence contemporary everydayness, was not his "bourn." His spirit was smitten with loftiness; it wanted to sing or rather to "carol." So it sprang back to the more spiritual, the more vertical middle ages, where time was but a candle in the cathedral of eternity. The Lady and the fool, tasseled fable, hearty rejoicings, middle earth, laurel woods, espaliered gardens, bones, prayers, tongues of fire, shadows, shadows—this poet took the whole kit and caboodle out of the trunk and propped it up to dote on it, stroking it like doll's hair. . . .

His pathos is somehow all prettiness—cold. These poems might have been penned for the lords and ladies of Byzantium; they are the spirit's cultured pearls.

True, Merwin's four more recent volumes are even spookier, hardly for human readers at all. Yet in manner they are somewhere in tomorrow. Instead of brocade, the barest, briefest threads that relate to—you scarcely know what. But you want to know; they get into you.

Calvin Bedient. SwR. Spring, 1977, p. 367

To the extent that Merwin's work has affinities with those poets we identify with specific schools of contemporary American poetry, he comes closest to Robert Bly, James Wright, Galway Kinnell, and the Deep Imagists, in his creation of a series of complex poetic images emanating from the depths of the psyche, often never emerging into consciousness in the poems. Merwin's unquestioning acceptance of perception serves paradoxically to call into question the very structure of perception as it is traditionally understood. In this he is like the poets named above. In his work the images often remain deeply submerged, awaiting the reader's intuitive, if not intellectual resolution. The reader climbs around amid the words, pauses, and images as one climbs rocks underwater; one is never certain where the next step will carry him. But Merwin is more spiritual and less down-to-earth than the Deep Imagists. . . .

Merwin is a visionary poet whose work reflects an engagement in the silence of the self, a receptivity to supranatural experiences, and, in the later work, an openness to participation in the lives of other creatures, and a questioning of the basic structures of perception. In pursuing the negative aesthetic, he opens the way for a poetry that is mystical without being effusive, intimate without being personal, formal without taking itself (or anything or anyone else) too seriously, a poetry that is inspired yet controlled in that it follows a regular, if elliptical, pattern of thought. . . .

In the final analysis, Merwin's recent poetry may not be monotonous or weak at all; it may not be attaining to the condition of silence; it may be misjudged. In actuality, some of the poems of *The Compass Flower* and the recent prose pieces may manifest a radical departure in the evolution of Merwin's writing. They may manifest a new literary perspective, even a new genre.

Cheri Davis. W. S. Merwin (Twayne, 1981), pp.<br>19, 21, 160

W. S. Merwin was a student of [John] Berryman's at Princeton. One night he called the drunken Berryman "pusillanimous," and the poet wanted to flatten him. Merwin, of course, was right, as he is about everything in his own book of childhood recollections, *Unframed Originals*. With stunning sense for detail, setting, character and situation, Merwin employs flashback and story-within-story to recreate his parents, aunts, uncles and cousins in rural Pennsylvania. His father was a Presbyterian minister in Union City and in Scranton, a loving extrovert with everyone but his only son. Withholding love in order not to spoil the boy, he surrounded him with a myriad of don'ts so that one marvels how little Billy did not break into smithereens. He looks back without anger at this man on the go, so typically American and yet so strangely alone.

Merwin's mother emerges in the last of the six family studies as a woman prepared to die with the developed concentration with which she lived. She is a warm, unselfish person who also finds it difficult to express her love. The poet is walking to Athos, in the midst of the monks' praise of the Virgin Mary, unaware that his mother is about to die far away. He prays for her, remembers lines from Dante's *Purgatorio*, and brings his book to a peaceful closing, reconciled to his own limitations and to the unfulfilled lives from which he has come.

Merwin is a staring eye that misses no gesture or sign; each word and motion points to the whole. What appears on the surface to be a list of trivial observations or a mere digression, helps illuminate the final portrait with a Flemish painter's light. He is master of color and line, and *Unframed Originals* belongs in the gallery of great word-portraits.

James Finn Cotter. *Am.* Jan. 29, 1983, p. 76

# MILLER, ARTHUR (1915–    )

For Miller, . . . writing in a secular society in which our society's structure related to materialism, the development of values came out of his heterogeneous experience, religious and secular. Given that his family and his roots were always with him, given that the fact and the image of his work experiences—as in "In Memoriam" and the half-finished play of 1936—were in his subconscious, it seems that an emotional-religious-psychological conflict raged just beneath the surface. In his early works he was able to dramatize those value conflicts that were close to him and almost on the surface. In his richer works, in *All My Sons* and *Death of a Salesman*, the past came rushing in. . . .

In his career up to and including *Salesman*, Miller's Jewish heritage was in conflict with his American present. Believing in the values he assimilated from his earliest years right through his University of Michigan years, when he was a Jewish boy from New York in Ann Arbor, it was the moral dilemma of his times that was his subject. As a man and playwright, he saw group identity smashed by external forces and by the demands of individualism and success. On the other hand, at the same time he perceived the ideal world as one in which "the individual was at one with his society; his conflicts with it were, in our terms, like family conflicts, the opposing sides of which nevertheless shared a mutuality of feeling and responsibility." In this sense, Miller proceeded from his roots. Not certain of who he was but certain of his values he tried to set forth what happens "when a man does not have a grip on the forces of life and has no sense of values which will lead him to that kind of grip . . . the implication was that there must be such a grasp of those forces, or else we're doomed." These are the reasons behind Miller's portraits of Willy and Joe Keller, for example, for at base Joe's trouble was not that he could not tell right from wrong, "but that his cast of mind cannot admit that he, personally, has any viable connection with his world, his universe, or his society." It seems undeniable that in attempting to deal with his moral dilemma, Miller's roots were the barb or spur reflecting his Jewish heritage and sensitivity, and responsible for his continuity of thought and treatment from Brooklyn to Broadway, from adolescence to *Death of a Salesman*.

Daniel Walden. In Critical Essays on Arthur Miller, ed. James J. Martine (G. K. Hall, 1979), p. 195

One might argue, with justice, that *Death of a Salesman*'s only peer as *the* American play of the twentieth century is Eugene O'Neill's *Long Day's Journey into Night.* . . . There are many thematic similarities in the two. They are, of course, "about" the same thing—life-long quest of a certain image of self and other, set in the twin frameworks of family role relationships and occupational success striving. Both demonstrate how these spheres interpenetrate, particularly the way in which a culturally enjoined success ethic informs and corrodes family life. The Lomans and the Tyrones, though unlike in many ways, are both nuclear families and almost totally self-absorbed. The family members, with few ties to any rich life outside, feed upon one another; demanding too much of one another and of themselves, they are embittered by the inevitable gulf between ideal image and functioning reality. Both families subsist on fictions, shared delusions that seem necessary to the preservation of any family life at all. Perhaps all families require the maintenance of certain myths about themselves; but the Tyrones and the Lomans are extraordinary in the pervasiveness and grandeur of their domestic myths. In each play, crises arise and create a breaking through of the delusive fabric. Thus Biff, at last determined to expose Willy's comforting lies for what they are, says, "We never told the truth for ten minutes in this house!" The dramas are also akin in that the action pivots on a troubled target member—Willy Loman, Mary Tyrone—whose torments throw the tangle of domestic affection and accusation into sharp relief.

In the end, Willy's tragedy lies as much in the bringing down of his dreams as in the bringing down of the man. In some curious way, perhaps the dreams were the best part of the man. Willy chased the same green light Jay Gatsby chased. Willy and Gatsby share the same epitaph—"nobody came to the funeral." Willy's whole being has been based on the moving power of a friendship and a presence that do not exist. . . .

The play is now more than a quarter of a century old, and Willy Loman's America has been in many ways transformed. Yet the values portrayed and betrayed are with us still, and the pain and terror are not diminished by a fraction. Linda and Charley, who see Willy unblinkered, affirm that he is a tragic hero. Their words are now familiar, engraved on the consciousness of those who care about the American theatre and care about the texture of our national life. . . .

Robert N. Wilson. *The Writer as Social Seer*
(Univ. of North Carolina Pr., 1979), pp. 69–70

One could say a playwright is not a great playwright unless he can use things—in themselves—thematically, not simply as properties to be touched then discarded on the way to discovery, but somehow as the discovery itself. At this point, drama extends itself into poetry, and metaphor swells with movement to a broader, historical reality. Arthur Miller operates in this vision with reserve and intelligence and surprise.

He operates such power initially. The touch of any world begins, of course, with what we first see; and in Miller's opening stage demands, we not only find the physical setting depicting time and place, we often are presented with objects that instruct us intuitively through their metaphoric quality. . . . With well chosen objects Miller tips us off to the inner substance of his characters, or at least what they appear to be to the main figures whose viewpoints often shadow the plays. . . .

In Miller's world, even dreams become absurd, their baggage at last, heavy and silly and seemingly impossible to get rid of. Willy's dream land of big games and diamond mines and assistant buyer positions might be more beautiful than his actual everyday life, but as Biff slowly realizes, its self-inflation is eventually fatal. Such a revelation holds us abruptly in *The Price* as the playwright forces us face to face with the accumulation of the past, both of its dream and reality life.

Marianne Boruch. *LitR*. Summer, 1981, pp. 548–
49, 555, 560

## MILLER, HENRY (1891–1980)

We have in Miller an ideal instance of the interested eye, one filled with more ego than light, an "I" which lives in a world of utility and blunt satisfactions. Since objects are reduced to their signs (I am edible, I am drinkable, I am bedable), such signs are surreally enlarged and related, so that a woman is simply a collection of hungry concavities which must be approached warily but always with phallus aforethought. . . .

In *The Tropic of Cancer* and *The Colossus of Maroussi*, where Miller is at his best, in spectacular bursts, in similar fits and starts throughout his *oeuvre*, there is an eager vitality and exuberance to the writing which is exhilarating; a rush of spirit into the world as though all the sparkling wines had been uncorked at once; and the language we watchfully hear skip, whoop and wheel across Miller's pages makes an important esthetic point, especially to those of us who are more at home with Joyce or Woolf or James or Proust, and that is that beneath all the quiet ruminations of the mind, the slendered sensibilities, the measured lyricism of finer feelings, even nearby the remotest precincts of being, is a psyche like quicksand, an omnivorous animal, the continually chewing self. . . .

Some styles are celebrational, as Miller's often is; some are penitential, like Joyce's, full of self-imposed barriers, hardships, ordeals and penalties; and some are excremental—where the idea is simply to get it out, to write like hell and never look back, as Mailer says, until the words amass and mount in books which resemble the rubble of a prolonged catharsis.

Henry Miller's works are not *written*, and do not belong to the page like Pynchon's; nor are they *spoken* as Gaddis's are; nor do they employ the more formal oral eloquence of Sir Thomas Browne; they are *talked*, yarned like a sailor, endlessly gabbed. . . .
William H. Gass. NYT. Oct. 24, 1976, pp. 1–2

Like so many American writers of his generation, Miller formed his artistic premises in the matrix of the subversive, on a fanatical commitment to a doctrine of total personal freedom and the most unsettling honesty about himself and his emotions—whatever, in fact, represented an engagement of life antithetical to the hypocrisies of official society. Also he was, as it seems now, fortunately placed in history to become the sort of man and writer his radical metaphysics required him to be. At a time when, for the provincial American, raw experience in and for itself seemed equivalent to ascension to Godhead, Miller became a supreme cultist and chronicler of the rawest experience conceivable. At a time when the prevailing bigotries deemed it obscene for writers to describe the bodily functions in the language commonly used for them, Miller dedicated himself to becoming the world's first artistically serious writer of pornographic novels. At a time when reason and repression were still the dominant features of established culture, Miller became a champion of the unfettered libidinous self and treated the sex act as if it were a triumphant dance on the grave of the righteous.

But what is perhaps most striking about Miller is that, in the service of his nihilism, he has been able to revert to a state of total infantile irresponsibility, existing in that state not only without the slightest twinge of conscience but with the most astonishing happiness. This more than anything may well be what has helped estrange him from American readers, for he has tended to play far too cheerfully and guiltlessly the complete bastard for us to love him very much. It would seem that we can accept such a man only so long as we have reason to suspect that in some as yet unpolluted part of himself he is conscious of violating principles he knows to be right. The quite honorable French tradition of the flaneur is alien to us, and particularly odious is one who is a professional idler in everything except copulation and the writing of filthy books. We may salivate over his descriptions of sex, yet despise him for refusing to treat sex with the requisite moral seriousness and respect. For Miller saw the sex act as one of the funniest routines in the human vaudeville, and he also saw it, in the form of its usual practice in the bohemian world he knew, as one of the most obvious symptoms of the emotional illness of modern culture, which had evolved from a state of miserable repressiveness to a state of moral anesthesia without ever attaining a genuine revolution of feeling. . . .

Yet Miller in his best work has always been able to transcend the sordidness implicit in this view. What saves him is his joyfulness in the face of the sordid, his power to find high pleasure in the sexual comedy and positively to revel in the detritus thrown off by the process of the world's dissolution. Unlike his French contemporary Céline, to whom the ugliness of the bodily functions was a prime indication that life was disgusting, Miller delighted in such ugliness because it was for him an affirmation of the vitality of life at a time when the forces of technology were hard at work regimenting, purifying, and intellectualizing life out of existence.

John W. Aldridge. *SR*. Nov. 13, 1976, pp. 26–27

It would be a pity to remember Henry Miller only as the man who made it possible for Americans to write about sex. If there had been no sex in *Tropic of Cancer*, Mr. Miller's first and best novel, it would have been an even better book.

Leon Trotsky said about Louis-Ferdinand Céline, who influenced Mr. Miller, that he walked into literature the way most men walked into their living rooms. The same is true of Mr. Miller, who was one of the earliest American authors to perfect a vernacular, conversational style and to use it to write an impressionistic, anecdotal novel about a comic, antiheroic character. In *Tropic of Cancer*, we can hear Céline's *Journey to the End of Night*, Dostoyevsky's *Notes From the Underground*, Walt Whitman and a smattering of Joyce and Rabelais.

Mr. Miller's reputation as a sexual pioneer tended to obscure the fact that he was a marvelous observer, a man with an infallible ear and a flair for finding symbolism in unobtrusive places. In one of the most successful scenes in *Tropic of Cancer*, he turned an encounter with a Parisian prostitute into a declaration of war: the war between the sexes, between nations, between man and his conscience.

It was not the joy of sex that animated Mr. Miller's books so much as the comedy of sex, a mood he may have borrowed from Rabelais. It might have been better if he had clung to that mood, for in his later books he showed an increasing fondness for philosophizing. In this, he was just the opposite of the man who said, "I wanted to be a philosopher but cheerfulness kept breaking in."

An easy and jubilant movement from the particular to the general, from the event to the symbol, had always been Mr. Miller's forte. After his first novel, however, the general began to crowd out the particular. As someone said about a ballet written by Salvador Dali, the dancers were so burdened with symbolism that they could hardly move.

There was not a great deal of fun in American fiction in the 30's. At his best, Henry Miller was wonderful fun to read. He was the poet laureate of expatriation, and his portraits of Americans in Paris may be the best that have ever been written.

Anatole Broyard. *NYTd*. June 9, 1980, p. D14

# ● MOMADAY, N. SCOTT (1934–    )

This first novel [*House Made of Dawn*], as subtly wrought as a piece of Navajo silverware, is the work of a young Kiowa Indian who teaches English and writes poetry at the University of California in Santa Barbara. That creates a difficulty for a reviewer right away. American Indians do not write novels and poetry as a rule, or teach English in top-ranking universities either. But we cannot be patronizing. N. Scott Momaday's book is superb in its own right.

It is the old story of the problem of mixing Indians and Anglos. But there is a quality of revelation here as the author presents the heart-breaking effort of his hero to live in two worlds. . . .

Young Abel comes back to San Ysidro to resume the ancient ways of his beloved long-haired grandfather, Francisco. Abel is full of fears that he has relaxed his hold on these ways, after living like an Anglo in the Army. He is our tortured guide as we see his Indian world of pollen and rain, of houses made of dawn, of feasts and rituals to placate the gods, of orchards and patches of melons and grapes and squash, of beautiful colors and marvelous foods such as piki, posole, loaves of sotobalau, roasted mutton and fried bread. It is a wantless "world of wonder and exhilarating vastness.". . .

Abel's troubles begin at once. He has a brief and lyrical love affair with a white woman from California seeking some sort of truth at San Ysidro. Then he runs afoul of Anglo jurisprudence, which has no laws covering Pueblo ethics. He is paroled to a Los Angeles relocation center and copes for a time with that society, neither Anglo nor Indian. He attends peyote sessions; he tries to emulate his Navajo roommate, who almost accepts the glaring lights and treadmill jobs, the ugliness of the city and the Anglo yearning to own a Cadillac. Abel cannot "almost" cope. Because of his contempt, a sadistic cop beats him nearly to death. But he gets home in time to carry on tradition for his dying grandfather.

There is plenty of haze in the telling of this tale—but that is one reason why it rings so true. The mysteries of cultures different from our own cannot be explained in a short novel, even by an artist as talented as Mr. Momaday.

Marshall Sprague. NYT. June 9, 1968, p. 5

As a modern, historical consciousness and a member of a largely desacralized society, [Momaday] knows that he cannot return to the mythopoesis and archaic ontology of his Indian ancestors, that the Kiowa verbal tradition "has suffered a deterioration in time," . . . and that the Kiowa culture can no longer establish identity and compel belief solely through the authority of its myths and rites. As a Kiowa who "feels Indian" in spite of all this, he is intent on reconciling his "primitive," tribal, "blood" consciousness with his modern, individual consciousness; but he is also bothered by a fear of presumption and sacrilege, a suspicion that he is evoking his dead relatives along with their myths, visions and rites without really being able to believe in them, or, to put it more precisely, to believe in what he has made them—in his imagination and through his art.

Put in yet another way, *The Way to Rainy Mountain* is one man's intensely personal discovery of what Joseph Campbell has called the collapse of traditional mythology and its displacement by creative mythology. But Momaday has gone one step farther, for he has sought to posit the essential continuity between these two kinds of mythology, insisting that both are acts of the imagination and both are capable of generating the same kind of belief. And he has done so in two ways: through the development of a complex structure in which to cast these many journeys he hopes to make . . . and through a series of memories or visions of his Kiowa ancestors through which he claims to have achieved a full sense of identification with them. . . .

[Momaday] is not only functioning as a creative mythologist, an indication of his modern, individualistic perspective; but he is also dramatizing the process whereby traditional mythology becomes creative—an indication that the two are continuous and reconcilable.

The last structural indication that Momaday has been moving toward the convergence of personal and cultural experience, poetry and myth, can be found in the poems which frame the entire work. Their positioning is itself an indication that creative art, that is the authority of the imagination, is most responsible for the integrity of the work, the journey it recalls, and the idea of the self which it reveals.

Charles A. Nicholas. SDR. Winter, 1975–76, pp.<br>149, 155–56

*House Made of Dawn* (1968) is the most complex and the most obscure novel written by an American Indian. Virtually every page of the text illustrates Momaday's fascination with structure: the novel makes use of multiple points of view, stream of consciousness techniques, abrupt changes of time and chronology achieved primarily through the use of flashbacks and flashforwards; it also incorporates ethnic materials (traditional oral tales, fragments of poetry), and historical documents, both oral and written. If there is one major problem with the novel it is its obscurity, which has resulted in a number of ambiguities about factual matters within the narrative. . . .

It is impossible to analyze *House Made of Dawn* without considering two relative points at the outset. First, the meaning or meanings of Momaday's novel are irrevocably bound up in the novel's structure: form and content interlock. Second, the novel should not be interpreted without reference to two other works published by the author: *The Way to Rainy Mountain* (1969) and *The Names* (1976). The first of these has a tripartite interwoven structure involving Kiowa legend, established facts about that legend ("historical" facts), and Momaday's personal experiences with these events or facts. *The Way to Rainy Mountain*, like Tosamah's sermon in *House Made of Dawn*, records the historic movement of the Kiowa people from the Northern to the Southern Plains. *The Names*, a kind of precocious autobiography, covers much the same material. . . .

What he is not . . . certain of, it seems to me, is what the American

Indian *was*. That past—the end in the beginning—forms the central quest of all of his prose works (*House Made of Dawn*, *The Way to Rainy Mountain*, *The Names*). Reading any one of these volumes is a frightening experience since in each one of them Momaday has created a painful image of his self: a man in search of his roots. I would further suggest that Momaday has yet to solve the dilemma of his own identity. The ending of *House Made of Dawn* . . . typifies this dilemma.

Charles R. Larson. American Indian Fiction<br>(Univ. of New Mexico Pr., 1978), pp. 78–79, 81–<br>82, 94

*House Made of Dawn* is a memorable failure. Some of its passages attain a prose surface brilliance and also a depth, not at all like the historic depth of Macaulay or the ancient, almost etymological depth of Hardy, but a kind of depth of physical perception simultaneous with a post-Romantic understanding of man's relationship to nature—an understanding and a sensory perception which are both great and unique. . . .

The novel falls apart rather than coming together: it remains a batch of often dazzling fragments, a kind of modern prose Sutton Hoo—perhaps because the young Momaday yielded to the deadly, fashionable temptation of imitative form in dealing with contemporary identity crisis, here specifically the fragmented personality of the misfit Abel. The book's own fragmentation is not quotable, since the problem is an incoherence of large parts, but any reader will readily grant that the sequence of items—say, the bear hunt and the murder that parallels it; the night scenes with Father Olguin; Abel's flashbacks; his encounter with the enemy tank; and his encounter with Angela—is without fixed order. The parts can be rearranged, no doubt with change of effect, but not always with recognizable difference. The fragments thus presented are the subject. The result is a successful depiction but not an understanding of what is depicted: a reflection, not a novel in the comprehensive sense of the word. . . .

The book is therefore an intelligent miscellany of more and less well-written facets that together represent a historical and contemporary situation of great importance, but it is not a successful understanding of or coping with that situation, and so it fails as a novel—right through its evasive ending.

What remains is nonetheless sometimes rare photography with scraps of great prose. The prose is often rhythmically distinguished: long in its rhythms, with neither the complex clauses of James and Macaulay nor the streams of Joyce and Faulkner, yet very far indeed from the syntactical and artistic simplifications of Hemingway. And there are other successes. The long unified description of the bear hunt is remarkable for its psychological perception of the sexual relationship between hunter and hunted (the prose, the psychology, and the bear owe something to Faulkner). And the great description of the Eagle Watchers Society . . . approaches the barren courage of Melville's *The Encantadas*.

But probably the most successful general feature of the novel is its landscape, which is both intensely sensory and symbolic in its implication of a human and historically specific relationship to that landscape. . . .

Roger Dickinson-Brown. *SoR*. Winter, 1978, pp. 30–32

Near the end of N. Scott Momaday's *House Made of Dawn* the old man, Francisco, in the fever of dying, recalls a solitary bear hunt from his youth. A preliminary and, it seems, self-imposed ritual to the hunt was a visit to a cave of the Old Ones. . . . The bear hunt which follows is a central tale in the novel, in the same way that Francisco, the protagonist's grandfather, is a central cohering character. The hunt was an occasion of great, self-conscious manliness, carried off through conscientious application of racial skills and virtues, and accorded, in the pueblo, well-earned esteem. But most interesting, I think, is the quiet trespass in the Anasazi cave—a terrifying sin of commission, according to the lawyer. A sacrilege, and therefore the height of bravery.

Francisco works as a structuring principle in *House Made of Dawn*. His lime-twig trap, his hope to snare the sacred, frames the eighty pages and thirteen days of Part One. His inexpressible grief sets the tone that broods behind every page. Until the last part, Francisco is inarticulate and peripheral, a still point against whom the story's violence brushes and whom it then leaves alone. But in this book peripheries are profound, delineating limbuses. Francisco—heroic, crippled, resonant with the old ways, impotent in the new—acts as a lodestone to the novel's conflicting energies. His incantatory dying delirium in Spanish fixes Momaday's symbolic compass: Porcingula, the white devil, the black runners. The commotions of the narrative gather and cool around the old man, and around his dying the book shapes its proportions. Francisco becomes at the end the lens for the single sharp image the novel has been struggling to focus on: Abel's convalescent, redemptive participation in the running. The direction, the structure of *House Made of Dawn* is toward proportion, toward a falling into place. The novel resolves into Francisco's recollections and is driven by tensions revealed to be his: sacrilege and sacredness, fear and courage.

It is a brave book. Momaday's ambition is enormous and untried; he is attempting to transliterate Indian culture, myth, and sensibility into an alien art form, without loss. He may in fact be seeking to make the modern Anglo novel a vehicle for a sacred text. . . .

The novel concerns survival, not salvation, enduring rather than Faulkner's sense of prevailing. The dawn runners physically manifest *the* Indian strength—they abide, "and in this there is a resistance and an overcoming, a long outwaiting." And Momaday is proposing not only a qualified hope for cultural continuity, but a holy endurance. The running is a sacred rite and an act of courage, thus a warding off of fear and evil, the specters (consolidated in such demons as Martinez and wine) that gnaw at Indian probity throughout the book. The race at dawn is additionally a sacrament of creation. As such it outlines the novel's purpose and achievement.

*House Made of Dawn.* Its subject is creation myth, the antithesis of Benally's "plan." The book's metaphysics build from a sequence of creation schemata: the diaspora of the Bahkyush, the feast of Santiago, St. John's Word, Tai-me, Benally's songs, his grandfather's story of the Bear Maiden. The book *is* a creation myth—rife with fabulous imagery, ending with Abel's rebirth in the old ways at the old man's death—but an ironic one, suffused with violence and telling a story of culture loss. Sacrilege repeatedly undercuts sacredness. Father Olguin constantly faces the corruption of his faith, from Angela's mockery, from the perverse vision of a Pueblo Christ child. The vitality of ceremony is juxtaposed to the helplessness of drunks. The peyote service is sullied, almost bathetic. But sacrilege impels sacredness here, as fear does courage, and loss survival. The series of myths, each variously imperfect, each with common corruptions and shared strengths, overlap, blend, and fuse as this novel. . . .

Momaday is a preserver of holiness in *House Made of Dawn.* He has transported his heritage across the border; in a narrative and style true to their own laws, he has mythified Indian consciousness into a modern novel.

Baine Kerr. SWR. Spring, 1978, pp. 172–73,<br>178–79

## MOORE, MARIANNE (1887–1972)

Marianne Moore is not an original thinker. Her "message" of freedom through sacrifice could not be more commonplace, as she herself would agree. Yet she may make it strike us with an original force because it is arrived at in the poems themselves only through difficulty. It is hard for her to sacrifice silence. Then again, it is hard for her to sacrifice speech. Sacrifice alternates with sacrifice, and the freedom with which we are able to put them together, reclaiming both speech and silence "in/the name of freedom" and as a taboo against psychical oppression, is the freedom of Moore's verse. We may take freedoms with her verses because she has given them to us. She covets nothing that she has let go.

What is commonplace as idea is not necessarily commonplace as a personally held and acted-upon conviction; in fact, commonplace, as Marianne Moore embraces it, is rare. It is for the intensely personal valuation that Moore has performed upon the common places as well as the exotic places of the world that we feel gratitude and enlightenment, if we are able to feel them. "In Distrust of Merits" shows us commonplace abhorrence of war and the Self who participates by not participating, yet it has a felt intensity, a "mountainous wave" of unconscious fastidiousness "that makes us who look, know depth." "He/sees deep and is glad, who/accedes to mortality" ("What Are Years?"). It is an easy thing to *say*, but difficult to *see*. . . .

Marianne Moore's work is a lifelong exposition of paradox, and no matter how much careful observation she lavishes on the objects that illustrate her various paradoxes, no matter how much precise illusion is given shape through her disarming rhetoric, the paradoxes still remain and are always interesting. Perhaps paradox itself is the rock crystal thing that the hero is seen to see. It is accuracy and mystery well married; it is naked in its objective transparence, but armored in the untouchable axial law that made it. . . .

There is only one poem called by Marianne Moore "The Hero," but in effect all the poems she wrote might claim this as some sort of subtitle. It is telling that the hero of the poem "The Hero" is an anönymous character, for the hero can be anybody at any time who shares the hero's devotion to vision and to the "rock crystal thing." Heroes have pasts and futures. This is clear from the poem; all her past sensations gather in her, preparing her with responses to her fathering fate, her apprehensions, her convictions. We must acknowledge the value of childhood and of limitations in general, turn the wishes born of both into actions. These actions are heroic when they express both the personal desire of the hero, fulfilling some need in her, and connect also with the desires of a community of potential heroes. Thus the wish and the limitation become a dance, a poem, a Brooklyn bridge or icosasphere, Bach's Solfegietto, or a knight in quest of modest armor. . . .

We shall always come back to "science" in the work of Marianne Moore, because science was to her a method of knowledge indispensable to her comprehensively evaluative mode of poetry. Moral sense may be uppermost, but it must be informed with the greatest possible exactitude about the state of things in the physical world. In order to make spiritual acknowledgment of creation, it must make technical acknowledgments— how it was done, how it is to be done. This technique links the past and the future as well as the matter and the spirit of all worldly phenomena. If "science" is accurate observation of the world's developing, temporary balance, and eventual dissolution, and "prophecy" the accurate observation of those processes on a spiritual level, then poetry, if it is to contain the truest of all observations, must put them together. The confusion is accurate and necessary. Confusion, submitted to poetry by unconfusion, confusion affectionately admitted, leads to the development and expression of the whole soul.

Pamela White Hadas. *Marianne Moore: Poet of Affection* (Syracuse Univ. Pr., 1977), pp. 213, 216, 219, 223–24

It holds true . . . of Marianne Moore's poetry at all times that the form, the instrument designed, varies with the intended point of view and the scope of experience looked into or out upon. Naturally she did not always succeed in these experiments; in some of her early poems (like "Snakes, Mongooses") discursiveness may defeat the shape of the whole. But she always obeyed a counsel that she offered younger writers: "Be just to initial incentive." If the subject had attraction, she would not desert it; and sometimes the effort of execution sets up a tension with the intended theme. The tension keeps even the lesser poems alive because the subject of the poem is never sought for but comes as an involuntary summons. The reader too becomes aware of the interaction between the beckoning subject—inhering not in any one theme or image, but in all the words together—and the objectifying figure of spoken sound.

Marianne Moore's poetry shares some technical qualities with the three modern poets most closely associated with her—T. S. Eliot, Ezra Pound, and William Carlos Williams. All these poets developed new rhythmic patterns, freeing verse from the over-use of iambic pentameter and the cul de sac of elaborate post-Swinburne stanzaic forms. All of them introduced a conversational tone, a greater proximity of poetry to spoken language. They could all convert seemingly "non-poetic" material into the substance of art.

At the same time, the differences among them are as marked; otherwise none would have been a true writer. . . . She does not juxtapose motifs from the past (of art, literature, history) with fragmentary present scenes in the way that Pound and Eliot had. Instead, if she uses past events or quotations from earlier writers, it is to bring them directly within the range of her observation. . . . Likewise, although she sometimes invokes myth for its suggestive power, she does not rely upon it for unifying heterogeneous subjects. Dialogue in her poems, when it occurs, sounds like people talking in the present, not being overheard or remembered. As she remarked, she never considered herself an "imagist," but every page of her work presents images for which alone the poem deserves to be remembered.

Lawrence Stapleton. *Marianne Moore: The Poet's Advance* (Princeton Univ. Pr., 1978), pp. 221–22

In Moore, sincerity is a blend of eagerness and restraint, of ambition and humility. She leaps, precipitously, into speech, and then checks herself, paradoxically producing more speech by recording her revisions. . . .

For Moore, integrity is the opposite of tedium, and sincerity and gusto are two sides of the same coin. As sincerity is connected with the urge for truth and accuracy, gusto is, as Hazlitt says, "power or passion defining any object." Moore's "gusto" is also like the classical *energeia*, which modernists appropriated. It is the emotional byproduct of the flux and tension of form. This flux and tension are set in motion by sincerity, which accepts no single-minded description of reality. But Moore's gusto is not, as is the energy in Pound's vortex, the eye of the storm, a perfect center created from the collision of perspectives. It is the feeling of pleasure accompanying bafflement, the energy released in the poem by the resistance of an object to each onslaught of form. Her acts of description and definition repeatedly give way to exclamation of delighted defeat. The desire for possession is displaced by passion and admiration. Gusto is an emotion connected with failure, not with mastery, with relinquishing, not attaining, "what one would keep." Few writers deal with failure so enthusiastically. Moore celebrates the world's elusiveness, its superiority to our acts of appropriation, seeing the world's freedom as intrinsic to our own. And "gusto thrives on freedom," on the repeated discovery of difference. Thus her poems do not seek a still center in the turning world; they are distinctly temporal, and turn with it in constant astonishment. . . .

Moore's greatest poetry does not deal directly with the major myths of our culture, with tragic or comic themes. Her truths, excerpted from her poems, may seem proverbial. But if we consider her subjects and themes as occasions for significant imaginative acts we can have no doubt about the value of her art. Like "impassioned Handel" in "The Frigate Pelican" who was "meant for a lawyer and a masculine German domestic/ career—" but who "clandestinely studied the harpsichord/and never was known to have fallen in love," Moore is "unconfiding" and "hides/in the height and in the majestic/display of her art." Like the frigate pelican and his fellows, without cosmic purpose ignoring the more obvious lures of the romantic sensibility, she "wastes the moon.". . .

Moore's poetry is opposed, above all, to complacency, inertia, dejection. Her objective in the aesthetic of sincerity and gusto is to keep the mind alert and free, the world large and abundant.

Bonnie Costello. *Marianne Moore: Imaginary Possessions* (Harvard Univ. Pr., 1981), pp. 3, 13–14

## MORRIS, WRIGHT (1910–    )

Wright Morris may well be the last of our novelists to write with a sense of the whole of America in his blood and bones, to possess a vision of the country as both a physical place and a metaphysical condition. The literary tradition from which he seems most directly to descend—and it is a tradition shared with some incongruity by James, Twain, Edith Wharton, and Sherwood Anderson—may have passed on to him the materials of this vision, and it may be said to have been reconstituted in his work with very little likelihood that it will survive beyond his work. . . .

But one thing is certain. The America of Morris's novels no longer exists as a territory of our collective imagination, and that is because the myth that brought it to life in our imagination is dead. We may think that the myth survives in the popular culture of our day, but we will be wrong. It is not even there in lessened mutated form. What we see in popular culture are imitations and prevarications of the myth, media entombments of artifact, cartoon facsimiles which may have the vague contours of the original with one essential element missing: they bring nothing to life; they no longer fire and transform our aspirations. . . .

There is much humor and a rare and genuine kindness in the novels of Wright Morris, but the dark strain has deepened in them. It is also to be found—in different guises and because of somewhat different provocations—in the works we consider most original and permanently valuable in the modern American literary tradition. It arises perhaps, as Philip Rahv once said, from a recognition of "the discrepancy between the high promise of the American dream and what history has made of it. [From Dreiser and Anderson to Fitzgerald and Faulkner] the inner feeling of [the modern American] novel is one of nostalgic love of nativity combined with baffled (and sometimes angry) disenchantment." That has been the troubled preoccupation of some of our finest novelists, and inevitably it is also Wright Morris's—although it should be said that he cannot tolerate without some amusement the faintest note of apocalypse.

Nevertheless, his somber awareness of what has happened to us in the past and is continuing to happen to us today cannot be entirely concealed behind the subtle locutions of his irony and wit. It is perhaps that he is holding in escrow the ultimate pessimism he clearly sometimes feels. For he has, after all, lived much, has found much cause for love and wonder, and has too much practical sanity to make final pronouncements of either hope or disaster.

John W. Aldridge. In *Conversations with Wright Morris*, ed. Robert E. Knoll (Univ. of Nebraska Pr., 1977), pp. 3, 6, 12–13

There are . . . two worlds in the fiction of Wright Morris, and any adequate conception of his work must make room for both. The first has an absolute reality; it is a playground of natural forces which do the work of time, destroying each moment in order to create the next. The second is the habitat of a supernatural force, imagination, which nevertheless grows out of the natural process of evolution.

The real-ideal dualism points to an emerging pattern of contrasts, or opposites, which can be found in Morris's work. They include physical conception and imaginative conception, life and art, flow and arrest, process and culmination, text (outside of space but experienced in time) and photo (outside of time but experienced in space), man and nature, hero and witness. . . . The relative weight Morris assigns to one side of the dualism or another varies from book to book depending upon the specific situation depicted, the side which other themes happen to give the greater stress, and the point to which his developing consciousness of the world has brought him. His reservation of absolute judgment grows first from an ambivalence toward his subject, an ambivalence which is the only legitimate and truthful reaction to a profoundly ambiguous world, and from his basic premise that life is process. His tendency to think in patterns of opposites on whose relative worth conclusive judgment is withheld is further evidence of his deliberate tentativeness; respect for the unfinished character of the world prevents him from emphasizing once and for all one side of a dualism when tomorrow he may find the other more cogent.

Morris has always been a strong spokesman for the importance of tradition in shaping the individual talent, and his own talent has been partially formed by two very different writers—D. H. Lawrence and Henry James—who are both singled out for praise in *The Territory Ahead*. Morris himself has said that his admiration for other writers is "remote from imitation"; it is rather an awareness of literary tradition as part of the total culture out of which any writer must write. Because, as he says, echoing James's judgment, "It is the fiction that shapes the fact," Morris was "influenced" by Lawrence and James before he ever knew their work. Like any good artist, he was attuned to his time and place, which owed a part of their sense of themselves to these men. . . .

In Morris's work, the treatment of choice more nearly resembles that of such doctrinaire existentialists as Sartre than that of Lawrence: characters are often confronted with very difficult dilemmas resulting from the nature of the contingent world in which they find themselves. Nevertheless, like Lawrence, Morris senses a creative presence in the universe that comes close to being God and that debars him from the radical states of anxiety, fear and trembling, and sickness unto death usually associated with existentialism. Impersonal forces are working their obscure ends in man, but there are ends, however obscure. Moreover, existentialism is an extremely self-oriented philosophy, while Morris's most sensitive characters, like those of Lawrence, have an instinctive sense of belonging among the larger forces of life in the cosmos and recognize that the universe is not a mere backdrop for their own self-absorbed little dramas.

G. B. Crump. *The Novels of Wright Morris: A Critical Interpretation* (Univ. of Nebraska Pr., 1978), pp. 15–18

A summary description of Wright Morris's new novel, his 19th, suggests that this sophisticated "regionalist" has forsaken the impressionistic visual emphases that distinguish his best fiction (*The Works of Love, The Field of Vision, Ceremony in Lone Tree*) for a more conventionally narrative picturing of life in Nebraska's "middle Western plains"; the method, let's say, of Conrad Richter or Willa Cather.

*Plains Song* follows through four generations a family "cursed" because its women "bear only daughters, if anything at all.". . . I think this novel is saying that the way women have changed is only part of a fabric of overall change; and that, in saying so, it makes the mistake of satirizing one of its major elements (women's liberation), while simply celebrating its counterpart (rugged individualism and uncomplaining toil)—thus creating a feeling of unequal empathies, an imbalance in the generosity that the book otherwise seems to breathe.

Nevertheless, it succeeds as both an insistently changed lament ("plainsong") and a sequence of vivid and revelatory images. . . .

This eloquent novel portrays the passage of time with remarkable concision, and its understated (plain) style carries surprising emotional force. We feel how these people age: how their habits subtly alter; how they grow apart from others, become set in their ways. Wright Morris knows the embattled regions within his people as well as the harshly beautiful landscapes that surround them; and it is this rich double focus that gives his novels their unique solidity and truthfulness.

Bruce Allen. *NR.* Feb. 9, 1980, p. 40

No American writer's style, I think, is as perfectly controlled as Morris's. Everything style has been trained over the centuries to do, Morris makes it do in his novels. . . . Morris's style—the American language in action—conveys the informal tone and feel of a man talking to men. He makes imaginative use of American slang, clichés, idioms, and especially of midwestern speech patterns and rhythms as a way of getting at the American character. He tunes us in on the resignation, the melancholy overtones, the subtle poetry, the humor, the shrewdness of insight of midwestern speech.

In any work of fiction, the point-of-view technique the writer chooses dictates style. The third person central intelligence point of view that Morris most often uses dictates a conversational, informal tone and style; Morris modulates between a simulation of first-person informality and the more formal syntax, diction, and tone of an omniscient voice. Filtering his character's experiences and reveries through the third person, Morris employs his unique ability to transform the clichés of American language and culture into expressions of wit, satire, and peculiar lyricism. Morris creates a congruence of outer and inner reality—a triumph of style. Examining the immediate emotional and intellectual intuitions and perceptions of his characters from within, as they move from one small, but highly charged moment to another, Morris has evolved a flexible style, based on a manipulation of clichés, that has proved effective in rendering the sensibilities of both articulate and inarticulate characters. . . .

Each of Morris's novels is an answer, given in the language of the cliché, to Crevecoeur's cliché question, "What is an American?" The cliché is symbolic of the American dream defunct, and it is in this "dead" language of clichés that Morris tells us of the sterility of modern life. But the special contexts he prepares for clichés simultaneously annihilate their phoniness and resurrect their original vitality; he suggests that the dead past can be made to live again.

Morris's characters share his efforts to salvage something from the cliché.

David Madden. *MQ.* Summer, 1981, pp. 319–20

# ● MORRISON, TONI (1931–    )

The tone of much black writing is forensic, a public tone that speaks across ethnic and political gaps, that at one time or another has been used to persuade or frighten whites into action and to cajole or exhort other blacks into solidarity and revolution. Toni Morrison's tone, in this lyrical story [*The Bluest Eye*] about growing up black and poor in a northern Ohio town, is a more private tone, the tone, as it were, of black conversation. All of which is not meant to imply that Mrs. Morrison has no political consciousness, far from it, but only that she has found a way to express that consciousness in a novel instead of a harangue. She has the skill to convince you that she is telling it like it is without constantly telling you that's what she's doing—and that you'd better pay attention to her.

This story commands attention, for it contains one black girl's universe: alienation from the white world in a candy store, a sad neighbor girl made pregnant by her father and eventually driven mad, class conflict among black playmates, deracinated adults fighting each other and splitting up, a father who denies his son, and most of all that sad little girl, who wishes her eyes were blue, the bluest eyes in the world.

The girl never got those eyes; she was spiritually destroyed instead, and no marigolds bloomed either that year. To the narrator, those twin losses seem connected: "I even think now that the land of the entire country was hostile to marigolds that year. The soil is bad for certain kinds of flowers. Certain seeds it will not nurture, certain fruit it will not bear, and when the land kills of its own volition, we acquiesce and say the victim had no right to live. We are wrong, of course, but it doesn't matter. It's too late. At least on the edge of my town, among the garbage and the sunflowers of my town, it's much, much, much too late."

Raymond A. Sokolov. *Newsweek*. Nov. 30, 1970, pp. 95–96

With the publication of *The Bluest Eye* in 1970 and *Sula* in 1974, Toni Morrison has laid claim to modern portrayal of the preternaturally sensitive but rudely thwarted black girl in today's society. *Sula* is more fully dominated by the title character, and Sula's characterization is the more complex; in both novels, however, the protagonist is forced into premature adulthood by the *donnée* of her life. Pecola's comprehension of her world is never articulated for either the other characters or the reader; Sula, too, remains a partial enigma both in and out of her narrative. But the pain that each experiences is made vivid and plain. Taken together, the two novels can—and I think must—be read as offering different answers to a single question: What is to become of a finely attuned child who is offered no healthy outlet for her aspirations and yearnings? Pecola escapes in madness; Sula rejects society for amoral self-reliance. For both, sensitivity is a curse rather than a blessing. Morrison's second novel, though richer in many ways, is essentially a reworking of the material of the first with an alternative ending. Though her characters' problems are conditioned by the black milieu of which she writes, her concerns are broader, universal ones. Her fiction is a study of thwarted sensitivity. . . .

Both Morrison's novels find beauty in sensitive response and show its inevitable doom in a world in which only the hard, the cagey, and the self-interested can triumph. Although both Pecola and Sula fill essential roles in their communities, it is not the admirable in their characters that has an influence. Pecola serves as the bottom-most societal rung whose lowliness raises the self-esteem of everyone else, while Sula's acknowledged "evil" encourages others' righteous sense of comparative superiority. Sensitivity is lovely, but impractical, says Morrison. It is a pragmatic outlook, if not a particularly happy one.

Joan Bischoff. SBL. Fall, 1975, pp. 21, 23

*Song of Solomon* by Toni Morrison is a fine novel exuberantly constructed and stylistically full of the author's own delight in words. Morrison has a strong narrative voice and much of her novel's charm comes from an oral tradition, her love of simply telling, for example, how places and people got their names and how these names—Not Doctor Street, Ryna's Gulch, a boy called Milkman, Mr. Solomon, women known as Pilate, Sing and Sweet—contain history. There is an enchantment in Morrison's naming, a heightening of reality and language. Though each name is almost mythical it can be explained factually, thus the grandmother named Sing was really part Indian, Singing Bird, but not quite, the illegitimate daughter of a white gentleman, she was Byrd. In *Song of Solomon* lives are as strange as folk tales and no less magical when they are at last construed.

Toni Morrison has written a chronicle of a black family living in a small industrial city on the shores of Lake Michigan, but the method of the book is to enlarge upon the very idea of family history, to scrape away at lore until truth is revealed. And so we see that all the fears and misunderstandings that have shaped, say, the hostile marriage of Macon Dead and his wife Ruth, are as open to interpretation as the influence of dialect and The Good Book upon an old ballad. Milkman Dead, their son, finds that he is burdened by the truth about his parents and elated by a trip to Virginia to discover the remote romantic tales of his family's past. Morrison's novel demythologizes the Dead family, but even as Milkman learns the truth—there was no gold hidden in a southern cave, no lurid scene in which his mother threw herself naked upon her father's corpse—the new myths are created. There was, in fact, Milkman's great-grandfather, Solomon, a prodigious Biblical lover who enters into legend. "O Solomon don't leave me," the black children sing in their play, a corrupt version of Solomon's story, but of course their game, their song has the vitality of life over legend and so does Morrison's novel.

*Song of Solomon* is so rich in its use of common speech, so sophisticated in its use of literary traditions and language from the Bible to Faulkner, that I must add it is also extremely funny. Toni Morrison has a wonderful eye for the pretensions of genteel blacks and the sort of crude overstatements made by small time revolutionaries. Like many fine artists she dares to be corny—there is a funeral scene worthy of Dickens in which a crazed old woman sings "Who's been botherin' my baby girl" over her daughter, a poor deluded creature who has died of a broken heart. And like many great novels at the core it is a rather simple story of a boy growing to maturity. On the day Milkman Dead is born a mad insurance agent, Icarus-like, is trying to fly off Mercy Hospital. Milkman is finally weaned from the romance of the past and his own self-concern, a grown man ready for life, ready to fly. As for myth, Toni Morrison knows it's dead material unless you give it life—that's art.

Maureen Howard. HdR. Spring, 1978, pp. 185–86

Toni Morrison's works are fantastic earthy realism. Deeply rooted in history and mythology, her work resonates with mixtures of pleasure and pain, wonder and horror. Primal in their essence, her characters come at you with the force and beauty of gushing water, seemingly fantastic but as basic as the earth they stand on. They erupt, out of the world, sometimes gently, often with force and terror. Her work is sensuality combined with an intrigue that only a piercing intellect could create.

Two of her three novels, *The Bluest Eye* (1970) and *Sula* (1974), reveal a consistency of vision, for they illustrate the growth of a theme as it goes through many transformations in much the same way as a good jazz musician finds the hidden melodies within a musical phrase. Both novels chronicle the search for beauty amidst the restrictions of life, both from within and without. In both novels, the black woman, as girl and grown woman, is the turning character, and the friendship between two women or girls serves as the yardstick by which the overwhelming contradictions of life are measured. Double-faced, her focal characters look outward and search inward, trying to find some continuity between the seasons, the earth, other people, the cycles of life, and their own particular lives. Often they find that there is conflict between their own nature and the society that man has made, to the extent that one seems to be an inversion of the other. Her novels are rich, then, not only in human characterizations but also in the signs, symbols, omens, sent by nature.

Wind and fire, robins as a plague in the spring, marigolds that won't sprout, are as much characterizations in her novels as the human beings who people them.

Barbara Christian. Black Women Novelists<br>(Greenwood, 1980), p. 137

Toni Morrison . . . has achieved major stature through the publication of only three novels. *The Bluest Eye* (1970) and *Sula* (1973) are brief, poetic works which explore the initiation experiences of their black, female, adolescent protagonists. *Song of Solomon* (1977) is a much longer but still lyrical story relating Macon (Milkman) Dead's search for familial roots and personal identity. Milkman's development is framed and illuminated by the maturation stories of three women important in his life, and the presence of these subplots in the tale of a male protagonist is a good indication of the importance of female initiation in Morrison's thought.

For Toni Morrison, the central theme of all her work is [beauty and love]. . . . Certainly, this theme is evident in *The Bluest Eye*, *Sula*, and *Song of Solomon*, their female characters searching for love, for valid sexual encounters, and, above all, for a sense that they are worthy. . . .

Morrison's early works explore the results for black women when the values are real and powerful but are designed primarily for middle-class whites. This concept certainly appears importantly in *Song of Solomon*, but that book also explores what happens to women whose values (and value) are determined by the men who control their lives. From the outset, these values are known by some of Morrison's female characters to be useless, even damaging, to them. . . .

In Toni Morrison's novels, she joins her basic theme with the initiation motif, and the initiation experiences, trying and painful as they are, fail. . . .

In her fiction, then, Morrison has united her theme, the explorations of love, and a traditional device, the initiation motif, along with a series of brilliantly dramatized foreshadowing events, skillfully made frames, and splendid characterizations. The resulting novels are compelling statements of the failure of human values. The inversion of a traditional motif—that is, the treatment of failed initiations—is successful, its effect devastating. The achievement is remarkable, making it clear that Toni Morrison is, indeed, a major American novelist.

Jane S. Bakerman. *AL*. Jan., 1981, pp. 541–42,<br>563

Because Toni Morrison is black, female, and the author of *Song of Solomon* . . . one expects from her a fiction of ideas as well as characters.

*Tar Baby* has both. And it's so sophisticated a novel that *Tar Baby* might well be tarred and feathered as bigoted, racist, and a product of male chauvinism were it the work of a white male—say, John Updike, whom Morrison brings to mind.

One of fiction's pleasures is to have your mind scratched and your intellectual habits challenged. While *Tar Baby* has shortcomings, lack of provocation isn't one of them. Morrison owns a powerful intelligence. It's run by courage. She calls to account conventional wisdom and accepted attitude at nearly every turn of her story. She wonders about the sacrifice of love, the effects of racial integration, the intention of charity. Continually she questions both the logic and morality of seeking happiness or what Freud said passes for it, freedom from pain, by living in social accommodation. Although Morrison tells a love story—indeed, she tells two or three stories about love—her narrative lines run to complexities far beyond those of physical or emotional bonding. . . .

To believe Toni Morrison's characters isn't to believe their dramatic behavior. They are real people—in a story. The reason we can't credit their behavior is that, except for the most minor of figures, their actions are determined by Morrison's convictions, not their histories. Such is the curse of novels of ideas.

Webster Schott. Book World. March 22, 1981,<br>pp. 1–2

All of Morrison's characters exist in a world defined by its blackness and by the surrounding white society that both violates and denies it. The destructive effect of the white society can take the form of outright physical violence, but oppression in Morrison's world is more often psychic violence. She rarely depicts white characters, for the brutality here is less a single act than the systematic denial of the reality of black lives. The theme of "invisibility" is, of course, a common one in black American literature, but Morrison avoids the picture of the black person "invisible" in white life (Ellison's Invisible Man trying to confront passersby). Instead, she immerses the reader in the black community; the white society's ignorance of that concrete, vivid, and diverse world is thus even more striking.

The constant censorship of and intrusion on black life from the surrounding society is emphasized not by specific events so much as by a consistent pattern of misnaming. Power for Morrison is largely the power to name, to define reality and perception. The world of all three novels is distinguished by the discrepancy between name and reality. . . .

Morrison's use of mythic structure, more and more overtly as her work develops, is central to her existentialist analysis. The heroic quest for identity achieved by conquest in and of the outer world embodies the human need for transcendence and self-definition; at the same time, the mythic sense of fate and necessity corresponds to the experience of facticity, both as irrevocable consequence and as concrete conditions for choice. Between those two poles—free heroism and determined role—move Morrison's characters. Further, mythic patterns are especially appropriate to her social concerns, since the mythic hero by his nature both embodies and transcends the values of his culture. These connections would be significant in most presentations of existential themes, but the special situations with which Morrison is concerned further complicate her use of myth. On the one hand, traditional myths claim to represent "universal" values and experiences; on the other, they clearly exclude or distort minority experiences by offering inappropriate or impossible models (e.g., Shirley Temple). . . .

Morrison, then, must capture "universal" aspirations without denying concrete reality, construct a myth that affirms community identity without accepting oppressive definitions. In the process, she must take the outline of the mythic structure, already so well suited to the existentialist quest for freedom and identity, and adapt it to the historical circumstances that surround this version of the quest. She values the myth as a way to design, not confine, reality; it remains to be seen how much further she can carry that notion.

Cynthia A. Davis. CL. Summer, 1982, pp. 323–<br>24, 341–42

## NABOKOV,   VLADIMIR   (1899–1977)

He makes his novels function on two frequently interpenetrating levels: the level of the "reality" they depict and that created by the way in which that depiction is organized. This second level will take on an increasing importance for Nabokov, and is most evident in the way in which he imposes artificial authorial patterns, overloading his works with obvious contrivance and coincidence. . . .

Increasingly one has to be aware of the role Nabokov's often delicate and scarcely perceptible patterns play in his books if one is to hope to make a full reading of them. Thus, early in *The Real Life of Sebastian Knight* we come across a list of books in Knight's library. The narrator detects a strange melody in the list; and so he should. The books, more or less in the order in which they are arranged, will have a series of echoes in the course of the work to come: some featuring in descriptions of Knight's novels, others in the main narrative, helping to bring about that inter-penetration of the two which is the whole point of that work. Thus, we find an echo of *Hamlet*, the first title on the shelf, in Knight's first novel, about a fat student who comes home to find his mother married to his uncle, an ear specialist, who has poisoned his father. Much of the echoing is a great deal subtler than this; and there are moments when the melody almost dies away, until it is finally rounded off with *King Lear*, the final title, since the death of a king, or checkmate, is a proper conclusion to a book that abounds in references to chess.

Echoing of this kind is much more than a gratuitous virtuosity. It is vital to Nabokov's conception of the form of fiction, of the novel as a self-reflecting form, circular rather than linear, constituting its own autono-mous and self-justifying world.

Alex de Jonge. In *Vladimir Nabokov—A Tribute:*
*His Life, His Work, His World*, ed. Peter
Quennell (William Morrow, 1980), pp. 60, 63

The difficulty of assessing Nabokov's achievement as a novelist writing about people obviously derives from the flagrantly artificial quality of his fiction. Current sophisticated theories of criticism notwithstanding, read-ers of novels have traditionally tended to identify the *artificial* with the *superficial*. The Nabokovian universe, we all know, is a construct of words, taking life from the page and pen of its author. Self-conscious artifice intrudes on the reader's awareness, signaling the discontinuities between Nabokov's fabricated worlds and the one we call our own. According to Nabokov himself, upon completing one of his novels the reader should experience "a sensation of its world receding in the distance and stopping somewhere there suspended afar like a picture in a picture." It is not only at the end of his novels, however, that Nabokov arranges his effects in this way. The continuous word-play, allusions, self-conscious references, and authorial intrusions all serve to interrupt the reader's sympathetic participation in the author's illusory world. In this way, Nabokov alerts us to the fictional status of his literary landscape; he impels us to recognize that all the apparent depth and dimension we perceive in this "picture in a picture" are achieved aesthetic effects. . . .

Instead of provoking indignation, our reading of Nabokov's fiction should encourage us to clarify some familiar distinctions. The freedom of a literary character is always illusory. A realist may attempt to make what "happens" to his character appear to rise inevitably out of his nature or the nature of the world posited by the fiction, but the form of a character's fate is always the author's choice. Plausibility is both natural and artificial; and while Nabokov's worlds declare themselves fiction, their author recognized the need for plausibility and consistency within their structure. . . .

What I am suggesting, then, is that we may be denying Nabokov's characters their reality because of a misreading of, or disenchantment with, his method. The lives of literary characters (and, indeed, our own lives) are a great deal less autonomous than we would often like to believe. What we may resent, when reading a Nabokov novel, is the loss of our illusions rather than any inherent lack of humanity on the author's part. Shattering such illusions was a feat Nabokov particularly enjoyed. Obviously anticipating the stir his pronouncement would create, he once told an interviewer, "My characters are galley slaves." The description is characteristically inciting; yet it contains more honesty than arrogance. Nabokov's love of puns is surely evident here in his use of the word "galley," which refers to the printer's proofs of a manuscript as well as to an ancient rowing vessel. Nabokov's characters serve their literary master; but slaves, after all, are puppets only in the social sense.

Ellen Pifer. Nabokov and the Novel (Harvard<br>Univ. Pr., 1980), pp. 4–5, 8, 11

In Vladimir Nabokov's works many of the characters who die do not simply disappear. Not only can the presence of their spirits be detected; the faint influence of these spirits upon the living can also be discerned. Nabokov has appropriately suggested such ghostly presences and influences as invisibly as possible. Yet the clues are provided: he characteristically gives us sufficient evidence to detect the ghostly activity concealed in his written world. . . .

Nabokov's ghosts are concealed by some of his favorite diversionary techniques. Many of his characters ridicule or scoff at what are actually genuine spectral presences and influences. Skepticism, facetious remarks, and even serious speculations presumed to be inaccurate all help to disguise Nabokovian ghosts. Another camouflaging factor is Nabokov's fondness for the pathetic fallacy, many uses of which tend to conceal the presence of spirits in faintly personified backgrounds. Yet such patterns, when finally detected, can actually help to locate some of Nabokov's most elusive ghosts.

Indeed, there is a remarkable patterning about both the presence and influence of Nabokovian ghosts. They consistently appear in, or act through, certain background elements such as wind, fog, lightning, sunlight, and water. These elements are typically featured in faintly unusual ways. It is even occasionally suggested within a given work that spirits lurk in the pertinent element. Moreover, these background elements often seem appropriate (for example, a warm wind or a raging one) in view of the deceased's personalities, their emotions just prior to death, and their logical objectives in trying to influence the living. Perhaps most important, the ghosts continually appear at times when their own logical objectives are furthered and promoted.

Nabokovian ghosts induce dreams in which their former selves appear. Such dreams, as suggested in *Transparent Things*, tend to be prophetic. Somewhat similarly, Nabokovian ghosts cause a person to remember (or to have visions of) their former selves when they are present. Such recollections are often surprisingly vivid and usually quite abrupt. The general patterning also includes details and phrases not necessarily associated with any individual ghost but recurring throughout Nabokov's works at times when ghosts are present. They may thus be considered characteristic background details attending Nabokovian spectral activity. In brief, these are: descriptions of sunsets and the low sun, illuminated or stained-glass windowpanes, and rising, whirling dust. Also quite frequently when a ghost is present, Nabokov describes what would be seen by a hypothetical observer or spectator with a lofty, unusual perspective.

Another aid in detecting Nabokovian spirits is that both their presence and influence are subtly confirmed in various encoded ways. Numerous casual, sarcastic, or joking references to ghosts, specters, spirits, shades, etc. fit a pattern of truth if taken seriously. Their unwitting accuracy thus resembles that of Gogolian remarks about the devil. There is even what could be termed a pattern of misunderstanding about Nabokovian ghosts. For example, when a character intensely (but apparently unsuccessfully) wills a deceased person to give some sign of continuing existence, that person's spirit typically *is* present.

Finally, the presence and influence of Nabokovian ghosts are confirmed by a complex system of encoded names and agencies. Not only are the names of the ghosts sometimes hidden in the text when they appear; these bodyless beings often concentrate their influence on, or act through, a particular living person (or even an animal or insect). In such cases, there is often a suggestive relationship between the names of the spirits and of the people they influence. When butterflies or moths are involved, the spirits' former selves were typically associated with similar creatures in some special way.

W. W. Rowe. *Nabokov's Spectral Dimension*
(Ardis, 1981), pp. 9–11

*Lolita* may be usefully scrutinized as a hermeneutic narrative, involving the proposal and solution of an enigma. The operations of the hermeneutic narrative are particularly legible in detective texts; the reader of detective fiction is propelled through the narrative by the guarantee of truth at the end of the line. Detective fiction is teleological in character. Expectation and desire are sustained in the hermeneutic narrative by various delays that postpone the solution of the enigma. To satisfy this expectation and desire, to reach the solution of the enigma, involves following the narrative line in its unfolding until the truth is deciphered. In *Lolita* the truth at the end of the line is the identity of the fiend who has purloined the nymphet, a truth that is absent for most of the plot. It might be said, then, that the line of Humbert's own journey in quest of the fiend doubles the line of the hermeneutic narrative, which ends with the truth, the name, the man, Clare Quilty.

David Packman. *Vladimir Nabokov: The
Structure of Literary Desire* (Univ. of Missouri
Pr., 1982), pp. 31–32

## NEMEROV, HOWARD (1920–    )

Howard Nemerov is one contemporary poet who has interested himself in the elaboration of a distinct tradition in English poetry, that of the secular contemplative lyric. For Nemerov . . . the sources of poetry lie "far out in the sea of tradition and the mind, even in the physiological deeps," as he puts it in *The Measure of Poetry*, a prose poem in his latest collection which explains a great deal about his attitude and method of composition.

For Nemerov, measure is an elemental order, which he compares to the rhythm of the tide, and which is acted upon in the process of writing by "the objects which are to appear in the poem." This dynamic working relationship between basal constancy and individual variousness yields "moments of freedom, moments of chaos," "relations which it may be that number alone could enrage into being"; that is, without the underlying, reassuring sense of order provided by rhythm, we perhaps could not afford to tolerate wildness, nonsense, fine excess.

This is not a reading of the world with which everyone will agree; but even a superficial appraisal of this witty and deft collection, Nemerov's ninth, will reveal that *The Measure of Poetry* is a distillation of long experience, and not empty theorizing. In more than seventy expertly lucid, pungent, and economically managed lyrics, Nemerov makes use of "the objects" of contemporary upper-middle-class life—its games, its gadgets, its intellectual enterprises—as well as of nature, as occasions for an unending flow of gently ironic observations on the flux of personality in the continuum of history. Nemerov is both urbane and humane—not always necessarily a congenial combination; he is Horatian in his perspective, academic in his precision. His poems do something we're not accustomed to these days; they aim at the articulation of what it is not unfair to call a kind of rarefied commonplace. . . .

Nemerov's modesty of diction reminds me at times of his contemporary, [Randall] Jarrell; but Jarrell's poetry, passionately involved with the theme of change, was prolix and effusive where Nemerov, who seems really to be writing about the *status quo* from a far more conventionally remote and professional vantage point, is felicitous and neat. This kind of calm straightforwardness goes against the noisy self-advertising mainstream of current writing, and it deserves praise and attention for that. There's genuine intelligence and feeling here, and the fact that the verse doesn't call attention to itself—except, perhaps, by dint of its polish—is part of the point. *The Western Approaches* affords pleasures close to those which belong to music that is playful, various, and elegantly resolved.

Jonathan Galassi. *Poetry*. Dec., 1976, pp. 164–65

Howard Nemerov's poetry in *The Western Approaches* is a poetry mostly of saying rather than singing, even when it speaks of the power of traditional, transcendent song. The saying includes some skilled modes of speech, in some of the best poems, notably "Learning the Trees" and "A Cabinet of Seeds Displayed" (the kinship of subject is nearer essence than accident), reaching a firm and fair contemplation, mastered in technique, with an important, reverberant something to say. The reverberation comes from understanding quietly won. The book also offers fine poetry of physical description, and some high song.

The book, then, is important in itself, and in its place in the development of one of America's best and most highly reputed men of letters. Since the book is important, I shall take it seriously and, thus, disapprove some. Mostly I shall attempt to define what cons itutes Nemerov's typical style, attitude, metrical convention.

His style, in deep intertwinings with attitude, is witty, analogical, speculative, and uncertain. Yet it is also nostalgic and reverential, especially toward great past poetry and music; also slangy, chatty, obscene; with some unusual combinings. The uncertainty underlies, interlaces, and unlaces much of the rest. . . .

The book may well be Nemerov's best book of poems, which ranks it high. Too much is still too ready of wit, merely and pointlessly if cleverly speculative, self-mockingly relaxed, curiously analogical. Who else but Nemerov would devote a whole, rather carefully written poem to asking whether the fishing hook or the question mark is upside down? But, then, who but Nemerov would be apt to notice the reversed likeness? It's the lively and observant intelligence that occasions the problem. Nemerov is conscious of the difficulty and has answered the charge "that my poems are jokes, even bad jokes" by saying "I incline to agree, insisting, however, that they are bad jokes, and even terrible jokes, emerging from the nature of things." The pun on *bad joke* is a pretty good joke, but not a sufficient defense. At least to me his jokes seldom sound expressive (as those of Randall Jarrell's sometimes do) of a desperate-absurdity-locked-into-the-tears-of-things. . . . The best work—excellent physical description; the controlled variety and feeling of "The Backward Look"; the intricate, precisely registered intelligence that in "A Cabinet of Seeds Displayed" reaches contemplative poetry of the first rank; the greatly haunting conclusion of "Boy With Book of Knowledge," the fine completeness of "The Consent"—requires high praise and much gratitude. For Nemerov more than most poets, his best is the enemy of his many-skilled normal; he is too near to poetic greatness to step modestly away.

Paul Ramsey. *Parnassus*. Spring/Summer, 1976,
pp. 130–31, 137–38

Introspection is not a mood in Nemerov's work. It is the very atmosphere of his world, which becomes finally a corridor of mirrors—like the great hall at Versailles—in which the mind is seen gliding through the void. Searching for friendship, the mind finds only itself. Trying on the shapes of the external world in an unending masquerade, the mind finds fascination and satisfaction, if not companionship, in creatures that are, metaphysically, at least, smaller than itself. The most abiding of these creatures are found in the natural world. Few of the poems concern Nemerov's relationship with people and even the novels and short stories portray people from a distance. Nemerov has discussed his reticence about drawing on personal relationships in the *Journal of the Fictive Life*. When he does write about personal relationships, as in the poem about his sister's suicide in *Gnomes & Occasions*, his approach is restrained and indirect—even if ultimately moving.

Nemerov's supposed narrowness is simply a reflection of his cultivated pursuit of what interests and preoccupies him as a poet and novelist. He is a contemplative writer whose primary interest is in the process of contemplation itself. No modern writer has more eloquently traced the subtle emanations of consciousness and its shadowy journeying through the fine membrane of language out into the strangeness of the external world. In this connection he told an interviewer in 1966 that possibly the "only significance that anyone was ever able to rely on, in thought at any rate, was the love of the world, terrifying as it is, that connected him to it by means of the word." In retrospect the novels, stories, and poems coalesce in the light of this observation. His interest has continually been in the excitement caused when the pliable but domineering mind comes up against the hard surface of the external world. With breadth of vision he has shown the results of this collision to be simultaneously pathetic and absurd. The pathos and absurdity are symbolic of a whole range of ambivalences that allow one to see Nemerov as a religious poet with no religion, a philosophical poet with no philosophy, and a satirist filled with compassion.

Nemerov's strength lies in the persuasiveness with which he articulates these ambivalences and in the clarity with which he brings the complex refractions of consciousness within vivid reach of the senses. Paradoxically, it is often his most cerebral poems that engage the senses most provocatively, as in "The Town Dump" and "Brainstorm." It is as if in his lifelong effort to unite inner and outer worlds he stretches himself on such occasions to sustain the fine balance between the sensible and the immaterial. In both poetry and prose he has shown an absorbing interest in the experimenting mind. Challenged by the monotony of their society and by the obdurate silence of the physical world, his fictional characters and poetic narrators react to their plight with originality and panache. Nemerov gives them depth, moreover, in revealing the disaffection and hunger that linger after their most brilliant intellectual excursions. In this respect as in others, Nemerov has, without especially trying to do so, trenchantly captured the spirit of his time.

Ross Labrie. *Howard Nemerov* (Twayne, 1980),
pp. 144–46

# NIN, ANAÏS    (1903–1977)

Like Anaïs Nin's fiction, her Diary is also a collage composition. The assembled elements are the bits and pieces of her life: fragile evocations of her feelings; her victories over herself; her occasional moods of despair; richly detailed portraits of the people who moved her, inviting friendship and compassionate analysis, or provoking her disapproval and critical analysis; passages from books and letters; passionate declarations of her aspirations as a writer; passages brilliantly describing the psychological problems of the artist; sharp observations of the cultural patterns of America; and fascinating accounts of Nin's own repeated journeys into psychoanalysis. Selected from the mass of materials of the unpublished diary, the passages that comprise each published volume are themselves a collage composition presenting a phase in the life of their creator.

Nin's Diary, a work of art in itself, possesses special importance for those who are intrigued by the creative process. Because this Diary exists, we can see exactly how Nin's fiction was made. Even greater insights may someday be available to those who are able to study the unedited manuscripts. But a comparison of the present version of the Diary with the fiction reveals first, and perhaps most strikingly, Anaïs Nin's insistent need to preserve her experience, the stuff of her life, by recording it with astonishing dedication, even passion. The intensity and power of this need explains why Henry Miller and Otto Rank were unsuccessful in their attempts to free Nin of the diary. The diary *was* her life, her inner life, which the circumstances of her outer life prevented from receiving full expression. This need to preserve her experience, to protect it from alteration, change, or loss, proves the depth and strength of Anaïs Nin's creative will and inadvertently demonstrates one of the theories of her most famous analyst, Otto Rank. . . .

As she has repeatedly told her readers, Anaïs Nin's most valuable resource as an artist is her own complex self. Picking and choosing from the many and varied experiences of this self, she has created her ingenious books by combining elements that would not be found together in traditional fiction. She welds odds and ends of experience into collage compositions with the intensity of her personal vision of self and reality. As she has grown and changed, so have her books, reflecting the life that gave rise to them, just as the life has fed upon and been nourished by the books.

The quest that is traced again and again in Nin's writings actually involves a very radical concept: the abandonment of the idea of the self as a given fixed entity or essence. We create ourselves as we live, Nin explains poetically in her books and in the example of her own life that is revealed in the Diary. The idea of the self as a collage of experiences is central to Nin's psychological vision. Max Ernst, in writing of collage, quotes André Breton: "'Who knows if we are not somehow preparing ourselves to escape from the principle of identity?'"

Sharon Spencer. *Collage of Dreams: The Writings of Anaïs Nin* (Swallow/Ohio Univ. Pr., 1977), pp. 6–7, 17

Approaching Nin's *Diary* is difficult; the fact that it consists of edited versions of her original entries places it somewhat in a category of its own. A curious blend of direct access to a younger psyche or self, but with elements deemed unimportant edited out by the same psyche grown older, Nin's *Diary* has as little affinity with the retrospective reminiscences of an older Benjamin Franklin as it does with the daily entries of a Samuel Pepys. Indeed, one sometimes wonders whether Nin's *Diary* is not closer to fiction than autobiography, since in view of her deliberate omission of certain figures and aspects of her life, what we are really given here is the life of a "persona" rather than that of the author herself.

At the same time, however, one could argue that the editing only enhances the value of the *Diary* as a document of the growth of a psyche: as the teleology of inflation or regression is more apparent to the finished personality, so in the *Diary* we have only those aspects of her younger self that the older Nin found to be most strongly incorporated within herself. . . .

The most striking aspect of the first *Diary*, for example, is the larger-than-life quality and the numinous force of the individuals Nin presents. The clue to this exaggeration is to be found in the psychological theory of projection, but not, however, projection of the reaction formation variety—projections that are merely opposite to unconscious feelings. Rather it is a matter of the projection of archetypes, configurations which are intrinsic in one's psyche and which when projected onto individuals in one's life empower these individuals with sacred or divine forces for one's self. The "inflation" is "pathological" in the sense that it "naturally depends on some innate weakness of the personality against the autonomy of collective unconscious contents," but it is also part of the process whereby one is enabled "to annex the deeper layers of the unconscious." In the *Diary*, the constellation of projections is like a star, with the Self (Nin) at the center, radiating energy into the figures around her while at the same time she gradually incorporates their power; as she takes back into herself the energy she has previously projected outward, the Self begins to gain in confidence and ego strength.

Stephanie A. Demetrakopoulos. *Mosaic*. Winter, 1978, pp. 121–22

For Nin, perhaps more so than with most writers, the significance of her achievement in twentieth-century literature is linked closely to her literary career. As a fiction writer she tried consistently to keep before her the same principles that she later sustained so effectively in the *Diary*, but the nature of her attempt to describe and simulate psychological reality was often not apparent to her readers during the late 1930s through the early 1960s and in fact was not made clear until she became one of her chief literary critics and analyzed her works in the *Diary* and in *The Novel of the Future*. . . . Only after she perceived that the *Diary* would be her most acclaimed contribution to letters did Nin seem to recognize that her mode of autobiography was as effective a vehicle for her ideas as the novels. It is not the first time that a writer has tenaciously subscribed to a particular approach or genre, only to find later that acceptance and literary success lay in quite a different direction. . . .

Her fiction, although kept in print, is, regrettably, generally not given great attention. Nin was too long neglected, and she has been praised to excess recently for the wrong reasons. Her greatest value is as a legitimate cicerone through the feminine psyche, as an author who shows both women and men that the pursuit of one's completeness is a difficult task that must be undertaken, even though it is unpleasant to do so and even though it might not be successful in the end. She was nonetheless an optimist in a landscape of psychological despair, and her vision was augmented by her dedication to moderation and understanding.

Benjamin Franklin V and Duane Schneider.
*Anaïs Nin: An Introduction* (Ohio Univ. Pr.,
1979), pp. 291, 294

## OATES, JOYCE CAROL (1938–   )

In Joyce Carol Oates's works three themes—woman, city, and community—merge into an all-too-real nightmare. Her cities are the settings for death, riots, and the violent wreckage of human lives. Her women are victims, raped physically and psychically by both men and the world. Not only is community an unrealizable dream, but few characters even aspire to it. . . .

Continuously, her fiction searches out and exposes the very root of violence: a sense of personal impotence. At the heart of violence in her world is the absolute and utter inability to affirm oneself—without which the person is unable to live fully as a human being, to define, affirm, and assert himself, and to enter satisfying relationships with other persons. . . .

One of Joyce Carol Oates's persistent concerns is to make the tragic vision real to the twentieth century. She seeks through her works to awaken contemporary society to its own destruction, to deepen the consciousness of her readers to the tragic dimensions of life. This task demands that her own perceptions of the times be sharply defined, that she confront—because resolution is impossible—the ambiguities of the day without trying to answer them, and that in so doing she offer to her readers something more than the sensationalism of the daily news. . . .

Oates's works are limited, and she pays a price for her lack of humor. The tragic burden of the lives of her characters at times becomes barely tolerable and excessively oppressive: unrelieved, catastrophic events strain, if not defy, the imagination. Oates's characters may be ordinary people in one sense, but they suffer an extraordinary number of misfortunes and endure unbelievable afflictions—factors which tend to limit the works.

Unless she can move away from the two-dimensional, often superficial characters to which she has thus far almost solely confined herself and more directly towards her announced stronger moral posture and affirmative, transcendent vision, Oates will be doomed to repeating herself—a criticism frequently leveled at her at present. She has richly exploited the resources of her thematic concerns and of her choice of characters, and unless she moves on, she will become derivative of herself. Her tragically diminished people have told their tales, and their power to raise our consciousness is fast becoming exhausted. Her response to the complex phenomenon of urban life amounts to a deeply sensitive witness, but unless she is able to go beyond this, she fates herself to monotony and redundancy.

Mary Kathryn Grant. *The Tragic Vision of Joyce Carol Oates* (Duke Univ. Pr., 1978), pp. 15, 32, 117, 140–41

As Oates's skills as a novelist have developed, her work has increasingly evoked the confusing experience of our time and, more importantly, related our chaotic and imperfectly apprehended experiences to wider patterns of significance. Her importance for us is seen partly in the seriousness with which she sees the writer's dual, and perhaps contradictory role of submerging herself in our age, and partly as well, in her struggle to achieve a transcendence of our time in her articulation of it. In Oates's most recent work one now discerns a movement, observable in her essays as well as her fiction, towards a fascination with Eastern renunciatory philosophical modes. It is as if the violence and egocentric destructiveness which have been such tragic outcomes of Western history and philosophy must somehow be transcended by embracing the opposite vision. Of course such a development in Oates's thinking is prefigured in Lawrence's own. Lawrence, too, came to despair at the cultivation of the uniqueness of the self which has been so fundamental to Western consciousness. His later vision is not unlike that of Oates in *The Assassins*, where we first see, in her novels, her espousal of something akin to Eastern renunciation, a growing interest which seems to be entering all her work in the mid-seventies. On the surface, such a development is strange in writers like Oates and Lawrence, so imbued with the possibilities of transcendence achieved through the flesh, and it may be that the next stage in her career will show her developing in surprising, even more experimental, directions.

Possibly more than any American novelist now writing, Oates has shown herself sensitive to the eddying feelings of living in the 1960s and 1970s. But of course we look to writers to respond to more than the intellectual or social fashions of their age. Oates sees the cultural roles of the artist as that of struggling with and articulating the underlying, ongoing movements of feeling, not merely its glittering surface.

G. F. Waller. In *Critical Essays on Joyce Carol Oates*, ed. Linda W. Wagner (G. K. Hall, 1979), p. 17

*Bellefleur* is the most ambitious book to come so far from that alarming phenomenon Joyce Carol Oates. However one may carp, the novel is proof, if any seems needed, that she is one of the great writers of our time.

*Bellefleur* is a symbolic summation of all this novelist has been doing for 20-some years, a magnificent piece of daring, a tour de force of imagination and intellect.

In *Bellefleur* Miss Oates makes a heroic attempt to transmute the almost inherently goofy tradition of the gothic (ghosts, shape-shifters, vampires and all that) into serious art. If any writer can bring it off (some will claim it's already been done), Joyce Carol Oates seems the writer to do it. . . .

Whatever its faults, *Bellefleur* is simply brilliant. What do we ask of a book except that it be wonderful to read? An interesting story with profound implications? The whole religious-philosophical view of Joyce Carol Oates is here cleanly and dramatically stated. She has been saying for years, in book after book (stories, poems, a play and literary criticism), that the world is Platonic. We are the expression of one life force, but once individuated we no longer know it, so that we recoil in horror from the expression of the same force in other living beings. "Don't *touch* me," Gideon Bellefleur keeps saying, as Yvonne Petrie said in *The Assassins*, Laney said in *Childwold* and a host of other characters said elsewhere. Blinded to our oneness, we all become assassins, vampires, ghosts. We are all unreflectable nonimages in mirrors, creatures of time, and time is an illusion; we are all sexual maniacs, lovers engaged in a violent struggle to become totally one with those we love (copulation and murder are all but indistinguishable); we are all crazily in love with the past—first our own Edenic childhood, second the whole past of the world. . . .

Joyce Carol Oates has always been, for those who look closely, a religious novelist, but this is the most openly religious of her books—not that she argues any one sectarian point of view. Here as in several of her earlier works the Angel of Death is an important figure, but here for the first time the Angel of Life (not simply resignation) is the winner. In the novel's final chapters Gideon Bellefleur turns his back on all he has been since birth, a sensualist; starves himself until we see him as a death figure; finally becomes his family's Angel of Death.

Joyce Carol Oates is a "popular" novelist because her stories are suspenseful (and the suspense is never fake: The horror will really come, as well as, sometimes, the triumph), because her sex scenes are steamy and because when she describes a place you think you're there. Pseudo-intellectuals seem to hate that popularity and complain, besides, that she "writes too much." (For pseudo-intellectuals there are always too many books.) To real intellectuals Miss Oates's work tends to be appealing, partly because her vision is huge, well-informed and sound, and partly because they too like suspense, brilliant descriptions and sex. Though *Bellefleur* is not her best book, in my opinion, it's a wonderful book all the same. By one two-page thunderstorm she makes the rest of us novelists wonder why we left the farm. How strange the play of light and shadow in her graveyards! How splendid the Bellefleurs' decaying mansion! How convincing and individual the characters are—and so many of them! In one psychic moment, when the not-yet-2-year-old Germaine cries "Bird—bird—bird!" and points at the window a moment before a bird crashes into it, breaking its neck, we're forced to ask again how anyone can possibly write such books, such absolutely convincing scenes, rousing in us, again and again, the familiar Oates effect, the point of all her art: joyful terror gradually ebbing toward wonder.

John Gardner. *NYT*. July 20, 1980, pp. 1, 21

*Angel of Light* demonstrates, perhaps better than any other Oates novel, what I think is the *real* reason for the critical unease surrounding her work: that she goes against the prevailing impulse in contemporary fiction toward the private and personal, a small-scale vision illustrated in the work of such a much-admired writer as Ann Beattie. As *Contraries*, Oates' thoughtful and illuminating collection of essays, makes clear, Oates' models are the 19th-century masters like Dostoevski and Conrad; like them, she is what I would call a "social" novelist, interested in creating microcosms of the world that reflect the moral and philosophical questions encountered by man as he is in conflict with society, nature, God, history. What she admires in those novelists is passion, energy, the courage to take artistic and emotional risks. . . .

*Angel of Light* is neither small nor tidy. It is a complex, dense, multi-layered work that unfolds with all the profound implications of Greek tragedy—in fact, the story is a modern version of the fall of the House of Atreus. Yet Oates seems at last to have in control two of the weaknesses that have sometimes been the result of her considerable ambition and energy—a feverish, overwritten prose style and a heavy-handed use of symbolism.

Susan Wood. *Book World*. Aug. 16, 1981, p. 5

Even when Joyce Carol Oates is in a playful mood, her writing fails to provide patches of sunlit ease; she's too self-mesmerized to tune out the racket in her head and clear away a pool of summery calm, preferring instead to heap on the rubble, the noise, the piles of broken glass. She doesn't write books now, the books write her. She's like an obsessive pianist who even in her sleep practices arpeggio runs, her fingers rippling up and down a phantom keyboard. Snap to, Ms. Oates. It isn't too late. Wake up, wake up, wake up! . . .

Although *A Bloodsmoor Romance* has the fixings of a provocative antinovel, Oates's inability to turn off the babble once again plunges her into the gumbo. In a typical Oates novel, the reader is treated—if that's the word—to a series of Big Scenes connected by a lot of flimsy, careless doodle. Her fans probably drum their fingers patiently during the drowsier passages, knowing that Oates will soon barbecue a new fright for their snacking pleasure. . . .

Perhaps the key to Joyce Carol Oates's fiction is her phantasmagorical fear of sex, her revulsion from the flesh's treacheriès. Sex in her fiction is seldom a tender idyll, a bit of lingering play, or even a collision of will and temperament. . . . Sex is instead a ghoulish prank, a corporeal meltdown. . . . Oates's books . . . are wonders of reckless energy and dishevelment. Although Oates's poetry is hardly ringing or memorable, it's easier to take than her prose because in writing poetry she's compelled to choose this word, that. But in writing fiction she doesn't seem to spiff up her sentences before dispatching them into the world; ragtag and motley, her phrases are thrown into the breach like waves of ill-prepared soldiers, a doomed multitude. She ought to spend more time revising and paring down, but she seems incapable of trimming away her wordy flab, or unwilling. Perhaps she *prefers* to drift high and free in the transcendental ether.

What *A Bloodsmoor Romance* makes clear is that writing, for Oates, is not a vocation or a calling but a semidivine compulsion. To her, the writer is a shortwave set receiving and beaming messages into the far reaches of dreamland.

James Wolcott. *Harper's.* Sept., 1982, pp. 68–69

## O'CONNOR, FLANNERY (1925–1964)

A major premise of O'Connor's thinking is that the realm of the Holy interpenetrates this world and affects it. It is the workings of this mystery that she was most concerned with demonstrating in her fiction. By her own explanation, the grotesquerie of her stories is directly related to her Christian perspective. This is a point that has bothered some critics, who feel that a Christian view of life ought to tend toward the reconciliation of opposites, toward wholeness and affirmation, whereas the grotesque is by definition distorted, incomplete, or incongruous. To these critics O'Connor might have responded that they were trying to claim what has not been fully achieved: while opposites might be reconciled in Christ, the world was not yet reconciled to Him; we may know of the existence of wholeness because of Christ, but we are not yet whole ourselves. O'Connor's Christian conception of wholeness gave her the background against which she saw man in his present condition as, at best, incomplete; even the good, she felt, has a grotesque face, because "in us the good is something under construction."

O'Connor found elements of her Christian vision of man in both the religion and history of her native region. The legacy of a revivalistic past has lingered longer in the South than in any other region of the country, and while O'Connor hesitated to describe the South as Christ-centered, she did feel it to be Christ-haunted. The South's history included a major experience—the loss of the Civil War—in which O'Connor found important theological implications. She saw the loss of the Civil War as the South's collective and personal experience of the biblical story of the Fall. . . .

While she was an artist of the highest caliber, she thought of herself as a prophet, and her art was the medium for her prophetic message. It was her intention that her stories should shock, that they should bring the reader to encounter a vision he could face only with difficulty or with outright repugnance. And she wanted her vision not only to be seen for what it was but to be taken seriously. She was confident enough of her artistic powers to believe this would happen, even if it took fifty or a hundred years.

Dorothy Tuck McFarland. *Flannery O'Connor*
(Ungar, 1976), pp. 1–2, 114

What *is* the serious religious writer to do in an age like ours? He cannot ignore his readers, nor can he bow before them. For Flannery O'Connor the solution was to shock them—to assault their modern rationalism and undermine it to the point where the readers themselves would have to admit its limitations. She wanted to make them *see*. In "The Fiction Writer and His Country," she considers the problem of the writer who is dealing with an audience whose beliefs are alien to his, and she asserts that such a writer "may well be forced to take ever more violent means to get his vision across . . . to the hard of hearing you shout, and for the almost-blind you draw large and startling figures." This comment may alert us to the rhetorical function of the grotesque elements in Miss O'Connor's work, but I think she meant a great deal more. When she spoke of "ever more violent means," I think she was referring to the total structure of her works, not just to one set of characteristics, however important. The plots themselves were carefully and deliberately structured to shake the reader's confidence in his own rational abilities, and thus to make him see Christ's suffering and man's redemption as the basic fact of human life. . . .

Flannery O'Connor wrote the way she did because that was the only way she felt she could write to make her readers respond the way she thought they should. She wanted the actual experience of reading to be itself a process of reorientation, a refocusing of the mind's light toward what she once told Robert Fitzgerald was that great "sense of Mystery that cannot be accounted for by any human formula." Every element in the stories and novels had to be carefully constructed so that the reader would be sure to be affected by it. His eyes would finally, she hoped, be burned clean, so that like Tarwater's at the end of *The Violent Bear It Away*, "they would never be used for ordinary sights again."

It would be no easy job to reorient these mulish modern readers, Miss O'Connor knew. She must build her stories out of steel, so they would be tougher than the reader's will to resist. But at the same time she could not be too direct, or the readers might find out what she was up to and stop reading before the book had a chance to affect them. Her primary strategy, in this assault on modern skepticism, was to entice the reader into believing that he was seeing things from the author's point of view, only to pull the rug out from under him at the story's end. This shock—the realization that the author actually saw things from a wholly unexpected perspective—would, perhaps, demonstrate to the reader that his rationalistic twentieth-century vision, which he had thought so sophisticated, was wholly inadequate to deal with the mysteries of divine grace at work in the world. By showing him some manifestations of that "amazing grace" in her fiction, Miss O'Connor hoped to have prepared the reader to look for it, and to welcome it as it occurred in his own life.

Robert H. Brinkmeyer, Jr. SoR. Spring, 1979, pp.<br>314–15

Flannery O'Connor never wrote a first-person narrative, nor did she ever completely surrender her third-person prose to the limitations of a subjective point of view. She undertook the offices of writer with all the freedoms of traditional storytelling, assuming the omniscient manipulation of fictional destinies with an unquestioning ease. One wonders if she could have written otherwise, for a subjective perspective in fiction writing narrows the authority of the given account; it implies that there can be another point of view, a different set of meanings to assigned events. In turn, this relativity suggests that one can live in doubt, that one can live, as Lionel Trilling has said, "by means of a question" instead of by an unassailable religious persuasion.

This was exactly what O'Connor did not want to do—to concede that there could be more than one viable interpretation of reality. In her opinion, conflicts between ways of being constituted a challenge to Christian truth that could not be brooked, and with this certainty of outlook, she reserved final narrative authority for herself. For the hard of hearing she would "shout," for the blind she would "draw large and startling figures."

Yet with all this allusion to rhetoric, to bold and unambiguous fictional strategies, O'Connor was curiously reluctant to exploit the potential of the omniscient voice. Rarely in all these tales of bizarre and violent experience does she reflect on the meaning of the grotesquery or give explicit value to fictional events. She infrequently enunciates in her fictional world what she had no trouble conveying in personal life—that Christian orthodoxy was the consistent measure of experience. This is usually left for the reader to infer, to come upon through the indirections of allusion, incongruities, and distorted hyperbole. . . .

To the extent that she called folly by its right name, she was a truth teller in both a doctrinally condoned and a more widely recognized sense. This is an accomplishment that remains unaffected by the limits of inference. Even when unembellished by revealed anagogical implications, Flannery O'Connor's work retains a weight of human concern that makes the reading of the fiction a disturbing encounter, valuable to readers of any persuasion because its haunting truth rests on sharable experience rather than prohibitive religious allusion.

Carol Shloss. Flannery O'Connor's Dark<br>Comedies: The Limits of Inference (Louisiana<br>State Univ. Pr., 1980), pp. 102–3, 128

# ODETS, CLIFFORD (1906–1963)

Clifford Odets was a complex man, nurtured in a complicated age, but out of his intense struggles with self and society were born six plays of continuing importance. The stock picture of Odets as the radical author of *Waiting For Lefty*, who later abased himself before the Un-American Activities Committee and sold out to the Establishment, makes classification easy for criticism at a gallop. Such a view fails to do justice, however, to the depth, intensity and relevance of Odets' plays. It is simply untrue, for example, that the later work of Odets is uniformly poor. *The Big Knife*, *The Country Girl* and *The Flowering Peach* can stand comparison with *Awake and Sing!*, *Golden Boy* and *Rocket to the Moon*. Indeed, the early *Golden Boy* and the late *The Flowering Peach* are probably—all parts considered—the two best plays Odets wrote in his twenty years as a major American dramatist. . . .

Like every play that has ever been written, *Golden Boy* bears the stamp of its decade. Nevertheless, this fine play also transcends the narrow interests of the thirties, for in Odets' depiction of a young man's struggle between self-realization and self-destruction, between idealism and materialism, *Golden Boy* persists in being meaningful. Similarly, the later plays project specific pre-occupations of the post-Second World War period; yet *The Big Knife, The Country Girl*—and, especially, *The Flowering Peach*—also reveal themes that have obsessed imaginative writers in every decade since, at least, the First World War. Odets, in other words, is very much in the mainstream of modern theater and literature. . . .

Even unsympathetic critics of Odets have acknowledged his verbal gifts. This talent has little to do with the accuracy of a tape-recorder, or with the ability to write stunning curtain lines. The Odets canon is full of quotable dialogue . . . , but no line in the best plays is there for its own sake. Odets told [Arthur] Wagner [in an interview] "there are playwrights who don't know their punctuation isn't very important in the recreation of the character they've written, or that, as we used to say in the Group Theater, their script is only a series of stenographic notes." Analysis of Odets' plays nevertheless reveals a highly sophisticated use of dramatic language, an employment of words that can bear close reading and analytical criticism. Dialogue in the best work of Odets performs a number of simultaneous functions: it expresses character; it forwards action; it creates mood; and it exposes theme. But in addition, Odets' language also possesses color, power and variety—that is, it has distinction aside from its service to character, structure and theme. Imagery in some plays—*Golden Boy*, for instance—is especially noteworthy. In short, Odets is one of the rare "poets" of the modern drama.

Edward Murray. *Clifford Odets: The Thirties and<br>After* (Ungar, 1968), pp. 219–22

The ear he brought to recording the idiom and rhythms, the substance, the lurking depths of communication below sheer words, all these come from an awareness of the social scene that could not have been contrived or assumed. Odets recorded the experience he lived, one way or another, one place or another. That experience may indeed not have resembled in fine detail the daily events in The Bronx of his heroes and heroines. But he did catch the intensity, however obliquely, the passionate spirit of a group of artists, actors, writers, intellectuals of various sorts, caught up in one of those periods in human history where public events force men to make their own private values, to find their own goals, to commit themselves to community enterprises that give one identity and provide one with a small area of meaning. His awareness of theatrical environment, with its articulately self-conscious and incessant self-expression, was carried over well to the highly verbal world of his striving families. The American economic depression of the 1930's, like the great famines and disasters of history, natural or man made, created a crucible in which forms of art were shaped not only as means for dealing with this specific and enormous enveloping event but also for dealing with oneself, for mapping out territories which had inner integrity and coherence without regard to large political generalizing. . . .

Odets quickly outgrew the tendency to preach and to intrude forced themes; more important, even his early plays rise above that weakness through their superior craftsmanship. It is a tribute to Odets' integrity as a dramatist that he constantly strove for newer and more expressive insights to advance his themes. This integrity helped Odets to survive the decade that had fostered him and to write at least two excellent plays many years later. *Awake and Sing* assumes its stature among the plays of 1935 not because the others were necessarily poor, but because Odets combined certain truths with effective dramaturgy in a manner that other social protest writers found difficult to accomplish. Economic determinism is there, but so are real people. Marxist stock phrases are much in evidence in all the early plays, but so are rich and accurate colloquialisms. Melodramatic clichés abound in the plotting, but these, too, are outweighed by the great number of honest, natural moments. For Odets was much more than merely "the little Jesus of the proletarian theatre," as one critic called him. His plays remain valid because they deal with universals.

Odets was determined to depict problems of inequality and repressed opportunity in American society. His principal medium for doing so was one often used by American dramatists—the family. . . .

But it is the family as a social organism (rather than specific marital problems) that most often occupied Odets' attention, and there seemed to be a marked calming in the playwright's attitude on this subject that makes a comparison of his early and late plays interesting. In Odets' early dramas, the family mirrors society and the playwright's emphasis is on rebellion. The process can probably be translated into a single axiom: the individual must liberate himself from the bonds of a repressive family; the people must liberate themselves from the bonds of a repressive society. Odets' basic attitude is not abnormal in a Western culture, where the emphasis has tended more and more toward individual achievement, less and less toward a family-oriented social structure. Still, Odets carries the idea to an extreme that is surprising, especially when viewed in the light of the traditional Jewish pattern of close family ties.

Michael J. Mendelsohn. *Clifford Odets: Humane Dramatist* (Everett/Edwards, 1969), pp. xiv–xv, 113–15

The impact of *Awake and Sing!* derives not from its social protest against the horrors of poverty, but from the potency of spirit in its people. At last, although the language was English, not Yiddish, Odets was substituting for the consolatory spectacles and sentimentality in the Yiddish theatre the first deeply felt and formally achieved realism in America. He was daring to put on the stage the lives of recognizable people struggling for life amidst "petty conditions." And he was hoping their conflicts—by reason of their universality—would reach an audience not limited to Jewish-Americans. . . .

Underneath the fiery political message, Odets is counseling himself in [Waiting for] Lefty not to wait passively for his personal success or salvation, but to join with his Group [Theatre] brothers and deliver an uppercut to "the enemy" responsible for all of their problems, ranging from betrayals by women to material deprivation, to his failure to get parts in plays. His indictment of a patently unjust social system is genuine; the personal steam, however, is supplied by his relationship to his parents and by his current yearning not only to overcome his loneliness, but also to deliver an "uppercut" to his surrogate fathers, the Group directors—most particularly to [Lee] Strasberg, who, unlike [Harold] Clurman, has not encouraged him in this project. He finds it a "blessed thing" to learn from the freedom of collaborative improvisation in working on this one-act play "how Bach must have felt sometimes". . . .

The rich, compassionate, emotional flow in Golden Boy, with its layers of meaning, its cornucopia of American image, of symbol, of character, and its ornamenting grace notes of oblique dialogue and humor, would perhaps never be surpassed by Odets. Although in his work he would again and again confront the same moral dilemma in a variety of manifest forms, all of them deeply humane, he would not again illuminate it as intensely and profoundly as here. . . . With Lefty, the invitation to become the spokesman for a righteous hatred of injustice had successfully allied his private rage to a socially shared and constructive end. In a subtler way this had happened with Awake and Sing!, celebrated by audiences for helping them to feel more "real." However, in the larger and more abstract canvases of Paradise Lost and in The Silent Partner he was unsuccessful in persuading an audience that his anger spoke for them. Perhaps it was because in both those plays he sacrificed his unique gift for detailed immigrant-American characterizations and dialogue to his conscious need to depart from this idiom and to make abstract formulations which would transcend his Jewish-American identity. He often said he wanted the respectability of a Sidney Howard, a Maxwell Anderson, a Robert E. Sherwood.

Margaret Brenman-Gibson. Clifford Odets, American Playwright: The Years from 1906 to 1940 (Atheneum, 1981), pp. 257, 305, 475

## O'HARA,   FRANK   (1926–1966)

So many of O'Hara's poems are playful, "casually insightful" celebrations of the esthetic autonomy of the creative act. The last stanza of "Autobiographia Literaria" (the serious, Coleridge-inspired title, of course, totally at odds with the spirit of the poem) specifically celebrates this esthetic ego involvement. . . . The wonder here is a mock-wonder—whimsical rather than Whitmanic—but it is aimed at calling our attention to the "action" of making the poem. Here, as elsewhere in O'Hara's work, the mock-heroic posturing is only superficially satirical. Underlying the casual chronicles of everyday events in his work is a deep commitment to the transformative qualities of poetry—its ability to open our eyes, sharpen our perceptions, involve us more totally with the world around us. O'Hara's whimsy is, if I may be permitted an oxymoron, a serious whimsy. . . .

O'Hara's work also has apparent affinities with Pop-Art: in poems like the one beginning "Lana Turner has collapsed" or the delightful poem called "The Lay of the Romance of the Associations" in which the Fifth and Park Avenue Associations in New York attempt to get together, only to be frustrated because "that bourgeois Madison Avenue continues to obstruct our free intercourse with each other." But the sense of playfulness and social satire O'Hara's poems share with Pop-Art seems to me less substantial than the "action" involvement of the writer within the poem and the relationship of that literary idea to the painterly esthetic of Abstract Expressionism. . . .

The achievement of O'Hara and the Abstract Expressionists shows us that transient matters can be dealt with in an enduring way. The art of the moment does not always have to be propagandistic and tied to rapidly changing social issues. When the moment-to-moment reality of the individual becomes the focus, the art becomes made up of the very stuff of life itself. Art has always been preoccupied with the universal, these artists seem to be telling us, but life continues to serve up a steady diet of particulars. It is as a careful chronicler of those particulars that O'Hara has made his mark on literary history.

O'Hara's best known and most often anthologized poem, "The Day Lady Died," illustrates how carefully controlled and drafted his "casual" art can be and how what is seemingly a random list of selected moments from a day in the poet's life is actually a tightly structured, artfully contrived series of effects. The poem records the deep impression that the news of Billy Holiday's death made on him. The emotional impact of that moment is heightened by its juxtaposition of trivial and impersonal details with O'Hara's recollection of hearing Billy Holiday sing. The poem begins with facts and figures—impersonal, trivial, routine. . . .

"Poem for a Painter" makes specific O'Hara's painterly sympathies and his inclination to view the art of painting as more able to capture fleeting emotional moments than poetry. In lines reminiscent of Hart Crane, he writes, "The ice of your imagination lends/an anchor to the endless sea of pain." The painterly imagination is frozen; the event captured on the canvas is its own enduring record. O'Hara wrote a great deal about painters in his poetry as well as his prose, and there can be no question, I think, that he attempted to consolidate the achievement of Abstract Expressionism in literary art.

Fred Moramarco. *JML*. Sept., 1976, pp. 441–46

The problem of influence is a major topic, for O'Hara assimilated an astonishing variety of styles. His best poems fuse what he called the "charming artifice" of Apollinaire (and of a host of other French poets from Rimbaud to the Surrealists) with the bardic voice of Mayakovsky, the colloquial speech of Williams or the late Auden, the documentary precision of Pound's *Cantos*, and the Rilkean notion of being "needed by things." O'Hara's equivocal response to the English Romantics is especially interesting. Generically, his major poems follow Romantic models, but he almost always injects a note of parody, turning the conventions he uses inside out. Aside from literary models, O'Hara's poetry also incorporates specific film techniques, phonetic and rhythmic devices modeled on the music of John Cage and Erik Satie, and such concepts of Action Painting as "push and pull," the "all-over," and the notion of the canvas as a field which the artist enters. The result of assimilating such varied influences is the creation of a new kind of lyric poem. . . .

O'Hara's poetry is characterized by a remarkable confluence of styles. Aside from the influence of painting, discussed in the last chapter, and the close bonds between O'Hara's lyric and the arts of film and music, the poems reflect an unusual combination of literary influences. Dada and Surrealism continue to stand behind O'Hara's distinctive imagery— an imagery inclining toward artifice and the landscape of dream. The colloquialism and celebration of ordinary experience recall Williams and, to a lesser extent, the later Auden; but the use of proper names and documentary "evidence" seems to derive from Pound rather than Williams. . . .

O'Hara's syntactic structures were influenced by Apollinaire and Reverdy, while his peculiar brand of Personism can be traced back to Mayakovsky, Pasternak, and Rimbaud.

The *Collected Poems* is, in short, a very learned (detractors would say, an eclectic) book. O'Hara's reputation as casual improvisator, unschooled doodler, could hardly miss the mark more completely. . . . One of the special pleasures of reading O'Hara's poetry is to see how the poet reanimates traditional genres. Ode, elegy, pastoral, autobiographical poem, occasional verse, love song, litany—all these turn up in O'Hara's poetry, although his tendency is to parody the model or at least to subvert its "normal" conventions.

Marjorie Perloff. *Frank O'Hara: Poet among Painters* (Braziller, 1977), pp. xiii, 138–39

O'Hara's primary achievement has been his use of himself in his own poems as something like the "visual-biographical emblem" that [Boris] Pasternak speaks of. The central figure in O'Hara's poetry is himself; but unlike Montaigne, the man is not the book, and there are hints of depths that are never fully sounded. There are no extended childhood memories, no memories of past love affairs, in general, no history of the self at all. One gets to know O'Hara through a series of moments, and one of his constant themes is his perception of himself as an array of separate selves, multifarious and unpredictable, constantly creating himself anew as if he were himself a work of art. Yet the poet as he appears in his own poems does have a recognizable personality, and it might be helpful to try to form some sort of composite description of this figure. . . .

O'Hara rejected the possibility of metaphysical truth. Because he did not believe a poet should seek to impose order on experience, he did not want to impose the order of an elaborate, carefully wrought prosody on his own verse. But though O'Hara claims not to "like" poetic devices such as meter, rhyme, assonance and "all that stuff," he nevertheless does seek a kind of shapeliness, the verbal equivalent of "pants . . . tight enough so everyone will want to go to bed with you." He does not want to be correct, but he does want to be attractive. His humorous reference to the importance of running, rather than turning to face his pursuer and assert his credentials reflects his dislike for a language that asserts its own authority. Poetic language, he believed, ought to come spontaneously to mind under the stress of immediate experience.

Alan Feldman. *Frank O'Hara* (Twayne, 1979), pp. 43, 45

## O'HARA, JOHN (1905–1970)

As a novelist and storywriter, John O'Hara is one of those figures who, while seeming less than entirely great, do seem entirely necessary, as a feature or a primary aspect of modern American fiction. What he represents is realism; praised by Allan Nevins as having given the necessary historical record of the 1930s, he has somehow become the best modern case of the writer as social historian. The critics were never quite easy with him, though, perhaps because the public swallowed him with enormous delight. . . .

O'Hara's novels and stories, found excessively frank in their time, postulate a coordinated, respectable and essentially monogamous society, held by code and habit and desire, and struggling within it an essentially adulterous humanity. His first novel starts in an unsatisfactory marital bed, and so, in a sense, does all life in the O'Hara universe. Caught between the two—substantial, virtuous society and practical sexuality and angst—is that recurrent O'Hara type, the respectable reprobate.

His work shares the dominant literary attitudes of his time; it is touched with that mixture of radicalism and nostalgia central to the mood of the early to mid-century American novel, and something of the self-made intellectuality also characteristic of the period. His temper was shorter than that of many of his peers, and his anti-intellectuality ("I'm not some hairy philosopher. I'm just an ordinary guy who happens to write well") more assertive, leading to stronger declarations that what he possessed was, well, ultimate craft: the gift of getting dialogue right, observation precise, structure under control. Even his sense of grievance was reasonably typical; there was arrogance and defiance as well as social aspiration that passed, as with Fitzgerald, deep into the tenor of his writing. Perhaps the most striking difference from the rest of his rather incestuous generation is in the rhythm of the career. O'Hara was the writer as worker, and the work intensified as time went on. The bulk of the production falls in fact in the post-war period; here came the intensive night writing spells that generated a story a month, enabled him to produce seven books, including three big novels, between 1955 and 1961, and leave a mass of posthumous work which continues to appear (he died in 1970), like the stories of *Good Samaritan*. . . .

But he could write with an extraordinary, clear purity, which is most articulate as a tone. It comes out as a mode of apparent indifference, a hard surface given to the text through a predominance of dialogue or a continuous functionality of scene, through the abstraction of psychological inwardness from the characters through a particular way of spatializing the public and the private, the narrative overview and the inward moves of being. This offended critics who made humanism a requisite of a fictional text. . . .

O'Hara worked best with a very special marriage of accumulated, dense social detail, a given wealth of society, and a sparse and limited mode of writing; this is why he so frequently succeeds most in the short stories.

Malcolm Bradbury. TLS. May 28, 1976, p. 633

*The Lockwood Concern* is the fourth of a series of novels that attempt not only to create a fictional region representative of America in the twentieth century, but also to study the American man of action during this period. From Sidney Tate onwards, though Joseph Chapin and Alfred Eaton to George Lockwood, O'Hara presents the psychology of the individual American who is engaged in society and commerce and who is an insider rather than an outsider. Because he did not belong in Pennsylvania, Tate was somewhat ineffectual in his role, while Chapin was his opposite, the product of a small community who had an inappropriately grand ambition. Alfred Eaton is Chapin on a large scale, but he is so external a man that when he is prematurely retired there is nothing for him to do. George Lockwood is more interesting than all of these: he is at once more aggressive and more thoughtful, and he is more introspective than any of the others. As his "concern" begins to collapse owing to the disaffection of his children, he begins to realize what has happened to his life and what the family obsession has cost in human terms. But it is too late. Like the others, Lockwood comes to his end with a sense of futility and emptiness. . . .

O'Hara sees that aside from money, modern America has no system of rewards that can engage a mature person's interest. An attractive reward must create a new involvement and a new kind of responsibility. The award or prize is useless unless it has a future life. . . .

Often compared to Anthony Trollope and George Moore, O'Hara was like them because he dealt with the ordinary realities of his society. He did not write about peripheral people as Hemingway often did, nor did he dwell in a world of grotesques with Faulkner. In the tradition of Lewis and Dreiser and Anderson, he confronted the materialistic world of middle-class America, and as the spiritual heir of Edith Wharton, he explored the world of society with an intensity few others have even attempted. Yet he was more than the social chronicler who comes to mind in a comparison with Trollope or Moore. He was a man of tremendous feeling who tried to understand how such forces as ambition, sexual passion and jealousy, as well as kindness and love, affect all human beings. There was a turbulence and violence in all his best work, just as there was in him. His vision of humanity was not hopeful, but he put value in loyalty, in communication between individuals and in imaginative kindness. He is a writer about people far more than a chronicler of society. O'Hara's world is not only a mirror of reality but a product of his own feelings and intelligence.

O'Hara's industry—his obsession with writing—was a curse as well as a blessing, for he wrote too much and the quantity of his work confused his public and caused him to be undervalued. His public statements and vanity turned people against him and he was resented and underrated, usually by his inferiors and often by his own associates. By now, however, it is clear what his best work consists of—thirty or forty short stories and novellas, for their artistic delicacy and a psychological acuteness unsurpassed in American literature; *Appointment in Samarra*, for its youthful vitality and honesty; *From the Terrace*, for its ambition, thoroughness and immense readability; and *The Lockwood Concern*, for confronting most completely the values that tormented him through his life. These works make O'Hara one of the half-dozen most important writers of his time.

Frank MacShane. The Life of John O'Hara<br>(Dutton, 1981), pp. 225–26, 238

Surprisingly for a writer whose work is sometimes crudely plotted or imperfectly realized, O'Hara's interest is to a large degree aesthetic. He is capable of very refined observation and great finesse in his handling of characters and their developing situations. His short stories reveal these qualities continually, but they appear in the novels too, and in one special quality he is approached by no one. Although his characters are characteristically two-dimensional, he creates a psychological atmosphere around them at times that is extraordinary. His ability to "sense" or "feel" a character within the context of an introspective mood can be seen in even his worst novels. Mildred Simmons and the party she gives, and Nina Stephens when she first appears, in *The Big Laugh*, have this special quality of being felt through a projected mood that is full of tones. The Eaton mother in her widowhood as she talks to her daughter-in-law in *From the Terrace* is captured with the same psychological inwardness. This power of projection, usually witnessed in O'Hara's women, might be called "depth of tone," and it is but one aspect of an aesthetic richness in O'Hara that has been slighted or ignored.

O'Hara cannot be called a major novelist, and his achievement is not at the level of Hemingway, Fitzgerald, or Faulkner. But if his best work in fiction is taken together—his short stories, nouvelles, and perhaps seven of his novels—he compares well with his contemporaries: with John Steinbeck, John P. Marquand, James Gould Cozzens, James T. Farrell, and John Hersey. Compared to Steinbeck, O'Hara produced a larger body of superior work, and his social intelligence is almost infinitely more mature. O'Hara is an elusive writer, but if he creates a tradition in American fiction, it is perhaps in the role he adopts as a musing observer of American middle-class despair. The writers who follow him, in his special concerns, are John Cheever and John Updike, who bring a similar sense of disquiet and subterranean anguish to the suburbs. Their characters are portrayed in a closely specified social dimension, and yet are always subject to the terrors that followed O'Hara—their isolation and entrapment within the abysses of themselves. O'Hara's career began with trauma and psychic fixation, from which he was unable to free himself; he could not write them out of his system or evade them. From the fly-by-night hotel rooms he occupied as a reporter to his "Linebrook" study outside Princeton, the terror of his loneliness was always part of him. But in his magical moments as a writer—and he has many—his haunting becomes everyone's.

Robert Emmet Long. John O'Hara (Ungar, 1983), pp. 173–74

# ● OLSEN, TILLIE (1913–    )

About Mrs. Olsen one is not inclined to say, as might have been said about Bernard Malamud or Philip Roth on their first appearance, that here, no matter what comes of it, is a rich outpouring of talent. Mrs. Olsen's stories [in *Tell Me a Riddle*] depend heavily on her own experience, and that experience seems to be narrow. But, to judge from the stories, it is also one that she has felt very deeply and pondered and imaginatively absorbed. The one remarkable story in her book, "Tell Me a Riddle," is a *tour de force* which pits aging and dying immigrant Jews against their native-born children, prosperous, troubled and helpless. Mrs. Olsen treats this familiar subject with balance, a cool humaneness, as if she were trying to see through the eyes of both generations and accept the self-pity of neither. . . .

Mrs. Olsen writes with steady hardness of tone, clinging to the one perception—the perception of loss and forgetting—which controls her story. In some passages she presses too hard, trying for verbal effects, intensities upon intensities, she cannot quite control, and not allowing her fable to move freely on its own. Nevertheless, the story is a remarkable piece of work, and one can only hope that Mrs. Olsen, having been possessed by the powers of memory, may now move ahead to fiction in which everything depends on the powers of invention.

Irving Howe. NR. Nov. 13, 1961, p. 22

Four stories make up this first book by a gifted, mature artist with an uncanny sense of compassion. Rarely, at least in recent years, has the literature of alienation been engaged in such devout service of the imagination. In writing which is individualized but not eccentric, experimental but not obscure, Mrs. Olsen has created imagined experience which has the authenticity of autobiography or memoir. With a faultless accuracy, her stories treat the very young, the mature, the dying—poor people without the means to buy or invent lies about their situations—and yet her writing never succumbs to mere naturalism.

Some critics will persist in finding analogies to Mrs. Olsen's work in the socially conscious literature of the thirties. They are there, if one wishes to be blind to everything else, but the truth is that Mrs. Olsen has been more daring. Sometimes she is able to compress within the space of a single sentence or a brief paragraph the peculiar density of a career, a lifetime, in the manner of lyric poetry. It follows that the poverty which she describes never strikes one as formulary or anachronistic, but as an image for contemporary experience. Although addicted to metaphorical language, she uses it flexibly and unself-consciously to record, to analyze, and then to judge, fusing it with thought and feeling in such a way that the prose becomes the central intelligence of these dramas. . . .

Some of these stories have their faults, but they are faults of enthusiasm. Occasionally the prose will get out of hand, or, in choosing to be on such intimate terms with her characters, Mrs. Olsen will descend to a literal-mindedness which is her humanity unrestrained. Even so, there are stories in this collection which are perfectly realized works of art.

The foremost of these is a dramatic monologue entitled "I Sit Here Ironing," in which an unnamed and physically nondescript woman (a voice really), after a lifetime of deprivation, explains as she does the day's ironing the growth of her estrangement from her homely, first-born daughter. As she describes the early slights and disasters which brought such a relationship about, one has revealed the many human forms which loss can take. Mrs. Olsen's woman is burdened with exhaustion, a victim of a world in which all the panaceas have been discredited. To say that she seems ordinary or without stature indicates only the costume she may be wearing, for her suffering is made extraordinarily vivid and historic. . . .

Although she had explored the possibility of multiple consciousnesses functioning within the same dramatic situation in the earlier "Hey Sailor What Ship," one feels that in the final story she has actually fleshed two protagonists of equal vigor, enmeshing them in a marriage which seems as real and as permanent as any one will encounter in recent fiction. "Tell Me A Riddle" is a modern day "Ivan Illych." The death of Mrs. Olsen's heroine is the death of social consciousness itself, gruesome, alienated, and without consolation. In the death-struggle of this old activist and her mate (with both continually pitting their dignities against the other), Mrs. Olsen has envisaged a true tragedy of human mortality. In the last grim acts of a social protest which sprang from love, not cant, she puts it more eloquently than I can, in the words of the desolated old man who has been left behind, when he says: "Aaah, children . . . how we believed, how we belonged."

Richard M. Elman. *Com.* Dec. 8, 1961, pp. 295–96

Tillie Olsen's *Yonnondio* is unfinished, but what we have is an extraordinary achievement. The book was begun in the early 1930s, and worked on intermittently until 1936 or 1937. A few sketches appeared in print during this period, and then nothing. The manuscript of *Yonnondio* was set aside while Mrs. Olsen began to take on "everyday jobs" and raise a family. . . .

Yonnondio clearly must take its place as the best novel to come out of the so-called proletarian movement of the '30s. The dogma and stilted characterizations that deform so many of the novels of that period have no place in Tillie Olsen's writing. She is a consummate artist who, in a paragraph such as the following one about the life of a miner, demonstrates just how searingly successful "protest" writing can be: "Someday the bowels (of the earth) will grow monstrous and swollen with these old tired dreams, swell and break, and strong fists batter the fat bellies, and skeletons of starved children batter them, and perhaps you will be slugged by a thug hired by the fat bellies, Andy Kvaternick. Or death will take you to bed at last, or you will strangle with the old crony of miners, the asthma." I know of no work that "bespeaks the consciousness and roots" of the 1930s as brilliantly as *Yonnondio.*

But it would be a terrible mistake to see *Yonnondio* as a work limited to, and bound by, the '30s. Mrs. Olsen's richness of style, her depth of characterization, and her enormous compassion make *Yonnondio* a work which must not—cannot—be restricted by any particular time or period. Its publication simply reinforces what we already know from *Tell Me a Riddle*: Tillie Olsen is one of the greatest prose stylists now writing. One can only think ruefully of what might have been had she not been "denied full writing life"—had those 40 years been hers, and so ours, not 40 years of "unnatural thwarting of what struggles to come into being, but cannot." Mrs. Olsen is quite right when she says (again, in "Death of the Creative Process") that a writer cannot be reconciled "for what is lost by unnatural silences." "*Yonnondio! Yonnondio!* The word itself a dirge," wrote Whitman. "Then blank and gone and still, and utterly lost." But now, with the publication of the found manuscript—unfinished as it may be—we can say: At least not that—not utterly lost. *Yonnondio* is a magnificent novel, one to be all the more cherished for the disruption it makes into the unnatural silence of Tillie Olsen.

Jack Salzman. *Book World.* April 7, 1974, p. 1

There is no more powerfully moving a piece of fiction in recent years than Tillie Olsen's long story "Tell Me a Riddle.". . . All of the stories of *Tell Me a Riddle* are superb but the title story is the one that remains most vividly in the mind. It will withstand repeated readings—and the sort of close, scrupulous attention ordinarily reserved for poetry. . . .

[*Silence's*] strengths lie . . . in its polemical passages. Olsen asks why so many more women are silenced than men; she asks why there is only one woman writer "of achievement" for every 12 men writers; why our culture continues to reflect a masculine point of view almost exclusively. . . .

One feels the author's passion, and cannot help but sympathize with it. Certainly women have been more generally "silenced" than men, in all the arts. But the book is marred by numerous inconsistencies and questionable statements offered as facts. . . .

Tillie Olsen must have felt justified in subordinating—or silencing—her own considerable artistic instincts during the composition of *Silences*, and I would not quarrel with her decision. It was a generous one: she wanted to reach out to others, to the living and the dead, who have, evidently, shared her own agony. One must respect such an impulse. But the thinking that underlies *Silences* is simply glib and superficial if set in contrast to the imagination that created *Tell Me a Riddle* and *Yonnondio*, Olsen's novel.

Joyce Carol Oates. NR. July 29, 1978, pp. 32–34

Tillie Olsen's remarkable power comes from having almost never written at all. A working-class woman who grew up in America in the 1930s, had children, and did "someone else's work" for years to support her family, Olsen was likely to have been silenced by daily struggle until, like the dying grandmother of her story "Tell Me A Riddle," she would want only the "reconciled peace" of a small, clean, empty house. Instead, through an incredible effort of will, Olsen, like Walt Whitman, used her enforced "long foreground" not only to write but to do so with extraordinary empathy. Part of Olsen's present high reputation in America admittedly springs from her role as heroine of her own life. The sheer grit that she needed in order to find the strength and time to write—and to believe she *could* write—has meant that she (usually implicitly) adds the argument of her experience to her discussion in *Silences* of the conditions of creative work: I am the woman, I suffered, I was there.

Olsen is far more than the token working-class writer whose presence soothes the middle-class American women's movement (though she is certainly also being used as that). First a silent, then a vocal conscience for American women's writing, Olsen writes with an elegance, compassion, and directness rare in any period. Though her politicized recognitions form a unique link between 1930s radicalism and the women's movement of the 1980s, Olsen has published little. . . . Olsen's great subject, the emotional life of the working-class family, has been so buried in American culture since the 1930s, that it looks completely new. . . .

Unlike Whitman, Olsen does not sublimate private despair into cosmic affirmation. The external circumstances of her characters generate ironies characteristic of nineteenth-century realism: poverty, dirt, tired bodies, heat, smells, drink, labour, recalcitrant objects and a toxic failure of will that manifests itself in violence or withdrawal. Only sex is left out; as Cora Kaplan remarks in her introduction to *Yonnondio*, Olsen sees neither fulfillment nor release there. Within such limits, family love (maternal passion in particular) is peculiarly generous, since it is felt in full knowledge of inevitable separation and probable crushing of hope. All of Olsen's narratives deal with two generations. . . .

In Olsen's subjective essays motherhood looms large as a cause of silence precisely because it does engage one's deepest emotions: "There is no one else responsible" for children's needs. "It is distraction, not meditation, that becomes habitual; interruption, not continuity; spasmodic, not constant toil." In her more objective fiction she sees motherhood as the experience which expresses continuity and separation simultaneously, a paradox which politicizes it: the mother, cut off from experience of the world by sexual division of labour, must nevertheless impart values to her children or see them fall.

Helen McNeil. *TLS*. Nov. 14, 1980, p. 1294

Olsen's importance to contemporary women who read and write or who write about literature is widely acknowledged. Yet although her work has been vital for feminists today, and although one article does discuss her background in some depth, few of Olsen's contemporary admirers realize the extent to which her consciousness, vision, and choice of subject are rooted in an earlier heritage of social struggle—the communist Old Left of the thirties and the tradition of radical political thought and action, mostly socialist and anarchist, that dominated the Left in the teens and twenties. Not that we can explain the eloquence of her work in terms of its sociopolitical origins, not even that left-wing politics and culture were the single most important influences on it, but that its informing consciousness, its profound understanding of class and sex and race as shaping influences on people's lives, owes much to that earlier tradition. Olsen's work, in fact, may be seen as part of a literary lineage so far unacknowledged by most contemporary critics: a socialist feminist literary tradition. . . .

On the whole, in spite of the Left's demands on her time and energies, the prescriptiveness of its more dogmatic criticism, and the androcentrism or outright sexism of many of its spokesmen, there is no doubt but that Olsen's Marxian perspective and experience ultimately enriched her literature. . . .

In the fifties, partly out of a spirit of opposition to the McCarthy era, and blessed with increased time as the children grew up and there were temporary respites from financial need, Olsen began to do the work that gave us the serenely beautiful but still politically impassioned stories of the *Tell Me a Riddle* volume. Olsen's enduring insistence that literature must confront the material realities of people's lives as shaping circumstances, that the very categories of class and race and sex constitute the fabric of reality as we live it, and that literature has an obligation to deepen consciousness and facilitate social change are part of her—and our—inheritance from the radical tradition.

Deborah Rosenfelt. *FSt.* Fall, 1981, pp. 373–74,
403–4

## OLSON, CHARLES (1910–1970)

Olson's argument throughout his poetry is that awareness is an event caused by multiple forces, setting multiple forces in action. No force is ever spent. All events are lessons. No event can be isolated.

Olson therefore evolved a kind of poem that would at once project historical ponderables (for history is the ground for all his poetry) and allow him free play for contemplation and response. The poems in *Maximus III* were written "in gloom on Watch-House Point" from 1963 to 1969. They constitute the third volume of perhaps one long poem, "Books VII and After" (Olson's working title), comparable in American literature to *The Cantos* and *Paterson*; perhaps a suite of poems (the early format of "letters from Maximus" allowing for the versatility and spontaneity of a correspondence) like *Leaves of Grass.* . . .

If we allow for the sections of these poems that quote historical documents, and for the occasional jeremiad, we can go a long way toward understanding them by noting that they are variations on Keats' nightingale ode. They are for the large part written at night (by a Timonish Endymion *en pantoufles*, or an insomniac bear with clipboard wandering about Gloucester, caught from time to time in the spotlight of a police cruiser), they share the imagery of bird and flower (cormorant and nasturtium here), fierce seas and bonging bells (buoys on Cape Ann), and they meditate on resonances of the past that can still be heard. . . .

I have not been able here to give any notion of the wideness of these new Maximus poems—the horizon they survey is vast—nor of their depth, which goes back into various histories (the Hittite, Egyptian, Greek, Roman, paleolithic)in new and bright ways (Olson's eyes were open to everything and very little got by him). Nor have I mentioned their religious concern. The best way to offer a summation is to note that a movement is closed by them, a movement that began with Thoreau and Whitman, when America was opening out and possibilities were there to be stumbled over or embraced. Olson is the other term of this moment. He is our anti-Whitman (like Melville before him). He is a prophet crying bad weather ahead, and has the instruments to prove it.

Guy Davenport. Parnassus. Spring/Summer,<br>1976, pp. 255–56, 259

Not only is Olson an unusually interesting theorist, but a case can be made that a study of his poetics should logically precede an examination of his poetry, that his poems cannot be adequately appreciated within the terms of recent poetic theory. . . . Olson deserves close attention precisely because his poems do not conform to what modern critics have argued is essentially poetic. His poetry raises questions of poetic theory with unusual directness, and these questions, rather than the poems themselves, are my subject. What are the attractions of an expository poetics? What ends are served by expository poems? Why should a didactic poet use so exclusive a rhetoric? . . .

In general, . . . Olson's poems and his understanding of the nature of poetry are hardly separable. He is commonly thought to have been one of the most influential American poets during the years following World War II, but influential more as a writer of manifestoes than as a poet. He himself, however, felt that his occasional remarks about poetry and his poetry itself followed from the same motives and envisioned the same goals: "Projective Verse" was meant to regroup forces—chiefly Olson's, but Pound's and Williams' too—after a barrage of rejection slips. . . .

Though his main distinction is the ability "to assimilate and coordinate a large number of preceding inventions," his own work significantly develops the range of post-Symbolist poetry. Specifically, his attempt to teach his readers is not burdened, as Pound's is, by a commitment to a nonrational psychology and rhetorical strategy; Olson addresses himself to his readers' understanding in a language unembarrassed by abstraction, and the sequence of his statements usually follows a formulable logic. This reclamation of abstract discourse and of logical organization is based in part on a refined epistemology derived from Whitehead; it is this part of Olson's work . . . that has had the most beneficial influence on contemporary poets, especially on those poets, like Imamu Baraka (then LeRoi Jones) and Edward Dorn, whose pedagogical ambitions are specifically political. . . .

American literary culture appears to have no way of handling a poet like Olson, committed to a pedagogical and rhetorical poetics, short of labeling him a shaman, and Olson perhaps had no experience at rejecting what was, after all, flattery. If this was the case, it is not hard to see why his later poetry was egocentric, though it is depressing to witness how, almost routinely, contemporary culture can corrupt so ambitious and so American a poet.

Robert von Hallberg. Charles Olson: The Scholar's Art (Harvard Univ. Pr., 1978), pp. 1–3, 216

Olson's canon has within it a potent utterance: life is strangled by systems. Existence has an order that cannot be isolated from nature; the order is continually changing and evolving. A system is a halting of change; it seizes upon a possible order and continues to duplicate it endlessly. As it entrenches in the midst of nature, its tyranny upon life grows, until the system is a prison of contradictions.

In his *Maximus* sequence, we are struck at once by the solitude of his protagonist. Olson portrayed himself as a lone adventurer in a world that other human beings have vacated. He celebrates the glory of direct experience, of awareness that is aroused by unmediated contact with nature beyond systematized thought. The poignance of this long, awesome poem comes from the sense that he cannot enjoy the splendor of earth alone; his words are the song that would lure humanity out of doors. Orpheus is one of his heroes. Fighters and redeemers are the gods of his personal mythology.

It may be difficult to accept Olson as a great poet. His poetic ideals were imperfection, the uncompleted, the process without the end, disordered vitality. He is a saboteur of the certainty that thrived in his era: his vision of man is that he is a wild and passionate creature who is being lured into a false Eden of systems and institutions and who barters the realms of nature and his own primal humanity for a few material possessions. As Olson argued throughout his writings, man only now wakes to the splendors of the real, still rubs from his eyes the primordial sleep, but already he is being driven back toward the dark again by a society that thrives on diminishing his awareness. Olson wanted the poet to be the measure of awareness, to be that lone human figure thrust deep into the uncertainty of the real, where he lives and expresses himself joyfully and is ultimately joined by others.

Paul Christensen. Charles Olson: Call Him Ishmael (Univ. of Texas Pr., 1979), p. 212

# O'NEILL, EUGENE (1888–1953)

Perhaps a better slogan for O'Neill than art for art's sake would be art for life's sake. He tried to convert the theater back into a church because he had a deep psychological need to do so. Only art could turn doubt into will and despair into acceptance. Only art could release his pain of spirit and allow him to transcend himself. O'Neill was driven by personal demons in all his work, demons that had to be exorcised over and over. The inward turn of his mind away from political or social preoccupations toward its own workings was the turn of his plays. The tension of his inner conflicts was his plays' tension. And this tension, this pain of spirit, could only be released if shared by an audience, by a body of fellow sufferers who in the sharing became father confessors. The exorcising could only take place through the performance of rituals that were communal in nature.

Yet O'Neill's plays amount to more than elaborate confessions or disguised autobiography. For his attempt to make of the theater a place where rituals were acted out had broad cultural significance. It was an attempt to restore to the theater the function it had possessed in ancient Athens and, in more sublimated form, in Elizabethan England—the function of life celebration. . . .

The purpose of the [Provincetown] Players, at least in an aesthetic sense, was religious. And O'Neill's own purpose was equally, if not more, religious. Remaining faithful to his purpose for over thirty years as a playwright, he realized drama on a higher aesthetic level than most American playwrights even contemplated. Not surprisingly, the way to the aesthetic heights was through the psychological depths, and for that reason, along with his personal need, he explored the psyche and its motives without quarter. To dramatize what he uncovered meant shattering genteel morality and conventional dramaturgy. Consequently, there were legal and artistic struggles, but he managed to shatter the morality and dramaturgy both. Through his passion, imagination and daring the American theater finally became three-dimensional in the tradition of the European.

Leonard Chabrowe. *Ritual and Pathos: The Theater of O'Neill* (Bucknell Univ. Pr., 1976), pp. 12, 14–15

I do not wish to present an argument that O'Neill is an absurdist dramatist, but would suggest that in his insistence that his realistic manner must also be expressive, must be "real realism," he did play a part in extending the limits and did assimilate into his form means of exploring areas of human experience which continue to be of pressing interest to us today. Retention of the realistic framework seems to have been essential to the functioning of his creative imagination. He did experiment with expressionist and symbolist techniques but . . . even within such experiments he constantly veered towards sets and situations in which the familiar and human, as opposed to the remote or metaphysical, could be recreated and explored.

And yet. Whilst O'Neill never does break the illusion he does go to the edge, does threaten it. Within the conventional performing of the play itself, his characters perform for each other and adopt a succession of different roles. . . .

Similarly, although in the late plays O'Neill does appear to keep to a sequential time span, there is, co-existent with the realistic rhythm of linear time, a different temporal rhythm: a strange recurrence and circularity of the kind that would be explicit in the drama of the post-war period. . . .

The fictional time span of each of O'Neill's late plays occupies only a day or a day and a half of fictional time, and each is limited to a single set. . . . In each, a linear plot drives the action forwards. *The Iceman Cometh*, with its revelations, act by act, about the death of Evelyn and the betrayal of Rosa, is modelled on the detective mystery; *Long Day's Journey into Night*, with its hints, its anticipated telephone calls, its trips to the doctor and drug store, its ominous predictions about the return of the fog, on the well-made play. *A Touch of the Poet* and *Moon for the Misbegotten*, the one with its duel, the other its intrigue over the old homestead and both with seduction plots, follow the course of the old melodrama. The linear plot is used in each case to hold the audience and stimulate their curiosity, whilst other elements slowly take possession at a deeper level, and meaning accrues to seemingly neutral words and images. Time and space are extended in these plays, within the firm structure of the linear plot, by a succession of vignettes of off-stage characters and events which are integrated into the dialogue in jokes, tall stories, reminiscences and involuntary memories. At their simplest, these present people or events from outside the stage setting but inside the play's fictional time span.

Jean Chothia. *Forging a Language: A Study of the Plays of Eugene O'Neill* (Cambridge Univ. Pr., 1979), pp. 188–89

If *Ah, Wilderness!* marks the high point of O'Neill's optimism about the potential for the achievement of humanistic goals in modern American experience, *The Iceman Cometh* appears to represent the depth of his pessimism. This work, like *Long Day's Journey into Night*, is an American interpretation of what critics such as Joseph Wood Krutch have described as a "tragic humanism." Although these late plays did succeed in revealing the contour of the universe in which modern man lives, they also exposed the failures of their protagonists to achieve humanistic goals. Through Hickey, Larry, and Parritt of *The Iceman Cometh* and the tragic Tyrones of *Long Day's Journey into Night*, O'Neill interpreted what he was finally to concede as humanism's limitations as a religion. They do not, however, seem to indicate his total rejection of a humanism as a social philosophy. Rather, these late plays suggest O'Neill's final acceptance of a tragic view of experience.

O'Neill's "tragic humanism" reaffirms the classical proposition that man's condition precludes forever the full realization of his ideals. It is, however, the individual's response to the tragic fact of his limitation that remains not only the measure of man's nobility but also of his humanity.

Esther M. Jackson. In *Eugene O'Neill: A World View*, ed. Virginia Floyd (Ungar, 1979), p. 256

# OZICK, CYNTHIA (1928–    )

Cynthia Ozick is a writer with a lot on her mind. Being American she worries about it and claims at one point that she is as ignorant as a writer must be and reads nothing but sensational newspaper accounts. Being Jewish and intellectual she doesn't push that pose very far and actually gives us [in *Bloodshed, and Three Novellas*] a thoughtful preface along with four substantial stories that contain or point at serious ideas without precisely succumbing to viewiness. What does she think about? About the conflict of cultures taking place in the minds and hearts of young Jews living just a generation past the time of the Holocaust; problems of conduct and belief for those who may want access to Jewish tradition yet who cannot accept the cultic aspect of the religion. . . .

Ozick's thoughts remain interesting even when the reader finds flaws in their logical process or finds them suffused with a sort of parochialism. . . .

All these stories have puzzling endings. That's because Ozick's imagination is adventurous, with a feeling for life as mystery and riddle. When she uses complex forms, as in "Usurpation," it's not for show but because the relationships to be defined between tradition and the individual talent are themselves complicated and morally perplexing. Her prose is often richly colored and nuanced, owing something to Woolf and Lawrence, and she also has an acute ear for the way the varieties of American character betray themselves in the many variations of American vernacular speech, including such "foreign" American vernaculars as that of the worker-rabbi in "Bloodshed" and the Bulgarian-American doctor in "An Education." Wherever American writing is going now, Cynthia Ozick is a distinctive and bright part of that movement into the future.

Julian Moynahan. NYT. April 11, 1976, p. 8

Cynthia Ozick could have been a scholar; a generation younger and she might have been a rabbi. What she has become, luckily for us, is a unique and challenging writer whose intellect is vivified by all the lively juices of a storyteller and a reveller in language. Most of Ozick's work is fraught with the tension between rationalist and holy thinker on the one hand, and talemaker, invoker of magic and miracle on the other. . . . So the action of fiction and the action of magic are identical for her—both proceed by a confounding of instances, a perception of the hidden symmetry in creation's parts. . . .

Ozick has no trouble finding ideas for her stories, it's her inventive powers that are less reliable, the inhibition against tale-telling has taken its toll. What she sometimes lacks is the insane, trusting, necessary willingness of the truly relaxed natural tale-teller to let her characters walk off just out of hearing of her commands and live lives that might surprise her, almost as though she were one of her own readers. Her desires for these stories and her overwhelming delight in conundra, at times overwhelm and inhibit them; then they move like Talmudic argument, not like stories on their way to a destination.

Rosellen Brown. NR. June 5, 1976, p. 30

Self-consciousness about writing fiction can lead to overindulgent prose and the substitution of egoism for ideas. Cynthia Ozick is the most self-conscious writer I know of. Yet she steadfastly shuns overindulgence of any sort, and instead does what too few contemporary fiction writers do on a regular basis—think. Ozick is obsessed with the words she puts on paper, with what it means to imagine a story and to tell it, with what fiction is. The result is a body of work at once as rich as Grace Paley's stories, as deeply rooted in Jewish folklore as Isaac Bashevis Singer's tales, as comically ironic as Franz Kafka's nightmares. . . .

A perfectionist, she has written just one novel, *Trust*, and three collections of short works: *The Pagan Rabbi, and Other Stories*, *Bloodshed, and Three Novellas*, and now *Levitation: Five Fictions*. Yet she is one of the best. Because she deals with ideas—many of them steeped in Jewish law and history—her stories are "difficult." But by difficult I mean only that they are not in the least bit fluffy. No word, emotion, or idea is wasted. They are weighty, consequential tales, lightened and at the same time heightened by their visionary aspects.

Ozick writes magically about magical events. But she distrusts sorcery, the stock in trade of fiction writing. This irony gives her work a thought-provoking dialectical quality. Her stories are elusive, mysterious, and disturbing. They shimmer with intelligence, they glory in language, and they puzzle.

In "Puttermesser: Her Work History, Her Ancestry, Her Afterlife" [in *Levitation*], we first meet Ruth Puttermesser—34, an unmarried lawyer, something of a feminist—while she is living in her family's apartment in the Bronx. . . .

"Puttermesser and Xanthippe," the longest of the five fictions, is an almost perfect novella. Ozick's character, Puttermesser, now 46, is still single. She is still working for the city government. . . . When the mayor ousts her boss, political appointees take over. And "in their presence the work instantly held its breath and came to a halt as if it were a horse reined in for examination." Patronage is in; Puttermesser is out; the city is falling apart.

Puttermesser, pushed beyond fantasy, creates a golem—an artificial creature of cabalist lore—out of the earth in her potted plants. When Puttermesser is fired, the golem, who insists on being called Xanthippe after Socrates's shrewish wife, gets her elected mayor of New York.

Under Puttermesser's rule, the city is transformed: Gangs of youths invade the subway yards and wash the cars; lost wallets are returned; muggers form dancing troupes, traffic grids unlock; out-of-work corrections officers take gardening jobs; litter vanishes; New York extends interest-free loans to the federal government. . . .

Like Ozick, Puttermesser is an intelligent rationalist. Puttermesser makes a golem; Ozick makes up stories. Ozick equates the magic in her stories with the magical process of writing fiction. So writing about rooms levitating and golems becomes writing about writing, about making magic. For Ozick, fiction *is* magic.

Robert R. Harris. SR. Feb., 1982, pp. 58–59

Once there was a "near-sighted, twenty-two-year-old young woman infected with the commonplace intention of writing a novel." In pursuit of this intention, she "became" Henry James. She exulted in his work, anguished over her own, and worshiped at literature's altar. . . .

Having been James, Cynthia Ozick knew his struggles with Europe and with his Americanness quite well, and this knowledge was of use when she set out to establish herself as a religious Jew amid and in opposition to Christian culture. We are not speaking of religion as metaphor—like that rigorous Catholic Flannery O'Connor, Ozick refuses atheist and agnostic readers such an escape hatch. The characters of both are filled with anxiety about their place and privileges in the world; the writers then put them through their social and spiritual (add intellectual for Ozick, racial for O'Connor) paces with high seriousness, low vaudevillianism, and assorted shades of irony. . . .

Cynthia Ozick's new novel, *The Cannibal Galaxy* . . . in a series of *As Ifs* that are bold, cunning, and wholly her own, examines motherhood, pedagogy, the premises of cultural and biological reproduction, assimilation, exile, ambition, idolatry, and immortality. . . .

Like a murder mystery, the book's title suggests the ferocity and tension that run through its story. The literal murders are history's province. Culture makes a place for the subtler ones in families and in schools; between parents, teachers, children, patriots, exiles, the privileged, and the dispossessed. All take their chosen or allotted place, drawing what they can from tradition, belief, and need. Those with more predatory urges join the cannibal galaxies, "megalosaurian colonies of primordial gases that devour smaller brother-galaxies—and when the meal is made, the victim continues to rotate like a Jonah-dervish inside the cannibal, while the sated ogre-galaxy, its gaseous belly stretched, soporific, never spins at all—motionless as digesting Death."

This is Ozick's first novel in 15 years, and its length allows her to draw out her themes and her language—to portray and parody the repetition of school years, school lessons, habits, ideas; to show children as prosaic as they are precocious and a Paris as full of detail as of tragedy. "The novel is long," Ozick wrote in her introduction to *Bloodshed*'s novellas, "because it is a process, like chewing the apple of the Tree of Knowledge: it takes the novel a while before it discovers its human nakedness." In that process, her gifts—a series of Dual Curriculums containing drama and didacticism, humor and passion, plain and highly enameled prose—are laid fully bare as well.

Margo Jefferson. VLS. Sept., 1983, pp. 1, 12–13

# PERCY, WALKER (1916–   )

In all of Percy's novels the hero inherits what amounts to an orthodox Christian view of man and his relation to reality, but the world inhabited by the hero is dominated by ideas that are powerfully twisted away from any orthodox view. In the first three novels the heroes finally achieve, despite the age they live in, a religious apprehension of their own stance in the world. In the fourth novel [*Lancelot*], however, the protagonist is maddened by what he sees as the ineffectuality of Christianity in a world he finds intolerable. Vowing to take matters into his own hands, Lancelot becomes a modern Gnostic. . . .

Two crucial aspects of Gnosticism are worth emphasizing here: (1) Man the creature is not responsible for the evil in which he finds himself. He has a right to blame it on someone or something else. The assumption that "In Adam's fall/We sinned all" is to the Gnostic pure nonsense. And (2) Man's salvation depends upon his own efforts. He must rely not upon faith but on gnosis, the secret knowledge that makes it possible for him to evade the snares and entanglements of the demon and to reunite his soul with the divinity from which he has come. . . .

A Gnostic impatience with human limitations can easily convert into a hubristic denial of one's own limitations and an amoral disregard for ethical systems demanding decency in the human community.

That seems to be what happens to Lancelot Andrewes Lamar, the character whom Walker Percy has presented as the complete twentieth-century Gnostic—a millennialist through and through—confident that he knows how to reform a corrupt world and willing to kill if he cannot cure. . . .

The ending of *Lancelot* is ambiguous, but I think that Percy juxtaposes the speaker and the auditor, the Gnostic and the Christian, in order to suggest that we are indeed in an either/or situation. *Either* we accept alienation as our necessary condition—acknowledging the world's evil condition and helping to ameliorate it, but never presuming to believe that we can eliminate it—and live in faith, *or* we will find our own theories inviting and condoning the Hitlers, the Idi Amins, and the Lancelots of the world.

Cleanth Brooks. SoR. Autumn, 1977, pp. 678,<br>680, 685–86

Despite repeated protestations that, *as a novelist*, he owes little to the South, Percy has not only located each of his novels in the region, but drawn poignantly of its "atmosphere"; there are passages in *The Last Gentleman* that reveal the author firmly the realist, as anxious as Zola or Flaubert to capture a limited part of what some of us these days call "the environment". . . .

Anyone who has spent time in the Mississippi Delta knows how exact, how fine and right Percy's writing is. He will repeatedly tell a Yankee visitor that unlike Faulkner, Eudora Welty, or Flannery O'Connor, he has spent little time with the region's "plain folk," black or white, and has followed the example of continental novelists, from Dostoevski to Sartre and Camus. Yet Percy loves the South, and if he doesn't give us the weird, bizarre, or overwhelmingly dreary people that many of the region's other novelists have made a point of putting before us, he at the very least evokes the atmosphere, the conditions of life which surround and define the lives of those who belong to a particular region. Not that he is a committed realist, either. Naturalistic observation gives way frequently to flashes of psychological subjectivity. Humorous, beguiling comedy, in no need of any heavy symbolic interpretation, and quite pleasing to the reader, gives way to densely abstract speculation, rendered through an obvious and not especially original literary device: the notebook left inadvertently but conveniently lying about. The notebook is Sutter's, and it is quite worthy of Marcel; and Heidegger, one believes, though he would not be capable of Sutter's earthy, blunt, Rabelaisian side, would certainly recognize the ideas of this wayward, distracted, near-suicidal doctor.

Robert Coles. *Walker Percy: An American Search*
(Atlantic-Little Brown, 1978), pp. 181–82

Walker Percy belongs among a small group of writers in our time who have done something for modern American literature that many people thought would never be done. He and novelists like Saul Bellow, Flannery O'Connor, and J. F. Powers—to name people from three regions—have given to contemporary American fiction an intellectual and even a philosophical tone lacking in classic modern writers like Hemingway and Fitzgerald. Percy and writers like him have become intellectually involved with European thinkers and novelists and have used insights gained from this involvement without losing their own native genius for writing fiction. They have not cut themselves off from their ethnic and regional traditions but rather have followed these traditions back to their sources in the Old World. They have derived benefits from being Jewish or Catholic or even Episcopalian that other and perhaps greater writers of the American past often did not know. Thus Percy cannot be pigeonholed as, say, a Catholic novelist. Instead, Percy is a novelist of profound intellectual curiosity and sensitivity. He feels himself more closely aligned with the continental novelists, for "the European novels are more philosophical, more novels of ideas" than English and American novels are.

The ideas in Percy's novels are basically Kierkegaardian, but the novels are not simply a framework for presenting the Danish philosopher's ideas. Instead, Kierkegaard is, for Percy, as Emerson was for Whitman, a kind of flame that brought the author to a boiling point. When one writer influences another the way Kierkegaard influenced Percy, it is not because one gives and the other takes certain ideas. It is because the older author brings the younger author face to face with one or more of the archetypes. It is Kierkegaard's encounter with the archetypal mythic quester, his "knight of faith," that helped to shake Percy out of his mental fixation on the general laws of science. Ideas usually inspire men and women to generate more ideas, but archetypes set flowing a stream of images in the psyches of artists who are receiving a torch from their masters.

Ted R. Spivey. In The Art of Walker Percy: Stratagems for Being, ed. Panthea Reid Broughton (Louisiana State Univ. Pr., 1979), pp. 273–74

Like so many existentialists Percy attempts in his theory of language, as well as his novels, to recover the human being from the Cartesian split of mind and body which dominates much of twentieth century thinking. Percy is, of course, influenced greatly by Kierkegaard in these matters; and his radical anthropology has its base in the Kierkegaardian insistence on individual sovereignty and choice as well as in the Judeo-Christian view of man as the fallen seeker.

As Percy has often said, he writes in "the Christian context," and his theory of man is also modeled after the Judeo-Christian anthropology. He believes that this theory is flexible enough to be adapted to the twentieth century, provided that those who adopt it confront the notion of the Fall. The Christian is always faced with the problem of an estrangement which goes beyond the estrangement attributable to technology, to capitalist competition, and failure to adapt to certain social structures. The "normal," common fate of human beings in the Judeo-Christian tradition is alienation. The human being is a seeker, *homo viator*, exploring its alienation from self, others and God.

Cecil L. Eubanks. In Walker Percy: Art and Ethics, ed. Jac Tharpe (Univ. Pr. of Mississippi, 1980), pp. 122–23

With *The Second Coming* (1980), Walker Percy is trying to deliver answers. In a recent interview, he suggested that the work, his "first unalienated novel," represents a departure or breakthrough in his literary career: "I'm convinced that in *The Second Coming* there's a definite advance, a resolution of the ambiguity with which some of my other novels end: the victory, in Freudian terms, of eros over thanatos, life over death." In *The Second Coming*, Percy is making a deliberate attempt to avoid ambiguity, to do more than merely satirize contemporary mores, to offer answers and state them plainly. In the past, critics have frequently complained of Percy's penchant for equivocation and especially of his tendency to write indecisive and even enigmatic endings. Such indecisiveness has given rise to diverse and sometimes contradictory critical opinions as to the fundamental world view that informs Percy's fiction. Some critics have interpreted Percy's novels as expressions of Christian faith, while others have maintained that Percy takes a despairing, even nihilistic view of life. With *The Second Coming*, Percy is responding to this critical confusion; he is trying to make his affirmations plain.

Despite Percy's effort in *The Second Coming* to state his answers clearly, his tendency to opacity is not entirely overcome. Try as he will to offer constructive criticism, to suggest alternative modes of living, to root out the source of the modern malaise, Percy's very manner of presentation frequently seems either to defuse or to invalidate his answers. A fundamental ambivalence polarizes his fiction. . . .

The force of Percy's answers are mitigated by equal and opposite strains in his novel. He advocates commitment to the world as it is, and at the same time he castigates the world for falling far short of his ideal. Percy counsels acceptance of limited knowledge, but his hero is by nature a seeker, for whom inquiry is inseparable from existence. In effect, each of Percy's affirmations is countered by an opposing philosophical position. The truth, he seems to suggest, is a collage of contradictions. Such contradictoriness, or philosophical tension, can perhaps best be understood as an expression of the conflicting demands of immanence and transcendence. . . .

Doreen A. Fowler. *Critique*. Winter, 1981–82,
pp. 13, 21–22

● **PIERCY,  MARGE  (1936–    )**

*Dance the Eagle [to Sleep]* is a novel deeply informed by experience with revolt and revelation during the past decade, but . . . it is not a happy, idyllic romp, a lyrical reassurance that the Generation Gap has opened into Happy Hollow. . . . The classics that Marge Piercy has chosen as models are those dark fantasies, like *Lord of the Flies* and *Lord of the Rings*, lord-books heavy with pessimism and persecution, and animated by the age-old Manichean struggle between Good and Evil in which winners are somehow always losers. *Dance the Eagle [to Sleep]* tells the story of some not-too-distant time in which a small army of youth, drawn together by mutual feelings of alienation and hostility towards an oppressive, dehumanized system, declare themselves a nation apart. Secession first takes the form of an armed takeover of a New York City high school and the establishment of a communal lifestyle during the ensuing siege. Though the initial revolt is put down, the rebels retreat to the New Jersey countryside for a prolonged period of communal experience, self-imposed and underground exile which is followed by a suicidal episode of guerrilla counter-attack. The resulting holocaust of repression by "them" scatters and decimates the rebels, but like an earlier Civil War, does not diminish the spirit of secession. The firestorm passes, leaving smoldering embers that are carefully nurtured by the surviving few. . . .

*Dance the Eagle [to Sleep]* is a frightening book, which will reassure only those who can take solace from the fact that it is cast as a futuristic novel. This is no real solace, since Marge Piercy has used the future only as a parabolic mirror of the recent past; her novel is indirectly about the Movement, more specifically about the rise, fragmentation, and fall of the Students for a Democratic Society. The future setting allows her a certain freedom of exaggeration and abstraction, so that she may elevate the rise and fall of Reich III into a Götterdämmerung of symbolic and tragic proportions, and by so doing extrapolate and give fabulous substance to the essential Myth of the Movement.

Seen from this angle, the novel leaves the reader with a devastating sense of how far apart the generations have indeed moved, that the Gap has become an abyss. It is obvious that Piercy feels that her compatriots have passed through a trial by fire, that they are scattered and diminished but that the encounter has been a confrontation of massive proportions and implication. They have gained more than they have lost, and what they have gained is the solidarity of identity, a new consciousness far more sombre in implication than a sappy love of bell-bottoms and peanut butter.

John Seelye. NR. Dec. 12, 1970, pp. 24–25

At the very beginning and the very end of this rambling novel [*Small Changes*] Marge Piercy powerfully covers that particular quality of lost identity and desperation which, once recognized as common experience, has sparked the rage and solidarity of the women's liberation movement and created the concept of women's consciousness. The novel spans the 1960's in the lives of two women: Beth, the provincial working-class girl who discovers that the ideal marriage she's always dreamed of is a living hell and gathers her strength to escape it; and Miriam, the brilliant, "independent" mathematician, who is caught, blinded and thoroughly trapped—at least for the moment—by a middle-class version of the same nightmare.

In exploring both of their lives against a blurry background of late 1960's youth culture and radical politics, Piercy means to show the cross-class experience of women's oppression, to demonstrate the situations in which it occurs and to show some of the ways in which it is confronted. She succeeds in the first, and that success is the novel's strength; but it cannot compensate for the wordy, rhetorical and often monotonous quality of much of the narrative, nor for the fact that its author forces highly unconvincing resolutions to situations that are described at such length that they deserve at least open-ended fates. . . .

A final problem. Many women radicals will understand this novel's hostility to political "heaviness" on the American left, and how one of its functions was to celebrate machismo at the same time it relegated women activists to the kind of subservient roles that a real revolution must banish. But I wonder if most non-movement readers of the book won't assume that the hostility is directed toward the general priorities of the 1960's left. Piercy has been careless about her targets, and her failure to integrate and unify the issues that float through the novel—feminism, the antiwar movement, the oppression of the working class, the Government's outrageous (and continuing) use of grand juries to harass and jail radicals—implies that most of these concerns should be discarded in favor of the more important struggle, sexual equality and freedom. On the basis of Piercy's first two novels, and her often eloquent poetry, I find it hard to believe that she means this; yet it's disturbing that, in a novel of this length, set among highly politicized people, almost all of the characters are obsessively self-concerned: with alternate life-styles, aspects of communal living, their own emotions. Neither poverty nor racism, for example, is more than casually mentioned.

The problem of how to transform the cultural conditioning of women, which is inseparable from transforming the lives of all the exploited and the structure of the society that keeps them that way, is a profound one. Piercy shows what happens when women struggle for themselves (Beth) and what happens when they give up (Miriam). But the context in which the author allows their lives to evolve is too rigid, too blurry and sometimes too downright confused to grant the characters she has created the reality and the strength they deserve.

Sara Blackburn. NYT. Aug. 12, 1973, pp. 2–3

Piercy's desire is for a world of wholeness and completeness, where natural growth and development can lead to a satisfying participation in the fullness of life. As individual poems recount instances in which a sense of wholeness is attempted or gained or lost, they also explore the attitudes and actions necessary for a state of sustained community. . . .

As a woman, Piercy is particularly concerned about women and their ability to participate with integrity in a fully-realized life. In a number of poems, she examines the female growing-up process in America; in each case, the young girl is shown to possess great potential strength and individuality which is slowly but surely diverted or covered over. . . . Traditionally, a male/female dichotomy has been assumed in which the male has been viewed primarily as an objective, rational, abstract theorizer, too busy with the important intellectual progress of the world to be bothered by daily problems. The female, on the other hand, has been viewed primarily as an emotional, subjective, grubby doer of ordinary tasks. Man equals mind equals significant mode of knowing and being; woman equals body equals lesser mode of knowing and being. What Piercy wants to do is to change the value assigned to these two modes; and, in addition, she wants to synthesize and unify the separate parts to form whole people: thinking, feeling men and women, confident in mind and body. . . .

Piercy views contemporary America as a dream turned nightmare. The fertile land which once offered a place of freedom and tolerance—a place of growth—has now become full of death and destruction. Possession, subjugation, and selfishness have violated the land itself and the people who live in this society.

Jean Rosenbaum. MPS. Winter, 1977, pp. 193–<br>94, 201–2, 204

Marge Piercy is a prolific novelist and poet, a one-time organizer for SDS, who has become a spokesman for radical feminism. Though she presents herself as a revolutionary, battling against orthodoxies of every kind—political, cultural, sexual—her novels are surprisingly conventional. In conception and style, in the grim determination of her didactic intentions, her work is reminiscent of the radical-proletarian fiction of the 1930's, in which the message outweighed the manner of its telling. In each of her six novels, Miss Piercy seizes upon a problem that she regards as symptomatic of a sick, unjust, patriarchal society, and builds a heavily documented narrative around that problem to drive her moral home.

In *Woman at the Edge of Time* she concentrated on mistreatment of the insane; in *Small Changes* on women trapped in repressive marriages; in *Dance the Eagle to Sleep* on the exploitation of radical women by their sexist comrades; in *The High Cost of Living* on the high cost of being a lesbian in a bigoted academic milieu. Through the exhaustive detailing of social and sexual atrocities, Miss Piercy turns her novels into indictments crackling with outrage. Now and then she has tried to leaven the heavy freight of actuality that is her stock in trade with utopian imaginings, in the spirit of Doris Lessing's more elaborate science fiction, as in the futuristic dream world envisioned in *Woman at the Edge of Time*. But these fantasies are just as programmatic as her realistic novels. . . .

In her most recent novel, *Vida*, Marge Piercy looks back with elegiac nostalgia to the 1960's and the exhilarations of the anti-war movement as remembered by Vida Asch, a Weatherman fugitive. . . .

What is in some ways most bewildering about *Vida* is the way Marge Piercy's ideological severity toward bourgeois values—"We can't make a new society in the shell of the old if we're living a middle-class existence"—is insidiously overwhelmed by her rather girlish enthusiasm for the good things of that life. . . .

*Vida* is crammed with . . . arcane trivia, the sort of padding that was left out of an earlier and far more affecting fictional account of the anti-war apostles of violence, M. F. Beal's *Amazon One*, published in 1975. In that powerful novel, Miss Beal captured the derangement, the complacency, the resentful and terrified confusion of the Weatherman mentality in fiercely compressed prose that had the authentic ring of imaginative and historical truth. Next to M. F. Beal's radical activists, Marge Piercy's pale into ideological cartoons. *Vida*, almost twice as long as *Amazon One*, is stale and self-indulgent, leaving no breathing space or room for thought between writer and protagonist. At the end of this revolutionary soap opera, our heroine is still free, still running, and charged with unfounded confidence, as she walks into the sunset, that "What swept through us and cast us forward is a force that will gather and rise again." Those who have no sense of history can believe anything.

Pearl K. Bell. *Cmty.* July, 1980, pp. 59–60

Marge Piercy is known in England mainly as a novelist. That the author of *Vida* and *Woman on the Edge of Time* is also a powerful, distinctively American poet may come as a surprise, even to her admirers. As might be expected, *The Moon Is Always Female* reflects the uncompromising bias of the committed feminist, of which some of us by now are weary. But Marge Piercy's poems are so energetic and so intelligent that weariness is out of the question. This is, in fact, her sixth book of poems, and it is an excellent one. A tough, often humorous, sometimes angry view of herself emerges from the poems, yet they are free of embitterment. They lack that harsh edge of hysterial accusation—as if with a few nasty words one could instantly abolish half the human race—which spoils so many poems by women these days. Here finally is a feminist artist for whom one need rarely blush.

*The Moon Is Always Female* is gratifyingly longer than most poetry volumes, and absorbing throughout. In effect, Ms. Piercy is still a novelist in her poems; she has perfected an easy flowing unrhymed line in which she says what she means with few frills. If you object to poems that tell you things, then you will not like this book. . . . It is possible, of course, to find all this feminist rabble-rousing annoying. However good the advice, poetry may not be the best vehicle for it. Indeed, if Marge Piercy were only a rabble-rouser she would not be a poet. The fact is, she can be as subtle as anyone writing today. . . . "At the well" alone would convince me that Marge Piercy is one of America's major writers. . . . The strength of Piercy's work is its outwardness, its frankness. Even if you do not agree with her, you have to meet Marge Piercy halfway.

Anne Stevenson. *TLS*. Jan. 23, 1981, p. 81

Perhaps no other poet of this generation has more consistently identified herself with the political and social movements of her own times. Her earlier involvements were with the civil rights and antiwar movements of the 60's, which generated in turn the women's-rights and antiwar movements of the 70's. For anyone interested in what's been happening on the cutting edge during the past two decades, she's clearly essential reading.

Miss Piercy has the double vision of the utopian: a view of human possibility—harmony between the sexes, among races and between humankind and nature—that makes the present state of affairs clearly unacceptable by comparison. The huge discrepancy between what is and what could be generates anger, and many of these are angry poems—which, for those who want poetry to be nothing but beautiful, will mean points off. Because her poetry is so deliberately "political"—which, for some, means anything not about ghosts and roses—how you feel about it will depend on how you feel about subjects such as male-female relations, abortion, war and poverty. Those who don't like these subjects will use adjectives like "shrill" to describe the poems. . . .

Taken as a whole—and I recommend you do so only slowly, as this is rich fare—this collection [*Circles on the Water*] presents the spectacle of an agile and passionate mind rooted firmly in time and place and engaging itself with the central dilemmas of its situation. . . .

If poets could be divided into Prioresses and Wives of Bath, Miss Piercy would very definitely be a Wife of Bath. Low on fastidiousness and high on what Hazlitt called "gusto," earthy, bawdy, interested in the dailiness of life rather than in metaphysics, highly conscious of the power relationships between men and women but seeing herself by no means as a passive victim, she is ready to enter the fray with every weapon at her command. She is, in sum, a celebrant of the body in all its phases, including those that used to be thought of as vulgar. Surprisingly, her poetry is more humorous than her novels, although not all of it is what you'd call funny. The Wife of Bath was sometimes a savage ironist, and so is Miss Piercy. Neither has much interest in being ladylike. . . .

Tidiness is not her virtue, but then in the hierarchy of virtues this is surely not at the top. Essentially her poetry is a poetry of statement and story, and metaphor and simile are, characteristically, used by her as illustration rather than as structural principle. This does not bother me very much, since it's a mistake for a reader to look for the same qualities in every poet.

Miss Piercy's emotional range is great, and at her best she can make you laugh, cry, get angry; she can inspire you with social purpose and open doors through which you may walk into lived reality. One effect she almost never achieves, because she almost never tries for it, is that touch of the cold hand at the back of the neck, that glimpse into the borderlands. The darkness she sees is human-created and therefore potentially correctable. . . .

Margaret Atwood. NYT. Aug. 8, 1982, pp.<br>10–11, 22

## PLATH, SYLVIA (1932–1963)

For Plath, poetry had always been symbolic action. In *The Colossus*, she had used language to impose an order upon experience, but the order in her poems contradicted her vision of reality as fragmented and perpetually disintegrating. Only in a poem could the world be composed and controlled, and so poetry was artificial; it lied. In the later poetry, she begins to tell the truth. When she comes to see that reality resides in her own mind, words and poems become as real as anything else. The expression of her vision in words unleashes reality, for her poems describe what is real: her own consciousness. The action that is poetry is recognized as symbolic action (she never ceases to know the *difference* between art and life), but the symbols now reflect rather than counteract her own life. . . .

There remains a gap between woman and poet.

As poet, Plath sees with increasing clarity this gap. She sees as well the existence of life and its inevitable corruption into death. The forces in her that gave rise to her awareness of and fascination with death are surely complex; but surely the fact that she existed for so long with a sense of her own self as disparate, bifurcated, contributed to a desire for wholeness that she could equate only with death. The pulse of life was the movement towards disintegration: the stasis of death brought integration. And perfection. For Plath had viewed perfection as a solution to her problem, a perfection that she had been led to believe was achievable through talent and sheer willpower. She needed to be good at everything because in that way she could *be* everything: woman and poet. Although this program proved impossible, she was left with a belief in, and a desire to achieve, perfection. There was perfection in death.

Suzanne Juhasz. *Naked and Fiery Forms: Modern American Poetry by Women—A New Tradition* (Octagon Books, 1976), pp. 102–3

If her poetry is understood as constituting a system of symbols that expresses a unified mythic vision, her images may be seen to be emblems of that myth. Red, white, and black, for example, the characteristic colors in her late poetry, function as mythic emblems of her state of being much as they do in the mythologies which she drew upon. A great many other particulars of her poetry are similarly determined by her system, and personal and historical details as well are subordinate to it. While a confessional poet might alter certain details to make them more fitting . . . Plath's alteration of details has a deeper significance. Her protagonist in "Daddy" says, "I was ten when they buried you," but Plath was only eight when her father died. A magical "one year in every ten" cycle, however, conveys the mythic inevitability necessary to define her state of being. It is precisely such details of confessional literalness that Plath most frequently alters or eliminates, when they are not sufficiently mythic. . . .

Without [the awareness of a mythic dimension in Plath's poetry], the elements of suffering, violence, death, and decay will generally be seen as aspects of a self-indulgent stance that is merely—albeit brilliantly—nasty, morbid, and decadent, the extremist exhibitionism. Were she a "confessional" poet, this might be the case. But her poetry is of a different order, and these details are absorbed into a broader system of concerns. To see the autobiographical details only as such is to regard Plath's vision of suffering and death as morbid, but to appreciate the deeper significance of her poetry is to understand her fascination with death as connected with and transformed into a broader concern with the themes of rebirth and transcendence.

To deal with the structure of Plath's poetry is primarily to deal with the voices, landscape, characters, images, emblems, and motifs which articulate a mythic drama having something of the eternal necessity of Greek tragedy. The myth has its basis in her biography, but it in turn exercises a selective function on her biography and determines within it an increasingly restricted context of relevance as her work becomes more symbolic and archetypal. . . .

Had Plath survived, it seems likely, given the nature of her concerns at the end of her life, that she would have further developed and further explored the overtly religious themes of some of the last poems, coming more and more to realize her power of what Ted Hughes calls her "free and controlled access to depths formerly reserved to the primitive ecstatic priests, shamans and Holy men. . ."; and, as in the case of her mythology, evolving a sensibility shaped by several traditions, but with a voice unmistakably her own. The unflinchingness of her gaze, her refusal to compromise the truth, her precision, her intelligence, and her passion—all of these would have qualified her uniquely in the discovery of her wholeness, to convince us that the achievement is possible.

> Judith Kroll. *Chapters in a Mythology: The Poetry of Sylvia Plath* (Harper & Row, 1976), pp. 4–6, 210–211

Romantic in its immediacy, her sharpened poetic was not quite typical of the sixties, and precisely to the extent that it was Poundian. Poundian in the first place as to eye. Her work unfolds perhaps for the first time the full dramatic potential of what T. E. Hulme called "the new visual art," an art depending "for its effect not on a kind of half sleep produced by meter, but on arresting the attention, so much so that the succession of visual images should exhaust one." (This rapid piling up of "distinct images" produces "the poet's state in the reader." Now, despite the avowed classicism of Hulme and Pound, Imagism was actually a centaur poetic of which the basic and stronger half was romantic sensation. To induce the poet's state in the reader when that state is visual ecstasy, a state in which the magic breath of metaphor ripples the dull surface of life, is to write romantically.) But though the new visual art set itself off from leisured traditional description by rapid-fire figuration, it was notorious for being static, limitedly pictorial. The instant fixing of a single impression, as by a jeweled pin, was its convention. Still, there was nothing to prevent its being thickcoming and developmental; it could be galvanized.

Or so Plath, more than any other, was to prove. She made images burst forth and succeed one another under acute psychological pressure, the dramatic crisis of the poem a generating furor. In violent import, color, solidity, and velocity her images are unsurpassed. Even when her spirit ebbs, her imagery ferments. In "Words," for instance, one metaphor instantly gives rise to two others, which are then elaborated in quick succession, each giving way and coming in again, but without any effect of haste. Proliferation has perhaps never been more subtle and vigorous, more constantly deepening.

But the most "delicate and difficult" part of the new art, so Hulme implies, is "fitting the rhythm" to the image—fitting *all* the sound, I might amend. And Plath's ear is no less gifted than her imaginative eye. For instance, she rivals Pound's hearkening ear for the calling back and forth and expressive rightness of sounds. . . .

With Pound, Plath also shared the decidedly modern ear for what she called the "straight out" rhythms and words of prose and colloquial speech; like Pound, if less ambitiously and more evenly, she assimilated them into poetry, creating new verse rhythms. . . .

Plath's poetic, then, is Poundian—romantic. True, classical simplicity shows up in passages, and classical grace and proportion sometimes govern whole poems. Then, too, her persistent use of stanzas reflects the same orderly habit of mind that made her list each morning what she wanted to accomplish during the day. Undeniably, moreover, certain associations of the word "romantic" shrivel when held up to her flame. The shriek of her ego, the sound of a tense holding on to little, drove off every softness. She maximized horror as if she lived on menace. All the same, her poetic is full of romantic presence. No retreat, no passivity, can harbor in it; it is the aggressive poetic of one buried alive but not ready to die. (Even in expressing revulsion from reality she reached obsessively and inconsistently for visual analogy, a language of rapport.) What is her struggle against fear, pain, isolation, if not romantic? Perhaps we would deny her reasons for writing at all to think of it as anything else or anything less.

Calvin Bedient. In *Sylvia Plath: New Views on the Poetry*, ed. Gary Lane (Johns Hopkins Univ. Pr., 1979), pp. 15–18

Plath's moving universe is animated at times by love but more often by the forces that dominated her emotional life, primarily rage and fear. Her importance as a poet depends upon how successfully she evolves strategies with language to make effective metaphors for the terrific experience of those murderous forces. She is fascinating because the "shape" of her psyche is peculiarly bottomless, a world of infinite plunge. . . .

This is perhaps the darkest form of romanticism—a form darker than Roethke's—the evocation of a series of horrors, each more horrible than the last, and of which no man knows the end. Plath's great and underlying terror is always the nausea of movement itself. Even Plath's pleasures crowd in on her this way, threaten to become too much if she cannot somehow bring them under control, slow their onslaught. It is true, as some have suggested, that the poems may be read as attempts to create a mythical self capable of withstanding the changes in her life, the betrayals and the losses. But it's the kinesthetic sense of pitch and roll, the stomach-tilting sensation of that bottomless series of plunges, that we experience most strongly. And the evocation of that sense is her particular genius. . . .

Plath uses many devices, not all of them subtle, to achieve the artistic effect of a world in violent motion. For one thing, many of the late poems make use of the motif of journeying: "Blackberrying," "On Deck," "Crossing the Water," "Ariel," "Getting There," "The Bee Meeting," "Totem," and perhaps "Words" as well. There are also poems like "Black Rook in Rainy Weather" and "Letter in November" that seem to indicate that the shapes of her thoughts, her intuitions, come to her in motion rather than when she is standing still. Another of her devices is the beginning *in medias res*. No one is better than Plath at giving her reader the experience of being swept up in an action that has been gathering momentum for some time. . . . Two devices seem to me a part of her medium not always sufficiently considered when critics have sought to unravel her message. One of them is the deliberate use of ambiguity, of elaborate puns (another of Roethke's intensifying devices), and the other is a manipulation of images that, in some of her better poems, makes her the poetic daughter of Wallace Stevens.

Richard Allen Blessing. In *Sylvia Plath: New Views on the Poetry*, ed. Gary Lane (John Hopkins Univ. Pr., 1979), pp. 59–61

Plath appears as a unique and disturbing figure in American poetry. She is a poet of enormous talent, who pushes toward a vitalistic account of human existence in its relation to a hostile external reality. Yet she fails to believe in her own theoretical and positive program sufficiently to overcome the corrosive effects of death-fear and death-longing. She enacts repeatedly a drama that can terminate in either life or death, using poetry as a means of playing out the alternate fates reserved for her by existence. The discrete moments of unity and ecstasy in her work anticipate a greater unity of thought and sensation, but that unification of diversity never emerges. As she returns again and again to the same symbolically charged landscapes and the same figures of death and suffering, she seems to lose faith in the ultimate triumph of the life force over the forces of negation. The process of self-transformation winds down into self-annihilation.

Yet it is perhaps absurd to expect that Plath by herself could present an integrated vision of body and mind, of life and death. Our culture has been riddled since Puritan times with intense divisions within its system of ideals and its versions of human purpose. Plath reflects a gigantic split within American culture between its positive valuation of a fierce selfhood and its radical denial of the body's sufficiency. Plath is unusual in the extremity of her rejection of the body, but her search for self-expansion through a denial of the surrounding physical reality—of the body, of the social system, of the limitations of time and space—is the essential American story. . . .

Plath's quest for initiatory change fails because the other cannot be brought under the domination of the self, even when the self wills its own destruction so as to merge with the world. Her fierce and brilliant language is all directed at the other whom she wishes to overcome, but the giants and colossi of her poetry fall down only to rise again; the body immolates itself only to return to its old, guilt-ridden shape. As Kafka says, the suffering the artist undergoes releases him—for more suffering. Plath's initiatory dramas release her from one state of suffering so that she may endure a new agony. For the briefest moment, though, she is set free from the imprisonment of selfhood; and it is this moment that her best poems, "Ariel," "Fever 103°," "Lady Lazarus," and "The Couriers," celebrate. If she could not sustain her liberation beyond the moment, she still provides an intense vision of the irreducible, entwined core of life and death.

Jon Rosenblatt. *Sylvia Plath: The Poetry of Initiation* (Univ. of North Carolina Pr., 1979), pp. 161–63

More than a decade of readers and critics have been deceived in reading and reacting to Sylvia Plath. She has been neatly positioned under that confessional umbrella where life's irrefutable direction is deathward, where certain emotions have become clichés of madness. Her poems have been petrified into a handful of graven ur-myths ("preexisting options that constitute a state of being") that attempt to normalize Sivvy at the same time that they rob her poetry of its full range of wit and vitality. . . . It is simply inaccurate to trace Plath's development to a final, glossy union of warring selves, woman and artist, or to place in a matrix the poet's sensibility in guilt over imagined incest with "Dad." Such resolutions betray the same limitation: ultimately they dismiss Plath the poet, who seventeen years after her untimely death we are only beginning to appreciate for her emotional pioneering and remarkably skilled poetics. . . .

In *The Colossus* Plath failed to incorporate a perfect, unitive, imaginative vision into the functioning of her poetic sensibility. By using the most intimate subject matter available to her—women's blood and birth myths, voluntary and involuntary creation—she evaluates her old poetic, its failures and its promises in *Crossing the Water*. While Plath is exploring a new freedom in form, rhythm, and sound, she is also revising inherited stereotypes about women. These simultaneous functions form a more intimate commentary on—and guideline for—her future development than the distanced world of art provided her in *The Colossus*. . . .

Thematically and technically, the last poems, defying both critical and psychological labels, argue for a positive, creative space for ambivalence. Plath demonstrates her mobility between the contradictory extremes of self-effacement and the diminished life on the one hand, and theatrical energy on the other. The speaker reminds us that her enlarged sensibility is always at work weighing, balancing, and combining. Her expansiveness is not a matter of diffused emotions out of control or schizophrenic inattention. Rather, it is a conscious love of motion. . . .

Certain themes are present in slightly altered forms throughout her writings: she counsels physical limitations, warns against the hazards of an exclusive imaginative life, mocks romantic illusions and later marital-love delusions, recognizes the failure of a simple identity. Yet these themes seem less important, less defining, than Plath's consciousness of her changing poetic and her explorations of the startling gamut of emotional options for the speaking voice. By *Ariel* and *Winter Trees*, she has turned "fatal equilibrium" into creative ambivalence, giving a dual artistic authority to passivity and motion in her final poems.

Mary Lynn Broe. *Protean Poetic: The Poetry of Sylvia Plath* (Univ. of Missouri Pr., 1980), pp. 180–81, 187–91

## PORTER, KATHERINE ANNE (1890–1980)

The most powerful tension in her work is between the emotional involvements and the detachment, the will to shape and assess relations in experience; and the effect of this is sometimes to make a story look and feel strangely different, unanalyzably different, from the ordinary practice. But there is a more significant difference. A great deal of the current handling of the psychology of motive is a kind of clinical reportage. In two respects the work of Katherine Anne Porter is to be distinguished from this. First, she presumably believes that there is not merely pathology in the world, but evil—Evil with a capital *E*, if you will. Along with the pity and humor of her fiction, there is the rigorous, almost puritanical attempt to make an assessment of experience. Second, she presumably believes in the sanctity of what used to be called the individual soul. . . .

It has been said that the work of a major poet, in contrast to that of a minor poet, possesses, among other things, a centrality of coherence—or even obsession. The more we steadily inspect the work of Katherine Anne Porter, the more we see the inner coherence—the work as a deeply imaginative confrontation of a sensibility of genius with the *chiaroscuro* of modern civilization, in which it is often hard to tell light from dark. It becomes clearer and clearer what she meant when she said that she had been working on one central plan "to understand the logic of this majestic and terrible failure of the life of man in the Western World.". . .

What we find in the fiction is a hatred of all things that would prize anything above the awareness of human virtue: that is the essence of the author's dissent and the core of the despair that sometimes appears for our future—a future in which the responsible individual disappears into a "nothing," a mere member of what Kierkegaard called a "public," a "kind of gigantic something, an abstract and deserted void which is everything but nothing."

Robert Penn Warren. In Katherine Anne Porter:<br>
A Collection of Critical Essays, ed. Robert Penn<br>
Warren (Prentice-Hall, 1979), pp. 9–10, 14–15

*Ship of Fools* is a brilliant book. Porter herself was fond of it, and she pointed out to carping critics that it developed a major theme present in most of her work—the theme of the life of illusion, of self-deception. But it is not a great novel. The structure is loosely episodic and the crowded cast of characters is far too large. Porter apparently did not have the ability to construct a satisfactory plot of novel length that would bring into a significant relationship a few fully developed characters. *Ship of Fools* cannot stand comparison with the great Victorian novels nor with the major work of Henry James (whom, incidentally, Porter greatly admired). Her true genre was the short story and the novella (or long short story), and her accomplishments in those forms can stand any comparison. Porter once said, "I don't believe in style: The style is you," and she didn't like being called a stylist. Nevertheless, she may be, in fact, the greatest stylist in prose fiction in English of this century. There is of course the aforementioned Henry James, but a comparison, for example, of the opening pages of her "Hacienda" with the opening pages of *The Ambassadors* would be instructive to a young writer learning his craft. Sentence by sentence, paragraph by paragraph, Porter is better. Compared to her precise perceptions and carefully modulated rhythms, James's prose is somewhat slow-moving, ponderous, and diffuse. . . .

As time goes by, the accomplishments in American fiction, poetry, and criticism between the wars take on more and more significance. Katherine Anne Porter's stories, especially those written during this period, will be given an increasingly high position in our literary heritage.

Donald E. Stanford. SoR. Winter, 1981, pp. 1–2

## POUND, EZRA (1885–1972)

Pound's significance, for those who are not principally concerned for poetry, his or any other, may be thought to turn therefore on what we understand by "a literary civilization"; whether we want any more of it; and, supposing we do, what chance we stand of getting it in any future that we can foresee.

In the first place, such a civilization will have as its avowed end, quite unashamedly, *pleasure*—John Masefield's "delightful spoil." Literature may instruct, and the poet of *The Cantos* certainly acted in the belief that it did; but if it instructs, it instructs only by pleasing—surreptitiously, through the delights that it brings. Moreover, if we trust Pound, the pleasure that literature brings is direct and as if immediate, like the pleasure of cool air brushing against one's bared and heated skin. This depends upon a sensuous aliveness in ourselves such as Pound had when he spoke of the "effect of a decent climate where a man leaves his nerve-set open, or allows it to tune into its ambience.". . .

To Pound it seemed, as it has to others, that in Protestant cultures it was the Hebraic component which instilled fear and distrust of sensuous pleasure; and so he threw his weight always on the side of the Hellenic voice which called on sculptors to make images of the gods, as against the Hebraic iconoclasm which was set against "graven images."

Donald Davie. *Ezra Pound* (Penguin, 1975), pp. 100–101

It needs no oracle to tell us that *The Cantos* are an extreme form of sequence. They are, in fact, a sequence of sequences, each growing out of the preoccupations and experiences of a limited period of time. It is ludicrous to imagine that the whole line of succeeding cantos, developing for almost fifty years, constitutes a single integrated work in any ordinary sense. The normal process of getting a work under way, discovering its form and bearings, and revising it so that all may emerge as organically as possible is simply not open to a poet who writes out of the succeeding phases of his experience, in the chronological order of his private spiritual and empirical history, without leaving time for recasting. . . .

Pound's genius in deploying documentary quotations and other data is extraordinary. He does lose aesthetic perspective and grow lengthy because of his love of the materials and of the sound of the human voice expressing, however drily and repetitiously, certain favorite doctrines that seem to him hard, vibrantly relevant kernels of perception. But he also makes a found poetry of these materials—rearranges them, creates internal rhymes, balances them against snatches of his own phrasing and pure imagistic flashes or other quick poetic notations. The intrinsic poetics of expository speech created a special music for him, so that a phrase like "every bank of discount" becomes a refrain in a lyrical sense, not merely a reiterated point of argument. One has only to compare his use of such materials with that of certain of his followers—Charles Olson, for instance—to see how much truer his ear is than theirs. Line by line he is superb, although page by page one does grow a bit weary.

Still, it is interesting that in these volumes written in the 1930's the passionate lyric centers, harking back to early work and usually based on the *Odyssey*, are indispensable. . . .

But it is clear that there is *no* Dantean or Homeric structure—just allusions to those structures that enter the recurring improvisational patterns in the separate volumes. Pound's mind teemed with the phrases and images and figures that populate the works that meant most to him. They are at once fixed points of reference and energizers of the associative process always at work in his imagination. He did not forget impressions or tones of any kind very readily, and all together they created a constant pressure on him not very different from that created by the insistent dead on Odysseus—too much to handle very neatly except in a single poem or passage.

M. L. Rosenthal. *Paideuma*. Spring, 1977, pp. 4,
10–11

As the reader comes to know Pound's poetry, he will increasingly recognize and go beyond the multifarious objects of knowledge that at first dominate the landscape of each poem, and he will become more interested in the poetic character of the presence, seer, protagonist who presents the data. The data are variously instructive, diverting, beautiful or awe-inspiring, and the patterns of emotion and moral value that they create are fascinating or rewarding. Eventually, however, it is the richness and quality of the mind, rather than the *virtù* of the objects it contains and which it salutes, that continue to fascinate and to instruct. It is only at first that Pound's purism of surface and form seem clinically to exclude the presence of a known human speaker. . . .

The *Collected Shorter Poems* can be . . . categorized by provenance or by form. As they are read through, volume by volume, in order of writing, a hardening of Pound's sense of society and of the artist's role in society is noticeable, especially in the modernization of his language in *Lustra*. When, finally, the early Pound is approached by means of such questions as, What does he have to say? What are his typical attitudes?—questions which do not seem often to have been asked—one notices a set of variations upon the theme of the poet, singer, seer or sage—the friend of nature, of beauty, of wisdom, of refinement—engaged in the study of beauty or society, or, more frequently, of both. The emotions are those of exile—aesthetic, ironic, elegiac or indignant. One speaks of emotions and attitudes rather than of thought, ideas or "message" in discussing Pound's verse before *Mauberley*. . . . Emotion, indeed, is the origin and end of Pound's poetry, despite his concern for "direct treatment of the 'thing,'" objectivity, technique, and despite his surgery of rhetoric and gush. What Pound "has to say" is "the world is thus and thus"; but what he communicates is always emotion and attitudes charged with emotion. . . .

The greatness of the *Cantos* is concentrated in the *Pisan Cantos*, though it is liberally scattered elsewhere. Only in the *Pisan Cantos* do the unerring rightness of style and the refinement of phrase have a great job to accomplish, namely the survival of the author's mind, with its extraordinary freight. Not that Pound becomes confessional or emotional—the pathos is largely inadvertent—it is simply that he has so much to tell us and himself, and a great number of interesting things going through his head, as he watches the guards, the clouds and the insects. . . .

The tendentiousness and unevenness of some of Pound's achievement make it difficult to settle squarely on a tolerable generalization about his place among the poets; he is perhaps the greatest of the moderns, since that term does not exactly fit Yeats, nor the Eliot of *Four Quartets*. However, his Promethean gifts are so original that the process of comparison with others does not seem very productive; perhaps he should not be placed among others.

Michael Alexander. The Poetic Achievement of<br>Ezra Pound (Univ. of California Pr., 1979), pp.<br>43, 47, 227–28

In spite of Pound's "mystical ear" (to borrow Williams' phrase) for the invention of new musical and rhythmic patterns, it is the daring confidence with which *The Cantos* are able to absorb so much prose narrative and historical documentation that remains one of their most decisive technical accomplishments. Pound himself realized that upon such a strategy depended poetry's chance to "donner une idée claire et précise," and thus to compete successfully with the novel as a significant medium for the expression of social, psychological, and historical judgments. . . .

It is part of the continuing fascination of Pound's work that it compels us to confront its ideas, including the "wrecks and errors," as deliberate social and historical judgments, just as it is part of the epic's aesthetic technique to base much of its rhythm on the inclusiveness of the "prose tradition." Ultimately, it is from Pound himself that the right to question the polemical content of his work on its own terms derives, since few poets have argued as forcefully against the aesthetic as a category necessarily distinct from and indifferent to the social and political spheres of human cognition. Yet I know that my own focus of attention has at times caused me to leave insufficiently analyzed those aspects of the poems, the syntactic and metrical inventions, the audacious use of patterned sounds and images, which attracted me as a reader long before questions of ethical sense or historical argument began to impose their own pressures. In many ways it would have been easier to write a quite different book, one concentrating far more exclusively upon the immediate aesthetic appeal of all three epics, but such an undertaking would undervalue just those features that separate *The Cantos*, *Paterson*, and *The Maximus Poems* from traditional lyrics, and impose a perspective that risks excluding the texts' specific intentions and governing conventions from scrutiny.

Michael André Bernstein. *The Tale of the Tribe: Ezra Pound and the Modern Verse Epic* (Princeton Univ. Pr., 1980), pp. 279–81

Of the four great American Moderns, Pound was the only poet to believe in what we now call ethnopoetics—the coupling of anthropology and poetry, the opening up of other, nonwestern cultural traditions—both as method and metaphor. In the *Pisan Cantos* Pound was fighting not only for his own personal survival, but for the survival of the Western world as well. For survival, he knew that the industrial West had to turn to cultures which were based on values other than that of profit, and ideals other than that of the economy of abundance with its concomitant disposable and interchangeable objects, its scorn of both masterpiece and craft. He turned to Provence and to Greece, but more significantly he turned to China, and Africa, and even, occasionally, to the American Algonquin.

Thus, to dwell on Pound as exile, as directing his major effort toward breaking the English tradition, represented by the pentameter, is to belittle his achievement. Pound was not so much an exile as he was a citizen of the world. . . .

[His] belief that the province of poetry is "the whole social order" is Pound's great strength, his source of optimism, and one of his major contributions. We have him to thank for his persistent affirmation throughout the first half of the twentieth century, a period in Western history preoccupied with its "heap of broken images," of the possibility of a "new sacred book of the arts," as Yeats called it. A sacred book which would heal the splits in culture, remove, in effect, the banks from the position of power and place the artists in the position of authority. . . .

The wisdom of the *Pisan Cantos* is the wisdom of one wise old man, Pound, who himself understands that we must listen to the wisdom of the old, internalize the old, and not fall prey to the tradition of the new (which is an economics of consumption and waste on all levels). "Philosophy is not for young men" . . . Pound wrote early in the *Pisan Cantos*. This is another way of saying that wisdom is reserved for, is the privilege of, the old. And as Simone de Beauvoir points out, the important thing to understand is that the status of the old is "never *won* but always *granted*."

Kathleen Woodward. *"At Last, the Real Distinguished Thing": The Late Poems of Eliot, Pound, Stevens, and Williams* (Ohio State Univ. Pr., 1980), pp. 92, 95–96

*The Cantos* may be incomplete, may contain errors, may be a rash attempt at epic in an age of experiment. It may be too bulky, too obscure, too idiosyncratic. Despite Pound's remark about Buckminster Fuller's similar geometric (or geodesic) vision—"'Buckie' has gone in for structure (quite rightly) / but consumption is still done by animals" (*Thrones 97*)—it may be too schematic. Such details as building the Constitution and measuring out the form of a civilization in one sense constitute an infernal machine that could have sunk Pound's effort in *l'esprit de géométrie*. Certainly it made him a servant to his conception and to whatever his historical destiny might bring. He could alter his poem no further than by shifting to the 120-canto alternative and selecting the proper subject that might come to hand. . . .

Such weaknesses may be unavoidable corollaries of Pound's strengths: of the scope of his subject, of the necessary submission to its claims, and of such ethical qualities as energy, purpose, endurance, and faithfulness to an epic vocation that could hardly have been a more exacting mistress. Error, from simple errors of fact to the cataclysmic error of allying himself with historical fascism, may have been part of the cost of trying to realize the motive "To build the city of Dioce whose terraces are the colour of the stars" in a poem that might become "reading matter, singing matter, shouting matter, the tale of the tribe" precisely *because* he had made his life the vehicle for trying not only to perfect the vision but also to make it fact. He made himself not only the poet of many voices seeking to constitute the mind and life of the normal man wishing to live mentally active in a complacent era, but also the champion of "these simple men who have fought against jealousy," of "the sensitive" (as he perceived Joyce when he first met him in 1920), of the artist-saint like Constantin Brancusi—both of what the simple heart feels and of what the intense mind does and might do. If he presumed to voice "The enormous tragedy of the dream in the peasant's bent shoulders," he did it by becoming "the last American living the tragedy of Europe."

Forrest Read. *'76: One World and the Cantos of Ezra Pound* (Univ. of North Carolina Pr., 1981), pp. 436, 438

# ● PRICE, REYNOLDS (1933–    )

A young Southerner, Reynolds Price, has written an exceptionally fine first novel, *A Long and Happy Life*, and, all told, Mr. Price looks like one of the most promising talents to have emerged for some time.

Mr. Price's opening did put me off; the writing seemed lush, and I feared that this might turn into a light trifle of Southern sweet talk and honeysuckle. But very quickly it became clear that this was no purveyor of gossamer sensibility but a very sure and adult writer with a firm grip upon his materials.

These materials are very modest. Mr. Price's people are simple rural folk in North Carolina, and his plot is slight: the seduction of a young girl by her young man, his return to discover she is pregnant, his proposal of marriage, and her acceptance. But this slight thread of plot is so interwoven with all the textures of family life, and Mr. Price's feeling for the girl and what passes in her mind is so sure, that by the time we have finished the book we have been involved in those major matters of life, death, and the dawning of truth upon the human mind that have always been the substance of great fiction.

The book moves toward its close at a beautiful pace. And the ending itself—the girl, about to have her young man at last, sees her future life with him suddenly deflated and common, and yet she must go forward to that future—is a wonderfully sustained portrayal of a delicate shift in perspectives that can stand comparison with Joyce's "The Dead." Romance has been punctured, but what remains, though more troubled, is more human and moving.

William Barrett. *At.* April, 1962, p. 160

Reynolds Price's first novel, *A Long and Happy Life* (1962), was an unusually distinguished performance, as impressive in the lyricism of its style as it was in the renewed vitality he brought there to his time-worn theme (the fearful and immense complexities of human love). Amidst a spate of pornographic and programmatic novels, it stood out like a beacon of life and light or, at the least, a breath of fresh country air. Price was not afraid to *narrate* (something many of our fiction writers have either forgotten how to do or now disdain to do), nor was he afraid to retell one of the oldest stories in the world.

Such, however, is not the verdict one must finally render on his second novel, *A Generous Man*. The *story* here is essentially the coming of age, both sexually and intellectually, of Milo Mustian, older brother of Rosacoke Mustian, the heroine of Price's first novel. . . .

Furthermore, Price's style, which seemed so powerful and moving in his first novel—shot through as it was with perceptions of natural beauty of the freshest intensity—seems to have degenerated here into a *manner*. His prose has become more modish, as his theme has become more muddled. A case in point is his fondness for the simple sentence with a simple subject but endlessly compound predicate, which has a certain hypnotic power but eventually becomes tedious and finally no substitute for a legitimate *style* which supports and reinforces the theme at every step.

This novel is supposed to present, apparently, a dramatic rendering of an elemental human experience, one fraught with pain and peril, which all men must finally undergo. Its possibilities for beauty and drama are certainly endless; but Price appears content to give us a fifteen-year-old North Carolina boy, wise both in speech and in thought far beyond his years—more a suburbanite Ivy Leaguer than a country boy whose folks raise tobacco. When he lets North Carolina speak and act for itself, Price is on home territory and safe. When he tries to impose a false intellectual and stylistic sophistication on his native material, it will simply not support this factitious superstructure, with a resulting loss of clarity and power. For all his implications about the necessity of both give and take in human love, Price's treatment involves largely the give and take of sex: his metaphysics becomes largely acrobatics. Finally, as Rosacoke remarks when Milo is discoursing on the dramatic events of "Death's" escape, "Just call it a snake. I'll know who you mean." Price might have done better if he had followed this advice more closely himself. His talent is a very fine one. Let us hope that he will not further abuse it.

Robert Drake. SoR. Winter, 1967, pp. 248–50

*A Generous Man*, perhaps better termed a romance than a novel, has suffered considerable indignities from reviewers and critics who have set it down as a playful allegorical quest for the great snake Death. That a part of the author's intention slipped past undetected is not surprising: Price's observation that he let the name Death "become one more nail in the coffin I was building for the great Southern hunt" might well come as news even to the attentive reader. Nature, the importance of man's relationship to nature, or, put another way, man's being a natural creature, shows not in the guying of such mythicized solemnities as the hunt but rather in a sense of place radically altered from the one communicated in *A Long and Happy Life*. . . .

Price's more recent novel, *Love and Work*, offers variations on and apparent contradictions to the thesis that the point of contact of man and nature, as of man and the supernatural, is important and may be crucial—that its informed perception could and does change whole lives. . . .

Nature of any description is little in evidence in *Love and Work*, the focus turned inward, the protagonist self-absorbed, living life at second hand or attempting to recreate it in charming vignettes of his parents' meeting and courtship, which his wife, who knows him, sets down as "easy lies". . . . Price clearly espouses no program after the manner of the Agrarians. In his fiction the naturalistic perspective receives no adherence; the pastoral mode, in so far as the term describes his first novel, was a point of departure. . . .

Price [is not] a Romantic, for he has already shown that the "literally human qualities" of life are best grasped, interpreted, and communicated in and through a place where man's status as created and creating being, where his amphibian nature and the more constant spectacle of his fall from grace, irresistibly present themselves.

Allen Shepherd. Critique. 15, 2, 1973, pp. 86,<br>92–94

When a work of fiction as compelling and original as Reynolds Price's latest novel [*The Surface of Earth*] comes along, it deserves evaluation in its own terms. Why should the reader worry if, in its relatively straightforward narrative, its rich, rhythmical and rather formal language and its brooding obsession with family as a kind of fate which a child must come to terms with before he can be free "to walk clean away into his own life," it seems to be out of step with the march of most contemporary fiction?

More important is the fact that it meets what seems to me the supreme test of a novel: it manages to recreate a world and people it with characters as complex and stubbornly mysterious as those in life, and it draws the reader into that world—sensually, emotionally and intellectually—to the point that he experiences those lives and earns whatever insights may be gained from them.

In this, his longest and most ambitious novel, which took ten years of planning and three years of writing, Reynolds Price focuses on the harm that parents do, through the flawed choices, emotional failures and unsatisfied hungers they pass on to their children unto the third and fourth generation. Indeed, the biblical estimate seems conservative here when one considers that although the action begins in 1903 on the evening of 16-year-old Eva Kendall's elopement with her Latin teacher, Forrest Mayfield, the book opens with a conversation in which the Kendall children are drawing from their father details of their maternal grandfather's suicide. ("What's shameful, sir, in wanting the truth?" Eva asks, "We're all nearly grown. . . . It's our own story.") And the novel ends, 491 pages later, with that suicide's great-great grandson, Hutch Mayfield, struggling to put his heavy inheritance behind him.

A narrow focus? Perhaps. But unquestionably an important one which takes the reader beneath the surface of events into the interior world, even the unconscious world, of the principal characters. . . .

Despite the book's length and what begins to seem toward the end a plethora of explanations and confessions from the characters themselves, the narrative remains, on the whole, surprisingly succinct, displaying Mr. Price's gift for catching whole landscapes in a few images, whole characters in a few telling gestures or fragments of talk. And what a luxury it is to be immersed in his majestic prose.

There is, however, a static quality to the novel as fragments of human experience are seized and held for microscopic observation, then analyzed at length from shifting points of view in dreams, in letters and in endless talk. This quality is suggested in the Blake-like image which the author has designed for the jacket of the book—a fixed sun face gazing with an intensity that threatens to burn through surfaces to the mysteries beneath them. . . .

Although this powerful novel seems in the end to be overweighted with wordy explanations of the emotional demands, debts and failures that constrict the Mayfields' and the Kendalls' lives, it represents a leap forward by a gifted novelist into visionary territory which few of his contemporaries have the courage to explore, territory which, if conquered, can yield the hard-won wisdom of the human heart.

Everyone who is interested in serious fiction ought to read it.

Anne Hobson Freeman. *VQR*. Autumn, 1975,
pp. 637–39, 641

Complexity may be of several types, not all of which are constructive or ultimately enriching to narrative. But in Price's novels one particular type of complexity, which he calls "dialogue" . . . does enrich his narrative; in fact Price's technique of "dialogue" equips his novels to speak on the multiple levels on which his listeners need narrative. Price's long and complicated novel *The Surface of Earth* is his most recent and most successful experiment in this kind of narrative. By quoting from Augustine's *Confessions* in the epigraph, Price initiates a dialogue that not only results in the enhancement of the theme, but is, in fact, the way the novel is finally told: a long and often fierce debate with Augustine. Complexity, then, is not to be found solely in what abstract statement might be made after the novel is read. It is to be found in the nature of narrative itself.

Invoking Augustine enables Price not only to talk about motion and rest as powerful shapers of human life but also to use them as elements of technique. The *Confessions*, echoing through the small but deliberate aperture of the epigraph, gives *The Surface of Earth* the capacity to generate an intelligible and complex world. . . .

The complex design of *The Surface of Earth* invokes Augustine as the great archetype of the human consciousness troubled in its very humanness. In the lives of three characters, seen in crucial moments, Reynolds Price answers Augustine's model with one of his own. In a "strong personal vision and voice," *The Surface of Earth* rings many changes on immense themes of the nature of mortal consciousness, of love, of the self, of life in motion. Price's accomplishment in the novel is the more amazing because he achieves multiple meaning for his characters, settings, and incidents without emasculating them with allegory. Through the novelist's faithful acts of attention, and through those of his characters, *The Surface of Earth*, from epigraph to Rob's final laugh, insists upon life as the primary experience. Theories, ideas, abstractions, and interpretations of life are appropriately secondary—risky departures from the ground of human existence, the surface of earth.

Michael Kreyling. SoR. Autumn, 1980, pp. 853–<br>54, 867–68

A fifth novel by an author who won fame with his first book, *A Long and Happy Life*, published nearly 20 years ago, *The Source of Light* continues a family saga begun in *The Surface of Earth* (1975). And there's much to admire in its pages. Reynolds Price has an unplodding imagination. . . .

*The Source of Light* is a 300-page narrative wherein absurdist savagery has no place and the idea of gentleness as a value isn't once mocked—which is to say, it's a rarity.

It's not, though, speaking bluntly, a compelling or exciting work of fiction. One failing is that the novelist merely assumes that the question whether his hero quits Europe or stays is momentous, but never demonstrates that it is. I was troubled too, by Price's difficulty in finding distinct voices for his characters. Nearly everybody in the book—from Southern preppies to Dilsey-style servants, to Oxford stonemasons, to liberated American women—speaks a lingo best described as Southern-clever-wry, and in time the sameness of the speech becomes disconcerting.

Finally there's the Faulkner problem. Significant differences exist between Hutchins Mayfield and Faulkner's young masculine heroes—and between Faulkner's old people and Price's—and between Faulkner's literary allusions (the Bible and Keats) and Price's (the Bible and Shakespeare)—and between Faulkner's conviction of the uniqueness of the Compsons and Price's conviction of the uniqueness of the Mayfield clan. But while the differences exist, I'm afraid they're not as noticeable as the resemblances. The overall impression left is that of a fictional world rendered indistinct by the spreading shade of the great Faulkner tree; no action or person or style of utterance quite manages to achieve energetically independent being. Dignity and intelligence are always visible in

*The Source of Light*; what's missing is the quality of freshness and surprise that makes novels novel.

Benjamin DeMott. *SR*. April, 1981, p. 72

## PURDY, JAMES (1923–　)

Purdy's major strength lies in his ability to take so-called repellent subject matter and so work with it that he turns it into a true work of art, much like the ugly driftwood which undergoes a change into something rich and strange when worked upon by a master. All this is accomplished in a style that is not only unique in its simplicity, but which is also characterized by clarity, force and beauty—the three chief qualities of good writing. In addition to Purdy's ability to write unforgettable parables of the way Americans have lived in the past two decades, Purdy's loveless view of life is rich in humor of various kinds—zany, "black," surreal or quietly reflective. . . . Purdy's . . . humor does not serve as a contrast to the dour actions that he usually narrates; instead, his humor is warp and woof of his style. . . .

Purdy's talent is a many-sided one; for, in addition to being an instinctive portrayer of the dark underside of human nature, he is also an excellent regionalist, as is seen in *The Nephew*, and a crack fantasist, as in *Malcolm*. Purdy's ability as a satirist has already been dwelt upon in *Cabot Wright Begins*, but *Eustace Chisholm and the Works* reveals his strength as a Realist who depicts the tragic world of homosexuality. But Purdy has, in fact, created many worlds; and each with its own discernible and distinct features. Each of these worlds is populated with a host of characters: orphans, thoughtless and cruel parents, failed artists, budding writers and actors, spinsters, grand ladies, teachers and professors, widowers and widows, financiers, homosexuals, and invalids—all of whom form a veritable gallery of typical figures of and for our time.

Henry Chupack. *James Purdy* (Twayne, 1975),
pp. 127–28

Purdy's literary career suggests the struggle of a dissenting individual voice to break through patterns of conformity. The earliest work was printed privately by friends and he was first published commercially in England. Though championed by writers such as Dame Edith Sitwell and John Cowper Powys, Purdy has never enjoyed the support or approval of the American literary establishment. Admittedly, when his work began to appear in the late fifties, its highly wrought style and proliferation of bizarre characters might have been expected to disturb popular critics who had ordained a diet of representational social realism with its "instant relevance". . . .

The author's distinctive formal and philosophic preoccupations need to be seen in a broader, more tentative perspective. Although it has an urgent bearing upon the present day, there is a timeless quality to his work. The avowed concern for the world of the spirit and its relation to language evokes the native tradition of Melville and Hawthorne with their passion for metaphysics and command of symbolist techniques. As might be expected, there is also an evident fascination with the hellenic age when speculations on human destiny were at an intense pitch. Purdy sees modern America as the enemy of the soul and would subvert the suffocating patterns its culture imposes upon the individual self by his own exemplary fictions. Thus his families and miniature societies are simultaneously the vehicles for an exploration of the national psyche. At another level he re-tells, in his own special idiom, the Christian story of how a being charged with life's spiritual or divine possibilities is denied kinship in the larger world. It is misleading, then, to insist on measuring the characters in such a drama by the criteria of social realism or by those of a strict psychological verisimilitude. They are projections of the inner life, put forward as hypotheses about existence and endowed with the reality of the author's innermost convictions. Regarded in this light, art is accorded the highest functions—it keeps alive the memory of those ingredients that have been excluded from everyday existences and Purdy might more profitably be seen as the "memorialist" of the qualities that have gone missing from his native culture. He is the self-styled prophet and chronicler of its omissions.

Stephen D. Adams. *James Purdy* (Barnes & Noble, 1976), pp. 7–9

James Purdy has the unmistakable voice and gently antiquated phrasing of a radio announcer. His stilted, lilting colloquialism infects each of his characters with a common tempera flatness of tone and gives his narration the rickety preciousness of a porch swing. The voice fits the timeless Midwest of Purdy's best stories—and of his new novel, *Mourners Below*—the way Damon Runyon's did Broadway; it cleaves to the rhythms proper to the world it creates, but keeps you aware, by its very pervasiveness, of the bemused, sardonic intelligence behind it all. Purdy may slip in references to "our town," but his sensibility is more like Grant Wood's; in the black humor of his artificial Americana, he seems sometimes as distanced as a puppeteer.

That feeling's reinforced by much of *Mourners Below*, an uneven, out-of-kilter, oddly satisfying novel. Though much of his best work was published before 1965, Purdy has recently been returned—however such things happen—to semivogue, with a selection of his stories available in paperback and the early novels *Malcolm* and *The Nephew* reissued in an omnibus edition by Viking. As if to commemorate his rediscovery, Purdy's come up with a plot that's disconcertingly like a super-imposition of those two works: the picaresque, slightly surreal adventures of an astonishing naif (à la *Malcolm*) add up to a self-revealing search for the truth about a boy killed in battle (à la *The Nephew*).

The Candide here is Duane, at 17 the youngest, slightest, shortest, and most dreamily abstracted of the Bledsoes, known for his figure skating and childlike attention span, and mourning the death of his brothers Justin and Douglas in the (unnamed) war. . . . Purdy's a master of the short story, and his best novels are brief and spare. *Mourners Below* comes in under 300 pages, but it's studded with tempting tangents that often prove defects of structure. . . .

Purdy winds up the novel with a deft change of scale; turning, by implication, the small end of the telescope on his characters, he transforms the grotesque and outlandish back into the mundane. In the context of history, after all, it was simply another Darwinian courtship dance. Casting shadows down the years, Purdy implies untold generations of Bledsoes, each scrambling for the survival of the next, visiting the shrines of women to secure their race of men. That makes them stubborn, heroic, hateful, foolish, and possibly doomed—much like any other family; the long view nudges *Mourners Below* past satiric contrivance and gives it, finally, life.

Debra Rae Cohen. *VV*. July 22, 1981, p. 37

## PYNCHON, THOMAS    (1937–    )

The single terrible possibility which underlies each of his books, which threatens whatever peace or sanity his characters might find, is that there may be no chance for living—and yet we continue to live, the novocainized and impotent products of a massive psychic prosthesis.

Pynchon's three novels explore this possibility with an obsessiveness that would seem psychotic, were it not for the very real social urgency of the question itself. In *V.*, *The Crying of Lot 49*, and *Gravity's Rainbow* his themes and situations continue to revolve around the major myths of the Conspiracy, the Quest, and what we can call the Unwilling Cyborg. The particular shape each of these terms may take is variable; indeed, Pynchon displays a profligate inventive genius in devising different manifestations, manically wide-ranging versions of them. There is always, in his book, a Conspiracy: a gigantic, subtle, murderous Plot contrived by forces too powerful and too remote ever to be fully known, a Plot which involves more and more of human history the farther one penetrates its ramifications, a Plot whose ultimate goal appears to be the automatization and subjugation of all things living and creative, ultimate control and ultimate soullessness. There is always, also, a Quest, an Investigation which attempts to bring the Plot to light, to solve and thereby foil its insidious intent. A character may be propelled on his investigation by the most minimal coincidences or clues, but once he embarks on his investigation he begins to discover relevant data and hints everywhere he turns. Between these two elements, Plot and Quest, conspiracy and counterforce, the characters of the novels find themselves caught in the position of being Unwilling Cyborgs; they discover, that is, how much and how secretly the Plot has succeeded, in their own lives, in transforming them into programmed, manipulated antiorganisms robbed of free will. As they struggle to solve the secret of the Plot, then, they struggle also to regain what the Plot has stolen from them. On the surface, this archetypal Pynchon situation owes a good deal to the controlling fiction of William S. Burroughs's junk-universe, from *Naked Lunch* to *Exterminator*—the "Nova Mob," extraterrestrial criminals forcing the people of Earth into addiction and living death. The difference—and, perhaps, the salvation—in Pynchon is that he, unlike Burroughs, admits the possibility of escape, freedom, and cure (though just barely) within the sanctions of ordinary humanity, which is to say within the social and passional purview of the novel form itself. For Burroughs, the only alternative to total enslavement is total, almost Buddhist suspension of ordinary human impulse. Pynchon's characters do what Burroughs's are past doing: they fight against their entrapment, and even win marginal victories over it.

The world Pynchon's characters inhabit is a strange one of half-light, half-truth, where moral choices continue to be made, but where the terms of the choices are never clear enough for anyone to understand why, or often when, a crucial decision has been reached. This is only another way of saying, finally, that they inhabit the world of all European fiction from *The Pilgrim's Progress* to *The Plague*, the world of our own daily attempts to lead a human life.

Frank D. McConnell. *Four Postwar American*
*Novelists* (Univ. of Chicago Pr., 1977), pp. 163–64

In its attention to the interior landscape, recent fiction has forgotten the density of the exterior one. Modernism prefers to speak of the world of politics and ethics in personal and aesthetic terms. Pynchon does the opposite. In his books, character is less important than the network of relations existing either between characters, or between characters and social and historical patterns of meaning. Pynchon also tries to attend to the force with which history, politics, economics, and the necessities of science and language shape personal choices and are in turn shaped by those choices. To see in this a deliberate turning away from novelistic realism . . . is to confuse certain mediating literary conventions with unmediated reality. For most of this century, fiction has located the origins of human action in the depths of personal psychology. Pynchon comes up for air and looks elsewhere. What he finds seems cold and abstract only to the extent that it remains unfamiliar in literature and art (if nowhere else). . . .

The ethical problems in *Gravity's Rainbow* have analogues in the linguistic and interpretive problems it raises as well. Language for Pynchon is not a system complete in itself but an ethically and socially performative (his word is "operative") system, one which can be altered by deliberate acts. The model of language in *Ulysses*, on the other hand, is characteristically self-enclosed. For Joyce, the history of language is, in effect, an embryological history (in the chapter known as "Oxen of the Sun"), a version of an unconscious cycle unaffected by personal or social choice. *Gravity's Rainbow*'s history of language (in the episode set in the Kirghiz) is instead political, "less unaware of itself," determined by conscious decisions. . . .

In Pynchon, unlike Joyce, the surface details are often incredible and baroque, while the underlying organization is all too plausible and disquieting. Beneath the fantasies and the paranoia, Pynchon organizes his book according to historical and scientific theory—according, that is, to an order independent of *literary* imagination, an order derived more from the realms of politics and physics than from the self-conscious Modernist reflexivities of language and literature. . . .

Pynchon's challenge to literary studies offers one means of turning away from this dead end—there are other means available as well, of course—and to turn instead to methods of reading that have . . . "a reason that mattered to the world." As with criticism, so with the act of reading itself: Pynchon challenges his readers to participate, not merely in the linguistic and philosophical puzzles of his books' interpretation, but in the choices that those books make plain. It is a challenge with special urgency, for it is offered by a writer who—in the judgment of this reader, and of many others—is the greatest living writer in the English-speaking world.

Edward Mendelson. In *Pynchon: A Collection of Critical Essays*, ed. Edward Mendelson (Prentice-Hall, 1978), pp. 4–5, 13–15

The most abused of [the] critical "keys" to Pynchon is the concept of entropy, a corollary to the second law of thermodynamics. According to this law, systems that produce work by the transfer of thermal energy cannot function at perfect efficiency; thus the perpetual motion machine does not exist for the simple reason that all engines run down. Entropy is the measure of inefficiency in such systems: the less efficient the engine, the higher the entropy. The literary mind would probably take little notice of such matters were it not for the fact that the world and the universe of which it is a part are themselves "systems" subject to entropy. . . .

Pynchon . . . less interested in the running down of the world or the universe than in the running down of the civilization into which he was born . . . uses entropy as a paradigm of the snowballing deterioration of the West. But unlike some of his characters and certain of his critics, Pynchon realizes that the concept of entropy can be applied to society *only by analogy*, and that, consequently, no "law" says that a society's decline must be irreversible. Indeed, civilizations do not decline perpetually, but rather wax and wane.

David Cowart. Thomas Pynchon: The Art of Allusion (Southern Illinois Univ. Pr., 1980), pp. 1–2

In *Gravity's Rainbow* Pynchon continues his trend of increasingly more profound analyses of fictions. In this novel he includes only one story. The only other possible story, about Morituri, does not qualify because it only switches narrators in order to carry on the same plot line as the rest of the novel. The only intercalated story, the account of Byron Bulb, resembles *Cashiered* in *The Crying of Lot 49* because it describes a character threatened by a force that certainly exists. Unlike that film, and even though its hero is a light bulb, this story is not merely a humorous caricature of the problem of a novel's main character. Somehow Pynchon maintains seriousness and makes Byron a paradigm of the alien in a hostile world.

At least a dozen of the characters in *Gravity's Rainbow* create fictions. Even some madmen, such as the man who thinks he is World War II, and some dead people, such as Walter Rathenau and William Slothrop, make fictions. Most noticeably, the characters in this novel make brief fictions—and usually only one apiece—that, compared to the many fictions in the book, offer little promise. Many of the characters construct fictions that explain Slothrop's experiences, but he constructs fewer fictions than does Oedipa. Pynchon makes it clear that she tries to discover whether positing the existence of the Tristero will explain her experiences. In contrast, Slothrop interrupts his search for the rocket, and he often tries to understand its technology rather than any larger, metaphysical meaning it may have. He meditates less and forges on against confusion less resolutely than does Oedipa. In *Gravity's Rainbow*, then, fictions have even more value than in the earlier novels, but constructing them appears to be nearly impossible. . . .

In short, Pynchon's examination of this artistic medium has reached an important juncture. Throughout his career he has speculated on its nature and its relation to other media, thereby casting a coldly intellectual light on his work. In *Gravity's Rainbow*, however, he has both found the understanding he sought and discovered how to make his writing more humanly important. By culminating the first process and beginning the second, his most recent novel achieves the status of a major work. He now stands ready to create even more impressive books. . . . Pynchon's conception of the mission of literature is distinctive. With great skill he manipulates the traditional elements of fiction in order to reveal the inadequacy of realistic literary conventions and commonsense epistemologies, and he builds small new constructs, using information from nonliterary fields, borrowing especially from science, psychology, history, religion, and film. Finally, he gradually creates a complex literary fiction that incorporates, interrelates, and evaluates nonliterary information and ways of organizing it.

John O. Stark. *Pynchon's Fictions: Thomas Pynchon and the Literature of Information* (Ohio Univ. Pr., 1980), pp. 171–74

By insisting upon the power of language in the world, Pynchon's writing helps preserve a critical distance between private thought and public vision. His writing keeps us in an uncertain but engaged equilibrium between the extremes of self and society. This is the reason he is the most compelling social writer we have. The complexity of his understanding prevents opposition from declining into false division. His fiction reminds us of what a true society would mean, and articulates a society of isolation that already exists. The paradox of Pynchon's career thus far is that a writer so vehemently communal should be so resolutely private; but this is only a seeming paradox, for publicity is not community and exchanges being known well for being well known.

It is in his isolation that Pynchon remains one of us. His perfect absence from the public view contributes to the scattered presence of his Orphic voice. His absence gives his books a curious autonomy they would not otherwise possess and assists them in blurring the readerly distinction between fiction and the real world. His disembodied voice gives vitality and importance to the neglected and private details of the life beyond his fiction. His writing therefore keeps us company and awakens in us the possibility that we are not alone. This awakening is the "physical grace" of Thomas Pynchon, at once communal and incomplete, a continuity of song that never resolves. Listen.

Thomas H. Schaub. *Pynchon: The Voice of Ambiguity* (Univ. of Illinois Pr., 1981), p. 152

## RABE, DAVID (1940– )

As a veteran, Rabe certainly had an advantage over most of his contemporaries in the theater, whose experiences were more likely to be of anti-war demonstrations than of combat. Curiously, however, *The Basic Training of Pavlo Hummel* (1971), the first fruit of [a] playwriting grant and the first of what was to become known as Rabe's Vietnam trilogy, actually offered little evidence of having been written by a veteran of anything but theater classes.

No doubt this apparent distance from personal experience resulted in part from conscious artistic decisions. To begin with, since Rabe conceived of his work as art and not advocacy, he deliberately eschewed any political "relevance" (perhaps tacitly acknowledging the superior polemical effectiveness of journalism). . . .

While scrupulously shunning these journalistic snares [such as "ineffectual haranguing" and the "autobiographical mode"], however, Rabe fell into a different trap: excessive familiarity. *The Basic Training of Pavlo Hummel* was one more variation of the pathetic but predictable rites of passage of the classic army misfit, trapped in a situation not of his making and far beyond his limited powers of understanding. All the stock characters and standard scenes were in evidence: the blustery drill sergeant, the squad bully, the uncaring family; the barracks-room banter, the ritual brawls and other crude tests of manhood, and finally the senseless death of the protagonist, a tragicomic climax to a perverse pilgrim's progress.

Perhaps Rabe was trying for a Vietnam version of *Woyzeck*. But instead of creating an agonized and extreme but nonetheless representative figure of humanity, Rabe deliberately designed the character of Pavlo to be a cipher—a literal nobody instead of an Everyman. The net effect was to make his brutalization and anonymous death almost meaningless: The progressive dehumanization of someone scarcely human to begin with involved so little dramatic motion that the play was less revealing of the cruel irony of Pavlo's empty existence than of the barrenness of Rabe's imagination. . . .

Rabe's resurrection of the form of symbolically heightened realism was nevertheless a remarkably audacious act of defending the sovereignty of the sensibility against the numbing assault of both the form and the content of media coverage of Vietnam. But one wishes that his talent had matched his courage, that his symbolism had been less trite or capricious or both. *Sticks and Bones* (1971), his next play, was a bit closer to home, at least in some ways; it had the potential of exhibiting the authenticity that was so woefully missing from *The Basic Training of Pavlo Hummel*. Instead, it took Rabe even further from his proclaimed intent: "to diagnose, as best I can, certain phenomena that went on in and around me."

Robert Asahina. *Theater*. Spring, 1978, pp. 35–36

In his Vietnam trilogy—*The Basic Training of Pavlo Hummel*, *Sticks and Bones*, and *Streamers*—Rabe confronts the radical disunities of the American experience and attempts to forge a means of expression to overcome alienation. The problem of language lies at the center of all three plays. In *The Basic Training of Pavlo Hummel*, which concentrates on the social roots of an individual rebellion, Rabe demonstrates the alienating effect of the debased American language. In *Sticks and Bones*, which analyzes the destructive impact of this alienation on a family group, he links this debased language to a characteristic American refusal to accept reality. In *Streamers* he treats the problem in a larger context, showing the nearly insurmountable barriers to human communication. While concentrating on the metaphysical conditions which engender the social alienation of the first two plays, Rabe struggles to create a new language based on awareness and human sympathy. Rabe perceives that, as Richard Poirier has observed, the contradictions of the American experience necessitate an essentially new vocabulary, a new style which can adequately express the connections between Ishmael's experience in the crow's nest and that on the deck below. Though Rabe has not yet perfected such a style, he has taken a major step towards it by blending an essentially realistic social revolt in his plays with elements of metaphysical revolt. His rebel characters ultimately fail, but they struggle to articulate their own experience and establish human contact.

Craig Werner. *ETJ*. Dec., 1978, pp. 517–18

*Sticks and Bones*, with its keen sensitivity to the venality of American society, is a savage satire of middle-class shallowness, smugness, and spiritual deficiency, and a pessimistic vision of the hellish condition of human beings on this earth. The play suggests that America's artificiality and superficiality lead us to narrow, ethnocentric behavior, to stonelike insensitivity, to savage and monstrous mistreatment of others, to the distortion of our lives, and to a condition in which death is better than life. The model from which this social criticism and existential pessimism is projected is a famous American television family, and the central event is the return from Vietnam of their wounded son, David. David drives his family to discover the ugliness and emptiness in their own lives, an ugliness and emptiness that, during the Vietnam era, caused devastation of a foreign land and the maiming of America's youth. . . .

Many critics have admitted difficulty in discussing this play; indeed, it is a difficult work to describe, paraphrase, and analyze satisfactorily. It is explosive; like a poem, its verbal and theatrical images are so associatively and spontaneously presented that it resists simple, direct retelling. Its essence lies in the dynamic interplay of world, stage action, and theatrical resource (props, lighting, costumes, etc.). However, its mixture of the savagely brutal, the hilariously funny, the softly poetic, the pointedly critical, and the darkly pessimistic clearly conveys Rabe's vision of human loneliness in a universe without meaning and of a hellish American ethos, where people destroy love for security, beauty for plasticity, freedom for material wealth, and humane feeling for petty satisfactions of group affiliation. David Rabe has written a major work of dramatic art: it is little wonder that he has been called the "best young playwright since Edward Albee," someone to be compared favorably, according to the critic John Simon, with America's greatest dramatist, Eugene O'Neill. . . .

Like Jean Claude Van Itallie in *America Hurrah*, Rabe cries out in savage tones against the ugliness of American culture, indeed of all Western culture. But Rabe goes on to project a truly poetic reflection of the dark, lonely condition of human beings; a condition in which materialism, war, ethnocentricity, and mass culture are the means—ugly and terrible—of selfish survival in the face of the void. Brilliantly, Rabe has fused episodic incident and linear plot, associative image and cause and effect development, poetry and prose, monologue and dialogue, comic and tragic impulses, in order to reveal a panorama of truths about American culture and about life and death itself. In *Sticks and Bones*, the intertwining of realistic and Absurdist aesthetic impulses is so effective and complete that we can hardly disentangle the rich linkage without distorting the delicately wrought dramatic arabesque Rabe has created.

Samuel J. Bernstein. *The Strands Entwined: A New Direction in American Drama* (Northeastern Univ. Pr., 1980), pp. 30–31, 34

# RANSOM, JOHN CROWE (1888–1974)

Ransom is . . . no poet of modern alienation. Rather, one of reconciliation. But the poet is hardminded and knows the inescapable biological, historical, and philosophical contexts which dictate that all reconciliation is doomed to be imperfect and fleeting, and that tenderness must ultimately exist in the long perspective of irony. If he is a poet of sentiment, he is a critic of rigorous mind, with an astute sense—in his own poetry as in his poetic theory—of the technical aspects of the literary art. And I should emphasize that for him the polarity of rigor of mind and warmth of heart, though generating an inevitable irony, represent inevitable dimensions of man's fully realized life. But rigor and tenderness, hardheadedness and love—these, in man and work, were united, beyond irony, in a sense of grave joy.

Robert Penn Warren. SoR. Spring, 1975, p. 249

Unless we understand that Ransom's penchant for logical argumentation, his relentless dialectic, was in part at least a way of organizing and systematizing an intense emotional life, a method of discipline for his strenuous imagination, we will miss an essential truth about this very passionate man and poet. For Ransom, as those of his fellow Fugitives who have written about him all attest, was by no means the friendly, avuncular man of reason that his genial manner and his courtly demeanor seemed to indicate; far from it. He did indeed have a formidable, analytical mind; he took ideas very seriously, and his thinking was methodical and rigorous. He was, as Thomas Daniel Young writes, always willing to debate almost any issue at any time; it was his way of thinking. But there was more to the man than the thought; the same mind that worked out the poetics and the theory wrote the poems. He insisted on poetry as a way of knowing the world, superior in its fullness of apprehension to the partial truths of science and philosophy, and there can be no doubt that he believed this because he perceived it thus in himself. Out of this amiable and unpretentious but ultimately very private and strong-willed man came some of the best poetry of the twentieth century, and also some provocative and creative thinking about poetry and society, and these were the product of passion disciplined by logic and made formally felicitous by strategy. Ransom was no sweet reasoner; that was only his tactical method. He held strong convictions, felt emotions powerfully; and when he took his stand, he meant it.

Louis D. Rubin, Jr. The Wary Fugitives: Four<br>Poets and the South (Louisiana State Univ. Pr.,<br>1978), pp. 62–63

## REED, ISHMAEL (1938–    )

The American search for a usable past began with our first writers. American historians, cultural critics, and artists have repeatedly rewritten our history in response to evolving philosophies and social issues. And novelists, both serious and popular, have followed close behind, infusing fictional human relations with historical reality to cultivate—or to create—myths about our past. The old, tenacious forms of historical fiction either glamorize the past, reinforcing old myths of greatness, or revise history by exposing the lust, greed, despair, or irrationality of ages or men once considered stable, moral, and vital. But although contemporary novelists like Roth, Doctorow, Pynchon, Barth, and Ishmael Reed still mine and recast history, they have renewed and transformed the once-belittled historical novel. These novelists go beyond mere revisionism, questioning the possibility of historical understanding, rejecting the limits of historical reality and even of verisimilitude, exposing the irrelevance of both revering and rejecting the past.

The most recent example of this new kind of historical novel is Ishmael Reed's *Flight to Canada*. Through parody, exaggeration, anachronism, and the juxtaposition of literary myths, Reed transforms the experiences of slavery and the Civil War into comedy. Reed's two previous excursions into the American past, *Yellow Back Radio Broke-Down* and *Mumbo Jumbo*, exploit eras more easily transformed into comedy: the American West and the Twenties. But slavery, the Civil War, the assassination of Lincoln? Although they furnish material for the countless contradictory theses of historians, essayists, poets, and novelists, these aspects of our past have always been considered either tragic or epic. However, Ishmael Reed has little use for the romanticism or social realism traditionally associated with the relations of slave and master. And in *Mumbo Jumbo* he rejected serious protest art, and art of subjection, as a form imposed on Black artists by Western civilization. . . .

Reed has made *Flight to Canada* a work of broadly comic satire. . . . Reed's slave masters expose their corruption in their own features and actions; they need no crushed and humiliated slaves to expose their guilt. Because Reed refuses to depict the abject misery and subjection of the slaves, *Flight to Canada* arouses neither sympathy and guilt nor pity and fear. Instead, Reed liberates the material of slave narratives from the form exploited and imposed by the likes of Harriet Beecher Stowe. He demands that his story be read as fiction rather than as bitter reality, and he demands that we consider him a novelist rather than a spokesman.

Linda Shell Bergmann. ChiR. Fall, 1976, pp. 200–<br>201

Among the important themes in Reed's fiction are the conflict of blacks and whites, the function of the white critic, the impact of the white man and black woman on the black man, the "field nigger" as political opportunist and the importance of self-reliance. In each instance the literary folklore involved varies in focus and intensity. In delineating the black/white conflict the ancient African past serves as the basis for explanation while the Afro-American slave experience plays a similar role in explicating the theme of the "field nigger" as political opportunist. Similarly, the role of "LaBas" varies: it may be fundamental and precise in making the role of necromancy clear as in *Mumbo Jumbo*; or it may be less crucial and more nebulous as in *The Last Days of Louisiana Red*. The literary folklore, especially necromancy and LaBas, are therefore variable. . . .

The scope, intent and method of Reed's literary folklore are what separates him from other black writers with similar concerns. His channeling of millennium old tales and history into an enlightening contemporary context is unique. His intent is not a flag-waving affair which asserts that "my culture is better than yours" but rather an attempt to let flow the stifled information and accomplishments of third world (nonwhite) cultures. The method is a structured innovation: all is said but it is said in an unpredictable fashion. The structure relates to historical parallels and the unpredictability to Neo-HooDoo.

Despite what I call "the political uniqueness" of Reed's literary folklore, his writing is not heavy in a pedantic sense. It is inclusive, but its inclusiveness is presented in a manner that is exciting. The aesthetic approach of Neo-HooDoo is what allows Reed's writing to cover so much ground without being tired.

Norman Harris. Obsidian. Spring/Summer, 1979,<br>pp. 41–42, 49

*A Christmas Carol, Dr. Strangelove, The Manchurian Candidate*, and Robert Coover's *The Public Burning*—all hover as influences over this latest production [*The Terrible Twos*] by Ishmael Reed, the novelist and poet who has been called the best black writer in America today.

Imagine an America—observed during the decade 1980–1990—in which the cities and the economy are collapsing, radical Catholic clergy do battle with Moral Majoritarians, and a top male model elected president to front for wealthy Western businessmen turns into a compassionate neo-socialist. So does Santa Claus (rebelling against the monopoly that owns "exclusive rights" to him), emboldened by the terror spread by "the Nicolaites, a local cult which believes that St. Nicholas is God."

Reed's mastery of crosscutting techniques and his extravagant inventiveness keep the madness on the boil and help disguise this novel's essential commitment to savage social criticism. It's a jeremiad against "the bosses, and the subzero people, the heartless Scrooges," a surrealistic accusation that America's prosperity was "built on the bones of blacks and the blood of injuns." In its (many) finer moments, this is matchless comic invective. Ishmael Reed is a one-of-a-kind writer.

Bruce Allen. *SR*. June, 1982, p. 72

## REXROTH, KENNETH (1905–1982)

[*An Autobiographical Novel* is] the detailed account of his first twenty-one years by a man who appears to have total recall of almost everything that has happened to him. It is easy to see why Kenneth Rexroth was regarded almost with reverence by a whole generation of West Coast poets, for he had exemplified in his youth their idea that all life is movement and that all movement should be free. . . .

*An Autobiographical Novel* is a wonderfully entertaining book. It is also a specifically American odyssey, which has no counterpart in any English life of the period. . . .

There are occasions when one feels that a later Rexroth is speaking for the youthful one, as when he says that at the age of nineteen or twenty he had "begun to feel that unedited Wyatt was better than Surrey, and that Marsden [sic] was better than Beaumont and Fletcher." It may be true, but is very surprising to be told that Wyndham Lewis had "a greater influence on Chicago painting in those years" (the very early 1920s) "than did the major Cubists and Expressionists," and when he adds that Lewis was "never a purely abstract painter," and that he used mostly a "color organization based on crimson and dark green," it seems that he can have seen little of Lewis's early work. There are other minor mistakes, and one feels that if dates had been given more might be evident. The title also is a little puzzling. Does it mean that passages in the book are deliberately invented? One would prefer not to think so.

When the words of reservation have been said, however, this remains a fine book, illuminating both about the author and the period in which he grew up. Kenneth Rexroth is a genial polymath (he has translated poetry in six languages) "who is also a bohemian and a mystic, a scholar and at times a bit of a bum." It is not likely that he will ever be widely regarded in England as an important poet, but nobody could read this autobiography without feeling that he is an admirable man.

Julian Symons. *TLS*. March 25, 1977, p. 332

His work for 40 years has moved among his passions for the flesh, for human justice and for the natural world. He integrates these loves in the long poems, and sometimes in briefer ones. *The Signature of All Things* may be the best of all. It is the strength of Rexroth's language that it proscribes nothing. Starting from his reading in a Christian mystic (Jacob Boehme, 1575–1624), he writes vividly of the natural world, he refers to *Pilgrim's Progress*, he ranges out into the universe of stars and focuses back upon the world of heifers and minute phosphorescent organisms. It is a poetry of experience and observation, of knowledge—and finally a poetry of wisdom. Nothing is alien to him.

Rexroth's characteristic rhythm moves from the swift and urgent to the slow and meditative, remaining continually powerful; his line hovers around three accents most deployed over seven or eight syllables. It is remarkable how little his line has changed over 40 years, in a world of changing poetic fashion. . . .

In temperament and idea Rexroth is close to D. H. Lawrence, about whom he wrote his first major essay, in 1947; but Lawrence's best poems take off from Whitman's line—and Rexroth's prosody is as far from Whitman's as it can get. Perhaps there is a bit of William Carlos Williams in his enjambed lines; maybe Louis Zukofsky. We could say, throwing up our hands, that he is a synthesis of Tu Fu, Lawrence and Mallarmé. To an unusual extent Rexroth has made Rexroth up.

Donald Hall. NYT. Nov. 23, 1980, p. 9


## RICH,  ADRIENNE  (1929–      )


The poem "Diving into the Wreck" [presents] adventures behind the common definitions of sexuality and beyond the damages done by acculturation and conditioning. It is here also that Rich makes her strongest political identification with feminism, in her attempts to define experiences unique to women or to define the damages done by false definitions of sexual identity. Into her images she has been able to concentrate much of what has always been in her poetry: what it is like to feel oppressed, betrayed and unfulfilled. The explicit identification with feminism sometimes sets poems off balance. But this is a matter of presentation and not—as some critics have suggested—because Rich has radically changed the direction or interests of her writing. . . .

Twinned with the anger in [her] recent poems, there is also an enlarged awareness—a new voice, I think, in Rich's work—of the tragedy wrought into human relationships and into the attempts at dialogue and exchange. There are two particularly important examples: on the level of social injustice, her "Meditations for a Savage Child" and, less general, a poem of blunted love, "Cartographies of Silence." "Meditations for a Savage Child" is a remarkable poem based on the documents Truffaut also used so movingly in his film *L'Enfant Sauvage*, the records of the French doctor, J. M. Itard (now published as *The Wild Boy of Aveyron*). Itard had observed and partly "civilized" a savage child in the late eighteenth century. Rich, perhaps following Truffaut, introduces excerpts from the doctor's accounts as points of departure for each of the five sections of her poem. Unlike Truffaut, who chose to play the part of Itard in his film, Rich often takes on the role of the child, or ponders what he has to teach her, as she engages in a series of meditative exchanges with the voice of Itard. The poem is partly a long historical register of Rich's own divided spirit. Itard is an adversary but not an enemy, as they gaze across the ambitious ruins of Enlightenment philosophy. In the solicitous elegance of his prose, she finds words which have been emptied of their meaning: humanity, administrators, protection of the government—the roots of much which would have once engaged her own ardor. But in the mysteries of childrearing, of miseducation, she locates everything which defeats that ardor. . . .

It is hard to know, now that some of Rich's force and passionate intelligence has been directed into prose, just what role poetry will come to play in her life and in her writing. Critics have in the past pointed out how much, in her commitment to the notation of present feelings, the pain of the moment, Rich has given up the traditional retrospective and shaping functions of verse. Poems like "Meditations for a Savage Child" and "Cartographies of Silence" show that whatever she has relinquished she has given up purposefully, that she understands the price of her ardor without giving up her rights to it.

> David Kalstone. *Five Temperaments: Elizabeth Bishop, Robert Lowell, James Merrill, Adrienne Rich, John Ashbery* (Oxford Univ. Pr., 1977), pp. 162, 165–66, 169

The interpenetration of psyche and history is . . . a major situation in Adrienne Rich's recent poems. She makes her analysis of individual consciousness and history by uniting the issues of sexuality and war in a way neither of the other poets does. The most intimate relations of love and marriage are traced out in her poems until they are revealed as a terrifying war, and war itself is seen as a fact originating in the patriarchal oppression of women. Domination, depersonalization, and dehumanization are the vectors of the patriarchal soul; multiplied and extended on a national scale, these male traits are, in Rich's view, an ur-political explanation for the Vietnam War and its atrocities. Social dislocation and war stem from an estrangement, at some original moment, between "male" and "female" components of the human psyche. Rich pursues this split, investigating its origins and its costs. In effect she is conducting a historical examination of the psychic life. . . .

The ultimate intention of *Diving into the Wreck* is to call this whole patriarchal myth into question. Rich does so by dramatizing the process of critique and self-exploration in a new myth that constructs her own version of the origin and history of consciousness. Nor is Rich's myth a simple reversal of [Erich] Neumann's model. For, unlike the fecund captive-treasure of the patriarchal myth, here the captive is dead, arrested in the strained posture of unfulfilled searching. Nothing can be won from this figure except the fact of death. The new "fruitful center" in Rich's myth has become the creative antagonism of the woman-hero to traditional consciousness and old patterns of myth—an antagonism motivated because that book of stories and explanations excludes her. So in the course of the journey an androgynous woman has been invented, one appropriating her own fruitfulness and power, and brought into being by her own creative momentum—that is, from the process of critique.

Rachel Blau DuPlessis. In *Shakespeare's Sisters: Feminist Essays on Women Poets*, ed. Sandra M. Gilbert and Susan Gubar (Indiana Univ. Pr., 1979), pp. 291–92, 295

*A Wild Patience Has Taken Me This Far* assembles in chronological order the poems Adrienne Rich wrote between 1978 and 1981. These poems, given to rhetorical excesses and political simplifications, are far from her best work; but a fair portion of the collection is important. For some time, Rich has been moving towards the extreme of radical feminism; in this volume she arrives humourlessly at its pole. The irony that tempered her depiction of the conflict of the sexes in *The Dream of a Common Language*, her one great book, is gone now. What has survived is a poetry that will, and should, discomfit many readers; it will sometimes move them as well. . . .

Missing from . . . most . . . poems in the book, is a sense of balance. In Rich's worst poems, such as "Frame," she wilfully misrepresents men, committing the same act of distortion that she complains about elsewhere. "Frame" stoops to vicious clichés, portraying men as incurable rapists, invoking the stereotype of the Boston policeman who has nothing to do other than pursue and maim young women.

Fortunately, Rich can do better. The self-obsession that characterized much of her earlier work, which was largely concerned with an evolving autobiographical *mythos*, has widened into a concern with the "selves," past and present, around her. While her dream of a common language has never been realized in her own poems, Rich approaches it in pieces such as "Culture and Anarchy" and "The Spirit of Place," both of which call up for inspection the lives of earlier women.

Jay Parini. *TLS*. Nov. 12, 1982, p. 1251

## ROETHKE, THEODORE (1908–1963)

The life Roethke loves is a process, a cosmic dance with Bird, Leaf, Fish, and Snail in which the Eye half-perceives and half-creates all of the dancers. The abiding Leaf, ever-decaying, never to be decayed, and the questing Snail, ever evolving, never to be evolved, are Roethke's partners. They suggest the rhythm (and the limits) of the dance. Nothing is ever lost; nothing ever fully arrives. And it is Love and the love of Love which moves them all.

Blake is evolved, both by name and by imitation, as the representative poet-mystic, the visionary who saw the sun to be a choir of angels chanting "holy, holy, holy." The eye of such a poet has the "altering power" in abundance, making Blake one of the mystical brotherhood of singers who, perhaps, are as one singer in the cosmic vision.

We come, at the end which is not an end, to One, which is where we began in "In a Dark Time." There *one* became *One*. Now "everything comes to One." The sense of Oneness has enlarged to include all of creation, all of the dancers. Some of the loneliness of the "dark time" has been dispelled, and the motion here is that of the dance, not of "the tearing wind." The third "dance on," like Gertrude Stein's third rose, suggests infinite repetition. The dance goes on, still and still moving, into the silence beyond the poem.

Like the aging instant which forever vanishes just ahead of us, each poem in *Sequence, Sometimes Metaphysical* has independent worth and identity, yet each is enlarged in meaning and value by its relationship to other of the poems and to the whole. And, like that vanishing instant, each poem in the *Sequence* destroys itself to make way for the next poem. Ever decaying, never to be decayed; ever evolving, never to be evolved, the poems of *Sequence, Sometimes Metaphysical* prove that each ending is a new beginning, and that endings and beginnings alike are "perpetual."

The sequence of twelve poems may not wholly master the complexities of a world in process, but, taken together, the poems represent a remarkable attempt to wed the motion of the creative mind to the motion that is life itself.

Richard Allen Blessing. *Theodore Roethke's Dynamic Vision* (Indiana Univ. Pr., 1974), pp. 218–19

If one were to search for the persistent pattern which unifies Roethke's work, making it such a coherent body of work, one would have to settle on the pattern of rebirth. . . . The starting point of Roethke's work is this passion for rebirth, to strip away encumbrances in order to get back to first things. This impulse might possibly be connected with the manic-depressive pattern of his own personal experience, with its violent oscillations between extreme states of joy when the sense of being gained greatest access, and unendurable anxiety which threatened the very stability of the self. These oscillations clearly undermined any sense of continuity of self which Roethke might have been able to secure. The self was for him something that had to be perpetually recreated. It was an extremely tenuous concept since it had to be based on assurances of spiritual identity, and confidence continually wavered. Roethke called himself a perpetual beginner. Each time in each new poem, it was as if he had to begin over again, no previous gain being sufficient in the arduous process of self-definition. His work is therefore completely autobiographical in the broadest sense—a compulsive and continual reassessment of the nature of identity. . . .

Roethke never claimed that he had reached the final stages of mystical illumination. He was interested in mysticism as a psychological process that terminates in an undefinable but somehow potent sense of illumination. Such an analysis offered him a means to objectify his search for spiritual identity within a structure that is universally recognizable, but this structure always had to be justified in personal terms. His mystical poems actually record the desperate struggle for belief, rather than a formularized ritual.

In both his early and late poetry, if Roethke took the problems of the self as his theme, he was neither egocentric nor narcissistic. The self in his poetry becomes a symbol, interesting to him only when it impinges on representative concerns and not otherwise. In fact he is the least confessional of modern poets. His poems are never private complaints, the record of domestic misfortunes which move for their human content but seem never to exceed themselves. Yet he never evaded the personal either. His poems show how the violence of the self—the problems of alienation, discontinuity, and homelessness—can be written about with subtlety and passion. . . .

With Theodore Roethke, the pressure of his own imagination, the inescapable presence of his own individuality, is always recognizable in the depth of his penetration into the interior processes of personality, and in his acute sensitivity to the subliminal, irrational forces of life.

Rosemary Sullivan. *Theodore Roethke: The*
*Garden Master* (Univ. of Washington Pr., 1975),
pp. 190–91, 194–95, 198

His sense of tradition encompassed not only a conscious historical attitude, but a psychological state, and his act of imitation was not a mechanical process, but a basic component of those imaginative faculties most directly involved in the creation of a poem. The degree to which his sense of tradition was an emotional attitude involving his whole psychological condition is most clearly demonstrated in his belief that while he was writing "The Dance" Yeats was in his presence.

The strongest single influence on Roethke's concept of his tradition, and one of the most important poets in that tradition, is T. S. Eliot. . . .

Roethke offers in his poems a number of metaphors marking his evolving conception of the relationship between "tradition and the individual talent." In his earliest book, the poetry of the past is viewed as an inherited burden. The pressure of the past is a sinister force against which the modern poet self-consciously struggles to assert his own originality. Later, Roethke begins to discover that a literary inheritance is not given as a birthright but must be created as a means for permitting the poet to realize his own abilities through imitation and finally assimilation—arts that at their worst are mimicry and blatant theft and at their best enable the poet to find "the accent" of his own speech and yet at the same time to overcome the limitations of the solitary talent unsupported by tradition. . . .

Had Roethke lived longer, it is likely that his most important metaphors for his sense and use of tradition would have developed into something like myths. If he had enlarged his metaphor of "rocking" into a concept of history explaining the reanimation of the past in the present, it might well have been similar to Yeats's gyres. "The dance" in which "everything comes to One," if extended, might have become, like Blake's *Milton* and *Jerusalem*, an all-encompassing myth for the total assimilation of past into present poets and the realization of self through absorption into the organic structure of the poem. Perhaps Roethke would have found the descent of Milton into the mind of Blake and the embrace of Creator and created at the end of *Jerusalem* prototypal myths for that process whereby the poet becomes his tradition and the tradition becomes the poet.

Jenijoy La Belle. *The Echoing Wood of Theodore Roethke* (Princeton Univ. Pr., 1976), pp. 166–68

There is no explicit mention of God in "The Lost Son," but there is "Father Fear," whom one can assume as a substitute, since God, house, and father often fuse their meanings in "The Lost Son" sequence in the *Praise to the End!* volume. In effect, God takes on the masculine qualities of a father in "The Lost Son," and the poem itself, as an act of creation, emphasizes the sense of hierarchy and order associated with the greenhouse. . . . "The Lost Son" is the only poem in the sequence that dramatizes the need for dying, and it is the only poem that perfects a sense of stasis, that is, a mystical sense of stillness for its own sake. . . .

The animism in the surrounding poems is affirmatively alive and more intense than that in "The Lost Son" . . . and for this reason there is very little or nothing of a quiet sense of stasis, of being on the edge between life and death that the last section of "The Lost Son" conveys so well. This central poem gives Roethke a way out, a "going-forward" in the journey out of the self that defines the Roethkean mode of identity, because "The last time I nearly whispered myself away. / I was far back, farther than anybody else.". . . One could say, then, that the animism from the surrounding sequence of poems is conditioned by the central poem, toned down in effect, and made to bear the burden of death. The poetry in "The Lost Son" carries this idea, not only by assertion . . . but also through the mood of stasis, especially by means of the slowed down, sometimes monometric, rhythms and the barren field imagery. This conditioned animism is what Roethke develops in the subsequent long poems, and brings to perfection in the last of these long poems, "North American Sequence." It is a kind of trope really, . . . a regenerative pattern in the poetry, and if it succeeds as a defining characteristic of Roethke's poetry, of the Roethkean mode of identity, it is because this regenerative animism is conditioned by the reality of death and stasis, the beginning expression of which is found for the first time in "The Lost Son."

Emphasizing the shifting nature of the mind in "The Lost Son" ("Tell me:/Which is the way I take"), Roethke lays much stress on repetition—repetition of images, of moods, of rhythmic forms (everything twice), and it is this repetitive form that supports the tragic element in this and subsequent long poems, for only in repetition is the epic theme manifest, the dance between life and death, joy and sorrow, pity and fear. One could say that the shifting nature of the mind that Roethke's repetitive forms create defines a real or dramatic sense of the edge between the lost son and the found father, between the empty house and the full house (flower filled), and between the false self and the true self.

Harry Williams. *"The Edge Is What I Have":*
*Theodore Roethke and After* (Bucknell Univ. Pr.,
1977), pp. 66–68

Roethke's poetry will never be properly understood unless read within the context of Romanticism in its American manifestation. The work of recent critics has been invaluable in showing the breadth and continuity of the Romantic movement from its origins in eighteenth-century Germany to the present. What seems constant in this nearly intractable movement is the recognition that every man is cut off from nature; given this state of affairs, art becomes indispensable in the process of reconciliation between self and nature (subject and object). Every man has either to make his peace with nature or wage his own "war between the mind and sky" (as Stevens called it). . . .

Roethke's specific connections were Romantic, especially with the American visionary side. More so than any other contemporary poet, he carried on an exhaustive dialogue with his precursors. . . .

In all, *The Lost Son* remains the central volume, this poet's most durable achievement, and the key to his work. This is not to dismiss the love lyrics of his middle period or the best of his later meditative sequences, which deepen and extend the autobiographical mythos at the core of all his best writing, the quest for the greenhouse Eden. The cycles of death and rebirth are crucial here, providing the contrarieties that generate creative energy. The long poem sequences, Roethke's favorite medium, make constant use of this pattern; the poet's most basic movement is from desolation and fear to consolation and joy. In this, Roethke becomes a meditative poet par excellence.

It looks clear now that Roethke has earned a permanent place in the literature of American Romanticism. Finally, it is Roethke's fierce honesty with himself that illumines his best work; when he succeeds, it is because he has managed to speak directly about his most personal and, often, disturbing experiences. When he fails, it is because of self-deception or affectation.

Jay Parini. *Theodore Roethke: An American*
*Romantic* (Univ. of Massachusetts Pr., 1979), pp.
4, 188

Despite the hard-won sense of reconciliation and joy that concludes *The Far Field*, Roethke was never completely at peace with himself. Death remained for him, until the end, a terrible consequence. For Roethke, as for the protagonist in his poetry, spiritual advancement was always accompanied by some slipping back, and the gains he made in the poems of his final volume were apparently only temporary, though that final struggle did represent, in Roethke's words, some progress. His push toward the Absolute was indeed among those experiences that are "so powerful and so profound . . . that they repeat themselves . . . again and again . . . each time bringing us closer to our own most particular (and thus most universal) reality." In his last poems, it appears that Roethke drew as near to his particular and universal reality as life would allow. To go further meant to go beyond life, to die.

If Roethke was haunted by a fear of death, he was also haunted by an attraction to it. From the very beginning, in *Open House*, those taut little poems of self-loathing such as "Epidermal Macabre" and "Prayer before Study" reveal something of a death wish. And therein lies the ultimate irony of Roethke's poetry, that his struggle for identity inevitably necessitated the loss of his identity. Roethke discovered that in order to find himself he had to lose himself, and the truth of that paradox produced in him the conflicting drives that are most clearly revealed in "Sequence, Sometimes Metaphysical." His desire was to attain ultimate union, but he could not bear to pay the ultimate cost, the loss of his own individual identity. What he passionately desired was an impossible contradiction, "to be something else, yet still to be!". . .

The remarkable unity of Roethke's work is attributable to Roethke's persistence, to his "spiritual toughness," for he never once grew lax in the pursuit of his ultimate identity. Like the mystic, Roethke's awareness of another level of reality, one more real and significant than that which is normally perceived, led him to dedicate himself to the attainment of the Absolute.

Neal Bowers. *Theodore Roethke: The Journey from I to Otherwise* (Univ. of Missouri Pr., 1982), pp. 208–10

# ● ROSSNER, JUDITH (1935–   )

*To the Precipice*, a first novel, is about love and marriage. Except that the Ruth of the novel doesn't marry the man she loves, it is a familiar tale, sure enough. But Mrs. Rossner makes it new, dramatic not sentimental, grown-up, not adolescent or sticky. Her people, buffeted by their feelings, act irrationally; but they can also show a maturity and a sense of responsibility that run counter to their previous behavior.

Ruth comes from New York's Lower East Side where she lives in a tenement slum. The toilet is outside; the shower (but no tub) is arranged over a cemented corner of the kitchen.

Her father is a violent, stubborn man, who expresses his feeling of failure and love of family by a continual, frightening belligerence. The mother is a stolid, suffering woman, old long before her time. The son, harried by the father and his own yearnings, feels hemmed in and caged.

And there is David, whom Ruth has known since they were children. David has been comforter, guide, confessor and later Ruth's lover. Without thinking much about it, she assumes that when she marries, it will be to David. A life without him would be unthinkable.

To get out of the city one summer, Ruth accepts a job as a tutor and companion to two children of a wealthy family, the Stamms, and she gets a taste of life denied her before. Mrs. Stamm is an interesting woman: biting, hard, very capable—nobody obviously to push around. Ruth does not like her, but the reader won't agree. Indeed, I wish Mrs. Rossner had told us more about her.

The husband, overshadowed by his wife, is diffident and retiring; in love as well as in life his character is "that of a small boy promised a reward he is too timid to accept."

He is also 18 years older than Ruth. Nevertheless, after his divorce from his wife, he asks Ruth to marry him and she does. Why? Mrs. Rossner tells us why and also why the relationship between David and Ruth does not stop at her marriage—a relationship that comes to a crisis. The ending is one the reader will acknowledge as reasonable though not necessarily as a happy one.

Her novel shows its apprentice side. She tends to overfurnish it for one. She can't step into a room without describing its contents or wallpaper. It is not enough for the mother to make tea. The author supplies a boiling kettle, a strainer, lemon, the works. And there is an ambiguity about some of her characters I'm not sure she intended.

Her greatest strength is that she carries off the big scenes, the climaxes and crises with a sure hand. Their tone is right; their language expressive. And she has a true novelist's understanding of human behavior—an understanding that comes by instinct, not by study. And, as her subject shows, she is willing to aim at big targets. She is a lady we will hear from again.

Thomas Lask. *NYTd*. Feb. 24, 1967, p. 33

Ms. Rossner says that she wanted to deal in her novel [*Any Minute I Can Split*] with "comparisons between the standard family and alternatives, from casual affairs to communes." The standard family is represented here by Margaret and her unloving, overbearing, shiftless, bed-hopping husband, and by his wealthy, mindless, heartless parents. Margaret's main casual affair is with a nineteen-year-old who feels no affection for anyone; it ends when he beats her up, rapes her, and walks off. The commune offers a spider web of crisscrossing tensions under superficial friendliness. As the novel's title suggests, every relationship is uneasy and tentative; the indication is that we are beginning to see in America the ironic triumph of situational existence.

Situational morality, which seemed such a bold and happy idea back in the bold and happy Sixties, asserted that moral judgments could not be general and absolute but had to be custom-tailored, had to give each particular situation its due. Similarly, in less significant areas, Americans learned to judge people, actions, jobs, and relationships relatively, with regard to particular situations. And of course they learned to appear, act, and relate to others situationally. We became merely the raw material of situations; context determined character. Ms. Rossner shows us the results: Relationships have no fixity; morality varies with the individual, his situation, and his mood; other people become mere stage props in the scene each individual stages for himself; emotional relationships are sadomasochistic; and human identity dwindles down to a self-centered bundle of memories, hangups, and desires. . . .

Ms. Rossner is too willing to write about ideas; instead of being incited to thought, we are too often obliged to hear Margaret's expository thinking. . . . But she evokes the commune well, and her unpleasant scenes are especially credible.

J. D. O'Hara. *SR*. Aug. 5, 1972, pp. 52–53

Judith Rossner has impeccable literary credentials. Her first three novels were beautifully reviewed and didn't sell. *Looking for Mr. Goodbar* is so good a read, so stunningly commercial as a novel, that it runs the risk of being consigned to artistic oblivion.

That would be a mistake. The sureness of Judith Rossner's writing and her almost flawless sense of timing create a complex and chilling portrait of a woman's descent into hell that gives this book considerable literary merit. . . .

Passivity is a theme that has been dealt with much of late. Sumner Locke Elliot's brilliant novel, *Going*, describes a Nixon-like United States where nobody acts until it's too late, and they're all dead. Erica Jong explored that emotional disease in women whose pathology is not only similar to cancer's but whose morbidity is greater. Passivity may kill more slowly, but it is more efficient; it kills a whole lot more people in the end. Judith Rossner gives passivity an added dimension of horror. She anatomizes its growth, step by chilling step, showing how it can be as effective a means of suicide as poison or a gun.

It is a measure of *Mr. Goodbar*'s richness and complexity that it can be read on many levels. Catholics might view it as a passion play; feminists might consider Theresa a political victim of rape. Men may focus on the book's sexuality. (Men have tended to overreact to the wider use of sex in recent writing by women, but I don't think there's all that much behind this new freedom; sex is simply another area of experience for the woman novelist to mime in the same sense that the freedom to write about being Jewish, say, is for Jewish writers.) What adds to my view of *Mr. Goodbar* as an exploration of passivity is the angry and frustrated reaction of a number of women who have read the book. *Mr. Goodbar* may, for them, have driven the final stake through the heart of the axiom that passive is a good way to be if you're a woman.

Another thing that has to go is the assumption that any book written by a woman about a woman who even vaguely resembles herself fits neatly into a genre labeled "women's fiction." You can bet that the current and upcoming novels by middle-aged men—Bellow, Heller, Roth, Styron—won't be labeled "male menopausal fiction."

Nor should *Mr. Goodbar* be shunted off into the genre of "commercial fiction," a convenience by which reviewers are able to measure literary merit simply as inversely proportionate to the number of people who buy a book.

If there is a genre into which *Mr. Goodbar* falls, it is a genre of uncommonly well-written and well-constructed fiction, easily accessible, but full of insight and intelligence and illumination. It is a noble genre. And Rossner's heroine, Theresa Dunn, in this tough and powerfully controlled novel, takes her place beside Henry James's Isabel Archer and Scott Fitzgerald's Nicole Diver as another victim of the American Dream, a woman who never roused herself enough to wake up from the nightmare.

Carol Eisen Rinzler. NYT. June 8, 1975, pp.<br>24–26

On pages 97 and 98 of *Attachments* we learn in one three-minute sweep of the eye all the "news" (for that is what *novel* means) that Rossner has to impart to us. On those two pages we are given in graphic detail the answer to the major question raised by the novel: How does a woman, the heroine, Nadine, "do it" with her Siamese-twin husband? And when her best friend, Dianne, marries the other twin, how do *they* do it? Once these momentous questions of logistics are solved, there remain a few others that ought to create curiosity, but somehow—because of the endless, flat terrain of language we have to travel across—they do not. Only one further question of consequence is posed: What happens to the two marriages when the twins decide to risk the operation and are separated? The predictable answer past, there is no nourishment left in the book.

Put aside the essential poverty of the sensational idea and the attenuated workings-out of the occasional complications. . . . Rossner uses words carelessly; she is deaf to the natural music of good sentences because she is so preoccupied with the ramifications of her catchy idea. . . . There is no grace, no imagery that is not tired and hackneyed. The prose has a tone-deaf quality ("Far from the rest of the house, in feeling if not in fact"). It proceeds doggedly along its synthetic paths.

Doris Grumbach. SR. Oct. 1, 1977, pp. 30–31

The backwoods of Fayette, Maine, and the cotton mills of Lowell, Massachusetts, in the mid-19th century where *Emmeline* takes place are worlds away from the New York City streets where Judith Rossner set *Looking for Mr. Goodbar*, the best seller that made her famous five years ago. But Rossner's literary leap is not as admirably adventurous as it sounds. *Emmeline* is not a full-fledged historical novel, but a historical romance, heavier on the petticoated swoons than on the subtle interweaving of public and private destinies in the newly industrialized America of the 1840s.

In setting her historical scene Rossner relies heavily on two elementary facts about 19th-century America: that religion was the dominant tradition and industrialization the alienating innovation. She adds historical detail—mill machinery, boarding-house routine, railroad building, exciting tales from the west, and ominous news from the south. But Rossner's old New England seems arranged from the outside rather than imagined from within.

This simplicity of vision is partly justified by Rossner's identification with her unsophisticated protagonist. When 14-year-old Emmeline is sent from the poverty-stricken family farm in Maine to make money in the Lowell mills, it is appropriate that she has only a crude understanding of the new world she enters and an unreflective attachment to the religion she brings with her. Rossner convincingly evokes Emmeline's initial horror at the monster mill and then her naive willingness to see the mill in familial terms; the lonely girl is easily and uncomprehendingly seduced by the fatherly Irish overseer in the weaving room who offers, briefly, the care and warmth she finds nowhere else.

However, as Emmeline's youthful shape takes on womanly contours, the historical perspective remains flat. The book turns into a predictable melodrama, which I won't quite give away, though it gives itself away almost immediately. The crux of the plot is that Emmeline's contours get even more womanly as a result of Mr. Maguire's attentions.

Illicit sex and incest are the supposedly shocking revelations of the book. "You have to kind of gentle down readers if you're using a subject like this," Rossner explained in a recent *Publishers Weekly* interview. Her strategy works too well. We flip through pages of her clear prose, our sympathies never really roused by her transparent plot or characters, our sensibilities barely jarred by the broken taboos.

Rossner, however, had a very different reaction when she heard about Emmeline's tragedy from a real-life Fayette resident, 94-year-old Nettie Mitchell (whom Rossner credits in the novel's epigraph). "Nettie's remembering gave me goose pimples," Rossner told the *Publishers Weekly* interviewer, "and that's a sure sign for me." Unfortunately that's not a sure sign for her readers. Rossner has not made her imagination work hard enough at transforming the melodramatic truth into more than shallow fiction.

Ann Hulbert. NR. Oct. 11, 1980, pp. 38–39

*August*, Judith Rossner's seventh, in many ways remarkable novel, is about a four-year psychoanalysis. The patient, Dawn Henley, a tall, beautiful Barnard freshman with considerable artistic talent, enters treatment at 18, after falling asleep at the wheel of her car and running it into a tree. We see Dawn exclusively during her sessions; the people who touch her life are glimpsed through her impressions alone. Among the principals are the women who raised Dawn: Vera, her father's sister and physical double, and Vera's lesbian lover, Tony. The child calls Vera "daddy" and Tony "mommy," until a teacher, who does not know both parents are women, explains that Tony is "daddy," because Tony is the one who goes to work. Dawn's search for information about her "birth parents," as she refers to them, particularly events surrounding her father's death, becomes the primary project of her analysis. She learns that her mother committed suicide when she was six months old, and that a year later her father, a homosexual, drowned in a boating accident. . . .

Rossner's depiction of the intimate, yet laboratory-like atmosphere behind the closed office door is masterfully real. Dawn's story is absorbing, partly because Rossner has invented an intriguing case history, but more importantly because she has plunged imaginatively into her character with the same freedom and abandon patients strive for in psychoanalysis. Dawn, who is intelligent and in pain, begins her probe on page one, and although pruned of the inevitable fogbound accounts and broken-record repetitions of actual analyses, her monologues capture their ragged, suspense-story tempo. With each association, a little dust lifts from the buried origins of personality. . . .

*August* is limited by its characters' (and author's) insularity, but the power of the analysis is never diminished. It is a moving, distinguished achievement, full of delight and surprise. Lulu fits her patient like a glass slipper, providing the young woman with a chance to gain her life. And the analyst, too, is rewarded beyond calculation.

Laurie Stone. *VV*. Sept. 6, 1983, p. 34

## ROTH, PHILIP (1933–    )

Sardonic wit is never at a loss for subject matter these days; we live in times so absurd that it is no longer necessary to read ponderous essays by French intellectuals. The evening paper provides plenty of material in the unlikely event that the normal events of the day do not. But this avalanche of human folly is as much a curse as it is a blessing to the writer of contemporary fiction, particularly if he has the satirical bent of a Philip Roth. In the years following *Portnoy's Complaint* it became increasingly difficult to find a congenial home for his sizable verbal talents. The grotesquery of the world chipped away at what a literary imagination might conceive, always threatening to outdo in life what one had patterned in art.

In Roth's case, the late sixties took a fearful toll. His next books were pitched on that shaky ground called the playful gimmick. For a writer without his reputation, the results, no doubt, would have been fatal. For Roth, however, even the slimmest straw can lead to a darkly comic drowning. . . .

*Our Gang* was written in the white heat of indignation and outrage. To call Roth's grasp of politics "puerile" would be like equating a temper tantrum with sophisticated diplomacy. But in the context of 1971—with the war in Vietnam still raging and American citizens still deeply divided about its moral justification—critics tended to respond to the righteousness of his position rather than the artfulness of his book. Granted, novels are never written in a cultural vacuum; they always contain some residue of the social environment, such as the baggage of special interest groups and competing claims about what the "representative" consists of. Novels pinned to a volatile political climate merely render the problem exasperating.

A post-Watergate rereading of the novel is even more fascinating than reading it during the days when Nixon dictated our foreign policy. What some were quick to dismiss as cranky paranoia in 1971 has surfaced as a highly prophetic reality four years later. If anything, Roth's outrageous parody of Nixon is not outrageous enough for the postimpeachment era. Such are the risks the political satirist runs in our time.

Sanford Pinsker. The Comedy That "Hoits": An<br>
Essay on the Fiction of Philip Roth</i> (Univ. of<br>
Missouri Pr., 1975), pp. 71–72

Philip Roth's tenth book [*The Professor of Desire*] is a thoughtful, even gentle, stylistically elegant novel about the paradox of male desire, that lacerating sexual passion which may lead to happiness but cannot survive it.

The effect of the book is more that of discourse than of fiction, high-level discourse adorned with wit, with rhetorical devices new and ancient, and with its piquant illustrations. Its form is that of monologue, rather than first-person storytelling, for the scenes are more often adumbrated than dramatized, the characters more often indicated than developed.

This method, designed to involve the reader intellectually rather than sensationally, is, of course, perfectly intentional—a remark that ought to be unnecessary. But we have been racing through a couple of decades in which the writers have so far outdistanced the critics that it is aggravatingly commonplace to see writing that is in fact subtle and resourceful dismissed as if it were a mistake by commentators whose perceptions simply haven't kept pace.

The monologist in Mr. Roth's novel is David Kepesh, a professor of comparative literature, two of whose enthusiasms are for Chekhov and Kafka. . . .

The author's control of this world seems perfect except perhaps, in one regard. The reader is not as certain as might be wished of the ironic distance between author and narrator, particularly at the end of the book, when Kepesh rages internally against the working-out of the desire-happiness paradox in himself, as if it were a black misfortune and his alone, "a ridiculous, vicious, inexplicable joke!" One wants to say to him, and to feel that Mr. Roth is saying of him, that it's a joke all right, but a sad, small, universal, necessary joke that cloaks a piece of folk wisdom David Kepesh is absurdly late in learning. . . .

If this reading is not indicated with absolute clarity, it seems at least a likely one, leaving us with *The Professor of Desire* as a fine display of literary skills, a challenging brief novel, moving when it needs to be, an erudite examination of the troglodyte within us.

Vance Bourjaily. NYT. Sept. 16, 1977, pp. 1, 50

*The Ghost Writer* is . . . a strangely unsatisfying book. These days one is too decently in awe, too empathetic (maybe too sophisticated, or lazy) to demand the Big C from every work of quality. Just the recognition of quality, as distinct from the okay delight, strains the rusty dynamo of critical intelligence. But Catharsis—or its modern impersonation, Insight, the Big I—is what *The Ghost Writer* seems to promise, seems to be rushing us toward, the grail of its endeavor, only we never get there. So at the end and afterward, one remains (not unhappily) in Roth's enticing grip, his thrall, but doesn't quite know why. Everything still impends, but the sense of purpose is diffused. . . .

It is probably clear that I do not think Roth can any longer be judged on the merits of his individual books—though, of course, that shall continue to happen as his individual books appear. *The Ghost Writer* is strangely unsatisfying; it grows less unsatisfying and more strange—more wondrous—as it is connected to what Roth obviously connects it to: his own work, previous writers, aesthetic and moral responsibilities that always threaten to collide and that he makes collide. Roth is stylistically the cleanest of writers, so his ire, and ours, is silhouetted. He plies, always, an abrasive grace; and mucking up the web of his endeavor is a by-now long history of coconspiratorial challenge and disappointment: Why doesn't he do the large, complete, major-theme, Big C novel we can all recognize as truly great?

The answer, I think, is that he has done it, or is doing it, however imperfectly, in all his work; that Roth can be read selectively (anyway will, who has time for anything else?) but not discretely. Is it a fault of *The Ghost Writer* that it requires some knowledge of where Roth has been before and how we have responded and (I think) a brushing-up with James? I suspect a "yes" reflects convention, a wish, maybe a practical necessity, certainly reviewer's convenience—and a moral ratio that is insultingly lopsided. . . . Roth's games are inseparable from his candor—his unquenchable yearning, at times of the mind, at times of the groin, to tell, in art, how the madness is. Zuckerman does his best, and it's still tentative; but it's the best, most rigorous (with exceptions), most human, most demanding of our better selves, *least* pulling down of the reader to some common vulgarity, least disinterested in spirit, of any contemporary essay-story I know. *Que sera, sera*, but Roth's uneasy, multifaceted worlds have, in *The Ghost Writer*, become my own, and I think writers' own, Jews' own, our own. The rest is the madness of apathy.

Eliot Fremont-Smith. VV. Oct. 8, 1979, pp. 33, 36

From the outset, Roth's fictional interpretation of American Jews as a regnant bourgeoisie disturbed as much as it amused. Jews of the parent generation, reacting with understandable pique to this parody of their aspirations and achievements, granted Roth what no American contemporary, not even Norman Mailer, had been able to provoke, and what no American author since Henry Miller has more enjoyed—a public antagonism, proof in the form of outrage that his work had hit a nerve. In protesting that he had not portrayed them fairly, these Jews offered the most tangible demonstration of his success. For the critic of bourgeois complacency, what sweeter response than his constituency's cry of "foul," exposing that very obsession with propriety that he has been ridiculing? It was not for Philip Roth to worry, as many other serious American authors have had to do, about artistic irrelevance: he has always had the fuel of audience reaction pumping. . . .

Roth's Jewish bourgeois comedy provided us, during our prolonged adolescence, with models of the lovable hero, whose fumbling attempts at direct self-gratification foiled the inhibited digestive tracts and spirits of his elders, and whose "honest" search for a better life exposed the hypocrisy of those with foreordained religious and ethnic guidelines. This was no small thing to owe a writer.

It is tempting to speak of Philip Roth as if he were the author of but a single creation, the chucked-beneath-the chin Jewish college boy who first appeared in *Goodbye, Columbus* and *Letting Go*, resurfaced in *Portnoy's Complaint*, and made his way through difficult marriages and into the difficulties of a literary career in *My Life as a Man* and *The Professor of Desire*. In truth, of course, Philip Roth's highly disciplined professional career included a good deal more. . . .

But though his work has ranged in setting and form, no one could have been surprised, or unhappy, to see the author returning as he has recently done to the fictional adventures of the lad from Newark. In Roth's two most recent novels, *The Ghost Writer* and *Zuckerman Unbound*, this young man has become a writer, in the first novel a fledgling writer visiting a Master, and in the second an all-too-renowned novelist trying to cope with his new fame. . . .

By his own suggestive references to his earlier work and to the cultural milieu from which it emerged, Philip Roth makes it possible to look back now on the development of the character who has become Nathan Zuckerman: indeed, he seems to invite such a consideration. Where the early heroes demonstrated their opposition to embourgeoisement by searching for sexual pleasure, their late counterparts pursue a more substantial form of self-realization through artistic creation. The initial resistance of the protagonist to the Jewish middle-class agenda has gradually expressed and justified itself in a successful writing career. Keeping pace with this thematic progression is the author's own technical development: far more than his previous works, *The Ghost Writer* and *Zuckerman Unbound* are models of compression and formal elegance. . . .

Reading Philip Roth remains pleasurable, but the pleasure has in it the element of predictability. Those who want literature to reassure them by fulfilling the expectations they bring to it will find in Philip Roth their comfortable assumptions of twenty odd years ago. In order to go beyond this, Roth would have to part with the formula that brought him undeniable success, but at the cost of that greater success his latest heroes espouse: the success of the artist unbound.

Ruth R. Wisse. *Cmty*. Sept., 1981, pp. 56–60

Much has been made of the ingenuity with which Roth spins out the dialectics of life *vs*. art and hedonism *vs*. convention, but *Zuckerman Unbound* has neither the concentration and feeling of necessity we expect in a book this short, nor the richness and breadth its many themes require. It's a protracted sketch, a rambling novella lit by some stunning moments—the death of Zuckerman's father is as moving as anything Roth has written—but whose last chapter in no sense flows from its first. What unity it possesses comes from Roth's voice, as always a marvel of fluidity and bite, and from the public persona of Roth, which gives Nathan Zuckerman a resonance and coherence he would not otherwise have.

For all Roth's declaimers of autobiographical intent, he counts heavily on our willingness to read his new book not as fiction but as a document in his ongoing debate with those who call his work, especially *Portnoy*, anti-Semitic, narcissistic and exploitative of those close to him. Thus, the real reason why Nathan's mother is a paragon of sweetness and patience lies outside these pages, in Roth's wish to refute accusations that Mrs. Portnoy, that strident Oedipal nightmare, must have been drawn from life. What holds the book together is not the connection its elements have with each other, but the connection each has with the author. A reader who had missed *Portnoy* and the surrounding brouhaha would have trouble figuring out why *Carnovsky*, the contents of which are barely mentioned, causes such a fuss.

Roth's subject has always been himself, and perhaps that's just not enough anymore. Having already catalogued his more interesting aspects—sexuality, upbringing, Jewishness, ambition—he's left with the infinitely more attenuated subject of his relation to his own literary reputation. Leaving aside the considerable vanity inherent in the assumption that this is a matter of wide concern, what is the reader supposed to do while Roth tap-dances around what seems to be considerable feelings of guilt? If 12 years later Roth is still obsessed by the attacks on *Portnoy*, maybe he *shouldn't* have written the damn book, already. By forcing him to place his enormous gifts in the service of an uneasy self-justification, the *vrai* is indeed having its revenge.

Katha Pollitt. *Mother Jones*. Sept./Oct., 1981, p. 66

From the beginning of his career, he has been explicitly seeking out one spiritual father or another, and though his publications (up until very recently) have each differed in their manner of presentation, he keeps returning to an established set of themes concerned with authority and individuation. It is as if he were ringing changes on Nietzsche's idea of man as "*das kranke Tier*," the sick animal—dis-eased by virtue of his self-consciousness and doomed to ever more ingenious attempts at curing himself. Roth makes much of his coming to maturity in the fifties, that decade of earnestness and of drifting, of "conformity" and incipient anti-establishmentarianism. His protagonists thrive on the cultivation of sin and polymorphous perversity, but at the same time their erotic adventures are informed by missionary, redemptive ideals and their transgressions made keener by an exquisite sense of propriety. Faced with temptation, his hero will usually give in—and then use the occasion to test his capacity for conscience. Never wasting, never in line, he synthesizes the stereotypes of pushy Jew and nice Jewish boy. For his parents, and for the women he loves, Roth reserves both his tenderest and his most scabrous outpourings. As he terms Kafka, so is he himself a "family-haunted son," and yet at all junctures he insists on being "on my own." Having hurt his loved ones, he will get a more vivid sense of himself, of human possibilities generally, through the consequent suffering and guilt he experiences. His ambivalence, in other words—his hesitating and pulsating between carnal and spiritual imperatives—is the ambivalence of Stephen Dedalus and Raskolnikov, only in a minor, bluesy key: tragedy verging on farce.

Howard Eiland. In *Critical Essays on Philip Roth*,
ed. Sanford Pinsker (G. K. Hall, 1982), p. 256

The fiction of Philip Roth, more than that of any other Jewish American writer, has been intertwined with his readers' responses to his work, with justification of his themes and methods, with literary theory, and with his Jewish identity. Beginning with the publication of *Goodbye, Columbus* in 1959, his satire of Jewish suburbia, and reaching sensational proportions with the publication of *Portnoy's Complaint* in 1969, the controversy about Roth's status, both as artist and as a Jew, has not abated. Roth's talent, according to Irving Howe, "has been put to the service of a creative vision deeply marred by vulgarity." Howe's criticism of Roth is based on his discerning in his writings an "unfocused hostility" stemming from his "thin personal culture." In other words, Roth "comes at the end of a tradition which can no longer nourish his imagination." In short, Roth assaults American Jewish life in his satires without being generally nourished or sustained by the culture which he chooses as his central subject. Thus, the critical observation is also an ethical indictment. Roth vulgarizes Jewish life in his fiction. . . .

Were the issue of Roth's loyalty or disloyalty to his people limited to a discursive tug of war between the writer and his critics, his career would pose interesting questions in the sociology of literature alone. But the drama between the Jewish writer bent on freely expressing his desires in his art and his moralistic family, friends, and readers has infiltrated his fiction and gradually has become his central subject, his characters, and his plot. The solely sexual drives of his earlier protagonists evolve into artistic longings, sensual pleasure alone evolves into a devotion to art for its own sake, uninhibited by social, ethical, or historical restraints. As Ruth Wisse has observed, "where the early heroes demonstrated their opposition to embourgeoisement by searching for sexual pleasure, their late counterparts pursue a more substantial form of self-realization through artistic creation." I do not believe, however, as Wisse does, that this reflects the recycling of an old theme into a stereotype that lacks the vigor of the original, that he is merely making the bourgeois Jew an easier and more automatic target of ridicule now that his protagonist is an artist. On the contrary. As his art begins to turn in upon itself, it also seems to be moving toward a stronger and more complex identification with Jewish life.

Hana Wirth-Nesher. Prooftexts. Sept., 1983, pp. 263–64

Philip Roth's new novel [*The Anatomy Lesson*] is more necessary than satisfactory. I'm glad he wrote it, but I'm also glad to hear he's now finished with his alter ego, that notorious and embattled Jewish writer, Nathan Zuckerman. Three novels have been enlisted to do the work of perhaps two and a half. *The Anatomy Lesson* offers an important variation on the theme of the trilogy and a few grand comic scenes, but signs of strain have begun to intrude. Roth is overworking his material, stretching it too thin, repeating himself. There's an irony here; in this story, Zuckerman has exhausted his writer's capital; having used up his life in his books, he's unable to write at all.

To recapitulate as briefly as possible; the central theme of the Zuckerman trilogy is "the unreckoned consequences of art." In *The Ghost Writer*, which remains Roth's best novel to date, the young Nathan Zuckerman is exposed to the perils of the life of a literary recluse. In *Zuckerman Unbound*, he must endure the perils of literary celebrity. In *The Anatomy Lesson*, Zuckerman confronts the perils of being a famous writer who is finished with writing. Forget fame and wealth, Roth seems to say, forget the women who pull up their skirts as soon as they enter a writer's room: the writer's life is not a happy one. It is, quite literally, a pain in the neck. . . .

The good stuff in *The Anatomy Lesson* survives a second reading. Both times I've read it, however, I've found myself pushing toward the end. Over the years, Roth has refined his tone of voice, his comedy and his mastery of fictional techniques, but if he's now incapable of conjuring up a dull scene, he's still fully capable of running a good idea into the ground. Flying high on Percodan, Zuckerman engages a limousine with a young woman driver. He says he's Milton Appel, a publisher of pornography. Talking nonstop—a consequence of the drug—'Zuckerman translates himself into another life. It's a marvelous scene until Roth carries it too far: Zuckerman has the details, even the rationale, of this pornographer's business just right. The episode reminds us of Zuckerman's persuasiveness in translating the enigmatic Amy Bellette into Anne Frank in *The Ghost Writer*.

It's impertinent to confuse the author of a book with its protagonist. Zuckerman is not Roth, though he shares some of his biography. Can Zuckerman's ghost have been exorcised with this novel? I hope so, but it's hard to shake the image of Sherlock Holmes crawling back from the brink of the Reichenbach Falls.

Peter S. Prescott. *Newsweek*. Nov. 7, 1983, pp. 132, 132D

## RUKEYSER, MURIEL (1913–1980)

Upon reading Muriel Rukeyser's latest volume of poems, upon going through *The Gates*, one feels silent, sad, instructed, grateful. No words of prose from a reviewer are needed to explain these poems; and to praise them is almost condescending. The woman who wrote them has been with us 20th century American readers almost a half a century: a gifted observer of this world; a person who can sing to us and make our duller, less responsive minds come more alive; and not least, someone who has proven it possible to be a sensible human being, a woman inclined to give, to extend herself toward others, and also a first-rate poet. We all struggle with the sin of pride; Muriel Rukeyser has been blessed with less narcissism than most of us—especially remarkable in such an introspective, sensitive, and self-aware person, who has for so long been committed to telling others what crosses her mind. She is saved from self-centeredness by a compassionate concern for others, all over the world, and by a wonderful capacity for self-mocking irony.

Robert Coles. *APR*. May/June, 1978, p. 15

The publication of Muriel Rukeyser's *Collected Poems* is an occasion for rejoicing. Not only is Miss Rukeyser one of those poets American literature would seem impoverished without, but, like William Carlos Williams, she has been an indestructible force for the good of poetry and poets for decades. For all that the poems have changed over the years, it is impossible to say that there has been a technical development. Miss Rukeyser seems to have been born poetically full-grown, and for this reason it is as rewarding to open the book at any point as to proceed systematically from beginning to end.

But wherever you begin, there is no sense in being niggling about Miss Rukeyser's rhapsodies in language. Yes, there are faults of construction. Yes, there are poems—such as "Tree of Rivers"—that begin, so to speak, in one key and end surprisingly in another. Never mind. However surprising, disturbing or rhetorically long-winded Miss Rukeyser's poems seem, they never bore you. It is always the same passionate and compassionate poet writing out of her extraordinary, iridescent imagination who confronts you, and although some of the earlier poems may seem dated (history itself is dated), what textbooks still pigeonhole as "social realism" makes for moving stories. Miss Rukeyser is fortunate in being among those poets who can tell stories in verse. . . .

Miss Rukeyser's collage method is effective, her indictment of war and American capitalism biting, and her feeling for the American wilderness and man's place in it is as fine as Faulkner's. . . .

Like Melville's, Miss Rukeyser's realism is really a bridge to an intensely visionary state of awareness. The line between world and world is indistinct. The threshold of the miraculous and mystical is never far away. It is as if life were always happening to her on two or three levels. Beneath her passion for social justice and her empathy with all sufferers lie deeper apprehensions of what existence and its paradoxes can lead to. . . .

It is inevitable that Miss Rukeyser will be compared with Whitman; indeed, *Leaves of Grass* must have shown her part of the way. Among modern poets she is the equal of Pablo Neruda, and like him, committed to a vision of humanity that acknowledges pain but leaves little room for despair. She is also patently a feminine poet—feminist but not bitchy. Love poems stud the volume. One of the most beautiful is "Song, The Brain Coral" (1939), which is more than a love poem. It condenses into one lyric a whole philosophy of linked humanity.

Anne Stevenson. *NYT*. Feb. 11, 1979, p. 12

Rukeyser is essentially a modern poet of possibility (a word which recurs in her writing and conversation) in the tradition of the transcendental writers of America's Golden Day: Emerson, Whitman, Thoreau. . . . Rukeyser's vision of possibility is . . . based in part on the marvels of technology, but her times—times of war, waiting for war, and living with the vast human devastation of the mid- and later twentieth century—and her personal exploration of the struggle of the individual in a corrupt society . . . caused her vision of possibility to rise from a more inclusive complexity than [Hart] Crane's. Yet the basic source of her vision is her self (in the Emersonian sense), which she sounds in poetic exploration and extends in human involvement thereby discovering the possibility to which all may aspire, despite repression, war, genocide, and the chorus of poets who sing . . . that "the humanistic way . . . has already been defeated." She believes that all her involvements, political, scholarly, artistic, are "ways of reaching the world and the Self," those two ever fertile sources of possibility. . . .

Words that come to mind after a reading of Rukeyser's lyrics are "strength" and "movement." Hers is not a tender but a strong lyricism that does not aim to distill or crystallize an emotion or an experience. Rukeyser's aim is to follow the powerful rhythms of experience in herself (and often in her imagining of another) in a world which in its fears about economics and war has conspired to be silent about the deepest human values and to repress impulses which interfere with "getting ahead." Rukeyser would not deny these rhythms, these impulses. She has said that talk about poetry which is "in terms of the start, the image, the crystallization" is inadequate. . . . In Rukeyser there is the no less rigorous, wide-ranging exploration of emotion and experience and the attempt to project them onto an imagined other, often a whole society; Rukeyser's world is always *there*, in her poetry. Dickinson is severely alone; there is little expression of an effort to reach another, through touch and speech, as in Rukeyser. Nor is there the expansive impulse (given form in Rukeyser's long lines) to reach the world, to include and transform an unfeeling other. There is no such impulse at exploration and inclusion in Rossetti and Brontë whose poetry is meditative—a distillation, again, a crystallization of very private emotions and experiences.

Louise Kertesz. The Poetic Vision of Muriel Rukeyser (Louisiana State Univ. Pr., 1980), pp. 46–47, 75–76

# SANDBURG, CARL (1878–1967)

As always in good poetry, it is language that does it. But Sandburg is very difficult in this respect, because his way of using language can be deceptive. It is much like prose in its syntax, and the colloquial vocabulary adds to an apparent casualness. In his best poetry Sandburg *uses* vernacular language, slang even; by this I mean that in Sandburg's instance it isn't the self-conscious employment of a "low" vocabulary to call attention to commonness, a vaunting of plebeian virtue (though later in his career Sandburg was prone to do just this, ad nauseam). An expression such as "the *crack* trains of the nation" is an organic part of his vocabulary, not an affectation, and he employs the adjective because it is simply the appropriate word to image what he wishes to convey about the train. As such it provides precisely the intensification of language, the heightened awareness of the texture of experience, that the best poetry affords.

I stress this because unless the way in which Sandburg employs vernacular imagery is properly recognized, his way of poetry will be misunderstood. . . .

The best poems in *Chicago Poems* (1916), *Cornhuskers* (1918), and *Smoke and Steel* (1920) succeed because of the tension between the idiom and the subject; their impact lies in the resolution, through language, of that tension. But from using vernacular language to intensify everyday experience into poetry it is an easy, and a fatal, step for one to begin assuming that because the experience is ordinary and the language is of the earth earthy, they are therefore inherently Poetic. To depict in compelling and appropriate language a train moving across the prairie is one thing; it is another and a considerably less interesting matter to assert that because it is a train on the midwestern American prairie, and because the language is avowedly vernacular, the joint appearance within a poem constitutes the poetry. On the contrary the instant that the tension between language and object is slackened, what is produced is not poetry but rhetoric.

This is what begins happening to Sandburg as poet very early in his career: following the *Chicago Poems* his poetry shows an increasing tendency thereafter in almost a kind of geometric progression, to substitute rhetoric about experience for evocation of his experience. Sandburg began to believe his press notices. He was now the Poet of Mid-America, and thenceforward he sought to live up to the title by cataloguing the everyday scene in the Midwest. His poetry had been likened to Walt Whitman's; now he proceeded to imitate the least attractive aspects of Whitman's verse, producing only hot air and chaff. . . .

Those who chronicle and interpret American letters are bound ultimately to rediscover for themselves the excellence of Carl Sandburg. When that happens, the fine poet and masterful biographer will at last reemerge from the dumps. There have been other poets who have written and spoken silly things—things far sillier and sometimes considerably more sinister than ever he wrote or spoke—and who have woven a public image of specious rhetoric and role-playing about their reputations, and yet been remembered finally because at their best they wrote well. Perhaps the centenary of Sandburg's birth, in 1978, will be made the occasion for his restoration. Very likely, however, it will take a little longer. But the time will come.

Louis D. Rubin, Jr. SwR. Winter, 1977, pp. 182–<br>83, 185–86, 189

Nobody in America could have written [the poems in *The People, Yes*] but Carl Sandburg. They have the thumbprint of his personality, his ear for a good yarn, his sense of the revealing detail, his empathy with folk wisdom, his unique ability to transform the raw materials of common speech into a lyricism with a swing and rhythm recognizably his own. Other poets may from time to time touch on his materials, but their touch is inevitably different from Sandburg's. . . . But each of these contemporaries of Sandburg's would have made a poetry quite different from his. Yeats or Stevens or Frost would assuredly have used regular meters, formal stanzas, rhymes. The free verse of Williams or Pound has an entirely different specific gravity compared to Sandburg's. These are matters of style—but as is ever the case with style, the differences are not merely on the surface. . . .

Much of his work is flawed, but in at least two periods of his long career he achieved a democratic art that lasts. Sandburg's best poems still speak of lives of people in small towns, in city ghettoes, and of the energy and broken patterns of industrial life with the force, the clarity, and the pleasure that first was found in them. And the poetic vision in *The People, Yes* is felt, not in the invention of a new language or a novel presentation for poetry, but in the poet's faith that "the bookless people" could, in their adversity, provide a thesaurus of idioms commensurate with their strength to endure and their will to survive.

Like the men who broke the plains in Illinois, Carl Sandburg was a pioneer. His vision of life was neither tragic nor cheery, but inclusive of defeat, of doubt, of despair even; these conditions he found life to transcend by its own resilience. He was deeply in the American grain in his pragmatism, his hopefulness. He once said, "The past is a bucket of ashes." He wrote of the present he knew. Now that that present and his work have become parts of our past, we can look back at Sandburg's best poems with gratitude for their capturing a portion of the reality of his time. We can thank Sandburg, too, for enlarging the possibilities of subject and language for other poets who came in our century.

Daniel Hoffman. GaR. Summer, 1978, pp. 392,<br>406

Sandburg certainly stands wide of the major thrusts of both the writing and criticism of poetry in our time. Many of the critical terms which condescend to him are indubitably right in their import. At the same time, I think it fair to suggest that their import is less than adequate to Sandburg's whole poetic achievement. He was engaged in the same pursuit of the native which occupied his two Chicago contemporaries [Edgar Lee Masters and Vachel Lindsay], but . . . unlike them he located a poetically constructive imagination of the land in and for which he wrote. His voice gains authenticity when it is considered across its breadth of utterance, and I would find it difficult to make this claim for either Masters or Lindsay. Unlike the latter, his is only occasionally the effort at poetic beatification, and unlike the former he is largely guiltless of ingrown maundering. Instead, . . . though Sandburg shared a certain tentativeness and openness with his contemporaries, he in fact fashioned and for the most part held fast to a close and living sense of the native, one congruent, finally, with his land's own aspect.

What emerges from the whole poetry, in this view, is a wholeness of perception, one rooted in a consistent feel for a land conditioned by a problematic history and filling a landscape difficult to redeem by transcendental gesture. His scene is peopled with the kind of minor movers and doers who in fact have so largely occupied it, and who have little choice but to take their character from the land's own spatial and temporal indeterminateness. The people and their work, or the poet's perception of the land itself, occasionally prompted him to a sort of overblownness, a raising of cities, the land, or the people to improbably conceived heights, . . . but such rhetoric, sharing something with Lindsay's or Masters' distention, is more occasional than pervasive. . . .

And such indifference of passage transfers from Sandburg's sense of time to his sense of space also. His landscape is no more a deliverer than his history. At such formative points as the perception of time and space, thus, he is the poet of a tolerable but clear disenchantment.

Bernard Duffey. CentR. Summer, 1979, pp.<br>295–97

## SARTON, MAY (1912–    )

Sarton's work is filled with the longing to touch someone else, and the simultaneous distaste for the unsatisfactory nature of human relations. Art becomes her substitute for human experience, a way of talking about life, not living it. Even art is "ultimately" unsatisfactory. Not only do the critics fail to applaud one enough, or at the right time, or for the right reasons, but for the sterile, lonely, childless woman, the work of art itself is only a poor substitute. The childless woman, and particularly the homosexual woman, does not realize that children, like poems, are never what one thought they would be when one created them. . . .

Much of Sarton's work is conceived with the journey as a metaphor for life, and it is a mark of Sarton's new maturity that she faults the journey contained in *Crucial Conversations.* . . .

For most of her central characters, the pain of love, the price, is not worth the joy. As a result, it is hard to care what happens to her characters. All of them have a bloodless quality. They must choose between head and heart, but their heads are not screwed on very straight and their hearts seem shriveled. Sarton's women are like so many "modern" women—too easily distracted yet with just enough talent to make them fretful and dissatisfied with themselves and their lives with others. . . . Too concerned with the function of her art for herself, she never asks what the function of her art is for the reader. Sarton's journals, poems, and novels all suffer from this sense of finding one's own center, but never communicating "these gifts" to her audience. If art is her surrogate lover, it betrays, as does the lover, because of the excess of her great expectations. That excess is directly connected to her unwillingness or inability to be "engaged" with her characters, or to have them "engaged" with one another.

We close her books with a sense of promise undelivered. Despite the fact that Sarton herself is not enamored of the novel, *Crucial Conversations* is a step forward, though only a step. The lives of Reed, Poppy, and Philip, or, more accurately, their conversations about their lives, may mark the beginning of a new stage in Sarton's development, where she no longer mistakes the signposts for the journey, and moves forward in her explorations of and commitment to human relationships.

Nancy Yanes Hoffman. SWR. Summer, 1977, pp.<br>259, 263, 266–67

Ostensibly a novel about dying, *A Reckoning* is actually about coming to terms with one's own life. May Sarton, a prolific writer of poetry, memoirs, and fiction, has published over 30 books in the last four decades. *A Reckoning* is her 16th novel and like much of her previous work, it reflects the inner life and passion of a woman, the private life revealed in all its intensity.

The heroine is a 60-year-old widow, Laura Spelman, who is told abruptly on page one that she has inoperable lung cancer. In this moment of crisis, Laura experiences a sudden clarity of vision: unafraid of death, but not of dying, she wants to "do it well" her own way. Laura faces death gracefully but her impassioned plea is less for dying well than for living honestly. . . .

Drawing deeper into an inner world of illness and reminiscence, Laura willingly "lets go her identity as a person in the world" and becomes "a listener to music, a watcher of light on the walls." Miss Sarton handles this transition well; it allows her to see the world from only Laura's perspective. This is Miss Sarton more as poet than as novelist, a single voice she is obviously most comfortable with. . . .

Cancer and homosexuality are, admittedly, difficult subjects to write well about; until recently, they were, for different reasons, unmention-able as well. But this novel does not deal effectively with either; it is marred by Miss Sarton's style, which tends toward the ready cliché and occa-sionally teeters on the edge of sentimentality. Miss Sarton is best at evok-ing the private sensibility of one person. But in *A Reckoning*, where sepa-rate voices and the fabric of other lives are necessary to create a world outside the main character, this kind of interior singularity approaches solipsism.

Lore Dickstein. *NYT*. Nov. 12, 1978, p. 14

Sarton confronts . . . the inhumanity of American society toward the elderly and imagines the old as embattled, giving up their lives at the same time as they are fighting for them. The ideal of graceful aging yields to guerrilla warfare. In *As We Are Now*, Sarton's most powerful novel, a frail, single woman in her seventies struggles against the repressive struc-ture of the nursing home and asserts the value of the total human being over the total institution. . . .

Sarton's portrayal of old age is a welcome departure from the West-ern literary tradition of gerontophobia—fear of aging and disgust for the elderly—particularly since over the centuries the most vicious satire of the elderly has been leveled at female characters. From Sarton's first novel *The Single Hound* (1938), whose heroine is an elderly Belgian poet, to *Kinds of Love* (1970), a passionate encomium to old age, her literary world has been populated with ideal portraits of aging characters and allu-sions to elderly persons—especially women, and often single women—whom she admires. Aging with grace and dignity has been a persistent, even obsessive theme in her work. . . .

The new complexity of Sarton's vision of old age is reflected in the quality of her writing. *As We Are Now* has a hardness to it that is lacking in her previous fiction, which is basically dominated by aphorism, not power or drama. . . . And Sarton has carried this new understanding of the tragedies of old age into her writing since then. As we have seen, Sarton's vision of old age in her earlier work is unrelievedly romantic. But her recent writing is more cautious and more cognizant of the real physical and mental disabilities of old age in general and of the vulnerability of elderly women in particular.

> Kathleen Woodward. In *Gender and Literary Voice*, ed. Janet Todd (Holmes and Meier, 1980), pp. 109, 124

Seldom in our time has a novelist so consistently and courageously defended human freedom against the historic patterns of violence and degradation as has May Sarton. Hardly a form of violence, from physical to psychological, escapes her concern. Stalinism, Communism, Fascism, racism, Nazi-ism, censorship, conscription, laws denying freedom to homosexuals, intellectuals, women, loom large in her work. Since she knows only too well that the power of the sword and the war machine have failed to achieve the freedoms for which each war was presumably fought, she uses the power of her pen to make a series of convincing arguments for the rights of individuals against repressive institutions and laws which deny human freedom. Hers is a rage for justice, for political and social change, and for international peace.

Sarton is concerned lest in failing to challenge the history of past and present tyrannies we may be condemned to repeat them on an ever more deadly scale in a not too distant future. Political, social, and psychological violence symbolize the forces of darkness against which her heroes and heroines test their moral fibre. By their resistance, passive as it is at times, their personal acts of refusal to serve, like civil disobedience itself, is the price conscience pays for its victory in seeming defeat.

> Mary Bryan. In *May Sarton: Woman and Poet*, ed. Constance Hunting (National Poetry Foundation, 1982), p. 133

May Sarton is a secular writer, but she draws freely upon a Christian tradition which has long contemplated the psychology of spiritual growth, the power to accept or to enact a change in one's life for one's inherent moral betterment. In both the Christian tradition and May Sarton's novels, this self-examination essential for growth can never occur productively in an intellectual vacuum of self-adoration but only against an awareness of genuine virtue. Using the language of scripture and liturgy, Sarton attempts to identify that indefinable and indispensable quality of virtue within the particular experiences of the characters in her novels, and presses new meanings both from the traditional emblems of language and from the experiences themselves.

Sarton finds elements of virtue in nature imagery, particularly in her close study of the plants and birds of New England. She treats these natural objects with observant realism, introducing religious terminology only as a common body of images to expose the mind's pondering these things. In *Kinds of Love* (1970) Jane Tuttle receives a dead owl as a love offering from the troubled Nick Comstock: she examines the bird first scientifically, using a reference book to distinguish the Barred Owl from a Great Gray, then mythically—"'Athene's bird,' Jane murmured. 'You can see why the owl has haunted men'"—and at last religiously—"She laid a hand gently on the incredible softness of the head, as if to bless it." Repeatedly Sarton's characters discover virtue in natural objects by contemplating them with this wholly attentive, admiring respect for the things as they are. . . .

May Sarton also redefines the traditional Christian role of the ministry in her novels of the seventies. Not ordination but response to human need determines a man's role as a minister—or more often, a woman's role. The author makes grave demands of her clergy; they are not mere counselors or administrators but divine comforters, saviors, agents of God. In *As We Are Now* Caro Spenser, left to die in a rest home, imagines a temporary housekeeper, Anna Close, as a "heavenly nurse [who has] come to be with me." Anna comes when Caro is most desperate for the palpable reassurance of a physical human presence. . . .

Although all of Ms. Sarton's seventies' novels are studies of this effort toward intellectual and moral growth, *Crucial Conversations* is the most bitter in its denunciation of society as a stifler of spiritual development. . . .

Christian humility, particularly the tradition of womanly tact, gains a new definition through May Sarton's novels. As the author perceives a widening gap between Christian virtue and public morality, she begins to define anger as a necessary part of virtuous behavior. More and more insistently as these novels develop through the seventies their author demands that her characters turn their moral growth into decisive actions. The self-losing, self-discovering surrender to natural forces and to human affection in *Kinds of Love* (1970) turns to a rebellious insistence on one's own moral integrity by *Crucial Conversations* (1975). Sarton does not use the language of scripture and liturgy as a private code or as a general symbol for goodness but as a means to explore self-conscious psychological experience. She always tests the language in a dramatic situation. This is her art: her novels are not treatises on morals or abstract studies of virtue but a vital working out of the consequences of personal moral decisions in the conscious inquiring minds of their characters.

Gayle Gaskill. In *May Sarton: Woman and Poet*,
ed. Constance Hunting (National Poetry
Foundation, 1982), pp. 157, 159, 162–63

## SCHWARTZ, DELMORE (1913–1966)

Whatever its particular failings, *In Dreams Begin Responsibilities* articulated the pervasive disillusion of that era in a voice charged with intellectual passion and self-conscious irony. Delmore's poems were dramatic utterances, full of the vivid inflections he had grown up hearing. Irving Howe's description of his prose could apply to his early verse as well: "the sing-song, slightly pompous intonations of Jewish immigrants educated in night-schools, the self-conscious affectionate mockery of that speech by American born sons, its abstraction into the jargon of city intellectuals, and finally the whole body of this language flattened into a prose of uneasiness, an anti-rhetoric." In the stories Delmore was starting to publish, these echoes would be more deliberate than in his poetry, but they were unmistakable all the same. And while "the discussion of the Jewish problem" may have been muted, as he insisted to [James] Laughlin, it was implicit in the poems' very tone. Where Jewish writers like Clifford Odets, Daniel Fuchs, and Henry Roth had confronted their experience directly, Delmore claimed as his imaginative province the cosmopolitan world of letters purveyed in the pages of *Partisan Review*. Faintly Marxist, imbued with a sense of history's fatal flaws in the wake of the Munich Pact and on the verge of World War II. Delmore was, Howe suggests, "the poet of the historical moment quite as Auden was in England." It was as if the self-constituted intelligentsia with which he had allied himself required a spokesman to dramatize its cultural dilemmas.

Delmore had a heroic conception of the poet, and shamelessly identified himself with what he took to be the sensibility of Modernism, calling on those precursors of modern consciousness, Marx and Freud, to guide him in the difficult quest of a "tradition of the new" (to use Harold Rosenberg's fine phrase). . . .

It was no doubt [a] Byronic element in his character, combined with the subtle tonalities of a wry Jewish ironist, that made his poetry so attractive to a generation whose intellectual style had been appropriated from

Europe. When *In Dreams* appeared, Robert Lowell, John Berryman, and Randall Jarrell had not yet published a line. It was Delmore's lot to take up where his predecessors had left off and define the temper of that uncertain era. No one was more surprised than he when his labors were heralded as the flowering of a new generation.

James Atlas. *Delmore Schwartz: The Life of an
American Poet* (Farrar, Straus & Giroux, 1977),
pp. 140–41

The . . . line ["while History is unforgiven"] is the key to understanding the themes of Delmore's work . . . , his lyric evocations of solitude, of great imaginative masters, of obsession with being caught in a twilight world between past, present, and future. He is constantly dissolving the distinction between universal and personal history. Shadowy philosophers (Plato, Socrates, Marx, Freud, James, Whitehead, Aristotle) are evoked throughout his work to bear witness to events and moods that in themselves appear mysterious, impulsive, melancholy, retrospective. They are appealed to, in effect, to impose intellectual order on a patchwork and exhausted self that yet has immortal longings for beauty, tenderness, grace, and power. Yet these longings too often appear to disguise a brutish, angry, and resentful self. . . .

Delmore's poetry consciously works with the themes of personal history set against the stream of universal history that he sees as deterministic. As a literary critic, he chooses his subjects and makes his emphasis in a similar direction. Part of this emphasis takes the form in the general essays of elucidating the phenomenon of isolation in modern poetry. Much could be said negatively about Delmore's elaboration of commonplace ideas. Yet the very fact that he takes pains to remind his readers of what they may take for granted is a sign of the importance the issues had for him. Modernism, in fact, is the condition which Delmore thought he must define and redefine, no matter if the subject be meter or metaphor or the themes typical of the pre-Romantic or post-Romantic imaginations. . . .

He argues with great precision and a sense of the importance of the commonplace, for instance, that from the "isolation of poetic sensibility the obscurity of modern poetry also arises.". . .

[Schwartz made a] conscious effort . . . as a critic to be generous to both the ideas and the particular forms that poets and poems took. He was faithful to his sense of history and to the infinite ways poets took in interacting with history. At the same time that he succeeded so admirably in the primary task of the critic to be a good elucidator and a generous spirit, he also succeeded in commenting indirectly on his own dilemmas as a poetic man. He saw his fellow artists as he saw himself—trying to find a language faithful to the particular torments of our time that his own life so tragically embodied.

David Zucker. *IowaR*. Fall, 1977, pp. 98, 101–3

Now that he is dead, the legend of the *poète maudit*—the doomed and sacrificial poet—has already claimed him. And before we submit to the distortions that current sentimentalities are likely to inject into this kind of legend, we had better attempt a cooler glimpse at the work he has left. It may, surprisingly enough, provide some very strong imperatives to revise our stock notions of the alienation of poetry and the poet today.

Delmore had a beautiful lyrical talent, and so long as he continued to write anything at all, this gift never left him altogether. It's too early to say what in our period, if anything, will be lasting; but my own judgment, perhaps partial, is that some of his lyrics will survive. But the great triumphs of modern poetry were nearly all in the lyric, and he wanted to help restore verse as a narrative medium. He admired Hardy's *Dynasts*, for example, before it became fashionable among some academic critical circles. But where Hardy had dealt with the fate of nations and empires, and the broad sweep of history, Delmore chose a very personal subject matter as the material for his own major narrative effort.

This work is *Genesis*, and the abstract design of it does not look too unpromising. It tells the story of the growing up of a Jewish boy (Delmore himself), of how his forebears came to this country, the strife of the parents and how it is inflicted as a trauma upon the boy. The narrative would be carried by the prose, but a rather cadenced and rhythmic prose that wouldn't be too glaring a contrast to its verse accompaniment. The latter would take the form of a poetic comment and explication of the narrative in the manner of a Greek chorus. Not bad as an idea, though the material is conventional: another version of the archetypal Making of an American. But the execution of the design fails badly. . . .

In fiction, he produced two stories that stand out amid all the writing of this kind in his period; and considering the vast volume of stories written during our time, this is no small accomplishment. One is the near-perfect story, "In Dreams Begin Responsibilities," which—significantly enough—uses a kind of surrogate lyrical form to express his inveterate family material. The other story, however, shows even more strikingly the specific powers of the fiction writer in bringing into compact focus a wealth of social and human observation. The story is "America! America!" and it says more in its few pages about the saga of the Jewish lower-middle class in American life than most of the genre novels we have had on this theme. . . .

For literary criticism he had great brilliance and potential, and I believe, had he given himself to it, would have become one of the foremost critics of our time. His early pieces give very alert and sensitive readings of Hardy, Auden, Tate, and others. He was starting from Eliot as a base, but his young man's mind was swarming with ideas, and he was working toward a position and point of view of his own. But the patience and concentration needed for this were denied him—for a number of reasons, partly because his energies were dispersed into other writing, principally perhaps because of his own psychological disturbances. . . .

When you add it all up, what have you? Certainly, not something at all negligible. To have written anything, however fragmentary, which stands out among the productions of one's time, and which may even lay some claim to permanence, is a higher achievement than to turn out a body of work fully formed but glittering only for the moment. But just as certainly, his achievement is a failure—and a failure all the more in relation to the power of the original gifts. For Delmore was not merely one of the many talented persons who go astray; nowadays talented people swarm all over the literary landscape; he happened to have major gifts, and in saying this, I weigh my words. And in the light of those gifts we have to judge his literary career as a human failure. It is that human failure that currently invokes the facile image of the *poète maudit*—the poet exiled and accursed by the tribe.

William Barrett. *The Truants: Adventures among the Intellectuals* (Doubleday, 1982), pp. 233–36

## SEXTON, ANNE (1928–1974)

If, as "The Double Image" and many of her early poems reveal, the cause of Sexton's madness and its accompanying desire for death has been her woman's situation, experience, identity, it is also true that the affirmation of life at which she arrives through the acts of her poems is founded in her womanhood. "Live," the final poem in her third book, *Live or Die*, helps her to locate the source of and reason for life in woman's situation, experience, identity. . . .

Being a poet causes Anne Sexton to understand herself as possessor of "the excitable gift," because the act of poetry unites understanding with experience; its vision is insight. Though her poetry begins as therapy for her personal salvation, because it is a public act it reaches out to others. Yet it is always rooted in her personal self, her private life, as is the sun. It does not, like much of the "confessional" poetry of men, abstract or generalize upon its own experiences, either explicitly or implicitly; nevertheless, it communicates to others and offers its gift. . . .

Sexton . . . tries to explain how this gift works. Commenting upon her explorations of self, of "that narrow diary of my mind," she finds their purpose to have been, not beauty, but "a certain sense of order there." If she had tried "to give [him] something else,/something outside of myself," he would not then know "that the worst of anyone/can be, finally,/an accident of hope." Generalizing, in other words, destroys the very meaning sought.

Suzanne Juhasz. *Naked and Fiery Forms: Modern
American Poetry by Women, A New Tradition*
(Octagon Books, 1976), pp. 124–25

To mourn the woman by telling less than the truth about the poet is to perform no service. She was, let it be said, a flawed poet who became more deeply flawed, as she made of her worst tricks a trade. I did not follow her career attentively. In a life filled with books to read and things to do, one may be excused for giving second place to a poetry that dwells irritably on the squalor of the everyday, without abatement or relief. Did no one acquaint this poet with [Matthew] Arnold's famous words?—that there are "situations, from the representation of which, though accurate, no poetical enjoyment can be derived? They are those in which the suffering finds no vent in action; in which a continuous state of mental distress is prolonged, unrelieved by incident, hope, or resistance; in which there is everything to be endured, nothing to be done. In such situations there is inevitably something morbid, in the description of them something monotonous. When they occur in actual life, they are painful, not tragic; the representation of them in poetry is painful also." The amused or wry tone of some of her poems was sheer ballast. She was sustained by a long argument, and a *private* one, which might well have been carried on in prose or in a diary, about whether life was worth its cost in suffering.

She decided not. And in her last book, together with much ballast, there is an evil spirit brooding, and something more hateful than bitterness. It is hatred. A lover is addressed as "Mr. Panzer-Man." He is the Nazi, she the Jew. Sylvia Plath had used the same analogy, in her celebrated attractive-repulsive poem, "Daddy." How far does it hold? Do fathers and lovers seek to exterminate women who are poets, is there a plan to wipe them out, are they hauled from their beds and beaten and killed? No, it is not sincere. Perhaps the subject ought to be dropped: it is too disgusting. Confessional poetry, we must see, has come to us historically in two kinds. There is the terrible secret (Baudelaire) and there is the beautiful secret (Wordsworth). The newer confessional poets touched neither of these bases. "I am desperate," they were saying. "Others are responsible. The world has done this to me. Look!" *Life Studies* inaugurated the reign of a personal and debased mode of the poetry of grievances; the author of that book [Robert Lowell] brought a few of his students with him; now they are gone, and his own poetry has grown indistinguishable from theirs.

David Bromwich. *Poetry*. Dec., 1976, pp. 170–71

Of all the confessional poets, none has had quite Sexton's "courage to make a clean breast of it." Nor has any displayed quite her brilliance, her verve, her headlong metaphoric leaps. As with any body of work, some of the later poems display only ragged, intermittent control, as compared to "The Double Image," "The Operation," and "Some Foreign Letters," to choose three arbitrary examples. The later work takes more chances, crosses more boundaries between the rational and the surreal; and time after time it evokes in the reader that sought-after shiver of recognition.

Women poets in particular owe a debt to Anne Sexton, who broke new ground, shattered taboos, and endured a barrage of attacks along the way because of the flamboyance of her subject matter, which, twenty years later, seems far less daring. She wrote openly about menstruation, abortion, masturbation, incest, adultery, and drug addiction at a time when the proprieties embraced none of these as proper topics for poetry. Today, the remonstrances seem almost quaint. Anne delineated the problematic position of women—the neurotic reality of the time—though she was not able to cope in her own life with the personal trouble it created. If it is true that she attracted the worshipful attention of a cult group pruriently interested in her suicidal impulses, her psychotic breakdowns, her frequent hospitalizations, it must equally be acknowledged that her very frankness succored many who clung to her poems as to the Holy Grail. Time will sort out the dross among these poems and burnish the gold. Anne Sexton has earned her place in the canon.

Maxine Kumin. Introduction to *Complete Poems of Anne Sexton*, ed. Maxine Kumin (Houghton Mifflin, 1981), p. xxxiv

Her poems tend, on the whole, to begin well, to repeat themselves, to sag in the middle, and to tail off. She had an instinct for reiteration; she wanted to say something five times instead of once. Her favorite figure of speech is anaphora, where many lines begin with the same phrase, a figure which causes, more often than not, diffuseness and spreading of effect rather than concentration of intensity. . . .

Sexton's poems read better as a diary than as poems. They then seem a rather slap-dash journal stuck with brilliant phrases. Even the most formally arranged poems have, underneath their formal structure, no real or actual structure: they run on, they chatter, they moan, they repeat themselves, they deliquesce. Or, conversely (as in the famous "Her Kind"), they stop without any particular reason—they could have been shorter, they could have been longer. If, as A. R. Ammons once said, a poem begins in contingency and ends in necessity, the trouble with Sexton's poems is that they lack that necessity—the conviction that they were meant to be just as they are, with just these words and no others, extending to just this length and no other, with each part pulling its weight. [Emily] Dickinson and [Elizabeth] Bishop often make us feel that necessity; Edna St. Vincent Millay—like Sexton a facile and prolific writer—does not. . . .

As Sexton passes into the anthologies, the more obviously "feminist" poems will no doubt be chosen, and there is no reason not to represent them. . . . But the evil eye (as Sexton put it) should be in the anthologies too. This "evil," unsympathetic, flat, malicious, gleeful, noticing eye is neither male nor female, but it is Sexton's most distinguishing characteristic. . . .

Sexton's chief flair [was] a knack for the flat, two-dimensional cartoon. Some of that shrewd caricature should make its way into the anthologies too.

Helen Vendler. NR. Nov. 11, 1981, pp. 34–36

## SHAPIRO, KARL (1913–    )

At 63, Shapiro has now published a new collection of poems, *Adult Bookstore*, in which he returns to the idiom and themes of earlier poems. The diction and rhythm are plainer and smoother, the verse possesses that simplicity called for in the *Essay on Rime* but missing in much of the subsequent work. Here at last is a volume worthy of that auspicious beginning, here is the mature poet in full control of his craft and his heart.

Shapiro puts aside his dreams of being the reformer of modern poetry and modestly sets out his own claim to speak in his own voice. In "My Father's Funeral," he contrasts his memories of his father with those of Dylan Thomas, Sylvia Plath and Arthur Miller. . . .

The poet does not spare himself in this realistic look around him. In "My Fame's Not Feeling Well," he takes an objective view of the reputation that has disappointed the critics. He does so with humor and in a straightforward style. Only a balanced man could write so balanced a poem. . . .

The title poem "Adult Bookstore" captures the mad world of pornography in a few spare sentences: "Every thing is sanitary, wrapped in cellophane." The poem ends with a quotation from Shakespeare: "The expense of spirit in a waste of shame/Is sold forever to the single stag/Who takes it home in a brown paper bag." The ironic omission of the reference to "lust in action" emphasizes how even our vices have been sterilized today. "Girls Working in Banks" offers the same idea in another context.

The final section of this book includes poems on Japan, translations of Catullus and a retelling of the myth of Philomela. The story loses none of its original horror and goriness in Shapiro's version, but such exercises are not what this poet will be remembered for. His mirror of society in wartime and in postwar America has been a unique contribution, and his individual voice speaking for the disenchantment and the dreams of his generation has been a generous gift to poetry as a source of human awareness. Now that he has hit his stride, we can look to more poems that reflect the many faces of man.

James Finn Cotter. Am. Nov. 20, 1976, p. 356

Shapiro succeeds where other poets fail (Robert Lowell is the most obvious example) in making history a part of his poems, showing the reader an event, a period, a world that is on the verge of disappearing, even as it begins to engage our attention. He is a surprisingly naturalistic writer (Delmore Schwartz once referred to Shapiro's "inexhaustible power of observation"), whose work provides one of the most accurate portraits we have of America from the late Thirties until the early Sixties. His poems tell us what it was like to be alive during those decades, just as his essays—written "with gusto and sassiness, with the delight of an amateur filling in," as he says—rage against the indignities and excesses of those years. . . .

What older contemporary poet, besides Theodore Roethke, has written so many necessary poems? Certainly not Lowell, John Berryman, Randall Jarrell, or a host of other writers often regarded as more "important" than Shapiro, people who, in spite of their achievements, have given few poems to the common heritage of American literature. Who, other than he, has written this many poems known and loved by an audience beyond the confines of academic courses and writers' workshops? . . . It may sound strange to speak of Karl Shapiro as a "neglected" writer. But in a peculiar way, he is. While critics and scholars rush to sort out the confused lines and tangled lives of confessional or suicidal poets his age and younger, in a torrent of scholarly articles, dissertations, and books, Shapiro remains persistently unstudied. . . . One obvious answer to the question about the lack of extended discussion of such an important writer is that his reputation rests on more solid ground than that rarified turf in the groves of academe. By the popularity of his books . . . [and] the authority of his essays, he continues to enjoy that happy condition of being read for pleasure rather than merely studied.

Long known for his biting wit and occasionally irascible temper, he may simply have scared away any commentators for whom poetry is merely academic.

By virtue of his range of subject matter and his skill, Karl Shapiro is our greatest living poet; and *Collected Poems* is, quite simply, the latest and best evidence for saying so.

Michael True. Com. Nov. 10, 1978, p. 725

Karl Shapiro is basically a loner whose poetry is related . . . to several movements and tendencies in modern poetry. The specific movements, quite well-defined in literary history, are the Fugitives of the early 1920s and the Beat Generation of the 1950s. The general "tendencies" are the Confessional disposition of many poets of the 1960s, and the Romantic impulse that has been with American poetry since the mid-nineteenth century. These are . . . "qualified influences." No other term is really possible. . . .

Shapiro's habit of managing his poetry in a manner that parallels existing movements, while somehow maintaining individuality, independence, and distance, is characteristic of his relationship with the so-called Beat Generation of Allen Ginsberg, Gregory Corso, Lawrence Ferlinghetti, Michael McClure, Gary Snyder, and Brother Antoninus. Jack Kerouac, the novelist, was also a member of this group. Shapiro's defiantly titled *Poems of a Jew* (1956) and *Defense of Ignorance* (1960) were published when the Beat Generation was at its height (1952–1960). . . .

Unlike the Fugitives and the Beats, the "Confessionals" are not, in a strict sense, a school or movement of poetry. Such inclinations in Shapiro, like everything else, also predate the beginnings of the so-called "Confessional school" in 1959–60, with the publication of Robert Lowell's *Life Studies*, Anne Sexton's *To Bedlam and Part Way Back*, and Sylvia Plath's *Colossus*. . . .

Shapiro's poetry partakes of the mentality of the Beats and the Confessionals (here identified with the academics), but with one paradoxical difference: his poetry ultimately acknowledges no "Innocence," and correspondingly confesses no "Guilt." From these qualities it derives an often stunning power, but by contrast and unfortunately, also the not-uncommon revulsion of so many readers—the price the author must pay for this so-called "honesty."

Joseph Reino. Karl Shapiro (Twayne, 1981), pp.<br>157, 160–63

# SHEPARD, SAM (1943–    )

Widely divergent in quality, all his plays reveal his affinity for aspects of popular culture. Whereas the Ridiculous playwrights capitalize on sophisticated trivialization of pop art, Shepard smiles gently at its stereotypes. His first play, *Cowboys*, is lost, but its very title announces his affection. In his first surviving play, *Rock Garden*, the three comic C's blend; the dialogue is easy and colloquial, the self-conscious positions are redolent of camp, and the characters talk past each other cruelly. Unlike Chekhov's plays, where communication can occur in the interstices between speech, or Pinter's, where dialogue can deliberately veil communication, Shepard's competing monologues delineate the isolation of each character. This technique becomes deft in the *Five Plays*, each one pivoting on a single event: Joy gets a job in *Chicago*; a plane signals to picnickers and then crashes in *Icarus's Mother*: a bookcase for the titular *Fourteen Hundred Thousand* books is begun and then dismantled; crab lice attack husband and then wife in *Red Cross*; Floyd needs a new hit song in *Melodrama Play*. There is much rhythm but little reason to these exploratory sallies. . . .

Shepard's extraordinarily inventive comic range needs the scope of longer plays. *The Unseen Hand* and *Mad Dog Blues*, with their different language blends and lonely agglomerations, outshine the briefer plays in their respective volumes. Preceding them was *La Turista*, a metaphysical farce before Shepard had heard of Ionesco. In later full-length plays Shepard again wields several kinds of colloquialism, cruelties born of isolation, and anachronistic legends that typify camp.

Ruby Cohn. In *Comic Relief: Humor in
Contemporary American Literature*, ed. Sarah
Blacher Cohen (Univ. of Illinois Pr., 1978), pp.
299, 301

*True West* seems to be Shepard's most realistic work to date; the dialogue is natural and colloquial; the characters, with the exception of Mom, psychologically motivated; the action, linear and casual. Despite certain structural strains, the play avoids the obvious surrealistic dislocations common in Shepard's earlier work, while his distinctive aria-like monologues are likewise virtually absent. Even the setting of *True West* seems intentionally mundane. . . . In short, it is as if Shepard were stressing the reality of his play in the same way that the magazine *True West* used to certify on its cover that the tales contained inside were "non-fiction.". . .

It is typical of Shepard to mix the real and the surreal in his work.

Unlike *The Curse of the Starving Class*, however, a play which it resembles in several ways, *True West* does not oscillate between fantasy and reality. Rather, the two levels co-exist; the one seems to displace the other even while the basic realistic framework of the play remains, more or less, intact. In other words, objective and subjective realities are not juxtaposed, they are superimposed; the "real" world is not simply challenged or questioned by "alternative levels of consciousness," it is suffused by them. Shepard attempted this technique less successfully or subtly in both *Suicide in B$^b$* and *Buried Child*. As a result, the reality of the play begins to vibrate with subjective energy and meaning; objects become symbols; characters, archetypes; actions, allegories. . . .

Despite its objective reality, and its universal ambiguities and implications, *True West* may, in fact, be Shepard's most subjective, most personal play to date. Like the conflict at its core, the play seems locked in battle with itself: essentially an autodidactic writer, Shepard nevertheless imposes a strict, self-conscious structure on his work; again and again, unaccountably, he tries to pin down his symbols; when he does, they die. And yet the play itself continually rebels, breaks free, comes back to life.

William Kleb. Theater. Fall/Winter, 1980, pp.<br>68, 71

Shepard's plays can be divided roughly into three categories. First were the early plays, mostly one-acts, from 1963 to the mid-seventies: They are abstract collages, consisting of lyrical monologues, stunning imagery, and a sense of paranoid despair. The second group deal with visionaries, who pursue their emotional identity and spiritual freedom, even if it results in isolation and betrayal. Finally, there are Shepard's two great "family plays," *Curse of the Starving Class* and *Buried Child*, in which the hero, *after* his visionary quest, attempts to discover if his new-found knowledge can redeem his past—and that of his country.

The difficulty most theatergoers had with the first group was that the plays didn't seem to be "about" anything, lacking easily identifiable characters and plots. But once one realized these plays were about pure emotional, psychological, or spiritual states—presented directly to the audience, rather than packaged in "character" and "story"—they became as lucid as dreams. . . .

The second group of Shepard plays, which includes *Melodrama Play*, *Tooth of Crime*, *Suicide in B Flat*, and *Angel City*, concern the artist as visionary. One of the popularized figures of this media century—from Franz Kafka to Woody Allen—has been the artist who publicly exposes his deepest feelings and conceals his private life.

Shepard's genius has been to see in this theme a metaphor for contemporary life, to transform what could easily become an artist's self-pity into an exploration of the conflict between the integrity of self and the compromises of community.

Again and again in Shepard's plays, the characters are shamans—cowboys, criminals, rock stars, screenwriters—or mythic American figures such as Paul Bunyan or Mae West who embark on a search for emotional freedom. Sometimes they reach a momentary ecstasy of self-fulfillment, but more often they are forced to surrender their private vision to the service of public commerce. They are spiritually kidnapped, their gifts corrupted, dreams merchandised, souls poisoned. . . .

In the last few years, the Shepard hero—who had frequently referred to himself as an "escape artist"—has begun to realize that his quest eventually and inevitably leads him back to the family. The monumental power of *Curse of the Starving Class*, the finest "family play" since *Long Day's Journey*, comes from Shepard's recognition that the hero has no choice but to confront his past, to accept his blood and transcend it.

Ross Wetzsteon. *NYM*. Nov. 24, 1980, pp. 22–23, 25

Shepard's protagonists only indirectly express an interest in the figures of historical time; rather than shape history and discover the names of their desires, they go after adventure, self-discovery and the authentic forms of play. Shepard's theatre incarnates the Cowboy of Interior Plains, the lumpen prole drifter, the shiftless suburban punk, the self-referential jazz artist, the violent and paranoid rocker, the ratiocinating detective, the off-the-wall madman. With his deeply ingrained Western sense of psychological rootlessness and space, Shepard's work is nonetheless prodded by a conflicting urge to make a home in the contemporary wilderness. Appropriately enough, Shepard himself entered the paradoxically open and enclosed space of the theatre not through the urban fastnesses of "literature" but through the ephemera of music, drugs, and the felt needs of an actor working in a decaying Eastern city during a time of intense theatrical experiment and social change. Successfully locating a place in the shattered yet still heroic American landscape, Shepard's theatre evinces a kind of passage home into the blood truths of second innocence.

In his rock plays of the early '70s—*Cowboy Mouth, Mad Dog Blues*, and *The Tooth of Crime*—Shepard approached rock as the extreme embodiment of his fascination with all theatrical forms. Rock was about much more than cheap thrills and expressionist license. In Shepard's view, America's "temporary culture" had defined and limited the terms of all performance, forcing the Self to act out the fortunes of limited identity in an atmosphere made feverish by the elusiveness of a more substantive freedom; rock offers a countering style of self-assertion, self-command, "full of fuckin' courage . . . flying in the eye of contempt," he writes in *Tooth*. In Shepard's theatre, characters who aren't clinging, paranoid or nostalgic, to some remnant of a real or imagined past attempt vivid projects of self-invention: immediate, exhibitionistic self-projections, an opening of the self to varying styles of risk, violence and escape. Angry and disappointed, seething with thwarted energy and lost patience, they become the wanderers, outlaws, gamblers and musicians— escape artists, seeking a home in the moment, where the heart lies, merging role-playing with iconoclasm, leaping into the void to find themselves on stage. These restless, liberated *personas* overlap in Shepard's imagination: it's the cowboy, Hank Williams (not Little Richard, for instance) who's the Gate Keeper to Shepard's rock 'n' roll heaven, and Bob Dylan, the self-invented Gypsy Cipher of Shepard's *Rolling Thunder Logbook*, who can vanish "like the Lone Ranger.". . . *The Tooth of Crime* . . . is one of the most extraordinary plays of the '70s, a sci-fi/primitivist vision uniting language, metaphor, action and intention at a level few American plays have achieved. Shepard begins with the assumption that rock is about violence, a sacred criminal violence with its own standards and values. *Tooth* applies the realization that if denied a living historical base, a continuity of myth, past and present, then such violence is empty, and ultimately self-destructive. Rock was the theatre in which an entire generation enacted precisely the same cultural disillusionment.

Robert Coe. In *American Dreams: The Imagination of Sam Shepard*, ed. Bonnie Marranca (Performing Arts Journal Publications, 1981), pp. 57–59

By retreating from the "carefully planned regurgitated event" and entering forcefully into the world as "play," Shepard cuts himself off from the strict social, economic, and sexual objectification that have always characterized American drama. For him drama is no longer a set of formulaic codes but rather an open field. Like the literature of Cooper, Hawthorne, Melville, Thoreau, Poe, and Whitman, Shepard's plays construct a homemade world where the building of something new is more important than the architecture of the past. In *Fourteen Hundred Thousand* it comes out in the construction of bookshelves and talk about a cabin. In *The Curse of the Starving Class* it is in the construction of an animal pen and a new door frame. The effort is something like Thoreau's retreat to Walden and to the solace of new imaginative space. In order for the world to be new, a new set of boundaries have to be struck. Like so much in early American literature, the effort in so many of Shepard's plays is to create protective environments that will insulate against the wild perils of the frontier. . . .

Going beyond the themes and conventions of Transcendentalism and Romanticism, and the telling verbal associations that link Shepard with Whitman, one final link needs to be made between Sam Shepard and 19th-century American literature. And that is his recourse to mythic impulses. On one level the reading of myth in his plays is quite classical: the agon between characters of huge proportion (*The Tooth of Crime*). On another level the reading takes a different classical bent: the grievance of son with father (shown in embryo in *The Rock Garden* and in more maturity in *The Curse of the Starving Class*). But for a writer like Shepard, imbued with a whole range of mythic preoccupations that take him as far back as folk and Indian lore, the correspondences run deeper. Shepard himself says: "Myths speak to everything at once, especially the emotions. By myths I mean a sense of mystery and not necessarily a traditional formula. A character is for me a composite of different mysteries. He's an unknown quantity." In fact, what Shepard seems to be saying is that his plays spring from the impulse to get inside this unknown quantity in order to *see* what's there. What's there, of course, is the play he is writing at any given moment. But through exercising the visual side of his imagination and sketching a scheme towards its conclusion, which in *The Tooth of Crime* took the form of Crow, a totally "lethal" and "savage" human who needed a victim, Shepard transforms the mystery into something approaching a known quantity. And yet only *just* approaching. For in no sense does Shepard seem to be writing out of some codified mythopoeic tradition but rather a naive American one that takes its savagery to heart and finds literary structures to exorcise it. As Hawthorne and Poe proved, the strategy need not be at all conscious but comes, instead, out of some deep emotional need to show fear in the face of the unknown and the unseen. In Shepard's dramatic romances and tales fear is a wilderness with no path leading out.

Like those American writers with whom I've tried to connect him, Sam Shepard takes it for granted that the mystery is insoluble and will forever leave its imprint strewn throughout the imaginative landscape of both mind and body. It is simply another feature of his complex and eccentric design.

Michael Earley. In *American Dreams: The Imagination of Sam Shepard*, ed. Bonnie Marranca (Performing Arts Journal Publications, 1981), pp. 128, 132

What is remarkable about Shepard's plays is the way they display the new raw unstable anguish and wit that marks the self seeking itself now, and that they display with such half-demented, half-lyrical force the things that oppose this quest, its exacerbated American circumstances, which

Shepard's own new raw questing sensibility has made its scene, obsession and poetry.

I believe that all Shepard's themes or motifs can be subsumed, even if loosely and with jagged projections everywhere, by this perspective. Consider the question of "roots," so stark or shadowy in his plays. To have roots is to have continuity and so a basis on which to act (a step to a step), to act in both senses of the word. Not to have roots is to risk acting on air. This is why I think the facts of Shepard's literal and cultural background are important. He couldn't have come from the East or North or at another time. In the West rootlessness is far more widespread and for many almost the condition of life. But at the same time the West, particularly California, is the place where, most acutely, visible success, gestures of self, personality, fame are means, conscious or not, of making up for or disguising the lack of roots. . . .

The very "rootlessness" of Shepard's theater, its springing so largely from a condition outside the continuity of the stage, is a source of the difficulty we have with it, as it is also a source of its dazzling disturbances. But inside his theater, within its own continuousness, a tragi-comic drama of names and selves unfolds. I think of the frantic efforts of so many of his characters to make themselves felt, often by violence (or cartoon violence—blows without injuries, bullets without deaths: dream or make-believe, something filmed), of the great strand in his work of the ego run wild, of the craving for altered states of being and the power to transcend physical or moral or psychic limitations—and the very alterations and transcendences of this kind carried out in the plays: the transformations, the splitting of characters, the masks, the roles within roles, the mingling of legendary figures with invented ones. And I think of the "turns," the numbers, the oratorios and arias, and especially the monologues or soliloquies that aren't simply contributions to the plot but outcries of characters craving to be known. . . .

Everything I've been discussing converges in *The Tooth of Crime*, which I think is Shepard's greatest achievement, the one play which is most nearly invulnerable to charges of occlusion or arbitrary procedures, the one that rests most self-containedly, that seems whole, inevitable, *ended*. It contains his chief imaginative ideas and obsessions at their highest point of eloquence and most sinewy connection to one another. It exhibits his theatrical inventiveness at its most brilliant yet most uncapricious and coherent, and it reveals most powerfully his sense of the reciprocities of art and life. A splendid violent artifact, it broods on and wrestles with the quest not simply to be known but to be known inexhaustibly, magically, cosmically: the exaltation and tragedy of fame.

Richard Gilman. Introduction to Sam Shepard,<br>
*Seven Plays* (Bantam, 1981), pp. xix–xxii

## SINGER, ISAAC BASHEVIS (1904–    )

"What can one do? How is one to live?" the narrator of *Shosha* asks, and though the setting of this novel is Warsaw of the Twenties and Thirties, before the war had given shape to the modern world, the existential dilemmas of philosophy and love behind these questions seem entirely modern. Love is so confusing that Tsutsik, the narrator, conducts affairs with five different women at once, and when he does settle down, it is with Shosha, the moronic and physically stunted sweetheart of his childhood, as if in demonstration of love's inner illogic. Matters of philosophy, which are closer to Tsutsik's heart, prove even more troublesome. He wishes he could find some universe of value and meaning in religion, wishes he could dig up out of the past some useful concept from Jewish mysticism, wishes he could salvage some significance from the old stetl. The only alternatives his friends can offer from the present are Stalin, or Trotsky, or the ideas of a cafe philosopher whose masterwork is a book called, marvelously, *Spiritual Hormones*. But none of this will do. Not unlike Isaac Bashevis Singer himself, one supposes, Tsutsik seems doomed to be a man at a spiritual loss.

All this makes for an entertaining novel, for though Singer is an earnest writer, his earnestness steps lightly, and in any case he provides plenty of amorous women and unexpected turns in Tsutsik's writing career to move things along. But entertaining or not, the novel labors under the growing shadow of Hitler, which ultimately overtakes the story and brings it to a grimly abrupt ending. There are no spiritual hormones, Singer seems to be saying. There are no solutions to existential dilemmas. There is not even a stetl to yearn for anymore, only the rootlessness of the modern world.

Paul Berman. Harper's. Sept., 1978, p. 94

Singer's ultimate reputation must rest on his short stories. Here his narrative quickness and philosophic depth show to best advantage, not marred by the structural flaws of some of the novels. "Gimpel the Fool," the title story of the first collection (translated by Saul Bellow), has already been widely anthologized and recognized as a jewel of modern letters. But perhaps the best series of stories, nearly perfect and highly distinctive Singer, fill the third volume of collected stories, *Short Friday*. "Taibele and Her Demon," "Blood" (a story widely praised, but also condemned), "Esther Kreindel the Second," "Jachid and Jechidah," "The Last Demon," "Yentl the Yeshiva Boy" (also dramatized) and "A Wedding in Brownsville" have justly been praised as among the most creative and innovative stories of recent times. *The Spinoza of Market Street* has its title story and "The Black Wedding," which Ted Hughes described as "a more alive, more ferocious piece of poetic imagination than any living poet . . . would be likely to get near." In *A Crown of Feathers* the lead story by the same name and the final tale, "Grandfather and Grandson," also represent the true vigor of Singer's imagination and thought.

Yet despite his storytelling prowess, the creation of special worlds to suit his artistic needs and moral tales, his theological quests, his bold characters both human and superhuman, his stylistic individuality and his poetic imagination, certain criticisms of I. B. Singer have at least limited validity. His oeuvre has undeniable diversity—it even includes widely hailed children's books—still, some questions must be asked about its range. So much reveling in the supernatural tends to create an impression, not altogether justified, of narrow sameness and repetitiveness. (Yet Singer deploys the supernatural for valid and *different* reasons every time he resorts to it.) More justified is the charge of the limited range of psychological states, partly caused by the predominance of obsessions. As one critic has put it, Singer has generally aligned the human will with sexual will. Also, Singer's fusion of the archaic with the modern cannot always succeed, and it doesn't. In his more recent books, especially the memoirs, the partnership between sexuality and spirituality has been baffling at times. But clearly Singer's chief failure—and it is a noble one— is the excess of his questions over the answers he is capable of giving. Skepticism, conservatism, humanistic balance, a poetic vision appear to be modest responses to giant questions. But the great theologians have also failed to find meaningful and sustaining answers to the same questions. The fact that Singer could even convincingly raise them in fictional terms is in itself a tribute to his enormous talent.

Lothar Kahn. WLT. Spring, 1979, pp. 200–201

In Singer's case we are dealing with a writer who adheres religiously to the goals of clarity and specificity, writing about only what he knows through some form of direct experience. This is a seminal reason why there is some degree of confusion on the question of his modernity or his contemporary relevance. For Singer is a writer, in an age of cultivated ambiguity, who *wants* us to perceive the epiphanies, doubts, and ambivalences of his characters. The other key term in his brief statement of aesthetics is "riddle"—for that is finally what the universe is for Singer. What he wants us to understand about his characters are their attempts to comprehend the structure and *modus operandi* of a universe that resists understanding. It is one of his special strengths that his characters are not disembodied creations who merely represent metaphysical problems, or their author's obsessions, but are invariably imbued with exceptional vitality and credibility. One could say without exaggeration that Singer feels and is able to dramatize characters in the same natural way that Kant saw the World in Ideas. The apparent contradiction, then, is of a writer who composes lucid, direct sentences about people and situations he knows, but whose metaphysics like Kafka's and Borges's are rooted and have never escaped from the interminable riddles of the modern world. It is clarity, then, in the service of illuminating our essential riddle of existence. . . .

Singer [is] spiritually akin to Borges, Kafka, Beckett, and Nabokov, for whom the problem of knowledge itself replaces the essential concerns of Tolstoy, Dostoyevsky, and Flaubert. This theme and its particular kind of modernism, or, if you will, post-modernism, are not unique to "The Bus." We find it in the novels *Enemies, A Love Story*, Singer's most recent novel *Shosha*, and to a substantial degree in *The Magician of Lublin*. Moreover, we find it in many of his stories from "Gimpel the Fool" to much of *Old Love*. . . .

This writer is somewhat baffled by those critics who relentlessly stress Singer's devotion to traditional literary and "moral" values while ignoring the meanings that are apparent behind the surface simplicity of his style, and his natural storyteller's gift. (Remember Joyce and Faulkner, Kafka, Borges, and Nabokov are all good, almost obsessive, storytellers.) "The Bus," then, like most of the fiction in *Old Love*, reveals a writer who manages to dramatize eternal paradoxes in a wholly contemporary fashion without making us overly aware of it. To my knowledge few fictionists have this gift and have demonstrated it so often.

Richard Burgin. ChiR. Spring, 1980, pp.<br>62–63, 67

*The Penitent* is a translation of a short novel called *Der Baal Tshuve* in Yiddish. Perhaps this title should have been translated as *The Master of Turning*, which would have been more literal and also a proper tribute to its distinguished author, who is a master of metamorphoses. But perhaps this book, first published in 1974, ought not to have been translated at all. It is a very unpleasant work, without any redeeming esthetic merit or humane quality. Singer's best book, retroactively worthy of the Nobel Prize he won in 1978, was his *Collected Stories*, published last year. *The Penitent*, a failed attempt at a Swiftian diatribe against the contemporary world, is his worst book, and yet it does expose limitations that are not Singer's alone, and so it sadly defines much that is uneasy and probably insoluble in the dilemmas of Jewish culture at this time.

Singer's strength in *The Collected Stories* is in a rare exuberance of narrative invention, rather than in the creation of character, but *The Penitent* has almost no story and invests itself in the character of its monologuist, Joseph Shapiro. . . .

Unfortunately, the reader can develop no interest in Shapiro because the author develops none. Shapiro is only a voice: negative, intense, apprehensive, fascinated by lust yet filled with revulsion toward it. The voice is indistinguishable from Singer's own, and there is no way to read this book except as Singer's tirade. . . .

How has Singer come down to this? I do not think that we have here only another episode in the decline and fall of practically everybody. Singer, like the somewhat subtler though equally pungent Cynthia Ozick, is representative of what might be called Jewish literary neo-orthodoxy. This attitude condemns as anti-Judaism or idolatry every acknowledged rupture or felt discontinuity that exists between the tradition and contemporary Jewish intellectuals.

Yet it is the illumination of the ambivalences and the ambiguities of such rupture that may have made Freud and Kafka, somewhat unwillingly, the authentic representatives of Jewish culture in and for our time. Miss Ozick has praised Singer as a moralist who "tells us that it is natural to be good, and unholy to go astray." Perhaps that praise is merited by *The Penitent*. Had Singer written often thus, he would indeed be remembered as a master of neo-orthodoxy, but hardly as a master of the intricate turnings of stories.

Harold Bloom. NYT. Sept. 25, 1983, pp. 3, 27

## SNODGRASS, W. D. (1926–    )

The question of how confessional poetry may be distinguished within the long tradition of first-person poetry on personal subjects leads us to a second question: How may Snodgrass's achievement as a confessional poet be distinguished within the confessional mode? . . . We can perhaps agree first on several qualities which tend to separate Snodgrass's work from that of other confessional poets.

First, much of Snodgrass's confessional poetry, like much of his more recent work, attempts what Snodgrass calls the poem of "becoming," the coherent, "place-centered," dynamic poem which is far more like a story than an *objet d'art*. Because Snodgrass's poems often dramatize the individual's ability (or inability) to choose, they accordingly have the particular merit of being able to accommodate and portray change, in the poet himself if need be. Partly as a result (a "story" must be clear to be effective), Snodgrass shows affinities with such poets as Frost, Auden, and Ransom, who, as Jerome Judson says, "seem to want us to know what they are talking about."

Second, as Alan Brownjohn has noted, Snodgrass generally avoids opportunities to generalize from his personal experiences; he withstands the temptation to make public pronouncements. Among those poets we call confessional, Snodgrass concentrates in his early work most exclusively on the examination of his own experience. His reluctance to generalize does not weigh against the universality of his best poetry, however. As we shall discover, Snodgrass's poetry achieves universality not by any explicit claim, but by the perceptiveness and honesty of its chronicle of private experience.

Third, as Paul Carroll has suggested, Snodgrass, unlike some of the other confessional poets, is not typically a poet of the extreme situation. In the first place, his experiences have in themselves not been particularly remarkable, and he has never attempted to convert the ordinary into the extraordinary. In the second place, Snodgrass has characteristically avoided as poetic material those of his experiences that are likely to have been, at least by objective standards, most dramatic. Thus, in "Heart's Needle," a sequence of poems about his loss of his daughter through divorce, Snodgrass treats the moment of initial separation only indirectly, by establishing a sense of felt inevitability in one poem, a sense of regret in another. His candor is balanced throughout his poetry not by reticence, but by gentleness; sincerity and decorum, the poetry of *Heart's Needle* shows, need not be incompatible. . . .

In summary, while Snodgrass is like the other "confessional" poets in his sustained close concentration upon the details of his own experience, his poetry at its best is distinctive for the lucidity of its descriptions, the modesty of its claims to public statement, and the respect it embodies for the depths of ostensibly "ordinary" experiences.

Paul L. Gaston. W. D. Snodgrass (Twayne, 1978),<br>pp. 20–22

*The Führer Bunker* consists of twenty monologues intended "to investigate the thoughts and feelings behind the public façade" of such personages as Adolf Hitler, Eva Braun, Albert Speer, and Joseph Goebbels. Hitler reminisces about a birthday cake his mother made him; Eva Braun sings *Tea for Two*; Goebbels recalls his many lovers. These revelations are meant to tell of character, though as a rule they come off as mere curiosities. . . . The personal revelations in *The Führer Bunker* make the characters seem more kinky than compelling: Hitler fantasizes about a woman urinating and defecating on him. These character sketches can otherwise be subversive because on their own momentum they often become justifications. . . .

Snodgrass once indicated that to render the death-camps even credible was almost beyond the power of literature; in this book, he focuses instead only on those people who visited Hitler's bunker between April 1 and May 1, 1945. The result is a book that is, in view of its ambition, disappointing.

Snodgrass intends this gallery of Nazi ghosts to be psychologically revealing, and the book does have telling moments. The best psychological portrait, "Hermann Fegelein," follows the frantic last thoughts passing through the mind of a mediocre man going to his execution. . . .

Snodgrass has always gone to some trouble to set even conversational diction and syntax to meters, but in this book his meters and stanzas seem to cause more trouble than anything else. The "visual" prosody of the Speer poems, set in cute triangular blocks of type, for the Nazi architect, is flat and arbitrary to the ear. . . . Snodgrass . . . resorts to limp redundancies and dislocated prepositions to get those clanking rhymes. Yet despite some stretches of lame exposition (as, for example, pp. 21–23) and flat verse, there are some good lines in the book. These seem to come easiest when Snodgrass's own irony finds a spokesman. . . . If more of his characters could speak with such vigor, the book would be more successful.

Robert von Hallberg. ChiR. Winter, 1980, pp. 117–20

## SNYDER, GARY (1930–    )

Writing, in the main, within the Imagist tradition of Pound, Williams, and the Orient, Snyder's poetry is not solely Imagistic. The gradual development of his work from the crafted to the visionary poem, his interest in primitive oral poetry, and his recent allusions to Whitman, Duncan, and other mystical poets attest to this. Significantly influenced early in his career by the demands of Oriental nature poetry for precision, sharpness, and spontaneity, Snyder's movement into Imagism and later toward the "visionary" was assured when he began his study of Buddhism in college. Its influence on the mind of Gary Snyder is profound, and it is deepening as he matures. From the sometimes "easy" references of *Riprap* to the basis of his later more mature work, *Regarding Wave* and the later sections of *Mountains and Rivers without End*, one finds this deepening of thought. However, since Buddhist theory is integral to these latter works, their richness and depth may be lost to those who do not have some knowledge of Buddhism. No poet in American literature has made Buddhist psychology so completely his own. Applied to the wilderness locale, found earlier in the work of Kenneth Rexroth, this Buddhist perception of oneness creates a poetry of immediacy and startling originality. . . .

Through Snyder's poems, one senses what archaic religion was all about. As Snyder states, "The primitive world view, far-out scientific knowledge and the poetic imagination are related forces". . . . Drawing on these wellsprings, Snyder attempts the creation in his own era of an ecological conscience. And although, as Sherman Paul states, "We cannot expect literature to cure us," it will ". . . hearten us by showing us new and true possibilities and how much may be achieved in life and art by conscious endeavor. Snyder's work . . . does this." Snyder's poetry truly influences one who reads him thoroughly to "see" in a startlingly new way. Presenting the vision of an integrated and unified world, this heroic poetic effort cannot but help to create a much needed change of consciousness.

Bob Steuding. Gary Snyder (Twayne, 1976), pp. 167–68

Snyder's roots are deep in Whitman and the Transcendentalists of New England, whose own roots were in German idealism, English romanticism, and Oriental (chiefly Hindu) mysticism. Like Whitman, Snyder celebrates nature, the simple, the animal, the sexual, the tribal, the self. Like Whitman, he speaks in the voice of a highly personal persona rooted in his own experience but by no means identical with it. Like Whitman, he sees man as an indissoluble part of the natural environment, flourishing when he accepts and adapts to that natural heritage, creating a hell on earth and within himself when he is separated from it by his intellect and its technological and societal creations. Like Whitman and Thoreau, though more thoroughly and intensely, Snyder wishes to live in nature and there to confront himself and the essentials, and like Emerson and Thoreau, he does not wish to be saddled with *things*. Like Whitman and Thoreau, he celebrates physical labor, its joys and its ability to educate one in the "true" sense. Snyder maintains truly though perhaps not all-inclusively that his poetics have been most influenced by the jobs he has held, that he has learned how to place words in a line by moving stones. Work, he says, is for him a form of play, and he has learned most from such work as he has performed. . . .

The major problem in Snyder's poetry is that he can rarely achieve the unity of thought and language required of a good poem. Usually, he is caught up in that poetic quicksand that swallows so much of the work of Whitman and [William] Carlos Williams and the "Beats": the cataloging of natural objects, mundane events, and sensory impressions until they are meaningless and boring. In short, there is a failure of poetic discrimination and organization which is in itself a failure of sensibility. . . .

If Snyder is by no means a great poet, he does have some important things to say about twentieth-century man's pell-mell progress toward environmental and societal disaster, toward destroying the place in which he lives, his home, the earth, as well as his mind, body and spirit; and occasionally, though only occasionally, he is able to embody what he has to say in memorable language, in striking form.

Abraham Rothberg. *SWR*. Winter, 1976, pp. 27–29, 36, 38

Among contemporary poets, no one has led us further back than Gary Snyder. His poetic quests thus include the reversal of popular (mis) conceptions of primitive people. . . .

This urge to get in touch with the virgin soil again, to intimately "know the ground you're on," is not original with Snyder, of course. It is a desire which pervades American literature, and is particularly intense in our post-frontier times. . . .

Gary Snyder . . . leaned west toward the Far East, leaving the mountain forests of America's northwest coast and actually going to Japan, to assimilate Oriental ways of perceiving; but, as the structure of *The Back Country* vividly demonstrates, he did come *back*. . . . His journey, then, took him (as the section titles of *The Back Country* indicate) from the "Far West" to the "Far East," but, firmly and finally, "Back"—east again to America's West. In *Regarding Wave* he reexplored the land, touched it affectionately, but not until *Turtle Island* did he make the radical descent, far below what America is, to what—long ago—it was.

Snyder, in his life and in his poetry, is the culmination of many essential American myths; he re-cycles us to our origins. He re-energizes, for example, both sides of the Christopher Columbus myth/quest: he has fulfilled Columbus' frustrated search for the mysteries of Cathay, and simultaneously he has sought to regain Columbus' initial vision of the New World, to re-envision and maintain that first glimpse of a green world of possibility, unencumbered by European history. Snyder, then, is the twentieth century extension and fulfillment of Columbus' dream; he merges East and West by bringing his Oriental insight to bear on the wilderness beneath present-day America. Snyder thus refers to himself as a "shaman/healer," for "shaman" is a term that applies both to North American Indian medicine men and to eastern Asian priests, and Snyder emphasizes the similarity in beliefs and attitudes, even in origin, of native Americans and Orientals. . . .

L. Edwin Folsom. *WAL*. Summer, 1980, pp. 104–6

# SONTAG, SUSAN (1933–   )

That Susan Sontag is philosophically oriented and has something of a metaphysical impulse to her thinking (although she would undoubtedly reject the word vehemently) is among the reasons why I think her one of the most interesting and valuable critics we possess, a writer from whom it's continually possible to learn, even when you're most dissatisfied with what she's saying, or perhaps especially at those times. For the past several years she has been the chief voice in America of one main tradition of French criticism, which is one of the reasons, I'm convinced, why she is disliked, where she's disliked, with such ferocity and xenophobic scorn. . . .

The truth is that Miss Sontag ought not to be examined under the prevailing American definitions of the literary or cultural critic, any more than the esthetic developments she has been talking about ought to be examined under the rubrics of the criticisms traditional in their realms. Ever since the New Criticism, its mission accomplished and its effects guaranteed, receded into history, we have been unable in America to come near agreeing on what esthetic intelligence is, although this kind of intelligence is surely what we should want to mean when we speak of criticism at all; and it is this kind that Miss Sontag possesses. . . .

The alarm that many people feel at the approach of Susan Sontag, the distaste, resentment and even fury she causes, has, it seems to me, two bases, both of them related to what I have been saying about esthetic independence or contingency. The cruder one is moral and "humanistic." She has been accused of being inhuman or anti-human for ignoring moral and spiritual elements in art, or rather for sanctioning and encouraging the immoral, pornography or camp, for example, violence or extravagance. To this the only answer is that no material, or data, or subject or, for that matter, mood in the esthetic realm has anything to do with being sanctioned or deplored, needs validation or, in short, lies in the moral universe at all. When Henry James said that the only immorality he had ever seen on the stage was the production of a bad play, he told us tersely about the way morality figures in the life of forms. The moral charge against Miss Sontag, which is mainly a charge against the kinds of art she has been interested in, issues from the same morale such charges always do: apprehension in the face of new consciousness.

Beyond this, Miss Sontag has marched, aggressively and with her great bristling apparatus of learning (an erudition at least as much philosophical and psychological as literary or technically esthetic), pointing every which way but most dangerously at certain processes of literary erudition itself, into some sacred realms, to the consternation of their guardians. At the least newcomers are expected to observe the rules. And one of the chief rules is that criticism is a province of the dispassionate (and fact-finding) intellect, which it is designed to serve and, so to speak, to fill out. . . .

For the problem of her sensibility is also the generating power of its interest and importance for us as she exemplifies and tests and expounds and shapes it into form in her writing. It is precisely classical ability to feel which, as it works itself out in our shibboleths and humanistic myths, means to feel *the way others have*, to feel certain emotions (in certain ways) that have been sanctified as properly human and necessary, that has come into question. One of the chief resistances put up by new literature, or new art of any kind, is to being told how and what to feel. Academic resistance to the new, on the other hand, is a balking at the notion that we don't already know and haven't already worked out the proper forms.

Susan Sontag has been engaged in trying to plot the course of her new feelings, which is to say her responses as a representative advanced consciousness. (She *is* advanced; would we want her laggard?) In doing this she has indicated all the debilities and irresolutions and compensatory aggressions and contradictions that are inevitable in consciousness in transition. The chief content of that transition now is the challenge to Western literary culture, or rather to the supremacy of literature *as* culture; the growing breakdown of the erstwhile separation between art and audience or, more strictly, between art as object for contemplation and as material for reabsorption into total experience; the claim of bodily experience to a place in esthetics; the more insistent relationship between politics and sensibility. These are Miss Sontag's themes [in *Styles of Radical Will*]; and she is the victim of their assaults, in their status as realities, upon our preparation, training, inheritance and need for continuity—on *what we were like before*—as much as she is their elucidator and master in awareness.

Richard Gilman. *NR*. May 3, 1969, pp. 23–25

There was a delightful innocence about Camp and its followers that I found intriguing. It was determinedly and doggedly antiintellectual, in a very, very intellectual way. Its devotees were trying so hard not to seem Profound, though there was really no danger at all of that, and yet they couldn't help but intellectualize everything, because they knew no other mode of perception. Miss Sontag's program was very simple: she was against thinking. But she was not really antiintellectual. Indeed in a way she was the very epitome of intellectuality: she was all ideas, and her emotions were not so much felt as thought. She got her thrills out of abstractions, which she reified into attitudes. The kind of thinking she was against was the kind that attempted to make sense of ideas. She did not want to make sense out of anything: she preferred to revel in concepts, treating them as if they were form-fitting silken garments, to be enjoyed for the snugness and the sheen. What she affected to be for was emotion, feeling, texture; she wanted her art to reveal the Thingness of the world, she said. . . .

What she wants is something she calls "transparence," which means "experiencing the luminousness of the thing in itself, of things being what they are." Interpretation ignores the sensory experience of art and attempts to squeeze as much content out of it as possible. Our culture of excess and overproduction has brought about "a steady loss of sharpness in our sensory experience." We must recover our senses, learn to see more, hear more, feel more. "The function of criticism should be to show *how it is what it is*, even *that it is what it is*, rather than show *what it means*." And finally, . . . "in place of a hermeneutics we need an erotics of art.". . .

For [Sontag], photography is an aggressive, appropriating act (one shoots/takes a picture) which "makes reality atomic, manageable, opaque . . . denies interconnectedness, continuity . . . confers on each moment the character of a mystery." Alienating us from direct experience, the photo provides a more intense second-hand experience, an illusion of knowledge; essentially discrete, disjunct, mute, ahistorical, the photo cannot tell the truth that comes only from words and narration. Photography levels hierarchies, fosters seeing for seeing's sake, "the didactic cultivation of perception, independent of notions of what is worth perceiving, which animates all modernist movements in the arts." Along with modernizing and surrealizing our perspective on reality, however, the camera also consumerizes it. The world becomes "a department store or museum-without-walls in which every subject is depreciated into an article of consumption, promoted into an item for aesthetic appreciation." And governments exploit the photographic image as another medium for capitalist ideologies—stimulating artificial appetites to consume, replacing real political change by a change of images, and keeping populations under surveillance.

Sontag's six essays [in *On Photography*]—really linked meditations or even prose poems—all take up these themes again and again, placing them in progressively more complex contexts, squeezing (now and then with visible strain) every bit of significance out of each disquieting aspect of the photographic image and its ambiguous but potent force in the modern consciousness. There are no illustrations here, just lean prose studded with tight-mouthed, provocative aphorisms (the intellectual's equivalent of the stand-up comic's one-liners). . . .

A splendid performance—intellectual pinball on the French model where the goal is to keep a subject in play for as long as possible, racking up a brilliant score of cultural references and profound (if somewhat obscure) *mots*. Yet *On Photography* is less self-consciously self-advertising than that; more disenchanted with pure esthetics, less against interpretation than one might have expected. It is, finally, a moralistic (Marxist persuasion) indictment of our common lot as "image junkies." The last sentences of Sontag's book call for an ecology of images without specifying the meaning of that term. Rather than mindless delight and preservation (save the seals! save the snapshots!) or puritanical proscription (only the pure may survive!), *On Photography*'s analytical exposé of the dynamics and extent of our addiction should serve as a definition by example of such an ecology.

Richard Kuczkowski. *Com.* Feb. 3, 1978, pp.<br>88–89

Miss Sontag claims (no doubt correctly) that illness as metaphor is used at the expense of the literally ill: it compounds their physical illness with a cultural judgment, moralizes their position as other, abnormal, ill-omened. Metaphor has a tendency to naturalize a given condition, to make it, through the play of comparison, reconnect with accepted ways of looking at the world, with a moralized network of ideas and beliefs which must always imply, in the case of illness as metaphor, that the disease is somehow chosen; if not deserved, somehow justified. . . .

When Miss Sontag argues that it is not morally permissible to use cancer as metaphor, we may find her ethically noble but utopian, caught in a Platonic dream of a language which would give direct access to realities rather than the displaced symbols of realities. No doubt she is not so naive as to mean this literally: really she wants us to get rid of metaphors whose implications we can't control, which are loosely used and come to be taken as literal. What is needed is not elimination of the metaphor, but the constant showing up of metaphor for what it is, through countermetaphor, through the rhetoric of exposure, which Miss Sontag so effectively manages.

*Illness as Metaphor* is wholly successful as polemic and as provocation to the rethinking of cultural metaphors. . . . Otherwise, I cannot help but feel that Miss Sontag could tell us much more about the subject, that she is in a position to undertake, somewhat in the manner of Michel Foucault, a more sustained "archeology" of the idea of illness in our culture. In particular, one would like to hear her at greater length on the perception that madness has become the modern glamour disease: what was originally a brilliant metaphor for the decentering of perception (in Rimbaud, for instance) has degenerated into an irresponsible literalness, so that one can find serious writers proclaiming that the discourse of schizo-phrenia is the only authentic language of our time.

Peter Brooks. *PR*. 46, 3, 1979, pp. 438–39, 443–44

It was the great virtue of *Against Interpretation* (1966) and *Styles of Radical Will* (1969), Sontag's two early volumes of essays, to have responded so authoritatively to the question of identity, defining modernist performances in their abdication from the whole variety of traditional aesthetic values: sublimity, disinterestedness, harmoniousness, completion, etc. . . .

Yet her criticism relied then (as it continues to rely) on a partial estrangement from the vagaries of radical modernism. She has never relinquished her strong sense of the incommensurability of modernism, speaking of it always as a problem or a crisis, never simply as a cultural advent comparable to others. . . .

All of her stories are in some sense productions of the will. They do not (as she once said of the greatest works of art) seem the ripened analogues of nature's forms, but rather *constructs* of an artificer whose hand remains unfailingly in view. Yet at their finest her fictions construct the drama of moral antinomy: the human longing for freedom *and* for bondage; for the completion of knowledge *and* for absolution from knowledge; for the parent's invincible purview *and* the naked need of the child; for an autonomy of self *and* for the dissolution of self into collectivity; for a historical past that is "arrangement," pregnant with meaning, *and* for a past that is heaped, broken—wreckage upon wreckage, pleading no tale.

To say her fictions are willed is only to say that she pursues by means of words what she has already understood to be in excess of their aptitude. . . . In *I, etcetera* her talent extends to a new kind of narrative that is precisely *not* inventive, that in fact tenders nothing that cannot be summoned from the documentary basis of her own life. These pieces—which seem to me the best of the book—may as well be called essays as stories. Identifying them by means of that sizable word, we do well to recall its inventor. "Project for a Trip to China" and "Unguided Tour" . . . wield an authority that has its sources not in fiction but, like the essays of Montaigne, in the perplexity of being only an individual, a subject, apart and without recourse to any of the forms of "total imagination," whether Calvin or the French Catholic League, Hegel or Reverend Ike. These works comprise the I of *I, etcetera*: in them Sontag has invented nothing save herself. And it is, in fact, not the storyteller's workshop but instead the bare by-room of an exigent self that serves as the gathering place for her best impulses. Resolved to write what she has done, seen, willed, endured, she persuades us again and again to take counsel. Disciplining the tangle of private experience into words, Sontag declares a persistent, if diminished, possibility of wisdom.

Benjamin Taylor. *GaR*. Winter, 1980, pp. 908–9, 911

In *Under the Sign of Saturn* Sontag is at work again reshaping the canon of modern European literature. Her particular polemic—a strong element in the general thrust of postwar New York literary criticism—is to celebrate the leopards in the temple of literature, not those cool and calm consciousnesses (like the Sophocles and Shakespeare of Matthew Arnold) who abided all questions and saw life whole, but those whose own derangement allowed them to explode the lies of order so that better forms might be discovered. In her criticism she labors to turn even the most self-isolating, uncompromising, and personally outrageous of such figures (I think here especially of Artaud) into humane teachers, whose flame, all the brighter for being trimmed, she will pass on to future generations. . . .

If *On Photography* is Sontag's belated neoplatonist turning away from that image of the critic in vogue, then *Under the Sign of Saturn* is her effort to reassess the public aspect of her pursuit of a career that has been defined historically by its distaste for public life and display. Searching for the shape of other careers, she implicitly meditates on her own: what am I to make of this pile of books that in some way is me? . . .

As always, her intelligence makes her essays refreshing, even though we may often learn less about her subjects than about what she thinks of them and how their ideas affected her. In pursuit of new connections she has fashioned a rhetoric of subordination that puts her forward as the humble lightning rod of culture. This is my tradition, she seems to say, these are my boys, and thus the Romantic project of finding the heart of a culture in its eccentrics winds up recommending instead the eccentricity of its own quest.

Leo Braudy. *NR*. Nov. 29, 1980, pp. 43, 45–46

## STAFFORD, WILLIAM (1914–    )

The imagination—its resilience, its stubborn and playful instinct for deriving meaning and awe from the world—is the central theme of Stafford's work. In this respect, despite profound differences in style, Stafford's poetry bears perhaps a closer affinity to the poetry of Wallace Stevens than to that of any other recent American poet. It exhibits a steady consciousness of Romantic tradition, particularly Wordsworth and Thoreau. Like Stevens's, Stafford's Romanticism is stylized, abstract, and always informed by a controlling intelligence. Stafford is not considered, as Stevens is, a "difficult" poet; his poems exhibit none of the studied, elegant artificiality of a Stevens poem. Most of them move with the apparent artlessness of a great centerfielder drifting back to make the catch of a slicing line-drive look routine. Stafford rarely seems to work hard in a poem, to contrive his results, to wring, as James Dickey often does, more adventitious significance out of a poem than its occasion warrants. In his interviews as well as in his poems, Stafford likes to promote a picture of himself as naïve.

In fact, however, his poems and his conception of poetry are extremely sophisticated. A deft, alert intellect exhibits itself everywhere in his work—through his frequent etymological use of words, through puns, through the construction of deliberate but carefully limited ambiguities and through a scrupulous New-Critical attention to consistency. . . .

Stafford's vision, although it comprehends paradox, is not particularly complicated. And it is precise—far more precise than Stafford's comments or prevalent critical opinion would have us believe. . . . By contemporary standards, Stafford's poems are relatively *closed*-ended and contain a relatively high proportion of didactic content. Stafford's didactic quality, however, does not immediately stand out, because his poems are frequently so cryptic. Without some grasp of Stafford's specialized vocabulary, it is impossible to make much of the ending of a poem like "So Long". . . .

Jonathan Holden. The Mark to Turn: A Reading of William Stafford's Poetry (Regents Pr. of Kansas, 1976), pp. 6–8

Stafford's poems reveal thematically a singular and unified preoccupation. The voice of his work speaks from a sheltered vista of calm and steady deliberation. The speaker looks backward to a western childhood world that is joyous and at times edenic, even as he gazes with suspicion and some sense of peril upon the state of modern American society. The crux of each volume by Stafford involves the search for that earlier age identifiable by certain spiritual values associated with the wilderness, values which can sustain him and his family as well as the whole of the technological and urban society which surrounds him. The means to this search come through a poetry of images, images frequently and profoundly mythic. . . .

In its larger context, his poetry is essentially Janus-faced: it looks back with nostalgia upon an idealized childhood, but never at a removal from a far more foreboding perspective of modern society. His poetry seeks to chart the connectives between these two worlds. What, then, is the relation between such a thematic preoccupation and the Emotive Imagination? It is precisely in the way by which the poetic imagination seeks to link up the two perspectives. The childhood world is extolled through images of the wilderness; the validity of that world and the accessibility of its values are revealed through a poetry of distinctly archetypal images. . . .

Perhaps William Stafford is equaled only by Theodore Roethke among American poets who cherish the memory of childhood. Stafford goes beyond even Roethke, however, in defining the father as the central occupant of that near-perfect world. . . .

The mythic quality of the childhood world is dominated by the figure of the father who appears in dozens of Stafford's poems. . . . The father who appears in the poems is heroic: he is provider and protector; his moral strength is steady and independent of worldly expectations; most important of all, he is the high priest of the wilderness. Like Sam Fathers to Isaac McCaslin or Natty Bumppo to the neophytes of the frontier, Stafford's father is initiator and instructor to the son, not only in relation to the wilderness itself, but in the moral values which inhere within it. . . . The figure of the father in these poems occasionally assumes the archetypal dimensions of the universal father.

George S. Lensing and Ronald Moran. *Four Poets and the Emotive Imagination* (Louisiana State Univ. Pr., 1976), pp. 178, 184, 187–88

Critics ought to talk more about tonality in Stafford. There are ways of seeing and saying which are, for good and bad, unmistakably his own: "If your policy is to be friends in the mountains/a rock falls on you: the only real friends—/you can't help it." Sometimes this kind of kookiness brings out statements which we have to take on faith if we are to take them at all. Still, when we ease into them they tend to make the sort of sense that the anomalous can make when it opens up part of our lives. In several poems in *The Rescued Year* Stafford attributes his bent for the apt but off-center phrase to "a turn that is our family's own." At his best, he makes this turn into a way of handling poems which combines the precise with the strange, fact with a quirky but frequently illuminating vision. I read through the collected poems [*Stories That Could Be True: New and Collected Poems*] to see what happens to this turn as well as several other characteristic Staffordisms. It grows less and less prevalent as he goes on, mellowing into a ripeness of distinctive seeing which produces row after row of brilliant poems in the later work. The relationship of those turns, early and mellow, to the quietness which everyone speaks of, is one of the bases of Stafford's voice. There are other recurrent elements in his tonality, such as the vast compassion which used to seem mainly for the forsaken but turns out, as the collected poems show, to be for all of us. Stafford can touch us with a delicate grace, bringing over to us an understanding of how others face the difficulties of their ordinary pains and places.

Frederick Garber. *APR*. Jan./Feb., 1980, p. 18

## STEIN, GERTRUDE  (1874–1946)

What distinguishes Gertrude Stein (b. 1874) from nearly all of her chronological contemporaries in American literature (e.g., Dreiser, Stephen Crane, Vachel Lindsay, *et al.*) is that, even a century after her birth, most of her works remain misunderstood. The principal reason for such widespread incomprehension is that her experiments in writing were conducted apart from the major developments in modern literature. Neither a naturalist nor a surrealist, she had no interest in either the representation of social reality or the weaving of symbols, no interest at all in myth, metaphor, allegory, literary allusions, uncommon vocabulary, synoptic cultural critiques, shifts in point of view or much else that preoccupied writers such as James Joyce, Thomas Mann and Marcel Proust. Unlike them, she was an empiricist who preferred to write about observable realities and personally familiar subjects; the titles of her books were typically declarative and descriptive, rather than symbolic or allusive. Like other modern writers, she was influenced by developments in the non-literary arts; yet Stein feasted upon a fertile esthetic idea that the others neglected—to emphasize properties peculiar to one's chosen medium and it alone. As her art was writing, rather than painting, Stein's primary interest was language—more specifically, American English and how else its words might be used. Indicatively, the same esthetic idea that seems so acceptable in modernist painting and music was heretical, if not unthinkable, in literature.

From nearly the beginning of her creative career, Stein experimented with language in several ways. Starting from scratch, she neglects the arsenal of devices that authors had traditionally used to vary their prose. Though she was personally literate, her language is kept intentionally unliterary and unconnotative. Her diction is mundane, though her sentence structure is not, for it was her particular achievement to build a complex style out of purposely limited vocabulary.

Richard Kostelanetz. *HC*. June, 1975, p. 2

There is probably no other writer who would be less comprehensible without reference to the time (the "composition") in which she wrote.

While it may be a tautology to say that writers reflect their time and milieu, there are still certain periods of the past in which cultural upheaval seems, in retrospect, so apparent and inescapable that the works of art created during that time become functions of that revolution. During such epochs, certain writers emerge who can be best appreciated only within the context of that release of cultural energy, just as there are others who, in following these pioneers, become writers for all ages. . . .

It does not seem outlandish to suggest that Stein occupies a similar position in Modernist literature. Like "an event in chemistry," she seems in retrospect to have been an inevitable product of cultural energy. Heir to a century of Romanticism and its implications for authorial subjectivity and experimentation, and versed also in modern psychology, Stein had the good fortune to be drawn to an environment, Paris, where innovators in the other arts were attempting experiments similar to hers that ultimately changed the way all civilized peoples were to see and create the world. Her relationship with Picasso was crucial in this regard: for beginning with *Melanctha*, Stein's writings quite often went through the same stages of experimentation as the paintings of her Spanish friend. . . .

[Stein is the] first writer in English that I know of who came to see writing as *purely* a problem in composition; and her explorations of the limits of the English language made it possible for a number of important writers to go to school to her. . . .

To reject Stein any longer is to reject Modernism. While this rejection may be a luxury that some people will continue to permit themselves, it is one that no serious reader can afford to indulge. To deal properly with modern letters, we must face the work of Gertrude Stein head on, in both its intrinsic and its cultural significance. She is too large a fact to be ignored any longer.

Michael J. Hoffman. Gertrude Stein (Twayne,<br>1976), pp. 132–35

Gertrude Stein's erotic works are demonstrations of disguised autobiography. For many of the lyrical and revealing pieces in her early oeuvre, *Painted Lace* (1914); *Pink Melon Joy, Possessive Case,* and *No* (1915); *Lifting Belly* (1917); and *Not a Hole* and *A Sonatina Followed by Another* (1921), Stein invented a witty code that played upon the details of her sexual and domestic self. In such a private autobiographical style she can tell everything—and she does. The works also have inherent literary qualities which would make them worthy of notice, even if they did not show so much of the author's personality and habits. They speak in her private but authentic voice—warm, teasing, with exaggerated flights of fancy and whimsy that point to the more radical developments of her later years. The subject and style are, then, both testing grounds; in a sense, her life-style would become her art. Erotic, subconscious elements are allowed to interact with conscious craft to produce documents of the interior life. . . .

In her repetitions, mimicking, role playing as "author," Stein has always tried on attitudes like hats in front of the bedroom mirror. She creates a magic theater, in which she plays actor and audience at once. Her attitudes surface and change, coalesce and fragment. If at first she seems to affirm her passion, later she questions and mocks, even denies the worth and quality of her relationship. Autobiographical themes of identity, self-justification, narcissism, and pride occupy her as well as moral questions of guilt, innocence, sin, security, risk, and certainty, and all of these are juxtaposed against frank homosexual statements and naive, totally positive images of her relationship. She finally seasons her text lightly with a straight-faced romantic vocabulary that might in other contexts pass for heterosexual. . . .

Since Stein is never far from humor in any of her pieces, her frankest are no exception. The joyfulness and humor of her treatment of sexual themes breaks down social and linguistic barriers. The shock of juxtaposition of her unusual style forces Stein, as an observer and participant, into new and unexpected perspectives. Pushed by her own temperament to solve certain technical problems of rhyme and diction, to make up new words, to join others together, to treat her lines as a virtuoso singer might, Stein charms by the sweetness of her melodies, her sophisticated naturalness, her complex simplicity, her careful cheerfulness, her precarious self-acceptance. These private writings constitute her interior theater; she is the hero of an appreciative audience and the villain when the boos begin; and she is finally the audience itself, alternately caught up in the hisses and applause.

Elizabeth Fifer. *Signs.* Spring, 1979, pp. 472–73, 483

## STEINBECK, JOHN  (1902–1968)

The fiction of John Steinbeck has had a special appeal to the scientist, for of all the major American writers of fiction in this century, Steinbeck alone has had an abiding interest in natural science and brought that interest to his writing. The marine scientist, in particular, has claimed Steinbeck for his own because of the writer's life-long attachment to the seashore and its animals. He was, according to several professional scientists who knew him, "a very good amateur biologist." Furthermore, if

Steinbeck does have a claim on the attention of future generations of readers, much of that claim will be based on his concern with science, since he alone, among American novelists of his time, saw man as part of an ecological whole.

At the same time, however, Steinbeck's scientific outlook created many problems for him as an artist and contributed significantly to a generally negative response to much of his work by literary critics. His use of science put him in a position of isolation—often the critics did not understand what he was doing. Further, his use of ideas associated with science brought him into conflict with the novel form and its traditions, leading him into difficulties with characterization, plot, and point of view which he was only partially able to overcome. While the modern novel as a whole has tended to drift back toward the poetic and mythic, Steinbeck's fiction, particularly during those years when he was most heavily influenced by his marine biologist friend, Edward F. Ricketts, was often infused with large doses of naturalistic philosophy. Thus, his example not only provides some interest as an exception to the general flow of modern American fiction, it throws into sharp relief the central scientific-poetic duality of the novel form itself. . . .

Steinbeck's greatest successes—*In Dubious Battle*, *Tortilla Flat*, *Of Mice and Men*, *The Grapes of Wrath*, and *Cannery Row*—are all triumphs of perception, so that his adoption of the non-teleological approach must be said to have had its advantages as well as its disadvantages. It provided that edge of differentness that every writer must have if his work is to make its mark and be remembered.

John Steinbeck's exact place in the history of the American novel and his contribution to the evolution of the novel form are yet to be determined. Too much prejudice is still attached to his life and too much confusion still surrounds his goals and methods for any kind of objective assessment to be made at this time. Nevertheless, when that assessment is made, I think those who make it will be bound to acknowledge that frequent use of scientific attitudes and methods in his fiction which took him beyond the tradition of Naturalism-Realism into an achievement purely his own. Perhaps no such thing as a novelist who is also a scientist is possible—a writer who consistently brings a thoroughgoing scientific philosophy and methodology to the writing of fiction. But John Steinbeck went further in this direction than any other modern American writer of distinction has, and as far, perhaps, as any writer can. His attempts led to some failures and some rather extraordinary successes. His work, in its own way, was often as experimental and daring as that of any number of other modern writers whom we honor for having extended the presumed limits of artistic expression.

Jackson J. Benson. *Novel*. Spring, 1977, pp. 248, 264

Instrumental in shaping [Steinbeck's] fiction . . . is [his] moral vision, which has been variously described, interpreted, praised, and questioned through the years. Steinbeck's pervasive compassion for human beings appears most characteristically in portrayals of the most vulnerable: the naive, handicapped, and disenfranchised . . . who rarely find the promised land, at least not as they dream of it. . . .

The fundamentally affirmative quality of the vision, however, tends on the one hand to minimize complexities and shadings of modern life, particularly in ethical values or choices, and on the other hand, to reveal more of group characteristics and ideas than of an individual's heart and mind. This is in keeping with the strong idealistic and intuitive elements in the vision.

The literary craftsmanship and skill with which the themes, symbols, and moral vision are expressed would seem to identify most definitely Steinbeck's fiction and ensure his place with the best writers of his generation. With them he shared a ceaseless dedication to mastering the art of fiction. . . .

No less effectively at times than Fitzgerald and Hemingway, Steinbeck experimented with nuances of dialogue and prose style and with varieties of point of view; and in diversity of works if not in richness he may have equalled Faulkner, creating not only stories and novels but also parables, plays, novel-plays, and nonfiction. . . .

Steinbeck's best works brilliantly expose mankind's "grievous faults and failures," alert us to social and economic dangers, and remind us of our forgotten commitments and dreams. Steinbeck's strongest convictions and passions appear in his fundamental belief in humanity, in his expectation that man will endure, and that the creative forces of the human spirit will prevail.

Paul McCarthy. John Steinbeck (Ungar, 1980),<br>pp. 141–43

## STEVENS, WALLACE (1879–1955)

For Stevens, the romantic meant the new, the vital, and above all the imaginative, and he looked to the British romantics for both illustration and sanction of his own values, even while jealously distancing himself from them to guard his own independence. He confronted romantic problems like the dualism between subject and object or the contradiction between life and art, and accepted key aspects of their aesthetic like the importance of imagination and the kind of defense of poetry to which imagination led. Yet in his drive to develop his own art and personality

Stevens saw the necessity of renewing romanticism and adapting it to modern times. He forswore mere repetition. Joyously welcoming the creative violence which Eliot feared, he redefined imagination to emphasize its ferocity while reformulating the cyclic quality of romantic experience. His poetry incorporated new strategies of image, syntax, and presentation of consciousness designed to create provisional rather than final fictions. In the process, he both extended romantic literary theory and reshaped romantic mental action into the poems of our climate. His profound relation to romanticism has been mentioned so much and systematically explored so little that its extensive investigation can open central approaches to both his aesthetic and his poetry. . . .

His startling appearance as a romantic in midst of the warring schools of Marxism or New Criticism in the thirties identifies the mature Stevens as his own man, able on occasion sharply to dissociate himself from his romantic forebears even while fighting through to a modernist art that continued and transformed their own.

George Bornstein. Transformations of Romanticism in Yeats, Eliot, and Stevens (Univ. of Chicago Pr., 1976), pp. 163–64

Forged in the crucible of Stevens' discontent with language is the solution to the linguistic dilemma: the "supreme fiction." To understand this important and persistent notion, we must first erase from our personal notions of "reality" anything but what we can point to or stomp on; we must, for example, try to think of the word "table," if spoken in a room which contains no table, as a *symbol*, because the word "table" has elicited something in our *minds*. As long as a word does not point to an actual object, we are in the realm of the mind: memory, imagination, anticipation, abstraction. And these are traits that set us apart from even the most intelligent animals; we are set apart by virtue of our preoccupation with symbols, "with images and names that *mean* things, rather than with things themselves," as Suzanne Langer says. . . .

For us, poetry is the closest approximation to Stevens' "supreme fiction." For Stevens, I think it was an imagined poet, a potential figure that he sketches again and again: "The Noble Rider" and "The Figure of the Youth as Virile Poet." Stevens' definitions of poetry are often bound up with delineations of this potential poet whose imagination Stevens thinks of as a kind of total faculty: imagination informed by reason. And as a merely "potential" figure, he seems to be a *collective* potential: less Stevens' than ours. Stevens is clear about his role: he helps people "to live their lives." This is, of course, all "make believe"—a supreme fiction. But, as I. A. Richards has wonderfully said, the poet's job is more than make-believe; it is making people believe. And what we find in Stevens' poetry, unique in the age of Eliot and Pound, is that make-believe in ourselves; we read Stevens to find the world robed in imagination's sequined harmonies, and to find ourselves, robing and disrobing the world around us.

Susan B. Weston. *Wallace Stevens: An Introduction to His Poetry* (Columbia Univ. Pr., 1977), pp. 5–6

To understand how diversity of diction in Stevens is dramatically motivated, we need to think of it in terms not of static patterns of contrast but of temporal unfolding. From this point of view, diversity is change, perceived as we read a number of poems or a single long poem—as we pass, say, from "The Idea of Order at Key West" to "The American Sublime" in the *Collected Poems*, or from "Chocorua to Its Neighbor" to "So-and-So Reclining on Her Couch" in *The Palm at the End of the Mind*, or from section IV to section V of "The Bouquet," or from section III to section IV of "Esthetique du Mal." Within such lines as "addicts/To blotches, angular anonymids/Gulping for shape" or "alive with an enigma's flittering," change is kaleidoscopic, the hand of the poet all but deceiving the eye. We may be aware of a pleasant strangeness in the proportion, without knowing exactly wherein that strangeness consists. . . .

Just as we see the Stevens of the *Collected Poems* turning from one metaphor, one analogy, one symbolic setting, person, or event to another, so also we see him turning from one expressive means to another, trying out now this kind of language, now that, now this kind of word, now that, in the incessant attempt to express what remains perpetually "beyond the rhetorician's touch." And in this same restlessness of mind, these same rejections not only of the past but also of the present which has already become the past, we can see a motive for his ransacking of the lexicon, his borrowings from foreign languages, his creation of new metaphorical meanings, the coinages and innovative formations that mark his diction. "It is never the thing but the version of the thing"; Stevens's poetic language is diverse, versatile, full of *divertissements*, in the root sense of all those words, knowing that "what it has is what is not" and turning from it "as morning throws off stale moonlight and shabby sleep." These turnings or shiftings at the verbal level are analogous to the changes with which the poems are concerned in their subject matter and descriptive detail. . . .

Marie Borroff. *Language and the Poet: Verbal Artistry in Frost, Stevens, and Moore* (Univ. of Chicago Pr., 1979), pp. 72–73

In the centennial year of Wallace Stevens' birth, Stevens' art still seems fresh and elusive, but less precious and less eccentrically modern than it did more than fifty years ago when his first book appeared. Since then, the rich and memorable language of *Harmonium* has been augmented by the equally memorable, if more abstract, phrases in the later books. It is now assumed that the imagery derives from eternal or universal human situations and reverberates with echoes of philosophic implications. The poetry still imparts its special quality of withheld thoughtfulness. The effect of its subtly qualified, seemingly abstruse statements is to suggest that the poet may be amused, even skeptical of their never quite formulated profundities. Along with this implicit questioning, each poem's discourse contemplates in exacting language the shadings of its idea. "Words are thoughts," Stevens says, and with this concept of language his poetry, as so many critics have noted, involves a movement of thought, an activity of mind. This activity is stimulated by intimations beyond the plain statements in poems. The poems exert the fascination of what may be recognized as theory and what may be realized at the same time as the poet's intuition of a person in a time, a season, and a place, a setting.

Stevens has taken his place among the other cherished figures of our literature as part of an inheritance rather than as the isolated phenomenon he seemed to be in earlier days. Many critics now regard him as one of the major figures in the romantic tradition, and his relationship to Wordsworth and Keats . . . will be easily accepted by most of his readers. Yet he has not receded into a general background of romantic poetry. He is still the individualist, the master of his own style. Stevens' individuality attracts and overcomes parody. And because he is inimitable, his influence has been minimal for a poet of his monumental reputation.

> Frank Doggett and Robert Buttel. Preface to
> *Wallace Stevens: A Celebration*, ed. Frank
> Doggett and Robert Buttel (Princeton Univ. Pr.,
> 1980), pp. xi–xii

Unlike Eliot, Pound, or Williams, Stevens was never passionately concerned with the quest for community. In the *Pisan Cantos*, the union of the weakest—the social bond forged by imprisonment—does foster wisdom. But for Pound, wisdom entails affection and humility, personal virtues, ultimately social virtues, which Stevens never believed essential to the hero. Of the four Moderns considered here, Stevens was the only one who never thought in terms of an ideal society or a utopia, but only in terms of *a* hero, *the* hero, the solitary mind. Only the Stevens hero stands alone and apart. Stevens posed questions of culture, certainly, but in epistemological, not political or social, terms. And it is perhaps as a result of this that we find his work, so elegant, so perfect, so deeply satisfying, yet so often chilly and curiously removed from the problems of twentieth-century industrial society. . . . But until *The Rock*, Stevens refused to accept an image of a man in the world as hero. In mixing the proportions between reality and the imagination, Stevens continually erred on the side of the imagination. Over and over he repeated the mistake he had cautioned against in "Examination of the Hero in a Time of War"—that the hero "be not conceived, being real."

His images of the hero were fabrications, projections, extrapolations, abstractions beyond man, preposterous shimmers or muscular giants, bare constructions in language that we certainly (to use Stevens' terms) do not recognize, much less realize, respond to, or accept. His art was conceptual; the idea, and the problem it reflected, often had more interest than the thing itself; the illustration of the definition was often less convincing than the formulation of the definition. For the irresistible transcendental pull was there. But this is not an Emersonian transcendentalism. It is the courage, hubris, and naivete of a radical humanism. . . .

What is the meditative mode for Stevens? The act of the mind? The act of the imagination? Speaking generally, it would seem reasonable to call all of Stevens' poems meditative, for it was Stevens' temperament to revolve an idea in his mind, to pursue it, muse on it. But . . . we must distinguish between *imagination* and *meditation*.

> Kathleen Woodward. *"At Last, the Real Distinguished Thing": The Late Poems of Eliot, Pound, Stevens, and Williams* (Ohio State Univ. Pr., 1980), pp. 100–101, 118

# ● STRAND, MARK (1934–    )

In Mark Strand's best poems [in *Sleeping with One Eye Open*] a fuzzy, peripheral, half-realized terror seems about to take shape. The tension is that if the terror materializes, becomes specific, the poet will be run out of the house of himself. Mr. Strand's poems are, therefore, new houses to dwell safely in. He builds them methodically, so they have strong textural walls with no loose joints or cracks. The tone is often flat and prosy, as if to diminish and control threatening feeling. The effect though is the opposite, to release feeling. Many of these poems are admirable houses.

> A. R. Ammons. *Poetry*. June, 1966, pp. 196–97

Mark Strand's *Reasons for Moving* is a marvelously haunted book. It is not clear whether the speaker of these poems is haunted by what he is, what he is not, or the obscurity of events. But this uncertainty is precisely the dramatic effect the poet seeks, and in most of the poems he achieves it. The theme that pervades the book (which throughout is unified in tone) is given in an introductory quotation from Jorge Luis Borges: ". . . while we sleep here, we are awake elsewhere and . . . in this way every man is two men." But Strand does not work this theme in the romantic vein. He neither longs nostalgically for past experience, wishing to recapture a lost pastoral self, nor imagines an amorous and adventurous ideal to dote upon in reverie or dream. Rather, his *Doppelgänger*, his other self, shares his own fate: neither one of them is complete, neither is sure of his own identity. From this ghostly confrontation a beautiful pathos arises. For example, in "The Accident" the victim and the train engineer are, in effect, the same character. . . .

If what a man does and what happens to him are, in some hidden sense, the same, then compassion and pity are also the same, and so too are responsibility and innocence. Thus the speaker and his other self are as much the victims of what they do as they are victims of what happens to them, and their identities have no fixed center. If anything is certain, it is merely the sense of "being swept away.". . .

Any poetic success runs the danger of becoming mannered, and occasionally the spookiness of these poems, their mysteriousness, seems perfunctory. At those times (as in "The Man in the Tree" or "The Whole Story") I would like to shake Strand by the lapels and say, "But experience is not that uncertain; events are more definable than you say; tell us who you are, where you have come from." Nevertheless, at its best Strand's art is sure. He has found his own voice and, for this book, his own theme: the elusiveness of the self and of reality. There are over a dozen poems in this small collection that are deeply moving.

Robert Pack. SR. Aug. 24, 1968, pp. 39–40

His fourth and finest book [*The Story of Our Lives*]—finest because the focus is so clear, the resonance of an already "placed" voice so unmixed and yet so unforced—begins with a sustained lament for the poet's father, for his father's life rather than for his death. Death is not to be mourned in Strand's thematics, of course, it is only to be identified. . . .

Strand insists, or broods, which is his brand of insistence, on the importance, for individual survival . . . , of rejecting that extremity of consciousness which process, which historical existence, cannot endure or transcend. . . .

Which is why Strand writes his lament not in verse but in the very dialect of negation, in prose, the one linguistic medium out to eliminate itself, to use itself up in the irrecoverable rhythms of speech rather than in the angelic (or ecstatic) measures of repetition and return. No recurrence, no refrain here, but the horror of knowing too much, of suffering more than is to be borne. . . .

What the book ends with . . . is that beginning: three long poems about utterance as enema, "The Story of Our Lives," "Inside the Story," and—crucially—"The Untelling." Evident in the titles alone is that concern with process, movement and trajectory which in even the most fragmentary lyric is felt to underlie the impulse to speak at all; even the wildest cry has a cause, even the weirdest lament has an effect. . . .

"The Untelling" is as vivid and unforgettable as a Bergman film, a Hopper landscape, with all the despairing notification those great names imply—but that is not what is new in Strand's book. What is new is his recovery of what might have seemed, to the merely finger-tapping critic, a lost art: the prosody of erasure. These astonishing poems remind us that originally the word *verse* and the word *prose* come from the same old Latin word, *provertere*, which in its prose past-participle means to *have moved on*, but which in its poetic infinitive means to *roll around again*.

Richard Howard. OhR. Spring, 1974, pp. 104,<br>106–7

Mark Strand is an outstanding poet. He *stands out* because, falling as he does between that generation of major American poets alive today (Ammons, Ashbery, Howard, Kinnell, Merrill, Merwin, Rich, Wright) and the younger poets who are just now gaining public recognition (Gluck, Hass, and Simic, to name three), he is both a transitional figure and a representative one. He is representative in his poetic influences (Stevens, Roethke and Bishop) and his translation of Latin American poets like Alberti; yet his first four books set him apart from the previous generation by their "plain-style" manner and from the following generation by their unmistakable authority of voice.

Strand, then, is unique in the context of contemporary American poetry. More importantly, the gradual development of his work, both in style and scope, signifies a major talent. In this age of abundance, if not over-abundance, when many poets seem to publish anything and everything they put down on paper, Strand is publishing "books of poems," not collections. . . .

*The Story of Our Lives* is not only one of the most original books of poetry to appear in years, but one of the most important, that is to say potentially influential ones as well. Out of all the pseudo-narrative and neo-surrealist poetry of the past few years, which Strand's work superficially resembles, only *The Story of Our Lives* is radical enough to make a significant contribution to a new American poetics, radical because radically simple in its use of syntax and metaphor, those two fundamental principles of American verse. . . . Although there is not the subtle lyricism of the earlier work, work influenced by the elegant lines of Richard Wilbur, nonetheless *The Story of Our Lives* is highly musical verse. . . .

Strand's real poetic debt . . . is to neither Whitman nor Eliot. The austerity of music and image, together with the mastery of tone, reminds one finally of the Stevens of "The Snowman". . . .

Robert Miklitsch. LitR. Spring, 1978, pp. 357–59

The deep underlying motive of Mark Strand's poetry is the solipsism or loneliness of the individual imagination, isolated from the world of memory, objects, the body, other people. This seems to me to be true even though his most poignant poems include "The Marriage," which fulfills its title, and "The Prediction," which in a courtly, painful way extends itself toward the young womanhood of someone long dead.

And though *The Late Hour*, Strand's new book, ends with a naming of people dear to the poet, they are hailed, characteristically, across a darkness that is not only intervening, but an infusing, negative quality. . . .

When Strand's striking imagination and compact, atmospheric style first came to notice ten or twelve years ago, the work gave a marvelous sense of freshness: discovery by the writer, and discovery by the reader. The poems also seemed enigmatic, in a way that was partly attractive, but also raised questions by leaving the shape and provenance of a poem uncertain, or merely vague. And somehow the style that was austere and tense in "Keeping Things Whole" and "My Life by Somebody Else" could turn—seemingly with only a little variation—into something too aureate and easy.

But in the best poems, the sense of freshness holds up: re-reading (in *Darker* and *Reasons for Moving*) poems first encountered in magazines, their virtues appear again. The poet has ideas, not merely sensations, and the ideas are animated by emotional conviction. The dreamlike natural landscape and the sense of the human body are distinctive. And all of this is held together by what can be called Strand's remarkable sense of the poetic: the voice is alone, and what it is alone with is poetry itself. Strand's accomplishment can be described by saying that his work exemplifies a central contemporary idea of poetry—or rather, of the poetic. And the limits of his accomplishment may be suggested by saying that his work is not of the kind that surprises the reader, by forcing us to revise our idea of what poetry is.

Certainly, that Strand's work depends upon a specific poetic diction is an understatement. (Does Mickey Cohen speaks Yiddish?) But the rhythms and syntax, too—litany, parallelism, the expert play of line-length and grammar—remind us that in its isolation, the imagination does not only speak to the world across the void: what it speaks is a poem. Other kinds of poem, even if conservative in form—Frost's "'Out, Out—'" might be an example—bring some sense of surprise that their materials, kind of word, rhythm, unity, can be poetic. Strand is an original wri*er, but not of the kind who challenges our idea of poetry. He confirms that idea, rather than enlarging it.

Robert Pinsky. *Poetry.* Aug., 1978, pp. 298,
300–301

Strand, too, conceives of the recognition of the Other as an elementary step for the emergence of the self: "consider how often we are given to invent ourselves; maybe once, but even so we say we are another, another entirely similar." *The Monument* locates the dialectic between self and Other in the complex relationship between the "author" and his hypothetical translator. If the author recognizes the Other as he constructs the text, so too the verbal text, as it emerges from the Imaginary, is founded, in [Jacques] Lacan's words, upon the "discourse of the Other." The author exclaims: "This word has allowed you to exist, yet this work exists because you are translating it." By extension, of course, we are all "translators" of the text, and the author initiates an endless chain of relationships; moreover, he himself seems to emerge from the diverse texts, sometimes two or three of them together, that act as epigraphs to many of the fifty-two sections, often rivaling the length of the "prime" text. So, for example, a citation from Unamuno seems to prefigure the "author" of *The Monument* by making him an Other projected by a precursor—"the desire to be someone else without ceasing to be myself, and continue being myself at the same time I am someone else." And so by analogy, it is the author of *The Monument* who makes the text of Unamuno or any other writer exist by "translating" it into his own work. *The Monument* thus establishes what [Michel] Foucault calls the endless referentiality, the infinite contextualism of texts that transcends and subverts the priority of any particular Other, and any particular "author.". . .

For Strand, *The Late Hour* is informed by an absence and otherness which creates the sense of a world and language so large and alien that their "presence" can be enunciated only through an indefinite, intersubjective mood. Somebody seems always to be saying something somewhere that seems to be somewhat significant. . . . In this context, the Other before which the self becomes anonymous can be seen as a principle upon which the self can, to use Heidegger's phrase, "throw itself upon the world" and reside in its possibilities. . . . The poet here is located at a point in time where the events described have already begun to occur, and as the past subjunctive implies, continue into the present. This mode of vision constitutes the basis for what Heidegger calls the "retrieve," a movement into the past to recover lost possibilities. Thus in "My Son" Strand reaches back towards a hypothetical son who seems to call "from a place/beyond,/where nothing/everything,/wants to be born." The poet of the retrieve attempts to locate those images from the storehouse of the Imaginary that suggest possible symbolic identifications. That is precisely the motive in "For Jessica, My Daughter"—"I imagine a light/that would not let us stray far apart,/a secret moon or mirror, a sheet of paper."

Richard Jackson. CL. Winter, 1980, pp. 139,<br>142–43

## STYRON, WILLIAM (1925–　)

Since the time he started writing, it seems to have been his conscious aim to perpetuate the great tradition in Southern literature, and to assume the throne left vacant by William Faulkner by producing something that, in terms of both its themes and its historical scope, could merit comparison with *The Sound and the Fury*, *Look Homeward, Angel*, and *All the King's Men*. Small wonder, then, that Norman Mailer, that supreme egotist and self-publicist, should see Styron as a kind of twin, and rival. Styron, it appears, wants to write the great novel of our time just as much as Mailer does; and this has necessarily led to a great deal of jealousy, and some back-biting, between the two of them. Small wonder, either, that Styron's first published book, *Lie Down in Darkness*, should have been treated with almost universal respect and had epithets like "brilliant," "major," and "tragic" showered upon it. *Lie Down in Darkness*, as befitted its author, had ambition written over its every page—it represented a deliberate stab at greatness—and the fact that Styron could back his ambitions up with an extraordinarily seductive style (by turns descriptive, lyrical, and elegiac) more or less guaranteed its initial success. It was almost too easy, thanks to the prodigious brilliance of its language and the intricacy of its narrative structure, to read more into the book than was actually there. . . .

The two books that Styron wrote during the next nine years register no significant advance on *Lie Down in Darkness*, at least as far as this problem of liberation from the past is concerned. His novella *The Long March*, for example, published in 1956, merely describes the same predicament as his first novel does, only this time in simpler terms, using the army as the institutional frame that tends to fix the movement of life and inhibit choice. And his second full-length novel, *Set This House on Fire*, does not so much find á solution as impose one. Cass Kinsolving, its hero, suffers up until the last pages just as Milton Loftis does, then assures us in the last pages, and several years later, that through his suffering he finally found a way out. . . .

Which brings us to *The Confessions of Nat Turner*: Styron's fourth book and the one, I think, in which he has begun to find the answers he needs—both to his own problems as a Southern writer of the second, post-"renaissance" generation, and to the larger questions facing anyone who inherits, however unconsciously, a particular way of organizing and figuring experience. Its subject is that ultimate victim of the past, and the roles and mythologies the past bequeaths, the American Negro slave. Its method, as Styron puts it, is that of "a meditation on history"; since the story is based on an actual slave revolt that occurred in Virginia in 1831 and the supposed "confessions" made by its leader, Nat Turner, after his defeat and eventual capture. In this way, Styron places himself squarely at the center of the Southern tradition—and not, as in *Lie Down in Darkness*, merely to commemorate that tradition but so as to develop it, carry it a stage further. History—the relationship of past to present in the writer's own experience and in the lives of his characters—is as much the motivating force in this book as it is in Faulkner's work, say, in Ransom's or in Warren's. The only difference is that it is now what James Baldwin has called the "common history" of white and black that comes under scrutiny; and this change, far from being a superficial one, signals other changes of approach and interpretation that enable Styron to achieve a radically fresh understanding of familiar material. In a sense the *Confessions* represents the most significant attempt made over the last twenty years to fashion something new out of the creative inheritance of the region. . . .

Richard Gray. *The Literature of Memory: Modern Writers of the American South* (Johns Hopkins Univ. Pr., 1978), pp. 285, 290–91

Although William Styron's fiction develops themes basic to all twentieth-century writing, a broad pattern of meaning in Styron's work is defined by his use of southern characters, settings, and themes, and by his relation to the southern literary tradition. Just as Faulkner found in his "little postage-stamp of native soil" universal meaning, Styron uses southern materials to construct his great drama of rebellion, despair, and the search for order. It is a developing vision. As one novel follows another, after Peyton's suicide in *Lie Down in Darkness*, Styron's protagonists seem to confront their adversaries and themselves with increasing dignity and power. Each work presents with growing effectiveness the traditional southern themes: the curse of racism, the influence of the past, the power of the social environment over individual will. In each novel there is greater understanding of the intimate relation between the black and white experience in southern history: A closer look at these themes as they are advanced in Styron's three long works of fiction—*Lie Down in Darkness* (1951), *Set This House on Fire* (1960), and *The Confessions of Nat Turner* (1967)—suggests that over the years Styron has been moving toward a coherent view of southern history, a kind of "myth.". . .

Nat Turner is the culmination of Styron's developing southern myth, and overall his three major works of fiction point to a tentative but growing optimism. *Lie Down in Darkness* reflects the young Styron's shame and despair for his own class and people; in *Set This House on Fire*, a different kind of hero—while nearly engulfed by the trials which test him—discovers the moral consistency and courage to survive in a chaotic world. *The Confessions of Nat Turner* presents a slave-hero's rebellion, defeat, and despair; yet it ends with spiritual resolution. Styron acknowledges the martyrdom which drove Nat Turner to violence; but in attributing to him a transfiguring final vision which qualifies all he had done, Styron affirms the resiliency of the oppressed spirit and his hope for the reconciliation of peoples whose separation has blighted southern history.

Jane Flanders. In The Achievement of William<br>Styron, rev. ed., ed. Robert K. Morris and Irving<br>Malin (Univ. of Georgia Pr., 1981), pp. 106–7,<br>121–22

Styron is not Elie Wiesel and could not have written an eye-witness memoir of what actually took place at Auschwitz as did Wiesel. Styron is a Southern Protestant who has written a *Bildungsroman*, a novel describing the hero's journey from innocence to experience. Styron did not experience the Holocaust at first hand and he chose not to write about it as if he had. His hero, who in many respects is his younger self, came to know and become involved with a survivor of Auschwitz. In the journey from innocence to experience the hero's encounter with a woman is often a decisive element in the process, but few heroines in literature have ever been responsible for so complex and multifaceted an introduction of the hero to the world of experience as is Sophie. Stingo's encounter with Sophie is absolutely crucial to his journey. Moreover, Stingo's sexual struggles are inseparable from the other components of the journey. Styron neither vulgarizes nor trivializes his subject by weaving together Stingo's sexual story with Sophie's account of what happened to her, the older narrator's reflections on Auschwitz, his younger self, and the many other elements—experiential, historical and ideological—of mature identity that he has been able to grasp as a result of his encounter with Sophie. . . .

*Sophie's Choice* can be seen as less a novel about the Holocaust than a novel about how the Holocaust affected a highly gifted young Southern writer. The Holocaust could not have affected Styron the way it did a Jewish writer. This does not mean that Styron's story is necessarily more or less significant than that of any other writer on the subject. Of necessity, Styron's story is different. Nor has Styron invaded anybody else's literary turf because his own literary tradition is "played out" and no longer offers a viable subject, as Alvin Rosenfeld has ungraciously argued. Styron came by his theme honestly and handles it with great artistry.

Richard L. Rubenstein. MQR. Fall, 1981, pp. 440–41

*Sophie's Choice* is a courageous, in some ways masterly book, a book very hard to review for the simple reason that the plot—even the double entendre in the title—cannot be given away. . . .

The novel's courage lies partly in this: After all the attacks on Styron, especially after *The Confessions of Nat Turner*, which some blacks and liberals (including myself) found offensive here and there, we get in *Sophie's Choice* the same old Styron, boldly and unmercifully setting down his occasional lapses (or his narrator's) into anti-Semitism, anti-feminism and so forth, baring his chest to whatever knives it may possibly deserve, even begging for it. Those who wish to can easily prove him anti-black, anti-white, anti-Southern, anti-Yankee, anti-Polish, anti-Semitic, anti-Christian, anti-German, anti-American, anti-Irish—the list could go on and on. No bigotry escapes him; the worst that can be said of humanity Styron claims for himself, wringing his hands, tearing his hair, wailing to all the congregation, *Mea culpa!* (Only in their taste in music are he and his favored characters faultless.)

Such all-inclusive, self-confessed sinfulness should absolve a man, and in a way, of course, it does; no reader of *Sophie's Choice* can doubt that Styron has put immense energy into trying to understand and deal justly with the evils in American history and the European holocaust, to say nothing of the evil (as well as the good) in his characters. Yet for all the civilized and, in the best sense, Christian decency of Styron's emotions when he's watching himself, the rabid streak is always ready to leap out and take command. . . .

As I said at the outset, Styron is very conscious of being one of the last to work a dying literary tradition—in effect, the Southern Gothic, the vein mined by, among many others, Walker Percy, Robert Penn Warren and, possibly, William Faulkner. (In my opinion, Faulkner has too much humor, even joy, to belong.) Styron makes a point, in *Sophie's Choice*, of naming his influences—Thomas Wolfe, Faulkner, Robert Penn Warren, etc.—and claims, in Nathan Laudau's voice, that he has surmounted them. In *Sophie's Choice* he does far more than that: He transfers, down to the last detail, the conventions and implicit metaphysic of the Southern Gothic—especially as it was handled by Robert Penn Warren—to the world at large. It is no longer just the South that is grandly decayed, morally tortured, ridden with madmen, idiots and weaklings, socially enfeebled by incest and other perversions: it is the world. . . .

In short, though I am profoundly moved by *Sophie's Choice* and consider the novel an immensely important work, I am not persuaded by it. Styron's vision may have humor in it—he tells us about Nathan's hilarious jokes, none of which turn out to be funny on the page—but if so, not an ounce of that humor is in the novel. Perhaps it may be argued that, in a book about American guilt and the holocaust, humor would be out of place. But it seems to me that humor is central to our decency. It cannot be replaced, as it is in *Sophie's Choice*, by great classical music or (a major concern in the novel) sex. If anything, classical music leads in exactly the wrong direction: it points to that ideal Edenic world that those master musicians, the Poles and Germans, thought in their insanity they might create here on earth by getting rid of a few million "defectives." I'm not, God knows, against Bach and Beethoven; but they need to be taken with a grain of salt, expressing, as they do, a set of standards unobtainable (except in music) for poor silly, grotesque humanity; they point our hearts toward an inevitable failure that may lead us to murder, suicide or the helpless groaning and self-flagellation of the Southern Gothic novel. [Originally published in *NYT*, May 27, 1979.]

*[The following is an excerpt from a note appended to the reprint of the above review.]*

Styron succeeded where many failed, and, more than that, that among the few who succeed he stands alone—if one does not count personal diaries or memoirs—as a writer who could fully dramatize the horror, the complexity, and something at least approaching the full historical and emotional meaning of the thing. He found the connections between the vast historical horror and the psychological equivalents in ordinary life, not to mention the eerie connection between what happened in Germany and what happens in these divided United States. But as I was saying, it is not just this subject matter that makes *Sophie's Choice* memorable. His descriptions of Brooklyn life and scenery have a vividness just as uncanny, and his analysis of the young writer's anxieties . . . to say nothing of his psychologically original and convincing analysis of Nathan and Sophie, make one look at people—and oneself—in a new way.

I'm not sorry to have pointed out that *Sophie's Choice* transmutes the old "Southern Gothic" to a new, universal gothic, and I'm not sorry to have claimed that the Southern Gothic is an inherently inferior form. But I would like to take this opportunity to say that the general implication of my remarks was ill-considered. What I suggested, I'm sure, was that, in following the gothic formula, *Sophie's Choice* was a castle built on sand. What is wrong with the gothics is not wrong with *Sophie's Choice*. When Dostoievsky published *Crime and Punishment* (I think it was), somebody important—I forget who—made a long trip to him (I think) to tell him, "You are the savior of all Russia!" After *Sophie's Choice*, I wish I had said, instead of what I did say, or at least in addition to what I did say, "You are the savior of all America."

> John Gardner. In *Critical Essays on William Styron*, ed. Arthur Casciato and James L. W. West III (G. K. Hall, 1982), pp. 247–49, 251–52, 245–47

## ● SWENSON, MAY (1919–    )

May Swenson, in her second book, *A Cage of Spines* . . . , is lively, ingenious, and fanciful. She enters the world of things, animate and inanimate, without self-consciousness and with a rare sense of play. She tells riddles, observes the weather, and turns her mind toward pebbles, birds, and small animals as readily as toward people. Her faults, by no means extensive, are perhaps too continuous a sparkle and an occasional lapse in the sense of scale, for some things *are* larger than others. She is an accurate naturalist, however, and an imaginative one.

> Louise Bogan. *NY*. April 27, 1958, pp. 237–38

May Swenson . . . is a poet who sees singly, and she is, to my personal taste, one of the most ingenious and delightful younger poets writing today (*To Mix with Time: New and Selected Poems*). She has, at any rate, probably the best eye for nature. . . .

Her attention to nature gives May Swenson's poems a directness of gaze that is sometimes lacking when she turns to other, apparently broader subjects. She needs, perhaps, the concreteness of things close at hand in order to see deeply; it is as though language, in her hands, responded naturally only to the actual and palpable. She has a staggering poetic equipment: visual acuity, a sense of form, a fine ear for rhythm and the colloquial. Among her recent poems there are too many with high pretensions, in the shapes of arrows or zigzags or earthquakes, dealing with the Scheme of Things. A series of travel poems—with the exception of one about a bullfight—strikes me as terribly self-conscious, as though someone had been Taking Notes. But even if, in her straining for fresh ways of saying things, this poet's sureness sometimes deserts her, she just cannot go wrong with her nature poems. They are *seen*; the husks and kernels of nature are *there*. And sometimes, at moments of great simplicity, her poems go almost as far in eloquence as poems can—as in a favorite of mine called "Question". . . . A poem like this, in its simple lyricism, makes us forget all questions about the direction of poetry, about schools and generations. It is, after all, a song; and songs hold their own secrets. This one may hold the secret of long life.

Peter Davison. *At.* Dec., 1963, pp. 84–85

No one today is more deft and lucky in discovering a poem than May Swenson. Her work often appears to be proceeding calmly, just descriptive and accurate; but then suddenly it opens into something that looms beyond the material, something that impends and implies. You get to feeling that if the world were different she would have to lie in order to make her point, but that fortunately the world is so various and fortuitous that she can be truthful and also marvelously effective.

So graceful is the progression in her poems that they launch confidently into any form, carrying through it to easy, apt variations. Often her way is to define things, but the definitions have a stealthy trend: what she chooses and the way she progresses heap upon the reader a consistent, incremental effect.

An example poem is "The Little Rapids." The words nimbly leap, at their best; they know what they are about. And the reader finds that they are about the heart, "its zest constant/even in sleep,/its padded roar/ bounding in the grotto of the breast." The words, vivid and apt as they are, are not enough to account for their success; the reader finds himself encountering adventures that converge into the one steady vision of the whole poem.

In the continuing work of Miss Swenson the question becomes: will her luck provide worthy encounters? Will she become distracted by this poking so interestedly in a dilettantish way into stray things? Sometimes, as in "The Secret in the Cat," you think that she is just clever, apt with diction, able to maintain a chosen topic and to rev it up. But that same cleverness often leads into wilder and more interesting regions, as in "A Bird's Life." Some of the cleverest poems, just through their intense unity, succeed in becoming greater things, as in the heart poem mentioned earlier, or in "Sleeping Overnight on the Shore," or in a wonderful poem about "The Watch." Partly, the most successful poems succeed through the ambition, the scope of the curiosity, of the writer; she pursues remote things, how the universe started, what will happen when . . . if. . . .

William Stafford. *Poetry*. Dec., 1967, pp. 184–85

May Swenson is the poet of the perceptible. No writer employs with greater care the organs of sense to apprehend and record the surfaces of the world. She is the exemplar of that first canon of the poet—*Behold!*

From the time her poetry began appearing in the early 1950s in such places as *New Directions in Prose and Poetry*, *Discovery*, the *New Yorker*, and *Poetry*, Miss Swenson's work in its concentration on the sensible has been very much her own. The preoccupation with perception dominates the poetry of her successive volumes—*Another Animal* (1954), *A Cage of Spines* (1958), *To Mix with Time: New and Selected Poems* (1963), *Poems to Solve* (1966), and *Half Sun Half Sleep* (1967). One can name, however, if not influences, at any rate some poets whose work runs parallel to hers. Her development of visual detail has some relationship to the accurate reporting of Marianne Moore. It is sometimes close to that other remarkable declarer of what is there, Elizabeth Bishop. Her interest in nature, its small creatures and their large implications, is reminiscent of Emily Dickinson. In form, her work may have had some relationship to the experiments of E. E. Cummings, though it has always been a distant one, her experiments having gone farther into the visual and less into the verbal than his. . . .

It is as an observer that May Swenson has become best known. Such a comment as Robert Lowell's "Miss Swenson's quick-eyed poems should be hung with permanent fresh paint signs" represents a common reaction. Miss Swenson achieves this freshness by a good eye enlivened by imagination. But however imaginative, her poetry is continually tied to accuracy of sight, to truth to the literal and concrete. This is so even when the truth is conveyed by metaphor or in a spirit of aesthetic play. From the beginning, Miss Swenson has demonstrated an unusual ability to set down accurate and detailed observations. . . .

Miss Swenson's involvement with the perceptibly solid is further seen in her placement of the poem on the page. Lines and spaces are carefully arranged in patterns appropriate to the subject. Some words are given typographical emphasis by being set off and repeated. Even punctuation and capitalization—or the lack of them—are arranged for visual effect. . . .

This linking of the parts of the poem, the care in its visual physical arrangement, is not related to form alone. It reflects the careful observation, the respect for the whole range of the senses, that goes into the language and concepts that Miss Swenson presents. Her poems are not limited to linear time; they are patterns in space as well. The shaped poem represents the poet's response to the aesthetic need for structure, a need met in other poets by the formal stanza or the syllabic or metric line. The enclosing of the poem within spatial boundaries rather than auditory-rhythmic limits is especially appropriate to the perceptual qualities of Miss Swenson's art.

Ann Stanford. SoR. Winter, 1969, pp. 58–59, 68–69, 71

She is known as a nature poet, "one of the few good poets who write good poems about nature . . . not just comparing it to states of mind or society," as Elizabeth Bishop has remarked. You can easily cull a bestiary from her work, which would include geese, turtles, an owl and its prey, a bee and a rose, frogs, fireflies, cats and caterpillars, landscapes and cityscapes, and always with a wondering, curious eye, an intense concern about the structure and texture of her subject, an extraordinary tactility. "The pines, aggressive as erect tails of cats," begins a poem on "The Forest." A poem called "Spring Uncovered" begins, "Gone the scab of ice that kept it snug,/the lake is naked," and ends where "a grackle, fat as burgundy,/gurgles on a limb" with "bottle-glossy feathers." She watches things over long periods, and tracks her metaphors through itineraries of implications, with pleasure.

But beyond the naturalist's patient observation lies something else. What critics have called Swenson's "calculated naïveté" or her ability to become "a child, but a highly sophisticated child," is actually that childlike ability to envision something freshly, to ask incessant questions and always be prepared for unexpected answers—required of the creative scientist. "What things really are we would like to know," she murmurs, and what else is the motive of the speculative intellect? Swenson's poetry asks as many questions as a four-year-old, and she wants to know not only how things are made and what they resemble, but where they are going and how we fit in. . . .

While Swenson does not write on feminist themes most of the time, she does so occasionally, with electrifying results. . . . Most often, she blends, she balances. Science, technology, the mental life of observation, speculation: she has invaded these traditionally "masculine" territories. Yet her consistent intimacy with her world, which contains no trace of the archetypal "masculine" will to conquer or control it, seems archetypally "feminine." So does the way she lets herself be precise yet tentative and vulnerable about her observations where a comparable male poet, perhaps driven by the need to overcome alienation, might be pretentious (Snyder?), pedantic (Olson?), nervous (Ammons? James Wright?) or agonized (Kinnell?); and her affinity for the small-scale object, like Emily Dickinson's, also reads like a feminine characteristic. . . .

Swenson has always had an individual style, though bearing traces here and there of Cummings, Marianne Moore, and especially Emily Dickinson. She has always been committed to formal experimentation, and she has often played with the shapes of poems. . . .

Swenson does not theorize on the subject, but her work shows some ways to express our relation to the natural world as we comprehend it. The shapes in *Iconographs* are shapes of speculation, balanced between the patterned and the random—for so we presently guess Nature to be— and attempting to capture both the ways we fit into the world and the ways we cannot fit. They are playful, quirky, eccentric, and imply that these are qualities intrinsic to the world as well as ourselves. But Swenson is modest as well as mentally fearless, and will not let us pretend that our model-building is more than that.

Alicia Ostriker. APR. March/April, 1978, pp. 35–<br>36, 38

These poems [in *New and Selected Things Taking Place*] mutter in the passive voice: "it is observed"; "it happens." The event, the text, stands out even as our guide to it steps back so as not to block the view. May Swenson indeed camouflages herself marvelously, and her protective coloration conveys respect. So we see "The World" clarified but glean only hints of "her world." For the poetry has no heroine and no heroics. In this she differs a great deal from so many modern women poets who attempt to find themselves—or at least such fragments of self as are retrievable—in their work. May Swenson, on the contrary, effaces herself, blends into the landscape. . . .

Swenson searches heaven and earth for a vantage point. The problem is, none exists. The meanings of God's spangled heavens have long since spilt out into the Einsteinian universe. Matter is motion. Fixed viewpoints swirl away and Swenson so much needs a firm footing and a clear view at first hand of things taking place. The sun, moon, and earth spinning in space are for her, and nearly everybody else, news—acceptable hearsay—third-hand reports. Remote. . . .

May Swenson derives her prime inspiration not from Mother Nature but from nature; she is too empirical to be classified as a "nature-poet." Her close, first-hand observation of the external world, coupled with scrupulous attention to the particular, labels her, wittingly or unwittingly, as a "naturalist." She is also a poet and may lay claim as such to a literary tradition and to her own particular forebears (e. e. cummings and Emily Dickinson for sure, probably Blake and Herbert, Apollinaire perhaps), but she covers her trail well. The book contains, I believe, no direct references to literature and in her particular field of inquiry, the outside or the outdoors, she blithely slips away from the formal, well worn path of the pastoral (there are a few exceptions; "Green Red Brown and White" is one) in order to plunge into new territory. She follows odd byways, stalking to catch the local fauna unawares. . . .

May Swenson can fairly be described as gun-shy. *Homo sapiens* makes her nervous. If she cannot declass man a notch or two, fur and feather him as it were, objectify him, she nerves herself and resorts to anthropomorphizing, as she does in the brilliant pot-calling-the-kettle-black, male-female dialogue of "Bleeding," with its text slashed diagonally by a white ribbon of alienation. Generally May Swenson fumbles whenever she has human preoccupations—sporting, social, whatever—on her mind. The voiced-interaction poems drum along, their cross-cutting repetition of words monotonous and mind-numbing, like a mantra. . . .

May Swenson lives on the Eastern seaboard, writes with a Western accent, and sees with a certain amused, clear-sighted naiveté. One has the impression most poetry written by women still is an interior matter and is set within four walls. Although she is not oblivious to the problems of being female, May Swenson is not indoors enough, let alone enough in her own skin, to accommodate herself to the woman poet's present persona. She does not want to "make waves" in the sense of stirring up trouble. She leaves the problem of gender pretty much alone, if only because it could be messy (cf. "Bleeding"). She edges away from the subjective, yet she holds with Romanticism, by which I mean an interest in the particular over the general, the single over the recurring. In selecting events, animals, men, scenery, topics, she is drawn to the non-nondescript, the unique occasion: a moon-landing, the strange animal (bison not cow), the odd man out (a blind man), the picturesque canyons, lakes, or into the gothic and the magical.

But when she is put on her mettle and forced to catch the meaning of the antithetically banal or the flux and flurry of water and snow, wind and weather, then she gives us poems such as "Working on Wall Street" and "Looking Uptown" and her *Iconographs*. Then she shines.

Rosemary Johnson. Parnassus. Fall/Winter,<br>1978, pp. 47–50, 52, 59

May Swenson's *New and Selected Things Taking Place* collects nearly thirty years of her remarkable poetry. At sixty, she may well be the fiercest, most inquisitive poet of her generation; certainly few are more brilliant or more independent of mien. Her poems . . . are characterized by an extreme reticence of personality, an abundant energy, and an extraordinary intercourse between the natural and intellectual worlds. She has always been as formal as poets come, demonstrating early and late a skilled employment of traditional verse as well as a passion for invented patterns. There are two central obsessions in her work: the search for a proper perspective and the celebration of life's embattled rage to continue. Her poems ask teleological questions and answer them, insofar as answers are ever possible, in every conceivable poetic strategy: she writes narrative, catalog, image, concrete, interrogatory, and sequence poems (often mixing these in a single work). Her language is generally sonorous, remarkable for its Anglo-Saxon stress, alliteration, extensive word fusions, and a devotion (now declining, it appears) to rhyme. She has made language an instrument for pursuit of ideas, but always ideas discoverable only in things of the experiential world. She believes, apparently, that the world functions according to some hidden final purpose, and furthermore, that a right apprehension ultimately reveals a Coleridgean interconnectedness of all parts. . . .

Nothing so excites Swenson's imagination or reveals her poetic investigation as that image of flight. In poems about airplanes, birds, insects, and especially space exploration, she celebrates the joy of flight. Motion is both her subject and her image, being life itself. Flight, however, rarely means escape; it is her means for exploration, penetration, for travel to and through the world; it is what humans cannot naturally do but . . . what becomes the passage toward and into vision. . . .

Vision, seeing, looking, recording are so pervasive in her poems that one almost forgets how active she makes all the senses in the service of penetrating surfaces. Flight is not only the revelation of human bondage, it is also the vehicle of imaginative and intellectual possibilities. . . .

Never a poet of ennui or cynicism, though often a poet of elegiac grief, she believes that all is beautiful if seen properly. . . .

Dedicated as they are to angles of vision, avoiding autobiography and personality, Swenson's poems necessarily emphasize structure—sometimes to the point of mannerism. Often enough they possess a wonderful lyricism that celebrates; but primarily they nominate, and this occasionally leads to an annoyingly indiscriminate series of similes; a thing looks like this. Or this, or this. This mannerism reveals a kind of "scientific" attitude in her work, an attitude also marked by often esoteric and technical terminology—not in itself a problem though it helps create the impression of a dispassionate stance when there is passion present and the need to show it. Swenson's reticence may sometimes mean the difference between a powerful experience and no experience, as in riddles or dry humor. Indeed, one of Swenson's characteristics is a wry wit which sometimes trails off into whimsy, into the glib and clever. . . .

If Swenson sometimes generates consternation and dismay, that fault is born of a poetry urgently trying to tell us that everything matters, a poetry so affirmative that we cannot escape knowing we matter. Even random reading here produces surprise, delight, love, wisdom, joy, and grief. May Swenson transforms the ordinary little-scrutinized world to a teeming, flying first creation.

Dave Smith. *Poetry*. Feb., 1980, pp. 291–95

## TATE, ALLEN   (1899–1979)

Most readers have long known that Tate has produced some of the finest poetry of his generation. This is true even of unsympathetic readers inclined to complain that the corpus is uneven in quality (as it is) and unfulfilled in promise (as it is not). Most consider the single novel a distinguished achievement, though few have recognized that it constitutes the great watershed in Tate's life as an artist, bringing into significant conjunction the insights, tendencies, and techniques of his early work and anticipating the masterworks that began to appear after 1940. As for criticism, no one—at least no one since the appearance of *Essays of Four Decades* in 1969—has doubted that in an age of critics Tate stands with the half dozen best and most influential. Now it is possible to regard the whole as a series of forays into the knowledge essential to our self-awareness as latter-day heirs of western civilization. Tate, we see, was never more than incidentally Fugitive, Agrarian, or even southern but was from first to last the colonial European, incidentally sired in Clark County, Kentucky, and doomed to live with the frustration of somehow having been born a legitimate spiritual child of Aristotle in a world dominated by children of Plato and Descartes.

Nevertheless the fact of Tate's southernness has often raised unwarranted expectations about his work, even in the minds of some who ought to have known better. This is especially true of *The Fathers*, a major novel. Arthur Mizener attributes its initial success to the possibility that readers thought it might be another *Gone With the Wind* and adds "whereas it is in fact the novel *Gone With the Wind* ought to have been." His "ought" is likely to be misunderstood. In one sense "the novel *Gone With the Wind* ought to have been" was Stark Young's masterful romance *So Red the Rose*, published in 1934; but Mizener is calling attention to the universality of Tate's work. He characterizes the action of *The Fathers* in the phrase "a terrible conflict between two fundamental and irreconcilable modes of existence," which, apt though it is, has had the unfortunate effect of inviting some readers to see the novel in Manichaean terms. The two modes probably are irreconcilable, but only as the parts of any paradox are irreconcilable; and together they constitute a paradox that characterizes all societies, American as well as those from which American society sprang, and will undoubtedly characterize the new societies into which America must dissolve long after our present body politic has vanished from the earth. To put it briefly, the world which Allen Tate describes is the perennial world of humankind, characterized by order and the appearance of stability on the one hand and by a restless dynamism on the other, both of which aspects seek to prevail as well as to exist in the face of a vast uncharacterized abyss which John Milton in another context called "the womb of nature and perhaps her grave."

J. O. Bryant, Jr. SwR. Spring, 1978, pp. 274–75

The body of Allen's poetry . . . is slim—as slim as Eliot's and Ransom's. He published one novel, *The Fathers* (1938). A remarkable work, it was never widely popular; but like Allen's best poetry, it remains in print, and I think it is destined to last.

Why did one so greatly and variously gifted write and publish so little? What he said of his friend John Ransom was not, I think, true of him: that he set out deliberately to be a Minor Poet. . . . My observation is that as an imaginative writer Allen had a gift that was highly and intricately autobiographical. This may seem odd, in that his poetics placed a premium upon achieved anonymity, classical restraint, the primacy of craftsmanship over subject—the antithesis of the romantic subjective artist whose work is the fervent unmediated outpouring of his own sensibilities. "As a poet I have no experience," he once remarked. Yet—and perhaps the paradox is the key—almost all that Allen wrote is drawn either directly from his own situation or from that of his immediate forebears. He used to speak of himself as having conducted his education in public, and if by that statement he meant that his writings consisted of his openly enunciated response to his own experience, it is quite appropriate.

As poet and critic Allen had impeccable taste. His literary coat-of-arms might well have borne the motto *nil admirari*—to be astonished at and by nothing. So fastidious was his literary sensibility that he could not tolerate blemish or imperfection, and this habit of mind no doubt served to lessen, or at any rate to restrict, his response to much work that was flawed but powerful. But whatever he admired was well worth the admiring, and he was almost never wrong in his enthusiasms. I believe that this fastidiousness was what inhibited him from publishing or even continuing to work for very long on anything of his own that did not seem absolutely right to him. His sensibility and his taste were whole and unified; had it been otherwise, he might have written more. Again, though, he would not have been Allen Tate. What he did write is not merely distinguished: it is unique in its distinction.

Louis D. Rubin, Jr. SwR. Spring, 1979, p. 270

The poetry of Allen Tate constitutes a body of work formidable not so much for its size, although ample enough, as for its demands on the intellectual tenacity of readers. These demands have been partially met by a small body of essays of considerable merit, informative and rewarding to the patient searcher for a full comprehension of Tate. The task of explication is never complete, of course, and the finest of commentaries will always display lacunae. Thus certain poems, crucial for an interpretation of Tate's achievement but almost totally neglected, have never received adequate elucidation. These unexplored texts, seemingly intransigent for the critic, constitute a serious barrier to the complete understanding of his poetry. Nevertheless, the principal gap in our knowledge of Tate lies elsewhere. The unity of his work, his poetry and prose together, has escaped the critical net. Despite some laudable attempts to demonstrate the integrity of Tate's career, its basis has remained obscure for most readers. As a result, few have grasped the magnitude of his achievement. . . .

Tate's skill as a craftsman of verse, his unusual style, his astonishing imagery, and his energetic syntax have been frequently noted and delineated. However, for all the dramatic intimacy and personal vigor that characterize it, Tate's is primarily a poetry of ideas. What keeps it from lapsing simply into an intellectual exercise in verse is his insistence that ideas are effective in poetry only when embodied in human actions and feelings. In Tate's work, then, personal intensity is inseparable from a commitment to intellectual integrity. His rejection of what he calls "romanticism" is a refusal to segregate the truth of the heart from that of the mind.

Thus Tate's work should be given the kind of consideration accorded other twentieth-century poets—such as Yeats, Eliot, or Pound—who combine an intimate focus on personal experience with an extensive grasp of the Western intellectual tradition. Though the play of ideas in Tate's writings is often limited to a small core of closely related themes, the range of his awareness is broad indeed. He can speak of Carneades, Proclus, or Iamblichus in one breath and of Mistral, Madame de La Fayette, or St.-John Perse in the next. He brings a well-informed mind to his criticism of Civil War histories and to his judgment of philosophies of history. He is a truly cosmopolitan author whose principal concern is European rather than American culture, even when the American South plays a central role in his meditations.

Robert S. Dupree. *Allen Tate and the Augustinian Imagination: A Study of the Poetry* (Louisiana State Univ. Pr., 1983), pp. xiii–xiv

## TAYLOR, PETER (1917–   )

Who, then, are Taylor's people—characters—individuals—the blood and flesh of the stories? It has frequently been noted that he writes only about upper middle-class Southerners who are not involved in acts of bloodshed, lust, or violence. Taylor's characters, therefore, put the author in a class apart from most contemporary Southern authors. His characters live in the city, function as a family unit in spite of a great many urban tensions, and display good manners at home and in the social circles to which they belong. . . .

What they possess and hold on to and practice is a set of formal country manners reminiscent of Jane Austen and eighteenth century England. It is as though the country house in Miss Austen's rural society had packed up and moved (servants and all) to the West End section of Nashville and settled in Elliston Place or Acklen Park or the suburbs and gone right on with established rituals. As a class these people may appear an isolated group in the modern Southern city and seem foreigners to its main currents. The truth is that they have not lost their close connections with the country. They have not cut themselves off from their background. That means that they retain an interest in an outlying county and keep in touch with cousins, friends, and older family servants in a small town somewhere beyond the periphery of the Nashville Basin. In other words Taylor's urban dwellers still cling, however futilely, to agrarian and feudal concepts of land and place. The Episcopal Church is so much taken for granted that it is seldom mentioned. . . .

What strikes us about Taylor on first reading is the almost casual understatement he gives to a theme as momentous as [the conflict resulting from the Southern shift from country life to city life]. The changes from a rural to an urban South are slow and quietly modulated in the stories, but they are indeed there to be acknowledged, dealt with, and somehow accommodated. . . .

Taylor's characters do not look ahead to a later, more complex time or consciously try to come to grips with what may be in store for them and their descendants in the Super-City. His people are simply not given to town-and-social planning, predicting the future, or intellectualizing on man's fate as a city-dweller. They may be concerned with Time Past and Time Present, but they are not ruffled by the omens of Time Future. They accept loneliness and separation and the loss of "Happy Valley." But they complain very little. Even while looking back, they do not howl over their losses; they present a fairly genial, good-natured face to a changing world and to each other. As a class they have not as yet been totally fragmented or assimilated into the ways of the city.

Unlike some of the people John Updike, Philip Roth, and Walker Percy write about, Taylor's Nashvillians are human beings who elicit compassion from us but do not strike us with terror. There is always the chance, however, that given another twenty years they will be just as terrible as the others. Perhaps Taylor is saying, finally, that by another generation these people will have outlived their Nashville period and come to the end of their uneasy period of Grace. As is the usual way of artists, Taylor has recorded a fragile company just in the nick of time.

Herschel Gower. Shenandoah. Winter, 1977, pp.<br>38–40, 47

As an author, Peter Taylor is more often praised than understood. The respect his work inspires frequently seems taken in by appearances, by the fact that in a formal sense, his material *seems* fixed. His stories usually take place in Tennessee—in Memphis or Nashville or Chatham; the characters are drawn from the upper middle class or from the Negro servant class; people are seen in terms of the family, rarely as isolated individuals or divorced ones or even single ones; the stories occur before 1960, and some take place around the turn of the century, while others are governed by the events and history of the 19th century, particularly, of course, the Civil War.

Yet the limitations Mr. Taylor sets on his work barely contain the shifting, probing attitude he constantly turns on his material. He is a great craftsman, but of a foxy sort, intent on working as much complexity as possible into the world behind his simple surfaces. In his best stories, his masterpieces, every detail is present in all its vital controversy; every part hums with its own inner fullness, as well as in its relation to every other part. He is a master of contradiction, though we have only to mention this quality when Mr. Taylor's singlemindedness must be accounted for. His work has always been concerned with the conflict between affectionate, civil society and chaos, regardless of whether the disorder is sexual, drunken, or natural. . . .

*In the Miro District* . . . invites us to look back. Tonally, particularly in the experimental prose poems, the book evokes the author's earliest stories when he wrote out of oneness with the domestic context he so lovingly described. . . .

The sources of tension in these stories are slowly transformed in a way which often emphasizes the futility of their having been distinguished in the first place. Mr. Taylor repeatedly raises moral dilemmas only to show they can't be solved because there are no black and white moral categories. Yet when we come to "In the Miro District," the equivalence of grandfather and grandson is ultimately what makes the story one of renewal. . . .

Human social life has always seemed precarious to Mr. Taylor, but at first its greatest threat was human violence. Gradually, his allegiance to a specific social order has yielded to his growing insight into the total insecurity in which custom must survive. In his most recent story, "In the Miro District," custom itself is questioned as a stable vessel, or rather our need for it to be fixed is questioned. "In the Miro District" is about the revolution in custom between the grandfather's day and his grandson's. Both live according to entirely different conventions, but the difference is one of detail. For both men, custom has not changed in its essential reference to love. The woman who once had all value vested in her honor still represents all that's important. Once her importance was expressed by not acknowledging her passionateness, now the opposite is true. . . . Where Mr. Taylor once seemed to fear chaos, he now seems to trust the order inherent in experience: an order that does not depend on social restraint for its existence. Through his career, he has altered and refined his questions, viewing the problem of order and disorder from different, even opposing, perspectives, testing the sanity of reason and the vitality of the irrational, mixing them until his questions have given way—not so much to answers as to moral sureness.

Jane Barnes Casey. VQR. Spring, 1978, pp. 213–<br>14, 227, 229–30

Taylor's dissatisfaction with the new (or the Northern or the New Southern) is untouched by the kind of revulsion or disgust which helped lead T. S. Eliot and Caroline Gordon to embrace religious faith. In fact, several of his stories—"A Spinster's Tale," for example—obliquely treat disgust of this sort as neurotic. At the same time, Taylor clear-sightedly places the retrogressive or escapist elements of Agrarian traditionalism. Only rarely are his stories merely elegiac (as in "The Elect," with its uncomplicatedly crude and unthinking New Southern politician and his comparably loyal and sensitive Old Southern wife); almost always they expose and complicate sustaining illusions or stereotypes. . . .

Taylor is most deeply and honourably Jamesian . . . in the compassionate ends to which he puts his objectivity: detachment in [his Collected Stories] facilitates sympathy, especially for the injured and the tainted, for the down-trodden wife, the fancy woman, the domestic (as in James, the victims are often women). This sympathy is also extended to the reader, through Taylor's welcoming, anecdotal manner, through the long, looping digressions, and a habit of unravelling mysteries or difficulties. Like James, Taylor locates character and significant incident in the subtlest details of speech and gesture. . . . The old ways are unsatisfying not because man's depravity or sinfulness has spoiled them (the pre-lapsarian South is an illusion too), but because they're limited and limiting. . . .

No moment in Taylor's fiction is richer or more complex than the end of "There," in which the two themes of home and death are woven together in a manner that reveals and ultimately refuses the tragic vision.

In other stories, though, the heroic gesture is seen quite differently. "Je Suis Perdu," for example, one of several stories set outside the South (but Southern in its themes and preoccupations), sees heroism as the *acceptance* of limitation; as a coming to terms with the constructions of relationships and the inevitability of ageing. This difference, though, pales in the face of a larger similarity: Taylor's understanding of and sympathy for the claims of both courses open to the protagonist; his sense that both defiance and acceptance are right, and partial.

The doubleness of this perspective belongs to tragedy. It also returns us to the myth of the South in Faulkner and the best of the Southern Agrarians. Coming to terms with "home" in much of the most interesting Southern writing means coming to terms with a history that includes poverty, guilt, defeat, and frustration. In this sense, it is a metaphor for the acceptance of human limitation, and the denial of false dreams of perfectibility. But at the same time it is also seen more positively: as a refusal of selfishness, a loving acknowledgement of kinship and relation. . . .

Though Taylor's output is slight, and in some ways narrow, it places him in the first rank of living American writers.

Zachary Leader. TLS. Jan. 22, 1982, pp. 75–76

# ● THEROUX, PAUL (1941–    )

That Paul Theroux's *Waldo*, for instance, is less than a stunning success may be the result of the twenty-five-year-old's desire to flap his literary wings too soon and fly too far. Perhaps he is impatient with the cloister, having left it, and yearns to explore the World at Large. In any event, Mr. Theroux forsakes his original reform school setting, follows his central character to Rugg College on a sexual fellowship of sorts, and turns him into a newly famous writer typing in a glass cage over the heads of enraptured nightclub audiences. Waldo is a disturbed gadfly who darts from crag to silhouetted crag, precluding the author's opportunity to dig beneath the complex surface he surveys. . . .

On the other end of the shelf, I wonder why Houghton Mifflin published *Waldo*. This is not to deny that Mr. Theroux has a book in him, it is simply to opine that this, like many a first novel, isn't the book because the author has not learned to control his chosen form, material, scope and style simultaneously. There are interesting moments and some of the comic images glance off truths like stones from a chisel—but the pieces don't fit together and the final sculpture doesn't fit the pedestal. . . . Mr. Theroux has not created a moving odyssey and the best elements of the book are the little sojourns of passing images, phrases and moments. . . .

I submit that the fault is not really the author's; he has an itch to write, literary ambition and some obvious talents that can grow with experience—but they need to be focused and distilled. The fault lies with the publisher who does a disservice to himself, the reading public and the author by publishing him too early. Some people ask why nobody reads fiction any more; one reason is that readers are put off by books that are not good enough.

Philip Kopper. AS. Autumn, 1967, pp. 698, 700

Narrative verve, the brightly sketched collection of urban desperadoes, and the extraordinary vividness of physical London will make *The Family Arsenal* a deservedly popular novel. For an American, Theroux has a remarkable ear for the rhythms and elisions of English underworld slang, and he even manages at this late date to make obscenity expressive. No foreign writer I've read has so skillfully caught the blend of coarseness, provincialism and bigotry that is one distinctive (and usually unexportable) brand of popular British humor.

In all these respects, *The Family Arsenal* is an assured success, like Theroux's fine travel book of last year, *The Great Railway Bazaar*; but Theroux has ambitions that go beyond the expert construction of a timely thriller. Opening with an epigraph from *The Princess Casamassima* and alluding a dozen times to *The Secret Agent*, he wants much of what happens in *The Family Arsenal* to play off against the two famous novels by James and Conrad that have shaped the way many people think about the anarchist impulse. . . .

Theroux's efforts to provide by implication an analysis of a historical situation and an ample sense of personal motivation are finally less successful than his handling of narrative excitement, satiric portraiture and the evocation of urban violence and distress. To ask for more power and analysis from an intelligent, absorbing thriller is not to debunk Theroux's achievement (or to grumble that he doesn't stack up against Conrad and James), but to suggest some of the critical issues raised by his work and the promises it holds out.

Lawrence Graver. NYT. July 11, 1976, pp. 1–2

Paul Theroux is simply a wonder, and this his eighth novel [*Picture Palace*] a remarkable piece of work. In reviewing his last one, *The Family Arsenal*, two years ago I spoke of how it (and its very fine predecessor, *The Black House*) each featured a desperate man endowed with great sensitivity, irony, and visionary or novelistic powers of forecast and apprehension. I also noted that both novels were consistently entertaining—I had not been so entertained since discovering Anthony Burgess in the middle 1960's. *Picture Palace* is even bolder and more daring than the last two, partly because its narrator (a first-person narrative Theroux hasn't used since *Saint Jack*) is a tough seventy-year-old photographer named Maude Coffin Pratt who is both desperately wrong about things—as we see from the tale of her life she unfolds, and which provides the course of the novel—and righter about them than anybody else can be, the way artists are "right" about things. In other words, Theroux has worked the metaphor of "visionary powers"—all those nineteenth-century heroines who saw so much—into a shutter-snapping wise-cracking ugly duckling of a narrator whose (hopeless?) passion for her brother Orlando is the determining fact of her life, and the reason she becomes a photographer in the first place. The book undertakes a very complicated and satisfyingly dialectical exploration of blindness, sight, insight, vision and revision—which exploration is the equivalent to the moral and political argument of *The Family Arsenal*, or the anthropological and mystical one of *The Black House*.

An exploration, but not an argument, for one never feels after reading Theroux that one has learned something about the Nature of . . . of whatever. An even better word for it is "entertainment," and some of the most entertaining things about *Picture Palace* are the set-pieces in which Maude encounters famous modern artists—like D.H. Lawrence or T.S. Eliot or Frost or Raymond Chandler—and "does them" (play is made with the sexual force of this expression) into art, storing them in an old windmill on Cape Cod, but more truly in the picture palace of her mind put on display by this novel. . . . It's all just a story, dazzlingly and intensely told, with the great modern fictional classics—James and Conrad and Ford and Faulkner, and Graham Greene too—giving Theroux ballast for the idea that the telling is enough. I think it is, because he never lets up, never writes a paragraph of filler or "transition" which has less than his full presence as a writer behind it. *Picture Palace* is another impressive testimony that as a steadily producing writer of long and short fiction, travel books, essays and reviews—of "letters" generally—no American writer matters more than this gifted and possessed word-man.

William H. Pritchard. HdR. Autumn, 1978, pp.<br>527–29

[*The Old Patagonian Express: By Train through the Americas*] is a sequel to the author's superbly entertaining *The Great Railway Bazaar: By Train through Asia*. Longer than its predecessor, and a good deal grimmer, it has fewer comic moments to divert us from the poverty Mr. Theroux everywhere encounters and which, since he speaks Spanish, is not so forgettably anonymous as the Asian distress that figured as little more than dusky scenery in the *Railway Bazaar*. I suspect that this book was also harder to write, since here Theroux was not inventing a form for a novel experience but uninspiredly following his old literary tracks. It is certainly harder to read. Theroux's prose is as sheerly enjoyable as ever and his insights into individual and social character are as fresh and penetrating, but the vagaries of rail travel in Latin America repeatedly tempt him to ramble from the main line of his narrative, and the book is a bit bloated in consequence. Theroux's padding, however, is always lively and intelligent, so it seems ungrateful to complain. What is it, then, that makes this book difficult, at once less entertaining and more interesting than the *Railway Bazaar*? It is, I think, the morally ironic contrast between the human misery Theroux observes and his will to make art and money out of rendering it, an irony that is echoed in our will to enjoy ourselves as much as we did on his earlier trip, and damn the disquieting disparity between us and the direly poor peasants we glimpse on every page.

Jack Beatty. *NR*. Sept. 22, 1979, p. 54

Drastic change indeed stalks the world of his fiction, that precisely rendered realm where cultures clash and characters encounter each other as society's pawns in a larger pattern. In a post-colonial world, in which Third World countries are struggling to exist in their own right (Africa provides the setting for five of the books, Malaysia for three), the only certainty is that such colonialist regimes "would be supplanted by an equal viciousness and that the Congo . . . would know more pitiless regimes." . . .

The encounters between East and West, between different cultures, and between the temperaments of different characters provide the formal antitheses of Theroux's fiction: "I often find that an alien landscape comes to me in sharper focus, and I like contrast: of character or situation." Nowhere is this more apparent than in the opening scene of *Girls at Play* (1969), in which the order of a hockey field at a girls' school is contrasted with the surrounding jungle. . . .

In one sense Theroux's novels and stories can be seen as fictions of manners. The characters often exist as products of a particular social and cultural milieu who are thrust into some alien landscape and must either come to some accommodation with it or muster a complete rejection of it. Theroux seems intent on exploring the essence of "American-ness" in many of his books and in debunking the older, colonial myths perpetuated by Graham Greene and Somerset Maugham in earlier novels. The anonymous Consul in the stories of *The Consul's File* (1977) wishes to disassociate himself entirely from the typically romantic image of the Consul as "drinker, a womanizer, reckless, embittered, a man with a past, an extravagant failure of some sort with a certain raffish charm. . . .I was pretty ordinary, in a place that saw little of the ordinary." It is the Maugham myth of colonial outposts the Consul wishes to eradicate . . . .

Theroux's fictional techniques are precisely those of the literary realist. His remarkably lucid and emblematic style is based on careful and precise observation, the seizing of sharp and clear images, and the documentary urge to record exactly what happens during the conflicts that ensue. . . . Exact impressions are caught like the moment in a photograph. In them the reader can drown, be swallowed up in the hard and clear reality of the image. . . . Theroux's precision in his style matches his eye for manners and customs—and the two reflect one another.

Along with the precise style—the almost documentary sureness and piling up of image and perception in a lucid sequence—must be included Theroux's plots. All his novels are meticulously plotted, embodying the same formal antitheses and structures as his themes. The novels are mechanical marvels of aesthetic balance and proportion, seeking out well-rounded patterns in all things. When these plots falter or seem less self-assured—as in the often tedious abstractions of *Picture Palace*, the somewhat fuzzy letdown at the end of *The Black House*, the almost too pat conclusion of *Jungle Lovers*—the novels seem to collapse: they lose that carefully "boxed" quality, that marvelous crafting of novelists like Kipling, Stevenson, Conrad, and Greene, whom Theroux has suggested inspired his own writing. . . . Many of Theroux's "willful and indpendent" characters may share his sense of a charmed life. They may also feel themselves possessed and mesmerized by an alien landscape which threatens to overwhelm them. In the middle of a long journey as yet incomplete but full of artistic promise and accomplishment, the writer may clutch his images and his observations to him as if holding on to his own evanescent consciousness and transforming it into palpable, recognizable shape. The tight precision of Theroux's literary realism—his style, his plots, his carefully balanced characters and customs, his searingly accurate perception of decay, the contemporary wasteland of much of the Third World and the American's ambiguous place in it—reveals a dedicated and thorough artist, perhaps like Henry James or, one of his own favorites, Joyce Cary. . . .

His awareness of the emptiness at the center of things seems to elicit not so much an ultimate vision but a sense of exhaustion and depletion, not a fullness of some existential dread but a lack of something, a black hole at the heart of the matter.

Samuel Coale. Critique. 22, 3, 1981, pp. 5–8,<br>13–15

One needs energy to keep up with the extraordinary, productive restlessness of Paul Theroux. He is alarmingly like the perpetual motion machine described in his new novel ("natural magnets . . . a thousand of them on a pair of wheels . . . you could light a city with something like that"), except that Theroux doesn't go in circles and has never moved in a predictable direction.

He is as busy as a jackdaw in the way he scavenges for forms and styles. In earlier novels he has taken conventional popular molds, like the ghost story (*The Black House*), the thriller (*The Family Arsenal*), the celebrity memoir (*Picture Palace*), and made them over for his own thoroughly original purposes. The geographic locations of his tales now make an almost unbroken ring around the globe. His train journeys (*The Great Railway Bazaar, The Old Patagonian Express*) are best read as freewheeling, impromptu fictions—the adventures of a picaresque hero who happens to bear the same name as his author and who shares his author's chronic cabin fever.

Theroux is 40 now—the most gifted, most prodigal writer of his generation. That statement begs a significant question. When, say, Malamud, Mailer, Updike, or Roth were 40, one could have spotted a stray paragraph from any of their books as "typically" Malamud, Mailer, Updike, or Roth. Can one do the same with Theroux? I couldn't. He has moved in skips and bounds, never staying long enough in one place for the moss of a mannered style to grow on his writing. . . .

Yet with *The Mosquito Coast* he has arrived at a temporary summation. This is not just his finest novel so far. It is—in a characteristically hooded way—a novelist's act of self-definition, a midterm appraisal of his own resources. It is a wonderful book, with so many levels to it that it feels bottomless.

In Allie Fox, Theroux has created his first epic hero. If one can imagine an American tradition that takes in Benjamin Franklin, Captain Ahab, Huey Long, and the Reverend Jim Jones, then Allie Fox is its latest, most complete incarnation. He is the King of Yankee know-how and know-all, an inventor of inspired gizmos—from a self-propelled, self-wringing mop to a machine that makes ice out of fire. He is a genius, clown, and monster, a commander of words, an angry demagogue. Listening to no one but himself, he leads his family out of the wilderness of modern America—its junk foods, imported plastics, and "hideola"—to create a new world in the bug-infested jungle of Honduras. . . .

Even in the barest outline, *The Mosquito Coast* sets up a whole series of suggestive ripples. Jonestown is there, of course: the foul clearing, the loudspeakers in the trees, the piled cadavers, the spools of recording tape. Beyond that, there is *the* original American story: the stale Old World, the sea crossing, the Indians, the "first Thanksgiving" as Allie Fox himself names it. Then there is a universal fable about the nature of godhead and belief. Finally, and much the most important, there is a tale here about the limits and possibilities of the creative imagination. Allie Fox is very like a novelist. He is an inventor. He makes and populates a world with an artist's totalitarian joy in his creation, bending everything and everyone in it to the requirements of his aesthetic design. At the end, it turns on him and he is literally consumed by it, as vultures tear out the very brains that set the world in motion. Fox's great imaginative enterprise both mirrors and mocks the creations of Theroux the novelist: The over-reaching hero and the writer are one and the same man.

I mustn't mislead here. These big themes (and one could hardly imagine bigger ones) are never proclaimed in the novel. They run deep, like subterranean rivers, nourishing the life of the book's surface. For, reading *The Mosquito Coast*, one is engrossed in a marvelously told realistic story. . . .

That is part of Theroux's secret. He has rooted his story deep in the reasonable—in sense impressions that we can all share, in knowledge we can ascertain. All the nuts and bolts are secure. And from that stable platform, the novel is able to take off like a rocket into the empyrean. From the dingy familiarity of a hardware store in stable platform, the novel is able to take off like a rocket into the empyrean. From the dingy familiarity of a hardware store in Northampton, Massachusetts, to a grotesque and tragic climax in the jungle, Theroux leads the reader cunningly on, step by reasonable step, reaching the exotic by means of the ordinary.

Jonathan Raban. SR. Feb., 1982,<br>pp. 55–56

Paul Theroux dedicates his book [*Kingdom by the Sea*] to "those friends of mine in Britain who, giving me a welcome I must ever gratefully and proudly remember, left my judgment free; and who, loving their country, can bear the truth, when it is told good-humoredly and in a kind spirit." At first, the dedication seems a sort of hubris; with the substitution of "Britain" for "America," and the deletion of a comma, it is Charles Dickens's dedication to his *American Notes*, and with it, Theroux announces that he's aiming for the company of the great. This is risky business, but not necessarily as foolish as it might seem; with his fondness for outrageously overstated humor, ghastly melodrama, and wickedly delineated backgrounds, Theroux is the most Dickensian of American novelists. "London Snow," a Christmas story so plum-puddingy it skates quite near the edge of parody, would not have been out of place had it appeared in *Master Humphrey's Clock*. . . .

Theroux is a conscious craftsman. In allowing England's present—its crushed and dispirited economy, its racism and classism, and especially the then-pervasive jingoism occasioned by the Falklands "war"—to work on him, to turn his spirit of adventure pinched and niggardly, he becomes the man of Britain's future, and perhaps our own. . . .

*Kingdom by the Sea* stretches the boundaries of the travel genre. Paul Fussell notwithstanding, when Robert Byron's *Road to Oxiana*—the long-forgotten "masterpiece"—was finally republished, its unquestionable charm rather undermined Fussell's claims for the grandeur of travel literature.

Theroux has done something else, and in doing so has surpassed *American Notes*. That smooth, righteous, and more than passingly naïve travelogue isn't the source of Dickens's reputation; had he written only *American Notes*, he would be as little remembered as Robert Byron. Theroux's situation is almost precisely reversed. For now, at least, the death-haunted *Kingdom by the Sea* stands as his best book. I'm not convinced that I've seen the future, but I have indeed seen some of Britain— and of Theroux. I hope the English repay the faith of his dedication, and treat him more kindly than we did Dickens.

Geoffrey Stokes. *VV*. Nov. 15, 1983, pp. 39, 41

# TRILLING, LIONEL (1905–1975)

To celebrate Lionel Trilling's work is not to advance any cause narrower than that of the cultivated literary and social intelligence addressed to the most generous conception of individual and social ends. Responsive as he was to the work of Freud, that fact no more defines him than does his allegiance to liberal democracy or his devotion to Wordsworth and Keats. If there is a characteristic mode of inquiry in his writing, it might be phrased: What, given the cultural situation with all its stresses, gaps, unarticulated oppositions, current shibboleths, are the appropriate objects of our attention at this moment? Among the foci he found revealing were the cultural fate of certain words, the shifts and permutations within a particular period of the significance attributed to certain books, poems, writers, social causes, human qualities, and—as in the notable essay, "The Fate of Pleasure," or his last book, *Sincerity and Authenticity*—the ways in which philosophy, history, and the arts recorded deep-running transformations in the culture in the course of the last two centuries.

When Trilling writes, he appears on each occasion to enter into the historical process as he conceives it, and by exposing the subject he has chosen for what it is and what it has become—for its contemporary resonance—asserts in the same breath our responsibility to facts and values of persisting importance and our responsibility to ourselves—readers who are tacitly urged to assume the implied burden of discrimination, judgment and action.

Quentin Anderson, Stephen Donadio, and
Steven Marcus. In *Art, Politics, and Will: Essays
in Honor of Lionel Trilling*, ed. Quentin
Anderson, Stephen Donadio, and Steven Marcus
(Basic Books, 1977), pp. vii–viii

Lionel Trilling has been variously described as a liberal, a conservative, a patriarch, an aesthete, a moralist, and so on. Though in his writings he consistently expressed a profound aversion to ideological thinking and was scrupulously fair and responsive to rival points of view, he came especially in his later years to be derided for various kinds of inflexibility and for downright obtuseness. Why so many literary people should have thought him vulnerable to their probings—malicious and otherwise—we cannot confidently say, but there is no doubt that a critic of his eminence was hurt in the eyes of many detractors by his seeming to operate so blithely, without benefit of theory or system. Though Trilling contradicted himself on occasion, and was of two minds on almost everything he touched, he knew what he was doing, or thought he knew. The pleasure we take in his enduring work is a pleasure in confronting a unified sensibility whose general absence our culture has persistently bemoaned through all the years of this century. . . .

There is a certain discomfort we must feel, confronted with Trilling's version of wisdom, with all it says of our collective diminution and of the ironic "knowing" gestures that are all we have in the way of legitimate response to the charge of inertia. Many of us may wish to resist Trilling, to insist that more is possible to us than he imagined, and that we need not be willfully deceived to take arms against what we feel ourselves encouraged to become. Some of us may even continue to feel that a politics is conceivable and legitimate at a time when every idea is converted to a cause and to be adversary is to be instantly authenticated even by one's ideological opponents. . . .

If we still find in his writings one of the consistent pleasures of literary experience, we must direct at his work that quality of aggressive engagement he honored in his own transactions with the writers he loved. Perhaps there is more of the "triumphal arch" and of the commemorative icon in Trilling's work than he would have liked to think; and perhaps, therefore, one cannot afford to be quite so aggressive in "attacking" his version of wisdom as he would have wished. Perhaps. What we can do, in thinking of Trilling's work, is to grant to it—in Trilling's words—"the complex fullness of its appropriate life."

Robert Boyers. *Lionel Trilling: Negative Capability and the Wisdom of Avoidance* (Univ. of Missouri Pr., 1977), pp. 1–2, 73–74

Trilling was unwilling, even in a grim time, to find the poetic experience in dissociation from the texture of society and . . . he insisted upon attaching even to an imperfect society an aura of inherited value. But if nearly every social institution harbors corruption, where is a scrupulous image of society to be found? He can hardly say, with Plato's disputant in *The Republic*, "Not here, O Ademantus, but in another world." And yet there is a sense in which, given such desperate conditions in practice, Trilling points beyond them not to any particular society but to the idea of a society, an idea sustained only by his need of such a thing. He can also point in another direction, toward Language: or, rather, toward a certain kind of language, a certain style, *eloquentia*. This is "the mind of the old European society" to which Blackmur referred, "taken as corrective and as prophecy." It is a corrective by virtue of the tradition it embodies, at once a rhetoric, a poetic, and a politics: it is a prophecy by virtue of its persistence as a working possibility. But of course it is beautiful only in its potentiality.

Normally we do not think of Lionel Trilling as a critic of language in the sense in which we apply that description to R. P. Blackmur, Leo Spitzer, or Erich Auerbach. Close intensive reading of a text is never the substance of Trilling's work, though it may have occupied his preparatory hours: he disposes of a poem's language before he deals with it in any explicit way. The poetic experience reaches him of course in language, but he does not settle upon it professionally until the language has ventured into the public world in the form of ideas. Indeed it may be one of the limitations of his criticism that its author is content with a strictly instrumental theory of language and that he has circumvented the questions raised by modern linguistics and hermeneutics. But the explanation is probably simple enough. Trilling values in language chiefly its self-forgetful character, the nonchalance with which it sometimes takes its nature for granted and turns toward something more interesting, the ideas and attitudes which make for life and death. He suspects any manifestations of language which call attention to themselves as constituents rather than as instruments, or which appeal to a particular class of reader rather than to readers in general. What Trilling values in language corresponds to what he values in society: reasonable energies at work, fair purposes and consequences, more nonchalance than self-consciousness, and just enough tension to foster and maintain vitality. For the same reason

Trilling distrusted every version of formalism: the forms he valued were transparent rather than opaque, functional rather than problematical. A form offers itself as a problem when its motives are not sustained by forces in the world at large and the available analogies are deemed useless. In both language and form Trilling values those procedures which can be construed as corresponding to a certain way of life, reasonable, cultivated, urbane. The rhetorical function of criticism is to maintain the correspondence.

Denis Donoghue. SwR. Spring, 1978, pp. 185–86

Rather than historian, philosopher, or theorist, Lionel Trilling was a sensibility who patiently cultivated thinking in order to subsume it to the rhythms of his search for wisdom. His worth, and his rare distinction, will outlive his individual essays. And his identity as a critic will, in time, be disentangled from the provinciality of his milieu. He is more than the narrow term "New York critic" can suggest. Like Edmund Wilson, he will be seen as a writer who sought always to rise above the conventions and shibboleths of his immediate surroundings. Both Trilling and Wilson, the two most important American literary critics of the mid-century, refused to let the art of criticism rest in the confines of academic specialization. Wilson, a decade Trilling's senior, represents a broader and more various achievement; his curiosity was greater, his learning more far-ranging. But Trilling went more deeply than did Wilson into the problems he took as his own. This difference noted, another similarity should be mentioned: both saw how attractive, and yet how delusory, organized political behavior could be.

Wilson surveyed more from his vantage point of dispossessed old-fashioned American cantankerousness and probity than did Trilling from his position as deracinated, aloof, and inquiring university teacher. But Trilling pursued more energetically than did Wilson the ways in which he could employ the terms of literary criticism to understand the struggle for self-knowledge his reading evoked in him. He will be seen in the future as a critic who, by examining certain aspects of literature, helped to enlarge his readers' sense of moral complexity. For that good and valuable reason, he will, I believe, outlive in importance other critics now deemed more fashionable. He reminds us all, and has reminded me for many months in writing this book about him, of something we can never wholly forget: literature is important by virtue not of its textuality but of its entry into our moral lives. That is an "old-fashioned" truth; Trilling, like Wilson, was old-fashioned.

Literature was, in Trilling's apprehension of it, the criticism of life in being the criticism of a life. That life, his own, never averted its attention from two extraordinary realities: the power of death and the corruption of doctrinaire politics. He was both eschatological and of his time and place. He judged present conditions, and the art and persons such conditions had placed in prominence, in the light afforded by the inevitability of death and the distinctly unforgettable barbarisms of Stalin. In being such a judge, Trilling worked always to define the mutable self within him, to recognize its enormous complexities and contrary imperatives. By his example, he helped to make more clear the same struggle of definition and recognition in his readers. His self demonstrated, in his prose, its affinities with those other selves. Literary criticism is a quiet, always imperfect, collective enterprise. It unites critic and reader. It was sustained, for years, by the drama of Trilling's self-critical examinations. His excellence is found in that drama.

> William M. Chace. *Lionel Trilling: Criticism and*
> *Politics* (Stanford Univ. Pr., 1980), pp. 187–89

Reacting to Lionel Trilling's insistent examination of all aspects of an issue, to his characteristic acknowledgment of the merits of quite contrary cases, Richard Sennett once accused him, "You have no position; you are always in between." Trilling's reply poignantly illustrates his fundamental critical stance. "Between," he said, "is the only honest place to be."

Trilling fashioned "between," the honest place within which he conducted his quiet but intensely dramatic dialectic, from two basic materials. One was his deep and enduring sense of human existence as a continuous struggle, of culture itself as "not a free creation but a continuous bargaining with life." The other was his conviction that the quality of personal experience results less from the outcomes of that struggle than from the comprehensiveness, the subtlety, and the energies of mind and imagination with which it is managed. These persuasions gave the distinctive color to his work as critic and as writer of fiction.

Because he invested the utmost seriousness in Matthew Arnold's conception of literature as a criticism of life, and because his consistent focus was on the destiny of the individual self in its often painful relationship to civilization, Trilling's consistent effort revolved around two poles: One was the honest, open exploration of the "variousness and possibilities" with which the inevitable and conflict-filled encounter between person and culture can be conceived. The other was an examination of the criteria by which the forms of variousness and possibility may appropriately be judged. Although a man of finely honed tastes with a disposition toward elegance, his aesthetic concerns always remained secondary. His fundamental interests were moral and therefore psychological and sociopolitical. Like the Arnold that he so richly understood and admired, he disliked and mistrusted systematic theories of literature as overly rarefied and as essentially irrelevant to the complexly related and central problems of how personal integrity may be achieved and how corporate life can be humanely arranged. More than that, he regarded these issues as inevitably recurrent. They cannot be resolved; they reject systemization. They can only be dealt with—*struggled* with—in the mind and imagination and then in the political marketplace, where individual wills contend with one another under social rules.

> Edward Joseph Shoben, Jr. *Lionel Trilling: Mind and Character* (Ungar, 1981), pp. 191–92

● **TYLER, ANNE (1941–    )**

One of the better things about *If Morning Ever Comes* is its title. It accurately suggests the unpretentious, mildly questioning quality, and the tentative little moral of Anne Tyler's first novel. . . .

The trouble with this competently put-together book is that the hero is hardly better defined at the end than he is at the beginning. Writing about a dull and totally humorless character, Miss Tyler has inevitably produced a totally humorless and mainly dull novel. That it isn't entirely dull is a tribute to Miss Tyler's restrained, unshowy style, a very pleasing niceness of observation (although an absolutely feminine one; what mind Ben Joe has is only vestigially masculine), and an excellent but unobtrusive use of symbols. Anne Tyler is only twenty-two and in the light of this her knowledge of what she is doing, her avoidance of obvious pitfalls and her refusal to take risks are a bit puzzling. I'd like to see what she could do if she stopped narrowing her own eyes and let herself go. It might be very good.

> Julian Gloag. *SR*. Dec. 26, 1964, pp. 37–38

The fact that 24-year-old Anne Tyler, who was born in Minneapolis and now lives in Toronto, grew up in Raleigh, N.C., must seem to her significant enough to make her publishers note on the jacket of this book that she "considers herself a Southerner." And this novel, in so far as it goes in for regional subject matter, does report upon life in still another rural Southern pocket. Her characters [in *The Tin Can Tree*] are the eight inhabitants of a three-family house on the edge of backwater tobacco fields—two bachelor brothers, two spinster sisters and the Pike family, whose small daughter has just been killed in a tractor accident when the book opens.

There are, indeed, some fine scenes and sounds of a regional sort, especially in one chapter in which a group of women talk over the Pike tragedy while tying tobacco. Here, as elsewhere in the book, she makes use of a nice specificity of local detail and neatly captures the casual and yet complex movement of Southern rural speech with its indirections and interruptions, its reticences and awkwardnesses which manage to express emotion.

Yet, rurality and Southernism are not really Miss Tyler's chief interest. Despite some obvious debts to the tradition of the Southern novel, she has none of the Faulknerian anguish over a present rooted in past wrongs. Nor does she share the late Flannery O'Connor's sense of a religious soil out of which characters are thrust forth into the withering present, taking grotesque and tragic shape—though Miss O'Connor's style, with its austere notation of scene and dialogue, may have taught her to make an eloquence of spareness. If she reminds me of anyone, it may be the Carson McCullers of 25 years ago—who, then as young as Miss Tyler, also wrote of human disconnection and the need for love in a stagnant community. . . .

Like [Sherwood Anderson's] Winesburg stories, *The Tin Can Tree* shows us human beings frozen into fixed postures. . . . Life, this young writer seems to be saying, achieves its once-and-for-all shape and then the camera clicks. This view, which brings her characters back on the last page to where they started, does not make for that sense of development which is the true novel's motive force. Because of it, I think, her book remains a sketch, a description, a snapshot. But as such, it still has a certain dry clarity. And the hand that has clicked its shutter has selected a moment of truth.

Millicent Bell. NYT. Nov. 21, 1965, p. 77

It's hard to classify Anne Tyler's novels. They are Southern in their sure sense of family and place but lack the taste for violence and the Gothic that often characterizes self-consciously Southern literature. They are modern in their fictional techniques, yet utterly unconcerned with the contemporary moment as a subject, so that with only minor dislocations, her stories could just as well have taken place in the twenties or thirties. The current school of feminist-influenced novels seems to have passed her by completely; her women are strong, often stronger than the men in their lives, but solidly grounded in traditional roles. Among our better contemporary novelists, Tyler occupies a somewhat lonely place, polishing brighter and brighter a craft many novelists no longer deem essential to their purpose: the unfolding of character through brilliantly imagined and absolutely accurate detail. . . .

Less perfectly realized than *Celestial Navigation*, her extraordinarily moving and beautiful last novel, *Searching for Caleb* is Tyler's sunniest, most expansive book. While etching with a fine, sharp wit the narrow-mindedness and pettishness of the Pecks, she lavishes on them a tenderness that lifts them above satire. Consider Daniel Peck. A cold and unoriginal man, aging gracefully but without wisdom, he is yet allowed moments in which we glimpse his bewilderment at a life that has been in the end disappointing. . . .

Reading *Searching for Caleb* one is constantly being startled by such moments: gestures, words, wrinkles of thought and feeling that are at once revelatory and exactly right. But at the center of Tyler's characters is a private, mysterious core which is left, wisely, inviolate. Ultimately this wisdom is what makes Tyler more than a fine craftsman of realistic novels. Her complex, crotchety inventions surprise us, but one senses they surprise her too.

Katha Pollitt. NYT. Jan. 18, 1976, p. 22

Anne Tyler's standards are high; she works both hard and fast. Of her earlier novels, this seems most similar to *A Slipping-Down Life*—the antagonists and circumstance and action are equivalent—but *Earthly Possessions* is far better done. If not precisely a sequel to her previous works, it's nonetheless a companion-text; the narrative is supple and the world a pleasant place. Violence and lust are rare, or offstage; the characteristic emotions are abstracted ones—anger comes to us as vexation, bliss as a kind of contended release.

Yet I do not feel this novel represents advance. The wheels are a touch too audibly clicking, and inspiration seems second-hand. It's as if her sense of continuity overruled the chance of change; the book is programmatic and the program feels over-rehearsed. Still, anyone who wrote the splendid *Celestial Navigation* and *Searching for Caleb* should be allowed to take a breather—and Anne Tyler's average work is more than good enough. *Earthly Possessions* is deft, good-humored and never less than engaging; one hopes its author, next time through, will once more be fully engaged.

Nicholas Delbanco. NR. May 28, 1977, p. 36

A marvel of a book deserving full critical recognition, *Morgan's Passing* covers twelve years in the life of its middle-aged hero, Morgan Gower, tracing the history and disintegration of his first marriage as well as his acquisition of a new wife and a new identity. As in Anne Tyler's other novels, the center of human interaction is family life with all of its perils, limitations, and rewards. . . . A man with and for whom life is difficult yet never boring, Morgan is a genuine eccentric in an urban setting, a comic anti-hero "acting out some elaborate inner vision" of himself.

In *Morgan's Passing* as in several of her previous novels, Anne Tyler shows her genius at creating such a figure. Morgan at once reminds us of other mild, at times tragicomic, eccentrics in *Celestial Navigation* (1974), *Searching for Caleb* (1976) and *Earthly Possessions* (1977); of Jeremy Pauling and Charlotte Emory and of Duncan, Justine, and the elusive Caleb Peck. Yet, like these other Tyler characters, Morgan is also unique, a highly individualized figure in a contemporary American land- scape. . . .

On the surface, *Morgan's Passing* is primarily the story of one man's handling of change and aging, although clearly the growth and change of Emily Meredith, the young puppeteer Morgan eventually marries, is also central to the plot. It is an elusive novel, however, at times zany, at times sad, a book preeminently concerned with marital mistakes and marked by Miss Tyler's characteristic sense of distance. . . .

It may be that . . . Tyler is holding back something of her narrative skill, but if there is a key to this distance in Tyler's work, it lies in the cen- tral metaphor of *Morgan's Passing*: puppetry. In many ways, Morgan Gower is a deliberate, conscious mask for the novelist. Like her, he is a small-scale impostor who laments having one identity, one life. . . .

It is precisely this sense of distance and respect for character and the privacy and inviolability of even fictional lives which Tyler invites her readers to share. She is, I think, remarkably successful. *Morgan's Passing* is a testament to that success.

Stella Nesanovich. SoR. Summer, 1981, pp.<br>619–21

New work by a young writer who's both greatly gifted and prolific often points readers' minds toward the future. You finish the book and immediately begin speculating about works to come—achievements down the road that will cross the borders defined by the work at hand. Anne Tyler's books have been having this effect on me for nearly a decade. Repeatedly they've been brilliant—"wickedly good," as John Updike recently described one of them. *Dinner at the Homesick Restau- rant* is Anne Tyler's ninth novel; her career began in 1964 with a fully realized first novel (the title was *If Morning Ever Comes*, and there are piquant links between it and her latest book); everything I've read of hers since then—stories, novels and criticism (Anne Tyler is a first-rate critic, shrewd and self-effacing)—has been, at a minimum, interesting and well made. But in recent years her narratives have grown bolder and her characters more striking, and that's increased the temptation to brood about her direction and destination, her probable ultimate achievement.

The time for such brooding is over now, though—at least for a while. *Dinner at the Homesick Restaurant* is a book to be settled into fully, tomorrow be damned. Funny, heart-hammering, wise, it edges deep into truth that's simultaneously (and interdependently) psychological, moral and formal—deeper than many living novelists of serious reputation have penetrated, deeper than Miss Tyler herself has gone before. It is a border crossing. . . .

*Dinner at the Homesick Restaurant* is, from start to finish, superb entertainment. . . . Much as I've admired Miss Tyler's earlier books, I've found flaws in a few—something excessively static in the situation developed in *Morgan's Passing*, for instance, something arbitrary in the plotting of *Earthly Possessions*. But in the work at hand Miss Tyler is a genius plotter, effortlessly redefining her story questions from page to page, never slackening the lines of suspense. There are, furthermore, numberless explosions of hilarity, not one of which (I discover) can be sliced out of its context for quotation—so tightly fashioned is this tale— without giving away, as they say, a narrative climax. There are scenes that strike me as likely to prove unforgettable. . . .

Seriousness does insist, in the end, that explicit note be taken of the facts of this career. Anne Tyler turned 40 just last year. She's worked with a variety of materials, established her mastery of grave as well as comic tones. Her command of her art is sure, and her right to trust her feeling for the complications both of our nature and of our nurturing arrangements stands beyond question. Speculating about this artist's future is, in short, a perfectly natural movement of mind. But, as I said before, I'm reluctant to speculate and I expect other readers, in quantity, will share my reluctance. What one wants to do on finishing such a work as *Dinner at the Homesick Restaurant* is maintain balance, keep things intact for a stretch, stay under the spell as long as feasible. The before and after are immaterial; nothing counts except the knowledge, solid and serene, that's all at once breathing in the room. We're speaking, obviously, about an extremely beautiful book.

Benjamin DeMott. NYT. March 14, 1982, pp. 1, 14

## UPDIKE, JOHN (1932–   )

Like Flannery O'Connor, who also studied art before she concentrated upon prose fiction, Updike pays homage to the visual artist's "submission" to the physical stimuli of his world far more than most writers. He transcribes the world for us, and at the same time transcribes the experience of doing so, from the inside. His world, like O'Connor's, is "incarnational"—vividly, lovingly, at times meanly recorded—perhaps because, in Updike, such a synthesis of fidelity and inventiveness allows an escape of sorts from the tyrannical, unimaginative cosmology of Calvinism. O'Connor was affirming her faith through allegorical art; Updike usually affirms it in words, but the act of writing itself, the free lovely spontaneous play of the imagination, *is* salvation of a kind. Does the artist require anything further? Updike's prose style resembles Nabokov's, of course, and yet it seems to me that in Updike the activity of art is never for Nabokovian purposes—never to deceive, to conceal, to mock, to reduce Nature to an egoistic and mechanical arrangement of words. On the contrary, Updike seems at times too generous, too revealing. His energies are American in their prolific and reverential honoring of a multitude of objects, as "Nature" is scaled down, compressed, at times hardly more than a series of forms of The Female. . . .

Out of contradictory forces that, taken very seriously, have annihilated other writers or reduced them to fruitless angry quarrels in the guise of literary works, Updike has fashioned a body of writing that is as rich, mysterious, and infinitely rewarding as life itself—which, in fact, it *is*, finally claiming no intellectual or moral excuse for its own being. It is uniquely Updike's, and uniquely American. Updike exiled from America is unthinkable, and America without Updike to record it—unthinkable as well. His special value for us is his willingness to be disarmed of perspective, to allow his intensely realized worlds to flower with something of the mysterious effortlessness of nature itself, and to attempt to spiritualize the flesh since, for many in our time, the "flesh" may be all that remains of religious experience. The charge that Updike is too fascinated with the near-infinitesimal at the cost of having failed to create massive, angry works of art that more accurately record a violent time is unfair, because it is far more difficult to do what Updike does. Like Chiron/Caldwell [in *The Centaur*], he accepts the comic ironies and inadequacies of ordinary life.

Joyce Carol Oates. MFS. Autumn, 1975, pp. 460,<br>472

He's a master of symbolic complexity, but one can't tell his women apart in a book like *Couples*; his characters' sexual preoccupations, mostly perverse, are too generously indulged; and the disparity between the surface and sub-surface of his novels is treacherous: to the naive reader . . . a novel like *A Month of Sundays* seems a merry, bourgeois-pornographic book about a minister who likes copulation, while to the subtler reader, the novel may be wearily if not ambivalently satirical, a sophisticated attack on false religion. . . .

Certainly he appeals, intentionally or not, to the two chief heart-warmers of the mindless in America, religion and sex. Protestant Christianity has always contained one great risk, a risk against which the best Christians always keep guard: like Marxism, it has a tendency to make light of reason and individual tragedy. . . .

The novels, properly understood, may be too much like sermons. No man can serve two masters, the artistic ideal, which makes its premise an essential and radical openness to persuasion, and the religious ideal, which, like Nietzsche's superman, is "deaf to even the best counter-arguments."

John Gardner. On Moral Fiction (Basic Books, 1978), pp. 98–99

John Updike flits among the various literary modes the way other people change dress: He has published four volumes of poetry and a play; when he is not writing novels he is turning out short stories; when he is not doing any of these you can catch him reviewing books in the *New Yorker*. He appears to aspire, indeed, to be every kind of writer—a man for all readers.

Yet while Updike is gifted at everything he puts his hand to, he is not equally gifted. Thus, although he is a first-rate miniaturist (his short stories are usually flawless, and his criticism can be truly remarkable—witness *Picked-Up Pieces*), he has failed to attain major status as a novelist. Perhaps his is a case of talent spread too thin to sustain the rigors of full-length fiction. Or perhaps something less tangible and more complicated is involved—a subtle clash between artistic ability and artistic inclination, between what John Updike is best equipped to write about and what he wants to write about. More specifically, he seeks to abandon his natural subjects—disgruntled marriages (*Couples, Marry Me*) and crumbling Wasp traditions (*A Month of Sundays*)—for darker, archetypal matters—alien accounts of wandering Jews (*Bech: A Book*) and militant blacks (*Rabbit Redux*). And these books of larger vision, despite not always being persuasive, are in fact the author's most interesting works.

With his latest novel, *The Coup*, Updike has heroically reincarnated himself in the form of one Colonel Ellelou, a crazed, anti-Western leader of the mythical African substate of Noire, now renamed Kush. . . .

*The Coup* is a very witty book about the merchandising of ideology. It is inventive in a Nabokovian way: nothing is too big—or small—to be poked fun at. The American scenes (Elleloû has conveniently spent some time at a small college in Franchise) have about them the pungency that last wafted through *Lolita*. It is almost as though Updike had to figuratively leave home—by impersonating the foreigner—in order to see most clearly into the frailties of home: "Everything in America, through that middle bulge of the Fifties, seemed to this interloper fat, abundant, and bubblelike, from the fenders of the cars to the cranium of the President. Franchise was a middle-sized city of 35,000. . . . The lake had been left, with that romantic *douceur* the Americans trail in the wake of their rapacities, its Indian name, Timmebago. . . ." Flecked with sobriety and whimsy, *The Coup* counters a concern for *temps perdu* with a muscular sense of presentness. More important, here John Updike comes closer than he has ever come before to matching the intention to the act.

Daphne Merkin. *NL*. Dec. 4, 1978, pp. 21–22

Two worlds, the natural and the supernatural, are present explicitly or implied in all of Updike's work, and they are basic to an understanding of it. In his writing there is always the physical, natural world, apprehended by the body through its senses and appetites. But there is also another, supernatural world (whether Christian, classical, or Islamic), apprehended by the soul, through faith.

Thus Updike sees man as a dichotomous creature, split between his physical desires on the one hand and his spiritual yearnings on the other. In Updike's fiction the protagonist's spirit cries out for expression. But because faith is so difficult in a contemporary world that is indifferent to spiritual values, the protagonist often loses his vision and devotes himself to the natural rather than the supernatural, the carnal rather than the spiritual. At moments of epiphany he may temporarily be transported by his body's physical action, to a sense of religious meaning. But these moments are rare and transient, and more often the Updike protagonist, in his desperate search for significance, finds that his spirit is suffocated by the material world. For in all the novels except *A Month of Sundays* the natural and the supernatural, the physical and the spiritual dimensions of man, stay stubbornly apart. They fail to integrate.

According to Updike, sex is the closest to a religious experience that the physical world provides, so the protagonist often searches for spiritual satisfaction in sexual encounters. He seeks the ideal lover who will provide for him the transcendent experience. But Updike is always aware that sex is, finally, a natural rather than a supernatural experience. The protagonist's search for spiritual satisfaction becomes futile and promis-

cuous, often resulting in his recognition of this futility and his acceptance
of one sexual partner. Such an acceptance signifies the resignation of the
protagonist's spirit.

While this acceptance of one woman, one job, and family responsibilities may seem ethically admirable to many, Updike is always suspicious of ethical action, believing that it hides an impoverished spirit. Thus
his novels are often peopled by altruistic Christians who substitute ethical, social, action for religious faith. While these characters might be
heroes for other writers, Updike consistently undermines their stature in
his own novels. Updike's novels suggest that involvement in ethical action
is a barrier to faith rather than a means to its fulfillment. . . .

For Updike the literary experience imitates the wished-for theological experience, in which the image exists as an incarnation of the author's
intention. In other words, by his repeated use of metaphorical language,
Updike is voicing the hope that the connection between the physical and
spiritual worlds can be made.

Suzanne Henning Uphaus. John Updike (Ungar,<br>1980), pp. 5–7, 133–34

Gifted with a pictorial imagination and poet's sensitivity to language,
Updike has taken as his subject the American middle class—with all the
sweetness and pain attendant upon its rituals of marriage and divorce and
child-raising—and defined, perhaps more persuasively than any other
American author, the emotional territory of memory and desire. At his
best, he invests the mundane with meaning and captures in the glimpse of
a moment the crises of contemporary life. . . .

It is not a pleasant book, this third Rabbit novel. Updike has always
been fascinated by the dark underside of American domestic life, and in
*Rabbit Is Rich* his scrutiny focuses on the guilt and resentments shared
between husbands and wives, fathers and their children. Both the sex
Harry engages in and the language he employs are considerably cruder
than before, and this change in his metabolism attests to a certain change
in the society around him. As documented by Updike's keen sociological
eye, America has become an ugly, materialistic place—defined by disco
music, television shows, and cheap hamburger joints—the controlling
metaphors of which are shortages of gas and runaway inflation.

Taken together, in fact, Updike's three Rabbit books constitute
something of an epic: They chronicle not only the maturation of one aging
athlete, but the evolution of an America through three remarkable
decades as well. And, in a sense, they also define Updike's own
philosophy and art, for while Harry bears little immediate resemblance to
his decorous creator, the two do share, as the author puts it, certain qualities of "Rabbitness.". . . Updike's characters are all afflicted by existen-

tial intimations of their own mortality. That fear is at once terrifying and restorative: It threatens to make everything they do meaningless and futile, but it also sends them running back to God. This theme, like so many others in his work, is rooted in Updike's own life.

Michiko Kakutani. SR. Oct. 1981, pp. 14–15, 20

Demonstrably filial in temperament, seriously threatened by the consequences of their own desires, many of Updike's male characters are like Piet [Hanema in *Couples*] in their growing estrangement from the modern world. The fathers—in nearly all their manifestations—have apparently receded or elected to keep silent; but rather than liberating their sons as might be expected, this leaves them shaky, unprotected, uncertain as to how to proceed: for Updike's typical protagonist is not able to adopt the perspective of the lonely but self-reliant existentialist, and looks to every quarter for the consolidation of some sort of authoritative, admonitory voice. It is because of such a filial, attentive consciousness, complicated by the withdrawal of paternal authority in a time of cultural transition, that many of Updike's characters are so unusually alert for signs. If one is not quite willing to rest on his own mental powers, if he is not able to live life without some kind of authoritative directive, the signs are necessary as personal and meaningful sources of direction. Recent Updike protagonists search for signs almost as a kind of divination. For what is the sign but a secret and divine message from some lofty authority outside the self, a directive beyond question which one need not dispute but is bound, humbly and filially, to obey? With the recession of fatherhood, the sign becomes crucial, not only as a source of guidance, but more significantly as a testimony that the universe is indeed meaningful, orderly, communicative, protective. Like their more orthodox forefathers, then, Updike's characters tend to look anxiously at nature and experience not as a blank and neutral surface, but as a fabric through which the divine imperative may at any moment be made manifest.

Kathleen Verduin. In Critical Essays on John<br>Updike, ed. William R. Macnaughton (G. K.<br>Hall, 1982), pp. 260–61

Henry Bech is John Updike's artistic demon made flesh. In his first appearance, in the 1970 *Bech: A Book*, we were introduced to a "graying and furtively stylish rat" of a New York-based Jewish writer in deep creative *tsuris*. Bech, "the last of the Joe Louis liberals," has a block after producing some well-received but poorly selling novels. So he fritters away his time lecturing at obscure colleges, wandering the world on State Department tours, and screwing everything in sight. . . .

The Bech saga is a more interesting in joke than it seems at first glance. What we have here is a quintessentially Wasp writer, Updike, who has always suffered from a kind of emotional constipation, relieving himself by conjuring up, out of his darkest anti- and philo-Semitic fantasies, a hairy, bearlike Jewish writer of approximately his age and travel-weariness who is productively constipated, pure and simple. Like most remakes and sequels, *Bech Is Back* is thinner stuff, with far too much padding for such a small book, but also with a more revealing subtext than the original, in which the writer just kept running from the dreaded prospect of commitment to one of the well-read but uninteresting women who chased him. . . .

In a 195-page book, only pages 104 to 179—"Bech Wed"—are worth reading. There's some pretty stale stuff at the front, involving Bech's "Third Worlding" it in Ghana, Kenya, and Korea. Dutifully, Updike sends Bech and Bea to Israel and Scotland, but he isn't too interested. As usual, his finest antennae rub together only when the lovers get trapped in the big house with each other's wayward, dueling sexual and money fantasies. Marriage turns on Updike like a certain kind of pornography.

Updike finds it hard to forgive women their existence, especially those who have given him/Bech any happiness. Bea, whom I actually liked, makes "gentle yipping noises when she f---ed." In Updike's moral universe, that puts her down among the beasts. It's an old trick, this, portraying your male hero warts and all but essentially with a self-satisfied pat on the back in order to have a license for mayhem on women. Updike is a better writer than this. Let him find a way to gently bury Bech and have another, more gracious look at the ladies.

Clancy Sigal. *NYM*. Nov. 1, 1982, p. 70

# ● VIDAL, GORE (1925–    )

Perhaps little more than a decade ago a novel dealing as frankly with male homosexuality as Gore Vidal's *The City and the Pillar* would have been labeled "freakish.". . . Unlike the usual characterization of the male homosexual in current novels, Jim Willard is drawn, with deliberate strokes, to appear the opposite of abnormal. Sympathetic as Mr. Vidal is to homosexuals and their precarious status in society, he has Jim express distaste for those more flamboyant groups marked by their mincing gait, loose-jointed wrists, and blatantly feminine voices. Jim Willard is sharply contrasted against these more obvious homosexual types by his outward virility, clean-cut features, and fine physique. Nor is Jim Willard an intro-spective or very sensitive young man. At first it would appear that the author purposely has chosen a most unrepresentative homosexual for his protagonist. But closer scrutiny will reveal that Gore Vidal is writing about the Jim Willards in every community. . . .

Gore Vidal has written his problem novel in a singularly flat, naturalistic style. It has already been pointed out that Mr. Vidal is gifted with that deadly competence typical of those very young writers who come up with three or four novels to their credit before they reach twenty-five. This is not entirely fair criticism. Vidal's novels are extremely read-able. They are the product of a facility for what we call slick writing as opposed to the more distinctive style of a craftsman mainly interested in his craft. But since he chooses to sacrifice, as he has done here, any possi-bility of his novel being hailed as a distinguished literary work in order to put over his message, perhaps it would be wiser to judge Mr. Vidal's novel mostly on its merits as a social tract. On this score Vidal is quite success-ful; but, here again, if we did not sense that there was a crusading spirit behind some of the challenging arguments put forth in the book, Mr. Vidal's blunt, dispassionate writing might easily send us off convinced that the Jim Willards can never expect anything of our times but hostility, or, at best, a tragic outcome to any attempt on their own part to solve their dilemma. And this is hardly the conclusion we believe the author intended to leave with us; not, certainly, in an age when we are taught that we can never be hurt by truths which help us to understand ourselves as well as our fellow men.

Richard McLaughlin. SR. Jan. 10, 1948, pp. 14–15

Gore Vidal, at twenty-five, occupies an enviable position in American letters. Not only is he the youngest of the group of new writers whose first books began attracting attention right after the war, but he has already produced as large and varied a body of work as many of his contemporaries may be expected to produce comfortably in a lifetime. Since 1946, when his first novel, *Williwaw*, was published, Vidal has written a novel a year—*In a Yellow Wood* in 1947, *The City and the Pillar* in 1948, *The Season of Comfort* in 1949, and now, in 1950, *A Search for the King*. He has a sixth novel, *Dark Green, Bright Red* completed and awaiting publication and a seventh already in progress.

*Williwaw*—written when Vidal was nineteen and still in the Army— was a slight and unpretentious book about the war. It was done in the clipped Hemingway manner; the sentences appeared to have been telegraphed and then pasted over the page. But there were no signs of Hemingway's purposeful understatement, his suggestion of hidden layers of immense unspoken meaning. The approach was literal and bald, the props had been carefully cut away rather than concealed, and the emotion was so rigidly controlled that one had the impression of reading a book which had only just managed to get written. Yet there was evidence of real, if premature, mastery in the handling of the central situation—the struggle of the men to bring their ship through the williwaw—and more than an intimation of potential insight in the brief characterizations. Vidal seemed to have learned early the trick of the narrow scope, the tight portrait. Where most young writers try to grapple with an outsized situation and too many characters and succeed only in revealing their youth, he apparently saw the advantage of leaving certain material alone until he grew up to it. His characters, consequently, were purposely unrealized, made up simply of a very few deft touches that gave the illusion of a total, although shadowy, outline. By concentrating on a single trait of a man, Vidal implied others. By yielding even scant information with reluctance, he forced the reader into a contest in which the winning of a single clue became—since it was won with such difficulty—more satisfying than complete revelation.

But the real power of *Williwaw* lay in the faithfulness of its intention to its impact, its tone to its material. In the williwaw—a violent storm common in the Aleutians—Vidal found the perfect instrument for making dramatic the emotion around which the novel was constructed and for which his terse style set the key. The truth of the war for the men who lived in its boredom but were denied its dangers was purposelessness. The contrast between the excitement and terror of the storm and the utter indifference of their reaction to it was thus the supreme, ironic example of that purposelessness. . . .

Right now Vidal is acutely aware of the need for values in both life and art. He is himself one of the best illustrations of the need, and his frantic productivity as a writer testifies to its urgency. The work he has produced up to now clearly shows his sincerity and his restless determination to explore every possibility that might lead him to his goal. But it shows just as clearly the reason for his recurrent failure. The only order Vidal ever found he found in the war, in the terse emotions and simple negation of the men of *Williwaw*. The moment he tried to move into larger and more complex areas of experience he was lost. His writing after *Williwaw* is one long record of stylistic breakdown and spiritual exhaustion. It is confused and fragmentary, pulled in every direction by the shifting winds of impressionism. It is always reacting, always feeling and seeing; but it never signifies because it never believes.

In this sense, Vidal is typical of his generation. He has lived through some of the most crucial events of history. He has read all the books, listened to all the psychiatrists, and been thoroughly purged of dogma and prejudice. The experience has left him with the great virtue of an open mind. But it has taught him one thing which it is sheer suicide for a writer to learn too well—that all things are relative and that there are at least twenty sides to every question.

Vidal's dilemma is wholly inseparable from the dilemma of his characters. As they search for a center of life, so he searches for a center of art. If they move forward, so must he, and finally they must succeed or fail together. For the goal they seek can exist only if Vidal can make it exist by discovering a way of giving it the maximum significance in his art, and that depends, of course, on his discovering a value and a morality for them and for himself.

John W. Aldridge. *After the Lost Generation*<br>(McGraw-Hill, 1951), pp. 170–71, 183

Gore Vidal will be recognized for speaking to his age in several voices. His voices have not always resounded clearly because he is still very actively a part of the age—an era that could do well to listen and then evaluate.

The first voice of Vidal is that of a former literary prince who has survived lionization and subsequent banishment. "Eight novels in eight years and still only twenty-nine years old!" Therein lie enough charges for banishment; but what of those eight novels, from *Williwaw* in 1946 through *Messiah* in 1954? Were they really worth any attention at all?

The heroes of these early novels, after the gray-gloomy soldiers of *Williwaw*, are young men who seem to be no more than mirrors to reflect what they see so clearly but understand so vaguely. In six novels, Vidal's protagonists are handsome, conventionally educated, taut-bellied but not muscle-bound fellows who move among stockbrokers (*In a Yellow Wood*), homosexuals (*The City and the Pillar*), Washington politicians (*The Season of Comfort*), medieval crusaders (*A Search for the King*), mercenary revolutionists (*Dark Green, Bright Red*), and tired European socialites (*The Judgment of Paris*). They are young men in search of life-centers, of worthwhile objects that promise final stabilization. Some among them settle on business, love, or power as temporary sustainers. The more unfortunate, who take these superficialities as absolutes, ironically are destroyed in their safe harbors; the wiser ones recognize that the quest is irrevocable once begun and that any safe haven is purely interim.

These heroes speak the author's rejection of absolute values or final judgments—of even the supposedly eternal verities of simple literary critics. They cannot find truths because an impersonal universe without even pretended justice has forced them toward merely human unabsolutes. But to Vidal the adventure of the human condition is fit motive for living and writing. *The Judgment of Paris* and *Messiah* are strongly humanistic: Paris rejects worldly power and abstract knowledge for love, a recognizably brief but nevertheless valuable human love; and Eugene Luther knows, as he dies old, that life, not death, is meant to be the great adventure.

But a philosophy of relativity is not sufficiently rewarding materially to sustain life, and thereby sounds the second voice of Gore Vidal—the voice of the tradesman. Academics prefer to see their novelists pure and starved rather than tainted by getting and spending, especially if the getting has been munificent. Vidal chose a trade that bears grudging proximity to literature—that of mercenary dramatist. . . .

The third voice audible in Vidal's writing since *The City and the Pillar* appeared in 1948 speaks of a reasonable respect for homosexuality—a subject of national fascination but of critical cowardice. Jim Willard still moves in *The City and the Pillar* through the strata of our society: the small-town childhood, the athletic prowess, the sophisticated and the untutored pederasts whom he meets, his baffled search for love—all have made the protagonist into a small-scale folk hero. The point of *The City and the Pillar* and of those tender stories in *A Thirsty Evil* is that there should be no point, no pointed finger, and no fascination at all.

A fourth voice reflects another role which Vidal has played—that of the reasonable man in an unreasonable society. Just as the subject of homosexuality received a reasonable treatment in *The City and the Pillar*, so has he spoken on the emotional excesses of his nation. The essays collected in *Rocking the Boat* show a mind at work criticizing the national preoccupation with Love the Panacea, the right-wing political paranoia, the erosion of civil liberties, and the danger to writers in assuming that the cornucopia of mediocrity excuses mediocrity when guised as serious art.

The civilized man must, as Vidal demonstrates, be mentor to his uncivilized brothers.

Finally, Vidal speaks as the voice of involvement to his age. A writer lives in his world of great unabsolutes and grubby human uncertainties; but he can, through the "understanding" that he so highly touts, be involved in shaping his nation, destined as it may be for cosmic nada.

Ray Lewis White. Gore Vidal (Twayne, 1968),<br>pp. 130–32

The fact is that Vidal Novelist had an unusually long apprenticeship. The early books, the eight that preceded *Julian*, are workmanlike enough, but they are curiously flat and undefined, without any of the zest and bitchy vitality Vidal shows in even the most ordinary conversation. Perhaps the years of thralldom to the tube were not such a waste after all, because when he did return to the novel a decade later in *Julian*, he brought to it the flavor and the energy of his own person. He is still an overly intellectual novelist, but now his subjects are more in keeping with his particular novelistic shtik. *Julian* is one of the best historical novels since Robert Graves's *I, Claudius*; it is a vigorous, authoritative re-creation of fourth-century Rome seen through several first-person accounts. *Washington, D.C.* is much less successful, partly, I think, because Vidal has always been uncomfortable with the conventional third-person narrative. Though he knows the Washington power game better than any other novelist, the plot creaks, and the characters move around awkwardly, self-consciously, and finally, unbelievably. He almost admits as much. "I don't know why," he says, "but the third person imposed a great strain on me, the constant maneuvering of so many consciousnesses through the various scenes while trying to keep the focus right."

In *Myra Breckinridge*, however, Vidal created a comic masterpiece, and what were faults in the earlier novels—a coldness and a passionless analysis of love and sex—became major virtues. Comedy, after all, demands "something like a momentary anesthesia of the heart," in Bergson's words. Its appeal is to intelligence, rather than feelings, and the intellect is where Vidal is most at home. American standards of sexual morality are turned inside out, and Vidal, with malicious glee, paints white black and black white. Not for nothing has he read and reread Evelyn Waugh, who laid down the rules of satire for Vidal's generation. Like Waugh, Vidal can create brilliant comic types, and he has an uncanny ear for absurd dialogue, which he reproduces with unfailing accuracy. In *Myra*, Vidal at last had found his voice as a novelist. . . .

It is not that Vidal's essays are better than his novels. It is rather that his essays are more consistently good and that the qualities that limit him as a novelist are precisely those that a good essayist needs: a forceful intelligence, a cool detachment, an unpretentious, graceful style, and a sense of perspective that distinguishes the big from the little. If most of his fictional characters seem unbelievable, his judgments on real people are both original and irrefutable.

Gerald Clarke. At. March, 1972, pp. 49–50

Despite its more or less foreclosed partisanship in favor of Burr, this latest and, with *Julian* and *Myra Breckinridge*, best of Vidal's 13 novels [*Burr*] is not designed merely to change the mind of anyone who has been brought up to venerate Jefferson and Hamilton at the expense of Burr. Because while the book is prejudiced against Jefferson, disdainful of Washington, and somewhat demonological about Hamilton, it nonetheless exhibits Vidal's characteristically 18th-century detachment about human follies, and this extends to the reader's presuppositions about the beginnings of our nation. . . . Necessarily the book is about treason; more significantly it is about the impossibility, when our society was small, dispersed, and yet interwoven in an extraordinarily complicated way, of deciding what specifically anyone could be treasonable about. . . .

If the novel is about treason . . . it is also about a much larger problem: to what does anything or anyone truly belong? The success and power of *Burr* derives from the ingenuity with which this question is probed, even to the point of making it a question about the legitimacy of writing such a book. . . .

Nonetheless, *Burr*, when taken with *Julian*, *Myra Breckinridge* and *Two Sisters*, suggests that Vidal is moving into fictional terrains more hazardous and more rewarding than ever before. He is working out ways by which characters from the past find versions of themselves in characters of later times and are then projected by Vidal as the manipulator of the material, in such a way as to make it all seem immediately contemporaneous and autobiographical. It doesn't matter if this effort isn't always wholly successful. What does matter is that Vidal, who now might lean on or merely transplant his laurels, is instead taking big and exciting chances. In *Burr* the chances have begun to pay off rather handsomely.

Richard Poirier. Book World. Oct. 28, 1973, p. 3

Any amount of biographical data cannot alter the fact that today *The City and the Pillar* is important as a mythic novel, not a homosexual one. . . . It is not entirely fair to say the changing times have given the book an antique veneer. *The City and the Pillar* was quaint in its day, although from some of the reviews that called it everything from "a male counterpart to *The Well of Loneliness*" to a "book on perverse practices," one would never know it was essentially an inversion of the American wilderness novel.

Far from proving that "all human beings are bisexual" (Jim Willard clearly was not), *The City and the Pillar* did prove that anyone who could crack the surface of *Huck Finn* and *The Last of the Mohicans* would eventually discover original sin. Vidal concluded it came into being when a pair of rebellious lads secularized the sacred rites of boyhood by enacting the forbidden parts of the rubrics. Read in the light of *Love and Death in the American Novel*, *The City and the Pillar* contains many of the recurrent themes [Leslie] Fiedler detected in Melville, Cooper, and Twain— the boyhood idyll, the intrusive woman, the miraculous sea, Cooper's redskin brother-surrogate for the white male in the guise of the red-haired Bob Ford, the lost frontier friendship. *The City and the Pillar* is the American wilderness novel demythologized; or rather it exposes the awesome truth the myth concealed.

> Bernard F. Dick. *The Apostate Angel: A Critical Study of Gore Vidal* (Random House, 1974), pp. 38–39

Sex is the issue on which Vidal has built his political reputation, but the larger part of his writing has dealt with the political labors of others. The characters of his early novels, withdrawn from any concern with the affairs of men, stand as so many adolescents before the heroes of the books that have marked the last decade. The narcissism of youth, the love of the body, is transformed into the narcissism of maturity and the love of power and reputation. His blade sharpened by personal combat, Vidal cuts into history with sharper irony than any contemporary novelist. The once solitary canvases are now crowded with figures trying to work their will.

The four novels are *Julian* (1964) and the loose American trilogy, *Washington, D.C.* (1967), *Burr* (1973), and *1876* (1976). They were underscored by a handful of essays and together they represent Vidal's reach for a lasting reputation of his own. They display an increasing preoccupation with the needless twists of history, and the lies that have given them substance. After *Julian*, they track native grounds. The American preoccupation coincides with Vidal's physical withdrawal from the United States. . . .

Even *Julian*, with its classical setting and its account of the war between Christianity and paganism, is a deeply American book. It has always been necessary for our national artists to come to terms with the religious impulse. This is because religion has been the traditional enemy of art in America, where the Catholic co-operation of Europe never took hold. It is not surprising that the American artist is customarily an agnostic. If he is a Lowell, his creations document the collision between the common sense and the immortal soul. If he is a Mailer, he wails at the inconvenience of people regarding a God more knowing than himself. . . .

The American novels feature no man so admirable, though Aaron Burr is even more engaging. It was typically perverse of Vidal to choose the least admired early American celebrity and present him as the central figure of the Founding Fathers' world. . . . For all the clarity and eloquence of its presentation, Vidal's vision of the past is little but a confused jumble of intuitions, postures, and crotchets. He has, in fact, no ideas about history at all, which is why he feels free to dress history in his plausible fictions. His theory of American empire turns out to be no more than an ill-tuned lament for innocence lost, without any accompanying statement to identify when innocence reigned, and of what it consisted. . . .

Vidal would like to tear down sex barriers, overrun the barricades of class, and refine the barbarous natives. I suggest that the accomplishment of the first two is unlikely to lead to the third. His liberal fustian is so badly out of key with his high-toned carping that his historical commentary, like his political commentary, is beyond redemption. It is clear that Vidal believes in iconoclasm, and after that it is very fuzzy. His heroes in history, Burr and Julian, were iconoclasts of a very superior sort. Beyond the fact that they were inharmoniously mated with their times, they are not all that alike—Julian, the ascetic philosopher turned general; Burr, the womanizer, the cutter of deals, the lawyer. History to them is a hurricane in whose eye they have landed.

Vidal is less a student of history than a student of human behavior. There is little to be learned, in his view, from the rise and fall of nations and empires, and much to be learned from the adaptation of individuals to life in the great world. In much the same way, Vidal the theater critic found it more interesting to watch audiences than to watch plays. Only by studying human reaction can we learn what are the true forces of a given time.

So Vidal, who emerged as the closest thing to a pure skeptic in contemporary America, has developed into the advocate of the self-conscious. His early novels hinted that this might be the direction he would take. Jim Willard, with his search for Bob Ford, and Blondel the troubadour, with his quest for a "center" in his life, represent the stirring of self-conscious feelings. Philip Warren refined them in *The Judgment of Paris* and Eugene Luther dramatized their apotheosis in *Messiah*. By the time he came around to writing the stories of Burr and Julian, Vidal was firmer than ever in his conviction. From describing the homosexual in the land of the heterosexual, he had grown to tell of the proud in the land of the timorous. Iconoclasm is the last refuge of the self-conscious man. . . .

Perhaps this is why Vidal has been ignored, for surely he is worthier of critical attention than the various serpents crawling in the grass today.

Vidal the artist is a detoured politician, and this is upsetting to those who like their art neat. Even so, as politicians have programs, artists have themes. A literary politician requires a theme that is somewhat programmatic. Mailer promotes the unabashed self, but it does not get him very far; I sometimes suspect he will die a forgotten man. Lowell has carved out his niche as the man of conscience, and there seems to be a rugged durability to it. But Vidal, the rationalistic narcissist, the advocate of the self-conscious but never the self, is the purest politician of the bunch. A Roman consul would understand him; so would an American senator. They would be inclined to accept him as a bird whose plumage enhances their breed.

Mitchell S. Ross. *The Literary Politicians*
(Doubleday, 1978), pp. 286–87, 289, 297–300

Few American writers can display the virtuosity of Gore Vidal: saline essays on popular arts and letters; our best political play, *The Best Man*; intimate analyses of politics, ranging from his observations chez Kennedy to the limitations of Ronald Reagan; futuristic visits to a small planet; revisionist appraisals of America's past imperfect in *Burr* and *1876*; and, of course, the sexual vaudeville of *Myra Breckinridge*, *Myron*, and, though he has shrewdly disowned it, the film *Caligula*, loosely based on his conceptions.

And yet . . . and yet, I know of no writer with comparable gifts who elicits so little critical response. . . .

A pity. In fact, Gore Vidal is a serious man and an almost solemn writer. No one who was not soberly concerned with values, morality, and history could have attempted *Creation*. . . .

Vidal has a purpose as lofty as the one in Thomas Mann's *Joseph* novels, no longer read and, in truth, not very much missed. . . .

In the remotest eras, Mann and Vidal suggest, the ancients had their own sense of history and prehistory, their own bewilderment about rival beliefs and impending catastrophe and the sense of God immanent in things and forever out of reach. . . .

Its central and grave flaw is typically Vidalian: if you wonder with Tolstoy how the poor die, or with Robert Coles, how they live, *Creation* offers not a clue. It does not, for that matter, tell how the middle class lived in the fifth century B.C. The book's style is panoramic and its populace notable—the sort whose names even then would have been worth an item in the evening papyrus.

Still, *Creation* is well worth the years of research and effort, and it rewards the hours of close attention it requires. In recent years there has been no historical novel remotely like it; nor has there been one which so effectively demolishes the author's carefully nurtured image of smiling mortician to the 20th century.

Stefan Kanfer. *NR*. April 25, 1981, pp. 34–36

The great charm of Vidal's writing is its auctorial audacity. The risqué, the demotic, and the left wing always threaten to bring down his elegant prose and mannered sophistication, and a devilish wit always counterpoints his angelically lucid style. It is a bravura performance withal, and in a sense Vidal is less a storyteller than a performer. His fictions do not tend to establish self-contained worlds independent of his mediation; rather, they constitute a juggler's feats, with Vidal compounding the most extraordinary materials not for the art of jugglery alone but for the opportunity to wear an audacious face. We are always aware of that face in Vidal's mature fictions. A quip, an outrageously sentimental *glissade*, an autobiographical indiscretion—all turn his jugglery into a performance, a *celebration* of auctorial selfhood. As I observed at the beginning of this study, Vidal's publicly crafted selves may not correspond to his private selves, but what matter? Selfhood is connoisseur's play in the novels, as stylish and entertaining a fiction as one could wish. The Vidalian persona, *con brio*, is the ultimate achievement of Vidal's art.

Robert F. Kiernan. *Gore Vidal* (Ungar, 1982),
p. 144

# VONNEGUT, KURT (1922–    )

Two themes predominate in Vonnegut's work—time as nonsequential (all moments in time exist simultaneously), and the yearning to reestablish the lost family. To see how closely these themes are related—to see this concept of time as a means of recovering his lost parents—is to understand much of Vonnegut's work. . . .

In both emotional energy and aesthetic achievement, Vonnegut's work describes a parabola, reaching its apex with *Slaughterhouse-Five* (1969), after which there's a steep decline to *Breakfast of Champions* (1973), and an even more precipitous decline to *Slapstick*, far and away his weakest book, flaccid in imagination, listless in execution, and evasive in theme. What happened, I would argue, was that as Vonnegut came closer and closer to the primal emotional impulse of his imagination, he had more and more difficulty finding metaphors with which to express it. . . .

Superficially one of our most complex authors, he is actually one of our simplest—behind the mask of the faux naif is a true naif, a believer in high school civics, in Jesus (one of his recurring characters), in the nuclear family, in the most innocent values. . . .

Superficially one of our most anti-technological anti-American authors, he is actually one of our most futuristic, our most patriotic—behind the mask of savage satire is a romance with the possibilities of science, with the American dream. No amount of scorn for either can obscure the fact that it's only scorn for the temporary deferral of the possibility, of the dream. . . . Vonnegut, in short, is perfectly in touch with the adolescent imagination: asking, as he himself admits, all the college sophomore questions. . . .

Ross Wetzsteon. *VV*. Sept. 27, 1976, pp. 77–78

"It is hard to adapt to chaos," Vonnegut writes in *Breakfast of Champions*, "but it can be done. I am living proof of that: It can be done." In a major sense, Vonnegut's novels represent just such an adaptation. He moves steadily away from old-fashioned stories of the sort that lead readers to believe that life has leading characters and minor characters, important details and unimportant details, lessons to be learned in order to pass tests of physical, psychological, or spiritual strength, beginnings, middles, ends. By the time Vonnegut gets to *Breakfast of Champions*, he has resolved to avoid storytelling in favor of a kind of writing in which all persons are equally important and the only moral is to learn to adapt oneself to the requirements of chaos rather than to the requirements of an orderly universe (the most laughable and also the most fatal of illusions). Vonnegut accordingly chooses to utilize a fictional technique that relies upon radical juxtapositions of space-age gimmickry, schizophrenic religions, and a nonspatial time sense for purposes of social satire.

Such a technique is uniquely successful in *Slaughterhouse-Five*, and its development certainly places Vonnegut in the center of postwar avant gardism. But to many, Vonnegut remains more of a phenomenon than a writer to be taken seriously, his success more of an accidental product of the 1960s than anything else. But even though there is some validity in this view, it is neither fair nor complete.

Vonnegut's popularity as a factor in his significance should be emphasized because it is one of the most important aspects of his achievement.

James Lundquist. *Kurt Vonnegut* (Ungar, 1977),
pp. 101–2

The moral drama between right and wrong loses all meaning if men are not free to choose and competent to act, and Vonnegut sees man as neither competent nor free. In his fictional world, there are no villains and, as well, no heroes to oppose them; both good and evil are beyond man's grasp. When he writes in the introduction to *Slaughterhouse-Five* that he learned in college "there was absolutely no difference between anybody," the ironic tone does not belie the accuracy of the words. Vonnegut does believe that all men are the same, and to read his fiction is to meet a cast of characters who are uniformly pathetic, helpless victims of a random, incoherent, meaningless existence, and whose suffering, unmitigated by any true higher purpose, is distinguished only by the self-delusions embraced to relieve it.

It is precisely this unrelievedly debased view of man that cripples Vonnegut's fiction and undermines his effectiveness as a moral critic. Caught in a conflict between what he wishes and what he believes, between what he wants for mankind and what he thinks mankind is fated to have, his fiction constantly exposes folly only to submit to inevitability. In Vonnegut's books, anger—which is, after all, a kind of hope—is always defeated by resignation, his criticism of society always emasculated by his final belief that man can do no better. . . .

*Vonnegut's problem, you see, is that although he abhors our mechanized culture, he believes the world view upon which it is based;* his vision of mankind—so many like individuals pushed by forces beyond their control—is really the same, nothing more than that same mechanistic metaphor misapplied again. And the result of that misapplication is always the same: pessimism, cynicism, resignation, despair. . . .

Vonnegut is, above all else, a compassionate man; he may not respect his characters, but he does care about them, is driven by an urge to ease their suffering. Given the pessimism of his outlook, however, all he can offer is the very solution he so often mocks: illusion, fantasy, the "harmless untruths" of Bokonism, of Tralfamadorian metaphysics, the soothing escapism of Billy Pilgrim's time-travel. As his recurring character, Eliot Rosewater, says to a psychiatrist in *Slaughterhouse-Five*, "I think you guys are going to have to come up with a lot of wonderful *new* lies, or people just aren't going to want to go on living." And there it is again, the same basic conflict resurfacing—between thought and feeling, between the artist and the humanitarian. Vonnegut wants to tell us the truth and at the same time spare us from it; he wants to ease our pain and at the same time show us that only "lies" can achieve that end. To comfort, he must lie; to tell the truth, he must hurt; for in the world as Kurt Vonnegut, Jr., sees it, happiness is utterly incompatible with truth. What he believes is what he hates; the peonies are still there, but now they are fake, manufactured illusions to ease our pain—only the excrement real.

David Bosworth. AnR. Winter, 1979, pp.<br>14–17

Kurt Vonnegut's position is very special. He has been not only a significant novelist in America, but an uncanny indicator of the way our
spiritual heartaches were heading, an unexpected "paperback writer" (in
the old Beatles tune) who magically rose from the supermarket stalls to
something like secular sainthood for 10 years or so. That he is no longer
quite so revered may be a relief. But the particular kind of fame that came
his way—"She was a freak," he writes [in *Jailbird*] about the genius bag-
lady, "that many people would have liked to photograph or capture or
torment in some way, or kill"—must have been as devastating as it was
amazing. The mere fact that he's survived as an ingenious story-teller and
not a down-and-out prophet (the brilliant Tim Leary) is a testament to his
staying-power and, perhaps, wry amusement at what happened to
him. . . .

It seems to me that Vonnegut now has to cope with his career as just
a regular brave language-and-guts-ahead novelist, like every other. History has its own crescendos that are surely out of the hands of men and
women. Vonnegut had a date with history that has been fulfilled, something that was denied to peers who persisted in the rich gloom like
Stephen Crane, Nathanael West, and Malcolm Lowry, to name just three
who never heard the roar of the crowd. Which leads one to think: Now
and in the future is when Vonnegut's real stuff will be tried, much more
than when he was a guaranteed best-seller and shaggy culture hero. *Jailbird* even turns a new corner, in its way. It's the best in some time. . . .

Seymour Krim. *VV*. Aug. 20, 1979, pp. 81–82

The narrator [in *Deadeye Dick*] is Rudolph Waltz, who tells the story of
his life vaguely chronologically, in the short installments that are a
hallmark of Vonnegut's style; he may strain your tolerance or credulity,
but never your attention span. Rudy's voice is mild and confiding, and
rarely wavers from the tone established in the opening pages, no matter
how grim the details he narrates.

And they are grim. The focal points of Rudy's story are two disasters:
at 12, he accidentally shoots a pregnant woman. When he is nearly 50 and
living in Haiti, his hometown, Midland City, Ohio, is the site of an
allegedly accidental neutron bomb explosion: Rudy and his brother Felix
can actually walk through an intact city of the dead, swept clean of corpses
by federal troops. It helps to know something about Vonnegut's past as a
survivor of the bombing of Dresden and a publicist for General Electric,
where "progress is our most important product." Progress, Vonnegut
intimates, is an ugly mid-American city left standing and corpse-free, a
technological improvement over the charnelhouse that was Dresden.

In its orientation toward disaster, *Deadeye Dick* looks back to
*Slaughterhouse-Five* and *Cat's Cradle*. But the technical innovations that

made Vonnegut an "experimental" writer in the '60s are gone: no Tral-
famadorean narratives, no intercutting from the land of fact to the terrain
of science fiction. What remains is a distilled sense of the doom always
impending in a world dominated by technocrats and military men; it is
palpable on every page, and permeates even events that have no direct
relation to Midland City's bomb factories. Whether routine or catastrophic, events are narrated in the patented Vonnegut style: plain to the
point of blandness, capable of large whimsy and small expressions of outrage that are almost immediately retracted with self-deprecating humor,
punctuated with the little aphorisms that are his most recognizable
trademark. It's a style that Vonnegut seems to think is both stoically
moral and, with its jinglelike refrains, appropriate for a mass readership;
he uses it to depict a world in which large mistakes, like neutron bombs,
are the only thing apt to put an end to the small mistakes that form the
grain and pattern of existence. His characters' lives are always shaped by
what they neither expect nor plan for. "It is too easy, when alive, to make
perfectly horrible mistakes," Rudy says, remembering that his father
helped keep young Hitler alive by buying a painting from him when he
was a starving artist in Vienna. Variations of this sentiment are
everywhere: small decisions balloon into large disasters, and Rudy
responds by saying, "this was quite a mistake"; then, because he is a cook,
he gives us a recipe. The book is full of them, presumably on the theory
that as formulas go, a recipe is less likely to result in something catastrophic than, say, Dr. Hoenikker's Ice-9 in *Cat's Cradle*.

*Deadeye Dick* is a much better book than *Slapstick* and *Jailbird*; in
fact, it serves to reiterate Vonnegut's implied claim that he is a competitor
(with Updike, Roth, and Mailer) for the right to dominate the large literary terrain between Sidney Sheldon and Thomas Pynchon. And yet it also
demonstrates what's fatally constricting about his work. I don't see in it
the squishy sentimentality attributed to him by most critics, maybe
because I think the skillfully disguised coarseness of thought and loutish-
ness of feeling in the work of someone like Bellow is more dangerous.
Instead, what never stops being problematic in Vonnegut is the calculated
naiveté and blandness of the style, coupled to the equally simplified
view—what used to be called the "absurd vision"—of the wrongness of
the world.

Khachig Tölölyan. VV. Feb. 22, 1983, p. 50

## ● WALKER, ALICE (1944–    )

Alice Walker's graphic first novel [*The Third Life of Grange Copeland*] delivers a powerful statement by letting the narrative, characters and episodes speak for themselves. In describing the lives of black sharecroppers from 1920 through the 1960s, the 26-year-old black novelist—author of a book of poems, *Once*, as well as a quartet of stories on insanity— could have taken the easy, tiresome way out by haranguing for militancy, revenge and separatism. Instead, she allows the reader to make his own assessment of Southern conditions and the desperate need for change. . . .

Miss Walker's novel—infused with poetic images that unfold visually as though performed on stage—is remarkably similar to Athol Fugard's excellent play, *Boesman and Lena*. In both works the black wives, constantly forced to move their few tattered possessions from one makeshift home to another, are tormented mainly by their husbands rather than the world. In both, the characters are castoffs lurking on the fringes of an oppressive white society, who see life as a perpetual cycle of hope and despair. . . .

Miss Walker deftly sculpts her people and delineates their relationships. Indeed, since they generally transcend the plot, the one episode involving civil rights workers seems an intrusion that neither advances the story nor enhances our understanding of the characters. Fortunately, it does not detract significantly from an otherwise compelling novel that emphasizes the humanity we share rather than the horrors of dehumanizing experiences.

Paula Meinetz Shapiro. NL. Jan. 25, 1971, pp.<br>19–20

In 1966 Langston Hughes commented on one of Alice Walker's short stories: "Neither you nor I have ever read a story like 'To Hell with Dying' before. At least, I do not think you have." Hughes's early recognition of the uniqueness of Walker's artistic voice is equally applicable to the 12 other stories in Walker's new book, *In Love & Trouble: Stories of Black Women*. This collection would be an extraordinary literary work, if its only virtue were the fact that the author sets out consciously to explore with honesty the textures and terrors of black women's lives. Attempts to penetrate the myths surrounding black women's experiences are so pitifully rare in black, feminist, or American writing that each shred of truth about these experiences constitutes a breakthrough. The fact that Walker's perceptions, style, and artistry are also consistently high makes her work a treasure, particularly for those of us whom her writing describes.

Blood and violence seem the everyday backdrop to her characters' lives—a violence all the more chilling because it is so understated. It affects the 10-year-old girl who discovers a lynched man's headless body just as surely and ruinously as it destroys the middle-aged wife trapped in a loveless marriage or the ancient black woman ousted from a white house of worship. . . .

I believe that the worst results of racism in this country have been to subvert the most basic human relationships among black men, women, and children and to destroy their individual psyches. It is on this level of interpersonal experience that Walker succeeds in illuminating black women's lives. Some of her characters are damaged by material poverty, but what they suffer from most often is emotional destitution. These portraits are not pretty. When the reality is prettier, as a result of the implementation of black *and* feminist goals and values, the stories will be prettier too.

Barbara Smith. *Ms.* Feb., 1974, pp. 42–43, 78

A close look at the fiction, especially the shorter pieces, of Alice Walker reveals that she employs folklore for purposes of defining characters and illustrating relationships between them as well as for plot development. By so doing, she comments on the racial situation in the United States and, in some instances, chastises her black characters for their attitudes toward themselves. The folklore materials Walker uses and the ways in which she uses them are especially evocative of Charles Waddell Chesnutt and Zora Neale Hurston. Therefore, interpretations of Walker's uses of folklore and folk culture place her in a tradition that goes back at least as far as the late nineteenth century. . . .

Alice Walker is assuredly in the literary and historical traditions of the recording and creative use of black folk materials. Like Chesnutt, she uses such material for social commentary. But her environment allows more freedom of usage than did Chesnutt's; where he had to embed his statements about slavery in an elaborate framing device and filtered them through the eyes of a white Northerner, Walker can be obvious, blatant, and direct about social injustices. Like Hurston, Walker reflects a keen insight into the folk mind. As Hurston reflected the nuances of relationships between men and women in *Their Eyes Were Watching God* (1937) through the use of the folk culture, so too does Walker use this culture to reflect relationships between the characters in *The Third Life of Grange*

*Copeland*. Like [Jean] Toomer, she feels that the folk culture is an inseparable part of the black folk at any level of existence—the college bred and the illiterate black are equal in their heritage. Although class and status may be allowed to distort how one views the culture, it can never be erased. Alice Walker does not attempt to erase it from her works.

Trudier Harris. BALF. Spring, 1977, pp. 3, 8

As a craftsman, Walker sorts out the throwaways, the seemingly insignificant and hidden pieces of the lives of Southerners, particularly black families, and stitches them into a tapestry of society. Who is to blame for the waste in our lives, she asks? Ourselves? The society that seems at every turn opposed to blossoming? The wrath of God? The question of responsibility for personal action and societal change is one recurrent motif in the complex quilts that Walker makes out of thrifty sentences, knotted questions, tight metaphors, terse sections. Her novels continually stitch a fabric of the everyday violence that is committed against her characters and that they commit upon one another in their search for regeneration, and regeneration is what they as black people desire.

The exploration, then, of the process of personal and social growth out of horror and waste is a motif that characterizes Walker's works. For her, the creativity of the black woman is essential to this process. . . . In searching for the means to her own artistic and political freedom, Walker investigates the legacy of the past. To deepen our understanding of the plight of her maternal ancestors, she not only calls upon her own personal history but upon Jean Toomer, who perhaps more than any other writer of the past had focused on the repressed creativity of black women. . . .

For this author, the black woman, as a result of her history and her experience, must be in struggle against these two distortions of life. Until she is free, her people cannot be free, and until her people are free, she cannot be free. Walker stresses the interrelatedness of these two obstacles to wholeness, for the struggle against them is not merely a question of replacing whoever is in power; rather it is a struggle to release the spirit that inhabits all life. Walker's quilts reiterate the basic concept that "the greatest value a person can attain is full humanity which is a state of oneness with all things," and that until this is possible for all living beings, those of us who seek wholeness must be willing to struggle toward that end.

Barbara Christian. Black Women Novelists<br>(Greenwood, 1980), pp. 180–81, 237–38

Alice Walker's unsparing vision of black women's victimization in sexual love—their isolation, degradation, or grotesque defeat by despairing or aspiring black men—has been a major element in her growing body of work. . . . Somewhat less prominent in defining her concerns has been Walker's active commitment to civil rights issues involving all black people. The commitment suggests a hope that societal change may help solve the type of private dilemma her fiction particularizes. The appearance of her second novel, *Meridian* (1976), did not so much negate this implied optimism as express a need to consider moral and philosophical issues raised by a political awakening.

At the same time, *Meridian* represents a shift from a preoccupation with commemorating black women's suffering to a concern with probing an individual black woman's situation for its roots and possibilities. Again Walker's optimism is less evident, however, than her need to explore questions of responsibility even, or particularly, among those with valid historic claims to having been victimized.

Martha J. McGowan. Critique. 23, 1, 1981, p. 25

It's true and important that a disproportionate number of people who seek out Alice Walker's sparsely distributed books are black women. She comes at universality through the path of an American black woman's experience and is even brave enough to write about such delicate fictional themes as interracial sex and the oppression of women by many cultures in Africa. . . . But white women, and women of diverse ethnic backgrounds, also feel tied to Alice Walker. The struggle to have work and minds of our own, vulnerability, our debt to our mothers, the price of childbirth, friendships among women, the problem of loving men who regard us as less than themselves, sensuality, violence: all these are major themes of her fiction and poetry. . . .

The storytelling style of *The Color Purple* makes it irresistible to read. The words belong to Celie, the downest and outest of women. Because she must survive against impossible odds, because she has no one to talk to, she writes about her life in the guise of letters to God. When she discovers her much-loved lost sister is not dead after all but is living in Africa, she writes letters to Nettie instead. The point is, she must tell someone the truth and confirm her existence. . . .

The result is an inviting, dead-honest, surprising novel that is the successful culmination of Alice Walker's longer and longer trips outside the safety of Standard English narration, and into the words of her characters. Here, she takes the leap completely. There is no third person to distance the reader from events. We are inside Celie's head.

In the tradition of Gorky, Steinbeck, Dickens, Ernest Gaines, Hurston, Baldwin, Ousmane Sembene, Bessie Head, and many others, Alice Walker has written an empathetic novel about the poorest of the poor. (In fact, her first two novels meet that high standard, too.) But, unlike most novels that expose race or class, it doesn't treat male/female injustice as natural or secondary. (And unlike some supposedly feminist novels, it doesn't ignore any women because of race or class.) Just as unusual among books about the poor and powerless, it is not written *about* one group, *for* another. The people in this book could and would enjoy it, too.

Gloria Steinem. *Ms.* June, 1982, pp. 37, 89–90

*The Color Purple* is an American novel of permanent importance, that rare sort of book which (in Norman Mailer's felicitous phrase) amounts to "a diversion in the fields of dread." Alice Walker excels at making difficulties for herself and then transcending them. . . .

Love redeems, meanness kills—that is *The Color Purple*'s principal theme, the theme of most of the world's great fiction. Nevertheless—and this is why this black woman's novel will survive a white man's embrace—the redemptive love that is celebrated here is selective, even prickly. White folk figure rarely in its pages and never to their advantage, and black men are recovered only to the extent that they buckle down to housework and let women attend to business. For Walker, redemptive love requires female bonding. The bond liberates women from men, who are predators at worst, idle at best.

Peter S. Prescott. *Newsweek.* June 21, 1982, pp. 67–68

## WARREN, ROBERT PENN (1905–    )

In Warren's cosmology, as in Heidegger's, man, confronting alternatives of world and idea, must choose neither. He must discover, through the awareness of limitation and the involvement of care, that these alternatives are false: that true being resolves these fragments into a new integrity. Is Warren an existentialist? The vagueness of the term makes the question fruitless. Hazel Barnes, striving to preserve the purity of the term, is forced to fall back upon such designations as "legitimate existentialists" to distinguish the true existentialists, like Sartre, who insists on the inevitable absurdity of man's condition, from the lapsed believers like Heidegger, who, in *Being and Time*, contends that absurdity is surmountable. Is Warren a disciple of Heidegger? Presumably not. Warren's metaphysic may in part reflect the work of any number of existential writers, or it may even be independently derived from a common source: that is, the Christian pattern of conversion. Heidegger's existentialism, after all, is an elaborate but unmistakable version of Christianity secularized, and Warren has called himself "an agnostic Presbyterian."

More important here than such pigeon-holing is the fact that Heidegger's philosophy helps us to define the quest for selfhood as it appears in all of Warren's fiction. Each novel takes its shape from the attempts of its major characters to cope with their own fragmentation. In *Night Rider* and *At Heaven's Gate*, Warren grapples with the problem of alienation and moves toward the solution which he articulates fully in *All the King's Men*; in the subsequent novels, he tests his vision with a variety of characters and situations.

Through all of the novels, the individual attains the true being of selfhood through self-awareness and the realization that, as Warren says in his essay "Knowledge and the Image of Man," he is "in the world with continual and intimate interpenetration, and inevitable osmosis of being, which in the end does not deny, but affirms, his identity. It affirms it, for out of a progressive understanding of this interpenetration, this texture of relations, man creates new perspectives, discovers new values—that is, a new self." The path to this new self begins, with *Night Rider*, in the darkness of Mr. Munn's broken world and ends, with *Meet Me in the Green Glen*, in the great awakening light of Cy Grinder's awareness as Cy discovers the unbroken web which is the world redeemed through knowledge.

Barnett Guttenberg. *Web of Being: The Novels of Robert Penn Warren* (Vanderbilt Univ. Pr., 1975), pp. xii–xiii

"Billie Potts" is probably Warren's best poem, and almost certainly his most important. Its brilliant imagery, its wide-ranging command of sound texture, and its novel synthesis of Warren's three master themes—passage, the undiscovered self, and mysticism—render the "Ballad" analogous to *Tintern Abbey* as the crucial poem in its author's maturation as a poet. From this point on Warren would be a "finished" artist, capable of very substantial technical innovations in later decades, but having essentially completed his formation of a fully developed point of view. Perhaps it was this sense of poetic self-completion that lay behind the ten year lapse between the "Ballad" and Warren's next publication in verse, *Brother to Dragons*. . . .

If, over the half-century span of Warren's verse, there is one quality that most unmistakably lifts him to the first rank of American poets, then that quality would have to be the remarkable power, clarity, and originality of his imagery, flowing copiously into every part of his poetic canon from the first part of his career to the last. By imagery we refer to that verbal construct which, beginning with simple pictorial power, may ascend to metaphorical, symbolic, and even mythic significance as it implies larger dimensions of meaning. . . . [The] cumulative power of Warren's imagery in his eleven volumes is incalculable.

Victor H. Strandberg. *The Poetic Vision of Robert Penn Warren* (Univ. Pr. of Kentucky, 1977), pp. 163, 273

The source of Warren's stunning power is *angst*, a kind of radiant metaphysical terror, projected outward into the natural world, particularly into its waiting waste expanses: open field, ocean, desert, mountain range, or the constellations as they feed into the eye a misshapen, baffling, and yearning mythology bred on nothingness. He is direct, scathingly honest, and totally serious about what he feels, and in approach is as far as can be imagined from, say, Mallarmé, who urged poets to "give the initiative to *words*." Warren gives the initiative to the experience, and renders himself wide open to it. He is not someone who "puts a pineapple together," as Wallace Stevens does, constructing its existence by multiple perceptions, by possibility and caprice rather than by felt necessity; he is not interested in the "ephemeras of the tangent," but in the unanswered sound of his heart, under the awesome winter presence of the hunter Orion. . . .

He is a poet of enormous courage, with a highly individual intelligence; he is fully aware of the Longinian pit that yawns for those who strive for Sublimity and fail to attain it. Precariously in balance, he walks straight out over the sink-hole of Bombast; his native element is risk, and his chief attribute, daring. . . .

If Wallace Stevens—to take Warren's most notable and obvious opposite—is "pure," Warren is impure; if Stevens changes reality by changing the angle of his eye, Warren fixes himself into it in wonder, horror, loathing, joy, but above all with unflinching involvement; if Stevens plays with it, tames it, and "understands" it, Warren encounters it nakedly, and without pretense, dallying, or skillful frivolity.

James Dickey. *SR*. Aug., 1980, pp. 56–57

No other writer, not even the explorers of American Studies or material folklore, has made so much out of our cultural artifacts: portraits of Signers, rifles, electric chairs, campaign trucks, hunting shirts and broadcloth coats, country graveyards, WPA murals, big houses and shotgun bungalows, letters and broadsides. If there has always been a particular verve in Warren's explicit exploration of the human past—what Jack Burden calls "the ash pile, the midden, the sublunary dung heap"—that verve is not noticeably lessened in the depiction of the human present. In both the past and present, warts and wens always seem to be plumper and brighter than those seen by other writers; expectorated phlegm is always more glittering, pus is yellower and more concentrated, mental defectives slobber more profusely. . . .

Warren has admitted his abiding interest in that grandest American dialectic, the moral and psychological tension between what is roughly identified as "Puritan dichotomies" and "Transcendentalism." Calling himself a "little footnote" in the long history of this intellectual tension, he suggests that the recurring theme of father and son in his own work expresses his urge to fuse the two halves of the dialectic—"the fact and idea," "the Emersonian and the Hawthornian." But to assume that Emerson and Hawthorne represent only the poles of the dialectic—that they are not sufficiently engaged by the ongoing interplay between those poles—is clearly an inadequate reading of both writers.

James H. Justus. The Achievement of Robert Penn Warren (Louisiana State Univ. Pr., 1981), pp. 328–30

Because Warren's poetry emanates from a mind that is deeply speculative, one which never refuses but rather cultivates obsessively the immanent meaning of all it has ever encountered, Warren is a pronounced thinker among poets. But he has not been so obviously in poems a thinker about poetry, about form, as have the majority of this century's poets. Among those who seem always to write as if the poem were beyond all else the subject at hand, Warren has seemed implacably committed to the tale, the story, the narrative—with an interlineated commentary which ranged from stage direction to head-shaking amazement to homiletic moralizing. He has seemed, that is, to be Conrad's Marlow. Marlow thinks and speaks about almost everything known to man. Except, it might be argued, form. But if we argue that the essential definition of form is feeling then it is clear that both Marlow and Warren deal in nothing else so passionately as feeling. Feeling is the form by which we know and understand whatever the world gives us. . . .

For while Warren has become that most lucid of thinkers, the dramatic observer of feeling, what he thinks about feeling is never simple and never conclusive. Moreover his thinking and feeling exist in such a tenuous balance as *lyric*, a formal existence no historian or philosopher can be quite comfortable with, that he has constructed a larger, subsuming form whose shape—in outline—is the tale and whose character is philosophy's dialectic. His purpose is, through the poetic enactment of feeling and the self-referential examination of that feeling, to confront the nature of human existence. He has tried and continues to try to find, develop, and refine a form in which he could make those direct, comprehensive statements Allen Tate called for. But not, I think, statements about "modern civilization" alone; rather about the condition and circumstance of men in the world. Excluding *Audubon*, Warren's most entirely successful poem, he has found his highest achievement in *Or Else*.

Dave Smith. In *Homage to Robert Penn Warren:*
*A Collection of Critical Essays*, ed. Frank
Graziano (Logbridge-Rhodes, 1981), pp. 36–37

In the later fiction (beginning as early as *Wilderness* but with *Flood* the apparent turning point) Warren's chief concern is less with self-knowledge per se—the need for it is not discovered here, but assumed—than with the manner and mood of man's conscious pursuit of understanding and verification of the meaning of life. In the later fiction Warren's concern is with knowledge as exploratory tool and with conscious need, sometimes pathetic and sometimes defiant, as vital fact. Ignorance and impulsiveness, idealism, impatience, and the obsessions of youth are no longer the urgent forces and major flaws of his characters. Rather, these men and women clearly, vexingly, possess the maturity of lives lived more than understood, lives understood more than accepted. Warren's later protagonists engage in probing, fitful, but patient quest of understanding and acceptance (often self-acceptance) while burdened with the ironies of maturity—their experience and "wisdom," their intelligence and habits of mind, the sardonic vision of lives suffered and endured (and sometimes inexplicably rewarded or blessed). At best they see themselves as survivors, their lives the curious legacies of others' passing; at worst they view their lives as existences merely muddled through. The urgency to *experience* has become in these people the commitment to *understand and embrace* that experience and to make it comprehensible and acceptable to others.

Neil Nakadate. In *Robert Penn Warren: Critical*
*Perspectives*, ed. Neil Nakadate (Univ. Pr. of
Kentucky, 1981), pp. 175–76

Robert Penn Warren is a major poet by any standard—perhaps even a prophet in some meanings of the word. He has had a sustained career as a poet for some sixty years. At an age when most are living and lecturing on the basis of their past creations, Warren continues to write profoundly, precisely, and beautifully. Since the *Selected Poems: 1973–1975* (published in 1976), he has published *Now and Then* (1978), *Being Here* (1980), and *Rumor Verified* (1981). Another volume is scheduled for 1982 and he has completed a longer poem on Chief Joseph. *Brother to Dragons* may be the best long unified single poem yet written in America. "Mortmain," "The Ballad of Billie Potts," and *Audubon* are significant and substantial. Warren is probably the most accomplished American narrative poet.

In the family and community poems considered in this volume, Warren has created a complex and extensive world. No American author seems to have started out with a design for the creation of his own literary community in several works, but many there are who have persistently developed works about their cultures and their places. Warren's people—even in this imaginary Kentucky community without a name—derive from and represent a world as recognizably Warren's as Yoknapatawpha is Faulkner's or Winesburg, Ohio, is Anderson's. The community exists in Warren's poetic works, although neither poet nor critic can pinpoint the time when he came to recognize its existence.

The poetic chronicle of Warren's family has a scope of more than a hundred years, not less than the time span of the Gant (or Webber) and Sartoris and Compson families or of the political and literary sagas of the Lowells and the Adamses. The joys and sorrows of the Penns and the Warrens are created with lyrical intensity and with national and historical implications. What Faulkner was perhaps groping for when he wrote *Flags in the Dust* is reflected in a different form in Warren's poems of the personal and community past.

The community past and the family past give the poems a texture different from that usually found in the fiction. The poems about the past reveal that the deep feelings almost always concealed beneath the hard exteriors of the narrators in Warren's best novels are indeed related to the personal and lyrical feelings of the poet.

In the diverse poems, the dominant theme seems to be the desire to know. The effectiveness of this motif is due in part to its final failure. There are moments of joy and even of reconcilement, but one cannot achieve ultimate joy in the labor of the frontier, the relationships of the family, the completeness of knowledge, and the beauties of art, or in the knowledge of the amazing grace of personal or religious salvation.

Floyd C. Watkins. *Then & Now: The Personal Past in the Poetry of Robert Penn Warren* (Univ. Pr. of Kentucky, 1982), pp. 169–70

## WELTY, EUDORA (1909–   )

Eudora Welty's fiction is the richest in human understanding and in power to shape and convey that understanding of any living writer known to me. In all of American fiction, she stands for me with her only peers— Melville, James, Hemingway, and Faulkner—and among them, she is in some crucial respects the deepest, the most spacious, the most lifegiving. . . .

Eudora Welty—in the wide centrality of her vision, in her fixed yet nimble scrutiny of what might tritely be called "the normal world" (the normal daily world of the vast country called the American South) and in the nearly infinite resourcefulness with which she has found means to convey the discoveries of that scrutiny—has opened to a whole generation of writers the simple but nearly unattainable possibility of *work*. We read her fiction, we recognized our world, we knew that our world was therefore the possible source of more good fiction. It had been done once; it could now be done again, and differently.

Reynolds Price. In *Eudora Welty: A Form of Thanks*, ed. Louis Dollarhide and Ann J. Abadie (Univ. Pr. of Mississippi, 1979), pp. 124–25

For Welty, as for most serious writers in English since James, the vision of the existence of man is not a simple relationship between stimulus and response. Behavior has its roots in history—not simply the history of the immediate past from which habits derive, but in an ancient, archetypal past. This dimension of history exerts a more basic, defining force on men, which over the course of human evolution has shaped the ways by which men have come to understand their relationships to nature, each other, and the universe. These shaping forces reside in the psyche but are more often than not unconscious. They are most clearly observed in outcroppings of myth and fantasy that to the artist's eye occur all around us. But the interest in myth and fantasy rests solidly in the present, real world. In "Place in Fiction" Welty writes that "the novel from the start has been bound up in the local, the 'real,' the present, the ordinary day-to-day of human experience". . . . It is significant, however, that the statements in which she seems to espouse allegiance to the photographic depiction of surfaces or appearances are quickly qualified. Place for Eudora Welty has a dimension of "mystery" because "it has a more lasting identity than we have." The "realism" that she finds essential to the novel applies equally to any kind of successful fiction. . . .

*The Golden Apples* can be seen perhaps as a merger of Welty's realistic method with the allegorical, but the notion hardly seems to do justice to so fine a book. It is more helpful to think of Welty's use of myth and fantasy in terms of three methods defined from a structural perspective. The demands she makes on her readers' imaginations are great no matter which sort of structure may be found. Her narrators may use myth and fantasy to define character; or with fantasy she may imaginatively create the interior of a mind or an allegorical landscape to investigate "the truth of the human heart"; or, finally, she may create characters who, like Virgie, are as aware of the dimension of myth and fantasy as the reader is asked to be.

Robert L. Phillips, Jr. In *Eudora Welty: Critical Essays*, ed. Peggy Whitman Prenshaw (Univ. Pr. of Mississippi, 1979), pp. 56–57, 67

Welty's constant theme is communication itself, the state of human existence in which individuals, because of some connection with each other in the natural world, become more than the simple integers they might seem. Every hero and heroine, from Mrs. Larkin to Laurel McKelva Hand, leaving the private, silent world of memory, grief, or dream, crosses a threshold into a real world that is enriched by that very entry, by that self so long withheld.

Also part of this passage is the reader of Welty's fiction. He must be attentive to the totally and artistically synthesized vision of the world that sustains her work. The moment of vision is built upon the particular world each fiction summons into existence. The climactic experience of each of Welty's fictions is not only the resolution of a plot but a denouement of the form, in which the world appears in its integrity before the reader, allowing him to realize how and when the parts become whole. . . .

Welty has given, and will continue to give (for these works are soundly made and will stand), a literature that reaches great stature in its theme of love. Few writers understand that the most complex human emotion, love, is also the most simple, and that a true treatment of the theme is both discussable and not.

Michael Kreyling. *Eudora Welty's Achievement of Order* (Louisiana State Univ. Pr., 1980), pp. 174–75

Placing Welty within the "Republic of Letters" is important in itself, but it has the greater advantage of focusing her final control of southern materials. Because of its vivid frontier settlement, its complicated plantation ethic entailing slavery, civil war, and the gradual decline of hereditary values, the South in general and Mississippi in particular present the modern literary imagination with unusually clamorous circumstances. As her fiction, essays, and interviews reveal, Welty's sense of a regional identity was deepened appreciably by the civil rights movement of the 1950s and 1960s and by the merging of distinctive American cultures which was accomplished in the following decade. Living continuously in Jackson, Welty observed closely this process of modernization, the small provincial capital of her birth transformed in the next seven decades into a metropolitan center with a diverse, highly mobile population approaching 300,000. But Welty's historicism has behaved admirably throughout. This ability to reconcile process and stasis, time and eternity, self and community, is, it seems clear, a reflection of Welty's citizenship in the modern "Republic of Letters." Relieved of the extremes of belief and rationalism, Welty discovered in this realm a suppleness of mind which is essential to the reconciler's art. More specifically, she discovered the means of forming an *image* of the South, one stripped of its historic defensiveness, romance, and ready applicability. There is finally a coolness at the core of Welty's work, a reserve or restraint that Walter Sullivan quite accurately notes, but it does not preclude her fulfilling the role of the modern vocation of letters. "The man of letters is primary in keeping open the possibility of man's apprehension of the truth of his destiny beyond time." Although etched in irony and pictured in displacement, Welty's preserved "Southern character" testifies to the strength of this moral "possibility." Her Mississippi chronicle is finally the outward shape of a passionate interior drama that has preoccupied all serious writers of the modern South and, before that, all chroniclers of Western culture.

Albert J. Devlin. Eudora Welty's Chronicle: A Story of Mississippi Life (Univ. Pr. of Mississippi, 1983), p. 212

## WEST, NATHANAEL (1903–1940)

It has become almost obligatory in any discussion of Nathanael West to mention his affinities with the current literary movement, "black humor." John Hawkes and Flannery O'Connor have directly acknowledged their indebtedness to him, and certainly he is to some extent a forerunner of such other novelists as Joseph Heller, Kurt Vonnegut and Thomas Pynchon. Yet his relationship to the theater of the absurd, which itself can be seen as closely connected to black humor, has not been explored, perhaps because West does not often work in the dramatic form. . . . Whether it has had any direct influence on the drama is uncertain; what is clear is that a close resemblance of motif exists. . . .

Not only are individuals lifeless or dehumanized in West's work, but even Nature, which in the romantic tradition has embodied life and vitality, is portrayed as dead or artificial as well. West emphasizes this particularly through imagery. On one occasion the sky is described as "canvas-colored and ill-stretched"; at another time its "luminous color seems to have been blown over the scene with an air brush." Yet at the same time that nature and humanity, which we normally think of as alive, are dead, inanimate things come ominously alive; so it seems that the inanimate and the animate have changed places. . . .

Showing the inanimate to be alive is a way for West to accomplish what several critics have pointed to as one of his primary goals—to emphasize the primacy of *things* in our lives, a primacy we have allowed and even encouraged at the expense of our humanity. Certainly West had an interest in presenting material objects of and for themselves, as his fantastic elaborations on the descriptions of the brothel interiors in *A Cool Million* suggest. . . .

It seems clear, then, that whether or not West exerted any direct influence on the dramatists of the absurd, a striking and not merely coincidental congruence of theme and technique can be traced in their works. They all use theatrical imagery in order to suggest the disjunction of appearance and reality, and perhaps even man's inability ever to *know* reality. They all imply the dehumanization of men by describing them as animals or things, and yet concurrently the inanimate comes alive. Of course, the absurdist dramatists have frequently gone a step beyond West in discarding completely any interest in plot or character development in the normally accepted sense. The circularity of the plays embodies the world view behind them—nothing really happens, no progress is made, no resolution is accomplished, either in the plays or in our lives. Yet it is also clear that, though West does not forgo plot resolution, which usually takes the form of violence, the fact that he employs caricature and not humanly recognizable people suggests that he, like the absurdists, believes it is impossible, given modern social and cultural conditions, for the individual to retain a whole, complete, integrated identity. Thus the fact that modern authors who write in different languages and genres have employed similar motifs in their works suggests a common response to features of modern life which make an impression on sensitive men everywhere.

Frank W. Shelton. SHR. Summer, 1976, pp. 225,<br>231–34

Words in the novel [*Miss Lonelyhearts*] fail to do the job West's characters assign them—to reveal a reality beyond themselves. But at the same time the words of the novel, West's words, manage quite successfully to do their job to reveal all they need to, the patterns their sound and sense make. . . . Words do not match reality, fit any empirical facts. Neither do they distort any facts or displace reality. They are not *about* something beyond themselves, an actual person's experience, a historical event. They constitute, rather, their own reality, and their only job is to be true to the structure of which they are a part, that is, to be right, self-consistent, aesthetically correct. . . .

West's novel does disturb us, threaten, because its form makes its theme intensely meaningful, utterly real. Here we witness words falling short of reality, and here, and here, and we watch their continual shortcomings compose an actual pattern of doom. We are unsettled because most of us are, like Dr. Johnson, rock-kickers—we ordinarily assume that our words signify something beyond themselves—and reading this story forces us to face the possibility that they do not. The story defines the issue that has become major in certain circles, "the problem of language." But West simultaneously solves the problem *in* the form, every word of the way. For unlike his characters, malpracticing empiricists all, and unlike most of us, West was, as an artist, a practicing idealist. We know that he got the idea for his novel from seeing actual letters to an advice columnist. Had he been concerned with historical-empirical fidelity, he could have used them more-or-less intact. But we also know that he changed them radically, that he in truth wrote his own letters, to make them right, aesthetically correct. All artists, of course, change things to suit their purposes, but their purposes have a single premise, that the work of art must be absolutely true to itself, self-integral, one. Then it can stand and unfold itself, an articulated body of ideas, an avatar of Being. . . .

We regard West loosely as a writer ahead of his time. I would say that it is specifically *Miss Lonelyhearts* that warrants this reputation, and that it anticipates in particular the work of Barth, Barthelme, Coover, Elkin, Gardner, Pynchon, of all those writers loosely bunched as comic whose humor, by trying its own limits, examines how language does and undoes us, what it gives and what it takes, what it may mean and what it may not, and if we are at last full of fear and wonder, we should be: Being is finally awful, no matter how we look at it.

J. L. Duncan. *IowaR*. Winter, 1977, pp. 124–25, 127

# WHARTON, EDITH (1862–1937)

In her major works Edith Wharton was able to evoke the metaphysical and symbolical implications of the situations which she was presenting. She knew how to maintain the single point of view while juxtaposing the narrator's varying depths of consciousness in order to achieve intense dramatic effects. She was also able to give moments of significant experience permanent form as viable works of art. She was adept at suggesting dimensions of experience that would ordinarily escape a literal transcription of it. As a result, she furnished the sensitive reader with fragmentary clues enabling him to divine implicitly her interpretation of her subject. . . .

Edith Wharton, seen in perspective, is a novelist who provides a link between the morally and psychologically oriented works of Hawthorne and James, who preceded her, and the later Realists like Sinclair Lewis or F. Scott Fitzgerald with their tendency toward the sardonic and iconoclastic. Edith Wharton may not have been capable of Hawthorne's moral inclusiveness, infinite perceptiveness, and imaginative reach which, as James said, made him "a habitué of a region of mysteries and subtleties" where he took as his province "the whole deep mystery of man's soul and conscience . . . the deeper psychology." She may also have been incapable of James's firm but infinitely subtle probing of the human mind and of his dissecting of the various nuances of behavior, conscious or unconscious, in any given scene.

But, like both Hawthorne and James, Edith Wharton was sensitive to the ambiguities in inner experience, in human behavior, and in many generally accepted ethical and metaphysical formulations. More than they, she, of course, understood the intricacies involved in living as a woman in a world set up for the social, economic, and sexual advantage of men. Sensitive as she was to the complications inherent in human motives and values, she tended in her work, as James did in his, to illuminate rather than resolve the complex issues and situations that she subjected to her scrutiny. She drew few simple conclusions about class, society, or individuals. More than James, she had the ability to assimilate natural landscape and urban milieu into her art and to make consummate use of such settings as active factors in the unfolding psychic drama in her work. In this respect she seems closer to Hawthorne than to James. . . .

She is a moralist as well as a mannerist. She transcends the realistic aspects of her world by striking intuitions into the psychic motivations of her characters. Though she did not herself use some of the later techniques of dream, association, distortion, and imagery that enable a writer to penetrate the innermost recesses of a character's psyche, she was, essentially and at her best, a psychologist in fiction. She continued the Jamesian propensity for disengaging "crucial moments from the welter of existence" to ascertain their true worth and significance and to determine how they affect the psyches and moral life of her characters.

Margaret B. McDowell. *Edith Wharton* (Twayne, 1976), pp. 142–44

The emotional problems that had dominated Wharton's earlier fictions—the sense of desolation, the need to place sexuality—had been problems that she knew at first hand. Now that is no longer the case. She may have felt driven to write repeatedly about the feelings of parents toward their children; however, she could only infer the nature of such feelings. She may have longed for family (the tone in fiction after fiction suggests as much), but she had none. In fact, although she made wholehearted efforts to get to know "les jeunes," she was more and more alone, and she felt increasingly alienated from the manners and practices of the younger generation. The inability to marshal her energy efficiently in these works bespeaks her uncertainty, and the tone in many of them is mixed. When she is at her best, Wharton captures the poignancy of aging. At other times, her management of the fiction grows less felicitous: increasingly, her satire lapses into an uncharacteristic querulousness, and everything about the postwar world is dismissed as vulgar and cheap. . . .

In her last novels, for the first time, if we do not read carefully, we might be misled into accepting the stereotype of "Edith Wharton: The Author" that has prevailed since her death: a haughty woman, cold, faintly supercilious, with the imperious remove that only breeding and great wealth can confer. That persona is there sometimes, on the surface; yet below, there is someone quite different. Defensive and wary, with desperate (and hopeless) longings, loneliness, and apprehension. Wharton's own epoch had passed, and she had never truly lived in it; now, too late for reconciliations, it was gone forever.

Cynthia Griffin Wolff. *A Feast of Words: The Triumph of Edith Wharton* (Oxford Univ. Pr., 1977), pp. 343–44

She moves beyond the subject of literal motherhood to meditation on the maternal principle itself and, combining literary, anthropological, and religious ideas, evokes the gods in which she believes the modern world stands in need. Those gods are female. They are the Mothers to whom Goethe had his Faust descend; they are the primordial maternal center of life whose loss to the Western world is recorded in Aeschylus's *Oresteia*, from which Edith Wharton at an early age took the image of the Furies that was to stay with her throughout her imaginative life but only in old age acquire the power of gender. They are—the Mothers of Wharton's last finished work, which she needed two volumes to contain—her mystical solution to a lifetime of tough-minded analysis, argument and debate on the subject of woman. . . . So when Edith Wharton directed her thoughts on motherhood and cultural continuity (or renewal) toward the mythic, toward the concept of the Great Mother of prehistory, she was moving into modern but not uncharted or untrod territory. Other writers were simultaneously engaged in the intellectual adventure that anthropologists and a few imaginative classicists had, before them, begun to explore. . . .

Wharton took the image of the Mothers from Goethe and then developed it into her own mystical philosophy of maternal wisdom, which she applies in her last two novels [*Hudson River Bracketed* and *The Gods Arrive*] both to the marital bond and to the artist's creative process. . . .

All of her life Edith Wharton saw men as weakly affairs. The most common criticism of her fiction has always been that her male characters do not compare with her women, and the charge is just. No man in Wharton's canon can come up to the mark of a Justine Brent or an Ellen Olenska or a Rose Sellars—to name only three out of many. In part the men do not measure up because Wharton's point, exactly, is that patriarchal society has made of men tyrants and fools. But lying even deeper, it must be admitted, has always been her gut-belief in the innate inferiority of men. Not until her last novel, however, in the figure of Halo Tarrant, who partakes of the strength and potency of the Mothers, did Wharton openly confront her own notion of inherent female superiority and develop it into an intellectually provocative, even if fundamentally conservative, concept. . . .

In her last two novels Wharton, it could be said, absorbed rather than feared the Furies. With them, so to speak, she tried to call America back to the ancient Mothers, the awesome matriarchs of Bachofen and then before him Goethe and then before either, so she seems to have believed, all human thought itself.

If this final, highly romantic vision of Wharton's is saddening—and in many ways it is: it conceives of women in totally maternal terms, it writes men off once and for all, it reverses rather than equalizes or eradicates the hierarchy of gender—it is also intriguing. . . .

It is tempting to imagine that she might have returned to the issues of power, creativity, and healing raised in her last two novels about modern Americans and found a way to harmonize her newly articulated mysticism about femaleness with her old concern for women's lives in the here-and-now. But that perhaps, given the vitality of her argument with America on the subject of women from *The House of Mirth* through *The Age of Innocence*, may be a little like wanting to modernize an old house. Maybe we don't need less than what we have.

Elizabeth Ammons. *Edith Wharton's Argument with America* (Univ. of Georgia Pr., 1980), pp. 189–91, 194–96

Wharton's greatest talent was the ability to recognize the secret gods of American society and to approach them with an air of irreverence, an attitude nearly sacrilegious, to expose them as the empty idols they are. She understood that what America worshiped more than anything else was wealth. She knew that her mother's dictum, "Never talk about money, and think about it as little as possible," reflected not a disdain for wealth but an attempt to hide an obsession. She watched (and chronicled) the rise of the Beauforts, the Rosedales, and the Abner Spraggs of the world to the position of national heroes, and she showed the results of this overwhelming materialism. Novel after novel depicts the consequences of regarding the world as a marketplace, describes the dehumanization of those frozen in materialism, especially of the women who become commodities. In old New York the most salable woman, Wharton perceived, was the virginal child bride, May Welland; later a taste developed for the more sophisticated but equally ornamental type of Lily Bart; in the twenties a more corrupted but equally decorative type, the flapper, Lita Wyant, prevailed. But each was the commodity demanded by a materialistic world—a woman without soul, without self, distorted and twisted from her true nature into a marketable product, one whose nightmare form was Undine Spragg.

Wharton knew it was not only women who suffered from this worship of wealth. If women lost their souls to become pretty things, men sold their souls—Ralph Marvell to attain his fantasy of egotistic escape, Selden and John Amherst to maintain secure positions in worlds they pretended to disdain. And the business of acquiring, protecting and increasing one's wealth, Wharton saw, kept one from the business of living. . . .

Money, that supreme American god, was Wharton's first target. This obsessive materialism degraded and destroyed many, and its power ruled in every period of American life that Wharton observed. But Wharton saw another American deity as almost equally dangerous, for she understood the consequences of the country's veneration of another false god—the idol of pleasure.

Pleasure is perhaps too strong a word to describe the secret god of old New York, for there the hidden idol was the milder goal of peace of mind, freedom from unpleasantness. Wharton knew that everyone seeks this peace, but she also perceived that what made old New York evil was its desire to achieve this peace at any cost. . . .

Conflict, tragedy, and pain were terrifying to Americans, and Wharton saw that their way of dealing with them was through belief in another god—the easy answer. Wharton knew that what America expected of life was "a tragedy with a happy ending". . . . America did not want to believe that "things are not always and everywhere well with the world," and preferred to retreat to the formula, to the answer that avoided conflict and required no thought. In Newland Archer's world the easy answer was the resort to the dictates of good form; for every problem there was an immediate and accessible rule to follow. When these rules fell apart, revealed as the empty conventions they were, Wharton identified a new set of panaceas that came to be worshiped in the twenties. These were the gurus, masseurs, rejuvenators, and spiritual advisers of the time, the people who sustain Pauline Manford's existence in "an atmosphere of universal simplification," who feed her need to believe that "America really seemed to have an immediate answer for everything, from the treatment of the mentally deficient to the elucidation of the profoundest mysteries." Whether the time was 1870 or 1920, Wharton satirized the folly of this retreat from the complexity of life's conflicts.

Carol Wershoven. *The Female Intruder in the Novels of Edith Wharton* (Fairleigh Dickinson Univ. Pr., 1982), pp. 164–67

## WILBUR, RICHARD (1921–    )

Let me try to list some of the virtues that distinguish the poetry of Richard Wilbur. First of all, a superb ear (unequalled, I think, in the work of any poet now writing in English) for stately measure, cadences of a slow, processional grandeur, and rich, ceremonial orchestration. A philosophic bent and a religious temper, which are by no means the same thing, but which here consort comfortably together. Wit, polish, a formal elegance that is never haughty or condescending, though certain freewheeling poets take it for a chilling frigidity. And an unfeigned gusto, a naturally happy and grateful response to the physical beauty of life, of women, of works of art, landscapes, weather, and the perceiving, constructing mind that tries to know them. But in a way I think most characteristic of all, his is the most kinetic poetry I know: verbs are among his conspicuously important tools, and his poetry is everywhere a vision of *action*, of motion and performance. . . .

Wilbur has been from the first a poet with a gymnastic sense of bodily agility and control, a delight in the fluencies we all admire in a trained athlete, in the vitality and importance of stamina and focused energy. . . .

This delight in nimbleness, this lively sense of coordinated and practised skill is, first of all, a clear extension of the dexterity the verse itself performs. If it were no more than this it might be suspected for an exercise in that self-approval which, like one of the poet's fountains, patters "its own applause." But it is more. For again and again in Wilbur's poems this admirable grace or strength of body is a sign of or symbol for the inward motions of the mind or condition of the soul. . . .

It is, I think, remarkable that this double fluency, of style and of subject, should be so singularly Wilbur's own, and that his poetry should exhibit so often the most important and best aspects of cinematic film: the observation of things in motion from a viewpoint that can, if it cares to, move with an equal and astonishing grace. But what these poems can do so magnificently that is probably beyond the range of motion pictures is, specifically, a transition, or, rather, a translation, of outward physical action (the heave of a weight, the bounce of a ball, the spirit of a runner) into a condition of the imagination; a dissolving of one realm of reality into another, for which the poem "Merlin Enthralled" might serve as an example.

Anthony Hecht. *TLS*. May 20, 1977, p. 602

There are poets . . . whose every major work is attended by a sense of stylistic experiment—Eliot and, more recently, Lowell come to mind. But there are poets as well who, having mastered their idiom, are content to spend a lifetime in its continued refinement, and in applying it to a handful of themes whose fascination never wanes for them. Poets as seemingly diverse as Emily Dickinson and Edwin Muir supply instances of such deliberately confined intensity. Wilbur is a poet of this, rather than of the former sort. His attention to his chosen subjects deepens without yielding often to passing distractions. This continuous deepening is more deservedly termed development, one might feel, than is a series of stylistic departures whose genealogical relations to one another are not easily to be traced.

Wilbur's chief recurrent theme is implicit in his approach to style. His intricately patterned poems reflect the discovery of patterns of natural beauty; and the poet's art thus strives to be an adequate analogy to the surrounding creation. The art of man mirrors the art of God. Creative energy finding its expression in natural and esthetic form is what Wilbur continually contemplates, praises, and seeks to realize in his own writing. . . .

His essays are meditative ventures, more inviting of the reader's participation than most criticism. Reading them does not merely augment our knowledge; it re-directs our attention, and cleanses our minds of much that is trivial and stale. Wilbur's prose, like his poetry, engages with an able lucidity "the whole of the world that is real to him," and does so with such persuasive eloquence that we see his world as one we would like to share. Such mutuality happily maintained between poet and reader has a simple name: civilization. One wishes there were more of it around.

Robert B. Shaw. Parnassus. Spring/Summer,<br/>1977, pp. 177, 185

Our strengths betray us. Nowhere in modern poetry is that axiom demonstrated more convincingly than in the case of Richard Wilbur. Elegance, sophistication, wit, learning, technical skill of a high order—these are the qualities that define the poet's current reputation. . . .

Wilbur is, in fact, aware of the darker elements of human experience, and he is in every way a more complete and a more significant poet than his detractors suggest. At the heart of his achievement is a willingness to face the full implications of our humanness, to confront not merely that paradoxical creature, man, but to encounter as well those structures—both physical and intellectual—that man has created for himself. Again and again, this requires that the poet respond to contradictions of the most disturbing sort. At the one extreme he discovers an immense, nearly heart-rending potential for beauty and love; at the other, mindless violence and inexplicable evil. In facing this paradox Wilbur explores its tensions and ambiguities with the careful attention only a poet can summon to such a task. If the result of such exploration seems controlled and poetically sure, that is, after all, what we have a right to expect from our artists. Wilbur's poems create beautiful shapes for the experiences they record; but often the very beauty of the designs may conceal from us the struggle and anguish of the experiences themselves.

Ejner J. Jensen. NER. 2, 4, 1980, pp. 594–95

# WILDER, THORNTON  (1897–1975)

The task Thornton Wilder sets himself in his novels is to find . . . a unity within the diversity of all life. Such a search necessitates a confrontation with the phenomenal world of apparent time. The resolution to the confrontation is for Wilder—inevitably perhaps—a mystical one. He affirms through characterization, through structure, through thematic development that there exist certain eternal verities which are unaffected by and which give meaning to the phenomenal world in which man exists. He repeatedly demonstrates that the concept of time and history usually accepted by man—that time can be divided into distinct periods and that events gain much of their significance because of their occurrence within certain distinct time periods—is illusory.

The novels deny by their circular structures the validity of the idea of time as absolute progression from one never-recurring moment to another never-recurring moment. Although within a circular structure there may indeed be progression, the fact that the end of the progression within the structure occurs at a point which has also been the beginning of the progression belies the concept of absolute linearity. Wilder has consistently employed this method. . . .

The themes which predominate in Wilder's novels arise from his overwhelming concern with the placement of man in universal time. His preoccupation with the theme of destiny versus chance—which receives major treatment in *The Bridge of San Luis Rey*, *The Ides of March*, and *The Eighth Day*—arises from his awe at the ultimate mystery of man's temporal existence. His attempts to resolve this problem lead him to a mystical acceptance of an unknowable but eternal ordering principle. The most frequently intuited evidence of a supraphenomenal reality in the novels is love, and love in its various guises is one of Wilder's major themes. That Wilder considers all kinds of love—the perverse and perverted forms, as well as the highest, selfless form—as reflections of a pure eternal love which gives meaning and direction to experience is evident.

Mary Ellen Williams. *A Vast Landscape: Time in the Novels of Thornton Wilder* (Idaho State Univ. Pr., 1979), pp. 103, 105

Like all Thornton's work, *The Eighth Day* narrates the journey of pilgrims through adversities. Awkwardly, comically, naively, painfully, heroically, they "seek the light." The narrator in *The Cabala*, George Brush in *Heaven's My Destination*, the Abbess in *The Bridge of San Luis Rey*, Chrysis in *The Woman of Andros*, Caesar in *The Ides of March*, Mr. and Mrs. Antrobus in *The Skin of Our Teeth*, the Ashley family in *The Eighth Day*—all endure the unalterable so that the unalterable becomes a source of strength. Each adapts to necessity as though it were a choice. This, Thornton believed, was the motif of Beethoven's last quartets: "es müss sein." He saw it in Kierkegaard's *Fear and Trembling*: "To transform the leap of life into a walk, absolutely to express the sublime in the pedestrian—that only the Knight of Faith can do.". . .

Ought we then to classify Wilder as a religious writer? He did not claim that distinction. Moreover, it is a mistake to equate an artist's convictions with those of his fictional characters. In *Our Town*, he had written that there is "something in all of us that is eternal," but that was far from an avowal of personal immortality. . . .

Yet in his preoccupation with the preciousness of ordinary daily life, in his figurations of faith, love and hope—especially hope—Thornton was not outside the mainstream of Christian teaching. The Crucifixion seemed to him the most magnificent metaphor ever found for mankind's imperfection. On the other hand, he thought that Christianity's involvement in blood and murder "reawakens the latent anguish of the infantile life and fills the inner mind with such vibrating nerves and such despairing self-abasement that the spiritual values can barely make themselves heard."

This can be said: Whatever the well-springs of his outlook, and they were many; whatever his personal doubts, shortcomings, anguish, or those of the world, he resisted the temptation to believe that the human race is going to hell. Mankind is like the planet Earth in *Our Town*, "straining away, straining away all the time to make something of itself." A melancholy Christmas greeting provoked an exasperated response: "The first Christmas also came into a world of anxiety and distress, hence the summons to be joyful—'rejoice, I say, rejoice!'" There were always sufficient pretexts in life for melancholy. "No, no—refuse that indulgence. Love life and be loved." The knowledge of imperfection was not to be carried on one's back like a load of stones.

Gilbert A. Harrison. *The Enthusiast: A Life of Thornton Wilder* (Ticknor & Fields, 1983), pp. 358–60

# ● WILLIAMS, JOHN A. (1925–   )

[John A.] Williams is a young Northern urban Negro whose characters [in *Night Song*] speak the jive talk of the big city, and his material generally has the desolate emptiness of warehouses and tenements seen at dead of night in east Greenwich Village, where much of the novel's action takes place.

*Night Song* deals with the life and death of a Negro jazz musician, Richie Stokes, who seems to be modeled after the late Charlie Parker (in the novel, Stokes is called "Eagle"; Parker was "the Bird"). But the human elements of the novel are two young people—Keel, a Negro, and his white girl, Della, who are in love with each other but caught in the paralyzing stalemate of the impossibility of their relationship. What comes across in the relationship of this pair is neither warmth nor love but an agonizing void.

Because the Negro writer can hardly escape being possessed by one theme, the problem of his own place in American life, he is always in danger of becoming abstract. This abstractness resembles, though it is far more humanly authentic, that of the proletarian novels in the thirties. Mr. Williams, for example, has the inevitable scene of the policeman, with no cause but his own insecurity, beating Stokes over the head with his club. It is not that such things do not happen; the trouble is that they have happened so often that they have become a cliché that must overpower a talented young writer like Mr. Williams, limit the possibilities of his imagination, and not permit him a place in the artistic sun, which his talent demands.

William Barrett. At. Jan., 1962, p. 98

John A. Williams is the author of the earlier *Night Song*, a novel about jazz. In his new work, *Sissie*, he draws in part on his authoritative knowledge of that world, but this novel is far richer and cuts deeper than most books about jazz. For *Sissie* is a chronicle of Negro life in transition, and it unites, as few novels do, the experience of the brutalized older generation of Negroes with that of the sophisticated young, who, one way or another, have made it in American life. As such, it is full of vivid contrasts, and it conveys memorably an image of the double war that Negroes wage—against their white oppressors on the one hand, and generation against generation on the other. In its portrayal of the conflict of generations, *Sissie* suggests the American-Jewish novel of a few decades ago in which the younger generation rebels against, but is emotionally wedded to, the experience of its parents.

Sissie is a proud, indomitable matriarch with two surviving children, Ralph and Iris. On one level the story is almost a sentimental saga of a Negro family that struggles against poverty and demoralization and finally achieves a tenuous respectability. Here the book is akin to the traditional American "immigrant" novel. But *Sissie* is steadily redeemed from sentimentality by the hard grain of its sensibility and by its implacable anger. There is none of the congratulatory tone of the usual up-from-the-slums story. The author is far too keenly attuned to the monstrous price of the victory. . . .

Inevitably, this novel invites comparison with James Baldwin's *Another Country*. *Sissie* is by far the better work. For all his platform polemics, Baldwin does not seem to possess the grasp of the Negro *milieu* that Williams displays. And where *Another Country* is shrill and noisy,

*Sissie* is permeated by a quiet anger that builds and builds inexorably. John A. Williams may well be a front-runner in a new surge of Negro creativity.

David Boroff. *SR*. March 30, 1963, p. 49

John A. Williams' *The Man Who Cried I Am . . .* has attracted considerable attention among the general public not so much for its literary excellence but because in the last pages of the novel its protagonist, Max Reddick, discovers a monstrous plot—code named "King Alfred"—to eradicate the black population of the United States. The plot, similar in many ways to Nazi Germany's "final solution," employs enough facts from everyday life to give the reader an uneasy feeling that perhaps this section of the book is not pure fiction: only slightly disguised, James Meredith, Malcolm X, Martin Luther King, Richard Wright, and James Baldwin all appear in the novel; so do numerous black organizations ranging from the Urban League to the Black Muslims. . . .

What has Williams accomplished by his use of bizarre and horrible metaphors for racial conflict and the plight of the black American? Perhaps his most important achievement is his escape from the protest novel tradition that has threatened to confine black writers within one narrow school. Since the publication of *Native Son . . .* , black novelists have either written naturalistic protest novels only to be compared unfavorably with Wright or have attempted to find a new form which would bring a freshness to their work but would still express their powerful moral indignation. Among the novelists of the fifties, only Ralph Ellison and James Baldwin stand out as achieving the latter goal. More recently, an impressive number of black writers have forsaken the old protest formula in favor of different subjects, structures, styles, or techniques. . . . Williams has demonstrated his ability to work with a type of horror tale which transcends mere documentation of ghetto conditions yet still carries the message he feels he must convey to his readers. The nightmarish scenes which emerge from his otherwise realistic novel startle the reader into attention and leave him with memories that he will not forget as soon as he may wish. Williams' success with this shock technique suggests one of the new directions that may be taken by the black novelist.

Robert E. Fleming. *CL*. Spring, 1973, pp. 186,
195–96

His subject is race, and his themes reflect the most advertised concerns of the revolution: the economic and psychological emasculation of the black man by the white, the struggle of the black man to preserve his manhood, the black will to survive and the enduring strength that brings victory. . . . He seeks to convince the reader that his picture of society, with its black ideological tilt, is accurate, bringing home to white Americans the extent of their crime and demonstrating to blacks the means by which they might triumph over white discrimination. . . .

Williams's novels are consistent in reflecting his ideological bias, but artistically they are quite uneven. *The Angry Ones*, dealing with discrimination against blacks who try to get specialized employment, and *Night Song* . . . , an excursion into the world of black jazz, indicate that from the beginning Williams knew how to put a novel together, but that he had not developed the emotional restraint or insight to put a *good* novel together. *Sissie* . . . , about the changing black family and the emergence of a new generation, is a great improvement. Williams, having learned much about himself and his subject, found a way to capture the complexities of both. *The Man Who Cried I Am* . . . rises to art, as if the three earlier novels were exercises of preparation. Its story of two black novelists makes one of the best novels of the 1960's. But *Sons of Darkness, Sons of Light* . . . and *Captain Blackman* . . . show a sharp falling off. The former, about the use of Mafia techniques in a "possible" future, and the latter, about the role of the black soldier in America's military history, are both thin and theme-ridden.

That he has not been more frequently successful is largely explained by the fact that he has expended his talents more on politics than on art. Perhaps more important, the course upon which his political and racial loyalties have guided him is not completely the course of his natural bent. The arena in which he is most comfortable is the world of the black intellectual. His prototypical character is the man of thought whose creativity is sapped by racism. The strength of the character and his interest for the reader lie in his powers of self-analysis and understanding. . . .

Though Williams resolves the paradox of "fortunate oppression" in *The Man Who Cried I Am*, he has perhaps gone too far on the road to polemics to turn back. He has chosen, more often than not, to use his art for the narrow rather than the larger political purpose, and it has led him into implausible exaggeration and offensive sentimentality. Unless a change in the times frees him of his deep sense of obligation to the narrower purpose, he will probably never write another novel as good as *Sissie* or *The Man Who Cried I Am*.

Jerry H. Bryant. *Critique*. 16, 3, 1975, pp.<br>81–82, 100

The corporate hero and the "cadences" are indeed appealing devices for rendering Black history in fiction, but my argument is that the point of the Afro-American novelists' theoretical project is not so much to be historically more accurate, though that is desirable, as it is to embody within the genre an exemplary self-determination. John A. Williams contributes to this project by boldly altering the conclusion of *Captain Blackman* into utopian fantasy, projected thirty years into the future. By that time 30 million light-skinned Afro-Americans playing the part of Trojan horses within the American establishment are able to short-circuit the Pentagon's nuclear attack system. Supported by African states American Blacks assume control over the military force, announcing that they have won the real war underlying American history, the war for racial supremacy instigated by white power that for hundreds of years has refused equality.

If genres were fixed, authoritative types, Williams's excursion into fantasy-utopia would be inconsistent with his otherwise realistic novel. . . . It is precisely the ending of *Captain Blackman* that completes its logic. Presenting the outcome of history in a version of fantasy, Williams jettisons the premise of realism—the assumption that a verbal text reflects an objective reality. Instead, he presents his novel as a creation frankly governed by the artist's imagination, replacing the domination of an old genre with the new control of the Black writer's consciousness. . . . The manner of writing in *Captain Blackman* constitutes the theme of entry into conscious shaping of narrative history.

John M. Reilly. *BALF*. Spring, 1979, pp. 5–6

In the 20-odd years that he has been writing seriously, John A. Williams has not had the satisfaction of being ranked among our first-rate novelists. Whatever the reasons for this, a lack of industry on his part cannot be one of them. Since 1960, when his first novel, *The Angry Ones*, appeared, he has stuck commendably to his task, publishing such notable novels as *Sissie* and *The Man Who Cried I Am* and a few volumes of nonfiction as well. *! Click Song* is his eighth novel. If that is not the largest output of any serious writer during the past two decades or so, it is impressive nonetheless—especially for a writer who, by his own account, has not always been encouraged by the treatment his books have received from publishers and critics. He is known to be a very proud man, with considerable confidence in his talent and beliefs, and the unfavorable treatment his work has received may simply have increased his determination to keep following the music he hears.

Much of the music that Williams hears springs from his abhorrence of racism and his devotion to the black struggle against it. He is surely not the only novelist who has made racism a matter of deep concern, but one can think of few others who have taken on the subject as regularly as Williams has, or with such directness of language and feeling. Williams, it can be said, pulls no punches. Still, whatever the necessities of his style and manner of attack—considering the urgency of the subject that occupies him—there are problems with his approach. He often throws more rhetorical punches than a general reader finds persuasive in fiction; and, related to that, he tends sometimes to lecture us bluntly about what troubles his characters, when we wish that he would—by an artful manipulation of his material—try to make us see it.

In *! Click Song*—which reflects some of the customary aggressions of his method—Williams returns to this attack on racism, extending it this time to the world of publishing and its satellites of literary evaluation.

Jervis Anderson. *NYT*. April 4, 1982, p. 12

## WILLIAMS, TENNESSEE (1911–1983)

*The Two-Character Play* is not a good play, but it is an important one. In this play, as in *The Gnädiges Fräulein*, *The Milk Train Doesn't Stop Here Anymore*, *In the Bar of a Tokyo Hotel*, and *Small Craft Warnings*, all recent works, Williams has used the theater to work out his personal and artistic problems. These plays are not intended to tell a story or to present a slice of life but to communicate—through a series of images, symbols, and clever language—his uniquely changing conception of reality. The effort, while admirable, has failed to produce good theater because the scope of his art, as the various versions of *The Two-Character Play* demonstrate, has become so narrow and so uniquely subjective that Williams is unable to communicate to his audience the significance of his vision.

Williams' recent plays, as illustrated by much of the opaqueness in *The Two-Character Play*, have become exercises in which he uses the actors as projections of his own mental anguish, with his personal psychosis serving as his thematic basis. Such a conception of drama, as in the case of Strindberg or Maeterlinck, can lead to powerful theater because the play provides a model by which the audience can come to recognize, through an examination of the dramatist's psychic state, its own or its culture's psychosis. Theater of this type returns drama to its origins and becomes a public ritual that is therapeutic for both the author and his audience. To succeed, as this form of drama does for the plays of O'Neill and for the earlier works of Williams, the psychosis must be so widespread with roots so deep in the psychocultural history of the audience that the malady is immediately recognized. Failing that, the work is nothing more than an exercise in ego.

Rexford Stamper. In *Tennessee Williams: A Tribute*, ed. Jac Tharpe (Univ. Pr. of Mississippi, 1977), pp. 360–61

Williams has his shortcomings. There is much lyrical excess in the earlier long plays, accompanied by occasional sentimental lapses and unresolved ambiguities of characterization. These faults stem from his unfortunate compulsion to invest a play with more "meaning" than its plot and characters can support—to strive pretentiously for deep significance through the complex use of myth and private symbol. But his virtues and strengths have also begun to stand out. He has a genius for portraiture, particularly of women, a sensitive ear for dialogue and the rhythms of natural speech, a comic talent often manifesting itself in "black comedy," and a genuine theatrical flair exhibited in telling stage effects attained through lighting, costume, music, and movement. More than many writers, he seems to have been obsessed by a need to write for his own survival, and he has continued through the years (except for a brief period in the late sixties when he suffered a mental breakdown) to complete or revise on the average a play a year. This too, however, has its price: recent plays like *Out Cry* (1973)—called in earlier and later versions *The Two-Character Play*—and some of the pieces in his *Dragon Country* collection of 1970 are deeply marred by his personal involvement in the desperate situations of his characters. This involvement may reflect his own growing despair during the late sixties, but if it is to become drama, it must be better distanced and universalized.

Stephen S. Stanton. In *Tennessee Williams: A Collection of Critical Essays*, ed. Stephen S. Stanton (Prentice-Hall, 1977), p. 2

"Moralist" may seem a perverse appellation for a playwright whose works concern rape, castration, cannibalism, and other bizarre activities, but in examining the plays of Tennessee Williams it is exactly this point—that he is a moralist, not a psychologist—that should be borne in mind. Williams' powers of characterization are real, but they are not his central gifts: witness *Cat on a Hot Tin Roof* which contains Big Daddy, one of Williams' most striking characterizations, but which fails nonetheless because in this play Williams' moral vision becomes blurred, and it is in the strength of that moral vision that his power as a playwright lies.

Admittedly, Williams' morality is a special one, but it is a consistent ethic, giving him a point of view from which he can judge the actions of people. Yet to say that Williams rewards those who, by his standards, are virtuous and punishes those who are evil is to oversimplify, for in the world of Williams' plays, good often has a curious affinity with evil. Beneath the skin of the Christlike martyr destroyed by the cruel forces of death and sterility lies the disease, the transgression that had made the author destroy him, while the character most fiercely condemned may at the same time be the one for whom pardon is most passionately demanded. From the self-lacerating desire simultaneously to praise and to punish stems the violence that agitates so many of Williams' plays. . . .

But Williams' best work derived its force from the strength of his moral temper, which led him to censure even what he most wished to exalt. Williams remains committed to the Romantic dictum inherent in his neo-Lawrencian point of view, that the natural equals the good, that the natural instincts welling up out of the subconscious depths—and particularly the sexual instinct, whatever form it may take—are to be trusted absolutely. But Williams was far too strong a moralist, far too permeated with a sense of sin, to accept such an idea with equanimity. However pathetic he made the martyred homosexual, however seemingly innocent the wandering love-giver, the moral strength that made him punish the guilty Blanche also impelled him to condemn Brick and Chance. Because he was condemning what he most desired to pardon, in order to condemn at all he sometimes had to do so with ferocious violence.

This violence, however grotesque, was never in itself the real problem in Williams' work. Nor were the disguises, transpositions, even evasions in his handling of the theme of homosexuality. They were, in fact, arguably a source of his strength, for they protected him from oversimplifications and encouraged the genuine ambiguity and complexity of his attitude to take symbolic form in his plays. Williams' problem is not that he dealt obliquely with homosexuality (the oblique view, after all, often reveals things that are invisible when the object is contemplated directly) but that he has expressed all too openly, especially of late but to some degree from the first, the impulse to sentimentalize. One of the central dangers confronting a Romantic writer is that his commitment to the idea of natural innocence will lead him not only to see this quality as inherent in the child or man in a state of nature (Kowalski is a curious late variant on the Noble Savage), but to affirm its existence in characters who have lived all too fully in the fallen world of mortal corruption. When this easy sympathy is extended without qualification, Williams' work slips over the edge of control into the maudlin just as it slips over the opposite edge into hysteria when the opposing impulse to punish—the self or others—is dominant. When these conflicting impulses are held in some degree of balance and Williams can judge his characters with perception, he is a moralist of some force, a playwright of some distinction.

Arthur Ganz. In *Tennessee Williams: A Collection of Critical Essays*, ed. Stephen S. Stanton (Prentice-Hall, 1977), pp. 123, 136–37

The underlying motive of many of his dramas is a search for purity. Whether Williams is primarily a sensation-seeker as some critics insist, or whether, as Williams says, his intention is "to illuminate the mainstream of life" with shocking material serving only to heighten the dramatic effect, he does tend to dwell on the sordid and the perverse. Yet no other American playwright has analyzed women with such subtlety and compassion. No other has come as close to creating a poetry of the theater embodied in dialogue, scenic environment, and in such theatrical devices as music, symbolic props, sound and lighting effects—all combining to create a seamless lyric impression. Despite the fact that he has written some of the most poetic lines spoken on the American stage, however, his poetry as such (two collections of poems: *In the Winter of Cities* and *Androgyne, Mon Amour*) is extremely uneven. . . .

Any thorough reader of Williams's work will note the constant reappearance of favorite images such as birds, cats, foxes, fox-teeth in the heart and in the gut, Don Quixote, a lamp or a candle at night, ice and snow, gauzy summer gowns, Arthur Rimbaud and his drunken boat, stairways and narrow passages, partitions and doors between people, ceremonial tea drinking, scavenging for food, and devices marking the passage of time. His themes . . . include: fear (of loneliness, of loss, of death), search for a lost ideal (youth, purity, involvement), honesty vs. mendacity, the need for compassion and tenderness among all people isolated in their separate skins. His compassion focuses most frequently on the elderly and the lonely, on women, artists, blacks, and helpless sensualists, and on any derelict whose luck has run out but who attempts to salvage a bit of dignity.

Felicia Hardison Londré. Tennessee Williams<br>(Ungar, 1979), pp. 23, 32–33

Passion is . . . the heart's blood of the theater, and Williams is to the stage what a lion is to the jungle. At its best, his dialogue sings with a tone-poem eloquence far from the drab disjunctive patterns of everyday talk. He is an electrifying scenewright simply because his people are the sort who are born to make scenes, explosively and woundingly. . . . Williams was also a moral symbolist. His earthy characters journey over a landscape that pulses with the strife-torn dualities of human nature. The duel is between God and the Devil, love and death, the flesh and the spirit, innocence and corruption, light and darkness, the eternal Cain and the eternal Abel. In the American tradition, this links Williams to three 19th-century moral symbolists: Hawthorne, Poe and Melville.

As a playwright, Williams had the minor defects of his major virtues. He sometimes ran a purple ribbon through his typewriter and gushed where he should have dammed. Occasionally, his characters were too busy striking attitudes to hit honest veins of emotion. His symbols sometimes multiplied like fruit flies and almost as mindlessly. His chief danger was the unhealthy narcissism of most modern art, whose tendency has been to gaze inward and contemplate the artist's ego, as well as his navel, to the point of myopia and hallucination. Almost inevitably, he suffered the attrition of dramatic power that afflicts most playwrights after the age of 50.

In the greatest drama, Greek and Shakespearean, there is a final reconciliatory acceptance of man's fate. Williams could not achieve that exalting serenity of vision. "Hell is yourself," he said more than once, and the only redemption he knew of was "when a person puts himself aside to feel deeply for another person." In the finest moments of his finest plays, Williams achieves the lesser, but genuine, catharsis of self-transcendence. In breaking out of the imprisoning cycle of self-concern, the playwright and his characters evoke a line from *Ecclesiastes*: "To him that is joined to all the living there is hope. . ."

Tennessee Williams is no longer joined to the living. At one point in *Streetcar*, Blanche pleads with her sister not to "hang back with the brutes," saying, "Such kinds of new light have come into the world since then!" Williams was one of the bearers of that light.

T. E. Kalem. Time. March 7, 1983, p. 88

## WILLIAMS, WILLIAM CARLOS (1883–1963)

Williams was probably the last important American poet to insist on seriously playing out the drama of cultural allegiance that had so much concerned the writers and artists of the nineteenth century. This issue, at least in its old terms, is no longer of moment, and we are now likely to consider it, as Randall Jarrell did in a review of *Paterson*, a "dreary imaginary war in which America and the Present are fighting against Europe and the Past." It was never that simple, though in depicting it even Williams followed the old melodrama by casting himself as an American village innocent and T. S. Eliot as a cosmopolitan sophisticate. His allegiance, however, was a matter neither of patriotic nationalism nor of sentimental infatuation, and it is not adequately accounted for by Pound's explanations: the poet's resentment of his father's English nationality, and the special advantage of his diverse immigrant background (he did not have "in his ancestral endocrines the arid curse of our nation").

Williams' allegiance is better assessed if one remembers that his own emergence as a poet was part of the American literary renaissance of the years of renewed cultural aspiration just before and after the First World War. He was one of the group of cosmopolitan cultural nationalists who recognized in the revolutionary crisis of society and sensibility called "modernism" a challenge to seek again on native grounds the promise of American life. America and modernism, he believed, were equatable, issuing in the new, and in a liberating conception of culture—that "culture of immediate references" of which he wrote so brilliantly in the essay "The American Background." For him the stake was freedom of self-origination: the recognition and sovereignty of the organic impulse that moves all living things. . . .

The necessity of a culture of contact is what Williams' life and work confront and exemplify. The conception of a dynamic, vital, relative (relative to us: related) culture underlies his art, which may be considered a flowering in imaginative forms of his perception of the particular and the local—a flowering of universal significance, he claimed, just because of this. This conception of culture required that he stay put (the practice of medicine helped), that he enter into immediate life (again by way of his "medicine" and the "*tactus eruditis*" of a physician), and that he discover the ground under his feet (historical America in *In the American Grain*, the recent past in the novels *White Mule* and *In The Money*, the present American scene in *The Great American Novel* and *Life along the Passaic River*—ranges of history that *Paterson* brings together). And it forced him to reconsider his art, its materials and formal means, the agency of imagination in its making, its personal and social ends.

Sherman Paul. *Repossessing and Renewing:*
*Essays in the Green American Tradition*
(Louisiana State Univ. Pr., 1976), pp. 183–85

As we have seen, the impulse of the long, meditative poem among these American poets is to find what will suffice in old age, or, as in the case of Eliot, what can be projected for an old age. And as a form it is impressive, primarily because its successes are hard won over a long period of poetic practice, but also because the emphasis is on process and becoming. Process: this by now has become a commonplace of criticism, but we must not let familiarity harden us to what should remain fresh. The meditative poem has a hidden dramatic form, and for this reason, insights can be revealed which are persuasive, moments can "occur" which are similar to Joycean epiphanies.

In *Paterson V* this is missing. For if Williams intended to adopt the meditative mode of the Stevens of *The Rock* and the Eliot of the *Four Quartets*, as indeed his allusions suggest and his age required, it is clear that he either did not understand it or his long life in poetry had not prepared him for an entirely new way of writing. Certainly the meditative mode was new to him. Earlier he had most often structured his poems in simple terms of anecdote ("This Is Just to Say," for example), portraiture ("Sympathetic Portrait of a Child"), the image ("Spouts") and/or combinations of the three, which tended to result in a fleshing out of the narrative line, upon which *Paterson I–IV*, however much it may look on the page like a modern collage, is bedrock built. Nor did "Asphodel, That Greeny Flower" provide him with experience in the strategy of the meditative poem (no matter how much we wish to be genuinely, not sentimentally, moved by it), being as it is a rather flaccid amble down an associational memory lane. . . . But *Paterson V* falls into none of these categories. Williams drops the structural methods of the narrative and association and substitutes—what? What is the process by which he would win the discovery of the uroboros, symbol of integrations, wholeness? Although the reader can point to an Eliotic question in section one of *Paterson V* and an Eliotic assertion in section three, it is much more difficult to locate an underlying dramatic or rhetorical logic which allows Williams to make this affirmation. The truth is this—that Williams does not so much experience as assert. His purpose was dramatic, but he could not escape the tyranny of the object. In *Paterson V* he continued his old habit of description: he chose a brilliantly defined object—the tapestry which weaves the narrative of the unicorn—for his symbol, not something ineffable, irreducible to an object, such as Eliot's notion of the still point. . . .

Williams, cut off from his lifelong concept of himself, divorced from the ground (the sexual) and thus divorced from his native culture (the American grain), sought himself outside himself, never reaching a still point from which he could include the universe. This was his failure, but his courage was also in this: the infirmities of age demanded that he do what he had not done before, and confronting those weaknesses, he invented something new.

Kathleen Woodward. *"At Last, the Real
Distinguished Thing": The Late Poems of Eliot,
Pound, Stevens, and Williams* (Ohio State Univ.
Pr., 1980), pp. 161–63

As an innovator, Williams shared many of his positions with Pound, but he may in the long run prove to be more influential. Pound to a much greater degree applied himself to, and found his material in, art and literature. Williams, likewise interested in simultaneity and interaction rather than casuality, suggests his own far different sense of experience in chapter 54 of the *Autobiography*. He refers to the exciting secrets of the "underground stream" of human experience itself, unselected. Attending closely to it, "there is no better way to get an intimation of what is going on in the world" (*Autob.*, 360). His whole objective, as it ultimately became clear to him, is to lift the "inarticulate" up to imagination. A sense of the common people as prime source of life, shared in the early

years with Eliot, seems never to have left Williams, despite a discourage-
ment made plain at least as late as *Paterson II*.

A "lifetime of careful listening" to the speech arising from his daily
tasks and contacts, convinced him that poem and life, also, are one—and
that each person is trying to communicate to the world the poem of himself. In many works, but particularly in *Kora in Hell*, *In the American
Grain*, *Collected Earlier Poems*, *Paterson* and the late poems, he
demonstrated the informing need for imagination, having realized early
that "The imagination transcends the thing itself." An explorer and discov-
erer, always conscious of the handful of men who had contributed positively to the shaping of the American spirit, he takes his place alongside
them.

> Charles Doyle. *William Carlos Williams and the*
> *American Dream* (St. Martin's, 1982), p. 178

## WILSON, EDMUND (1895–1972)

For all of Wilson's alert modernity, *Patriotic Gore* has . . . a curiously old-
fashioned flavor reminiscent of that of the nineteenth-century bibliophile
who wrote about ignored books that intrigued him from the assumption
that his task was not so much to call the attention of scholars to them as to
attach them once again to the consciousness of a reading public. In providing this flavor Wilson is implicitly correcting the widening battalions of
professors of American literature who in unearthing minor authors and
exposing them in monographs written in a quasi-scientific academic code
are, in effect, moving those authors from a simple earthen tomb to a hideous plastic crypt. Wilson's voice is for the ears of the general reader, in
whose existence he believed because his career had been devoted to
creating him, and it says to him, here in my pages that which flowered so
briefly may still be recaptured, but, despite my efforts, the fading is
inevitable; my final justification is that it has accounted to me for some
part of myself and may so serve you.

Only American writing seems to have tempted Wilson to so personal
an approach, to have brought him so close to the authorial glance from
the library window or the undramatic melancholy of a cleric of the past
century contemplating the paling rhetoric of a once consequential synod
of yet an earlier century. He unhesitatingly used the pronoun "our" when
talking of that writing; he was an American addressing Americans about
a wider reality they could share if they would but take care. Although *The
Shock of Recognition* and *Patriotic Gore* have informed readers beyond

America, and, it can confidently be assumed, will continue to do so, unlike Edmund Wilson's work in other areas these books have a further meaning for Americans. They are the literary equivalent of a message to the faithful which the ecclesiastical outsider understands and may even admire but which assumes for its fullest effect a common cultural experience as much as an intelligent mind. . . .

Leon Edel reminds us of Wilson's impatience, tempered with sadness, at being praised as an expositor at the expense of his novels. The elegiac note in his writings on Americans whose names have faded may have been struck from him by this: that he as well as Fitzgerald was a novelist of the twenties; that he as well as Lawrence pushed back the fences that cramped the representation of sexual love in literature. His undoubted sovereignty as a critic and historian may not have sufficed to balance the neglect of his fictions, and in his criticism, therefore, he developed a corresponding sensitivity to the neglected.

Perhaps Wilson in his image of himself as the man by the fire was unfair to the animals that crouched outside the circle of light and so unfair to himself. He may have underestimated their desire to perpetuate him. We thank him for the minor men he has restored to us but we lack reason to number him among them.

Larzer Ziff. In *Edmund Wilson: The Man and the Work*, ed. John Wain (New York Univ. Pr., 1978), pp. 51–52, 58–59

Edmund Wilson's view of American society—of any human society, perhaps—was ultimately a tragic one. While some of the more glaringly obvious outrages might be put right, social reform could go no further without running into insoluble problems. In America the conflict between North and South, between industrial and pre-industrial, had ended by stamping out the Southern way of life, which included getting rid of the degrading institution of slavery; but, after all, the forces that had triumphed were not much better. . . .

This being the pattern of his thinking, it was inevitable that sooner or later his purview of American history should come to include the lonely figure of the Red Indian. The nudge that actually started his active interest in Amerindian history appears to be described in the opening paragraph of *Apologies to the Iroquois* (1960). . . .

As a critic, as a man of letters generally—and, quite simply, as a man—Edmund Wilson was at bottom a historian. The imagination that guided him was the historical imagination. In his relationship with the world, he was aware that countries, institutions, languages, ideas, people, and he himself, were ceaselessly changing and that to comprehend anything is to comprehend the ways in which it is being altered.

Hence his relationship with all the major elements in his world—America, Europe, large political ideas, forms of art, the notion of literature itself—was a continuing drama, always unfolding, towards a dénouement that could come only with his own death. Everything he wrote was, in a sense, a progress report; or, as in the case of the brilliant short essay "A Preface to Persius," a kaleidoscope. He recognized this himself as he got into middle age.

John Wain. In *Edmund Wilson: The Man and the Work*, ed. John Wain (New York Univ. Pr., 1978), pp. 143–45

I have tried to show that Wilson cannot be simply dismissed as lacking a coherent point of view. He early adopted a version of Taine's determinism and when he was converted to Marxism assimilated the Marxist approach, deprived of its dialectic, to a general historical view of literature and literary study. Marxism became a variety of genetic explanation alongside psychoanalysis. Judicial criticism, the decision of what is good and what is bad in art, remained reserved to a judgment of taste independent of history.

I am aware that Wilson cannot be judged merely a theorist. On many questions he has nothing to say, for he has not thought them worthy of his attention. He is, and never claimed otherwise, a practical critic who has fulfilled his aims in reporting and judging books and authors from many countries on an enormous variety of subjects. He has opened windows, and not only to Russia. His human sympathy is almost unlimited. It extends, as he justly remarked, "even to those [manifestations of the American literary movement] of which, artistically, he disapproves," because he wanted to assert the dignity of the literary vocation in America. . . .

Still, there are definite limits to the reach of his mind. I am not thinking only of his obvious lack of technical skill in analyzing narrative modes or poetic structures. More disturbing is the coarseness and even sentimental vulgarity of his dominant interest in sex, displayed in some of the fiction and, obsessively, in the early notebooks. He shows hardly any interest in the fine arts or music. He lacks understanding not only for religion, which he treats as a "delusion," but also for philosophy. The early enthusiasm for [Alfred North] Whitehead, his "crystalline abstract thought," seems to be based on a misunderstanding. It supported Wilson in his limited sympathies for symbolism and made him discount the "two divisions of mind and matter, body and soul," also in his polemics against the Neohumanists. But he could not share Whitehead's neoplatonic idealism or his concept of God and soon abandoned him for Marxism. But as Wilson's Marxism discarded the dialectics, it meant rather a return to a basic positivism and pragmatism, a commonsense attitude to reality. One sees this also in the comment on existentialism, which Wilson ridiculed for its assumption that "the predicament of the patriotic Frenchmen oppressed by the German occupation represents the condition of all mankind." Wilson seems not to know that *L'Être et le néant* was published in 1936 and that existentialism goes back to Heidegger and ultimately to Kierkegaard. Wilson thus could not escape from the limitations of a world view fundamentally akin to his early masters, Bernard Shaw and H. G. Wells, however much he transcended their provincialism. In spite of his cosmopolitism, the wide range of his interests, there is a closeness and even crudity about his self-assurance and air of authority. But as public critic he dominates the early twentieth century with a resonance unmatched by any of the New Critics.

René Wellek. *CLS*. March, 1978, pp. 118–19

Wilson continues to be difficult to place intellectually. Some pointed out that he had forsaken his great promise as a literary critic, had traveled too far afield to contribute to any narrowly specialized field of scholarship. Some found Wilson lacking in aesthetic depth and sensitivity. . . . Still others have been turned off by the later Wilson who seemingly became remote from American life, responding to it with peevish and atrabilious disdain.

Such criticisms, however, missed the most important truth about Wilson, namely, that he never abandoned his own fiercely individualistic reading of literature, his idiosyncratic vision of things, which had always been the source of his powers. Throughout his life Wilson refused to respond to a publicly circumscribed body of problems, to an intellectual framework dictated by an impersonal community of scholars. He did not want to attack the problems that were expected of him, only those he agonized over himself. His lifelong desire was to learn all he could about what interested him, to dig deeply into those things, always putting every scrap of new information through the alchemy of his own sensibility, giving all the stamp of his own authority. If Wilson is one of America's great men of letters, it is because from his earliest years he insisted on seeing the world from a kind of introspective and self-willed patrician detachment. He was an intellectual who had to feel the world for himself, and an often frenzied introversion, a loneliness, a personal honesty, is what he offered to the world outside. . . .

If we Americans have something to be grateful for in the achievement of Edmund Wilson it is undoubtedly his steadfast devotion to the literature, history, and culture of the United States. There are, of course, those who said that Wilson went sour on the United States, that with the passage of time he became more remote from things American. Wilson often seemed to do little to dissipate this wrongful notion, as when he remarked, in *The Cold War and the Income Tax*, that "this country, whether or not I continue to live in it, is no longer a place for me." But such assertions, found in many letters and utterances of Wilson's later years, are the products of mood and moral outrage, rather than substance and conviction. Wilson had always been out of phase with the America of the twentieth century. He took his strength from being solidly rooted in the early republican America of his forebears. But he was at one and the same time the most assiduous and contemporaneous of Americanists. He never had a desire to live abroad. When he learned foreign languages and read foreign literatures it was always as grist for the mill of American experience. He traveled through America first; he read American books first and devoted most of his energies to these books. His very individualism and elaborate irritability hints at why he was first and foremost an Americanist. He wrote of and for his own needs and ours; he addressed mainly his fellow countrymen experiencing similar pains and joys of living in America in the middle of the twentieth century.

If Wilson is remembered several generations from now, it will certainly be as one of the most enlightening and original critics of American life. Already there is good reason to suspect that his work stands favorably in comparison with other critical historians of the American experience—men like Tocqueville and Henry Adams. Sometimes opinionated, sometimes even wrongheaded and perverse, often cantankerous in expressing his dislikes; nonetheless his views of the American scene remain clear, powerful, and penetrating. Wilson's writings are historical syntheses on the highest plane, and over the years they will continue to reveal to Americans more and more truths about themselves.

George H. Douglas. Edmund Wilson's America<br>(Univ. Pr. of Kentucky, 1983), pp. 221–24

Edmund Wilson's work provides an exception to Alexis de Tocqueville's prophetic remarks about the direction of literature in a democracy. In the 1840s the French sociologist predicted that American writers would be "fantastic, incorrect, overburdened, and loose" in style; that they would aim at imaginative effects rather than profundity of thought and erudition. The solidity and classicism of Wilson's style, his balance and clarity, and his earnest dialogue with his time and with other cultures set him apart from the wild and often provincial strain in American literature. He is our enlightenment figure, a *philosophe* in an age of world wars, depressions and class conflicts, rising taxes, lowering standards, intellectual bewilderment, bombs, revolutions, and bureaucracies. While our greatest writers from Poe to Faulkner and Mailer have immersed themselves in the destructive element—and have created bizarre styles to rep-

resent the fragmented and convulsed America they gave themselves to—
Wilson cultivated the aesthetics of plain communication: in the manner of
an eighteenth-century man of letters, he believed that words could right
wrongs, unconfuse issues, and unclog the minds of his fellow citizens. He
lived and worked to further the cause of rational inquiry and scorned mys-
tics, doomsayers, and others who claimed to commune with darkness and
light. He took possibility, not ecstatic transcendence, as his territory. His
characteristic literary form, the extended essay, reflects his rationalist
commitment to limited exploration and personal judgment; it also reveals
a kind of artistic bravery and individuality in a country gone mad in pursuit of the Great American Novel and other spectacular performances.

For the better part of our century Wilson practiced the writer's profession with an astonishing steadiness of purpose and diversity of activity.
He wanted his readers to understand modern art, politics, and culture,
and he assumed various roles to show them what he had discovered about
the texture of life and the tendencies of ideas and books since the French
Revolution. Basically a journalist, he took the nineteenth and twentieth
centuries as his beat. But in order to do his reporting fully and accurately,
he became a social critic, literary critic, observer of pop culture and the
lively arts, historian, travel writer, linguist, poet, playwright, and
novelist. He managed to fall in love with each role without losing his sense
of unity. His way of being a professional seems diffuse and difficult in our
age of specialization. Without establishing a resting place for his talents—
without committing himself to a fixed professional function—he became
a figure whose authority and insight are national resources. A professor
without a university, a critic without a "field," a historian without a
"period," he became the exemplary intellectual of his generation. He left
a wheelbarrow full of books on subjects diverse enough to challenge the
ambitions of a Renaissance humanist, and he supplied American literature with a talent unique in range, intelligence, and lucidity.

David Castronovo. *Edmund Wilson* (Ungar,
1984), pp. 1–2

# ● WILSON, LANFORD (1937–    )

A number of talented young playwrights either worked or started at La
Mama, among them Lanford Wilson, whose *This Is the Rill Speaking* used
sound patterns, movement, intertwining time and song to paint a picture
of a hillbilly town, its people and its rhythm. A sugar-free *Our Town*, it
found loved life in a dramatic collage of back porches, cars—everywhere.

Moreover, it was an early example of a movement away from the intelligibility of dialogue. This sounds silly, but if you listen carefully there is an overlap to daily conversation that turns meaningful words into the beat and music of existence itself. Wilson grasped the feel and rhythm of human conversation. But while the technique was exciting, it was also unresolved. Yet that's all right; that's exactly what La Mama and the far left wing are for—the new, the ambitious, the still-being-born and experimental. And a year after *Rill*, Wilson had developed the style for viable, full-length drama—*The Rimers of Eldritch*.

Martin Gottfried. *A Theater Divided: The*
*Postwar American Stage* (Little, Brown, 1967),
pp. 300–301

With his new play *The Hot l Baltimore*, Lanford Wilson's message to the American theater is: look, theater is *plays*—remember them? And so he goes back and writes a play so old-fashioned in its humanity that it's the freshest play—the best American play—I've seen this season. Wilson is a good young playwright who's been around a long time, he's never had a Broadway smash, but he hasn't gone sour or frantic or corrupt or paranoid. He just keeps writing, and a lot of his writing is for the Circle Theatre Company, the absolute epitome of the tiny, dedicated, poverty-stricken, repertory group, with real playwrights who write new plays for its permanent acting company.

The *Hot l Baltimore* is a daring play. In it Wilson dares to remind us of what writers once were in this country. His play is not an imitation of, say, the young Saroyan of *The LaSalle Hotel in Chicago*; it is an authentic rebirth of that kind of writer's spirit—open, compassionate, loving, hard-boiled, soft-boiled, scrambled—all the kinds of egg a writer could be in those days. Wilson's characters are the beautiful losers—the deadbeats, walking wounded, crippled up-the-creekers, along with their inevitable muse, the golden whore. They're living in a decayed Baltimore hotel, once grand but now slated for demolition. In their interweaving end games we meet them—the old lobby-haunters; the young brother and sister, health food freaks who are trying to get to the mail-order land they've bought in Utah; not one but three whores, one golden and two gilded; the young hotel clerk who glumly and ineffectually loves the golden whore.

Wilson not only loves these characters—creatures of his brain who represent what moves him about human beings—but he loves the play itself, and so he treats it the way you're supposed to treat something you love, building, developing, cultivating, being honest with it until he and the play are speaking to each other in a warm transfer of energy and good faith.

Jack Kroll. *Newsweek*. Feb. 26, 1973, p. 91

[*Talley's Folly*] is a duologue between Matt and Sally, from sundown through moonrise and thence to the start of three decades of married happiness. In the distance there is occasional band music holding out promises, but also the barking of threatening dogs of the kind that tear Tennessee Williams heroes into Orpheus-like pieces. Nearer by is the croaking of frogs, a discreet natural obbligato against which Matt and Sally can play out their duet of pursuit and evasion, hopefulness and disillusion, until revelations of their pasts to each other bring better understanding, absolution through mutual compassion, and final tremulous affirmation of love. It is a curious love that slowly emerges from a protective husk of banter, teasing, even pugnacity. Once out, however, it can match the moon in its zenith—hold its own even under the coming scrutiny of long sunlight.

Gradually, with the double assurance of a master of psychology and dramaturgy, Wilson unfolds not so much a series of events as a conversation that will last two joint lifetimes. . . .

Wilson has written some of the most tender, wisely funny, chargedly understated dialogue I have heard from a stage in many a moon, dialogue fraught with the essence of the greatest drama on earth: that of two pitiful yet glorious human beings clumsily and splendidly staggering toward each other.

It is dialogue that, like most exalted stage dialogue, skirts the ridiculous only to stumble triumphantly onto the sublime. . . .

Wilson is the only American playwright I can think of who is steadily growing, improving, paring himself down to essentials. *Talley's Folly* is—in range, mood, scope—a minor work, although a broad social background is suggestively sketched in; but the fineness of its details makes up in penetrancy and pervasiveness for what it may lack in weight and impact. Its small, insistent truths, like sand in a beach house, seep into every cranny of our awareness.

John Simon. *NYM*. May 21, 1979, pp. 76–77

The wounded and the wistful, those who cling to their illusions as if they are identity cards, who never stop searching for solutions, are the people who inhabit the landscape of Lanford Wilson. Undiscouraged by disappointment, they continue to nurture private dreams. Often these people are misfits—the girl in *The Hot l Baltimore*, Matt in *Talley's Folly*—but they are not necessarily outcasts. They project such a purity of spirit—idealism honed to perfection—that in comparison, conformists seem like aliens.

Wilson is sometimes labeled a traditionalist—and certainly he is more readily accessible to an audience than his contemporary, Sam Shepard—but one might say that he is as old fashioned as Chekhov. It is character, not action, that dominates his plays. Events may seem small, but they are consequential, and they can be filled with portent. . . .

In his nine full-length plays and some thirty one-acts, this major American playwright has created a unified body of work that speaks with eloquence about individualism and the importance of personal history: we are what we have been. His characters reach back to the past not for nostalgia but for anchors, for a lineage with those who have preceded them, for sustaining values. In his art, there is a quest for durability, for attachment. Personal relationships are his religion—if only people would make contact. Even when his characters are immersed in an urban environment, they retain an incorruptible pioneer spirit. In thinking about his American artistic forebears, one looks less to playwrights than to novelists such as Willa Cather, William Faulkner, and Eudora Welty. Wilson begins as a regionalist but becomes national. He is definably an American playwright, rooted in the farms and hills of his Ozark birthplace and also in the streets and cafés of his adopted city, New York. Though he might conceivably choose to write about a foreign culture, he has given no indication of leaving native soil. It seems to offer him constant replenishment. In his plays, he does go home again.

Mel Gussow. *Horizon*. May, 1980, p. 32

Lanford Wilson marries the playwriting strategies of a George S. Kaufman to the sensibilities of a Tennessee Williams, and the consequences are by turns hilarious and heartbreaking, which is to say intensely Wilsonian. Kaufman used to like nothing better than to fling together on a stage half a dozen disparate individuals, each of them possessing an attribute that could be emphasized with an increasing assurance of recognition, and therefore with increasing comic effect, throughout the evening; Williams, though he has a gift for ingenious plotting (think of the opening passages of *Sweet Bird of Youth*!), tends to lose interest in inventing actions, preoccupying himself instead with nuances of character. The latest of Wilson's plays to reach Broadway is *Fifth of July*, and in the course of it Wilson proves to be as busy a plotmaker as Kaufman and as sedulous a prober of the Southern psyche as Williams. His setting is a small town in Missouri, and his hero is Ken Talley, Jr., a young man who, having lost both legs in Vietnam, has come home to make a new life for himself as a teacher in one of the local schools. Ken owns and occupies the ramshackle old Talley homestead, in the company of a devoted male lover, a sister, and the sister's thirteen-year-old daughter. . . .

Because he started at the Caffe Cino and was part of off-off-Broadway's heroic era, because he wrote about homosexuals before it became commonplace to do so, and because he has steadfastly based himself at the Circle Rep off-Broadway, Mr. Wilson has won and kept the respect of people who would not give Lillian Hellman or William Inge the time of day as playwrights, but he is nevertheless a writer very much in their tradition. *A Tale Told*, the third play in Mr. Wilson's cycle about the Talley family of Lebanon, Missouri, has a great deal in common with *The Little Foxes*—even beyond a shared tendency toward melodramatic confrontations and climaxes.

Both plays generate a rich sense of individuals in a family in a community in the United States at a particular time in its history. Mr. Wilson has spoken of his concern with the economic context of his story; Miss Hellman—never the mere melodramatist she has been made out to be—put her economic concerns at the center of her play. And both writers are keenly aware of the connection between economics and morality. Mr. Wilson's Talleys exploit the poor people of their little Missouri town much as Miss Hellman's Hubbards "grind the bones" of their little Alabama town. In both plays a lonely middle-aged woman and a strongminded young one are aware of the family crassness and venality; in both plays the older woman is trapped, but the escape of the younger one provides hope for the future. . . .

Mr. Wilson is not a formal innovator or a deep thinker; his images of America, though evocative and cogent, are not startlingly original. He doesn't see to the heart of things, as O'Neill, Williams and Miller have sometimes done. But the people of his trilogy go on living when they are offstage. The Talleys have begun to take on the solidity of characters in a good old-fashioned novel. We have gone fulfilling journeys with them. We sense that there are more to come.

Julius Novick. *VV*. June 17–23, 1981, p. 77

In the background of Wilson's plays is an "Our Town" where sex drives are repressed, strangers are viewed with suspicion, and no one is allowed to ruffle surfaces. *The Rimers of Eldritch* (1966) dramatizes the evil in the town of Eldritch, with a suspense that is rare for Wilson. Not until a late scene is it clear that a frustrated spinster has shot the town derelict in the act of rescuing a crippled young woman from a sexual assault she provoked. On the false testimony of the crippled woman and her attacker, the murderess is acquitted. The respectable members of Eldritch town, the rimers of Eldritch, close ranks to defend their frozen surface—frozen, too, in a conventional theatre mould. . . .

With *The Fifth of July* (1978), Wilson embarked on what promises to be a series of plays about the Talley family of Lebanon, Missouri—respectable, intolerant, but sprinkled with Wilson's beloved deviants. The first Talley play opens not on the fifth but the fourth of July, 1977, a symbolic year after the United States Bicentennial. The family members are Aunt Sally, her nephew Ken, whose legs were shot off in Vietnam, his sister June, and her illegitimate daughter Shirley. Visiting the Talleys is not only Ken's lover Jed but also a childhood friend, John Landis, his rock-singer wife Gwen, and her composer. The frail plot hangs on Ken's ambivalence about selling the family estate, and Gwen Landis's intermittent desire to buy it. John Landis wants to "adopt" Shirley, whose father he may be. Indignantly repulsed by June Talley, he leaves, and fourteen-year-old Shirley realises: "I am the last of the Talleys. And the whole family has just come to nothing at all so far." But Wilson hints that this family in America's heartland may be pregnant with change; they will keep their land which Ken's lover will teach them to cultivate and which will be nourished by the symbolic ashes of Aunt Sally's Jewish husband Matt.

*Talley's Folly* (1979) backtracks to Matt on 4 July 1944. The play recounts rather than dramatises the courtship of Sally Talley by Matt Friedman. Like earlier Wilson characters, Matt functions both as narrator and protagonist. Aging misfits, thirty-year-old Missouri Wasp Sally strains against the family code, and forty-two-year-old Jewish Matt has no family or allegiances. Loners, they are attracted to one another, but Wilson delays their union for some hundred minutes of playing time. Talley's Folly puns on the Victorian boathouse setting and Sally's commitment to leave her family so as to share Matt's life. Wilson's forthcoming plays about the Talleys may move forward or backward in a tepid glow of traditional family drama comfortably ensconced—where else?—on Broadway.

Having begun Off-Off-Broadway, Lanford Wilson has steadily increased his characters' charm, making them acceptable in spite of their quirks. Both on and Off-Off-Broadway, he has been the consistent depicter of apolitical, uncommitted deviants. Unlike the stage people of his predecessor Tennessee Williams, Wilson's misfits rarely resort to violence, and they carry no mythic burden.

Ruby Cohn. *New American Dramatists: 1960–
1980* (Grove, 1982), pp. 23–26

Lanford Wilson's *Angels Fall* . . . seems to touch on an important subject, but that's only a mirage created by the hot shimmering desert climate in which the action unfolds. The setting is a mission in northwest New Mexico; there has been a potential nuclear accident in a nearby government uranium mine that provides the occasion for five travelers, stranded by a roadblock, to unburden themselves to each other and to the resident priest. The least of their problems seems to be their impending annihilation which, although it inspires jocular comments, functions mostly as a way of collecting unrelated people on the stage to do their hip contemporary numbers. Why should I be so annoyed by a mere dramatic device? Wilson's weakness for authorial manipulation, usually a harmless quality of his plays, gets downright intolerable when serious issues and genuine fears are used primarily for theatrical exploitation.

Anyway, the real purpose of the play is to introduce us to colorful characters plagued with psychological problems. . . .

There is a sense of artificiality and contrivance about the evening that is only underscored by its realistic pretensions. One waits in vain for just one unusual perception, just one unique moment, just one unexpected gesture; even a mistake. But the smooth humming of unruffled professionalism buzzes in our ears throughout the whole evening without a single hint of risk or danger. One hesitates to criticize competence in an art form so often characterized by carelessness and blunder, but if this well-organized and empty exercise represents the current aspirations of our off-Broadway companies then the theater is in a depressed state indeed.

Robert Brustein. NR. Year-End Issue, 1982, pp.<br>26–27

## WINTERS,  YVOR  (1900–1968)

Yvor Winters surrendered in a most extreme way to romantic ideas and subsequently tried to cure himself of the romantic malady. I suspect that, the testimony of his criticism notwithstanding, he did not succeed. In his late twenties, he was still writing poems premised on a romantic view of experience. He was able to *think* his way out of the romantic position and, with the help of a poetic discipline, was able to reform his sensibility. But the change came late. A man of twenty-seven is pretty much what he is going to be. He can study himself, discover his weaknesses and strengths so as to realize his potentialities, but he is not likely to change in any fundamental way. John Stuart Mill said that Wordsworth's poetry provided him with a "culture of the feelings." For Winters, the function of poetry is that of recultivating the feelings. In either case, it is the feelings that count. And a new—or postromantic—kind of poetry must have as its function leading the feelings away from the romantic abyss.

Winters was concerned with realized fullness of potential being, and he saw poetry as the most civilized and effective technique for realizing such being. But he also felt that there are limits on what we can know and judge: transcendence is a regress and leads to no wisdom. Winters was a theist, but he was not a Christian. He tells us that he arrived at his theistic position through studying poetry, that he did not begin with it but came to it as an inevitable conclusion—almost an unacceptable one. He felt, however, that man cannot make any inferences with reference to the existence or nature of immortality or as to the nature of the Divine plan, if any, for man.

Although Winters believed in a unified universe, he also held a Manichaean position with regard to the influence of the supernatural on human experience. He felt that we are beleaguered in some undefined way by evil. He could not determine whether this evil is merely a product of our minds or whether it is, in some sense, demonic. It is largely because the supernatural and the nonhuman otherness of nature seemed dangerous to Winters that he calls his own theoretical position a moral one, and it is the reason why he is distrustful of any mystical position. Although his preoccupation was with man's relationship to a supernature that he could not define, he was more concerned with protecting man from it than in merging with it.

> Grosvenor Powell. *Language as Being in the
> Poetry of Yvor Winters* (Louisiana State Univ.
> Pr., 1980), pp. 165–67

The most naïve critic feels urged to identify, analyze, and assess—even with Mr. Winters' help—the very special addition that he has made to contemporary poetry within this cryptic quantitative and qualitative self-judgment. His poetic practices and his theories coincided; his style and his techniques of verse were—for the most part—meticulously "moral" for both his early experimental and his later traditional poetry; above all, he took his responsibility for being this "moral" aesthetician with total seriousness. His unique contribution to twentieth century American poetry was his insistence on the artist's particular "morality." He expected it of all good poets; he demanded it of himself. It is the basis of his poetic and critical career—a philosophical *raison d'être*. For him, the word "moral" had a very special meaning in its artistic context, and it stemmed from his basic humanistic faith. He believed that within quite large limits man is the unique being with choice; therefore the true poet will feel himself obligated to make those "moral" choices which are aesthetically proper for the complete artistic synthesis of the poem at hand. He saw no reason why poetry in a directionless period must be formless. The good poet's faculties will govern his choices within his range in accordance with his beliefs, emotional controls, intelligence, and perceptions. He will control the various technical aspects of poetry by his "moral" judgment, and thus create order out of chaos. It was a stringent judgment that he made for himself as an intelligent and "moral" human artist. He applied it to his own poetry and to that of others whom he criticized. In one passage in *Maule's Curse*, he used the term "human" as a parenthetical expression for "moral." For him it was a total, complete position involving every faculty of the dedicated poet-teacher-critic. It provided him in all of these capacities with an intelligent way of thinking about poetry, and it contained important directives for its creation and criticism.

As such, his small, carefully selected body of poetry represents a certain tragic force in the dissection of this age. He had faced the "brink of darkness" in his personal contemporary chaos, had known the menace of unreason as an invader to be confronted and subdued. In his one short story, the sane narrator remembered with bitter precision every stage of his delusion as he had suffered it, and he had come back to record it with the cool voice of restored reason. So in Winters' life and his poetry he records and accounts for each quiet terror that he faced in the development of his art, his teaching, and his criticism. He strove for clarity and form against critical tides of unreason and unconsciousness. His poetic odyssey ends with the power of unreason recognized and conquered. His personal life and public career ended after he was quite capable of definition and of measuring what had happened to him. His later poetry and his last book of criticism make that quite clear with their self-revelations. He was confident that his Post-Symbolist school would vindicate him in the future. Perhaps it is the case that his erudite efforts as critic somewhat limited his public production as poet, and that his *Collected Poems* provides an overselective handbook for his students. But he would have it no other way. . . .

Yvor Winters cannot—indeed, need not—be "placed" in the history of poetry. Granted that he was an enigma in his era, he represents the totality of the classical tradition set down in modern times. He has remained above the storms of contemporary "schools" in his calm, if somewhat haughty tradition of dignified reason and resultant form. His iconoclastic critical views have often seemed prejudiced and at times even savage; his stance, patronizing and pedagogical. But his *poetry* remains clearly serene, refined, and reflective.

Elizabeth Isaacs. An Introduction to the Poetry of<br>
Yvor Winters (Swallow/Ohio Univ. Pr., 1981), pp.<br>
195–97, 202

Though Winters's version of the poet (after 1929) was always of a man embattled with reality, the metaphysical battles of the criticism of his thirties—with time, death and the "invasion of the impersonal"—were often replaced, as he became more concerned with ethical and social issues, by battles with the "dead living." Yet his achievement remains, when all is said and done, major. The best of his early verse has a freshness and limpidity, and a sensitivity to rhythm, unequaled save in the best work of William Carlos Williams. What he considered to be his major important poetry—that written after 1929—has been unjustly neglected, largely I suspect because of his reputation as a pugnaciously antimodernist critic, rather than for reasons intrinsic to the verse itself. To live with these poems is to be aware of a mind intensely sensitive to the reality of both the life of the intellect, and the nature of the physical world in which that intellect must live. The consciousness that informs the poetry is perpetually attuned to the claims of both spirit and world; it works toward balance, toward a just vision, toward a true and clear understanding of the nature of our life. The "massive calm" of these poems is intensely moving to one who has experienced the reality of their premises and who can sympathize with Winters's temperamental need to define the limits of our understanding with lapidary certainty. His best poems, "Apollo and Daphne," "The Slow Pacific Swell," "The Marriage," "On a View of Pasadena from the Hills," "John Sutter," "The California Oaks," "Sir Gawaine and the Green Knight," present us with sensory experience—a sense of the mind drenched in the physical reality of the world—and, simultaneously, an intellectual passion for understanding rarely equaled in the poetry of this century. . . .

In fact, Winters's concern with individual ethical responsibility, with his view of poetry as a process of moral evaluation whose chief end is the modification of the reader's sensibility so that he understands more clearly and fully the nature of human existence in the world, both point to a moral sensitivity hardly compatible with either the glorification of violence or the demand that the individual merge his being in that of a greater whole, be it state or race, endemic in fascism. Further, as we have seen from his own poetry, his ideals of human existence in the world were deeply imbued with notions of self-restraint, dignity and moral decorum. He viewed all suggestions of violation, spoliation, and trespass beyond natural and abiding limits with horror. The whole tenor of his writings indicates that the individual is responsible for his own spiritual state—his ideal is the rational man who understands and chooses, and he frequently seems impatient with determinist psychological models of human behavior which concentrate on the neurotic and the child, both categories in which the role of reason is diminished.

My chief concern in mentioning this aspect of Winters's work is not to refute the absurd charge of his potential fascism—a charge which his own actions and writings amply refute without outside help—but to draw attention to the fact that Winters's classicism and concern for reason and ethical probity were of a piece and prevented his being deluded, either in part or wholly (as so many of the major literary figures of this century have been deluded) by any of the versions of totalitarianism and moral and political nihilism peddled in his lifetime. This in itself should give significant pause to those readers who would dismiss his message and preoccupations as outmoded or trivial. His concern was with the centrally and perennially human, with the individual's apprehension of the nature of his life, here, in time and in the flesh. The focus of his vision was unwaveringly clear, undisturbed by notions, whether political or literary or both, of what Borges has called "energetic barbarism."

Dick Davis. Wisdom and Wilderness: The<br>Achievement of Yvor Winters (Univ. of Georgia<br>Pr., 1983), pp. 233–36

## WOLFE, THOMAS (1900–1938)

In many respects the most massive and impressive of the efforts to fashion an American epic was that of Thomas Wolfe. The vast, incomplete, and imperfect work on which he labored and which he persisted in calling simply "the book," was an effort at the "Great American Novel" that surpasses even Dos Passos' *U.S.A.* in scope, ambition, and intensity, although it is badly flawed in parts. At the time of his death in 1938, just before his thirty-eighth birthday, Wolfe had published two long novels, a collection of short stories and short novels, and an essay on literary method. He left behind an enormous mass of manuscript out of which his editor quarried two more novels and another collection of short pieces. All these works have a common subject and one almost universally recognized as Wolfe's own experience in his world presented under the transparent disguises of two protagonists, Eugene Gant and George Webber. Although this subject is treated in a variety of literary modes, forming a potpourri of dramatic scenes, narrative passages, lyrical descriptions, tone-poems, rhetorical incantations, and satirical social sketches, the works are all portions of one vast effort much like Whitman's attempt, as he expressed it, "to put a *Person*, a human being (myself, in the latter half of the Nineteenth Century, in America,) freely, fully, and truly on record."

To look at Wolfe's "book" as an attempt at an American epic helps us see what he is about and appreciate at least some of the causes for his successes and his failures. He felt a compulsive need to "sing America.". . .

In addition to this epic urge, the nature and content of his work was shaped by the quality of his personal experience, by the influence of John Livingston Lowes's theory of the imagination, and by the special way in which he wrote. Out of the interactions of these things with his powerful rhetoric and his dramatic talent came a body of writing which corresponds with remarkable accuracy to the special shapes and tensions of the American epic. . . .

However flawed as novels and imperfect as art his books may be, Thomas Wolfe's works constitute a major and remarkably successful effort to write his autobiography as that of a representative American and to embody in the record of his time and deeds on this earth a vision of the nature and the hope of his democratic land.

C. Hugh Holman. *The Loneliness at the Core: Studies in Thomas Wolfe* (Louisiana State Univ. Pr., 1975), pp. 161-62, 167

Thomas Wolfe was born *in*, yet was not *of* the South. More than any other major Southern writer, his reputation has gone into decline. In his lifetime critical opinion was divided over his achievement, though rarely over his genius. The criticisms of Wolfe—a woeful inconsistency, the lack of differentiation between authorial voice and protagonist's sensibility, the unwillingness to discriminate between the essential and the trivial, the failure to tell the reader very much about his protagonist, Eugene Gant–George Webber, and the shallow emotional and narrow intellectual reach of his fiction—all seem to me essentially just. Sympathetic observers would have it that Wolfe achieved a new maturity and stability near the end of his life . . . and Wolfe himself promoted this notion quite avidly. But like the legendary Southern Bourbons, with whom he otherwise shared so little, Wolfe never really learned or forgot anything. He was always starting over again. Even his moments of isolation were noisy; and he was never able to halt that inexorable march through his own experience or to control his desire not just to experience everything, but to devour it. . . .

It is perhaps this overpowering orality which marks Wolfe's essential narcissism, his swings between a desire for union and oneness and a deep suspicion of others, his inability to maintain stable ties, his lack of interest finally in the autonomy of the people and objects in the world that fascinated him, the shallowness of his sensibility. It was all for *him* and not for itself. One searches his fiction for the measured and calm discourse with friends or acquaintances from whom nothing is demanded. His fictional world fails to remain in our memory as does Faulkner's; rather what we remember is a central figure moving through a world which exists only insofar as it has to do with him. Unlike Faulkner's characters who are plagued by too much, Wolfe's never get enough. Recollection leads only to repetition. . . .

His tragedy was that he lived beyond any cultural tradition except that which he could piece together on his own. It was not a matter of believing or not believing in a religious faith or sharing certain ideas and ideals or manners. Wolfe was no different from many others there. The problem rather was that he had little sense of what had been lost and what might have once provided coherence. Like Jay Gatsby, Wolfe could finally only believe in the "green light," the world of infinite possibility. As a result he was continually re-creating his innocence. The protagonist of his later work could not have been "Eugene Gant," since the late fiction was less an elaboration than a repetition of the early novels. To be sure, emphasis was shifted and new episodes introduced, but nothing much developed. It was a replay. Had Wolfe actually gone back home earlier, he might have realized that he could not "go home again," could not retrieve it all in memory and relive it. This might have given him the necessary distance to let the present and past world be, and to let others come alive.

Richard H. King. *A Southern Renaissance*
(Oxford Univ. Pr., 1980), pp. 198–99, 202–4

## WRIGHT, JAMES (1927–1980)

Certainly the subject of death—except for *The Branch Will Not Break* (1963), Wright's most important volume—has been a constant one for Wright; in fact, one is correct in saying that of all American poets (Edgar Lee Masters excepted), past or present, there is no one obsessed with death to the degree evident in the poetry of Wright. . . .

"A Blessing" is Wright's finest poem, not only in the manner of the Emotive Imagination, but in the canon of his poems to date. This judgment is not an isolated one, for the poem, since its 1963 appearance, has won the admiration of critics of every stance, anthologizers, teachers, students, and other poets. It is a poem very simply posited until the concluding three lines when the metaphoric leap approximates the condition of absolute joy. "A Blessing," as its title implies, is one of the most positive of Wright's poems, demonstrating the long distance from darkness he is capable of moving. . . .

The speakers of a number of Wright's poems in *The Branch Will Not Break* seem to want to transcend the human into the purely natural, as indeed, James Dickey's speakers do, the difference being that Wright always recognizes that it is finally impossible to do this; Dickey merely does it. Wright acknowledges his limits as a human; Dickey refuses to recognize that distinctions between the human, natural, and other animal states exist. Theodore Roethke, under whom Wright studied at the University of Washington, has, like Dickey, found it easier than has Wright to achieve this transcendence. . . .

Apparently the James Wright of *Two Citizens* accepts into his poetry any strongly felt emotions, so long as they serve to illuminate his transformation. We believe Wright could have profited by exercising his editorial prerogative; many of these poems demonstrate emotion sentimentally and thus are ineffectual. For the personal poem to succeed as more than merely a recording of emotion, it needs to engage the reader's sensibilities. It is not enough just to tell, as Wright has elected to do in too many of these poems, what he feels and has experienced. One of the lasting values of the Emotive Imagination, when it is effectively used, is the ability to make the reader respond to the sensations and thoughts the poet is attempting to convey through images. . . .

Wright is not a poet whose subject interests can yet be called heterogeneous, yet the changed perceptions of self, the past, and America augur well for the prospect of Wright's challenging new concerns.

> George S. Lensing and Ronald Moran. *Four Poets*
> *and the Emotive Imagination* (Louisiana State
> Univ. Pr., 1976), pp. 88, 111–13, 129–30

I said earlier that James Wright was not death-haunted. Still, Death is the main character in our fictions. Wright was like most of us God-haunted and self-isolated. This risked the refusal of life and the debasement of creation which he had described. Wright allows us to see that if we choose not to undertake our destiny and choose not to front life, which the choice to employ habitual language and gesture means, we effectively ignore communal responsibility. This is the responsibility each bears to all. It is the responsibility of courage. Wright's courage consists in his willingness to communicate the truth of his feelings at the risk not only of public failure but of failure before his masters, Dickens and Horace. Wright continuously praised writers for telling the truth boldly and powerfully but shied away from such claims for himself. The irony, though it is not very ironic, is that the more he brought his life into his poems, his emotional and ethical and biographical and mythical life, the more truth he made us feel in ourselves, the more courage he gave us. The one story he tells proceeds from the conviction to which he was always faithful, that however tragic life may be there is the beauty of joy within it and we must seek tirelessly for it.

> Dave Smith. Introduction to *The Pure Clear*
> *Word: Essays on the Poetry of James Wright*, ed.
> Dave Smith (Univ. of Illinois Pr., 1982), p. xxvi

James Wright, who died in 1980 at the age of 52, was a poet of enormous verbal resources and skills engaged in a complex and deeply human quest to write—in his own terms—"the poetry of a grown man" in the style of

"the pure clear word." He was one of our great poets of the lost and desolate, feeling his way emotionally into the lives of the cheated, the drunk,
the lunatic. He was also a Horatian craftsman for whom craftsmanship
was never itself enough, continually struggling for clarity and against glibness in his work, and somehow capable of revealing what Robert Hass
calls "the aboriginal loneliness of being." But if Wright was an explorer of
our specifically human social darkness, he was also a poet of lyric ecstasy
and radiant natural light. Over the years his work increasingly evoked the
external natural world. Now in his last, posthumous collection [*This Journey*]—virtually completed before his death—Wright returns to his primary concerns, particularly exploring the terrible harshness and beauty
of nature, but with a luminous depth and intensity. . . .

The transforming moments in Wright's work are characteristically
either moments of human exchange or moments of the isolated self's ecstatic communion with nature.

Edward Hirsch. *NYT*. April 18, 1982, p. 15

## WRIGHT, RICHARD (1908–1960)

It is evident . . . that one of the outstanding characteristics of Wright's fiction is the ease with which the reader can identify with his anti-heroes.
Wright has been able to establish this relationship primarily through a
controlled point of view whereby the reader is privy only to the thoughts
and experiences of his narrator. As a consequence, although many secondary characters are developed incompletely, each major hero emerges as
a fully conceived personality: each man's motivations are explored and
his background sketched in. . . .

But having looked in detail at the heroes in Wright's major fiction, it
is also clear from such a study that a heroic model emerges—that,
although the books can unquestionably be read as separate entities, they
can also be read as parts of a whole. Therefore, instead of narrowing in on
a particular book's individual hero, we can, by reversing the process,
expand our perspective and discover a sort of mega-hero, a paradigm of
all Wright's heroes. This archetypal figure is best described as [the critic
Ihab] Hassan's rebel-victim, the innocent whose radical vision forces him
to reject his slavery. Marked from birth as an outcast, this anti-hero continues to be alienated from society until he dies; if he is stubborn he can
create his own identity by refusing first of all to accept the one society
brands him with, and then by actively seeking experiences that will help
form his character. In his stories, Wright chose the Negro not only to be
emblematic of all oppressed peoples but also to be the metaphor for mod-

ern man. Isolated, alienated, and haunted by a sense of dread, modern man and the black man have much in common. . . .

All his life, in and outside of his fiction, Richard Wright struggled to improve the black man's condition by protesting against the dreadful injustices he witnessed and experienced. For he felt that the community of man could only be strengthened by admitting all men as equals into it. Moreover, because he was attempting to present a realistic picture of the depths of despair and degeneracy so prevalent in black lives, he was forced to attribute certain undesirable characteristics to his heroes. Therefore, although he could not help but disapprove of their violent crimes, he recognized the need to have his heroes reveal their desperation through asocial means in order to shock society into an awareness of what it had done. His autobiography and last novel present the disgraceful initiation of black youth, his other fiction reveals the extremes to which the disinherited can go to claim their rights as men. Wright was too aware of how close he had come to being a Bigger Thomas to ever let society forget it. The final impression of his hero that one takes from reading his fiction, therefore, is that of a man beaten to the ground but determined to rise from his subjugation to join his fellow men in perhaps a godless world, but one where mutual respect gives life some dignity.

Katherine Fishburn. *Richard Wright's Hero: The Faces of a Rebel-Victim* (Scarecrow, 1977), pp. 192–95

Even if one discounts the positive, at times heroic, quality of characters ranging from Tyree Tucker in *The Long Dream* to Aunt Sue in "Black and Morning Star," the most cursory appreciation of *Lawd Today*, not to mention later humorous stories like "Man of All Works" and "Big Black Good Man," reveals that Wright's preference for realism did not prevent him from creating funny and congenial figures and situations. Nor indeed from incorporating into his writing many elements characteristic of black folk culture. Although in *Lawd Today* Wright does not turn to Southern pastoralism but to what rural folkways have become after a generation in Northern ghettos, he recreates in passing the whole context of verbal creativity which explodes in songs, jokes, the dozens, toasts and bombast. When contrasted with the uptight utterances of the whites, this makes for a warm image of black life even if it is also pathetic in the light of the facts of economic oppression. As he expressed it at the time, Wright's interest lay in exposing the system which imposed a "cheap" quality of life upon lower-class blacks, but his desire for authenticity made him emphasize those cultural rituals and interchanges that ensured cohesion and solidarity in the day-to-day struggle of ghetto existence.

Wright's style appears at times as visceral, inspired and naturalistic as it is supposed to be, yet he is by no means the innocent and interesting neo-Dreiserian primitive some critics have contrasted with Ralph Ellison's virtuosity and technical flexibility. The unequalled emotional power Wright attains in his best stories stems just as much from an extremely skilled *poetic* realism, in which intense suffering is achieved through symbolic connotation, as from the climaxing of comparatively short and self-contained dramatic episodes. This poetic, even prophetic, dimension should not be overlooked. In many ways, Wright's art was vision just as his writing was force, meaning and direction. His quest was largely and ultimately an attempt to establish a political and cultural context for the birth of the (black) man in world-wide terms. His vision rested both upon his confidence in the individual self and upon his belief in the power of writing.

Michel Fabre. In *Richard Wright Reader*, ed.
Ellen Wright and Michel Fabre (Harper & Row,
1978), pp. xxiii–xxiv

Richard Wright found that the meaning of life was in meaningless suffering. The reasons behind his suffering were racial, familial, educational, economic, and philosophical; no other highly regarded writer has ever had to break through so many restrictions. What Wright accomplished is a monument to the vitality and toughness of his ego; for, in conditions that would suppress or destroy other men, he made himself into one of the most important American writers of the century. While much of his work is undeniably weak and unsuccessful, three of his books, *Uncle Tom's Children*, *Native Son*, and *Black Boy*, will always be read. How he managed to write three such books, given his background, is hardly imaginable; because, though the Deep South should have destroyed him and was designed to do so, it created instead an author with a unique mastery of the subject of humanity's attempts, so often successful, to shatter its own.

Wright's great theme, which he expresses in varying levels of abstraction, is that the oppression of mankind causes the moral, psychological, and physical degradation of the tyrannical as well as that of the tyrannized. This thesis, admittedly not a pretty one, is resisted even today by white and nonwhite readers alike, because of its very correctness—its implications are too painful. How then was Wright, whose life was ever afflicted by the societal hatred of his race, his atheism, and his Marxist idealism, able to bore away to the philosophical essence of oppression and then present it with such urgent immediacy? It was his immense resilience, his will, his imaginative powers, and his ability to use literature as a bulwark against insupportable reality that permitted his insights and his artistry.

The species of oppression that Wright is unsurpassed at limning is, of course, racism, because it was that particular demon that so nearly annihilated him. His exorcism of the blight of racial prejudice was two-fold: he described the horrors that devolve upon blacks and whites alike from a warped description of his race; and he further militated against America's scorn of blackness by celebrating the beauty and strength of that spurned culture in his writings and, indeed, in his very existence—his success is eloquent testimony to the extreme toughness and endurance of the Afro-American tradition.

Wright is not only the virtual father of the post-World War II black novel, he is also the dominant precursor of the Black Renaissance of the 1960s: by rejecting the exotic Bohemianism of the Harlem Renaissance in favor of a literature gorged with authentic black experience, Wright gave to his recent literary descendants the legacy of a body of writing important not so much for technical innovation as for the presentation of themes now joyous, now gut-wrenching, but always genuinely, proudly black. And he bequeathed to all his readers a crudely powerful exhortation to look unflinchingly at his themes—and then beyond them, into the heart. Though he is perhaps not an author who appeals to the weak-spirited, it is undeniable that artistic greatness is the lot of this man who never wavered from his vision of the truth or compromised his integrity. Because of what he accomplished, to name a twentieth-century American writer of more urgency and moral power is difficult.

Robert Felgar. *Richard Wright* (Twayne, 1980),
pp. 174–75

## ZUKOFSKY, LOUIS (1904–1978)

His criticism is of the highest order; indeed, it may well be the subtlest and most profound criticism of poetry to have been written in this century.

I have been reading Zukofsky for 20 years and flatter myself that I have begun to understand how to read him; his work, as [William Carlos] Williams has said, cannot be thought of as "a simple song," rather, his song is more like Mozart's. There is no way of making him simple. As does all great art, his work resists cheapening, and it must be experienced in the full range of its intellect, craft, and music in order to be understood, even a little bit. The dedication is to art as a kind of supreme search for the clarity of the understanding. As with so much art that is not for sale, the drive toward clarity often makes for a difficult end result. We are left, as it were, with no help except from the poet's other poems, the tradition of the art of poetry, and our own intelligence. The handles are missing. . . .

Zukofsky, with his wife, Celia, a musician and composer, completed and published some few years ago a translation of Catullus that must stand as the most remarkable execution of that poet's verse into English that has ever been attempted. Not only do the translations succeed in carrying over the content of the poems and their music, they render into our tongue the actual sound of the Latin. It is a strange Catullus, granted; yet it also is, in a way that is hard to define, truer to him than all the modern attempts at translating his colloquial yet elegant lines—most of the contemporary tries at him have rendered his work into limp slang, a fearful butchery. . . .

Zukofsky is 72 now. It is clear to anyone who is seriously engaged with poetry that his work stands alongside that of Pound, Williams, and Stevens, as among the most authentic body of poetry to have been written by an American poet in this century. Those of his generation who may be considered his peers are [Charles] Olson and [George] Oppen. He has proffered us an enormous gift; somehow, we have refused to accept it, blundering after false gods and prophets. It is his own gift, pure and intense, his entire life, the rhythm and meaning of it, that is available to us in his books. To "place" him succinctly, then: He always was the real thing and always will be.

Gilbert Sorrentino. *VV*. June 7, 1976, pp. 77–78

I think that what makes good poetry is always the same, the use of words in such a way that "the thing is in the word." Empty words are empty, whether they are arranged according to modernist or traditional tenets. The defence of modernist technique is the vitality of the work it produces. In the work of Louis Zukofsky there is considerable vitality. The publication of Zukofsky's "A" is completed with these two new sections ["A" 22 & 23] (the musical conclusion, "A" 24, was published three years ago). The poem that began with "A Round of fiddles playing Bach. . ." reaches here a kind of musical speaking in which sound verges on a total displacement of meaning. But it is not that simple. A language reduced to sound would be no language at all. Zukofsky does something else; he uses words in ways that make their meaning appear tenuous, a momentary crystallizing of the flow of sound. The effect is one of discovery and surprise, of *initial speaking*. And that seems to be the burden of the opening, stanzaic section of "A" 22: "sweet treble hold lovely—initial." The middle section is an undivided passage (it runs for twenty-two small pages) constructed on a principle stated this way at the start: "word time a voice bridled/as order, what is eternal/is living. . . ." It is a history of a sort, but Zukofsky says, "History's best emptied of names'/impertinence. . . ." It is geological history, or a history embedded in geology. The asides that point to that understanding are only asides; the main thing is in the words moving in rhythm that represent historical growth-as-presence. Part of that process is the growth of language, and the rising of thought out of language, through methods of recording, like knots in the rope that the Incas used for communication: "new knots renewed ink anew." Midway through, Zukofsky begins to give his Book of Proverbs—lines and fragments from the Presocratic philosophers, the Hellenistic commentators, Epicurus, the Buddha, some of them charmingly translated: "Man featherless two-legs." Charm must be the frailest of poetic qualities. Much of the poetry here, and all through "A", depends on it: "little horse can you speak/won't know till it speaks." But it holds its place in the poem, as its signum. Interspersed with fragments from the philosophers are passages that mouth the original words, the way his *Catullus* mouths the Latin, and, in keeping with his principle, none of them is named in other than punning ways: "Pith or gore has 4/seasons. . . ." What his thinkers thought is not important to the poem; that is, it is not *thought* in the poem. What was once recorded is unearthed here, caught still in the substance of human speech. Language is to thought as the earth is to history: the "anachronous stone" is there in your hand. That is the nature of Zukofsky's historical materialism, which he sets in opposition to the historicism of the "scribes" who "conceive history as tho/sky, sun, men never were.". . .

The charm of his writing imparts a human warmth, a lived-in quality to the whole of "A", which, for all its length, remains a small poem, enclosed, a household. To place it alongside the *Cantos*, as some readers have done (speaking rather indiscriminately of "the long poem"), is to realize that the two are opposites, that *"A"* is the anti-epic *par excellence*, that the epic is the poem of unhoused mankind but that this poem has always been what it becomes here: a spiritual canticle of human habitation, "beginning ardent; to end blest."

Richard Pevear. HdR. Summer, 1976, pp. 315–16

Louis Zukofsky was a total poet: during a long life he practiced the craft of poetry with a single-minded passion. In his first maturity, he took the ideas of Pound about phanopoeia, melopoeia, and logopoeia as a point of departure for his own art. He also took Pound's ideas of composing in the musical phrase and the rhythms of great bass and such larger musical structures as the fugue. But Zukofsky extended Pound's range to include other musical patterns such as the sonata, the quartet, and the ballade and developed them in practice for over fifty years until he became not only the inventor but also the master of a new tradition.

He was and is a poet's poet. Although his work circulated in mimeographed sheets and little magazines, it was published in book form so rarely and in such limited editions that the public at large as well as academia could not hear of it through traditional channels. But practicing poets knew about it and found both Zukofsky and his work. Many of his followers and devotees, more widely known and anthologized than he, owe much of their music and polish to hard study of his premises and practices.

Thus as with the work of Pound and many innovators before him, we have with Zukofsky a tragic rehearsal of an old story: their inventions put them beyond the reach of most critics and readers who are trained to respond only to more traditional forms. With the mature work of Pound, almost all critics now find what they call "lyric passages" to praise, but the music and harmonies of much of *The Cantos* still remain much too subtle to reach the ears of many. Since Zukofsky went far beyond Pound in refining his lines until often only the harmonies are left, an even greater barrier exists which will take even more time for the poetry-reading public to cross. But since we have in Zukofsky the work of the greatest poet born in this century, cross it they will in time. Like Dante, Pushkin, Whitman and many another inventor/master before him, Zukofsky will inevitably have his day.

Carroll F. Terrell. In Louis Zukofsky: Man and<br>Poet, ed. Carroll F. Terrell (National Poetry<br>Foundation, 1979), p. 15

"Poem Beginning 'The'" carries itself with perfect assurance, as if this were the logical mode of expression for a young New York Jew. It is a triumph, and not just technically so. The author's passions come through strongly. His anger and frustration over displacement, poverty, injustice, intellectual corrosion, and so forth tally exactly with the broken, spotlit, warped contortions of the verse. His emotions *are* the lines of "The": intense, self-centered, ardent, and swift in their alternation.

The poem's obvious predecessor is "The Waste Land." In an attempt to surpass Eliot, Zukofsky pushes formal details to an excessive, but liberating, limit. Eliot numbered every tenth line, Zukofsky numbers all of them; Eliot appended witty notes, Zukofsky confounds us at the start with his daunting dedication; Eliot divided his poem into five parts; Zukofsky has six movements. Zukofsky stretches and pummels the modern idiom until he can call it his own. This seizure and recalibration of "The Waste Land" is consistent with "The"'s feverish engorgement. Zukofsky seems to want his poem to devour everything within range.

But "The" could also be described as an introspective's house of mirrors—potentially a deceptive, dangerous locale. Someone less intelligent and less ambitious might have spent years pursuing the same vein before discovering that investigations of the self require constant invention. But Zukofsky had found a voice something like his own, and he wasted no time in expanding his range. As soon as he had finished with "The," he started planning a more comprehensive work.

Barry Ahearn. *Zukofsky's "A": An Introduction*
(Univ. of California Pr., 1983), pp. 36–37

# BIBLIOGRAPHIES

The bibliographies list the major works of the authors included in this volume. The dates, including those for plays, are of first publication, unless otherwise noted. Pamphlets, one-act plays, and other minor publications are included only selectively. Stories and articles in periodicals are not included.

The bibliographies of authors included in the three-volume Fourth Edition and in Volume 4, Supplement to the Fourth Edition, have been updated through 1984.

The bibliographies of authors included in the three-volume Fourth Edition but not in Volume 4, Supplement, and who are reinstated in the present volume, have been updated from 1968 through 1984.

The bibliographies of the authors added in this volume (each of whose names is preceded by a bullet) are complete through 1984, with the exceptions noted above.

## GENRE ABBREVIATIONS

| | | | |
|---|---|---|---|
| a | autobiography | misc | miscellany |
| b | biography | n | novel or novella |
| c | criticism | p | poetry |
| d | drama | r | reminiscences |
| e | essay(s) | rd | radio drama |
| h | history | s | short stories |
| j | journalism | t | travel |
| m | memoir | tr | translation |

**EDWARD  ALBEE**
**1928–**

*Counting the Ways, and Listening*, 1977 (d); *The Lady from Dubuque*, 1980 (d); *Lolita*, 1981 (d); *The Man Who Had Three Arms*, 1983 (d)

**NELSON  ALGREN**
**1909–1981**

*The Devil's Stocking*, 1983 (n)

**A.  R.  AMMONS**
**1926–**

*The Snow Poems*, 1977; *Selected Poems, 1951–1977*, 1977; *Selected Longer Poems*, 1980; *A Coast of Trees*, 1981 (p); *Worldly Hopes*, 1982 (p)

● **MAYA  ANGELOU**
**1928–**

*I Know Why the Caged Bird Sings*, 1970 (a);

*Just Give Me a Cool Drink of Water 'fore I Diiie*, 1971 (p); *Gather Together in My Name*, 1974 (a); *Oh Pray My Wings Are Gonna Fit Me Well*, 1975 (p); *Singin' and Swingin' and Gettin' Merry Like Christmas*, 1976 (a); *And Still I Rise*, 1978 (p); *Poems*, 1981; *The Heart of a Woman*, 1981 (b); *Shaker, Why Don't You Sing?*, 1983 (p)

## JOHN ASHBERY
### 1927–

*The Double Dream of Spring*, 1970 (p); *Houseboat Days*, 1977 (p); *Three Plays*, 1978; *As We Know*, 1979 (p); *Shadow Train*, 1981 (p); *Apparitions*, 1981 (p); *Fairfield Porter*, 1982 (c); *A Wave*, 1984 (p)

## LOUIS AUCHINCLOSS
### 1917–

*Reading Henry James*, 1975 (c); *The Winthrop Covenant*, 1976 (n); *The Dark Lady*, 1977 (n); *The Country Cousin*, 1978 (n); *Life, Law, and Letters*, 1979 (e); *Persons of Consequence: Queen Victoria and Her Circle*, 1979 (b); *The House of the Prophet*, 1980 (n); *The Cat and the King*, 1981 (juvenile); *Three "Perfect" Novels—and What They Have in Common*, 1981 (c); *Unseen Versailles*, 1981 (t); *Narcissa, and Other Fables*, 1982 (s); *Watchfires*, 1982 (n); *Exit Lady Masham*, 1983 (n); *The Book Class*, 1984 (n)

## W. H. AUDEN
### 1907–1973

*Collected Poems*, 1976; *The English Auden*, 1978 (p, e, d); *Selected Poems*, rev. ed., 1979; (with Paul B. Taylor) *Norse Poems*, 1981 (tr)

## JAMES BALDWIN
### 1924–

*The Devil Finds Work*, 1976 (e); *Little Man, Little Man: A Story of Childhood*, 1976 (juvenile); *Horse Fair*, 1976 (juvenile); *Just Above My Head*, 1979 (n); *Evidence of Things Not Seen*, 1983 (j)

## AMIRI BARAKA (LE ROI JONES)
### 1934–

*Three Books*, 1975 (n, p, s); *The Creation of the New Ark*, 1975 (a); *Hard Facts*, 1978 (p); *The Motion of History, and Other Plays*, 1978; *What Was the Relationship of the Lone Ranger to the Means of Production?*, 1978 (d); *Selected Plays and Prose*, 1979 (d, e, s); *Selected Poetry*, 1979; *Reggae or Not!*, 1982 (p); *The Autobiography of LeRoi Jones*, 1984; *Daggers and Javelins: Essays 1974–1979*, 1984

## DJUNA BARNES
### 1892–1982

*Vagaries Malicieux*, 1974 (e); *Greenwich Village as It Is*, 1978 (t); *Smoke, and Other Early Stories*, 1982; *Creatures in an Alphabet*, 1982 (p)

## JOHN BARTH
### 1930–

*Letters*, 1979 (n); *Sabbatical: A Romance*, 1982 (n); *The Literature of Exhaustion*, 1982 (c); *The Friday Book; or Book-Titles Should Be Straightforward and Subtitles Avoided: Essays and Other Nonfiction*, 1984

## DONALD BARTHELME
### 1931–

*Amateurs*, 1976 (s); *Great Days*, 1979 (s); *Sixty Stories*, 1981; *Overnight to Many Distant Cities*, 1983 (s)

## ● ANN BEATTIE
### 1947–

*Chilly Scenes of Winter*, 1976 (n); *Distortions*, 1976 (s); *Secrets and Surprises*, 1978 (s); *Falling in Place*, 1980 (n); *The Burning House*, 1982 (s)

## SAUL BELLOW
### 1915–

*To Jerusalem and Back*, 1976 (t); *The Portable Saul Bellow*, 1977 (s, n); *The Dean's December*, 1982 (n); *Him with His Foot in His Mouth, and Other Stories*, 1984

**THOMAS BERGER**
**1924–**

*Who Is Teddy Villanova?*, 1977 (n); *Arthur Rex*, 1978 (n); *Neighbors*, 1980 (n); *Reinhart's Women*, 1981 (n); *The Feud*, 1983 (n)

**JOHN BERRYMAN**
**1914–1972**

*The Freedom of the Poet*, 1976 (s, e); *Henry's Fate, and Other Poems*, 1977

**ELIZABETH BISHOP**
**1911–1979**

*Geography III*, 1976 (p); *The Diary of "Helena Morely,"* 1977 (tr); *The Complete Poems, 1927–1979*, 1982; *The Collected Prose*, 1984 (m,s)

**R. P. BLACKMUR**
**1904–1965**

*Poems*, 1977; *Henry Adams*, 1980 (c); *Studies in Henry James*, 1983 (m,s)

**ROBERT BLY**
**1926–**

*Old Man Rubbing His Eyes*, 1975 (p); *Leaping Poetry*, 1975 (c); *The Morning Glory*, 1975 (p); *This Body Is Made of Camphor and Gopherwood*, 1977 (p); *This Tree Will Be Here for a Thousand Years*, 1979 (p); *Talking All Morning*, 1980 (e); *Truth Barriers* by Tomas Tranströmer, 1980 (tr); *Selected Poems of Rainer Maria Rilke*, 1981 (tr); *The Man in the Black Coat Turns*, 1981 (p); *The Eight Stages of Translation*, 1982 (c); *A Voyage to the Well*, 1984 (fairy tales, d)

**LOUISE BOGAN**
**1897–1970**

*Journey around My Room: The Autobiography of Louise Bogan*, ed. Ruth Limmer, 1980

**JANE BOWLES**
**1917–1973**

*Feminine Wiles*, 1976 (s, d, letters); *My Sis-*

*ter's Hand in Mine* [expanded edition of *Collected Works*], 1978 (n, d, s)

**PAUL BOWLES**
**1910–**

*Three Tales*, 1975 (s); *Things Gone & Things Still Here*, 1977 (s); *Collected Stories, 1939–1976*, 1979; *Next to Nothing: Collected Poems, 1926–1977*, 1981; *Points in Time*, 1982 (s)

**WILLIAM S. BURROUGHS**
**1914–**

*Mayfair Academy Series More or Less*, 1973 (s); *Book of Breeething*, 1975 (e); *Cobble Stone Gardens*, 1976 (p); (with Brion Gysin) *The Third Mind*, 1978 (c); *Blade Runner: A Movie*, 1979 (screenplay); *Ah Pook Is Here*, 1979 (n, e); *Roosevelt after Inauguration*, 1979 (e); *Port of Saints*, 1980 (n); *Cities of the Red Night*, 1981 (n); *The Place of Dead Roads*, 1984 (n)

**JAMES M. CAIN**
**1892–1977**

*The Institute*, 1976 (n); *Hard Cain*, 1980 (s); *The Baby in the Icebox*, 1981 (s)

**ERSKINE CALDWELL**
**1902–**

*Afternoons in Mid-America*, 1976 (e, t)

**TRUMAN CAPOTE**
**1924–1984**

*Music for Chameleons*, 1980 (s, e, a)

**RAYMOND CARVER**
**1938–**

*Winter Insomnia*, 1970 (p); *Put Yourself in My Shoes*, 1974 (p); *At Night the Salmon Move*, 1976 (p); *Will You Please Be Quiet, Please?*, 1976 (s); *Furious Seasons*, 1977 (s); *What We Talk About When We Talk About Love*, 1981 (s); *Cathedral*, 1983 (s); *Fires: Essays, Poems, Stories*, 1983

**WILLA CATHER**
**1876–1947**

No new publications

## RAYMOND CHANDLER
### 1888–1959

*Chandler before Marlowe: Raymond Chandler's Early Prose and Poetry, 1908–1912,* 1973; *Notebooks,* 1974; *The Blue Dahlia: A Screenplay,* 1976; *Raymond Chandler Speaking,* 1984 (letters, e); *Selected Letters,* 1984

## JOHN CHEEVER
### 1912–1982

*Falconer,* 1977 (n); *The Stories of John Cheever,* 1978; *Oh What a Paradise It Seems,* 1982 (n)

## ROBERT COOVER
### 1932–

*The Public Burning,* 1977 (n); *Hair o' the Chine,* 1979 (screenplay); *A Political Fable,* 1980 (n); *After Lazarus: A Filmscript,* 1980; *Spanking the Maid,* 1982 (n); *In Bed One Night, and Other Brief Encounters,* 1984 (s)

## MALCOLM COWLEY
### 1898–

*And I Worked at the Writer's Trade,* 1978 (m); *The View from Eighty,* 1980 (a); *The Dream of the Golden Mountains,* 1980 (h)

## JAMES GOULD COZZENS
### 1903–1978

*Just Representations: A James Gould Cozzens Reader,* 1978 (misc); *Selected Notebooks, 1960–1967,* 1983; *A Time of War: Air Force Diaries and Pentagon Memos, 1943–45,* 1984

## HART CRANE
### 1899–1932

*Hart Crane and Yvor Winters: Their Literary Correspondence,* 1978

## ROBERT CREELEY
### 1926–

*Thirty Things,* 1974 (p); *Away,* 1976 (p); *Selected Poems,* 1976; *Later,* 1978 (p); *Hello: A Journal, Feb. 29–May 3, 1976,* 1978; *Mabel: A Story, and Other Prose,* 1979 (s); *Was That a Real Poem?, and Other Essays,* 1979; *Charles Olson and Robert Creeley: Complete Correspondence,* 5 vols., 1980–82; *Mirrors,* 1983 (p); *Collected Poems, 1945–1975,* 1983; *Collected Prose,* 1984 (n, s, rd)

## E. E. CUMMINGS
### 1894–1962

*Complete Poems,* 1979; *Etcetera: The Unpublished Poems of E. E. Cummings,* 1983

## PETER DE VRIES
### 1910–

*I Hear America Swinging,* 1976 (n); *Madder Music,* 1977 (n); *Consenting Adults; or, The Duchess Will Be Furious,* 1980 (n); *Sauce for the Goose,* 1981 (n); *Slouching towards Kalamazoo,* 1983 (n)

## JAMES DICKEY
### 1923–

*The Zodiac,* 1976 (p); *Poems, 1957–1967,* 1978; *God's Images: A New Vision,* 1978 (p); *The Strength of Fields,* 1979 (p); *Falling: May Day Sermon,* 1981 (p); *A Starry Place between the Antlers,* 1981 (t); *Puella,* 1982 (p); *Night Hurdling: Poems, Essays, Conversations, Commencements and Afterwords,* 1982 (p, e, interviews); *The Central Motion: Poems, 1968–1979,* 1984

## JOAN DIDION
### 1934–

*A Book of Common Prayer,* 1977 (n); *The White Album,* 1979 (e, t); *Salvador,* 1983 (j); *Democracy,* 1984 (n); *Essays and Conversations,* 1984

## E. L. DOCTOROW
### 1931–

*Drinks before Dinner,* 1979 (d); *Loon Lake,* 1980 (n); *American Anthem,* 1982 (t); *Lives of the Poets: Six Stories and a Novella,* 1984

## HILDA DOOLITTLE (H. D.)
### 1886–1961

*A Tribute to Freud, Writing on the Wall, and Advent*, 1974 (e); *An End to Torment: A Memoir of Ezra Pound*, 1979 (m); *HER-mione*, 1981 (n); *Notes on Thought and Vision, and The Wise Sappho*, 1982 (e); *The Gift*, 1982 (n); *Collected Poems, 1912–1944*, 1983

## JOHN DOS PASSOS
### 1896–1970

No new publications

## THEODORE DREISER
### 1871–1945

*Letters to Louise*, 1959; *Notes on Life*, 1974 (e); *American Diaries, 1902–1926*, 1982; *An Amateur Laborer*, 1983 (n); *Sister Carrie*, definitive ed., 1983 (n)

## ROBERT DUNCAN
### 1919–

*Writing, Writing*, 1971 (p); *Dragons at the Gate*, 1976 (n); *Kiss*, 1978 (e); *Catalyst*, 1981 (p); *Collected Plays, Vol. 1*, 1981; *Selected Poems*, 1981; *Unpopular Poems*, 1981; *Ground Work: Before the War*, 1984 (p)

## RICHARD EBERHART
### 1904–

*Collected Poems, 1930–1976*, 1976; *Selected Prose*, 1978 (e, c); *Of Poetry and Poets*, 1979 (e, interviews); *Ways of Light*, 1980 (p); *Florida Poems*, 1981; *The Long Reach: New and Uncollected Poems, 1948–1983*, 1984

## T. S. ELIOT
### 1888–1965

No new publications

## ● STANLEY ELKIN
### 1930–

*Boswell*, 1964 (n); *Criers and Kibitzers, Kibitzers and Criers*, 1966 (s); *A Bad Man*, 1967 (n); *The Dick Gibson Show*, 1971 (n); *Searches and Seizures*, 1973 (n); *The Franchiser*, 1976 (n); *The Living End*, 1979 (n); *Stanley Elkin's Greatest Hits*, 1980 (s); *George Mills*, 1982 (n)

## RALPH ELLISON
### 1914–

No new publications

## JAMES T. FARRELL
### 1907–1979

*The Dunne Family*, 1976 (n); *Literary Essays, 1954–1974*, 1976; *Olive and Mary Anne*, 1977 (s); *The Death of Nora Ryan*, 1978 (n); *Eight Short, Short Stories and Sketches*, 1981; *On Irish Themes*, 1982 (e); *Sam Holman*, 1983 (n)

## WILLIAM FAULKNER
### 1897–1962

*The Marionettes: A Play in One Act*, 1975; *Selected Letters*, 1977; *Jealousy and Episode*, 1977 (s); *Uncollected Stories*, 1979; *Mayday*, 1980 (juvenile); *Helen: A Courtship, and Mississippi Poems*, 1981 (p); *Sanctuary: The Original Text*, 1981 (n); *Faulkner's MGM Screenplays*, 1983; *Father Abraham*, 1983 (s); *Vision in Spring*, 1984 (p); *The Sound and the Fury*, new and corrected ed., 1984 (n)

## F. SCOTT FITZGERALD
### 1896–1940

*The Cruise of the Rolling Junk*, 1976 (s); *Notebooks*, 1978; *F. Scott Fitzgerald's St. Paul Plays: 1911–1914*, 1978; *Screenplay for "Three Comrades" by Erich Maria Remarque*, 1978; *The Price Was High: The Last Uncollected Stories of F. Scott Fitzgerald*, 1979; *Correspondence*, 1980; *Poems*, 1981

## ROBERT FROST
### 1874–1963

Reginald L. Cook, ed., *Robert Frost: A Living Voice*, 1974 (contains twelve lectures by Frost in addition to text by Cook)

**WILLIAM GADDIS**
**1922–**

No new publications

● **ERNEST J. GAINES**
**1933–**

*Catherine Carmier*, 1964 (n); *Of Love and Dust*, 1967 (n); *Bloodline*, 1968 (s); *The Autobiography of Miss Jane Pittman*, 1971 (n); *A Long Day in November*, 1971 (juvenile); *In My Father's House*, 1978 (n); *A Gathering of Old Men*, 1983 (n)

**JOHN GARDNER**
**1933–1982**

*The Construction of the Wakefield Cycle*, 1974 (c); *The Construction of Christian Poetry in Old English*, 1975 (c); *Dragon, Dragon*, 1975 (juvenile); *October Light*, 1976 (n); *A Child's Bestiary*, 1977 (p); *In the Suicide Mountains*, 1977 (fairy tales); *The Life and Times of Chaucer*, 1977 (b); *The Poetry of Chaucer*, 1977 (c); *On Moral Fiction*, 1978 (c); *Freddy's Book*, 1980 (n); *The Art of Living*, 1981 (s); *Mickelsson's Ghosts*, 1982 (n); *On Becoming a Novelist*, 1983 (e); *The Art of Fiction: Notes on Craft for Young Writers*, 1984 (c); (with John R. Maier and Richard A. Henshaw) *Gilgamesh*, 1984 (tr)

**WILLIAM H. GASS**
**1924–**

*On Being Blue*, 1976 (c); *The World within the Word*, 1978 (c)

**ALLEN GINSBERG**
**1926–**

*The Gates of Wrath*, 1973 (p); *Gay Sunshine Interviews*, 1974 (interviews); *The Iron Horse*, 1974 (p); *First Blues*, 1975 (p); *Chicago Trial Testimony*, 1975 (court testimony); *Sad Dust Glories*, 1975 (p); *Madeira and Toasts for Basil Bunting's 75th Birthday*, 1977 (misc); *Mind Breaths*, 1977 (p); *As Ever: The Collected Correspondence of Allen Ginsberg and Neal Cassady*, 1977; *Journals: Early Fifties, Early Sixties*, 1977; *Poems All Over the Place, Mostly 'Seventies*, 1978 (p); *Composed on the Tongue*,

1980 (p); (with Peter Orlovsky) *Straight Hearts' Delight*, 1980 (p, letters); *Plutonian Ode: Poems 1977–1980*, 1981; *Mostly Sitting Haiku*, 1981 (p); *Man Loves*, 1982 (p); *Collected Poems, 1947–1980*, 1984

**ELLEN GLASGOW**
**1873–1945**

*Beyond Defeat: An Epilogue to an Era*, 1966 (n)

● **GAIL GODWIN**
**1937–**

*The Perfectionists*, 1970 (n); *Glass People*, 1972 (n); *The Odd Woman*, 1974 (n); *Dream Children*, 1976 (s); *Violet Clay*, 1978 (n); *A Mother and Two Daughters*, 1982 (n); *Mr. Bedford and the Muses*, 1983 (n)

**WILLIAM GOYEN**
**1918–1983**

*Arcadio*, 1983 (n)

● **JOHN GUARE**
**1938–**

*Something I'll Tell You Tuesday, and The Loveliest Afternoon of the Year*, 1967 (d); *Cop-out, Muzeeka, Home Fires: Three Plays*, 1970; *Kissing Sweet, and A Day for Surprises*, 1971 (d); (with Milos Forman) *Taking Off*, 1971 (screenplay); *The House of Blue Leaves*, 1972 (d); *Two Gentlemen of Verona*, 1973 (d, adaptation); *Marco Polo Sings a Solo*, 1977 (d); *Rich and Famous*, 1977 (d); *Landscape of the Body*, 1978 (d); *Bosoms and Neglect*, 1980 (d); *Three Exposures*, 1982 (d); *Gardenia*, 1982 (d); *Lydie Breeze*, 1982 (d)

**DASHIELL HAMMETT**
**1894–1961**

(with Alex Raymond) *Secret Agent X-9*, 1983 (collected comic strips)

**JOHN HAWKES**
**1925–**

*Travesty*, 1976 (n); *The Passion Artist*, 1979 (n); *Virginie*, 1982 (n); *Humors of Blood & Skin: A John Hawkes Reader*, 1984 (misc)

## ● ROBERT HAYDEN
### 1913–1980

*Heart-Shape in the Dust*, 1940 (p); *A Ballad of Remembrance*, 1962 (p); *Selected Poems*, 1966; *Words in the Mourning Time*, 1970 (p); *Angle of Ascent*, 1975 (p); *American Journal*, 1978 (p); *Collected Prose*, 1984 (misc)

## JOSEPH HELLER
### 1923–

*Clevinger's Trial*, 1974 (d); *Good as Gold*, 1979 (n); *God Knows*, 1984 (n)

## LILLIAN HELLMAN
### 1905–1984

*Scoundrel Time*, 1976 (m); *Three* [includes *An Unfinished Woman*, *Pentimento*, and *Scoundrel Time*], 1979 (m); *Maybe: A Story*, 1980 (m); (with Peter Feibleman) *Eating Together: Recollections and Recipes*, 1984

## ERNEST HEMINGWAY
### 1899–1961

*The Enduring Hemingway: An Anthology of a Lifetime in Literature*, 1974 (misc); *88 Poems*, 1979; *Selected Letters, 1917–1961*, 1981; *Ernest Hemingway on Writing*, 1984 (misc)

## CHESTER HIMES
### 1909–1984

*My Life of Absurdity*, 1976 (a)

## ● JOHN HOLLANDER
### 1929–

*A Crackling of Thorns*, 1958 (p); *The Untuning of the Sky: Ideas of Music in English Poetry, 1500–1700*, 1961 (c); *Movie-Going*, 1962 (p); *Various Owls*, 1963 (juvenile); *Visions from the Ramble*, 1965 (p); *The Quest of the Gole*, 1966 (juvenile); (with Anthony Hecht) *Jiggery-Pokery*, 1967 (p); *Types of Shape*, 1968 (p); *Images of Voice*, 1969 (c); *The Night Mirror*, 1971 (p); *Town and Country Matters*, 1972 (p); *An Entertainment for Elizabeth*, 1972 (d); *The Head of the Bed*, 1973 (p); *Tales Told of the Father*, 1975 (p); *Vision and Resonance*, 1975 (c); *Reflections on Espionage*, 1976 (p); *Spectral Emanations*, 1978 (p); *The Figure of Echo*, 1981 (c); *Rhyme's Reason*, 1981 (c); *Powers of Thirteen*, 1983 (p)

## RICHARD HOWARD
### 1929–

*Fellow Feelings*, 1976 (p); *Misgivings*, 1979 (p); *Alone with America*, enlarged ed., 1980 (c); *Baudelaire's "Les Fleurs du Mal,"* 1982 (tr); *Lining Up*, 1984 (p)

## LANGSTON HUGHES
### 1902–1967

*A Langston Hughes Reader*, 1981 (misc); *Jazz* (rev. ed.), 1982 (juvenile)

## ● ZORA NEALE HURSTON
### 1901–1960

*Jonah's Gourd Vine*, 1934 (n); *Mules and Men*, 1935 (s); *Their Eyes Were Watching God*, 1937 (n); *Tell My Horse*, 1938 (e); *Moses: Man of the Mountain*, 1939 (n); *Dust Tracks on a Road*, 1942 (a); *Seraph on the Suwanee*, 1948 (n); *I Love Myself When I Am Laughing . . . & Then Again When I Am Looking Mean & Impressive: A Zora Neale Hurston Reader*, 1979 (misc)

## ● DAVID IGNATOW
### 1914–

*Poems*, 1948; *The Gentle Weight Lifter*, 1955 (p); *Say Pardon*, 1961 (p); *Figures of the Human*, 1964 (p); *Earth Hard*, 1968 (p); *Rescue the Dead*, 1968 (p); *Poems, 1934–1969*, 1970; *Notebooks*, 1973; *Selected Poems*, 1975; *Facing the Tree*, 1975 (p); *The Animal in the Bush*, 1977 (p); *Tread the Dark*, 1978 (p); *Open between Us*, 1980 (c); *Whisper to the Earth*, 1981 (p); *Leaving the Door Open*, 1984 (p)

## ● JOHN IRVING
### 1942–

*Setting Free the Bears*, 1968 (n); *The Water-Method Man*, 1972 (n); *The 158-Pound Marriage*, 1974 (n); *The World According to Garp*, 1978 (n); *The Hotel New Hampshire*, 1981 (n)

## RANDALL JARRELL
### 1914–1965

*Fly By Night*, 1976 (juvenile); *Kipling, Auden & Co.: Essays and Reviews, 1935–1964*, 1980

## ROBINSON JEFFERS
### 1887–1962

*The Beginning and the End*, 1963 (p); *Not Man Apart*, 1965 (t); *The Alpine Christ*, 1974 (p); *In This Wild Water: The Suppressed Poems of Robinson Jeffers*, 1976; *The Double Axe, and Other Poems, Including Eleven Suppressed Poems*, 1977; *"What Odd Expedients,"* 1981 (p)

## ● ERICA JONG
### 1942–

*Fruits and Vegetables*, 1971 (p); *Half-Lives*, 1973 (p); *Fear of Flying*, 1973 (n); *Loveroot*, 1975 (p); *Here Comes*, 1975 (p); *The Poetry of Erica Jong*, 1976; *How to Save Your Own Life*, 1977 (n); *At the Edge of the Body*, 1979 (p); *Fanny*, 1980 (n); *Witches*, 1981 (e); *Ordinary Miracles*, 1983 (p); *Megan's Book of Divorce*, 1984 (juvenile); *Parachutes and Kisses*, 1984 (n)

## JACK KEROUAC
### 1922–1969

*Scattered Poems*, 1971; *Pic*, 1971 (n); *Heaven*, 1977 (p)

## GALWAY KINNELL
### 1927–

*Walking Down the Stairs*, 1978 (interviews); *Mortal Acts, Mortal Words*, 1980 (p); *Selected Poems*, 1982; *How the Alligator Missed Breakfast*, 1982 (juvenile)

## ● ARTHUR KOPIT
### 1937–

*Oh Dad, Poor Dad, Mama's Hung You in the Closet and I'm Feelin' So Sad*, 1960 (d); *The Day the Whores Came Out to Play Tennis, and Other Plays*, 1965; *Chamber Music, and Other Plays*, 1969; *Indians*, 1969 (d); *Wings*, 1978 (d); *Good Help Is Hard to Find*, 1982 (d); *Nine: The Musical*, 1983 (d); *End of the World*, 1984 (d)

## JERZY KOSINSKI
### 1933–

*Blind Date*, 1977 (n); *Passion Play*, 1979 (n); *Pinball*, 1982 (n)

## STANLEY KUNITZ
### 1905–

*Poems, 1928–1978*, 1979

## ● URSULA K. LE GUIN
### 1929–

*Rocannon's World*, 1966 (n); *Planet of Exile*, 1966 (n); *City of Illusions*, 1967 (n); *A Wizard of Earthsea*, 1968 (n); *The Left Hand of Darkness*, 1969 (n); *The Tombs of Atuan*, 1971 (n); *The Lathe of Heaven*, 1971 (n); *The Farthest Shore*, 1972 (n); *From Elfland to Poughkeepsie*, 1973 (e); *The Dispossessed: An Ambiguous Utopia*, 1974 (n); *Dreams Must Explain Themselves*, 1975 (e); *The Wind's Twelve Quarters*, 1975 (s); *Wild Angels*, 1975 (p); *The Word for World Is Forest*, 1976 (n); *Very Far Away from Anywhere Else* (British ed. titled *A Very Long Way from Anywhere Else*), 1976 (juvenile); *The Water Is Wide*, 1976 (s); *Orsinian Tales*, 1976 (s); *The Language of the Night: Essays on Fantasy and Science Fiction*, 1979; *Leese Webster*, 1979 (n); *Malafrena*, 1979 (n); *The Beginning Place*, 1980 (n); *Hard Words, and Other Poems* 1981; *The Compass Rose*, 1982 (s); *The Adventure of Cobbler's Rune*, 1982 (n); *The Eye of the Heron*, 1983 (n)

## DENISE LEVERTOV
### 1923–

*Life in the Forest*, 1978 (p); *Collected Earlier Poems, 1940–1960*, 1979; *Light Up the Cave*, 1981 (p); *Pig Dreams*, 1981 (p); *A Wanderer's Daysong*, 1981 (p); *Candles in Babylon*, 1982 (p); *Poems, 1960–1967*, 1983; *Oblique Prayers: New Poems with 14 Translations from Jean Joubert*, 1984 (p)

## SINCLAIR LEWIS
### 1885–1951

No new publications

**ROBERT   LOWELL**
**1917–1977**

*Selected Poems*, 1976; *Day by Day*, 1977 (p); *The Oresteia*, 1978 (tr)

**ARCHIBALD   MACLEISH**
**1892–1982**

*New and Collected Poems, 1917–1976*, 1976; *Riders on the Earth*, 1978 (e); *Six Plays*, 1980; *Letters, 1907–1982*, 1983

**NORMAN   MAILER**
**1923–**

*Some Honorable Men*, 1976 (j); (compiler) *Genius and Lust: A Journey through the Major Writings of Henry Miller*, 1976; *A Transit to Parnassus: A Facsimile of the Original Typescript*, 1978 (n); *The Executioner's Song*, 1979 (j); *Of Women and Their Elegance*, 1980 (b, m); *Pieces and Pontifications*, 1982 (e); *The Essential Mailer*, 1982 (misc); *Ancient Evenings*, 1983 (n); *Tough Guys Don't Dance*, 1984 (n)

**BERNARD   MALAMUD**
**1914–**

*Dubin's Lives*, 1979 (n); *God's Grace*, 1982 (n); *The Stories of Bernard Malamud*, 1983

● **DAVID   MAMET**
**1947–**

*Lakeboat*, prod. 1970, pub. 1981 (d); *Sexual Perversity in Chicago, and Duck Variations*, prod. 1974 and 1972 respectively, pub. 1978 (d); *American Buffalo*, prod. 1975, pub. 1978 (d); *The Water Engine: An American Fable, and Mr. Happiness*, prod. 1977 and 1978 respectively, pub. 1978; *The Revenge of the Space Pandas; or Binky Rudich and the Two-Speed Clock*, prod. 1977, pub. 1978 (d); *A Life in the Theatre*, prod. 1977, pub. 1978 (d); *The Woods*, prod. 1977, pub. 1979 (d); *Reunion, and Dark Pony*, prod. 1976 and 1977 respectively, pub. 1979 (d); *The Poet and the Rent: A Play for Kids from Seven to 8:15*, 1981 (d); *Short Plays and Monologues*, 1981; *Squirrels*, 1982 (d); *The Frog Prince*, 1983 (d); *Edmond*, prod. 1982, pub. 1983 (d); *Glengarry Glen Ross*, 1984 (d)

**MARY   MCCARTHY**
**1912–**

*Cannibals and Missionaries*, 1979 (n); *Ideas and the Novel*, 1980 (c); *Hounds of Summer*, 1981 (s)

**CARSON   MCCULLERS**
**1917–1967**

No new publications

● **LARRY   MCMURTRY**
**1936–**

*Horseman, Pass By*, 1961, later reissued as *Hud* (n); *Leaving Cheyenne*, 1963 (n); (as Ophelia Ray) *Daughter of the Tejas*, 1965 (juvenile); *The Last Picture Show*, 1966 (n); *In a Narrow Grave*, 1968 (e); *Moving On*, 1970 (n); *All My Friends Are Going to Be Strangers*, 1972 (n); *It's Always We Rambled: An Essay on Rodeo*, 1974; *Terms of Endearment*, 1975 (n); *Somebody's Darling*, 1978 (n); *Cadillac Jack*, 1982 (n); *Desert Rose*, 1983 (n)

**H.   L.   MENCKEN**
**1880–1956**

*The Young Mencken: The Uncollected Writings*, 1973 (misc); *A Choice of Days*, 1981 (a); *The American Scene: A Reader*, 1982 (misc)

**WILLIAM   MEREDITH**
**1919–**

*The Cheer*, 1980 (p)

**JAMES   MERRILL**
**1926–**

*Divine Comedies*, 1976 (p); *Mirabell: Books of Number*, 1978 (p); *Scripts for the Pageant*, 1980 (p); *From the First Nine: Poems, 1946–1976*, 1982; *The Changing Light at Sandover*, 1982 (p)

**W.   S.   MERWIN**
**1927–**

*Vertical Poems*, by Roberto Juarroz, 1976 (tr); *Houses and Travelers: A Book of Prose*, 1977 (s); *The Compass Flower*, 1977 (p); (with Jeffrey Moussaieff Masson) *Clas-*

*sical Sanskrit Love Poetry*, 1977 (tr); (with George E. Dimock, Jr.) *Euripides' Iphigenia at Aulis*, 1978 (tr); *Selected Translations, 1968–1978*, 1979; *Unframed Originals: Recollections*, 1982 (m); *Opening the Hand*, 1983 (p)

### ARTHUR  MILLER
### 1915–

*The Portable Arthur Miller*, 1977 (misc); (with Inge Morath) *In the Country*, 1977 (t); *Theatre Essays*, 1978; (with Inge Morath) *Chinese Encounters*, 1979 (t); *The American Clock*, 1980 (d); *Collected Plays*, 1981; *Salesman in Beijing*, 1984

### HENRY  MILLER
### 1891–1980

*Genius and Lust: A Journey through the Major Writings of Henry Miller* [compiled by Norman Mailer], 1976 (misc); *Gliding into the Everglades*, 1977 (e); *Sextet*, 1977 (e); *Some Friends*, 1978 (r); *My Bike and Other Friends*, 1978 (r); *An Open Letter to Stroker!*, 1978 (e); *Joey: A Loving Portrait of Alfred Perles, together with Some Bizarre Episodes Relating to the Opposite Sex*, 1979 (b); *Murder the Murderer*, 1979 (e); *Notes on "Aaron's Rod," and Other Notes on Lawrence*, 1980 (c); *The World of Lawrence: A Passionate Appreciation*, 1980 (c); *Opus Pistorum* [authorship denied by Miller], 1983 (n); *From Your Capricorn Friend: Henry Miller and the "Stroker," 1978–1980*, 1984 (letters, c)

### ● N.  SCOTT  MOMADAY
### 1934–

*House Made of Dawn*, 1968 (n); *The Way to Rainy Mountain*, 1969 (legends, h); *Colorado*, 1973 (t); *The Gourd Dancer*, 1976 (p); *The Names*, 1976 (m)

### MARIANNE MOORE
### 1887–1972

*The Complete Poems*, rev. ed., 1981

### WRIGHT  MORRIS
### 1910–

*About Fiction*, 1975 (e); *Real Losses, Imaginary Gains*, 1976 (s); *The Fork River Space Project*, 1977 (n); *Earthly Delights, Unearthly Adornments: American Writers as Image Makers*, 1978 (e); *Plains Song: For Female Voices*, 1980 (n); *Will's Boy: A Memoir*, 1981 (m); *Photographs & Words*, 1982 (photos, e, t); *Picture America*, 1982 (photos, t); *Solo*, 1983 (m, t)

### ● TONI  MORRISON
### 1931–

*The Bluest Eye*, 1979 (n); *Sula*, 1973 (n); *Song of Solomon*, 1977 (n); *Tar Baby*, 1981 (n)

### VLADIMIR  NABOKOV
### 1899–1977

*Details of a Sunset*, 1976 (s); *The Portable Nabokov*, 1978 (misc); *The Nabokov–Wilson Letters*, 1979; *Lectures on Literature*, 1980; *Lectures on Russian Literature*, 1981

### HOWARD  NEMEROV
### 1920–

*Collected Poems*, 1977; *Figures of Thought*, 1978 (e); *Sentences*, 1980 (p); *Inside the Onion*, 1984 (p)

### ANAÏS  NIN
### 1903–1977

*Diary*, Vol. 5, 1974; *A Woman Speaks: The Lectures, Seminars, and Interviews of Anaïs Nin*, 1975; *In Favor of the Sensitive Man*, 1976 (e); *Diary*, Vol. 6, 1976; *Delta of Venus*, 1977 (s); *Waste of Timelessness, and Other Early Stories*, 1977; *Linotte: The Early Diary of Anaïs Nin, Vol. 1, 1914–1920*, 1978; *Little Birds*, 1980 (s); *Diary*, Vol. 7, 1980; *The Early Diary of Anaïs Nin, Vol. 2, 1920–1923*, 1982; *The Early Diary of Anaïs Nin, Vol. 3, 1923–1927*, 1983

### JOYCE  CAROL  OATES
### 1938–

*Crossing the Border*, 1976 (s); *Childwold*,

1976 (n); *Night-Side*, 1977 (s); *The Triumph of the Spider Monkey*, 1977 (n); *Son of the Morning*, 1978 (n); *Women Whose Lives Are Food, Men Whose Lives Are Money*, 1978 (p); *All the Good People I've Left Behind*, 1978 (s); *Unholy Loves*, 1979 (n); *Cybele*, 1979 (n); *Three Plays*, 1980; *Bellefleur*, 1980 (n); *Contraries*, 1981 (e); *A Sentimental Education*, 1981 (s); *Angel of Light*, 1981 (n); *Invisible Woman: New and Selected Poems 1970–1982*, 1982; *A Bloodsmoor Romance*, 1982 (n); *Mysteries of Winterthurn*, 1984 (n); *Last Days*, 1984 (s)

## FLANNERY O'CONNOR
### 1925–1964

*The Habit of Being*, 1979 (letters)

## CLIFFORD ODETS
### 1906–1963

No new publications

## FRANK O'HARA
### 1926–1966

*Early Writing, 1946–1951*, 1975 (p, e); *Poems Retrieved*, 1977 (p); *Selected Plays*, 1978

## JOHN O'HARA
### 1905–1970

*The Good Samaritan*, 1974 (s); *"An Artist Is His Own Fault": John O'Hara on Writers and Writing*, 1977 (e); *Selected Letters*, 1978

## ● TILLIE OLSEN
### 1913–

*Tell Me a Riddle*, 1961 (s); *Yonnondio: From the Thirties*, 1974 (n); *Silences*, 1978 (e, c)

## CHARLES OLSON
### 1910–1970

*Olson-Den Boer: A Letter*, 1977; *The Fiery Hunt, and Other Plays*, 1978; *Muthologos: Collected Lectures and Interviews*, 2 vols., 1979; *Charles Olson and Robert Creeley: Complete Correspondence*, 5 vols., 1980–82

## EUGENE O'NEILL
### 1888–1953

*Ten "Lost" Plays*, 1964; *Children of the Sea, and Three Other Unpublished Plays*, 1972; *Poems, 1912–1944*, 1980; *Eugene O'Neill at Work*, 1981 (manuscripts); *"The Theatre We Worked For": The Letters of Eugene O'Neill to Kenneth Macgowan*, 1982; *Chris Christophersen*, 1982 (d)

## CYNTHIA OZICK
### 1928–

*Levitation: Five Fictions*, 1982 (s); *The Cannibal Galaxy*, 1983 (n); *Art and Ardor*, 1983 (e)

## WALKER PERCY
### 1916–

*Lancelot*, 1977 (n); *The Second Coming*, 1980 (n); *Lost in the Cosmos*, 1983 (e)

## ● MARGE PIERCY
### 1936–

*Breaking Camp*, 1968 (p); *Going Down Fast*, 1969 (n); *Hard Loving*, 1969 (p); *Dance the Eagle to Sleep*, 1970 (n); *4-Telling*, 1971 (p); *To Be of Use*, 1973 (p); *Small Changes*, 1973 (n); *Living in the Open*, 1976 (p); *Woman on the Edge of Time*, 1976 (n); *The Twelve-Spoked Wheel Flashing*, 1978 (p); *The High Cost of Living*, 1978 (n); *Vida*, 1979 (n); (with Ira Wood) *The Last White Class: A Play about Neighborhood Terror*, 1980; *The Moon Is Always Female*, 1980 (p); *Circles on the Water*, 1982 (p); *Braided Lives*, 1982 (n); *Parti-colored Blocks for a Quill*, 1982 (interviews); *Stone, Paper, Knife*, 1983 (p); *Fly Away Home*, 1984 (n)

## SYLVIA PLATH
### 1932–1963

*Johnny Panic and the Bible of Dreams*, 1977 (misc); *Collected Poems*, 1981; *Journals*, 1982

## KATHERINE ANNE PORTER
### 1894–1980

*The Never-Ending Wrong*, 1977 (m)

## EZRA POUND
### 1885–1972

*Letters*, 1974; *Collected Early Poems*, 1976; *Ezra Pound and Music: The Complete Criticism*, 1977; *"Ezra Pound Speaking": Radio Speeches of World War II*, 1978; *Letters to Ibbotson*, 1979; *Ezra Pound and the Visual Arts*, 1980 (c, e); *Pound/Ford: The Story of a Literary Friendship*, 1983 (letters); *Ezra Pound and Dorothy Shakespear: Their Letters, 1909–1914*, 1984

## ● REYNOLDS PRICE
### 1933–

*A Long and Happy Life*, 1962 (n); *The Names and Faces of Heroes*, 1963 (s); *A Generous Man*, 1966 (n); *Love and Work*, 1968 (n); *Permanent Errors*, 1970 (s); *Things Themselves: Essays and Scenes*, 1972 (e, d); *The Surface of the Earth*, 1975 (n); (with William Ray) *Conversations*, 1976 (interviews); *Early Dark*, 1977 (d); *A Palpable God: Thirty Stories Translated from the Bible, with an Essay on the Origins and Life of Narrative*, 1978; *The Source of Light*, 1981 (n); *Vital Provisions*, 1982 (p); *Mustian: Two Novels and a Story* [includes *A Generous Man* and *A Long and Happy Life*], 1983; *Private Contentment*, 1984 (d)

## JAMES PURDY
### 1923–

*A Day after the Fair: A Collection of Plays and Short Stories*, 1977; *Narrow Rooms*, 1978 (n); *Two Plays*, 1979; *Mourners Below*, 1981 (n); *On Glory's Course*, 1984 (n)

## THOMAS PYNCHON
### 1937–

*Slow Learner: Early Stories*, 1984

## ● DAVID RABE
### 1940–

*Nor the Bones of Birds*, prod. 1970; rev. as *The Orphan*, prod. 1973, pub. 1975 (d); *The Basic Training of Pavlo Hummel*, prod. 1971, pub. 1973 (d); *Sticks and Bones*, prod. 1971, pub. 1973 (d); *In the Boom Boom Room*, prod. 1973, pub. 1975 (d); *Streamers*, prod. 1976, pub. 1977 (d); *Hurlyburly*, 1984 (d)

## JOHN CROWE RANSOM
### 1888–1974

*Selected Essays*, 1984

## ISHMAEL REED
### 1938–

*Flight to Canada*, 1974 (n); *A Secretary to the Spirits*, 1978 (p); *Shrovetide in Old New Orleans*, 1978 (e); *The Terrible Twos*, 1982 (n); *God Made Alaska for the Indians*, 1982 (e)

## KENNETH REXROTH
### 1905–1982

*Sky, Sea, Birds, Trees, Each, House, Beasts, Flowers*, 1971 (p); *The Silver Swan*, 1976 (p); (with Ikuto Atsumi) *The Burning Heart: Women Poets of Japan*, 1977 (tr); *The Love Poems of Marachiko*, 1978 (tr); *The Morning Star*, 1979 (p); *Li Ch'ing-chao: Complete Poems*, 1979 (tr); *Selected Poems*, 1984

## ADRIENNE RICH
### 1929–

*Of Woman Born: Motherhood as Experience and Institution*, 1973 (e); *Twenty-One Love Poems*, 1976; *The Dream of a Common Language*, 1978 (p); *On Lies, Secrets, and Silence: Selected Prose, 1966–1978*, 1979 (e, c); *A Wild Patience Has Taken Me This Far*, 1981 (p); *The Fact of a Doorframe*, 1984 (p)

## THEODORE ROETHKE
### 1908–1963

No new publications

## ● JUDITH ROSSNER
### 1935–

*To the Precipice*, 1966 (n); *Nine Months in the Life of an Old Maid*, 1969 (n); *Any Minute I Can Split*, 1972 (n); *Looking for Mr. Goodbar*, 1975 (n); *Attachments*, 1977 (n); *Emmeline*, 1980 (n); *August*, 1983 (n)

## PHILIP ROTH
### 1933–

*The Professor of Desire*, 1977 (n); *The Ghost Writer*, 1979 (n); *A Philip Roth Reader*, 1980 (misc); *Zuckerman Unbound*, 1981 (n); *The Anatomy Lesson*, 1983 (n)

## MURIEL RUKEYSER
### 1913–1980

*The Gates*, 1976 (p); *Collected Poems*, 1979; *Outer Banks*, 1980 (p)

## CARL SANDBURG
### 1878–1967

*Ever the Winds of Chance*, 1983 (a)

## MAY SARTON
### 1912–

*The Small Room*, 1976 (n); *A Walk through the Woods*, 1976 (p); *A World of Light*, 1976 (a); *The House by the Sea*, 1977 (a); *A Reckoning*, 1978 (n); *Selected Poems*, 1978; *Writings on Writing*, 1980 (e); *Recovering: A Journal*, 1980 (a); *Halfway to Silence*, 1980 (p); *Anger*, 1982 (n); *At Seventy: A Journal*, 1984 (a)

## DELMORE SCHWARTZ
### 1913–1966

*What Is To Be Given: Selected Poems*, 1976; *I Am Cherry Alive, the Little Girl Sang*, 1979 (juvenile); *Last and Lost Poems*, 1979; *Letters*, 1984

## ANNE SEXTON
### 1928–1974

*45 Mercy Street*, 1977 (p); *Anne Sexton: A Self Portrait in Letters*, 1977; *Words for Dr. Y.: Uncollected Poems with Three Stories*, 1978; *Complete Poems*, 1981

## KARL SHAPIRO
### 1913–

*Adult Bookstore*, 1976 (p); *Collected Poems, 1940–1978*, 1978; *Love & War, Art & God*, 1984 (p)

## SAM SHEPARD
### 1943–

*Angel City, and Other Plays*, 1976 (d); *Suicide in B*$^b$, 1976 (d); *Curse of the Starving Class*, 1976 (d); *Rolling Thunder Logbook*, 1977 (journal); *Buried Child*, 1978 (d); *True West*, 1979 (d); *Seduced*, 1979 (d); *Four Two-Act Plays*, 1980; *Chicago, and Other Plays*, 1981; *Hawk Moon*, 1981 (s, p, d); *Sam Shepard Play Collection*, 1981; *The Unseen Hand, and Other Plays*, 1981; *Seven Plays*, 1981; *Fool for Love, and The Sad Lament of Pecos Bill on the Eve of Killing His Wife*, 1983 (d); *Motel Chronicles*, 1983 (s, p); *Paris, Texas*, 1984 (screenplay)

## ISAAC BASHEVIS SINGER
### 1904–

*Naftali the Storyteller and His Horse, Sus, and Other Stories*, 1976 (juvenile); *A Little Boy in Search of God*, 1976 (a); *Shosha*, 1978 (n); *A Young Man in Search of Love*, 1978 (a); *Old Love*, 1979 (s); *Nobel Lecture*, 1979; *The Power of Light*, 1980 (s); *Reaches of Heaven: A Story of the Life of the Baal Shem Tov*, 1980; *Lost in America*, 1981 (a); *Collected Stories*, 1982; *The Penitent*, 1983 (n); *Love and Exile*, 1983 (m); *Stories for Children*, 1984

## W. D. SNODGRASS
### 1926–

*The Führer Bunker: A Cycle of Poems in Progress*, 1977 (p)

## GARY SNYDER
### 1930–

*The Old Ways*, 1977 (e); *Songs for Gaia*, 1977 (p); *On Bread and Poetry*, 1977 (e); *He Who Hunted Birds in His Father's Village: The Dimensions of a Haida Myth*, 1979 (legends); *The Real Work: Interviews and Talks, 1964–1979*, 1980; *Axe Handles*, 1983 (p)

## SUSAN SONTAG
### 1933–

*On Photography*, 1977 (e); *Illness as Metaphor*, 1978 (e); *I, etcetera*, 1978 (s);

*Under the Sign of Saturn*, 1980 (c, e); *A Susan Sontag Reader*, 1982 (misc)

## WILLIAM STAFFORD
### 1914–

*Stories That Could Be True*, 1977 (p); *Writing the Australian Crawl*, 1978 (e, interviews); *A Meeting with Disma Tumminello and William Stafford*, 1978 (interviews); *Sometimes Like a Legend*, 1981 (p); *Roving across Fields*, 1982 (interviews); *A Glass Face in the Rain*, 1982 (p); *Smoke's Way: Poems from Limited Editions, 1968–1981*, 1983; (with Marvin Bell) *Segues: A Correspondence in Poetry*, 1984

## GERTRUDE STEIN
### 1874–1946

*How Writing Is Written: Previously Uncollected Writings of Gertrude Stein*, 1974 (misc); *Dear Sammy: Letters from Gertrude Stein and Alice B. Toklas*, 1977; *The Yale Gertrude Stein: A Selection*, 1980 (misc)

## JOHN STEINBECK
### 1902–1968

*The Portable John Steinbeck*, rev. ed., 1976 (misc); *The Acts of King Arthur and His Noble Knights*, 1976 (n); *Letters to Elizabeth*, 1978

## WALLACE STEVENS
### 1879–1955

*Souvenirs and Prophecies: The Young Wallace Stevens*, by Holly B. Stevens, 1977 (misc)

## ● MARK STRAND
### 1934–

*Sleeping with One Eye Open*, 1964 (p); *Reasons for Moving*, 1968 (p); *Darker*, 1970 (p); *The Story of Our Lives*, 1973 (p); *Another Republic*, 1976 (p); *The Monument*, 1978 (p, e); *The Late Hour*, 1978 (p); *Selected Poems*, 1980; *The Planet of Lost Things*, 1982 (p)

## WILLIAM STYRON
### 1925–

*Sophie's Choice*, 1979 (n); *This Quiet Dust, and Other Writings*, 1982 (e, m)

## ● MAY SWENSON
### 1919–

*Another Animal*, 1954 (p); *A Cage of Spines*, 1958 (p); *To Mix with Time: New and Selected Poems*, 1963; *Poems to Solve*, 1966 (p, juvenile); *Half Sun Half Sleep*, 1967 (p); *Iconographs*, 1970 (p); *More Poems to Solve*, 1971 (p, juvenile); (with Leif Sjöberg) *Windows and Stones* by Tomas Tranströmer, 1972 (tr); *New and Selected Things Taking Place*, 1978 (p)

## ALLEN TATE
### 1899–1979

*The Literary Correspondence of Donald Davidson and Allen Tate*, 1974; *The Fathers, and Other Fiction*, 1977 (n, s); *Collected Poems 1919–1976*, 1977; *The Republic of Letters in America: The Correspondence of Allen Tate and John Peale Bishop*, 1981; *The Poetry Reviews of Allen Tate, 1924–1944*, 1983

## PETER TAYLOR
### 1917–

*In the Miro District*, 1977 (s)

## ● PAUL THEROUX
### 1941–

*Waldo*, 1966 (n); *Fong and the Indians*, 1968 (n); *Girls at Play*, 1969 (n); *Jungle Lovers*, 1971 (n); *Sinning with Annie*, 1972 (s); *V. S. Naipaul: An Introduction to His Work*, 1972 (c); *Saint Jack*, 1973 (n); *The Black House*, 1974 (n); *The Great Railway Bazaar*, 1975 (t); *The Family Arsenal*, 1976 (n); *Picture Palace*, 1977 (n); *The Consul's File*, 1977 (s); *A Christmas Card*, 1978 (juvenile); *The Old Patagonian Express*, 1979 (t); *London Snow*, 1980 (juvenile); *World's End*, 1980 (s); *The Mosquito Coast*, 1982 (n); *The London Embassy*, 1983 (s); *The Kingdom by the Sea*, 1983 (t); *Sailing through China*, 1984 (t); *Half Moon Street: Two Short Novels*, 1984

## LIONEL   TRILLING
### 1905–1975

*Collected Works*, 12 vols., 1978–80; *The Last Decade: Essays and Reviews 1965– 1975*, 1979 (e, j); *Of This Time, Of That Place, and Other Stories*, 1979; *Prefaces to "The Experience of Literature,"* 1979 (c); *Speaking of Literature and Society*, 1980 (e, c)

## ● ANNE   TYLER
### 1941–

*If Morning Ever Comes*, 1964 (n); *The Tin Can Tree*, 1965 (n); *A Slipping-Down Life*, 1970 (n); *The Clock Winder*, 1972 (n); *Celestial Navigation*, 1974 (n); *Searching for Caleb*, 1976 (n); *Earthly Possessions*, 1977 (n); *Morgan's Passing*, 1980 (n); *Dinner at the Homesick Restaurant*, 1982 (n)

## JOHN   UPDIKE
### 1932–

*Marry Me*, 1976 (n); *Tossing and Turning*, 1977 (p); *The Coup*, 1978 (n); *Too Far to Go: The Maples Stories*, 1979 (s); *Problems*, 1979 (s); *Rabbit Is Rich*, 1981 (n); *Bech Is Back*, 1982 (n); *Hugging the Shore*, 1983 (c, e); *The Witches of Eastwick*, 1984 (n)

## ● GORE   VIDAL
### 1925–

*Williwaw*, 1946 (n); *In a Yellow Wood*, 1947 (n); *The City and the Pillar*, 1948 (n); *The Season of Comfort*, 1949 (n); *Dark Green, Bright Red*, 1950 (n); *A Search for the King*, 1950 (n); (as Edgar Box) *Death in the Fifth Position*, 1952 (n); *The Judgment of Paris*, 1952 (n); (as Edgar Box) *Death before Bedtime*, 1953 (n); (as Edgar Box) *Death Likes It Hot*, 1954 (n); *Messiah*, 1954 (n); *A Thirsty Evil*, 1956 (s); *A Visit to a Small Planet, and Other Television Plays*, 1956; *A Visit to a Small Planet: A Comedy Akin to Vaudeville* [Broadway version], 1957 (d); *The Best Man*, 1960 (d); *Rocking the Boat*, 1962 (e); *Romulus* [adaptation of play by Friedrich Dürrenmatt], 1962 (d); *Three Plays*, 1962; *Three: Williwaw, A Thirsty Evil, Julian the Apostate*, 1962 (3n); *Julian*, 1964 (n); *Washington, D.C.*, 1967 (n); *Myra*

*Breckinridge*, 1968 (n); *Sex, Death, and Money*, 1968 (e); *Weekend*, 1968 (d); *Reflections upon a Sinking Ship*, 1969 (e); *Two Sisters: A Memoir in the Form of a Novel*, 1970 (n); *An Evening with Richard Nixon*, 1972 (d); *Homage to Daniel Shays: Collected Essays, 1952–1972*, 1972; *Burr*, 1973 (n); *Myron*, 1974 (n); *1876*, 1976 (n); *Matters of Fact and Fiction, Essays 1973– 1976*, 1977; *Kalki* 1978 (n); *Three by Box*, 1978 (3n); *Dress Gray*, 1979 (screenplay); *Views from a Window*, 1980 (interviews); *Creation*, 1981 (n); *The Second American Revolution, and Other Essays (1976–1982)* (British ed. titled *Pink Triangle and Yellow Star*), 1982 (e); *Duluth*, 1983 (n); *Lincoln: A Novel*, 1984 (n)

## KURT   VONNEGUT
### 1922–

*Slapstick*, 1976 (n); *Jailbird*, 1979 (n); *Sun, Moon, Star*, 1980 (retelling of the Nativity); *Palm Sunday*, 1981 (misc); *Deadeye Dick*, 1982 (n)

## ● ALICE   WALKER
### 1944–

*Once*, 1968 (p); *The Third Life of Grange Copeland*, 1970 (n); *Revolutionary Petunias*, 1973 (p); *In Love & Trouble: Stories of Black Women*, 1973 (s); *Langston Hughes: American Poet*, 1973 (b, juvenile); *Meridian*, 1976 (n); *"Goodnight, Willie Lee, I'll See You in the Morning,"* 1979 (p); *You Can't Keep a Good Woman Down*, 1981 (s); *The Color Purple*, 1982 (n); *In Search of Our Mothers' Gardens: Womanist Prose*, 1983 (e); *Horses Make a Landscape Look More Beautiful*, 1984 (p); *Good Night, Willie Lee, I'll See You in the Morning*, 1984 (p)

## ROBERT   PENN   WARREN
### 1905–

*Selected Poems, 1923–1975*, 1976; *A Place to Come To*, 1977 (n); *Now and Then: Poems, 1976–1978*, 1978; *Brother to Dragons: A New Version*, 1979 (d); *Being Here: Poetry, 1977–1980*, 1980; *Jefferson Davis Gets His Citizenship Back*, 1980 (b); *Robert Penn Warren Talking: Interviews*, 1980;

*Rumor Verified: Poems 1979–1980*, 1981 (p); *Chief Joseph of the Nez Perce*, 1983 (p)

### EUDORA WELTY
### 1909–

*The Eye of the Story*, 1978 (c, e); *Twenty Photographs*, 1980; *Moon Lake*, 1980 (s); *Collected Stories*, 1980; *One Writer's Beginnings*, 1984 (r); *Conversations with Eudora Welty*, 1984 (interviews)

### NATHANAEL WEST
### 1903–1940

No new publications

### EDITH WHARTON
### 1862–1937

*Ghost Stories*, 1973 (s); *Fast and Loose: A Novelette*, 1977; *The Edith Wharton Omnibus*, 1978 (misc)

### RICHARD WILBUR
### 1921–

*The Mind-Reader*, 1976 (p); *Responses: Prose Pieces, 1948–1976*, 1976 (e); *H. H. Stevens*, 1977 (b); *The Learned Ladies* by Molière, 1978 (tr); *Andromache* by Racine, 1982 (tr); *The Whale, and Other Uncollected Translations*, 1982

### THORNTON WILDER
### 1897–1975

*The Alcestiad: or, A Life in the Sun, with a Satyr Play, The Drunken Sisters*, 1977 (d); *American Characteristics*, 1979 (e)

### ● JOHN A. WILLIAMS
### 1925–

*The Angry Ones*, 1960 (n); *Night Song*, 1961 (n); *Africa: Her History, Lands, and People*, 1962 (h); *Sissie* (British ed. titled *Journey Out of Anger*), 1963 (n); *This Is My Country, Too*, 1965 (m); *The Man Who Cried I Am*, 1967 (n); *Sons of Darkness, Sons of Light*, 1969 (n); *The Most Native of Sons: A Biography of Richard Wright*, 1970; *The King God Didn't Save: Reflections on the Life and Death of Martin Luther King,*

*Jr.*, 1979 (b); *Captain Blackman*, 1972 (n); *Flashbacks: A Twenty-Year Diary of Article Writing*, 1973 (e, j); *Mothersill and the Foxes*, 1975 (n); *Minorities in the City*, 1975 (e); *The Junior Bachelor Society*, 1976 (n); *!Click Song*, 1982 (n)

### TENNESSEE WILLIAMS
### 1911–1983

*The Theatre of Tennessee Williams*, 7 vols., 1971–81; *Tennessee Williams' Letters to Donald Windham, 1940–1965*, 1977; *Androgyne, Mon Amour*, 1977 (p); *Where I Live: Selected Essays*, 1978; *Vieux Carré*, 1979 (d); *A Lovely Sunday for Creve Coeur*, 1980 (d); *Something Cloudy, Something Clear*, 1981 (d); *The Bag People*, 1982 (e); *It Happened the Day the Sun Rose*, 1982 (s); *Clothes for a Summer Hotel*, 1983 (d)

### WILLIAM CARLOS WILLIAMS
### 1883–1963

*Interviews, William Carlos Williams: Speaking Straight Ahead*, 1976; *A Recognizable Image: William Carlos Williams on Art and Artists*, 1978 (e); *The Doctor Stories*, 1984 (s)

### EDMUND WILSON
### 1895–1972

*A Window on Russia for the Use of Foreign Readers*, 1972 (e); *Letters on Literature and Politics, 1912–1972*, 1977; *The Nabokov–Wilson Letters, 1940–1971*, 1979; *The Thirties*, 1980 (diaries); *The Forties*, 1983 (diaries); *The Portable Edmund Wilson*, 1983 (misc)

### ● LANFORD WILSON
### 1937–

*So Long at the Fair*, 1963 (d); *Home Free*, 1964 (d); *The Madness of Lady Bright*, 1964 (d); *Balm in Gilead*, 1964 (d); *The Rimers of Eldritch*, 1965 (d); *This Is the Rill Speaking*, 1965 (d); *The Rimers of Eldritch, and Other Plays*, 1967; *The Gingham Dog*, 1968 (d); *Lemon Sky*, 1970 (d); *Serenading Louie*, 1970 (d); *The Hot l Baltimore*, 1973; *The*

*Migrants*, 1974 (d); *The Mound Builders*, 1975 (d); *The Fifth of July*, 1978 (d); *Talley's Folly*, 1979 (d); *A Tale Told*, 1981 (d); *Angels Fall*, 1982 (d)

## YVOR WINTERS
### 1900–1968

*Collected Poems*, rev. ed., 1978; *Hart Crane and Yvor Winters: Their Literary Correspondence*, 1978

## THOMAS WOLFE
### 1900–1938

*Beyond Love and Loyalty: The Letters of Thomas Wolfe and Elizabeth Nowell, together with "No More Rivers,"* 1983; *My Other Loneliness: Letters of Thomas Wolfe and Aline Bernstein*, 1983; *Welcome to Our City: A Play in Ten Scenes*, 1983; *The Autobiography of an American Novelist* (includes *The Story of a Novel* and *Writing and Living*), 1983

## JAMES WRIGHT
### 1927–1980

*Old Booksellers, and Other Poems*, 1976; *Moments of the Italian Summer*, 1976 (prose poems); *To a Blossoming Pear Tree*, 1977 (p); *This Journey*, 1982 (p); *Collected Prose*, 1983 (e)

## RICHARD WRIGHT
### 1908–1960

*Black Power*, 1954 (t, e); *Savage Holiday*, 1954 (n); *The Color Curtain*, 1956 (e, j); *Pagan Spain*, 1957 (t, e); *White Man, Listen!*, 1957 (e); *American Hunger*, 1977 (a); *A Richard Wright Reader*, 1978 (misc)

## LOUIS ZUKOFSKY
### 1904–1978

*"A" 1–24*, 1978 (p); *A Test of Poetry*, 1980 (p, tr); *Prepositions: The Collected Critical Essays of Louis Zukofsky*, expanded ed., 1981

# COPYRIGHT ACKNOWLEDGMENTS

VIRGINIA QUARTERLY REVIEW. From articles by Louis D. Rubin, Jr., on McCullers, Anne Hobson Freeman on Price, Jane Barnes Casey on Taylor.

AUSTIN WARREN. From article on Auden in *The Southern Review*.

ROBERT PENN WARREN. From article on Ransom in *The Southern Review*.

MARY ELLEN WILLIAMS WALSH. From *A Vast Landscape: Time in the Novels of Thornton Wilder*.

THE WASHINGTON POST. For generous permission to excerpt numerous reviews and articles in *Book World*.

BRIGITTE WEEKS. From article on Godwin in *Ms. Magazine*.

GEORGE WEIDENFELD AND NICHOLSON, LTD. From article by Jacques Barzun in *The World of Raymond Chandler*, Miriam Gross, ed.

WESTERN AMERICAN LITERATURE. From article by L. Edwin Folsom on Snyder.

ROSS WETZSTEON. From "The Genius of Sam Shepard" in *New York Magazine*.

WHITSON PUBLISHING CO., INC. From Henry C. Lacey, *To Raise, Destroy, and Create: The Poetry, Drama, and Fiction of Imamu Amiri Baraka (Le Roi Jones)*.

BRENDA WINEAPPLE. From article on Coover in *Iowa Review*.

WOMEN'S STUDIES: AN INTERDISCIPLINARY JOURNAL. From article by Jaqueline Ridgeway on Bogan.

THE YALE REVIEW. From articles by Vincent Miller on Pound, Frank Kermode on Auden, Louis L. Martz on Hollander, Maureen Howard on Barthelme, David Thorburn on Beattie, John Hollander on Merrill. Reprinted by permission of *The Yale Review*, copyright by Yale University.

YALE UNIVERSITY PRESS. From Robert A. Bone, *The Negro Novel in America* (Hurston); Kimberly W. Benston, *Baraka: The Renegade and the Mask*; Cleanth Brooks, *William Faulkner: Toward Yoknapatawpha and Beyond*, by permission of Yale University Press.

DAVID ZUCKER. From "Self and History in Delmore Schwartz's Poetry and Criticism" in *Iowa Review*.

# INDEX TO CRITICS

*Names of critics are cited on the pages given.*